CONSTRUCTION EQUIPMENT AND MANAGEMENT

S.C. Sharma
Former General Manager
THDC India Limited

KHANNA BOOK PUBLISHING CO. (P) LTD.
Publisher of Engineering and Computer Books
4C/4344, Ansari Road, Darya Ganj, New Delhi-110002
Phone : 011-23244447-48 **Mobile:** +91-9910909320
E-mail : contact@khannabooks.com
Website : www.khannabooks.com

Dear Readers,

To prevent the piracy, this book is secured with HIGH SECURITY HOLOGRAM on the front title cover. In case you don't find the hologram on the front cover title, please write us to at contact@khannabooks.com or whatsapp us at +91-99109 09320 and avail special gift voucher for yourself.

Specimen of Hologram on front Cover title:

Moreover, there is a SPECIAL DISCOUNT COUPON for you with EVERY HOLOGRAM.

How to avail this SPECIAL DISCOUNT:

Step 1: Scratch the hologram
Step 2: Under the scratch area, your "coupon code" is available
Step 3: Logon to www.khannabooks.com
Step 4: Use your "coupon code" in the shopping cart and get your copy at a special discount
Step 5: Enjoy your reading!

Price : ₹ 399.00

ISBN: 978-93-82609-05-6

Construction Equipment & Management by S.C. Sharma

First Edition: 2016
Revised Edition: 2019
Reprint: 2022

Published by:
Khanna Book Publishing Co. (P) Ltd.
CIN: U22110DL1998PTC095547

Visit us at: www.khannabooks.com
Write us at: contact@khannabooks.com

To view complete list of books, Please scan the QR Code:

Printed by Vaibhav Products, Delhi (India)

PREFACE

With the increasing emphasis on infrastructural development in the country and adopting latest technology for fast development, there had been need for more mechanisation. Realising this fact, it has been felt by Technical Universities and Boards to introduce the subject on "Construction Equipment and Management" in their syllabi. There had been the necessity of a good book on the subject which covers the full syllabus for the students preparing for Graduation and Diploma Courses.

By adding the topics on wall plastering machine, use of drones and robots in construction industry, the book now covers AICTE model curriculum fully.

The book will help the students to understand various equipment used in different types of construction works, and aspects related to the management of these construction equipment. The book will meet the requirement of construction engineers to become thoroughly familiar with the working, application, upkeep, and optimising the production of the wide range of modern construction equipment.

Though every effort has been made to eliminate all types of errors, yet some errors might have been left unnoticed. Readers are requested to bring any mistake observed by them to the notice of the publisher for improvement.

— S.C. Sharma

With the rapid economic development of the country and technological advancement in Construction Equipment, there had been need for more skilled manpower. It has been felt by Technical Universities and Boards to introduce the subject on "Construction equipment and Management" to their syllabus. There had been the necessity of a good book on the subject which covers the full syllabus for the students appearing for Graduation and Diploma Courses.

By adding the chapters on Soil stabilizing machine, use of Drones and robots in construction industry, the book now covers AICTE model curriculum fully.

The book will help the students to understand various equipment used in different types of construction works and aspects related to the management of these construction equipment. The book will meet the requirement of construction engineers to become thoroughly familiar with the working, application, selection and optimizing the production of the wide range of modern construction equipment.

Though every effort has been made to eliminate all types of errors, yet some errors might have been left unnoticed. Readers are requested to bring any mistake observed by them to the notice of the publisher for improvement.

— S.C. Sharma

CONTENTS

Part - I : EQUIPMENT MANAGEMENT

Part - III : CONCRETE AND ASPHALT PLANTS

Part - IV : OTHER CONSTRUCTION EQUIPMENT

Part - I

EQUIPMENT MANAGEMENT

Part I

EQUIPMENT MANAGEMENT

Chapter 1

Equipment Management in Construction Projects

1.1 Introduction to Construction Equipment

As we know, construction activity is an integral part of a country's infrastructure and industrial development. It includes buildings such as hospitals, educational institutions, townships, offices, commercial complexes, etc.; urban infrastructure such as water supply, sewerage, drainage etc.; highways, flyovers, tunnels, ports, railways, airports; power systems; irrigation and agriculture systems; telecommunications, industrial plants.

Construction has become the basic input for socio-economic development. Besides, the construction industry generates substantial employment and provides a growth impetus to other sectors through backward and forward linkages.

The upswing in the Indian Economy has enhanced the demand for the construction and material handling equipment. The demand for construction and material handling equipment is correlated with the growth of other segments. Prior to 1960s, domestic requirements of construction equipment were entirely met by the imports.

During last 3 to 4 decades, construction industry has made enormous progress and has grown both in terms of size and diversity. The construction and mining industry are the primary users of the heavy earth moving equipment in India. The organised construction sector accounts for about 55% of the total construction equipment industry.

Construction equipment plays a significant role in the execution of modern high cost time-bound construction projects. These produce output at accelerated speed, and enables completion of tasks in a limited time. The equipment saves manpower which is becoming scarce, costly and more demanding day-by-day. In addition, equipment improves productivity, quality and safety. Thus, the construction equipment have become indispensable item of resources and their role continues to grow steadily.

In most cases, a piece of equipment does not work as a stand-alone unit. Pieces of different types of equipment work in groups, therefore, the optimization in the management of an equipment spread is critical for a contractor, both in achieving a competitive pricing position and for arranging the capital required to finance the project.

The project planner/engineer on the job is required to match the right machine or combination of machines to the job at hand. For this purpose, he is required to identify the construction equipment for executing the project tasks, assessing equipment performance capability, forecasting datewise requirement of numbers and types of equipment, and then selecting the equipment to be acquired.

The production tasks which can be performed with equipment include excavating, hauling transporting, compacting, grading, hoisting, concreting, precasting, trenching, pipe-laying etc. In addition, the support equipment are also required, at the project site, which include generators, compressors, pumping sets and other utility services equipment.

1.2 Classification of Construction Equipment

Construction equipment can be broadly classified on the basis of their functions as under :

1. Earthwork Equipment

(i) *Earth cuting and moving equipment* : Bulldozers, Scrapers, Front-end loaders, Motor graders.

(ii) *Excavation and lifting equipment* : Backhoes, Power Shovels, Draglines, Clamshells.

(iii) *Loading equipment* : Loaders, Shovels, Excavators.

(iv) *Transportation equipment* : Tippers, Dump Trucks, Scrapers, Conveyors.

(v) *Compacting equipment* : Tamping Foot Rollers, Smooth Wheel Rollers, Pneumatic Rollers, Vibratory Rollers, Plate Compactors.

2. Concreting Plant and Equipments

(i) *Production equipment* : Batching Plants, Concrete Mixers.

(ii) *Transportation equipment* : Truck mixers, Concrete dumpers.

(iii) *Placing equipment* : Concrete pumps, Conveyors, Hoists, Grouting equipment.

(iv) *Concrete vibrating equipment* : Needle vibrators, Plate compactors.

3. Material Hoisting Equipment

(i) *Hoists* : Fixed, Mobile, Fork-lifts.

(ii) *Mobile Cranes* : Crawler-mounted, self-propelled rubber-tyred, truck-mounted.

(iii) *Tower Cranes* : Stationary, Travelling type.

4. Special Purpose Heavy Construction Plant and Equipment

(i) *Aggregate production equipment* : Crushing plants, Rock blasting equipment, Screening plants.

(ii) *Concrete paving equipment* : Concrete paver finishers.

(iii) *Pile driving equipment* : Pile driving hammers.

(iv) *Asphalt mix production and Placement equipment* : Asphalt plants, asphalt pavers.

(v) *Tunneling equipment* : Drill jumbos, Muck-hauling equipment, Rock bolters, Tunnel boring machines.

5. Support and Utility Services Equipment

(i) Pumping and Dewatering equipment.

(ii) Pipe laying equipment.

(iii) Generators.

(iv) Welding equipment.

1.3 Introduction to Equipment Management

The cost of equipment in a project varies from 10 to 30% of the total cost of the project, depending upon the extent of mechanisation. In modern fully mechanised projects the cost of equipment goes upto 30%. Proper planning, selection, procurement, installation, operation, maintenance and equipment replacement policy plays an important role in equipment management for the successful completion of the project. With the growing use of machinery it has become necessary for construction engineers to be thoroughly familiar with the construction application and upkeep of the wide range of the modern equipment.

Equipment manager's main task is to reduce downtime, achieve optimum equipment utilisation and increase production at minimum cost. The cost analysis and the will of adopting proper techniques suited to the situation are the basic factors for the success and therefore, there is a need for a rational planning, proper selection, and judicious deployment of equipment in relation to the conditions so as to achieve optimum utilisation. Equipment engineer should coordinate with various wings of the organisation in discharging his job of equipment planning, balancing, selection of equipment and its utilisation, personnel selection and training, financial planning, preventive maintenance and general supervision. Thus, equipment management integrates and continuously interacts with human, technical, financial and production systems in order to achieve top efficiency and cost effectiveness.

Equipment engineer must be familiar with the handling of different types of equipment and remain in touch about the latest developments in the field. Utility of the equipment can be enhanced and it can be made versatile by providing certain attachments and accessories. A proper selection of equipment can solve large number of problems which may occur in future.

Evolution of Construction Equipment Industry

After the World War II, construction industry surged. To support these efforts certain development also took place which included development of torque converter and the power shift transmission to enhance the capacity of diesel engines and also that of heavy earth moving equipment the front-end loader replaced the old "dipper-stick" shovels. Concrete batching and mixing plants, and hot mix plants changed from slow manually controlled machines to hydraulically operated and electrically controlled equipment.

In India, the history of construction equipment industry is only about four to five decade old. Prior to 1960s domestic requirements of construction equipment were entirely met through imports. Domestic production begin in 1964 with manufacturing of bulldozers, dumpers, graders, scrapers etc. by Bharat Earth Movers Ltd. (BEML) a Public Sector Undertaking (PSU).

In the private sector Hindustan Motors established its Earthmoving Equipment Division in 1969 at Tiruvallur, near Chennai. In 1974, L&T began to manufacture hydraulic excavators under licence from Poclain, France. Telco also began production of hydraulic excavators under license from Hitachi Japan.

In late 1980s and early 1990s due to liberalization of economy with increased construction activities earthmoving and road construction equipment, concrete equipment, drum mix asphalt plants, and material handling equipment started manufacturing in India. During the last about two decades, construction industry has made enormous progress and has grown both in terms of size and diversity due to large scale infrastructure developments. Major thrust on infrastructural sectors of construction industry was on roads, power, ports, airports, mining, telecom, railways, urban infrastructure, real-estate etc.

1.4 Equipment Planning

Modern construction projects are complex in nature and success of a project depends greatly on proper and scientific planning. Before starting every project, its planning is done with great care, as the efficiency of the whole project largely depends upon its planning. While planning each and every detail should be worked out in anticipation and should be considered carefully.

The task of the project planner/engineer on the job is to match the right machine or combination of machines. For planning the equipment requirement, it is necessary to first determine machine productivity. After studying the plants and specifications, and visiting the project site, the planner must visualize how to best employ specific pieces of equipment to accomplish the work. Is it less expensive to top-load trucks with a wheel loader or a shovel? Several such questions must be analysed and then answered by the planner. To perform such analysis, the planner must consider both machine capacity and methods of employment.

Since no two projects are exactly alike; therefore, it is important that the planner begins each new project with a completely open mind and reviews all possible options. He should also consider new improved equipment available in the market.

Planning of a construction project involves deciding about the extent of mechanisation, equipment planning, execution planning etc. While planning a project we must very carefully decide about the extent of use of construction equipments. On major construction projects mechanisation is indispensable, while for middle and minor construction projects a compromise between manual and mechanical means has to be made. In a country like India, where man-power is cheaply and easily available, we can take advantage of this facility specially for the activities which can be easily carried out by the manpower. However, a combination of manual labour and machines is preferred. Now the question arises before the planner that : to what extent mechanisation is desirable?

1.4.1 Extent of Mechanisation

Extent to which mechanisation in a project should be planned, depends upon the following main factors :

1. **Manpower :** Type of manpower required by the project for its execution, is first decided and whether this type of manual labour is cheaply and sufficiently available round the year. In case the manual labour is costly or available only for limited duration or required type of labour is not available in the area, then the solution is only mechanisation. To decide whether the labour is costly or cheap, planner must consider the output given by the labour and overhead expenditure for the labour like accommodation, transportation to be provided to them etc. on one hand and output of the equipment and expenditure on the equipment on the other hand.
2. **Completion Period :** Every project is required to be completed in a particular duration, since delay in completion of project means increase in the construction cost due to rise in prices, payment of overhead for more period, imposition of penalty for delay etc. The overhead expenses include depreciation of equipments, supervisory expenses, accommodation expenses, light, water, power and insurance expenses etc. This completion period plays a deciding role about the extent of mechanisation, since less the completion period more the mechanisation. By employing more number of construction equipment project can be completed in lesser duration.
3. **Nature of Work :** Where the nature of work is such, which is beyond the scope of human labour to perform, use of construction equipments is unavoidable. Nature of work includes adverse weather, climatic conditions, topography, toughness, handling of large quantities of construction material for long distance.
4. **Availability of Money :** Since cost of equipment is too high and to be spent initially, it needs heavy investment in the beginning. Therefore, availability of money is main factor in deciding the extent of mechanisation.
5. **Availability of Indigenous Equipment :** The import of costly equipment and of spare parts proves a drain on foreign exchange resources of the country. After-sales-service, repair facility are also considered where equipment manufactured in our own country are not available, because time required for importation, shipment, installation and commissioning of the equipment and thereafter lead time for the purchase of repair spares will hamper the progress of the project adversely.
6. **Social Objects of the Project :** Some times projects are sanctioned with the object of providing employment opportunities, to improve the economic

condition of the masses in addition to the development in the area. In such cases manual labour is preferred over the use of machines unless otherwise any particular activity is beyond the capacity of manual labour.

7. **Labour Relations :** In certain areas, past experience indicates labour unrests, strikes, absenteeism, uncertainty, unavailability of labour or seasonal fluctuations. In such circumstances machines are preferred being more reliable to complete the project in time.

8. **Overseas Projects :** In cases where large number of projects are in hand in other countries, it is difficult and expensive to send large number of man-power required in adopting the manual means in these projects, therefore only, alternative left is to execute the project using construction equipment only.

9. **Quality and Performance :** The work carried out by means of construction equipment is of high standard of quality and performance. The quality is consistent, execution is fast, work is more durable, maintenance and repair will be very limited if projects are executed by using the construction equipment.

10. **Development of Industries :** In countries like India where industries are in developing stage, it is the need of time to use construction equipment for the development of manufacturing industry and faster industrialisation of the country.

Use of Machines V/s Use of Manual Labour

The advantages and disadvantages of using machines and manual labour in construction projects are briefly described hereunder :

	Points in favour of machines	***Points of favour of manual labour***
1.	It can handle tough works which can not be performed otherwise.	Initial heavy investments are not required to be made.
2.	It is cheaper when quantum of work is more and material is required to be transported for long distances.	Valuable foreign exchange is saved by employing manual labour instead of using machines which are to be imported.
3.	Machines when used in the project, it delivers better quality of work.	Small and short duration projects are sometimes found to be economical with manual labour.
4.	It is possible to adhere to schedules.	Direct advantage to considerably large number of people by way of employment which help in social and economical betterment.
5.	It is easy to predict the behaviour of a machine as compared to that of man, hence planning is easy.	No problem due to delay in procurement of spares for the repair of machines. The delay (lead time) is substantially high in case of imported equipment.

(Contd...)

6.	Being lesser number of persons, (operators only), it is easy to supervise and control.	Project can be started immediately, which is not possible in case machines are used. Since importation, shipment, transportation, installation and commissioning of equipments require a substantial time.
7.	It helps in development of technical know-how, skill and industrial development of the country.	Disposal of equipment and its balance spare parts poses a problem after the project is completed.
8.	Availability of Manpower and seasonal fluctuations will not affect the project's progress.	
9.	Effect of climate and topographic conditions is less when machines are used as compared to that when manual labour is used.	
10.	No problem for housing and transportation of persons and also for the arrangement for supply of food, water, light and medicines etc.	

1.5 Forecasting Equipment Requirement

As discussed earlier extent of mechanisation depends upon the nature and quantity of work to be handled, the specifications to be adopted, time period of completion, availability of skilled and unskilled labour. There are certain types of works where man cannot work and the only alternative is to use construction equipments, *e.g.*, earthwork compaction, construction of bridges, working under-water, concreting, dewatering, construction of bituminous/rigid pavements, working in steep slopes etc.

Considering above mentioned factors, planners are required to decide the extent of mechanisation, which means out of large number of activities involved in the completion of the projects which are the activities which should be completed by using the equipments. With the identification of the activities to be carried out with the help of equipments, work of equipment planning starts.

Following are the main points planner has to decide in equipment planning :

1. **Working Shifts :** By increasing the number of shifts we can reduce the number of equipment required, as the same equipment can be used in second and third shifts. This helps in reduction in initial investment of capital. But the number of shifts in which work can be executed depends upon the nature of work, the area in which the work is spread over etc. While planning the number of shifts it must be kept in mind that in double shifts, only 60 to 70% (nearly) extra work can be achieved and not really double. Similarly in triple shift only 100 to 125% of extra work, as compared to single shift can be achieved. This is because the efficiency in

the evening and night shifts is less as compared to that in day shift, besides maintenance also becomes difficult.

Since repair facility for the break downs occurred in the night shift is not fully available, provisions for standby equipment is desired. Experience has shown that this provision should be as below :

(i) For equipment used in single shift 10% standby
(ii) For equipment used in double shifts 20% standby
(iii) For equipment used in triple shifts 30% standby

2. **Number and Size of Equipment :** For deciding the number and size of the equipment, following factors should be considered :

   (i) Quantum of work.
   (ii) Working days available for completion of projects.
   (iii) Number of shifts planned.

   When quantum of work is too much then bigger size equipment are selected. The average rated output of these equipment will help in deciding number of the equipment required keeping in view the number of working days available and number of shifts planned per day.

3. **Matching Units :** There are certain equipments, which are used together in a team with other equipments, like scraper with pusher dozer, concrete batching plant with truck mounted concrete mixers, paver finisher with road roller, asphalt mixing plant with tipper trucks, wheel loaders with dumpers/ dump trucks etc. These numbers and size of the matching equipments should be planned for each activity, keeping in view that complete matching set must be utilised at the maximum and combination must be optimum.

4. **Procurement Scheduling :** Procurement scheduling is done considered procurement time required and time when equipment is required.

5. **Workshop and Stores Planning :** While planning for the purchase of equipments, it is necessary to plan for the workshop and stores for carrying out the repair and maintenance.

6. **Man-Power Planning :** Planning for manpower in order to operate the equipment and to carry out the repair and maintenance is also necessarily be done sufficiently in advance. In case skilled and trained manpower for the operation, maintenance and repair is not available than efforts should be made to train them before the arrival of equipments in the project.

7. **Site Conditions :** Site conditions play an important role in deciding the type of equipment. The type of equipment selected mainly depends upon soil available, and valley conditions, surface and strata where work is to be carried out. This helps in deciding whether to use wheeled equipments or crawler type equipments, to use dragline excavator or power shovel, to use crane or cable ways, to use rear-dump trucks or side-dump trucks or bottom dump trucks etc.

Rear-dump trucks are suitable for dumping to hoppers or fills, side-dump trucks are suitable for dumping in long length or on sides of roads, *i.e.*, on shoulders, while bottom-dump trucks are suitable for discharging free flowing materials like sand, gravel, dry earth etc. while moving, *i.e.*, in windows. Dragline is used for digging water saturated material from below footing level, while power shovels are used for loading hard soil or rock into the vehicle and digging above footing level. Thus, the type of equipment should be selected after knowing the type of work required to be done by the equipments.

Scientific Planning

As discussed earlier the success of a project depends greatly on equipment planning, it is therefore most essential to follow scientific and rational planning techniques. This means that the data or basis taken should be based on past experiences gained in various projects and on work studies carried out in various conditions at various places. Planner should use the mathematical models of the operation of equipments. The examples of such models are mathematical programming, queueing, simulation and other techniques. He should not use the assumptions, which may mislead the results.

Quantum of Work

The first stage of planning is to calculate the total quantity of work involved in each operation. For correct planning it is very much essential to ascertain quantity of work as accurate as possible. This should be found out by using the detailed drawings, designs and surveying the site. This estimate should be made using all scientific methods and not on merely assumptions. Care should be taken in categorising each operation according to its characteristics for example, earth cutting can be cutting of ordinary soil, hardsoil or soil mixed boulders, or rock cutting operation. This categorisation is necessary to know the machine hours required to do a particular operation, since each category requires different machine-hour efforts, *i.e.*, output rate for each category is different for the equipment.

While calculating the quantity of work involved it is necessary to take a note of various constraints, for example, (i) limitation of working space, which may affect the efficiency of the machine, so as to assess the output rate of equipment to be used, (ii) location of quarries and amount of material available in each of them, so as to know the correct lead and to assess the efforts involved in shifting the crusher location.

Output and Capacity of Equipment

Next phase of planning is to decide the equipment on the basis of its output and capability. The equipment must be capable to handle the work efficiently on which it is to be engaged. The output of the equipment so decided should be determined on the basis of past experiences on similar works. As we have discussed earlier that the same equipment gives different output in different conditions of work, therefore, it is very essential to use the past output data of similar works handled by the equipment in similar conditions.

Output of the equipment varies with various conditions. Following are some of them :

(i) Different type of soil needs different amount of effort and hence equipment engaged on them gives different output.

(ii) Reduction of horse power of engine due to altitude.

(iii) Time spent on servicing and inspection varies with the working conditions.

(iv) Output of the equipment also depends upon the operator's efficiency.

(v) Output of dumper etc. depends on the condition of haul road.

(vi) Time spent on the unproductive works.

(vii) Changing weather conditions are also responsible for variation in output.

(viii) Capacities of the matching machineries working in the same group.

While selecting an equipment care must be taken that the equipment should neither be of too big size nor of too small size than required for the work. It should be able to complete the work economically in completion period. Since too big size equipment will complete the work before time and its residual value (initial cost minus depreciation) will be high, which may not be gainfully used after completion of the job. Similarly with too small size of equipment, more number of equipment will be required for completing the quantity of work involved, which means un-economical proposition. Therefore, most economical planning is to select an equipment which can be fully depreciated by the time project is completed. It means the equipment must complete its economical life as soon as the project is completed.

Utilisation and Time-Period

It is always a good practice to utilise equipment to the limit of its useful life on one particular project. For a project of nearly 4 years or more duration, it is possible to use the equipment to its full economic life. The number of shifts per day should be decided, keeping this factor in view.

Experience have shown that an yearly utilisation for an equipment under average working condition in our country is as follows :

Single shift operation	—	1500 hrs.
Double shift operation	—	2500 hrs.
Triple shift operation	—	3200 hrs.

Thus, an equipment with an estimated economical life of 10,000 hours, when used on a 4 years project should work for 2500 hours per year. The means the equipment must be engaged on double shift, so that it can be depreciated fully to keep the production cost as lowest. In case the same equipment when used on 6 years project, it must be used on single shift operation.

When the project duration is less than 3 years, the equipment should be used in triple shift, so as to depreciate fully. This will not only avoid wastage in terms of residual value of the equipment but shall need lesser number of equipment with lesser investment on the capital items.

Two shift operation of equipment is economical and should be employed whenever possible. Three shift working results in frequent breakdowns and low availability, which means more standby and increase in cost. The three shifts should be used only when project duration is less, immediate repair facilities even in the night are available, proper lighting facilities in the area exists. Single shift should be used only when project duration is more than 5 and 6 years or where works are located in difficult terrain, or when equipments are scattered over a long distance where it is difficult to provide supporting facilities for a multishift operation.

1.6 Selection of Equipment

Proper selection of equipment for a construction project is of vital importance for its speedy and economical completion. Problem of equipment selection has become more complicated, because large variety of equipments are being manufactured now-a-days. For proper selection of equipment, a considerable experience in the operation and maintenance in the field is essential. Records kept for operation, maintenance and actual output obtained under comparable conditions of previous projects will greatly help in taking decision for equipment selection.

Following are the main points which should be considered in the process of equipment selection :

1. **Suitability of Job Conditions :** The equipment must meet the requirement of work, climate and working conditions.
2. **Size of the Equipment :** Size of equipment should be such that it must be able to be used with other matching units. If the equipment selected is of larger size, that will remain idle for most of the time or shall work on part loads, which means production cost will be more. On other side, if the equipment is of smaller size than desired, the equipment will not be able to work with the matching equipments and hence other equipments will have to remain idle or to be allowed to work on part loads, which shall again be uneconomical.
3. **Standardisation :** It is better to have same type and size of equipments in the project. It means lesser spare parts reserve, more interchangeability of parts if required, easy for the operators to understand it, mechanics will be able to maintain and repair better as they become expert by handling similar type of equipment.
4. **Availability of Equipment :** The equipment which is easily available in the market should be purchased. It should also be ensured that the equipment is of repute and is likely to be continued to be manufactured in future also. This is necessary for future standardisation and ensuring spare parts supply. It is easy to dispose off such equipment after completion of projects.
5. **Availability of Spare Parts :** While selecting a particular type or make of equipment, it should be ensured that the spare parts will be available at

reasonable price throughout the working life of the equipment. It should also be ensured that the downtime of the equipment for want of spare parts may not be more. This is all the more necessary in case of imported equipments.

6. **Multipurpose Equipments (Versatility) :** There are certain types of equipments which ae not utilised fully. Therefore, if possible, they must be capable of performing more than one function for example, excavator with wheel loader bucket arrangement or with rock breaker attachment.
7. **Availability of know-how :** The equipment selected should be satisfactorily handled by available operators and mechanics. A sophisticated equipment may give excellent performance but it may be difficult to handle and maintain it through available know-how.
8. **Use in Future Projects :** When equipment completes only a part of their useful life in a project, it should be kept in view that the equipment can be used in future projects and may not become obsolete.
9. **The Economical Aspects :** While selecting the equipment, it should be considered that the cost of unit production should be minimum.
10. **Reliability of the Equipment :** Equipment selected for the project must be reliable one.
11. **Service Support :** Service support should be available in the area of project where the equipment shall be used. Service after sales is a major criteria for selection of equipment.
12. **Operating Requirements :** The equipment selected should be easy to operate and maintain, acceptable to the operator and should have lesser fuel consumption.
13. **Past Performance :** If the equipment being purchased is of new make and model, it is desirable to enquire about its performance from other users, who are using this make and model.
14. The size and numbers should be such that full life is utilised in the project with very little residuals.
15. Reputation of the manufacturer.
16. Warranty or guarantee offered by the manufacturer.
17. Use of standard components in the equipment.
18. Adequacy of drive mechanism or power of the primemover.
19. Versatility of the equipment should be given due priority. This means a machine which can be used for many jobs. The versatility promises extra profit from two directions : (i) allows one machine to do the job of several machines and thus cutting into ownership and operating costs associated with additional plant and labour, and (ii) it increases utilization, which means a machine earns money when it might otherwise be idle. Now-a-days attachments can be fitted or changed quickly with the help of couplers.

A balance between reliability, investment cost, and operating cost should be found, since a policy of selecting the lowest priced equipment can often lead to overall higher costs.

1.7 Management Concept

Since equipment management should be an integral part of overall management of the project. Therefore, here we are discussing the management concept in brief. Detailed management aspects of various issues of the project may be referred in the book on "Construction Engineering and Management of Projects" by this author.

In any organisation there is a group of persons who manage its affairs for the attainment of its objectives. Management is the primary force within the organisation which tends to lead it towards the group goals. **Management** is the process of designing and maintaining an environment in which individuals, working together in groups, efficiently accomplish selected aims.

Some other definitions of management are :

- Management is principally a task of planning, coordinating and controlling the efforts of other people towards a specified objectives. It involves the combining of the traditional factors of product (men, machines, and materials) in an optimum manner paying due attention to the particular goals of the organisation.
- Management is science and art both. Management is a science in the sense, that it adopts a systematic approach through knowledge acquired by continuous and vigorous efforts in the field of management science. Management is an art, as it is an application of some skills to achieve the desired results, and utilise the talent of the people, and also because it manages the human beings.

1.7.1 Principles of Management

1. Division of work.
2. Authority and responsibility should always go together.
3. Discipline.
4. Unity of command.
5. Unity of direction.
6. Subordination of individual interests to the interests of the organisation.
7. Remuneration to workers should be fair and some proper method should be adopted.
8. Centralisation of power to control overall work.
9. Equality.
10. Stability.
11. Initiative.

1.7.2 Functions of Management

Various pioneers in the field of management including Fayol, Urwick, Koontz, Davis and θ'Donnel has given different management functions. A comprehensive list of all such functions is given hereunder :

1. Planning
2. Organising
3. Staffing
4. Directing :
   — Leadership
   — Communication
   — Motivation
   — Supervision
5. Controlling
6. Coordinating

Ralph Davis has divided the managerial functions in only three categories, namely, planning, organising and controlling. He considered directing and coordinating as a part of controlling, while staffing as part of organising. Some authors have classified these functions as planning, organising, leading and controlling. They considered staffing as a part of organising, whereas leading included motivation, communication and supervision. Some authors have considered decision-making also a separate category of function.

1. Planning

Planning means "thinking before doing". Before actual work is started, it is decided that what is to be done, how much to be done, how and where to be done, when to be done, and who will do it etc. The planning should aim at eliminating the wastage of material, idleness of men, machine and capital. Planning is necessary to ensure proper utilisation of resources (*i.e.*, man, material, machine, time and money) to achieve the objectives of the enterprise. In planning, a manager searches for the alternative courses open to him, and then selects best alternative.

2. Organising

In organising the human power is combined with other resources to give desired output. Organising includes formation of structure of authority and responsibility among the people to achieve the objective of the organisation.

Organising involves grouping of tasks necessary to carry out plans, assigning activities to departments and making provisions for coordination through delegation of authority. Organisation structure mean the systematic arrangement of the people working for the organisation, their positions and the relationships between positions. The organisation structure varies with the organisations and the functions to be performed and depends upon the goals and objectives established, the resources availability, the communications and the working relationships of the individuals, motivational and other factors.

Major principles of organisation which assist in arriving at the final structure are :

1. Consideration of objectives.
2. Responsibility and authority.
3. Span of control.
4. Delegation.
5. Chain of command.
6. Division of labour (or work).
7. Balance, stability and flexibility.

3. Staffing

Staffing is a managerial function which involves selection, training, promotion and retirement of personnel. For a new enterprise, staffing function is followed by planning and organising. After planning and organising the total activities, management is in position to know the man-power requirement at different levels. Management than starts with recruiting, selecting and training.

For an on-going enterprise, staffing is a continuous process for new jobs or to fill up the vacancies created by retirement or leaving the employees.

4. Directing

Directing is a function which includes all those activities which are designed to encourage subordinates to work effectively both in short and long run. Directing involves guiding, inspiring, overseeing and leading people for the accomplishment of predetermined objectives.

Directing can also be defined as, "telling people what to do and seeing that they do it to the best of their ability".

Directing function involves leadership, communication, motivation, supervision and coordination.

(a) *Communication*

Communication is a process by which ideas are transmitted, received and understood by others for the purpose of achieving desired results. Communication may be verbal or witten orders, reports, instructions etc. It may be formal (official or recognised system of communication) or informal (other than official communication, generally verbal conversation).

Therefore, main objective of a communication system is to exchange facts and informations in a manner which is acceptable to all concerned.

Principles or guidelines which must be followed for achieving effective communication in the organisation are :

1. Principle of clarity.
2. Principle of objective.
3. Principle of understanding.

4. Principle of consistency.
5. Principle of completeness.
6. Principle of feedback.
7. Principle of right time.

(b) *Leadership*

Leadership means to inspire confidence and trust so that there is maximum cooperation from the employees within the control of a manager. Leadership can also be defined as the ability to persuade others to seek defined objectives enthusiastically.

Success of a leader depends upon his qualities and characteristics. In the organisation, the leaders may be authoritarian (or autocratic leaders), democratic (or consultative leaders), persuasive leaders, functional leaders, and free – rein leaders (who gives high degree of independence in their working).

(c) *Supervision*

Supervising and overseeing his subordinates is an important part of "direction" function of every manager. Supervision means observing the subordinates at work to see that they are working according to plans and policies of the organisation and keeping the time schedule and to help them in solving their work problems.

Managers at the lowest level are known as supervisors. They are directly in touch with their operative employees or workers. The functions of the supervisors are :

1. Planning the work.
2. Issuing orders.
3. Providing guidance or leadership.
4. Controlling schedule.
5. Controlling output.
6. Motivate.
7. Maintaining records.
8. Liaison between management and workers.

(d) *Motivation*

It is a psychological concept and it relates to those forces operating within the individual employee or subordinate which impels him to act or not to act in certain ways. Motivation is a psychological act which attracts the workers to do more work and instigates.

Thus, motivation is a general inspiration process which gets the members of the team to do their task effectively, to give their loyalty to the group, to carry out properly the tasks they have accepted and generally to play an effective part in the job that the group has undertaken.

5. Coordination

Coordination is an orderly arrangement of group efforts to provide unity of action in pursuit of a common purpose. Coordination integrate and harmonise the workers to achieve a common object. Coordination helps in smooth working of enterprise by promoting team spirit.

6. Controlling

Controlling means to watch actual performance and compare with plans and to point out short comings, to rectify and to prevent recurrence. Some of the important controls are : quality control, budget control, cost control, production control, inventory control etc.

Controlling is a continuous process of measuring actual results in relation to those planned.

1.7.3 Types of Management

Managements are of different types depending upon their application. Some of the common types of management are :

1. Industrial management.
2. Construction management.
3. Safety management.
4. Financial management.
5. Production management.
6. Maintenance management.
7. Purchase management.
8. Personnel (Human resource) management.
9. Office management.
10. Materials management.
11. Inventory management.
12. Quality management.
13. Equipment management.
14. Project management.
15. Contract management.
16. Environment management.

QUESTIONS

1. What is equipment management? Discuss factors which decides extent of mechanization in a project.
2. Explain advantages and disadvantages of using machines and manual labour.
3. Explain construction equipment selection criteria. Discuss the criteria for recommending a construction equipment.
4. How equipment planning is done for a project of large size?
5. How would you forecast the equipment requirement for a construction project?

6. Describe various criteria for deciding two shift or three shift working in a construction project.
7. Discuss the factors considered while forecasting the equipment requirement for a construction project.
8. Discuss the factors which affects the output of construction equipment.
9. Discuss important points which should be considered while planning for equipment operation.
10. Discuss various factors which should be considered in the process of equipment selection for a construction project.
11. Construction and National Development are linked in separately.
12. Define construction management and also discuss its necessity.
13. Discuss different functions of management, in detail.
14. Define management. List out various principles of management.
15. Name different types of machinery required for the construction of infrastructure (civil engineering) projects.

□□□

Chapter **2**

Maintenance Management

2.1 Introduction

Whenever a machine is used, it is subjected to wear and tear hence proper attention should be given to protect the machine and its components from undue wear and thus protect them from failures. A proper attention means lubrication, cleaning, timely inspection and systematic maintenance. Maintenance of a machine means efforts directed towards the up-keep and the repair of that machine.

Every machine will require repairs even if it is best designed, hence the repair must be done at such a time when it may have least disruptions, *i.e.*, machine may be repaired when it is not being used or its use may be postponed without affecting the production of the project. Therefore, checking of the machine is generally done when it is not in operation, so that the defect, if any, can be immediately and easily rectified without causing extensive damage.

In this way, we say that maintenance is responsible for the smooth and efficient working of an equipment and helps in improving its productivity. It also help in keeping the machine in a state of maximum efficiency with economy.

Success of any organisation largely depends on proper selection of persons engaged for the operation work. Production in the concern depends largely on the maintenance of plant and equipments. Hence, the organisation of the maintenance wing should be such that a proper maintenance and overhauls etc., can be done economically and effectively. Maintenance wing is generally given an important position in the project.

2.2 Objectives of Maintenance

Main objectives of maintenance are :

1. To maximise availability of plant, equipment and machinery for productive purposes.
2. To extend the lifespan of plant, equipment and other facilities by minimising their wear and tear.
3. To ensure operational readiness of equipment at all times.
4. To reduce the cost of lost production due to breakdown.

5. To provide information to the management on the cost and effectiveness of maintenance.
6. To ensure safety through regular inspection and maintenance of plant, equipment and other facilities such as compressors, elevators, material handling equipment etc.

2.3 Maintenance Organisation

For effective maintenance, the maintenance workload of an organisation has to be matched with the available maintenance resources. For this purpose a balanced maintenance organisation setup is required to be developed. Following factors are considered for determining the appropriate form of maintenance organisation :

- Maintenance workload and its pattern depending upon type and conditions of machines.
- Amount of emergency maintenance work.
- Cost of non-availability of plant and machinery.
- Location of plants and machinery.
- Maintenance resources.

Functions

1. To develop maintenance policies, procedures and standards.
2. To schedule planned maintenance work in consultation with concerned departments.
3. To carry out maintenance, repairs and overhauls to ensure good operational status and availability. If necessary, arrange training for operators and maintenance workers.
4. To ensure scheduled inspection and lubrication of plant, equipment and machinery.
5. To maintain a record of maintenance work.
6. To prepare inventory of spares and other materials needed for maintenance.
7. To control inventory of spares and others materials.
8. To prepare maintenance budget and control it.
9. To develop proper management information system about the maintenance activities.
10. To help in selecting process and equipment from maintenance point of view.

Controlling Functions

11. To control men, spares and maintenance.
12. Monitoring and controlling of all failures so that causes of recurrent failures can be identified and diagnosis.
13. To coordinate with the plant and equipment manufacturers with reference to collection of maintenance information.

14. Spares inventory control for identifying abnormal spares usage.
15. To carry out failure analysis by constituting inter-disciplinary teams. Failure analysis includes frequency of failure, cost of resultant lost production, and cost of resultant maintenance resources used. The result of this analysis is useful for corrective maintenance decision-making.
16. To carry out maintenance cost control through :
    (a) identification of high cost area of maintenance.
    (b) monitoring the trend of maintenance effectiveness, and
    (c) proving information for maintenance decision-making.

2.4 Types of Maintenance

Generally maintenance can be done in the following two types :

1. Breakdown maintenance
2. Preventive maintenance

In the first case of maintenance, repair is done after the breakdown occurs, while in the second case maintenance is done on the basis of prediction or on the basis of periodical checking.

2.4.1 Breakdown Maintenance

Breakdown of a machine can occur due to the following two reasons :

(i) Due to unpredictable failure of components which cannot be prevented;
(ii) Due to gradual wear and tear of the parts, which can be eliminated to a large extent by regular inspections, known as preventive maintenance. From experience it can be decided that, when a part should be replaced, so that breakdown can be avoided.

In breakdown maintenance, defects are rectified only when the machine cannot perform its function may longer, and the production department is compelled to call on the maintenance engineers for the repairs. After repairing the defect, the maintenance engineers do not attend the machine again until another failure occurs.

In this type of maintenance, repair shall have to be done on failure, thus it may disrupt the hole production, if it is performing an important work. This method is much expensive also due to increase of depreciation cost, payment to idle operators, overtime to the maintenance staff for doing the emergency repairs, and idling of matching equipment.

2.4.2 Preventive Maintenance

Preventive maintenance is sometimes termed as "planned maintenance" or "scheduled maintenance" or "systematic plant maintenance" etc. It is an extremely important function for the reduction of maintenance cost and to keep the good operational condition of equipment and hence increases the reliability. Preventive maintenance aims to locate the sources of trouble and to remove them before the breakdown occurs.

Thus it is based on the idea "prevention is better than cure". Scheduled maintenance is always economical than unscheduled maintenance, as we all know that,"a stitch in time saves nine."

Best safeguard against costly breakdowns is to inspect, lubricate and check up the equipment as frequently as possible. To take full use of equipment and to maintain it in reliable condition, necessary measures should be taken to prevent overloading, dampness, negligence and misuse of machines. Frequency of inspection should be decided on the basis of the importance of the machine; wear and tear of the machine and its delicacy. Thus, periodic inspection or checking helps to find out the reasons leading to breakdown and to rectify them, when they are in minor stages. Thus, the repair can be done when one wants to do it, *i.e.,* when it has least effect on the production schedule. Further this repair requires lesser time as compared to that of breakdown repair and thus down time is reduced by doing preventive maintenance.

Objectives of Preventive Maintenance

Preventive maintenance has following main objects :

1. To obtain maximum availability of the equipment by avoiding breakdowns and by reducing the shutdown periods to a minimum.
2. To keep the machine in proper condition so as to maintain the quality of the product.
3. By minimising the wear and tear, preserve the value of the equipment.
4. To ensure for the safety of the workers.
5. To keep the plant at the maximum production efficiency.
6. To achieve all the above objectives with most economical combination.

Functions or Elements of Preventive Maintenance

Following are some of the important functions of the preventive maintenance programme :

1. Inspection or check-ups.
2. Servicing including cleaning, cooling and lubrication.
3. Planning and scheduling.
4. Records and analysis.
5. Training to maintenance staff.
6. Storage of spare parts.

1. Inspection or Check-ups

Inspection is an essential function of the preventive maintenance programme. Crews kept for this purpose should be well-trained. These crews carry out both the external and internal inspection. External inspection means to which for an detect defects from abnormal sound, vibration, heat, smoke etc. when machine is in operation; while internal inspection means inspection of internal parts, such as gears, bushes, bearings, tolerances in the parts, etc. during the period when the machine is under preplanned shutdowns.

Frequency of inspection should be decided very carefully, as too less inspection may cause breakdown, as defects could not be traced out and rectified immediately; while too much inspection means wastage of machine time and labour productivity. Hence, frequency should be decided on the basis of past experiences and accordingly the scheduled programme for inspection is chalked out.

For the purpose of inspection machines can be categorised as :

(i) Important Machines : These are those machines which can disrupt whole of the production, are delicate and require much time for the repair. More stress should be given for the inspection of these machines, and schedule for inspection, cleaning, lubrication, should be followed too rigidly.

(ii) Ordinary Machines : Frequency of inspection can be kept as low as they do not effect the production considerably.

2. Servicing

Mechanical components like gears, bearings, bushes and other friction surfaces give good performance for long periods, when they are systematically lubricated. Systematic lubrication means the application of right type of lubricant at the right time, at the right place and in right quantity. For servicing, a schedule should be prepared and followed strictly. Servicing includes cleaning, lubrication and check-ups.

3. Planning and Scheduling

Every preventive maintenance work should be pre-planned in detail on the basis of the analysis done on the past records. A scheduled programme thus prepared should be followed strictly. Thus, programme should be in detail specifying the points requiring daily, weekly, monthly, half yearly or yearly attention. Recommendations of the equipment manufacturer should also be kept in view.

4. Records and Analysis

Good record keeping is essential for good preventive maintenance as it helps in forecasting maintenance. For this purpose following records are generally maintained (i) Operation manual, (ii) Maintenance instruction manual, (iii) History cards and History registers, (iv) Spares procurement register, (v) Inspection register, (vi) Log books, (vii) Defects register etc. with the help of these records possible cause for major repetitive failures can be examined and rectified so as not to repeat so early.

These records help the managers to take decisions and plan maintenance.

5. Training of Maintenance Personnel

For the success of preventive maintenance a sound training is essential for the maintenance personnel. Hence the technicians and supervisors are trained to carry out maintenance, inspection and repairs in a systematic way.

6. Storage of Spare Parts

Sometimes machine remains idle for want of spare parts for a considerable time and thus it results in considerable loss of production. Hence, it is essential to keep the spare parts so as to avoid loss of production. But the judgement and experience of high order is required for deciding the number of such parts, as storage of a large number of parts will mean blocking of capital. The level of spare parts must be determined by considering different factors such as source of supply, delivery period and availability of that spare parts in the market.

Standardisation will help to reduce the spare parts inventory and will also help in specialisation of maintenance of particular type of equipment.

Advantages of Preventive Maintenance

Following are some of the important advantages of efficiently planned and well executed preventive maintenance programme :

(i) Reduction in production downtime.
(ii) Lesser overtime payment for maintenance personnel.
(iii) Lesser number of standby equipments are needed.
(iv) Less expenditure on repairs.
(v) Due to planned spare parts replacement, lesser spare parts are needed to remain in store at all-times.
(vi) Greater safety to employees because of reduced breakdowns.

2.5 Economics of Preventive Maintenance

Extent of preventive maintenance should be such that it may not become uneconomical. For this purpose cost of break-downs and cost of scheduled maintenance are to be studied. This cost should include expenditure of idle men, cost of idle machine, spoilage etc. It is natural that when the cost of scheduled maintenance increases, the cost of breakdown decreases. But after some extent, increase in the expenditure on scheduled maintenance becomes uneconomical. For this purpose these two costs should be plotted in a graph and cumulative costs of both types of maintenances are superimposed in this graph, as shown in the following Fig. 2.1, from which on optimum point can be determined,which gives the quantum of maintenance.

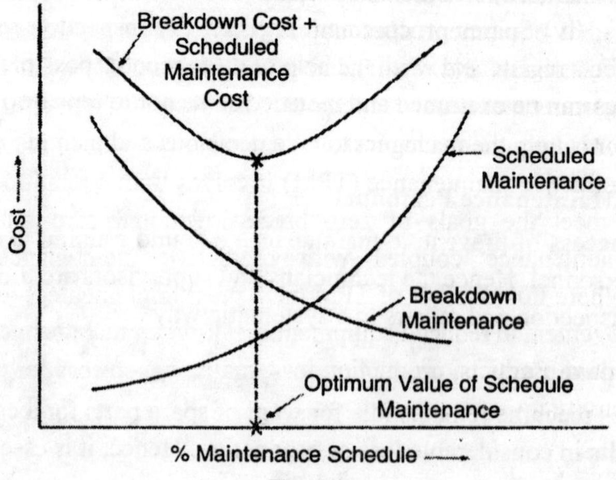

Fig. 2.1

From the economic point of view, it is also necessary to decide the quantum of inspection very carefully on the basis of past experience and records analysis as explained earlier. As over inspection costs more and results in large loss in production time, while under inspection results in more break-downs.

Care should also be taken, while preparing maintenance programme, so that as far as possible inspection and lubrication schedule should coincide, so that machine idle time and production disruption may be less. Inspection and lubrication schedules must be communicated to the production department, so that it may be able to free the machine as per programme.

Daily maintenance is done by the operators themselves. Before starting the work of their shift, cleaning, oiling and greasing should be done by the operators. For this purpose manufacturers used to issue maintenance instructions for their machines, which should strictly be followed.

Preventive maintenance of the machine depends largely on the operators. Hence, as far as possible, one operator for each machine be allotted; and when the same machine is used in more than one shift, one operator for each machine for each shift be allotted.

Periodic Maintenance is generally conducted by the maintenance crew, specially trained for this purpose. The period should be decided on the basis of past experience as explained earlier. Apart from this, operating instructions should carefully be followed by the operators. In case any abnormal sound or behaviour is noticed in machine, he should immediately bring this to the notice of maintenance crew, so that the defect can be rectified immediately. Care must be taken that it may not be left for the later date.

2.6 Latest Maintenance Management Techniques

2.6.1 Total Productive Maintenance (TPM)

In this system operators are incharge of all maintenance works. Just as man looks after his own health, operators look after the well being of their own equipment and carry out daily maintenance work such as clean up, lubrication, tightening and external inspection so that equipment does not fall sick. Whereas Maintenance Deptt. is responsible of overhauls and repairs,and gives advice and guidance to the operation department regarding maintenance methods. This system can be compared with the job of car driver and garreage mechanics.

Total productive maintenance (TPM) involves both operation and maintenance personnel to meet the goals of zero break-down and zero-defects by adopting preventive maintenance coupled with predictive maintenance and condition monitoring. Where this concept of TPM have been implemented, results have shown sizeable improvement in reduced equipment break-down maintenance costs, inventory costs, substandard products, production loss, maintenance cost per unit and increased labour productivity.

TPM covers the following :

(a) Restoring TPM is aimed for maintaining equipment at optimal levels.

(b) Understanding failure modes and controlling the source of their cause.

(c) Planning maintenance based on actual equipment condition.

(d) Improving reliability, maintainability and operability.

(e) Applying predictive and condition based monitoring.

Main Functions of TPM

(i) Eliminate unnecessary and unplanned downtime.

(ii) Eliminate equipment related quality problems and improve machine operability and maintainability.

(iii) Rigorous preventive maintenance programme, coupled with predictive and condition monitoring, be adopted to control deterioration with the cooperation of operation and maintenance personnel.

(iv) To impart training to upgrade operation and maintenance skills.

(v) Quality and maintenance teams to identify and control the equipment conditions to assure key product quality characteristics.

(vi) Information system be developed for operation, adjustment and maintenance with higher reliability.

Losses to be Prevented by TPM

(a) Losses of production and in repair due to breakdown.

(b) Set-ups and adjustment loss after shutdown is over.

(c) Idling and other minor stoppages less after shutdown.

(d) Loss due to slow performance of equipment because of its poor condition.

2.6.2 Zero Break-down Concept

As we know that breakdowns occur due to equipment disorders, *i.e.,* defects which remain invisible for one or the other reason and remain unattended. If defects are exposed and corrected in time, break-downs can be reduced to zero. This is the principle behind the zero defect concept. For zero break-down following actions are necessary :

1. Maintain equipment in good condition by cleaning, lubrication, bold tightening and carrying out other adjustments.
2. Adhere to good operating conditions.
3. Correct the design weaknesses.
4. Restore deterioration.
5. Improve operating and maintenance skills.

For achieving zero break-down object the operator should be given more responsibilities. He should be responsible for :

(a) Maintaining equipment in good condition through cleaning, lubrication, nut-bolt tightening and carrying out timely adjustments.

(b) Carrying out proper operation and visual inspection.

(c) Detecting deterioration through visual inspection, sound and other abnormalities noticed during operation.

2.7 Corrective Maintenance

Although this is broadly a preventive maintenance. While carrying out repairs on an equipment, either some minor modification work is done so that it may work little better than it was working before break-down, or some remedial action is introduced in such a way that it does not happen again, such works fall under the category of corrective maintenance.

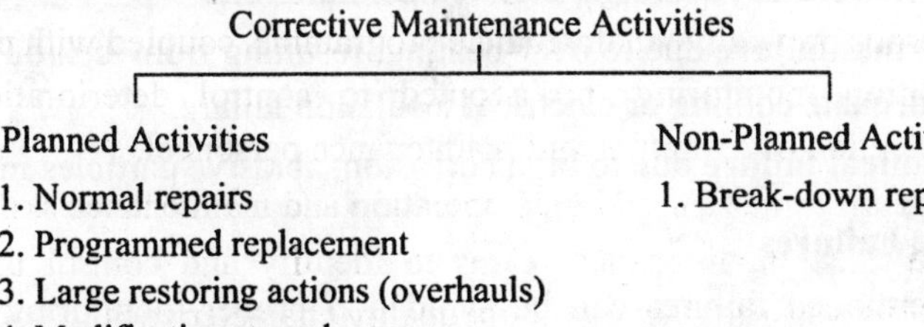

Whereas Preventive maintenance is responsible for cleaning the equipment, lubrication to prevent wear, programmed replacement and it also indirectly deals with condition monitoring, failure statistics, and adjustments to limit wear. Corrective maintenance deals with normal repairs, programmed replacements, modifications to reduce requirement of maintenance, and overhauls in addition to break-down repairs.

2.8 Condition Monitoring (Preventive Maintenance)

This is also used alongwith preventive maintenance. In this system, health of the equipment is regularly monitored and recorded in the form of mechanical vibrations, noise, acoustic, thermal emissions, changes in chemical composition, smell, pressure, relative displacement etc. This helps in diagnosis and detection of faults. Vibrations and noise are most valuable signals. Conditions monitoring can be applied in following three ways :

1. Qualitative checks based on look, sound and feel through simple inspection.
2. Condition checking by measuring some parameters regularly.
3. Trend monitoring by making measurements and plotting them in order to detect gradual departure from a norm.

Condition monitoring is the **condition based maintenance** and is concerned with extracting information from machine to indicate its condition and to enable them to be operated and maintained with safety and economy. The use of condition monitoring and non-destructive testing is the part of maintenance strategy with the aim to maximise the availability of the equipment.

With the advancement that has taken place in recent past in the field of **predictive or diagnostic maintenance** system, it is possible to predict the failure of machine much before they occur, so that maintenance staff can prepare themselves and arrange necessary parts required and skilled manpower for repairs to put the machine back on work.

Types of Failures

In order to study the failure we must understand the type of failure, which can be classified as follows :

(a) **Mechanical failure** due to vibration, mis-alignment, imbalance, fatigue, bad or worn out bearings, high temperatures etc.

(b) **Thermal failure** due to over-heating, resulting from lack of lubrication or in-adequate cooling or electrical insulation failure.

(c) **Chemical failure** due to high corrosion, abrasive particles in the fluids.

Monitoring the Failures

Above mentioned failures can be avoided if proper monitoring is done. For monitoring, various devices employed are :

1. Monitoring, Mechanical Failures

(i) **Shock Pulse Meter :** It detects the defects in rolling elements, like ball and roller bearings well in advance.

(ii) **Vibration Meter :** It measures vibration level to assess whether it is within the safe limits.

(iii) **Vibration Analysis :** It measures amplitude of vibration at different frequencies so as to know the reason for undue high vibrations.

(iv) **Ultrasonic Flow Detector :** It detects minor cracks.

(v) **Mechanical or Electrical Strain Gauge :** It measures deflection of foundations, columns etc.

2. Monitoring Thermal Failures

(i) **Infra-red Thermometer :** It detects hot spots for bearing and other parts of the machinery by the remote sensing.

(ii) **Thermo-vision :** This displays the hot spot detected by above device on the video screen.

3. Techniques for Maintenance

Latest techniques adopted by the engineers for correction are :

(i) **Plasma Spraying of Metal/Alloys : It helps in restoring worn-out parts to original dimensions and make them corrosion and erosion resistant.**

(ii) **Metalock system of repairing of cracks prevent its spreading further.**

(iii) **Eutectic Welding Techniques :** For depositing hard surfacing materials on worn-out parts, which can be later on machined to the required dimensions and tolerances.

(iv) **Heavy chromium plating** techniques for restoring worn-out shafts, bearings etc.

2.9 Reclamation of Equipment

Heavy earthmoving and other construction equipment are subjected to vigorous service conditions with impact, abrasion and heat as main wear factors. The vital parts which wear-off very fast need replacement. In view of high costs, inventory holding costs and poor availability these are beneficial to be reclaimed. Reclaimation is done with the object to restore a worn area to its original dimensions and improve its wear-resistance.

So as to select a proper material for relaimation, it is essential to understand the **type of wears.**

1. **Corrosion :** It is deterioration of material due to chemical action of gases or liquids.
2. **Erosion :** It is wasting away of materials by prolonged contact with an unfriendly environment like acid, heat etc.
3. **Friction :** It is the rubbing of one surface against the other. In extreme cases it leads to freezing or seizing.
4. **Impact :** It is sudden shock loads causing localised compression or deformation.
5. **Abrasion :** It is the grinding action by a solid sliding or rubbing against a surface.

2.9.1 Reclamation Techniques

Worn out parts are required to be reclaimed, but conventional process of welding may generate stresses, which causes distortion, cracks, warping or weakening of metal parts. Therefore, it is necessary to control heat input and obviate its detrimental effects on the base material.

1. Low Heat Input

The term welding means heating two pieces of metal until they melt and fuse together into one mass. This high heat necessary to produce fusion also produces many other undesirable changes in the molecular structure of the material and other defects as mentioned in the previous paragraph.

For fusion welding in cast iron it is necessary to heat the metal at its melting point (1150°C approx.), while by adopting 'Low heat input' method, it can be joined at around 800°C. This can be achieved by the diffusion of the atoms of the base metal into the filler metal, using a solvent. By adding this solvent melting point is reduced.

Similarly by using a solvent copper which melts at 1083°C can be made to melt at 720°C.

In this way, we can combine the advantages of brazing temperatures with the strength and homogeneous joints achieved with fusion welding. Due to low heat input, the distortion, brittlement, porosity and cracking etc. encountered with conventional fusion welding are minimised.

Advantages of Low Heat Input Concept

1. It minimises distortion, warping and cracking.
2. It minimises effect on grain structure of base metal.
3. It covers wide range of base metals weldability with increased service life before failure.
4. It helps in reducing shock.

Low heat input type electrodes are being marketed mainly under the trade names 'Eutectic' and 'Oerlikon Fon'.

2. Powder Coatings

Powder is comprehensively deposited through a low heat input process. This process effects a metallurgical solid state bond with the base metal at temperatures well below the melting point of the component. Variety of powders are available for deposition on different materials. The selected powder is flame sprayed, by means of an oxyacetylene delivery system, on to the work piece surface to bond with the base metal. This enable to deposit the coating evenly and in controlled thickness.

Oxyacetylene system which is used for spraying the powder, carry this powder through the, partial vacuum created by passage of oxygen through an injector aspirator, and is controlled by a lever activated by the operator. Acetylene is introduced after the powder is injected in the oxygen supply.

3. Cold Application Compounds

This is a revolutionary step in the field of repair and protective maintenance, as these compounds are stable, form a strong bond with almost all base metals, offer quick, simple, very economical, requires no welding equipment, power or gases, can be applied at room temperature, no heat input is required and very easily to apply. The compound is applied after mixing with the 'reagent'. This attains the properties to combat abrasion, impact, corrosion, cavitation and erosion after it is cured. Preparation required before applying is only to clean for freeing the surface from grease, oil etc. and removes oxides, rust, paint and other foreign matter. After the compound is cured and hardened, finishing can be done to make the item of required size.

4. Welding Techniques

Types of Materials : Majority of equipment components are manufactured from :

1. Plain carbon and alloy steel
2. Cast iron
3. Stainless steel
4. Manganese steel

Following parameters should be considered for metal deposition by welding.

(a) Plain Carbon and Low Alloy Steel

1. **Weldability :** Weldability decreases with the increase in carbon components and alloying elements.
2. **Thickness and Pre-Heat Temperature :** Higher the thickness more the heat discipation and accordingly higher the preheat temperature is to be maintained during heat deposition.
3. **Selection of Electrodes :** This depends upon material composition, amount of wear, and economics of the process.

(b) Cast Iron

Welding of cast iron is very difficult and complicated task, because the metal is prone to structural changes during heating and cooling, poor ductility, tensile strength, graphite flakes in structure, and practically zero impact value, pour weldability and sensitive to section, size and shape which cause sudden failure and appearance of cracks. Cast iron components generally need either deposition of metal on worn out surfaces or joining of broken or cracked components. Following steps and precautions should be taken for welding on cast iron.

1. Components should be free from cracks and dust and then should be cleaned with kerosene.
2. Locate two ends of cracks and drill 20-25 mm at both the crack ends. Prepare V groove by grinding.
3. Pre-heat the location by indirect heating upto 150-250°C.
4. Deposit buttering run on the side wall V groove with special type of low hydrogen, mild steel electrode. It gives sound, crack free base or subsequent nickel deposit by pure nickel electrode.

(c) Stainless Steel

Following steps are taken for stainless steel :

1. Identify base material composition.
2. Select Electrode nearest to the base material composition.
3. Pre-heat base and maintain the temperature during welding.
4. Anneal after welding (heating to 700-750°C, keeping for 10 minutes followed by slow cooling).

(d) Manganese Steel

In this material, it is better to put a cushioning run of crack-free weld deposit preferably with 16% Cr, 4% Mn or 29% Cr/9 Mn type of electrode.

5. Thermal Spraying Technology

Thermal spraying is an advance technology for repair and salvage of components. In this, processes and materials offer a very large scope to repair or salvage components with superior surface property for wear resistance due to alloy properties of sprayed material. To achieve good results a proper selection of thermal spray procedure and spray coating material is important.

Following are the basic thermal spraying processes which are widely used with certain variations :

(a) Oxy-acetylene flame spraying

(b) Electrical arc spraying

(c) Plasma arc spraying

(a) Oxy-Acetylene Flame Spraying : This is one of the earliest development in the field of Thermal Spraying Technology. In this process oxy-acetylene flame was used to heat low melting metal like Zinc, Aluminium, and their alloys to their molten state and an air jet from compressed air was used to atomise the molten item into fine particles and carry particles with some velocity through a thermal spraying gun, to strike a roughened surface of base metal, producing a sprayed coating. The bond between sprayed coating and sub-state was purely a mechanical one and the adhesion of coating to sub-strata varied depending upon the type of surface cleanliness and roughening.

(b) Electric Arc Spraying : This process utilises the heat of electric arc produced between two metallic wires, which melts the wire tips, and the molten metal so produced is then atomised by a compressed air jet and accelerated to strike at great velocity with sub-strata and thus forming a sprayed coating.

(c) Plasma Arc Spraying : This is the most advanced thermal spraying process representing the highest degree of automation to produce newer grades of sprayed coatings for the aero-space, aircraft and engineering components. In this process a non-transferred arc plasma of extremely high thermal capacity, with a flame temperature of 15,000°C, heats and melts high melting materials like ceramics, *viz.* oxides, cements, carbides and accelerates these molten particle to velocity as high as 1200 ft/sec to produce highly dense and strongly adherent coatings.

2.9.2 Advantages of Reclamation

1. Downtime due to replacement delays minimised.
2. Extends working life and reduces downtime.
3. Wastage is minimised.
4. Greater utilisation of equipment and manpower through minimised downtime and rejects.
5. Saves the cost of new parts.
6. Inventories of replacement parts can be reduced substantially.
7. Repair is easy and can be carried out by average skilled workmen in own workship.

8. Reclaimed item is reliable.
9. There is very less chances of warpage, distortion and other stresses in the original parts as reclaimation techniques to not required high temperature.

2.10 Maintenance Planning

Maintenance management is basically a system for planning and controlling the accomplishment. Since over-maintenance and under-maintenance, both are uneconomical, it is necessary to have optimum maintenance. To control down time, maintenance planning is very important, which means planning of spares, machines, craftsmen for the job, and the time in consultation with production department.

Following procedure should be followed for establishing a maintenance plan for a plant or equipment :

1. Determine critical units of plant and equipment.
2. Classify the plant into constituent items.
3. Determine the effective maintenance procedure for each item.
4. Establish a plan for the identified maintenance work.
5. Establish guidelines for items which fail randomly and without warning.
6. Establish a schedule for maintenance work.

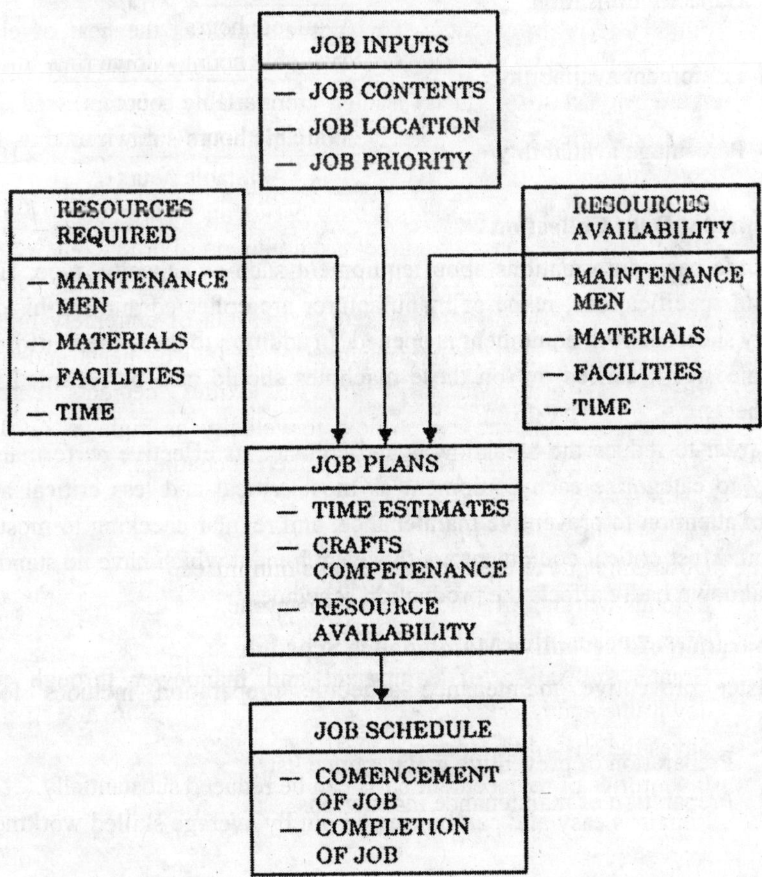

Fig. 2.2

Maintenance Planning Approach

Maintenance planning is required to be carried out in following phases :

(a) Equipment availability and utilisation study.

(b) Equipment data collection.

(c) Preparation of master preventive maintenance schedules and routine inspection check lists.

(d) Development of maintenance information system.

These are discussed hereunder :

(A) Equipment Availability and Utilisation

An analysis of past data can provide information regarding equipment performance. Equipment utilisation indicates the performance of production department and gives capacity utilisation for a section/plant. Whereas equipment availability indicates the performance/effectiveness of maintenance. In mathematical form these can be expressed as follows :

(a) Equipment utilisation factor $= \dfrac{\text{Operating hours}}{\text{Availability hours}}$

or Capacity utilisation $= \dfrac{\text{Operating hours}}{\text{Available hours}} \times 100$

(b) Equipment availability $= \dfrac{\text{Available hours} - \text{down time}}{\text{Available hours}}$

or Percentage availability $= \dfrac{\text{Available hours} - \text{down time}}{\text{Available hours}} \times 100$

(B) Equipment Data Collection

All the basic informations about equipment such as capacity, type, H.P., and other main specifications, name of manufacturer are collected and the history card (or history sheet) of each equipment is opened. In addition to these basic informations, maintenance work carried out on these machines should also be recorded in these history sheets.

In order to reduce the breakdowns and enhance its effective performance, it is necessary to categorise each equipment as most critical and less critical and give maximum attention to preventive maintenance, and regular checking to most critical equipment. Most critical equipment are those equipment which have no stand-by and their breakdown badly affects the production schedule.

(C) Preparation of Preventive Maintenance Schedule

Master preventive maintenance schedule preparation includes following activities :

(i) Preparation of preventive maintenance list.

(ii) Preparation of maintenance instructions.

(iii) After preparing the preventive maintenance list and preparing cards for each machine, the master schedules are prepared for all the similar machines. The master schedules are prepared in such a way that the work load is distributed uniformly in all the weeks of the year.

(D) Development of Maintenance Information System

Maintenance information system should be developed in such a way that, proper follow-up, control, data collection and updating of history sheets can be easily and regularly done.

Maintenance Manpower Planning

Manpower is main resource and hence demand maximum attention. Manpower planning involves following activities :

(i) Define overall company objectives and then convert them into man-power objectives.

(ii) Design the manpower information system and undertake a manpower inventory.

(iii) Analyse manpower requirement.

(iv) Analyse manpower availability and improve manpower utilisation.

(v) Identify training needs and arrange training.

(vi) Control labour costs on maintenance.

Manpower Requirement

Following factors are considered for deciding the manpower requirement :

(i) Complexity of job.

(ii) Periodicity of activities and time required for each of these activities.

(iii) Quantum and type of work.

(iv) Layout and locations of equipment.

(v) Allowances for leave, holidays, shifts etc.

Job description of each category of manpower is then prepared considering all the jobs to be performed. Total crew strength requirement is calculated considering total work contents in planned maintenance as well as the breakdown maintenance work. The work content are found out by applying any of the work measurement techniques.

Total crew size can be calculated on the basis of total work content and the available hours/year per person. Provision is also made for shift relief and leave reserve.

2.11 Maintenance of Construction Equipment

Maintenance of construction equipment can be done in two ways : (i) Maintenance at a central place, or (ii) maintenance at the work site by using mobile servicing units. The projects located at one place only prefer central maintenance centres, whereas large projects where equipments are distributed over a large area prefers maintenance at the work site by using mobile servicing units. The maintenance work of an equipment is carried out after the working hours, *i.e.*, when it is not used. Maintenance broadly includes following aspects :

1. Servicing　　2. Field repairs　　3. Inspection

1. Servicing

For the purpose of servicing, mobile servicing trailors having facility to store all the oils and lubricants, with pumps, grease guns, air compressor, water tank etc. are employed to attend the equipments at work site. The servicing includes following works :

(a) Cleaning　　(b) Cooling

(c) Lubrication　　(d) Check-ups.

(a) Cleaning : Dirt is a major cause of breakdown in the equipments, and damages bearing due to its abrasive action and the clog ventilation passages. It should be blowed with dry compressed air or using water under pressure.

(b) Cooling : Entire cooling system should be checked and adjustments are made wherever necessary. Cooling system checking includes, checking of fan belt and its tension, water pump, pump seals, radiator etc. For the purpose of cleaning the radiator, always use compressed air or soft and clean water.

(c) Lubrication : Lubrication is an important function of servicing and is meant for applying right type of lubricant at the right place, at the right time and in right quantity. Manufacturers used to recommend a lubrication schedule and type of lubricant to be used. Since construction equipments are required to work in adverse conditions, *i.e*, in dirt, mud, water, extreme weather conditions etc., these should be provided full attention for proper lubrication to reduce breakdowns and to improve performance. Following types of lubricants are generally used :

(i) Engine oil　　(ii) Gear oil　　(iii) Hydraulic oil

(iv) Heavy duty grease　　(v) Track roll grease.

(i) Engine oils have anti-wear properties, protection from rust and corrosion. The oils are defined by S.A.E. numbers. The S.A.E. numbers refer to the viscosity of oil. Viscosity is a measure of resistance to flow. When an oil loses its ability to perform any of its functions, namely, to lubricate, cool, seal and clean, it is said to be worn out. The oil gets contaminated in the engine with unburnt and partially burnt fuel, fuel combustion products including water, dirt and dust. This destroy the oil's ability to function efficiently and therefore the oil should be drained and discarded before it reaches to this stage. Therefore, the oil changing is recommended at particular interval to run the engine better and longer.

The manufacturer recommends the schedule after carrying out various experiments on the oil samples taken at various intervals. The experiments are conducted to measure microscopic wear particles, which pass through oil filters. These particles indicate the position of wear of different parts of the equipment : like 'iron' particles indicates oil pump wear,shaft wear and liner wear : 'chromium' shows wear of piston rings, bearings, valve stems; 'aluminium' represents piston or bearing wear; 'silicon' indicates dirt entry.

(ii) Gear oils cling to tooth surface even at high pressures, temperatures and peripheral speeds, and absorb shock loads and prevent scoring under heavy loads. These have anti-wear and anti-corrosion properties. These also perform the function of cooling, lubricating and cleaning the gears. Periodic changes of gear oil safeguards against future gear failures by eliminating dirt, water and wear metal contamination which may otherwise cause abrasion, corrosion or wear of gears and bearings. Equipments operating in deep mud or water should be checked frequently for contamination.

(iii) Hydraulic oils are used to act as medium of transmitting power and also provide for lubrication and cooling of the system components. Hydraulic oils are light mineral oils and are used to prevent wear and rust and resist oxidation. Foam is caused by entrained air or water. The hydraulic oils should, therefore, have antifoam property, over extended use or poor condition of the equipment or a localised hot spot sometimes 'burn' the oil and may turn the hydraulic oil to dark and thus makes it ineffective.

(iv) Heavy duty greases are used in bearings and gears and are capable of withstanding heavy wheel bearing loads and has water resistant properties.

(v) Track roll greases are used for track-roller bearings, and has good mechanical stability and anti-oxidant properties.

Oils and Lubricants : Oils, lubricants and greases are used for reducing friction between rubbing solid surfaces or moving parts and also for carrying away heat from surfaces. Lubricants of recommended grade and brands of good companies should only be used.

(d) **Check-ups :** While doing servicing, it is necessary to check-up all components which are sensitive. All nuts and bolts found loose during servicing should invariably be tightened. Loose chains and belt drives should also be tightened. Inflation pressure in the tyres, proper adjustment of the track, checking of ropes, cutting blades etc. are important aspects of servicing. A check list for each type of equipment should be made available to the servicing crew so that a thorough and systematic check-up of all the important systems is done by the crew.

A servicing station should have following equipment for servicing :

- Car lift
- Axle stand

- Battery charging and testing equipment
- Lubrication bay .
- Valve reseating kit
- Fuel injector test
- Fuel pump tester
- Tool box
- Compression gauge
- Old and grease guns
- Oils and grease in suitable size containers
- Hydraulic jack
- Air compressor with hoses
- Plug cleaning and testing equipment
- Wheel balancer
- Vacuum gauge
- Nozzle and needle grinding and lapping machines
- Bench nozzle testing and cleaning equipment
- Tyre repair equipment.

2. Field Repairs

A field maintenance workshop should be established to cater for day to day needs of the entire fleet of the equipments working in the work area. It should have sufficient space for keeping field stores and tools, and should be supplied with electric power, water, servicing station and compressed air. Workshop should be equipped with benches, vices, hand drills, grinders jacks, tyre repair facilities, welding equipment, gantry crane and a blacksmith's shop etc. Necessary machine tools, like small lathe, pillar drilling machine etc. are provided in a separate machine shop or in a mobile workshop mounted on a truck. This workshop helps to carry out miner repairs in the equipment.

3. Inspection of Equipments

Equipments should be inspected at regular specified intervals to detect faults which can be rectified in time to avoid breakdowns. The purpose of the inspection of equipment by the inspection crew is to bring into light about—defects in operation, change in adjustments, wear and tear, cracks or any other indication for likely breakdown in near future. If the defects are of minor nature, it can be rectified by the inspection crew at the work site itself, otherwise equipment has to be repaired in workshop.

The frequency of inspection should be decided on the basis of importance of the activity on which the equipment is used, manufacturer's recommendation, age of the equipment, nature of work and environment. A scheduled programme for each equipment with a checklist is prepared and given to the inspection crew.

It is very important to decide, when to inspect? How to inspect? and what to inspect? Inspection covers all important components including battery, electric line, fuel supply line, water cooling system, tyres, wire ropes, engine sound, colour of exhaust, oil pressure, engine cooling, water temperature, working of brakes, clutches, cutting edges, hydraulic oil pressure etc. It must also be thoroughly checked for the abnormal heating, noise and vibration of any moving part.

2.12 Maintenance of Main Components

The maintenance team should be formed in such a way that it includes the skilled mechanics to attend various components of the equipment, like, the engine, power transmission system, hydraulic system, electrical system etc. Here we are discussing main important components of equipments from maintenance point of view.

1. Engine

Sound of the engine during working is the the best indicator for its condition, and enables the mechanic to know which part needs his attention. All the engine manufacturers supply maintenance manual recommending the maintenance schedule and procedure for maintenance. These instructions should be adhered to strictly for better performance and trouble free operation. When engine gets clean air, fuel, water and lubrication, most of the problems would not arise.

Properly serviced air filters remove dust and dirt from the air which would otherwise results in wear and thus reduces engine life. This wear increases fuel dilution and decreases the viscosity of the crank case oil and also causes more fuel consumption and less power. Recommended oils should be used in oil type air cleaners. During servicing it should be ensured that all the joints between air cleaner and the engine are tight.

Oil and fuel filters should be serviced and changed as per recommendations of manufacturer. Fuel used should be of recommended grade and brand and should be free from dust, dirt, water and other suspended impurities. The oil filters remove the solid particles formed due to wear and other reasons and thereby reduces wear and thus increases the life of engine. Whereas the change of oil at specified schedule flushes very fine solid particles out. During operation it is necessary to keep a watch on oil pressure.

Any good brand of coolant should be used, or otherwise, clean soft water should be used as coolant in the engine so that scales are not formed and deposited on the cylinder walls or in the radiator. Fan belt tension should be checked and adjusted for proper circulation of water by running the pump at proper speed. Cooling water should be replaced periodically. Operator must watch the temperature in the temperature meter.

For proper running of engine, starter, battery and other electrical items should be checked and serviced as per recommendation. In petrol engines carburator, spark plugs, distributor etc. whereas, in diesel engines, fuel injectors and fuel pumps should be cleaned, checked and adjusted at specified intervals.

2. Power Transmission

Power transmission comprises of engine clutch, torque convertor, gear box, braking, hydraulic system for power shift. Proper adjustments of clutch plate and the pedal ensures long life of clutch. The oil system of the torque converter should be checked for leakage and ensure that oil is clean. Recommended oil should only be used in gear box and should be changed periodically as per manufacturer's instructions. The periodic changes of gear oil avoids future gear failures by eliminating dirt, wear metal and water which may otherwise cause abrasion or corrosive wear of gears and bearings. When the construction equipments are operated in deep mud or water, the gear oil should be checked frequently. If any contamination is found, change the lubricant and check the oil seals for leakage.

3. Hydraulic System

This includes pump, relief valve, hoses and oil tank, which should be checked regularly as per recommendations so as to get better performance. The wear in the hydraulic pump reduces the volume of oil handled by the pump which means reduction in oil pressure and effects the efficiency of the equipment. This problem can be solved by removing one or more thin shims (thin gaskets) from the pump head. Hydraulic oil of specific grade only should be used for change at specified intervals to get better service. Oil level should be regularly checked.

Different filters provided in the system should be changed as per frequency as recommended by the manufacturers. In extreme moisture condensation, hydraulic fluid should be changed annually. Proper routing and the ambient conditions in which the hydraulic system works, affect the life of its hoses. All hose lines must be routed to prevent sharp bends, kinks or twists.

4. Tyres

Tyres should be maintained, stored and used as explained in the chapter on 'tyres'.

5. Excavation Attachments

Booms, wire ropes, buckets etc. used with excavators, cranes, power shovels and other excavation and handling equipments should be inspected frequently for avoiding possibility of accidents. The wearing of pins, bushes and bucket teeths should be inspected regularly. Sudden shocks, excessive loads, corrosion and rust should be minimised.

6. Track

Operators must exercise daily check for visual checking of loose bolts, leaking seals or abnormal wear. The tracks and rollers must be clear of mud or stones. Excess speed of the machine raises wear by 20% on pins, bushings etc. The machine must be parked on level surface to relieve the strain on roller seals that causes leakage. Undercarriage pins and bushings must be replaced when the bushing outside diameter wear reaches 0.32 m or chain pitch increases by 7.32 cm, which ever occurs first.

7. Blade and Rippers

Be sure that the bolts of cutting edges are tight. Reverse or replace cutting edges when inspection reveals wear. Dozer blades and rippers get rugged use and so are ruggedly made. Weekly inspection of these is essential. Replace broken, loose or missing bolts at once to avoid more serious repairs. Rotate cutting edges and replace end bits regularly. Replace ripper tips and shank guards before damage occurs.

8. Undercarriage of Crawler Equipments

Since these are used in different soil conditions their life fluctuates. Their life can be increased by proper maintenance and operation. This is the single unit which performs most hazardous duty and absorb approximately 50% of a machine's repair and maintenance costs, and therefore should be given maximum attention for maintenance. Following are the few important, most common and effective maintenance practices :

(i) Shifting sprocket segments from one side to another when sprockets are worn on one side only.

(ii) Turning and cleaning pins and bushings as part of the overall services programme.

(iii) Rotating center rollers with those at the front and rear of the track to ensure even wear.

(iv) Use roller guards, since these are more effective in keeping material out.

(v) Track alignment influences wear of crucial undercarriage components including sprocket teeth, idler flanges, and track roller flanges. Alignment problems are normally the result of wear, improper parts replacement or damaged track frame (by accident). Special care should be taken to prevent the adjusted track rom being too right or too loose. A tight track will impose increased wear on pins, bushings, links, sprockets and idlers etc. A loose track can be harmful to final drive bearings and gears, idler center flanges, roller flanges, pins, bushings and sprocket teeth.

2.13 Maintenance Facilities

1. Mobile Workshop

Major construction projects having equipment deployed in large area, should have mobile workshop to attend immediate repairs of the equipment. The equipment and tools included in these workshops are selected according to the kinds of work to be done and the machinery to be serviced. The workshop should be equipped with carefully selected multipurpose equipment and tools to correct most field machinery problems while occupy a limited space. A proposed list of such tools and equipment is :

(i) Engine driven generator (about 4 to 5 kW).

(ii) Engine driven arc welding machine (about 5 kW, 40-250 amps).

(iii) Gas cutting and welding set.

(iv) Air compressor (about 1 kW and 50 lit. receiver).

(v) Hydraulic jacks (10, 15 and 30 tons), chainblock (2 tons), sling chain and wire rope set.

(vi) Lubricating equipment.

(vii) Tyre service tools.

(viii) Electric tools (Drill-13 mm, bench grinder-150 mm, hand-grinder).

(ix) Engine repair tools, including nozzle tester, and compression gauge.

(x) Battery quick charger (12-24 V, 100 Amp.).

(xi) Measuring tools.

(xii) Hand tools.

(xiii) Work table and mechanic vice.

(xiv) Fire extinguisher.

2. Service Station

A service station must have following items :

(i) A hydraulic garage servicing lift. A mechanical lift can be provided for light vehicles.

(ii) A high pressure pump.

(iii) Air compressors. These may be stationary or with portable arrangements driven by electric motor or diesel engines.

(iv) Tyre inflators.

(v) Hand operated grease pumps and oil pumps.

(vi) Spark plug cleaner and tester.

3. Central Workshop

The central workshop is established in project to carry out major repairs of the construction equipment. Various facilities of the central workshop are arranged in such a way that the repair can be carried out efficiently and with minimum delay. Plants and equipments maintained, serviced and operated in a proper manner are sent to the central workshop for overhauls in a phased manner. The central workshop should have following main shops/sections so as to enable to carry out all types of repairs :

1. Machine shop, with lathe, bench grinder, drill machine.
2. Fitting shop.
3. Blacksmith shop.
4. Welding shop.
5. Electric shop.
6. Tin and coppersmith shop.
7. Carpenter and uphostry shop.

8. Engine shop with cylinder connecting rod and line boring machines.
9. Assembly and track shop.
10. Transmission, differential repair shop.
11. Hydraulic pump and hydraulic system repair shop.
12. Painting shop.
13. Foundry shop.
14. Stores.
15. Time office and record section.
16. Fuel pump test bench.
17. Service station.

Tools and Accessories

The workshop should be fully equipped with necessary tools and other accessories. A central workshop also have following main tools and other machines to carry out repair/inspection in a proper method :

1. Cylinder boring and honing equipment.
2. Connecting rod boring and aligning equipment.
3. Valve grinding.
4. Tyre test tank and vulcanizer.
5. Brake drum turning and relining machine.
6. Chassis alignment.
7. Wheel alignment tools.
8. Brake testing equipment.
9. Portable electrical equipment for testing alternator, distributor, ignition and timing etc.
10. Head lamp beam checker.
11. Drilling machine (Pillar and hand).
12. Grinding machine (Bench and hand).
13. Centre lathe.
14. Welding set (Electrical as well as gas).
15. Jib crane.
16. Battery charger.
17. Nozzle grinder.

4. Medium Size Workshop

Central workshop for medium size project (project having about 100 construction equipment) must have all the tools mentioned above, *i.e.*, in the second paragraph under heading 'central workshop', in addition to a service station.

QUESTIONS

1. Write an essay on the "importance of the maintenance".
2. Explain how the preventive maintenance is better than break-down maintenance.
3. How will you evaluate maintenance performance?
4. Explain different functions of preventive maintenance.
5. Explain the statement, "Extent of preventive maintenance should be such that, it may not become uneconomical".
6. Discuss planned maintenance strategies.
7. What are the requirements of a good preventive maintenance?
8. Write short notes on :
   (a) Total productive maintenance.
   (b) Corrective maintenance.
   (c) Maintenance information system.
9. How will you measure various types of equipment failures?
10. (a) Describe maintenance planning approach.
    (b) How will you carry out maintenance manpower planning?
11. How will you plan for maintenance system?
12. (a) What are the objectives of maintenance?
    (b) Explain the "zero break-down" concept.
13. What is condition based maintenance? Explain in detail.
14. What is "reclamation of machinery"? Explain, how it is done?
15. Discuss advantages of reclamation.
16. Discuss various activities involved in maintenance.
17. Distinguish between "break-down", "preventive", and "predictive" type of maintenance strategies, clearly stating the type of management decisions involved in each of them.
18. What are the different types of maintenance systems? Could you give some examples for each alternative system?
19. Write short notes on :
    (a) Field repairs.
    (b) Servicing of equipment.
    (c) Maintenance of engine of a heavy earthmoving equipment.
20. Explain the necessity of a machine workshop in a major project. List out the tools and other items which should be provided in it.

21. What is the importance of a central workshop in a major construction project? List out the machine tools to be provided in it?

22. Explain the following in brief :
    (a) Economical aspects of preventive maintenance.
    (b) Predictive maintenance.
    (c) Servicing of a construction equipment.

23. Discuss important reclamation techniques generally adopted for construction equipment.

24. Write short notes on the following :
    (a) Storage and handling of lubrication.
    (b) Maintenance of hydraulic system.
    (c) Maintenance of undercarriage of crawler equipments.

Chapter 3

Economics of Construction Equipment

3.1 Introduction

Principles and techniques of engineering economics are utilised while making equipment selection and planning of finances for the purchase of construction equipments. Economics of construction equipment deals with the study of working of the equipment and to compute the unit costs of production. This economic evaluation helps in taking a decision to select an equipment or to retire it. Unit cost of production is calculated after estimating the best of production by calculating hourly ownership and operating cost of the equipment and knowing hourly production of that equipment.

Equipment selection is a decision-making from various alternatives which gives least cost of unit production considering various factors of economics being described in this chapter. It should consider the rate of interest on the equipment, time required to complete the project and effect of time on the project, as we know that time is money.

First we should understand the term economics, and engineering economics.

Economics : Economics is the science which studies human behaviour and aims at meeting maximum objectives with the help of limited resources. Economics deals with the economic problems of the people living in a society. Economics is a subject of interest to the engineers, as they have to deal with the economic problems related to increasing the production, reducing the efforts, increasing the wealth, improving the living standard, reducing the cost of products etc.

Engineering Economics : Engineering economics is the economics applied to the engineering problems and is based on economic analysis for identifying engineering problems and evaluating various alternatives utilising the economic concepts.

Engineering are required to use economic concepts for improving productivity, increasing wealth by maximising profit, cost control and cost saving, helps in decision-making, *e.g.*, selection of site, selection of equipment and their replacement analysis, material handling system selection etc. providing number of tools and techniques to solve engineering problems, resource allocation etc.

Following are the important **tools of engineering economics** which are used for solving economic problems of engineering concerns, may it be related to construction, manufacturing, mining, service or other engineering firms :

1. Models
2. Operation research
3. Break-even analysis
4. Value engineering
5. Make-buy analysis
6. Economic ordering quantity
7. Locational analysis
8. Economic theories/principles
9. Cost control and cost saving areas
10. Benefit-cost ratio.

3.2 Hourly Working Rate (Equipment Cost)

Hourly working rate of construction equipment comprises of the following components :

1. Owning Cost : It is made up of the following costs :

(a) Investment cost, (b) Depreciation cost,
(c) Major repair cost

2. Operating Costs : It includes the following costs :

(a) Cost of fuel (or power), (b) Cost of lubricants,
(c) Servicing and maintenance cost, (d) Labour cost,
(e) Cost of field repairs, (f) Various other overheads.

3.3 Owning Costs

(A) Investment Costs

This is a kind of fixed cost and continues to be incurred whether the equipment is used or not. Investment costs comprises of the following :

(a) Interest on the money invested in the procurement of the equipment
(b) Various taxes on the equipment.
(c) Insurance expenses.
(d) Storage costs.

If the money spent on the purchase of the equipment, was invested in the bank or similar other agencies, it would have earned an interest. Now this amount, equivalent to the interest, should be recovered from this equipment. The rate of interest should be equal to the prevailing bank rates.

Taxes pertaining to ownership of the equipment are those paid by the owner for the equipment. Similarly owner is also required to pay the insurance premium for the equipment, in order to cover the risk of the equipment and any other loss caused due to any accident by the equipment. Storage cost is the cost of space required by the equipment and other expenses to be incurred by the owner for keeping the equipment.

Generally these investment costs are taken as about 10 to 15% of the total cost of the equipment. This total cost comprises of the following :

(a) F.O.B. price of the equipment with all attachments and accessories.
(b) Insurance and freight charges.
(c) Expenses on un-loading, clearance and custom duty.

(d) Cost of transportation to the project site including loading and unloading.

(e) Errection and commissioning charges.

(B) Depreciation

Due to use and obsolescence every equipment loses its value. This loss is accounted for by depreciating the equipment every year. The depreciation, and obsolescence are described in detail hereunder :

1. Depreciation

Whenever any machine or equipment performs useful work its wear and tear is bound to occur. This can be minimised upto some extent by proper care and maintenance but can't be totally prevented. Its efficiency also reduces with the lapse of time and at one time it becomes uneconomical to be used further and needs replacement by new unit.

Therefore, we can say that efficiency and value of machine or asset constantly reduces with the lapse of time during use, which is known as "Depreciation". Some money must be set aside yearly from the profits, so that when an equipment becomes uneconomical, it can be replaced by the new one. Therefore, the initial cost of machine plus installation charges + repair charges—scrap value is charged against overheads and spread over the machine's useful life.

For this purpose depreciation account for an individual equipment is opened in the Company's Books and is known as "Depreciation Fund", or "Sinking Fund". This amount is deducted yearly from the profits and kept separately to have sufficient money for replacement at the end of useful life.

2. Obsolescence

Suppose a contractor purchases a machine for his production but after some duration a better machine comes in the market, whose production rate is very high and is more economical. Although the old machine is efficient but becomes out of fashion and uneconomical due to the new better machine which has come in the market. This is known as "Obsolescence". Consideration of this factor is of much importance and some money should also be set aside from the profits for this cause.

Hence, "Obsolescence" is the depreciation of existing machinery or asset due to new and better invention, design of equipment or processes etc.

It is very difficult problem for estimator to provide for the on cost on obsolescence, because no body can predict when a revolutionary change in the machine is coming in the market. But it is a general practice to reduce the life of a machine so as to account for the effect of obsolescence. The depreciation and obsolescence charges are then calculated for the reduced life.

Suppose an estimator expects the life of machine as 10 years when the depreciation rate will be 100/10 = 10%. By considering obsolescence also, its life may be taken as 8 years. Then the combined depreciation and obsolescence charges will be 100/8 = 12.50% instead of 10%. Therefore, the difference 12.50 – 10.00 = 2.50% will be obsolescence charges.

The other causes of depreciation are physical decay, accidents, deferred maintenance and neglect, inadequacy etc.

3.3.1 Types of Depreciation

For Further understanding depreciation can be classified as under :

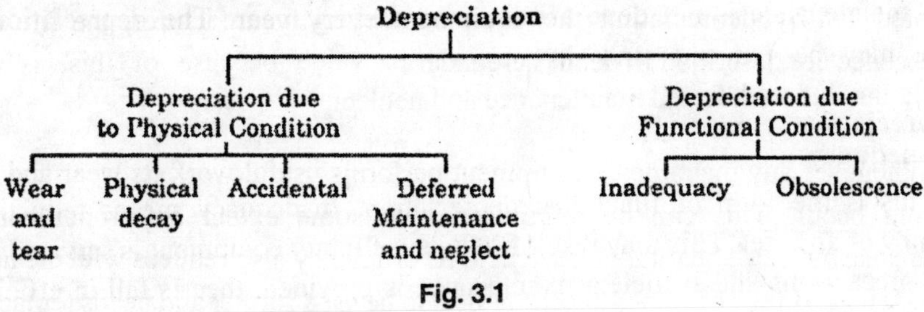

Fig. 3.1

Now, each type of depreciation is explained in short below :

(a) Depreciation Due to Wear and Tear

Everybody knows that when any machinery performs work, wear and tear of certain components takes place, although sufficient precautions are taken, *i.e.*, proper lubricating and cooling is done, which minimise wear and tear but it cannot be totally prevented. The cost of replacement because of this cause; it is the value of depreciation due to wear and tear.

(b) Depreciation Due to "Physical Decay"

There are certain items which get decay, because of climatic and atmospheric effect, with the result the value of these articles goes on reducing with the lapse of time. Although every effort is made by the owner to keep them in serviceable condition, even then because of climatic and atmospheric effect, there will be reduction in their value. This reduction in cost is depreciation due to physical decay.

(c) "Accidental" Depreciation

Although, the machine might have installed even few days back and sufficient care taken to prevent accident, even then, accident may occur due to some wrong operation, or some loose component or some other cause, which may result in a heavy damage. The depreciation in machine caused due to this reason is called accidental depreciation.

Now-a-days, to cover this risk most of the owners get their equipment insured with the insurance companies. For that owners have to pay certain premium yearly. The amount of premium depends upon the cost and life of equipment.

(d) Depreciation Due to "Deferred Maintenance and Neglect"

Every manufacturer supplies certain instructions for the smooth and efficient running of an equipment. For example, in the case of a vehicle, a manufacturer gave the following instructions :

(i) Lubricating oil 20 W 40 should be used in Engine.

(ii) Oil should be drained and new 20 W 40 oil should be refilled after prescribed running.

(iii) All the bolts and nuts should be re-tightened after recommended running.

(iv) Decarbonising after recommended running, and so on.

Now, if these instructions are not properly followed because of neglect and proper maintenance is not done as recommended by manufacturer, the life of the vehicle may be reduced, and depreciation in value because of this, is called depreciation due to deferred maintenance and neglect.

(e) Inadequacy

This is the form of functional depreciation. Inadequacy means reduction in efficiency of an asset. This may result firstly, even if any equipment is serviced under proper precautions and sufficient maintenance is provided, thee is fall in efficiency, with the lapse of time.

Secondly, suppose after 2-3 years of running, the work requirement is increased, but the plant cannot cope-up with the increased demand. This needs additional money either to replace with the bigger size plant or installation of additional similar plants. This is what is called depreciation due to inadequacy.

(f) Depreciation by Obsolescence

Now-a-days because of scientific advancement, there are large changes every day. If a new machine comes in the market which is more efficiency because of new invention and better design than the existing one, and the production by the new one is much cheaper and better then the existing machine has to be replaced to withstand market competition. This is called depreciation by obsolescence and is of functional type.

3.4 Methods of Calculating Depreciation

The following are the methods for calculating depreciation :

1. Straight line method
2. Diminishing balance method
3. Sinking fund method
4. Annuity charging method
5. The insurance policy method
6. The re-valuation or regular valuation method
7. Machine-hour basis method
8. The sum of the year's digits method

First two methods are commonly used and are described here.

(1) Straight Line Method

This method assumes that the loss of value of machine is directly proportional to its age. It means one should deduct the scrap value from the original value and divide the remaining value by the number of years of usual life.

Let C be the initial cost of a machine.

S be the scrap value.

N be the number of years of life of machine.

and D be the depreciation amount per year.

Then
$$D = \frac{C - S}{N} \text{ Rupees}$$

This method of calculating depreciation fund is also known as "Fixed Installment" method, because every year some (fixed) amount is deducted and no consideration is made about the maintenance and repair charges, which gradually increases as the machine is getting old.

■ EXAMPLE 3.1

(a) A machine was purchased for ₹ 45,000 on 1st January, 1976, the erection and installation work costs ₹ 7000. This was replaced by a new one on 31st Dec. 1995. If the scrap value was estimated as ₹ 15,000, what should be the rate of depreciation and depreciation fund on 15th June, 1985.

(b) If after 12 years of running, some assemblies are replaced and the replacement cost is ₹ 15,000, what will be the new rate of depreciation?

SOLUTION :

(a) Total cost = Machine cost + Erection and installation charges

∴ C = ₹ 45,000 + ₹ 7,000 = ₹ 52,000

Scrap value S = ₹ 15,000

Life of machine = From 1st January, 1976 to 31st Dec., 1995.

= 20 years.

∴ Rate of depreciation;

$$D = \frac{C - S}{N}$$

$$= \frac{52{,}000 - 15{,}000}{20} = \frac{37{,}000}{20} = ₹\ 1850.00$$

∴ Depreciation per year = ₹ 1850 only. **Ans.**

Now, depreciation fund on 15th June, 1985, *i.e.*, 9 Installments (from 1st January, 1976 to 15th June, 1985) could be accumulated.

∴ Depreciation fund collected upto 15 June, 1985

= ₹ 9 × 1850 = ₹ 16,650.00 only **Ans.**

(b) As after 12 years, assemblies have been replaced and cost of replacement is ₹ 15,000.

Now, book value in 12 years will be ₹ 52,000 – 12 × 1850 = ₹ 29,800.

and replacement cost = ₹ 15,000.

Hence, new book value ₹ 29,800 + ₹ 15,000 = ₹ 44,800.

As scrap value is same, *i.e.,* ₹ 15,000,hence the depreciation for the rest 8 years will be (₹ 44,800 – 15,000)

$$= ₹\ 29{,}800$$

$$\therefore \text{ New rate of depreciation} = ₹\ \frac{29{,}800}{8} = 3725$$

∴ New rate of depreciation per year = ₹ 3725. **Ans.**

(2) Diminishing Balance Method

This is also called "Reducing Balance" Method. The diminishing value of machine is greater in the early years. It depreciates rapidly in the early years and later on slowly. Therefore, it is better to depreciate more during the early years, when the repair and renewals are not costly.

So under this method, the book value of the machine goes on decreasing as its existence continues. A certain percentage of the current book value is taken as depreciation. Therefore, this is also called "Percentage on Book Value" method.

In this, let x be the fixed percentage taken to calculate the yearly depreciation on the book value.

then $$x = 1 - \left(\frac{S}{C}\right)^{1/N}$$

where, C = Initial cost, S = Scrap value, N = No. of the years of life.

It will be more clear by the following solved example.

■ EXAMPLE 3.2

A lathe is purchased for ₹ 80,000 and the assumed life is 10 years and scrap value ₹ 20,000. If the depreciation is charged by diminishing balance method, calculate the percentage by which value of the lathe is reduced every year and depreciation fund after 2 years.

SOLUTION : Here,

$$C = 80{,}000$$
$$S = 20{,}000$$
$$N = 10$$

We know that $$x = 1 - \left(\frac{S}{C}\right)^{1/N}$$

Substituting the given values in the above formula

$$x = 1 - \left(\frac{20{,}000}{80{,}000}\right)^{1/10} = 1 - (0.25)^{1/10}$$

Solving $(0.25)^{1/10}$ we get

$$(0.25)^{1/10} = 0.8706$$

$$\therefore \quad x = (1 - 0.8706) = 0.1294 = 12.94\%$$

$$\therefore \quad \text{Required \%} = 12.94$$ **Ans.**

$\therefore$ Value of lathe after 1 year = 80,000 (1 – 0.1294) = 80,000 × 0.8706
= ₹ 69648.00

$\therefore$ Depreciation fund after 1 year = 80,000 – 69648.00 = 10352.00

Now, value of lathe after 2 years = 69648.00 (0.8706)
= ₹ 60635.50

$\therefore$ Depreciation of 2nd year = 69648.00 – 60635.50 = ₹ 9012.50

$\therefore$ Depreciation fund after 2 years = 10352.00 + 9012.50 = ₹ 19364.50 **Ans.**

(3) Major Repair Cost

While minor or field repairs are carried out during the day to day working of the equipment, the major repairs are carried out after the substantial use of the equipment. Major repairs and overhauls are the replacement of major parts of the equipment because of the excessive wear through a long period of use. Since these repairs require a heavy amount of expenditure, they are met from the major repair fund. The major repair cost is spread out during the entire life span of the equipment and a flat rate is levied per working hour in order.to have a uniform rate. The amount thus collected in the pool is known as major repair fund, and major repairs and overhauls are carried out from this pool.

Usual practice is to consider this major repair cost as a percentage of straight line depreciation cost and is generally taken as 80 to 200% of the cost of depreciation depending on the type of equipments.

3.5 Operating Costs

(A) Cost of Fuel

Prime-moves for construction equipments are generally diesel engines or electric motors. The actual consumption of fuel or electricity in these construction equipment depends upon :

(i) Engine B.H.P.

(ii) The load factor, which means the extent to which the engine will operate at full power. Load factor generally very from 30% to 70%.

(iii) The condition of the engine.

Optimum fuel consumption in litres per hour per H.P. may be calculated using following formula :

Fuel consumption = 0.27 × load factor.

Equipment used in the construction industry seldom operate at a rated output, except for a short period of time.

During the balance part of its cycle the demand on the engine will be reduced substantially, resulting in decreased consumption of fuel. To allow for this the value of load factor (C) may be taken as follows as recommended by the "construction plant and machinery committee-1972 (central water and power commission)", taking into consideration the job conditions also.

S. No.	Type of equipment	Excellent	Average	Severe
1.	Wheel type equipment (Highway)	0.25	0.30	0.40
2.	Wheel type equipment (off-Highway)	0.50	0.55	0.60
3.	Track type tractors	0.50	0.63	0.75
4.	Excavators	0.50	0.55	0.60

Construction equipment is seldom operated for 60 min. In an hour and therefore, the actual fuel consumption is calculated by multiplying utilisation factor to the fuel consumption arrived from above formula.

(B) Cost of Lubricants

(i) Engine oil
(ii) Air filter oil
(iii) Transmission oil
(iv) Hydraulic oil
(v) Greases etc.

The quantity of lubricating oil depends upon various factors. Some of these factors are :

(i) Capacity of the crank case.
(ii) Condition of piston rings.
(iii) Number of hours between oil changes. This depends on the operating conditions and the manufacturer's recommendation. In extreme dusty conditions oil is required to be changed after every 50 hours of working, while in normal conditions it may vary from 100 hours to 200 hours.

Lubricating Oil Consumed : Requirement of lubricants including engine oil, air cleaner oil, transmission oil, greases and hydraulic oil, can be assessed on the basis of informations supplied by the equipment manufacturer. Although actual consumption of lubricants depend on the condition of equipment, but as a thumb rule expenditure on the lubricants can be taken as 30% of the fuel cost in diesel engine and about 20% of the fuel cost in petrol engines.

Following formula is used for estimating the quantity of oil required per hour :

$$Q = \frac{\text{H.P.} \times f \times 0.006 \times 4.5}{7.4} + \frac{C}{t} \text{ lit/hr}$$

where, Q = Quantity of oil consumed in lit/hr
H.P. = Rated horse power of the engine
f = Operating factor
C = Capacity of crankcase, in lit.
t = Number of hours between oil changes.

(C) Servicing and Maintenance Cost

Regular servicing and maintenance of each equipment is very essential in order to have the equipment in reliable and perfect condition of working. This cost includes :

(i) Change of lubricants.

(ii) Checking and servicing of fuel and lubricating systems, including change of filter elements.

(iii) Care of tyres and tubes.

(iv) Care of battery and electrical system.

(v) Cleaning of the equipment and other similar works.

(vi) Salaries of staff engaged on maintenance and servicing.

(D) Labour Cost

Labour cost is an important element of operating cost and contributing a major part of it. Labour cost element includes the salaries of operators, and helpers engaged on the equipment. Provision for leave reserve (may vary from 10 to 12%) is also made under the head of labour cost. A percentage of the wages of supervisory staff, depending upon the attention required on that particular equipment, is also to be added.

(E) Cost of Field Repairs

This is the cost incurred on minor repairs which are carried out on the site or in field workshops. These repairs include replacement of minor parts, such as fan belts, filters, bearings, wire ropes etc. and other adjustments required to be carried out during normal working of the equipment.

(F) Overheads

These are the charges which are incurred on complete fleet of the equipment. Therefore, proportional expenditure is booked under this head on each equipment. These charges includes the pay on watchman, light and water charges in the storage yards, uniform to the operating and maintenance staff etc.

Repair Reserve Fund

A provision for the repair of an equipment for its entire life is made by charging a percentage of the book value (excluding the value of tyre). The equipment earns this fund during the working of the equipment in order to carry out the repairs subsequently during its course of operation. Percentages for some of the major construction equipments are mentioned hereunder :

- Crawler tractor/Dozer 240
- Wheeled tractor/Dozer 200
- Shovels/Draglines, hydraulic excavators, vibratory compactors, wheeled loaders motorised scrapers 150
- Dumpers, tractor trailors 140
- Crawler and mobile cranes, transit mixers 120
- Air compressors and water pumps with diesel engine 100
- Air compressors with electric motors, wagon drills, concrete mixers 80
- Batching and mixing plants, towed scrapers 75

3.6 Determination of Owning and Operating Costs

To determine the cost of owning and operating, following procedure is adopted.

I. Ownership Charges

1. Depreciation

(A) Total cost of equipment less cost of tyres ₹ ______

(B) Deduct salvage value (generally 10% of A) ₹ ______

(C) Total investment to be depreciated (A – B) ₹ ______

(D) Economic life in hours ₹ ______

(E) Depreciation per hour (C/D) ₹ ______

2. Interest, Insurance, Taxes and Storage

(F) Annual expenditure on these items ₹ ______

(G) Interest, Insurance, Taxes and Storage charges/hr

$$= \left(\frac{F}{\text{Annual use in hrs.}} \right)$$ ₹ ______

Total Owning Costs = E + G ₹ ______

II. Operating Charges

3. Fuel charges

(H) Consumption in lit. per hour ₹ ______

(I) Cost of fuel per lit. ₹ ______

(J) Fuel charges/hr. (H × I) ₹ ______

4. Lubricating and filters charges

(K) Engine oil (Consumption/hr × rate) ₹ ______

(L) Transmission (Consumption/hr × rate) ₹ ______

(M) Final drive oil (Consumption/hr × rate) ₹ ______

(N) Hydraulic oil (Consumption/hr × rate) ₹ ______

(O) Grease (Consumption/hr × rate) ₹ ______

(P) Filters (Consumption/hr × rate) ₹ ______

(Q) Total lúb. and filter charges (total of K to P) ₹ ______

5. Cost of tyres

(R) Price of 1 st of tyre ₹ ______

(S) Estimated tyre life ₹ ______

(T) Cost of tyres $\left(\frac{R}{S} \right)$ per hr. ₹ ______

6. Repair charges

(U) Repair factor × Depreciation per hr. ₹ ______

7. (V) Operator's and helper's hourly wages ₹ ______

8. (W) Special items (like cutting edge, rippers, drill rods, bits etc.) ₹ ______

Total Operating Costs = J + Q + T + U + V + W ₹ ______

Total Hourly Owning and Operating Costs ₹ ______

3.7 Cost Control

Cost control is a method of comparing actual costs with predetermined standards or targets. Whereas the cost-reduction is meant to take drastic actions, sometimes by changing rigid boundaries laid down by the standards or targets. Cost control is therefore a continuous process,while cost-reduction measures are adopted only with a well-knit programme.

Costs are generally controlled through :

1. Standard costing
2. Budgetary control

1. Standard Costing

This is the set of techniques which involve the establishment of standard cost, measurement of variations of actual cost from such predetermined standard cost, analysis of reasons for variations and indicating ways to maintain and improve efficiency.

Standard cost is an estimated cost of a job or project prepared in advance of execution. This is prepared considering normal cost of normal production within normal capacity and under normal conditions and efficiency. The standard cost is determined following a systematic and scientific study of each element of cost and is for a given period and within assumed set of working conditions.

The standards should neither be unattainable nor should be such that which can be attained without any efforts. The standards are decided by using past experience and by taking the help of experiments or previously fixed norms.

Where feasible the standard costs should be developed jointly by the estimating, planning, equipment and finance departments. The standard cost of a work-package, a work-item or an activity are developed using past experiences or "time and motion studies", with all-in costs being priced at the then prevailing rates, some of the government construction agencies and established contracting firms publish their basic cost standards in the form of "standard schedule of rates".

2. Budget and Budgetary Control

Budget is a tool of management for planning its future activities including production, expenditure etc. Budget estimates are based on past experiences, present conditions and expected results and are projected in financial terms or in numerical terms, like units of production, man-hours, machine hours etc. Budget provides predetermined standards of performance which become the basis for control.

The project budget is the well coordinated and management approval financial plan of operations, indicating the amounts required for achieving assigned targets, and the expected receipts from sales or the value of work done. The project budget includes budgets at each responsibility/construction centre.

Budgetary control is the process by which the managers of responsibility/construction centres exercise control through continuous appraisals of actual expenditure and income with budgeted costs and revenue receipts. Budgetary control involves continuous checking and evaluation of actual results compared with the budget goals, thus helping in corrective action.

Standard Costing V/s Budgetary Control

(A) Common Principles :

(i) Establishing predetermined standards, target or yardstick of performance.
(ii) Measuring actual performance as compared to yardstick.
(iii) Locating variances between actuals and standard performances.
(iv) Disclosing reasons for such variances.
(v) Suggesting corrective actions, where necessary.

(B) Differences :

	Standard Costing	***Budgetary Control***
(i)	Applicable only to production, operation and project costs.	Applicable to all functional areas of an enterprise.
(ii)	More intensive in nature.	More extensive in nature.
(iii)	It is project's cost accounts.	It is project's financial accounts.
(iv)	More improved system.	Elementary system.

3.8 Cost Reduction

As discussed earlier cost-reduction measures are adopted only with a well-knit programme in various cost saving areas.

Cost Saving Areas

As we know that cost of the production consists of (i) materials cost, (ii) labour cost, (iii) overheads. Therefore, to reduce the cost, it is necessary to bring down the expenditure on these elements. Some of the areas, in which saving can be achieved are : material, labour and overheads, by way of judicious and rational distribution of manpower mainly operators, deployment of machines, increasing the utilisation and reliability of equipment, selection of right size and type of equipment and their accessories. Decision whether to use equipment or to do work with manpower also helps in reducing cost. These are illustrated hereunder :

(a) Reduction in Material Cost :

(i) Ensure purchase of right quantities of right quality at right time from right source and at right price.
(ii) Avoid overstocking or inventory build-up.
(iii) Planning material procurement in advance, scientifically and from practical consideration.

(iv) Decision regarding whether to purchase aggregate etc. or to manufacture.
(v) Minimum handling of material be ensured.
(vi) Utilise scrap and waste material.
(vii) Avoid wastage of material.

(b) Reduction in Labour Cost :

(i) Judicious and rational distribution of workmen.
(ii) Labour rate should be decided considering actual norms of output.
(iii) Suitable inspection and supervision methods be introduced.
(iv) Decision for single shift, double, shift, triple shift, or extended shift (one shift of 10 to 12 hrs.) be taken considering overall economy.
(v) Operators should be trained from time to time to make them well conversant with the latest technology to enable to achieve maximum productivity.

(c) Reduction in Overheads :

(i) Overhead expenditure should be maintained in a proper record and compared with estimates or standards from time to time.
(ii) To keep control on direct labour.
(iii) To have versatile machines with different accessories to have optimum utilisation.
(iv) Reduction in avoidable unproductive expenditure to the maximum.
(v) Construction of colonies, office etc. be made by utilising the local material for economy and location be decided after careful considerations.

3.9 Financial Ratio Analysis

Financial or accounting ratio may be defined as relating one accounting figure to another to provide better comparison. Different financial ratios are :

(A) Activity Ratios

(i) Inventory Turnover $= \dfrac{\text{Cost of material consumed}}{\text{Average inventory}}$

(ii) Average inventory period (months) $= \dfrac{\text{Average inventory}}{\text{Consumption per month}}$

(B) Cost Ratio (Percent)

(i) Employee expenses as percentage of production.
(ii) Fixed costs as percentage of production.
(iii) Variable costs as percentage of production.

(C) Profitability Ratios (Percentage)

(i) Gross Operating Margin

$$= \frac{\text{Gross operating profit before depreciation, interest and tax}}{\text{Turnover}} \times 100$$

(ii) Return on Equity

$$= \frac{\text{Net profit after tax and preference dividend}}{\text{Equity paid up and free reserves}} \times 100$$

(D) Return on Investment (R.O.I.)

$$\text{R.O.I.} = \frac{\text{Net profit}}{\text{Capital employed}} = \frac{\text{Net profit}}{\text{Turnover}} \times \frac{\text{Turnover}}{\text{Capital employed}}$$

$$= \text{Net profit ratio} \times \text{Capital turnover ratio}$$

Uses of Financial Ratio Analysis

Financial ratios provide useful indications to appraise financial health of a concern and overall efficiency of the project. Computation of ratios often leads to a further enquiry into various aspects of project, and which enables to bring out some important facts, which ultimately helps in :

(a) Planning : short, medium, and long range.

(b) Diagnosis of financial ills or industrial sickness.

(c) Decision making of all types.

(d) Keeping a continuous watch on the financial trends and taking corrective actions well in advance.

3.10 Replacement of Equipment

Equipment replacement decision plays an important role in the economic running of any concern for years. The reasons for replacement of equipment are : deterioration, obsolescence and inadequacy. The equipment is replaced in order to reduce production cost, to reduce fatigue, to raise quality, to increase output, to secure greater convenience, safety and reliability. The capital needed for the replacement of the equipment is recovered during its life cycle through depreciation realised every year.

The main reasons for the replacement of the equipment are :

(a) **Deterioration :** It becomes necessary to replace the machine when it wears out and does not function properly. Such machines start lowering the quality of product, decreasing the production and increase in labour and maintenance costs.

(b) **Obsolescence :** Whenever new equipment comes in the market, which is capable of producing more products of good quality with less labour and has more efficiency, the existing machine is to be replaced with this machine although its was functioning well. Generally this necessitated because the produce manufactured by new machine will be cheaper.

(c) **Inadequacy :** With the change of product design to meet the customers demand or quantity to be manufactured, old machinery becomes inadequate and, therefore, call for different manufacturing equipment.

Equipment Replacement Policy

Equipment replacement decision plays an important role in the economic running of any concern. A firm has to face three types of replacement decisions :

(a) The replacement of capital equipment, as it wears out.

(b) The capital equipment required for expansion.

(c) The replacement of old technology by the new, *i.e.,* the introduction of an improved equipment in the market which may produce cheaper products. It is also known as replacement of obsolete equipment.

Equipments are used to produce at profitable rate, so that the production can stand competition. Replacement decision is not an easy job, it requires several considerations. As it involves large capital investment, hence a wrong decision may adversely effect the profitability of whole concern. Therefore, a scientific approach to solve this problem is essential. For this purpose the theory of "Break-Even-Point" is very helpful.

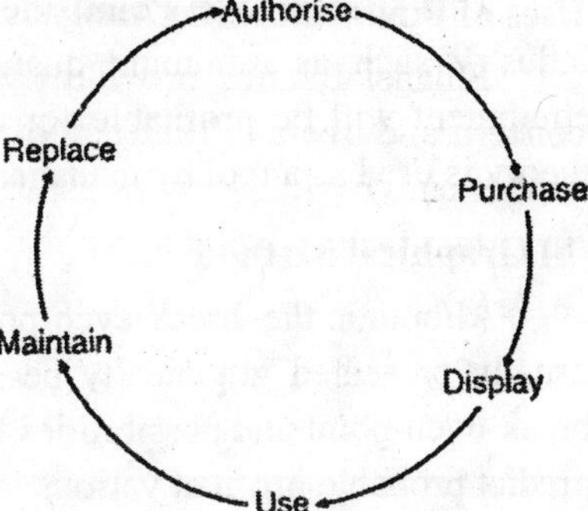

Fig. 3.2 Equipment life-cycle.

Large number of factors are responsible to replace the equipment before the expiry of the estimated life, namely :

(i) To reduce production cost.

(ii) To reduce fatigue.

(iii) To raise quality.

(iv) To increase output.

(v) To secure greater convenience, safety and reliability.

3.11 Break-Even Point (Equipment Replacement Analysis)

Break-even point means the level of output or sales at which no profit or loss is achieved. In other words, a business is said to be break-even when the income equals its expenditure. When production exceeds the "break-even point" the business makes a profit and when it is below the "break-even point", the business makes the loss.

Break-Even Point Theory

The break-even point of any two variable situations, is the point or the value at which they become equal as a result of the common variable.

(a) Mathematical Method

Let cost be common variable in two situations (i) and (ii), then cost equations will be

$c_1 = f_1(x)$ a function of (x) ...(i)

$c_2 = f_2(x)$ another function of (x) ...(ii)

c_1 — may be as total cost, cost per item or cost per day etc. for situation (i)

c_2 — same as c_1 but applicable to situation (ii)

x — a variable effecting c_1 and c_2 to solve for the value of the x.

Let $c_1 = c_2$

$$f_1(x) = f_2(x) \quad \text{...(iii)}$$

Equation (iii) can be solved for obtaining the value of (x). The value of x making the cost equal in both the situations, is called "Break-Even Value". Below this value of x one situation will be economical while above it another situation will be economical.

This "Break-Even Point" theory can be applied to solve several problems of an industry such as minimum quantity to be manufactured to avoid losses, which equipment will be profitable for a particular production etc. The break-even-point theory is used as a tool by management to aid in making decisions.

(b) Graphical Method

Although the break-even-point may be calculated mathematically, but it is usually presented graphically because it enables manager to see more clearly, the break-even-point and possibilities for profits and losses. By using these charts one can predict probable profit at various levels of output.

A break-even-chart given in Fig. 3.3 is used to determine break-even point and amount of loss or profit under varying conditions of output and costs. Income and expenditure in rupees is represented on vertical axis, while output (either in quantity or in percentage capacity) is represented on horizontal axis. Line A represents the fixed expenses. Line B represents total expenses, while line C represents revenue and indicates income at various levels of output. The point, where lines B and C intersect each other, is break-even-point. The space between lines B to C to the right of the break-even-point represents potential profit, whereas to the left of the break-even-point potential loss as represented. The amount of loss or profit can be measured on vertical scale.

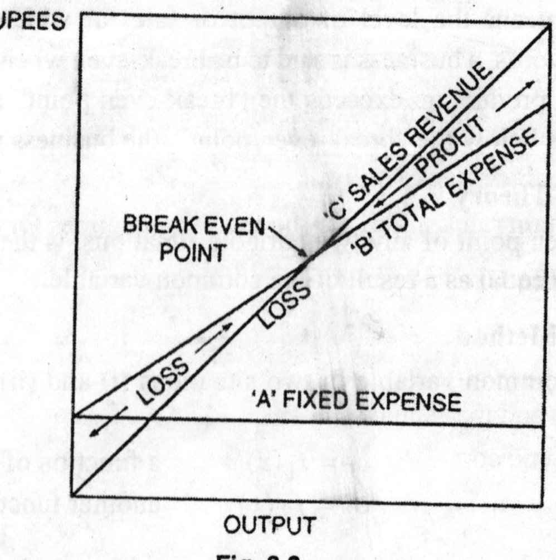

Fig. 3.3

This method can be applied to various problems. For example, a manager wants to replace an old machine by a new, then he must first know whether it will be profitable or not for which the must adopt break-even-point theory and construct the chart as explained above, shown in Fig. 3.3. The figures shows that for a production less than Q, it must not be changed whereas for production more than Q new machine will be economical.

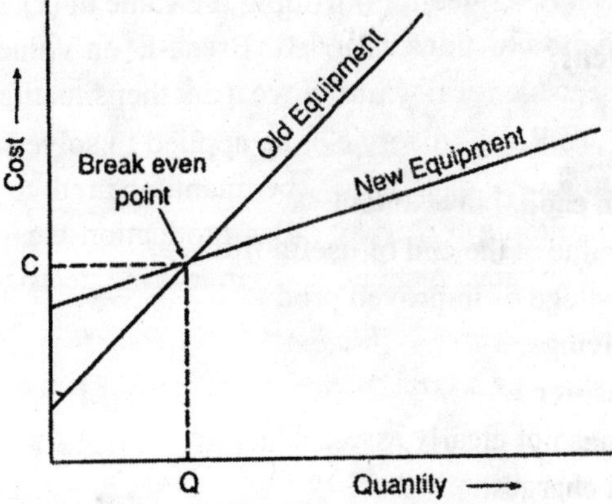

Fig. 3.4 Break-even-point theory.

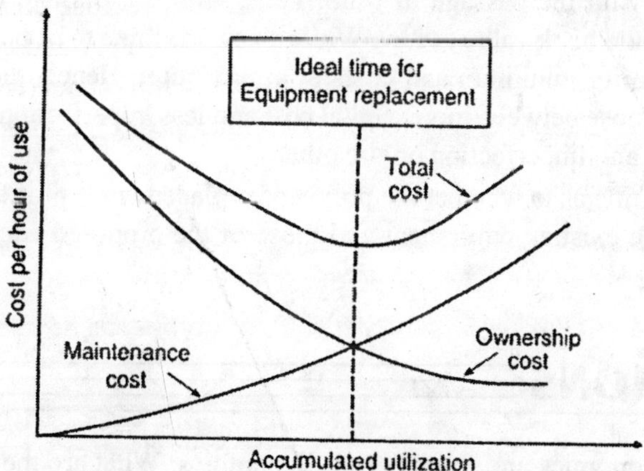

Fig. 3.5 Ownership v/s maintenance cost.

Guidelines for Replacement Analysis

There are certain rules which may be used as guidelines for replacement analysis.

1. For Equipment in Use

(a) Do consider :

(i) Operating cost.

(ii) Repairs and maintenance cost.

(iii) Down time cost.

(iv) Salvage value.
(v) Rebuilding cost.

(b) Do not consider :

(i) Original cost.
(ii) Money already spent on repairs and maintenance.
(iii) Unrealistic book value.

2. For New Equipment

(a) Do consider :

(i) Initial cost.
(ii) Interest on capital investment.
(iii) Salvage value at the end of useful life.
(iv) Cost advantage of improved product.
(v) Labour savings.

(b) Do not consider :

(i) Any savings not clearly assessable.
(ii) Overhead charges.

Almost all the equipments are subjected to deterioration and obsolescence in varying degree with the passage of time. Thus, with the passage of time operating inferiority high and book value as low. While a new machine to be purchased will have operating inferiority minimum and costs at a maximum. Hence, the problem before manager is to choose between more capital cost and less imperfection on one hand, and less capital cost and imperfection on the other.

For estimating as to whether the proposed replacement is profitable, the 'adverse minimum' of the existing equipment and those of the proposed equipment are found and compared.

QUESTIONS

1. Define Economics and Engineering Economics. What are the different tools of engineering economics?
2. Explain 'hourly working rate' of construction equipments.
3. How would you calculate (a) owning costs, and (b) operating costs of a construction equipment?
4. Explain the terms :
   (a) Depreciation (b) Obsolescence
5. Explain (a) Straight line method, **and** (b) Diminishing balance method of calculating depreciation.
6. (a) Explain the term break-even point.
   (b) Write a short note on "**break**-even point analysis, a tool for decision-making".

7. Explain "break-even point theory". How does it help in equipment replacement decisions?
8. (a) Illustrate some of the applications of "break-even point".
   (b) Draw a break-even chart and indicate the minimum economic production on it.
9. (a) Explain the term cost control? Explain its importance.
   (b) What is cost-reduction? List out various cost saving areas.
10. What is "standard cost"? Explain the term "standard costing"?
11. Differentiate between "cost control" and "cost reduction".
12. Discuss, how the cost control measures should be taken.
13. How standard costing is used as controlling tool?
14. Compare standard costing with budgetary control as a controlling tool.
15. What is budget? Justify the statement, "budget is a means for planning, coordination and control".
16. Explain the term "term-cost trade-off". What is its importance in a construction project?
17. Write short notes on :
   (a) Major repair cost.
   (b) Financial or accounting ratio analysis.
   (c) Equipment replacement.
   (d) Rent and lease considerations for acquiring equipment for a construction project.

Chapter **4**

Safety Management in Construction

4.1 Introduction

Millions of industrial accidents occur every year. In these accidents, lacs of workers lose their lives every year in the world. Accidents may cause injury which sometimes result in death or permanent total displacement. Accidents can be defined as "any occurrence that interferes with the orderly progress of activity". Statistics shows that 98% accidents can be avoided any only 2% can not be pre-assessed. The cost of accidents can not be expressed in money terms only. It also affects the individual and his family. Its social aspects is very tragedic because for a family an accident may mean economic dependence from independence, and which adversely affects the social relations of the family. After the accident, the mental attitude also changes.

Everybody in the construction industry must remember that, "Precaution is always better than cure". Accident do not happen they are caused, and most accidents can be prevented. Various measures should be adopted before and during the construction is undertaken. These measures include design, choice of technology, and education and training.

Types of likely hazards/accidents during construction include : falling of person from height, falling of materials from height, exposure to heat/cold; exposure to or contact with potentially harmful substances, contact with electrical current, over-excertion, injury due to project reinforced rods, striking against objects, accident due to lifting equipment, loose scaffolding machinery, tunnelling work, toxic material, impact noise, trench and embankment failure, collapse of temporary structures or failure of structure under construction.

Diseases caused during construction include; deafness due to noise impact, bone fracture, metal stress, diseases due to vibrations, muscle strain, skin diseases, tuberculosis, injuries due to burns, during welding etc.

Safety is very important aspect in any construction work as an accident free work environment boots the morale of the team members working in any hazardous situation. Recognizing these facts, construction projects involving various hazards and risks during construction prepares their own safety policy, safety manual and have a separate department or section for safety so as to create proper awareness and provide the know how about the importance of safety during project construction, operation and maintenance.

Adherence to the useful information, rules and mandatory requirements governing safety and guidelines will help prevent occupational injuries/diseases and accidents which constitute unavoidable and needless waste of human and material resources. Compliance of safety measures during construction stage invariably leads to efficient execution of works.

Safety means continuing and healthful living without injury. Safety is freedom from harm or the danger of harm. The word 'safety' refers to the precautions people take to prevent accidents, harm, danger, damage, loss and air/water/environmental pollution. Safety also deals with improvements in working conditions for better health. Safety is necessary everywhere and at all times, in homes, on roads, in offices, public places and while working.

Accidents can be defined as "any occurrence that interferes with the orderly progress of activity", or "an unforeseen event which causes personal injury or property damage". Accident can also be defined as an unforeseen and unaccepted/undesired event and it usually produces unintended injury, death, ill health or other losses to the persons and losses to the property.

It has been observed that most accidents can be avoided through the application of an effective safety programme. To combat the health hazards and accidents, a qualitative change in the area of safety and health management is needed during implementation of a construction project. A three-old strategy of action should be undertaken, which consist of :

(a) An efficient accident prevention programme.

(b) Immediate attention in case of accident.

(c) Comprehensive plan for rehabilitation of victims.

4.2 Losses Due to Accidents

Now-a-days serious attention is being paid the this matter, because now it has been clearly understood that these accidents cause heavy losses. In these some are direct losses and others are indirect losses.

The accident during construction may effect :

(a) man (b) material (c) machine

(d) equipment, and (e) time.

Direct Losses : These are the losses to the employer, which he pays to the workers for compensation. Employer also pays for medical expenses incurred on the worker. These type of losses can be measured in terms of money.

Indirect Losses : These indirect losses arise due to the :

1. Loss of time of this injured person.
2. Loss of time of his fellow workers, who stop work all the time of accident to help him or to show sympathy or for curiosity.

3. Loss of time of supervisors :
   (a) in assisting injured worker;
   (b) in investigation and preparing of report of accident;
   (c) in making alternative arrangement; and
   (d) in selecting and training the new worker to fill the vacancy if accident causes death or permanent disablement.
4. Loss due to damage caused to the machine.
5. Loss due to reduction in the efficiency of the workers which be returns after recovery.
6. Loss due to reduction in the efficiency of fellow workers due to fall in their morale.
7. Loss to the injured worker. Injured worker suffers the following losses :
   (a) Loss to his income.
   (b) Loss due to medical expenditure.
   (c) Pain felt by the worker, which cannot be compensated.

4.3 Causes of Accidents

As discussed earlier construction is an accident and injury prone sector due to various reasons such as nature of work, difficulty is implementation of safety measures due to scattered work and seasonal employment. The accident occur because of :

(i) lack of training,
(ii) breach of rules and regulations,
(iii) overwork/overtime by workers, and
(iv) negligence/not alertness.

Implementation of many projects are sometimes adversely affected due to unsafe operations and working conditions causing accidents, environmental pollution, health hazard, damage to buildings and other structures, property and machinery. Such **safety hazards** occur due to various reasons, some of which are given below :

1. Negligence on the part of workers or supervisory staff.
2. Faulty operation.
3. Exposure of harmful substances.
4. Accidental fall from a height.
5. Flash flood in bridge construction in hilly areas.
6. Sudden subsidence of overhead structures.
7. Inflow of flood water in underground operations.
8. Accident with construction equipment.
9. Earthquake, severe storm, tornado or cyclone.
10. Failure of forms, scaffolds, ramps, ladders etc.

To minimise the accidents, it is necessary to know about the cause of accidents.

General causes of accidents are given below :

1. **Accidents Due to Dangerous Machines :** These accidents occur from boilers, pressure vessel, prime moves, transmission system etc.
2. **Unsafe Physical Conditions :** It includes improper guards, improper illumination, improper ventilation, unsafe clothings.

   Some of the **unsafe mechanical or physical conditions** are :
   1. Inadequately guarded/unguarded machines/equipments.
   2. Defective conditions (rough, sharp, slippery, decayed, corroded, frayed, cracked etc.).
   3. Unsafe design or construction.
   4. Hazardous equipment, process etc.
   5. Unsafe method, process, planning etc.
   6. Unsafe dress or apparel or PPE.
   7. Inadequate or improper ventilation.
   8. Inadequate or unsuitable illumination.
3. **Moving Objects :** Sometimes moving object or falling object causes accidents.
4. **Personal Factors :** Sometimes accidents occur due to some personal factors like lack of knowledge, physical weakness, temperature, hours of work.
5. **Unsafe Acts :** It is violence of commonly accepted safe procedure. These include (i) working at unsafe speed, (ii) loading machines beyond capacity, (iii) not using safety devices, (iv) adopting unsafe procedure.

   Accidents can be prevented by stopping unsafe acts and removing unsafe mechanical or physical conditions. The unsafe acts of workers can be removed by proper supervision, instructions, training awareness campaign etc.

   Some of the **unsafe acts** :
   1. Working without authority.
   2. Operating at unsafe speed or at unsafe load.
   3. Making safety device un operative.
   4. Using unsafe/inadequate equipment or using equipment unsafely.
   5. Taking unsafe position or postures.
   6. Unsafe placing, missing, combining, operating etc.
   7. Working on moving or dangerous equipment.
   8. Failure to use safe dress or personal protective equipment (PPE).
6. **Human Causes :** These include age, experience, health, training, attitude, fatigue, etc.
7. **Electrical Causes :** Some of the important causes are :

   (a) Not providing proper protecting devices.

   (b) Not obeying proper instructions and not following safety precautions.

   (c) Failure to use insulated pliers, screw-drivers and rubber gloves etc.

8. **Exposure to Harmful Substances :** Injuries are also caused due to exposure to harmful substances, like toxic gases, fumes, dust, vapours, and mist.

   For removing the unsafe conditions, engineering measures are adopted by thorough analysis of job to make it safe by identifying the hazard of potential accidents and then developing a solution for each hazard that will either eliminate or control the exposure. All accidents occurred should be analysed to find the cause of the accident and taking remedial measures for preventing similar accidents.

   As unsafe condition constants the potential to injury someone. It is the unsafe act that leads to an accident. Hence, the first attack should be on the unsafe condition because it is controllable. The next important attack has to be on unsafe acts of workmen.

Other causes of accidents may be :

(a) *accidents due to dangerous machines*; such as pressure vessel, prime movers, transmission system, etc.

(b) *Moving objects or falling objects*.

(c) *Personal factors* like lack of knowledge, physical weakness, temperature, hours of work.

(d) *Human causes* such as age, experience, health, training, attitude, fatigue, etc.

(e) *Electrical causes* such as not providing proper protecting devices, carelessness, failure to use insulated tools.

(f) *Exposure to harmful substances* like toxic gases, fumes, dust, vapours, mist etc.

4.3.1 Factors Contributing to Accidents

Following are the main factors which are responsible for accidents :

1. Mechanical Factors

These are related to the defects and inadequate safeguards of machinery to unsafe conditions of equipment, these may be :

(i) Inadequately guarded.

(ii) Unguarded.

(iii) Unsafe design or construction.

(iv) Hazardous arrangement (piling, overloading, etc.).

2. Environment Factors

The environmental causes of accidents refer to inadequate physical and atmospheric conditions of work. They are distinguished from mechanical causes by the fact that they do not cause the accident directly, but indirectly contribute to its occurrence by virtue of their adverse effects upon the individual. These factors are also, sometimes, designated as 'external' to the individual and 'general' where all the workers are affected by them.

Some of the environmental factors which contribute to accident causation are :

(i) Bad illumination.

(ii) Bad ventilation.

(iii) Temperature of the place (too high or too low).

(iv) Speed of work.

(v) Hours of work.

(vi) Spreadover of work period.

3. Human Factors

It is the most important category which is responsible for accidents. Following are the main factors which constitute the human causes in various groups as under :

(A) *Individual Factors* :

(i) Age	(ii) Marriage
(iii) Education	(iv) Health
(v) Length of service	(vi) Work performance

(B) *Psychological Factors* :

(i) Attitude towards job	(ii) Interest and difficulties
(iii) Machine habits	(iv) Attention
(v) Fatigue	

(C) *Personality Factors* :

(i) Intellectual level	(ii) Emotional maturity
(iii) Adjustment	(iv) Anxiety level

(D) *Sociological Factors* :

(i) Size of family	(ii) Number of dependents
(iii) Financial position	(iv) Social status
(v) Interpersonal relations	(vi) Home environment

4.4 Accident Prevention

Accident prevention represents, control of man performance, machine performance and physical environment. For controlling accidents, **preventive procedures** are grouped in following four general classifications :

1. **Discover Accident Causes :** This consists of finding out of (a) the causes of previous accidents, and (b) the existing hazards that may cause accidents. This is necessary for accident prevention and should be treated as continuous process.
2. **Controlling Environmental Causes :** These are related to the machinery and equipment. Control of environmental causes (or hazards) is the most essential factor in many accident prevention programme, as it proves the sincerity of the management in its desire to prevent accidents.

3. **Controlling Behaviouristic Causes :** These can be controlled through the application of :

(i) Job analysis	(ii) Job training
(iii) Supervision	(iv) Discipline
(v) Physical examination	(vi) Proper placement of workers

These causes are the result of such complicated factors as heredity, emotion, diet, habits etc.

4. **Supplementary Activities :** These activities are valuable in arousing and maintaining interest in safety. These include posters booklets and other literature, films, contests, meetings, committees, suggestion system, employee magazines, safety handbooks etc.

Preventive Measures

Some of the preventive measures are explained hereunder :

(A) By Controlling the Performance

Accidents can be prevented by controlling the performance of men, machine and physical environment. Accidents can be prevented by :

(a) Discovering the causes, *i.e.*, hazards,

(b) Controlling the environment causes, as all the environmental causes have something to do with machinery and equipment,

(c) Controlling the behavioural causes through the application of job analysis, job training, supervision, discipline, proper placement, etc. and

(d) Awareness programme, *i.e.*, using posters, literature, films meetings, committees, suggestion system, safety handbooks, employees magazines etc.

(B) By Accident Prevention Programme

An accident prevention programme is aimed to reduce the number of accidents and thereby the cost of construction. The following are the objects of accident prevention programme :

(i) To reduce the human life sacrified.

(ii) To reduce the temporary and permanent injuries to labourers.

(iii) To avoid loss of materials resulting from accident.

(iv) To avoid unsafe practices of individual workers or personal hazards resulting from the carelessness of the workers.

(C) By Actions Taken for Preventive Accidents

Following actions are generally taken for preventive accidents at construction site, using equipments, plants, machineries, tools, materials etc.

1. **Safety Inspections :** Safety inspections are that monitoring function conducted in the project to locate existing potential hazards which has capacity to cause accident in the work place. The aim of safety inspections

is locating and correcting the hazards, and enforcing the safety regulations. The inspections are mainly of following types :

(a) Continuous/regular inspections

(b) Special inspections

(c) Surprise inspections.

2. **Legal Measures :** Legal aspects of the safety is mainly guided by the Central Government/State Government/Local Bodies Acts and Rules.

3. **Personal Protection Equipment (PPE) :** Though the PPE do not eliminate the hazards but they inter-pose an effective barrier between the persona nd the harmful objects and substances. The PPE may be respiratory protective equipment or non-respiratory protective equipment for head protection, eye and face protection, foot and leg protection, body protection. These may be rubber boots, hard toe safety boots, hard hats, safety belts, goggles for stone and metal grinders, stone chippers, gas welding aprons, respirator shields, manila ropes and slings for life lines, gloves, flash lights, battery lamps, magazine shoes, safety nets, helmets, life and ring buoys. Similarly protective clothings are used by workers engaged on cement handling, steel handling, concreting works, etc.

4. Training for safety.

5. Safety programmes.

6. Safety Audit.

(D) Implementation of Safety Measures

There is a need for consistent implementation of safety measures. Some of the such measures are :

1. Safe Workplace and Working Conditions :

(a) *Good layout* : Good layout includes sufficient space for movement, non-skid type floors.

(b) *Reduced noise level* : Use of such machines which produces less noise, provide separate space for such works which produces noise, make efforts for reducing the vibrations to help in minimizing harmful effects of noise.

(c) Inflammable materials should be stored separately.

(d) By providing proper safeguards to the machines, accident can be prevented. Some guards are built into a permanent casing, while some are attached afterwards.

(e) Machines or their parts should be fenced when it is not possible to provide safeguards.

(f) All boilers and other pressure vessels must be kept in proper condition. Safety valves, pressure gauges and water gauges etc., must be examined thoroughly at regular intervals.

(g) *Physical conditions* : Sufficient illumination, ventilation and height should be provided. Floor should be free from oiliness and kept clean.

2. Safe Material Handling :

(a) Hoists, cranes, lifts, etc. must be of sound construction. They must be tested periodically and well maintained.

(b) Avoid fatigue of workers, use handling devices where possible.

(c) Good house-keeping.

(d) Ensure safety during handling.

(e) Separate passages for men and handling equipment.

3. Personal Protection Devices :

(a) Use of goggles, helmets, gloves, apron, safety shoes, safety belts is necessary where required.

(b) Safety measures include special clothing for the protection of body, such as gloves, apron, mask, goggles, etc. loose clothing may be a source of danger.

(c) Repair work on machines should not be done when it is running.

(d) All the tools should be kept at their proper places.

(e) Chips should not be removed by hand.

(f) Workers should be trained about correct procedures and they should be educated about safety precautions. Constant warning, publicity and play cards carrying slogans (as 'Safety-First', 'Danger 440 Volts' etc.) are also helpful to reduce accidents.

(g) Fire hazard. To avoid the danger, inflammable materials should be kept away from general storage at a safe distance (minimum 50 ft. or 15.25 m). Fire extinguishers should be kept at suitable places.

(h) Prevention of electric accidents. To prevent electric accidents, following measures should be taken :

(i) Electrical insulation should be periodically tested.

(ii) Use proper tools for testing and repairing.

(iii) Work should be done after switching the power off.

(iv) Use such safety equipments as insulated tools and rubber gloves, etc., whenever necessary.

4. Safe Activities in the Organisation :

Each organisation has some peculiarities. On the basis of working methods, its process and other conditions accident-prone activities, and places, etc. identified. Past records also help in identification of such activities or areas. All out efforts must be made to reduce chances of accidents in these accident prone areas or activities.

5. Good House-keeping :

House-keeping means cleanliness in buildings, work areas, rest areas, equipments, machinery tools, etc., cleanliness include keeping them free from dirt, dust, filth, etc., and keeping things in pleasant and systematic manner :

(a) This minimize fatigue and discomfort to the workers and motivate them.

(b) It reduces the chances of accidents.

(c) Reduces the fire and other hazards.

(d) Increase the life of machinery, equipment, tool etc.
(e) Improves productivity.
(f) Improves quality of the product.
(g) Enhances the morale of workers.
(h) Material handling and internal transport become faster.
(i) Better utilization of floor space.

Good house-keeping includes :

(i) Clean and tidy working premises.
(ii) Clean and clear passages/aisles.
(iii) Well stacked and neatly placed material.
(iv) Proper illumination.
(v) Clean, well drained and well maintained roads.
(vi) No dangling of electric or phone lines in the working area.
(vii) Sufficient and safe clearances for aisles, at loading docks, through doorways, and wherever turns or passages are made.
(viii) Clearly marked aisles in factories or warehouses wherever mechanical equipment such as fork lift trucks, pallet jacks, tractor-trains, tow conveyors and other similar moving equipment are used.
(ix) Storage areas should be kept free from accumulation of materials that constitute hazards from tripping, fire or explosion.
(x) Covers and/or guard rails should be provided to protect personnel from the hazards of open pits, tanks, ditches etc.

4.5 Safety Programme

Safety programme in construction industry, must receive the full support of an entire organisation, beginning with top management and continuing down through the ranks to include the project managers, supervisors and workers.

In any safety programme, following are essential :

1. Secure the full support of top management.
2. Designate one person in the organisation to direct safety programmes.
3. Give publicity to the safety programmes.
4. Develop a safety programme for each job.
5. Install the safety programme, creatingthe competition with appropriate rewards for outstanding performance.
6. Train new employees with the safety programmes.
7. Safety practice the made effective.
8. Promote goods house-keeping.
9. Maintain adequate first-aid facilities.
10. Seek assistance from insurance companies.

Now-a-days, safety committees are formed including executives, supervisors and workers. This also helps in creating safety consciousness.

Safety programmes analyses causes of accidents and takes remedial measures. Safety programme is a continuous process. Special training are imparted to employees on safety aspects.

In order to create awareness, safety weeks are organised, safety instructions are displayed. It is also necessary to make necessary safety rules and enforce them.

It is advisable to produce a employee safety handbook, and gives to employees when they are first appointed.

It is necessary for every employer to appoint a safety officer in every project, to as to satisfy his legal duties to provide for the safety of the employees and others from risk arising out of work activities. This duty may be affected by doing the safety appraisal of every site, especially when the contract has been awarded. On sites this is pressure to ignore safety procedure to save time or to improve productivity, therefore, it is necessary to carry out safety audits at intervals by the employer's safety officer.

Due to variety of equipment, their use, site conditions etc., each construction company must develop their own safety programmes. These must be in two parts, (a) general, which is applicable for all works, (b) specifies which should be different for each type of equipment and for different types of works, like, tunnelling, steel erection, drilling and blasting, excavation, pile driving etc.

Safety programme is carried out in following three phases :

1. **Safety awareness :** This includes educational, onthe job training, behaviours, ergonomics, job safety analysis techniques.
2. **Safety implementation :** Implementation should be carried out by all concerned.
3. **Safety programme maintenance :** This phase is necessary to maintain enthusiasm and energy level which do not deteriorate with time.

4.5.1 Safety Policy

As per rule 39 of the "Building and Other Construction Workers Central Rules, 1998", every establishment employing fifty or more construction workers shall prepare a written statement of policy in respect of safety and health of construction workers. This policy should contain the following :

1. The intention and commitments of the establishment regarding safety, health and environmental protection of workers.
2. Organisational arrangements made to carry out the policy referred to above specifying the responsibility of different levels of hierarchy.
3. The responsibilities of the principal employer, contractor, sub-contractor, transporter or other agencies involved in the building or other construction work.

4. Techniques and methods for assessment of risk to safety, health and environmental and remedial measures therefore.
5. Arrangement for training of workers, supervisors or other persons engaged in the construction work.

The intention and commitment referred to at (1) above shall be taken into account in making decisions relating to plant, machinery, equipment, materials and placement of construction workers.

A copy of the policy should be displayed at the conspicuous places in Hindi and a local language understood by the majority of workers at a construction site.

The safety policy should have the following **objectives** :

(i) Zero fatal accidents.
(ii) Zero dangerous occurrence.
(iii) Should aim at an accident frequency rate of less than 0.5 per 1,00,000 hours worked.

4.5.2 Safety Manual

Every construction company should prepare a detailed safety manual complying with the statutory requirements, manufacturer's recommendations, Bureau of Indian Standards (BIS) and any other relevant standards and codes.

For similar projects, a common safety manual can be prepared and made applicable, however, site specific safety aspects should either be covered in the common safety manual or be issued separately. The safety manuals should cover all the aspects of safety.

4.6 Emergency Preparedness

Construction agencies should formulate an emergency preparedness plans for each of the sites. These plans should address forceable emergencies that may arise during the construction activities. Examples of activities for which plans should be prepared include amongst other things :

1. An accident which results in death or major injury.
2. A serious fire that threatens life.
3. A flood that threatens life.
4. Leakage of any dangerous materials or chemicals.
5. Major engineering failure.

The construction project should establish, implement and maintain procedure(s) for emergency preparedness and response is plan for contingency in advance and to periodically test these plans through practice drills (mock drills). This should include :

(a) Establishment of first-aid facilities that are matched to the site hazards and availability of further assistance like transportation to medical assistance etc.

(b) Rescue operation.

(c) Fire fighting etc.

The results of these practice drills should be evaluated and necessary changes, if any, should be incorporated in the system.

Emergency equipment like alarm system, emergency lighting and power, means of escape, critical switches, cut-outs etc. should be provided in adequate quantity. These should be tested at specified intervals for continuing operability.

An emergency preparedness plan should include details of the following :

1. The name, location and phone number of the emergency coordinator, and designated personnel.
2. Details of the emergency response teams with location and phone numbers.
3. Functions of the emergency response team.
4. Means of escape.
5. Communication with emergency services, such as :
   (a) Police
   (b) Fire services
   (c) Ambulance and hospital services.
6. First-aid facilities.
7. Site plans, indicating locations of the facilities available.
8. Suppliers of emergency equipment.

4.6.1 Accident Investigations

Accidents and dangerous occurrences which result in death, serious injury or serious damage must be investigated immediately to find out he cause of the accident/occurrence so that measures can be taken to prevent any recurrence. The purpose of an accident investigation is to discover hazardous conditions and practices so that accidents of similar causes may be prevented. Investigation should be carried out, as far as possible, immediately after the accident.

Each executive is required to personally investigate every accident of workmen under his jurisdiction in order to improve his own supervisory performance as well as to make sure that he is thoroughly acquainted with accidents that occurred under his jurisdiction. The investigation of accident is necessary :

1. To learn accident causes so that similar accidents can be prevented by mechanical improvement, better supervision or employees training.
2. To determine the change or deviation that produce an error which in turn resulted in an accident.
3. To publicize the particular hazard among the employees and supervisors so as to direct attention for accident prevention.
4. To estimate extent of loss/damage in terms of man-hours and machine-hours, and money.

5. To make suggestions for prevention of recurrences of similar or related nature of accidents.
6. To the extent possible, fixation of responsibility.

In case of all major/fatal accidents investigations should be made either :

(i) by an expert outside the concerned department,

(ii) by a committee having safety officer and executive of the department in which accident occurred, along with other members.

4.7 Safety through Legislation

The provisions of "The Building and Other Construction Workers (Regulation of Employment and Conditions of Service) Act, 1996" are applicable to any establishment which employees ten or more building workers either directly or through contractors in any building or other construction work.

Here, the "building and other construction work" means the construction, alteration, repairs and maintenance or demolition, of or, in relation to, buildings, streets, roads, railways tramways, airfields, irrigation, drainage, embankment and navigation works, flood control works, generation, transmission and distribution of power, water works, oil and gas installations, electric lines, wireless, radio, television, telephone and overseas communications, dams, canals, reservoirs, water courses, tunnels, bridges, viaducts, aquaducts, pipelines, towers, cooling towers, transmission towers, but does not include any building or other construction work to which the provisions of the Factories Act, 1948 or Mines Act, 1952, apply.

Besides above, there are other Acts and Rules, some of them are listed hereunder :

(i) The Electricity Act, 2013.

(ii) Indian Electricity Rules, 1956.

(iii) The Explosives Act, 1884 and Explosive Rules, 1983.

(iv) The Motor Vehicle Act, 1988.

(v) The Factories Act, 1948.

(vi) The Mines Act, 1952.

(vii) Workmen's Compensation Act, 1923.

As we all know that legislation alone cannot ensure safety in operations, unless effective approach to prevention of accidents and promotion of safety consciousness is achieved. The is possible by adopting proper control measures including safe design of machines and processes and use of protection devices and personal protective equipments and also effective safety procedures and practices as well as creation of self-regulating system on the shop-floor.

Government has set up National Safety Council in 1966 to promote safety consciousness among workers to prevent accidents, minimize dangers and mitigate safety sufferings and conduct programmes.

To assure safety to workers and elimination of damage to machinery and equipments, Indian Standards Institute has done commendable job. It lays down :

(i) Safety precautions to be taken during working operations.

(ii) Requirements for effective maintenance of tools and equipments.

(iii) Guidance on safe welding and cutting, use of powered industrial trucks, belt conveyors and fire-fighting equipments.

(iv) Standards and specifications of safe industrial operations and practices.

(v) Safety requirements for personal protective equipments.

(vi) Standards for fire safety in workshop and safety procedures to be followed in electrical work and use of electrical appliances in hazardous area and explosives atmosphere.

(vii) Specifications for protective clothing, safety helmets, face shields and safety equipment for eyes, ears, lungs, hands, feet and legs. These includes eye and ear protectors, gas masks, gloves, safety boots and shoes for mines etc.

4.8 First-Aid

Although sufficient safety measures are taken to minimise accidents but accidents cannot be totally avoided and hence, proper first-aid facilities for common accidents such as fire, heat stroke, cuts, minor injuries etc. must be provided in every work area by the employers.

A first-aid box must be provided in the charge of a responsible person, who must always be available in working hours and he should be trained in first-aid.

The workers as human being, are entitled to every consideration at the hands to the management and it lies in the administration to institute adequate precautionary and prompt first-aid towards its workers and hence it is essential that the management should be fully equipped to offer first-aid to the workers.

The contents of a first-aid box in workshop employing more than 50 persons has been specified in the Factories Act.

First-Aid Treatment for Electric Shock

1. If the casualty is in contact with or inclose proximity to the 'live' apparatus or line DO NOT TOUCH him until the electric supply has been isolated switch off electric supply. If this is not possible protect yourself with DRY insulating material and pull or push the casualty clear of the apparatus or line.
2. Then send for qualified medical assistance, and in the mean time, give the casualty first-aid treatment as follows :
   (a) Make the casualty as comfortable as possible.
   (b) Loosen any tight clothing.
   (c) Given tactful reassurances.
   (d) DO NOT give any liquid to drink.
3. If the casualty has stopped breathing, mouth-to-mouth resuscitation must be started immediately.
   (i) Clear the throat of fluid or any other item by sweeping around the mouth with finger.

(ii) Place the head in the extended neck position.

(iii) Close the nostrils by pinching lightly with thumb and forefinger.

(iv) Take a deep breath and then make an air tight scale with your mouth over the casualty's mouth and breath into the casualty. Watch the chest rise.

(v) Remove your mouth, and watch the chest fall.

(vi) Repeat as in (iv) and (v) above about 12 times every minute until casualty begins to breath.

4. If mouth-to-mouth resuscitation is not practicable follow 'Holger-Nielson Method' of respiration as follows :

(i) Lay the casualty face downwards, head to one side, forehead resting on the hands, placed one above the other.

(ii) Remove any artificial teeth or other matter from the mouth.

(iii) Kneel on one knee by the casualty's head, one foot by casualty's elbow.

(iv) Place the palm of your hands on the casualty's shoulder blades. Lean forward until your arms are vertical. Press lightly, force of about 10 to 14 kg is sufficient for about two and a half seconds.

(v) Release the pressure by allowing your hands to slide along the casualty's arms to his elbows. (taking one second), then raise the casualty's arms and shoulders slightly, pulling at the same time by facing yourself backwards (taking two and a half seconds). Lower the casualty's arms and return your hands to the casualty's shoulder-blades.

(vi) Repeat the movements, taking seven seconds for each complete respiration, until the casualty breaches of his own or qualified medical help arrives.

4.9 Fire Protection

1. Following precautions should be taken to avoid fire hazards on all oxy-acetylene cutting and welding :

(a) Keep hose and cylinder valves from from grease and oil.

(b) Keep cylinders away from stoves, furnaces and other sources of heat.

(c) Only 'Gas Lighter' should be used to light the torch.

(d) Avoid use of oxy-acetylene flame in confined spaces.

(e) For testing of leakages use only soap water and watch for bubbles.

(f) Value protection caps should be in place when cylinders not in use.

2. Gas cylinders should be kept up right in approved safe places where they cannot be knocked over, and well separated from furnaces and combustion materials. Loaded and empty cylinders should be kept in separate places.

3. Oxygen cylinders should not be stored in close proximity to acetylene cylinders. In no circumstances oxygen or acetylene cylinders should be

stored under direct rays of sun or in places where excessive rise of temperatures is likely to occur.

4. Following precautions should be taken during electric are welding and cutting :
   (a) Welder and all persons working in the immediate vicinity should wear suitable coloured goggles unless the work is completely shielded.
   (b) Persons should never look at an electric arc with the naked eye, as it may cause serious eye injury.
   (c) Only heavy duty electric cable with unbroken insulation should be used, an all connections should be water-proof. Frequency inspection should be made.
   (d) Before leaving the work, welder should switch off the power supply to the equipment.
5. Packages containing paints, varnishes, lacquers or other volatile painting materials should be kept tightly closed when not in actual use, and should be placed where they will not be exposed to excessive heat sparks, flame or direct rays of the sun.
6. Dirty wiping rags, paint scrapings and paint saturated debris, should not be allowed to accumulate but should be collected and disposed of at frequent intervals.
7. Smoking, open flame, exposed heating elements, and other sources of ignition of any kind should not be permitted in paint stores or areas where spray painting is done.
8. Fire extinguishes of appropriate capacity should always be at hand where flammable paint materials are being mixed, used or stored.
9. All combustible waste material, wood sealings, soiled rags etc. should be removed daily and burned in suitable burning areas. The saw mill and lumber yard be kept free from accumulation to combustible debris.
10. Smoking should be prohibited in all flammable storages viz. carpentry, paint shops, garrages, service stations etc. "No Smoking" signs should be posted on all such areas.
11. Flammable liquids, lubricants etc. should be handled and transported in safety containers and drums which can be tightly capped.
12. All electric installations should be properly earthed.
13. Following fire fighting arrangements should be made :
   (a) Fire extinguishers and fire buckets, pained red, be provided at all fire hazardous locations. The extinguishers should be inspected, serviced and maintained in accordance with manufacturer's instructions.
   (b) In isolated locations (away from the cities), it will be necessary to provide for an install complete the fighting facilities including provision for fire tenders commensurate with the numbers, size and importance of equipments, buildings or supplies to be protected.

(c) Since portable hand extinguishers have limited capacity, full reliance should never placed on them. Water in ample quantity and under adequate pressure should always be available for fire fighting.

(d) Fire exit and fire alarm arrangements should be provided at all locations featuring hazards.

(e) All staff should be conversant with the use of all types of fire extinguishing apparatuses. Demonstrations and training in fire fighting should be conducted at sufficient intervals.

4.10 Fire Extinguishers

Based on contents of extinguishing media, fire-extinguishers are classified into following categories :

1. Water-type extinguishers.
2. Foam-type extinguishers.
3. Liquefied gas carbon dioxide-type extinguishers.
4. Dry chemical powder-type extinguishers.

1. **Water-type Extinguishers :** These are of following types :

   (a) **Water gas cartridge type :** These are filled with water, and non-corrosive anti freeze agents are added to it. The gas required to expel the water is stored in a cartridge fitted with a sealing device which is pierced when the extinguisher is operated.

   (b) **Water (stored pressure) type :** In this air is introduced into the water filled container. To operate these extinguishers a safety pin is withdrawn, a valve lever depressed and the water jet is directed by a small length of hose.

2. **Foam-type Extinguishers :** These are of two types :

   (a) **Foam (chemical) type :** These have two containers, one inside the other. Outer container is filled to an indicated level with an aqueous solution of sodium bicarbonate, while the inner container is filled with a solution of aluminium sulphate in water. When the extinguisher is actuated by inversion, the two solutions are mixed and produces the form and a gas which sets as an expellant.

   (b) **Foam (mechanical) type :** This is similar to earlier one, except that this has no inner container. The foam is produced from a foam compound and water. The foam compound is stored in a sealed plastic bag which is ruptured on the release of carbon dioxide from cartridge. The water and the foam compound are mixed and expelled by the gas.

3. **Carbon Dioxide-type Extinguishers :** A steel cylinder filled with liquid carbon dioxide to approximately two-thirds of its capacity. A special discharge horn is fitted to direct the gas on to the fire. CO_2 is a gas at ordinary temperatures but when compressed for storage in cylinders, it liquefies. The liquid vapourises when released.

4. **Dry Chemical Powder-type Extinguishers :** These are also known as dry chemical extinguishers and are filled with a free-flowing non-toxic, non-conductive dry powder. Sodium bicarbonate is generally used for the purpose. The expellant gas is stored either in the extinguisher body or in a cartridge.

QUESTIONS

1. What is the importance of 'safety'? Explain various losses which may occur due to the accidents in construction projects.
2. Enumerate common causes of accidents. Describe various measures to prevent them.
3. How 'safety education and training' will help in safety? Explain.
4. Explain different factors which causes/enhances the chances of accidents.
5. Write short notes on :
   (a) First-aid (b) Efforts by Government towards safety.
6. What are the safety measures? Suggest different ways to minimise the accidents.
7. Explain in brief about :
   (a) Personal protective equipment (b) Fire protection.
8. Explain different types of fire-extinguishers.
9. Explain as to how the employer and employees both are affected by accidents.
10. Comment on the statement, "safety promotes productivity".
11. Describe safety control measures during construction.
12. Explain the contractual requirements on safety during construction.
13. What are the accidental hazards? Explain different types of hazards.
14. Discuss different types of accidents, in detail.
15. Discuss the procedure for prevention of construction accidents. Mention various preventive measures.
16. Write short notes on :
   (a) Safety Policy (b) Safety Manual
17. Explain the following, with reference to construction projects :
   (a) Safety (b) Unsafe acts
   (c) Unsafe physical conditions (d) Factors contributing to accidents
18. How will you classify accidents? Discuss.
19. Discuss the follow in brief :
   (a) Hazards control (b) Good house-keeping
   (c) Emergency preparedness for construction projects.

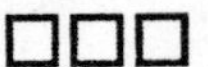

Part - II

EARTHWORK EQUIPMENT

Chapter 5

Earth-Moving Equipment

5.1 Introduction

Modern mechanical earthmoving really started when the crawler tractor was adopted from its agricultural antecedent. To meet the growing demand of minerals particularly coal, the earthmoving equipment was first introduced in 1940's in open-cast coalmines in our country. Shovels of about 2.2 cum capacity with dumpers of 12 to 15 tonnes capacity were introduced in these mines. Bhakra Nangal Dam started in 1950's used higher capacity and sophisticated earthmoving equipment like dozers, scrapers, shovels, draglines and dumpers. Almost same time in 1950's shovels of 1.5 to 2.5 m^3, front-end loaders, dozers with rippers, and 15 to 25 tonnes dumpers were introduced in iron ore mines, replacing manual mining and locomotive traction. With the introduction of heavy earthmoving equipment, bigger size operations were taken up in construction of Hydel dams, irrigation schemes, coal and metal mining. Kudremukh Iron Ore Project in late 1970's used 15 cu m shovels, 120 tonnes diesel engine dumpers, 15 cu m front-end loaders and dozers of over 600 H.P.

The equipment of various sizes used for various projects were imported from various countries. The indigenous manufacturers in the country are now planning to manufacture 10-12.5 m^3 shovels, 85-120 tonnes dumpers,about 450 H.P. class dozers, 30 m^3 scrapers, 30 m^3/90 m draglines etc. With indigenous manufacture, it will save high cost of importation and also help in standardisation which will solve the problems of spare parts stocking, maintenance and downtime.

With the application of heavy earthmoving equipment (H.E.M.), production of coal has increased from 25 million tonnes, similarly hydel power has also increased manifolds in last 30 years. All these activities involve movement of rock, earth and minerals in such a huge quantities that these works of irrigation, hydel, and mining (coal and mineral) projects can not be undertaken manually within the time schedule set for the projects.

Types of Earth Moving Equipments

Earth moving Equipments can be classified into following two types :

(i) Production Equipment : Equipment used for digging, moving the material to the site of construction (may be dam, irrigation project, road project, mining project or building construction project) or to the crushing plant.

(ii) **Service Equipment :** These are for the help of main production equipment to achieve optimum capacity. For small works dozers can be used as productive equipment. Motor Grader is used as production equipment in road construction projects, while it is used as service equipment for keeping proper gradient of service road for dams, mines and quarries.

5.2 Earth-Work Operations

Earth-work operations include pioneering, clearing, grubbing, stripping, draining, dredging, cutting and filling, and excavating. These operations are done primarily with heavy construction equipment such as, Dozers and Graders, Scrapers. Before taking up the earth-moving operations, it is often necessary to remove overgrowth, boulders and other obstructions, and developing a drainage system.

New projects are generally set-up on agricultural or waste land, which often requires filling and cutting for levelling the undulated areas. Various operations involved in earthwork are discussed, in short, hereunder :

1. **Pioneering :** It refers to the working over an over-grown or rough area, making it accessible for equipment needed for the project.
2. **Clearing :** It is an operation consisting of clearing a designated area of trees, brushes and other vegetation, removing surfaces boulders and other materials embedded in the ground, and disposal of all material cleared.
3. **Grubbing :** It consists of uprooting and removing roots and stumps.
4. **Stripping :** It is removal and disposal of objectionable top soil. Deeply embedded rocks and large boulders may have to be blasted before they can be removed.
5. **Drainage System :** Drainage system is primarily meant for carrying storm water, waste water etc. The drains should have a proper gradient for smooth flow.

5.3 Earth-Moving Operations

Earthmoving is the process of moving soil or rock from one location to another and processing it so that it meets construction requirements such as location, elevation, density, moisture content etc. Earthmoving operations involve processes such as excavating, loading, hauling, dumping, spreading, compacting, grading, finishing, crushing etc.

An earthmoving operation consists of the preparation of material, the loader/truck loading cycle, haulage of trucks to the disposal place, the deposition of the material and the trucks return trip to the loading station to start another load-haul-unload and return cycle.

Depending on the scope and working conditions of each project different operation methods and machine types should be selected to maximize the overall performances of the operation. Earthmoving operations require technical knowledge and skill to operate and maintain a variety of heavy equipment such as dozers, scrapers, motor graders, shovels, hoists etc.

5.4 Tractors

Tractors are the machines which change energy of the engine into tractive energy. The tractors are primarily used to pull or push loads, but they are also used for mounting many types of accessories like, bulldozer blades, rippers, front end shovels, hoes, draglines, clamshells, trenchers, winches, side booms, frontend bucket loaders, pipe layers etc.

As mentioned above,the tractor is a basic equipment and available in two types; namely (i) crawler or track type, and (ii) rubber-tired or wheel-type. The tractor is a multi-purpose machine, light models of which are used for agricultural or short haulage works, whereas heavy models are employed for earth moving works, cranes,shovels or special rigs. Wheeled units are employed for light but speedy jobs, whereas crawler units are rugged machines and are used for heavy duty works, where more tractive power is required.

Tractor Construction

Main constituents of a tractor are : Engine, clutch, transmission system, ground drive and controls.

A diesel engine is generally used as prime mover and mounted on the tractor frame and delivers the power through a clutch to the main power shaft. The power is transmitted from the engine to the final drive through engine clutch, torque convertor, change speed gear box transmission to rear differential and then finally to the rear drive axle. The drive is also transmitted through front differential to the front axle.

Engine clutch is provided to disconnect the engine from the rest of the transmission system so that gears can be changed to change the speed of the tractor. Care should be taken while changing the gears that the engagement of the clutch should be gradual to avoid undue strain on the surfaces of the clutch plates. The clutch control in small and medium sized tractors is through pedal like that of a truck, but in large tractors it is through lever operated by hand.

Transmission system provides speed reduction and multiplication of torque of the engine shaft, since final drive needs a high torque at low speed. The reduction in speed is done by means of a change speed gear box. Now-a-days torque converters are also used for the purpose. The power is then given to the drive axle through the differential, which changes the direction of the drive to 90° by using bevel gears and also reduces the speed upto some extent. Differential also facilitate in steering. As tractor changes its direction, one of the rear wheels must travel faster than the other, and this is achieved by the differential. In the wheeled tractor the steering is done through the front wheel. The outer ends of the two half shafts carry pinions which mesh with larger gears of the final drive, resulting variation in speed when the tractor is taking a turn. The change in the speeds of the track is made directly by stopping power supply to one, while the other continues to rotate.

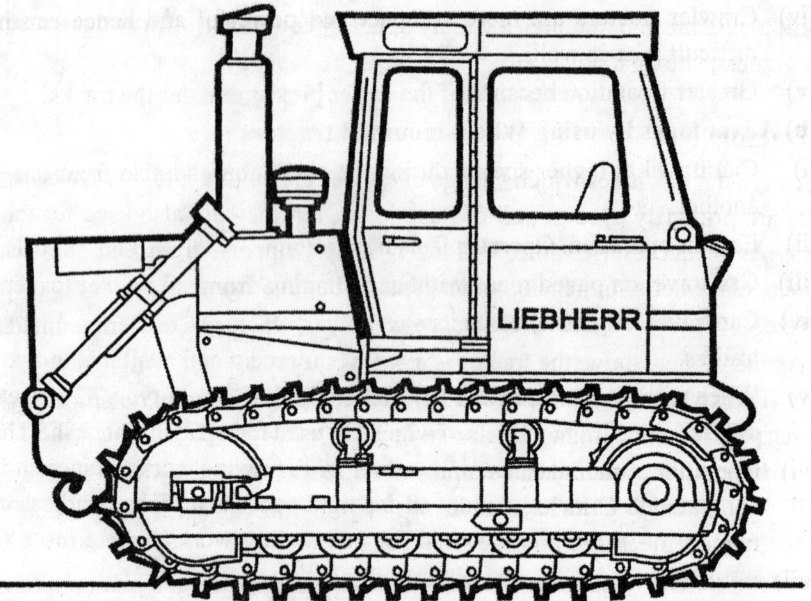

Fig. 5.1 Crawler tractor (Courtesy : Liebherr).

The power from drive axle is transmitted through wheels or crawler chains in wheeled tractors and crawler tractors respectively. Wheeled tractors generally have two large wheels in the rear and two smaller wheels in the front. For better traction under adverse load and ground conditions two wheels are fitted on each of the rear hubs. To make rear heavy for better stability of the tractor rear tyres are filled with water. The tread of the tyre should be selected carefully as it greatly affects its tractive efforts on a particular type of soil where it operates.

In Crawler tractors, live axles rotate large toothed wheels, known as drive sprockets, located at the rear of the track frame. In the front of each track frame, an idler is provided. An endless track chain is mounted on the sprockets and idlers. The chain is made of flat shoes pinned together end-to-end.

5.4.1 Crawler v/s Tyred Tractors

Each type of tractor has certain advantages in certain conditions. A comparative study of both the types of tractors is given hereunder to help in deciding that which of the two will suit more in a particular set of conditions.

(a) Advantages by using Crawler mounted tractors :

(i) More tractive efforts,hence can also operate on loose or muddy soil.

(ii) In absence of tyres, can easily operate in rocky conditions, as there is no danger for the damage of the tyres.

(iii) Where maintenance of haul roads is difficult, it can easily travel, specially in rough terrains.

(iv) Crawler tractors are more compact and powerful and hence can handle difficult jobs as well.

(v) Greater floatation because of the lower pressure under the tracks.

(b) Advantages by using Wheel-mounted tractors :

(i) Can travel at higher speeds during the operation and also from one job to another.

(ii) Ease in operation. Operator feels less fatigue.

(iii) Can travel on paved roads without damaging them.

(iv) Can travel long distances at its own power, whereas Crawler mounted needs trailers.

(v) When work is spread over long area, these are found to be producing more output.

(vi) Operation, maintenance and repair costs less in wheeled tractors as compared to Crawler tractors. As large number of track parts are subjected to more wear.

(vii) Initial cost of the Crawler tractor is higher than the wheeled tractors, due to expensive track system.

(viii) Easy to manoeuver.

5.5 Bull-Dozers

Dozers are machines designed primarily for cutting and pushing the material over relatively short distances. They consist of a tractor with a front mounted blade, controlled by hydraulic cylinders to very the depth of cut and rate of levelling depending on the material and application. Rear mounted hydraulic sacrifiers and rippers can be fitted to loosen hard material prior to dozing. A dozer is a frame mounted unit which a blade, curved in its section, extending in front of the tractor.

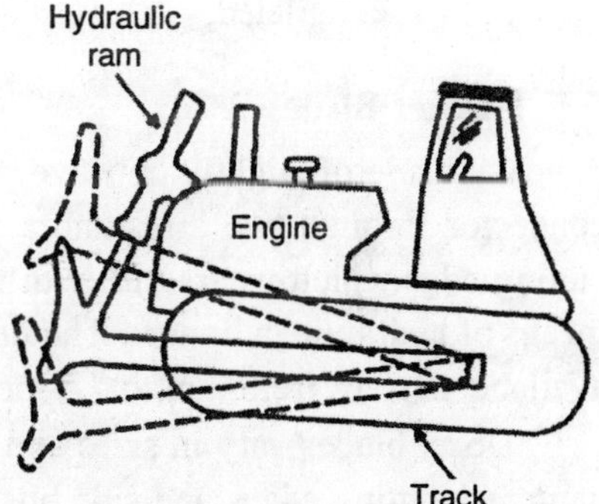

Fig. 5.2 Bulldozer with blade.

Bulldozer is a most versatile and most important equipment on construction projects. Basically it is a pushing unit, but is widely used as a multipurpose equipment and can perform large number of operations with minor changes under different names like; angle dozer, tilt dozer, tree dozer, and push dozer. Bulldozer scraps soft and granular material, pushes it in front or stock-piles. These are used for short hauls upto 100 metres only.

Angle dozer is used to push its load at an angle of nearly 25° to the direction of travel of the dozer. This is helpful where the material is pushed down the slope on hill work or where the material to be collected in a long windraw on one side of the line of travel of the dozer. The tilt dozer is used where blade is required to be tilted by raising one end upto 25 cm above the other, so as to start excavating a ditch or a trench or for excavation in hard ground. The push dozer is used to push the scraper unit during digging or loading operation by means of a rectangular plate, called the pusher plate. The tree dozer is used to remove the trees.

Dozer Specifications

At the time of purchasing of dozens following points should be clearly specified after examining the exact job requirements and the manufacturer's limitations.

Engine horsepower at the flywheel, total operating weight, speed range in various gear positions; blade type and size and also maximum tilt position or angle position; number, type and size of rippers; turning radius, fuel tank capacities. In case of wheel dozer also mention, number and sizes of the tyres, wheel base, ground clearance etc.

Following main factors should be considered while selecting and tractor dozer :

(i) Size of the dozer for a given job.

(ii) The type of work expected from the tractor dozer, *e.g.*, bulldozing, ripping, land clearing, pulling a scraper etc.

(iii) The type and condition of haul road.

(iv) Gradient of the haul road.

(v) Distance to be moved.

(vi) Type of work expected to be taken from the equipment after the present job is completed.

5.5.1 Dozer Blades

A heavy blade of slightly concave profile is attached in the front of the tractor. It is connected through two arms and a yoks to the tractor. The blade has a replaceable cutting edge,which wears out with the use of the blade. The blade is controlled by means of hydraulic cylinders. The dozer blades are also known as moldboard and are available in sizes from 2 m to 7.5 metres wide and 0.8 m to 1.5 m in height.

Dozer blades vary in sizes and design based on specific work applications. The hardened cutting edges and side bits are bolted, as it enables easy replacement when worn out.

Dozer blades can have three types of movements, namely; tilt, pitch and angling. All these three features are not available to all blades,but any two of these may be incorporated in a single mount.

1. **Tilt :** In this case dozer can raise or lower the either end of the blade in the vertical plane. Tilting permits concentration of dozer driving power on a limited portion of the blade's length.
2. **Pitch :** In this case the top of the blade can be pitched forward or backward varying the angle of attack of the cutting edge. This is a pivotal movement about the point of connection between the dozer the blade. When the top of the blade is pitched forward, the bottom edge moves back which increases the angle of cutting edge attack.

3. **Angling :** In this case blades mounted on a C-frame can be turned from the direction of travel. In angling the blade is turned so that it is not perpendicular to the direction of travel of the dozer. This results in pushing the material to roll of the trailing end of the blade.

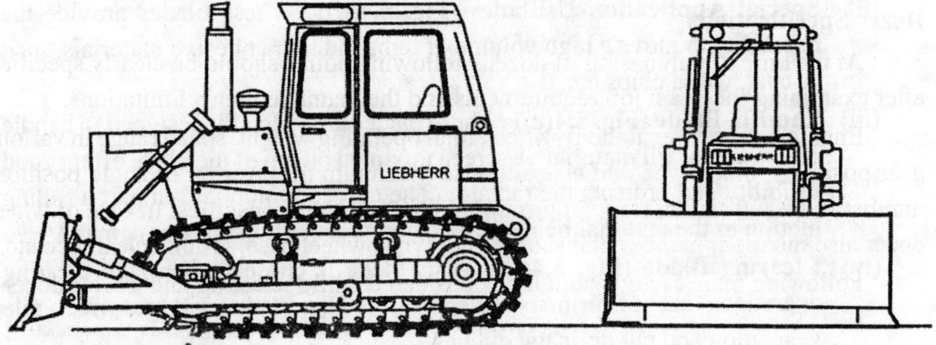

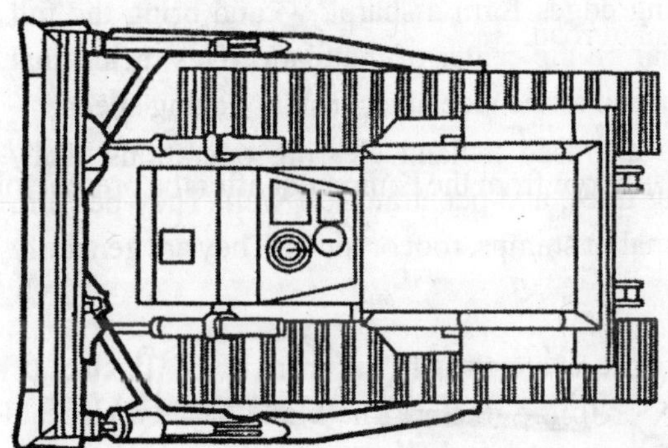

Fig. 5.3 Crawler dozer with blade (Courtesy : Liebherr).

Types of Blades

1. Blades for Production Dozing

(i) **Universal U-Blade (Fig. 5.4(a)) :** U-Blade should be selected for moving large amount of materials over long distances, and is appropriate for moving easily dozed material. These blades are used for stockpile work, trapping for loaders,and land reclamation.

(ii) **Straight or S-Blade (Fig. 5.4(b)) :** being smaller than the U-blade, it is easier to manoeuver. This blade penetrates material easily. Addition of a tilt cylinder increases the versatility of this blade. It can move heavy materials more efficiently. These have no curvature in their length, are mounted in a fixed position, perpendicular to the line of travel.

2. Blades for Special Applications

Some of the more familiar special applications of dozing blades are described below :

(i) **Angle Blade (Fig. 5.4(c)) :** The angle blade can be mounted straight or angled 25° to either side. It is designed to move material towards the sides of a cut, as required in road construction, backfilling or cutting ditches, and substantially reduces the amount of maneuvering.

(ii) **Special Application U-Blades (Fig. 5.4(d)) :** These blades provide the capability to move a high volume of light and non-cohesive materials, such as coal, wood chips etc.

(iii) **Landfill Blade (Fig. 5.4(e)) :** These blades are specially designed to handle refuse and/or fill material. A screen mounted on top of the blade offers good visibility and protects the radiator. The curved moldboard impart a rolling motion to the material being pushed and reduces horsepower demand.

(iv) **Clearing Blade (Fig. 5.4(f)) :** This blade is chosen when land clearing operations are of primary importance. The blade will cut tree, pile vegetation and cut drainage ditches.

(v) **V-Blade (Fig. 5.4(g)) :** This is used to shear trees, stumps and brushes at ground level. The two cutting edges form a sharp 'V' and bring the full machine power output to bear on the center of the blade. This means that vegetation can be cut and pushed to the side at a constant dozing speed.

(vi) **Rake (Fig. 5.4(h)) :** These are used in land clearing operations. They remove vegetation, including trees, and penetrate soil well. They perform efficiently when removing smaller stumps, root or rocks. They are generally replaceable.

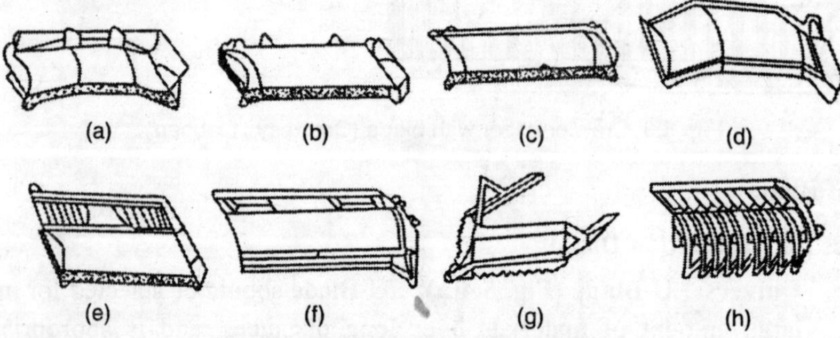

Fig. 5.4 Different types of dozer blades.

5.5.2 Rippers

Crawler-tractor, mounted with ripper is finding increasing use in construction, mining and quarrying. Cost of ripping vary from material to material to be ripped and some times very hard rock formations cannot be ripped. Cost of ripping should be compared with the cost of 'drilling—blasting' to consider economical way of excavation. While considering ripping cost, life of ripping type as well as shortening of life of undercarriage should be considered.

Characteristics of the material to be ripped influence the selection or ripper type; number of shanks required, ripping speed and amount of ripper penetration. For hard material single shank is preferred, but where material is easily penetrated and fractured into small pieces, a two or three shank ripper is used.

Ripper Types

Various types of rippers are used with the dozers. These may be towed units, integrated units, back rippers. Towed units are generally cable operated and are hard to manoeuver, whereas integrated ripper units are hydraulically operated. With crawler mounted tractors these integrated units are easy to manoeuver and provides a more compact and efficient units,while damage to tyres is expected in rocky conditions. Integral rippers are of two types—hinge or parallelogram. Back rippers are mounted on dozer blades, so that as the dozer proceeds forward, the back rippers pivot in the mounting brackets and drag over the ground. Those are used in light duty works.

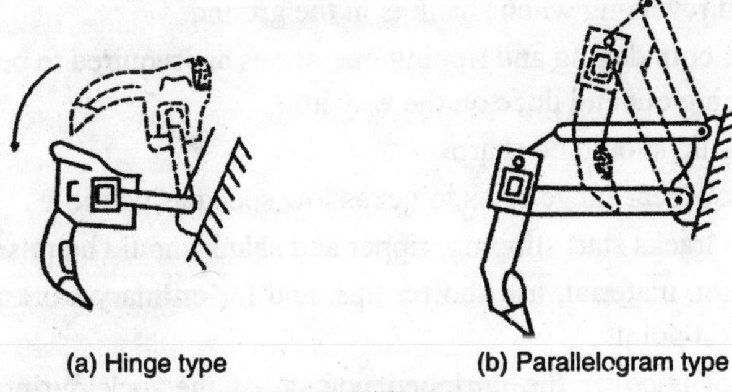

(a) Hinge type (b) Parallelogram type

Fig. 5.5 Rippers.

The construction of ripper is shown in Fig. 5.5 and 5.6. The tip can be replaced whenever it break, and protects the shank and adopter from damage. When adopter is breaking frequently, use the next shorter tip so as to reduce the load on the adopter. The protector is provided to support the tip as well as to provide wear protection for the adopter. This protector is replaced when it is worn out to 6 mm, so that any likely protector failure (which may cause adopter damage) may not occur.

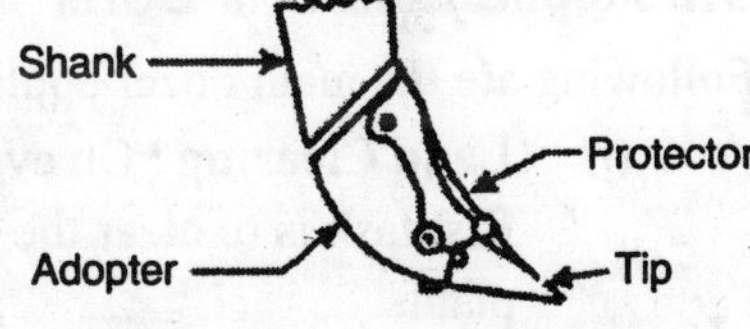

Fig. 5.6 Ripper shank with tip.

Rippers can also be classified as follows :

(i) Fixed Multiple-shank Ripper.

(ii) Variable Multiple-shank Ripper.

(iii) Fixed Giant Ripper.

(iv) Variable Giant Ripper.

The fixed multiple shank ripper is used for comparatively simple ripping operations. The shank moves only up and down during digging operation. Digging depth is adjustable by changing shank pin position or shank. Fixed giant ripper has only single powerful shank, but is not common as compared to variable giant rippers.

The variable multiple-shank ripper can change the angle of its shanks by means of ripper tilt cylinders. These are used where there are many boulders, or where the quality of rock is not consistent. The variable giant ripper has a single power shank. The angle of this ripper can be changed according to the ground requirements.

Ripping Efficiency

In order to achieve high ripping efficiency, following suggestions should be considered during ripping operations :

(i) When material is not broken, loosen the surface in one direction, then cross-ripping should be adopted.

(ii) If material is soft, use more than one shank ripper.

(iii) Ripping should be done downhill.

(iv) Avoid reversing when shank is in the ground.

(v) When both dozing and ripping operations are required to be done, it should rip going out and doze on the way in.

(vi) Shank tip should be sharp.

(vii) Use low gear range so as to get as low speed as possible.

(viii) When tracks start slipping, ripper and shank should be raised.

(ix) For hard material, use shorter tips, and for ordinary work use longest and sharpest point.

(x) Do not uncover the unripped portion of the rock during dozing of the material loosened by ripping. This will reduce the wear of under-carriage parts.

5.6 Applications of a Dozer

Following are the main dozer applications :

(i) Land Clearing : On every project, a bulldozer is the first equipment and its first task is to clear the ground for camp-site, and site or installing various plants.

Clearing of the land involves several operations depending upon the condition of soil and topography, the amount of clearing required, type of vegetation and the purpose for which clearing is done. The operations may include, removal of soil to remove unevenness of the ground, removal of trees and stumps including roots, removal of vegetation etc. For this purpose various types of equipment can be used. These may be tractor mounted bulldozers, tractor mounted special blades in which the stringer penetrates the ground to cut the main horizontal roots of the tree or a blade which slides along the surface of the ground for cutting vegetation, tractor mounted rakes to be used to grab and pile trees, boulders etc. without transporting excess amount of soil, tractor mounted clamp rakes to pick up felled trees and transport them to a place of dumping.

(ii) **Striping :** It is the removal of top soil that is not usable. Stripping is planned in such a way so that haulage is for minimum distance. Upto the distance of 100 meters dozer itself is used, but for more distances scrapers should be employed.

(iii) **Sidehill cuts :** Sidehill cuts should always be started from the top and then worked downward.

(iv) **Backfilling :** In backfilling material is pushed ahead of the dozer over embankments into ditches or against a structure. Angle dozers are found more suitable for this job as they can drift material into the trench while maintaining forward motion.

(v) **Ditching :** The rough ditches can be prepared by the dozers. These are constructed with a straight blade by working at right angles to the length of the ditch.

(vi) **Spreading :** These are also used for spreading the material hauled by trucks, scrapers etc. Depth of spread is adjusted considering the thickness required.

(vii) **Dozing rocks and frozen ground :** Rocks are generally removed by using one corner of the blade, as the full power is thus applied on this section of the blade. Large sections of rocks are removed by using the blade to lift the rock, simultaneously applying power to the tracks.

(viii) Maintaining haul roads.

(ix) Clearing of the floors of borrow and quarry pits.

(x) **Digging :** A dozer while moving forward with the blade inserted in the soil digs it. If the blade is lowered further, more work can be done, thereby resistances will increase, as a thick slice requires more digging power than a thin one. The blade, during operation should be lowered or raised gradually to avoid bumps in the path.

(xi) **Breaking Pile :** A pile may be knocked down by walking into it with the blade at the desired grade, after which it may be spread or piled elsewhere. If the heap is too large, it may be cut away in parts, either directly, or if it is not possible, the side cut should be repeated from different angles.

5.7 Output of Dozers

The production of bulldozers mainly depend upon the following factors :

(i) Size and condition of the bulldozer.

(ii) Distance travelled by the bulldozer.

(iii) Speed of operation.

(iv) Characteristics of soil being handled.

(v) Surface on which bulldozer is operating.

(vi) Efficiency.

When dozing the materials that tend to stick together and remain in front of the blade during dozing, the efficiency is higher as compared to that when dozing loose granular earth or shattered rock. Whereas hard and cemented material needs extra efforts in preblasting or ripping.

Output of a dozer in bank-volume/hr.

$$= \text{Loose volume handled/trip} \times S \times \frac{60}{t} \times \text{efficiency}$$

where, S = Swell factor,

and t = Cycle time (time required/trip) in minutes.

Swell Factor : As we know that, loosening of earth causes an increase in volume,which if expressed as a % of original undisturbed volume gives the percentage of swell earth. The ratio of volume of original earth to the loose earth is known as swell factor.

Loose volume handled/trip = Production per cycle

$$= \text{Blade width} \times (\text{Blade height})^2 \times \text{Blade factor}$$

Blade factor depends upon the type of soil and generally taken between 0.4 to 1.1, depending upon difficulty to easy dozing work.

$$\text{Cycle time (in minutes)} = \frac{D}{F} + \frac{D}{R} + G$$

where, D = Haul distance (metres)

F = Forward speed (m/min)

R = Reverse speed (m/min)

G = Gear shifting and manoeuver time (minutes)

Volume Conversion

The volume measure varies with the state of the soil. States of soil encountered in earthmoving operations are : (a) in-phase natural soil (known as bank soil), (b) loose excavated bulk soil, and (c) compacted soil. The bank volume swells when heaped in a loose state after excavation, and shrinks when compacted.

Volume conversion of common natural soils into three states is given hereunder :

Natural of soil	*Bank volume*	*Loose volume*	*Compacted volume*
Common earth	1.00	1.25	0.90
Sand	1.00	1.12	0.95
Clay	1.00	1.27	0.90
Rock (blasted)	1.00	1.50	1.30

For a given soil, the swell factor and shrinkage factor are defined as under :

(i) Swell factor = Loose volume/Bank volume.l

(ii) Shrinkage factor = Compacted volume/Bank volume.

Dozer Production Estimating

The major factors that control dozer production rates are :

1. Blade Type

As discussed earlier, straight (*S*) blades roll materials in front of the blade, and universal (*U*) and semi-universal (*SU*) blades control side spillage by holding the material within the blade. The blade capacity is a function of blade type and physical size. Manufacturers specification sheets provide information in this regard.

2. Job Conditions and Condition of Material

The type and condition of material handled affects the shape of the pushed mass in front of the blade. The volumetric load a blade will carry can be estimated by following methods :

(a) Manufacturer's blade rating.

(b) Previous experience (similar material, equipment, and work conditions).

(c) Field measurements.

Correction Factors		
Operator	1. Highly skilled	1.00
	2. Average	0.80
	3. Unskilled	0.65
Material	1. Loose stockpile	1.20
	2. Easy to dig : loam, sand, gravel	1.00
	3. Medium dig, common earth in natural state	0.80
	4. Hard to push, dry riped or blasted rock	0.67
Slot dozing	Ditches	1.20
Visibility	1. Clear	1.00
	2. Darkness, fog, rain, snow or dust	0.80
Efficiency	1. 50 min/hr.	0.84
	2. 40 min/hr.	0.67
Blade	1. Straight blade	1.00
	2. U-blade for light material	1.20
	3. Angle blade	0.50–0.75
Grades	Favourable (– 30%) to unfavourable (+ 30%)	1.25–0.40

Traction Coefficient : The available push power and drawbar pull of a crawler tractor depends on the traction between the ground and tracks. The traction is determined by the weight of the machine and the type of ground surface. The available push power and drawbar is derived from the following formula :

Available push power/drawbar pull (in kg)

= Machine weight (in kg) × traction coefficient.

Following table shows the values of traction coefficient for different materials :

Material	*Traction Coefficient*
1. Concrete	0.45
2. Dry clay, loam	0.90
3. Wet clay, loam	0.70
4. Dry sand	0.30
5. Wet sand	0.50
6. Quarry pit	0.55
7. Gravel road (loose)	0.50
8. Packed snow	0.27
9. Firm earth	0.90
10. Loose earth	0.60
11. Coal, stockpiled	0.60

3. Cycle Time

As discussed earlier, one dozer production cycle is the sum of the time required to push a load, back track and manoeuver into the position to push again. Dozing, is generally performed at low speed, 2.5 to 4 km/hr. The lower figures is suitable for very heavy cohesive materials. Return speed is usually the maximum that can be attained in the distance available.

5.7.1 Output of Rippers

Output of rippers depend upon the characteristics of soil, size of the tractor dozer, speed of the machine, shape and size of the ripper tooth, number of shanks used, and depth and width of ripping pass. However, following are the formulae used in general for calculating the output of ripper :

Production per hour

= (Bank-volume ripped per pass) × (Number of passes per hour)

Fig. 5.7 Crawler dozer in operation.

where, Bank-volume ripped per pass

= Length of pass × Width of ripping pass × Depth of penetration × Efficiency

Number of passes per hour

$$= \frac{60}{\text{Time for making one pass (in min)}}$$

and time taken in one pass $= \frac{\text{Length of pass}}{\text{Travelling speed}} + \text{Turn round time.}$

How to Increase Ripping Production

1. Rip downhill.
2. If material is not broken in one direction, cross-ripping should be adopted.
3. Ripping can be made easier by adding water to the area.
4. Do not reverse when shank is in the ground.
5. Use shorter points when ripping hard material.
6. For reducing wear of undercarriage parts, traction should be reduced by leaving a thin layer of loose material over the unripped rock.
7. As soon as tracks starts slipping, ripper and shanks should be raised.
8. Use low gear while ripping a rock.

5.8 Scrapers

Scrapers are the devices to scrap the ground and load it simultaneously, transport it over the required distance, dump and then spread the dumped material over the required area in required thickness level, and return to the pit for the next cycle. Thus, the scrapers are designed to dig, load, haul, dump and spread and some times called as carry all.

The scrapers are of three types : (a) towed type, (b) self propelled or motorised or conventional type, (c) self loading or elevating scraper.

Scrapers can also be classified as : 1. Crawler tractor scrapers or Wheel tired tractor scrapers, 2. Pusher loaded or self loaded scrapers.

The towed scrapers are provided with either cable or hydraulic control. Although these are becoming obsolete but even then some contractors use them because when coupled to a suitably powered crawler tractor, they can operate in extremely adverse conditions.

Self-propelled or motorised or conventional scrapers are most popular now-a-days. These are generally manufactured in ranges from 10 to 25 cubic metres. A motorised scraper needs push loading by a crawler mounted or a wheeled tractor. Wheeled scrapers have more fauling speed and hence are suitable for long distance hauling while crawler-towed scrapers travel at slower speed and can be used for short hauls only.

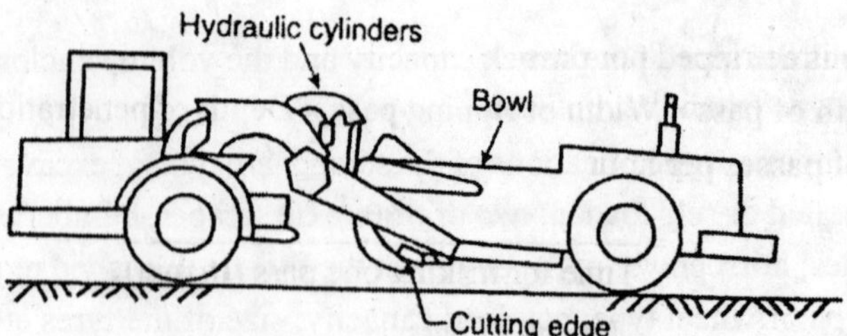

Fig. 5.8 Self propelled scraper.

The problem of loading by a pusher is overcome by the third type of scraper known as self-loading or elevating scrapers. These are twin engine scrapers and can work completely independently of all other plants. It does not need a pusher. To make them more effective and competitive with dump trucks, some of the manufacturers are producing three axle-scrapers of 40 cubic meter pay loads. However, these have certain limitations, firstly, the elevator cannot load particularly free flowing sands or handle rock infested soils. Secondly pay loads are restricted because of the additional weight of the loading elevator and its drive system. Thirdly, increase in loading time, the inability to obtain a full load, indicates that for powerful units a pusher is still required.

Construction

A self-propelled or motorised type scraper has following main parts :

(i) **Bowl :** The bowl is a pan to hold the scraped dirt. It is hinged at the gear corners to the rear axle inside the wheels, and is capable of tilting down for digging or ejecting. The bowl size is specified to indicate the size of the scraper.

(ii) **Cutting edge :** The bowl has a cutting edge attached at the bottom. The cutting edge is lowered into the dirt to make a shallow cut.

(iii) **Apron :** This is a wall in front of the bowl, which opens and closes to regulate the flow of the earth in and out of the bowl. This can open or closes in carrying position as well.

(iv) **Tail gate or ejector :** These are the rear of the pan which is capable of forward and backward movement inside the bowl. During loading it remains at its rear wall, while moves forward to help in ejecting the load during dumping.

All these items are controlled by the hydraulic system. Movements of these parts are controlled hydraulically. In hydraulic system, oil pressure works in the double acting rams provided separately for bowl, apron, and tail gate. The flow of oil in these rams is controlled by valves.

Specification of a Scraper

Usually the capacity of a scraper is given in terms of cubic metres struck and cubic metres heaped. Struck capacity of a scraper is the actual volume enclosed by the bowl and apron, struck off by a straight line passed along the top edge of the side plates. In other words it is the volume of the material levelled with the top edges of the bowl.

Heaped capacity is the sum of the struck capacity and the volume enclosed by the four plates at a 1 : 1 slope extending upward.

The other important specifications of the scraper are type of excavator, *i.e.*, towed type or self-propelled or self-loaded; two or three axle scraper, number of engines, *i.e.*, one or two engines; horsepower of the engine at the flywheel; pushed required with the scraper; track-type or wheel type; pay load capacity; size of the tyres etc.

Operation

Operation of a scraper is described hereunder for an earth work application :

(i) **Loading or digging :** Operator moves to the cut with the ejector at the rear and the apron raised approximately to 40 cm. The bowl is then lowered to the desired depth of cut, increase engine speed, move forward in first gear keeping optimum depth of out. When the bowl is full, the apron is closed and the bowl is then raised.

(ii) **Transporting :** The bowl is transported in high gear in raised position to provide sufficient clearance. during transporting, apron should be fully closed to prevent loss of the material, and the ejector should remain in the rear position.

(iii) **Unloading :** Unloading in a scraper is also termed as 'dumping and spreading'. The bowl should be positioned to spread the material to the desired depth during this operation. A partial opening of the apron during the initial unloading will help in even spreading. For wet and sticky material, the apron should be raised and lowered repeatedly until the material behind it is loosened and drops out of the bowl. Then the ejector is moved forward to push the remaining material out of the bowl at a uniform rate.

When the dump is complete, the tail gate is fully retracted, the apron dropped and the 'bowl' raised to transporting position. The finishing touch during spreading is done by grading it with the cutting edge, and the unit then hurries back and starts next cycle.

In hydraulic system the operations as described above are affected through oil pressure working in double-acting rams, usually two for apron and one for tail gate.

For better efficiency in the scraping operations following points should be taken care of :

(i) Depth of cut should commensurate with the power available for the cut.

(ii) Keep the haul roads maintained.

(iii) Pushers should utilise their waiting time in dressing the cut.

(iv) Loading operation should be carried out downhill wherever possible.

(v) Excessive turning of a pusher should be avoided, and scraper pusher balance should be maintained.

Economics of Scraper Operation

To examine the economics of scraper operation two main factors need detailed consideration, they are : material and haulage distance.

(i) **Material :** Scrapers can conveniently be used in all types of soils, like sand, gravel, silt, loam clay and their mixtures.

(ii) **Haulage distance :** It is generally seen that for very short distances say 50 to 100 metres, a bulldozer is most economical earth moving equipment, whereas a scraper is most economical when the haulage distance is less than, say, 1500 metres and more than 100 metres.

Number of Scrapers per Pushdozer

For attaining the maximum hauling capacities,wheel type tractor-pulled scrapers need the assistance of pushdozers during loading to reduce the loading time. Similarly crawler-type tractor pulled scrapers, which are claimed to be self loading can also be loaded by means of push dozers. If the use of push dozer is found to be economical, *i.e.*, the increase in production is sufficient enough to pay back the cost of the tractor dozer, it is better to use it.

When pusher dozer is used, it is desirable to match the number of pushers with the number of scrapers. Waiting of any one, reduces its efficiency and increases the production cost. The cycle time for a pusher includes the time required to load one scraper plus the time needed to move into position to load another scraper. It depends on the conditions in the loading pit, sizes of the pusher and scrapers and loading method.

Following formula should be used to determine the number of scrapers that a push dozer can serve :

$$\text{Number of scrapes served} = \frac{\text{Cycle time for scraper}}{\text{Cycle time for pushdozer}}$$

5.8.1 Elevating Scrapers

Scrapers described earlier depends upon a pusher tractor for loading, the elevating scraper is self loading one in addition to self propelled capabilities. It is similar to a conventional scraper except that its apron has been replaced by an 'elevator', also known as 'ladder'. This ladder is made up of chains with buckets bolted to it. The chain is rotated by power independent of the travel of the scraper. It has a variable speed and also reversing of the chain and buckets is possible. Loading of this scraper is done by forcing incoming earth over the cutting edge and subsequently ladder will carry it up into the bowl. They are capable of loading most materials except rock and boulders which are too large to pass between the cutting edge and the elevator buckets, and cohesive material with high moisture content.

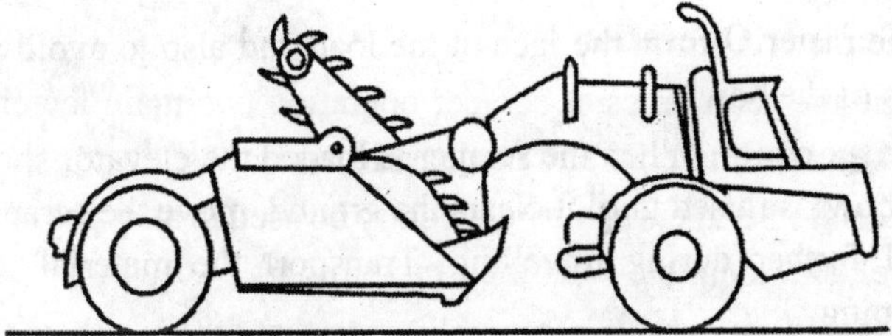

Fig. 5.9 Elevating scraper.

By using elevating scraper, cost of a pusher and its operator is eliminated. Elevating scrapers also have very good finishing ability, and hence very useful in preparing final layer of earth work in road or airfield construction work.

The operating cost and maintenance cost of the elevating scraper is higher by nearly 30% as compared to that of conventional scrapers. Due to dead weight of the loading mechanism, its transportation efficiency is reduced.

Fig. 5.10 Elevating scraper (Courtesy : John deere).

Operation

Operation of an elevating scraper is described hereunder. The working cycle is similar to that of conventional scraper.

(i) **Loading :** For making a cut, the bowl is first lowered to a depth which can permit the elevator and tractor to operate at high and constant engine speed. The cut will force material towards the bowl and elevator buckets will sweep the material into the bowl. The elevator has 4 forward and one reverse speed. Soft surfaces like, sand, silt and topsoil are dug and loaded at high speeds. Low speeds are used for loading tough materials, like, hard clay etc. When the bowl is fully loaded, stop the elevator to avoid sweeping of the material from the face of the load and also to avoid spilling over to sides of the bowl.

(ii) **Transporting :** When the scraper is loaded,the elevator should be stopped and bowl is raised until it clears the ground, move the scraper and raise the bowl further during travelling. Transport the material to the place of dumping.

(iii) **Unloading :** The bowl is lowered to allow the desired depth of the spread. With the machine in motion, the ejector floor is opened, thus allowing the bowl to unload itself and the loading edge of the ejector floor will strike off the unloaded material in the bowl, in a smooth and even layer.

When unloading is complete, the bowl can be raised, ejector floor is closed and the scraper is returned for the next cycle.

Optimising the Scraper Production

Following are the some of the suggestions which will increase the scraper production :

(i) Construct and maintain smooth haul roads for faster and safer travel with less driver fatigue.

(ii) Depth of cut should be according to the type of soil being handled.

(iii) Use ripper teeth in hard or abrasive materials for easy loading. While ripping a rock, the depth ripped should be more so as to leave a loose layer of material under the tracks and tyres to provide good traction and reduced wear.

(iv) Where possible, loading be done in down grade.

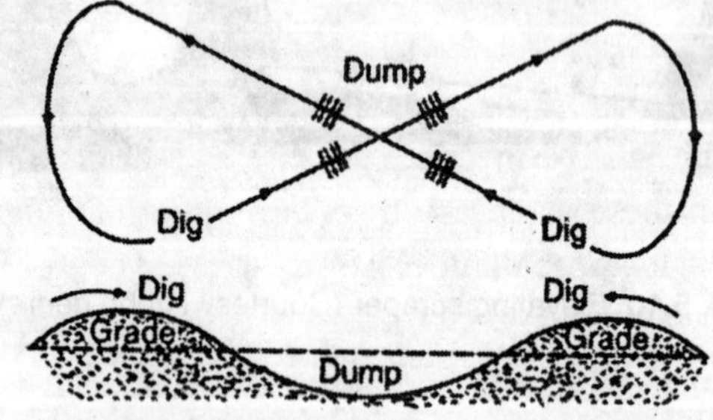

Fig. 5.11 Method of loading and hauling.

(v) To increase stability of the scraper during travel, carry the bowl as close to the ground as possible.

(vi) If necessary, pre-wetting of the soil is done so that soil is reasonably moist, since some soils will load more easily when they are moist.

(vii) Whenever possible, plan the work to eliminate all avoidable turns. For example, 'Figure 5.8' loading, hauling and unloading can be used to great advantage. By using this method, only two turns are required while two full loads are delivered, whereas normally two turns are required for each load.

(viii) Dumping should be done in an orderly pattern in the lifts of desired thickness so that compaction equipment work in an effective manner.

(ix) A spotter should always be employed to eliminate confusion and traffic congestion and coordinate the movement of scrapers for spreading the soil in the fill and that of compacting equipment.

Advantages of Elevating Scrapers

Following are the main advantages of elevating scrapers :

(a) Better loading ability in loose free flowing materials.

(b) Good finishing ability.

(c) Can be operated independently.

(d) Smooth and complete unloading of bowl by reversing the elevator rotation.

(e) Pusher tractor dozer is not required.

(f) Addition of ripper teeth to the cutting edge permits self loading in hard compacted material.

(g) Pulverising and mixing action by the elevator places material in uniform and homogeneous state for compaction.

Special Types of Scrapers

Other then the tractor towed, motorised, and elevating scrapers explained earlier, following are the other types of scrapers :

(i) **Tandem Scrapers :** In this type of scraper two bowls are attached to a single prime mover unit. It gives higher capacity per cycle.

(ii) **Twin Engine Scrapers :** This type of scraper has two engines with single bowl. This has the advantages of, (a) greater acceleration due to higher power, (b) higher speeds under sever conditions, (c) less chances for getting struck.

(iii) **Multi-Engine Multi-Bowl Scrapers :** This is the combination of the above two ideas. In these scrapers power is supplied to each wheel. These are generally self loading; number of axles varies between 3 to 6, number of bowls 3, capacity upto 80 cu m. This eliminates the need for a pusher.

5.8.2 Output of Scrapers

Output of scrapers depends upon the following main factors :

(i) Size and mechanical conditions of the scraper.

(ii) Hauling distance.

(iii) Condition of the haul road.

(iv) Characteristics of soil and work area.

(v) Efficiency.

Heaped capacity of scraper out of the two scrapers having more length or width and less height is higher even if the struck capacity is same.

Output of a scraper in bank-volume/hour.

$$= \text{Optimum loose volume loaded/trip} \times S \times \frac{60}{t} \times \text{Efficiency}$$

where, S = Swell factor.

and t = Cycle time/trip in minutes.

Cycle Time for a Scraper

Cycle time for a scraper is the time required for loading, hauling to the fill, dumping, and returning back to the loading position. This cycle time is divided into : (i) Fixed time, which includes loading, dumping, turning, accelerating, retarding. These elements are reasonably constant under uniform operating conditions. Generally time study data of such elements are available for three type of conditions, namely favourable, average and unfavourable conditions. (ii) Variable time, which includes hauling and returning; it depends on the distance travelled and the average speed of the vehicle. This time is generally required to be determined.

5.9 Loaders (Front-end Loaders)

A bucket is attached to the arms and capable of being raised, lowered and dumped through mechanical or hydraulic controls. The loaders having bucked in the front, known as 'Front-end loaders' are very common. The loaders are versatile, self propelled equipment mounted either on crawler or wheel type running gear. These loaders are fitted with front mounted general-purpose bucket operated through hydraulic rams, with which they dig, scoop, lift, transport, carry, dump or load into hauling units, bins, hoppers, conveyors and stockpiles. With the help of additional front and rear mounted attachments these can doze, scrap, grub, fork-lift, trench, grade, ditch rip, clamp, and winch. Applications of a loader very from handling coal, sugar, sand, salt, stone-etc. to earth moving and digging work in quarries.

Types of Loaders

Loaders are of the following types :

(a) Crawler loaders (b) Wheel loaders

(a) Crawler Loaders

Crawler track types are generally preferred for digging and loading jobs where ground conditions are poor and low pressure characteristics are required, and are preferable for applications involving rock and sharp stony ground as there is no possibility of tyre damage. These are best employed for short moves between loading and dumping points. These should be transported from one site to another after loading on the trailers.

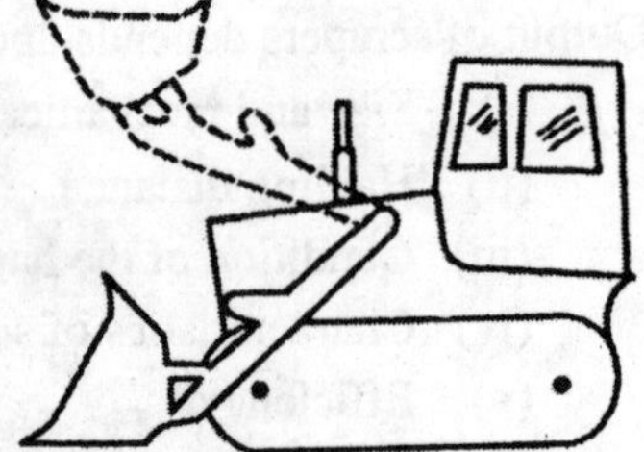

Fig. 5.12 Crawler loader.

(b) Wheeled Loaders

As a result of the development of more capable power trains (axles and tires), there was a steady and towards wheel loaders at the expenses of crawlers. Protective chains for tires, that considerably increases tire operating life, even in quarry applications, additionally favoured the wheel loader against the rather more difficult to manoeuver crawler.

Wheeled loaders are generally four wheel drive. However, for handling light jobs on good ground conditions two wheel drive variants are also used. Four wheel drive loaders are generally used for construction job, whereas, two wheel drive loaders are used for bulk handling of coal, cement, fertilizer etc. into hoppers and trucks.

From manoeuverability point of view, wheel loaders are of following types :

(i) Articulated type (Pivot steer).

(ii) Rigid frame-two wheel steer or all wheel steer.

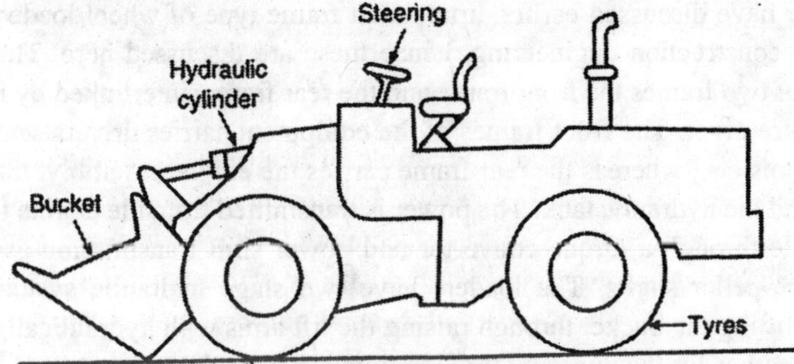

Fig. 5.13 Line diagram of wheel loader.

1. **Articulated type of loaders :** This type of loader is hinged in the middle of the front and rear axles, as shown in Fig. 5.14(a). Due to their operational characteristics and capability of working in limited spaced and short turning radius, resulting higher speed of work, these have become very popular. Because of the advantage of quick maneuvering and thereby easier spotting of loads, less rolling resistance on turns, better mobility on soft surface, these loaders give better performance and high productivity. The articulation permits the loader to pivot 30-45 degree either side of the centre.

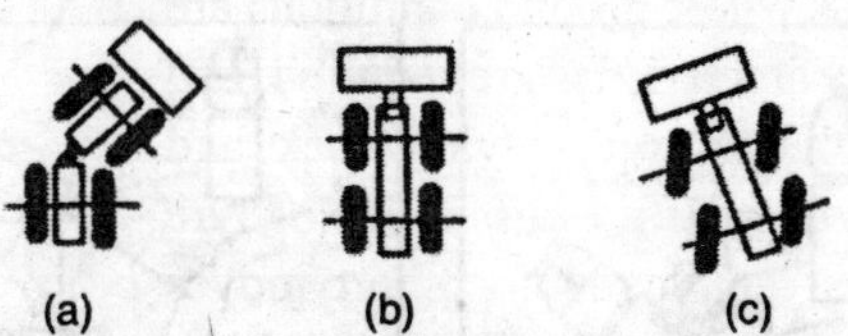

Fig. 5.14 Types of loaders : (a) Articulated, (b) Rigid frame-two wheel steer, (c) Rigid frame 4 wheel steer.

2. **Rigid frame type-loaders :** These are comparatively cheaper than articulated frame type of loaders. With this type of loader sometimes operators misjudge hopper or truck body width and therefore he has a manoeuver back and forth before dumping. Rigid frame loaders are of two types, namely two wheel steer and all wheel steer. By designing all wheel steer loader, manoeuverability is gained along with the advantages of rigid frame construction. In all wheel steer loaders, operator can switch from 4 wheel to 2 wheel steer or *vice-versa* by using a lever. On stockpile operations, all wheel steering allows the operator to align the bucket in the pile quickly to ensure a heaped load in the minimum possible time. While moving on the roads operator can set his loader on front steer only and then handles it like a normal road vehicle.

Construction

As we have discussed earlier, articulated frame type of wheel loaders are very common in construction engineering, hence these are discussed here. The loader is consisting of two frames,the front frame and the rear frame, interlinked by means of a vertical centre pivot. The front frames of the equipment carries drivers seat, bucket's hydraulic rams etc., whereas the rear frame carries the engine assembly, transmission assembly and the hydraulic tank. The power is transmitted from the engine to the front and rear axle through a torque convertor and power shift transmission assembly by means of propeller shafts. The loaders have two stage hydraulic system, one for hoisting or lifting the bucket through raising the lift arms with hydraulically-operated rams, and another for the dumping through dump arms which are operated by another set of arms.

The hydraulically actuated loader lift mechanism is located in front of the operator for safety reasons. Lift control provides raise, hold, lower and float positions. Bucket control has roll-back, hold and dump positions. Additional hydraulic controls are also provided for optional attachment.

Applications

Loaders with its general purpose bucket and with additional attachment can be used for :

(i) Loading the dump trucks in quarries, mines and industries.

(ii) Loading the material in the hopper of crushers, conveyors etc.

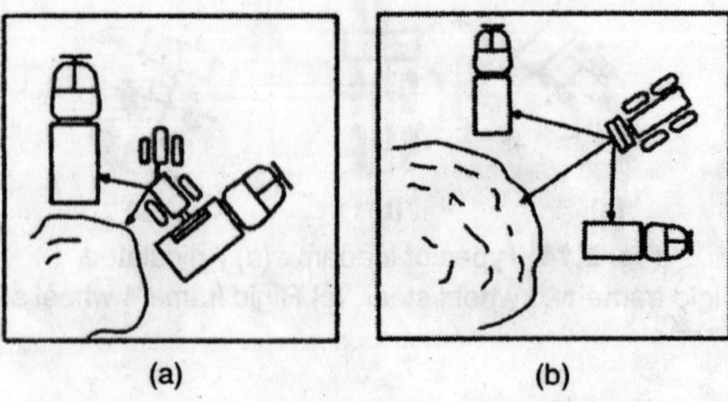

Fig. 5.15 Loading arrangement with (a) Articulated, (b) Rigid frame loaders.

(iii) Loading the waste material, clearing debris.
(iv) To move bulky objects.
(v) Removing snow.
(vi) Clearing the areas.
(vii) For forklifting.
(viii) For dozing, trenching, ripping etc. with the help of suitable attachments.

Thus the loader is a very useful equipment and is used in mining, quarrying, industrial work in addition to the construction engineering works.

Operations

Loaders are used to carry out following main operations :

1. **Loading :** Loading operation is the main operation performed by the loaders. Loading consists of scooping, lifting, turning and dumping materials such as sand, gravel and crushed materials from stockpiles, bank or construction site into the hauling units. For better output the bucket should be filled full and the number of hauling units deployed for the work should be such that there is no waiting time for the loader and there should not be more than one hauling unit in the queue.

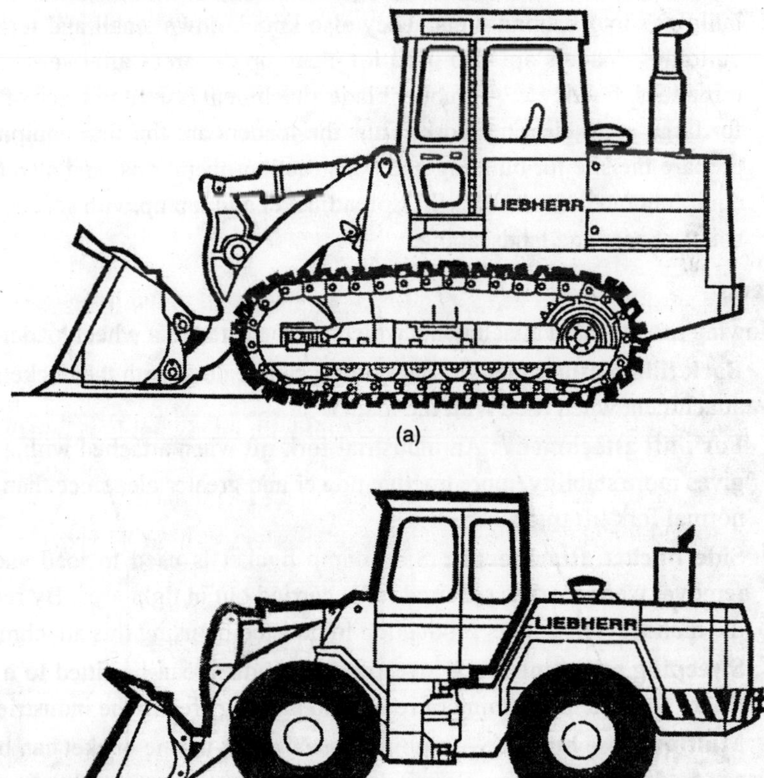

Fig. 5.16 Loaders : (a) Crawler (b) Wheeled, types (Courtesy : Liebherr).

2. **Hauling :** Wheel loaders are excellent for moving loose materials over short distances to dump into hauling units, hoppers, conveyors, bins or any other place of work in the construction sites.

   A *cycle time* for a loader consists of the following :

   (a) Time for scooping, lifting and dumping the bucket along with time required for changing the directions and taking the turns.

   (b) *Hauling time* : It is the travel time for load carrying and empty returning. Generally the high reverse speeds reduce the returning time enabling the reduction in cycle time and thus more work in one hour.

3. **Excavating :** Crawler loaders and heavy duty wheel-loaders are excellent for many excavation jobs, like basement digging etc. With excavator attachment it can also handle several other types of excavation works. These loaders can excavate as well as lift the excavated material and dump it into trucks or on the stockpiles. Incase surface is hard for excavating and scooping, the earth ripper or sacrifier attachment is mounted on the year of the loader to loosen such surface. The operator can then easily dig and load the material into bucket for removal.

4. **Clearing :** Loaders can scoop up and load the debris of demolished buildings into hauling units. They also knock down small and temporary buildings; loaders are also used for clean up the areas after snow-storms, tornadoes, floods etc. A grubber blade attachment is used in place of bucket for large-scale clearing work. Thus the loaders are the first equipment to prepare the site for building and construction operations; and also the last equipment in order to backfill, spread, level and top up with selected good soil for grass and landscaping.

Attachments

Following are the main attachments which can be fitted to a wheel loader :

(i) **Back filling attachments :** Backfilling can be done with the bucket of this attachment when used with the loader.

(ii) **Fork lift attachment :** An industrial fork lift when attached with a loader gives more stability, more tractive power and greater clearance than with a normal fork lift truck.

(iii) **Side bucket attachment :** Side dump bucket is used to load snow for removal when work is required to be carried out in tight area. By reducing the manoeuvering time, production in boosted by using this attachment.

(iv) **Sweeping attachment :** A sweeping attachment can be fitted to a wheel leader for general cleaning of roads and parking area in the industries.

(v) **Multipurpose bucket :** A multipurpose or four-in-one bucket can be used as a dozer, scraper, clamshell and general purpose loading. The multipurpose bucked is much heavier than the general purpose bucket, and therefore a loader equipped with it will generally need more counter-weight for the same operating load rating.

(vi) **Ripper-scarifier attachment :** These are mounted on rear of the loader to loosen hard surfaces such as compacted earth; hardpan, shale, slate, decomposed rock; to tear up old brick, asphalt or broken concrete pavement, that do not readily yield to direct bucket loading.

(vii) **Miscellaneous other attachments :** A large number of attachments for specialised job are also available for fitting to the loaders. Some of these are pipe laying attachments, wooden log or concrete pipe handling attachments, pole handling attachments, boom for loader crane set up.

(viii) **Stacking rake :** Stacking rakes are designed for follow-up clearing, racking and piling after trees and brushes have been cut by other attachments. The teeth are curved and of extra long length to carry a full load up into the fine line pile or windrow.

(ix) **Snow removal attachment :** Snow-removal V-plow is normally used for high speed plowing of snow on long stretches of highway, airport runways and places where there is ample room to throw the snow.

Fig. 5.17 Snow removal attachment.

(x) **Protective chains :** These chains offer the protection for wheel loaders where tires are exposed to sever wear, cuttings, and sudden failures due to punctures. Typical applications for the use of these chains would be in quarries, mines, or heavy rock.

Loader Buckets and Their Application

(i) **Standard bucket (Fig. 5.18a) :** This is most universally used loader attachment and can be used to particularly every type of material encountered during earthmoving operations. Applications of this bucket includes loading, excavation, scraping and level grading.

(ii) Rock bucket (Fig. 5.18b) : It is designed primarily for quarry operations and is very rugged. To achieve good penetration it has a V-shaped cutting edge. This V-shaped cutting edge also enables the operator to concentrate breakout forces on one point.

(iii) Side dump bucket (Fig. 5.18c) : This is designed for loading operations in extremely confined quarters, such as subway tunnel, etc. It is available with the opening on either or both sides, material is dumped to the side.

(iv) Log grapples (Fig. 5.18d) : This is designed for log loading operations. It consists of a loading fork and a hydraulically powered clamp, keepingthe logs from shifting or rolling out.

(v) Stockpile bucket (Fig. 5.18e) : This performs best when loading relatively light and non-cohesive materials. It weights less than a standard bucket and offers greater volumetric capacity. Since it is used in stockpile environment, it is not equipped with teeth.

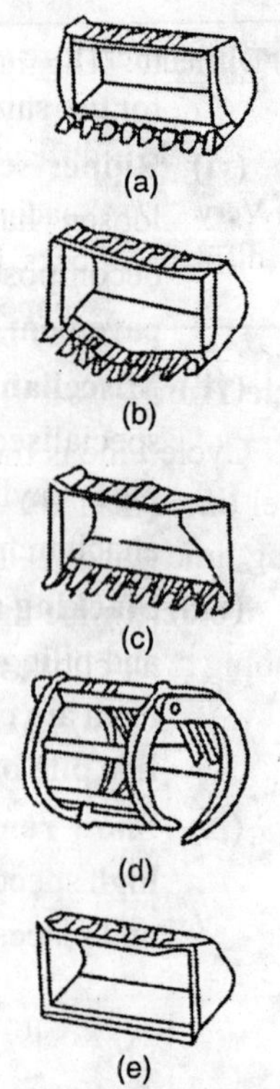

Fig. 5.18 Loader buckets.

5.10 Output of Loaders

Hourly production in m^3/hr $(Q) = q \dfrac{3600}{C} \times$ Efficiency

where, q = Production per cycle (m^3)

= Heaped Capacity × Swell factor × Bucket factor.

and C = Cycle time (in secs).

Bucket Factor

Bucket factor vary from 1.0 to 0.4 depending upon the height of bench, nature of fragmentation, efficiency of the bucket mechanism, operator's skill. Loading conditions affect the bucket factor as mentioned in the table given below :

	Loading conditions	***Bucket factor***
(i) Easy :	Digging and loading from stockpiles or from where no-digging power is required and the material which can be heaped in bucket. Sand, sandy soil with a moderate moisture.	1.0 to 0.8
(ii) Average :	Digging and loading from stock piles which is more difficult to penetrate and scoop but which make nearly a fully heaped bucket. Dry sand or only soil, clayer soil, clay, unscreened gravels or digging and loading of soft gravels directly from hill.	0.8 to 0.6

(Contd...)

(iii) Difficult :	Digging and loading of finely crushed stones, hard clay, gravity sand, clay etc. with high moisture content. It is difficult to fill the bucket with these materials.	0.6 to 0.5
(iv) Very difficult :	Loading of bulky, irregular shaped or rugged rocks, blasted rocks, boulders, sand mixed boulders, soils which can not be scooped up into the bucket.	0.5 to 0.4

Cycle Time

Cycle time is the time required for loading into the bucket, swing time (loaded), travel time (loaded), dumping, back swing and travel time (with empty bucket). The swing time (loaded) and back swing are generally termed as manoeuver time.

To determine the number of loads per hour the loader cycle time must be known combing these above mentioned timings,which are governed by the following factors :

(a) Loading time :

Material	*Minutes*
(i) Uniform aggregates	0.03 – 0.05
(ii) Moist, mixed aggregates	0.04 – 0.06
(iii) Wet loam	0.05 – 0.07
(iv) Roots, large rocks, soil	0.05 – 0.20
(v) Extremely cohesive material	0.10 – 0.20

(b) Travel time : In loader operation, travel time is a combination of haul and return travel. For estimating the travel into manufacturer's chart is used.

(c) Swing time is the time required for moving the bucket from one position to another keeping the height same. This time depends on the degree and speed of swing and the skill of the operator. Swing time are generally adopted as below :

Degree of swing	*Swing time, in seconds*
45° to 90°	4 – 7
90° to 100°	5 – 8

(d) Dumping time is the time required for unloading the bucket, and depends on the proper spotting of transport equipment, and the operator's skill. Dumping at a fixed area requires 5 to 8 seconds, while at an area not fixed requires 3 to 6 seconds.

5.11 Safety Precautions

5.11.1 General Precautions

Following safety precautions should be strictly followed by the equipment operator for preventing accidents :

1. Always remain alert and in proper physical and mental condition.

2. Always wear right clothing for the job, wear safety glasses, gloves, footwear, hard hat. Do not wear ties, rings or watches which can be caught by moving parts of the equipment.
3. Keep hands away from moving parts such as fan, V-belts, gears, drive shafts etc.
4. Before operation, make sure you know the equipment signal flags, sign and markings fully and also from where to get assistance and first aid.
5. Give warning to nearly people that you are about to start up your equipment.
6. Follow maintenance precautions suggested by the manufacturer and laid down in the operator's manual.
7. Keep the inside of the cab tidy. Keep windscreen, mirrors and lights clean. Clean any grease, oil etc. off hand rails, footsteps, pedals etc.
8. Never allow unqualified people to operate your machine. Operator should be familiar with the capabilities and limitations of the equipment.
9. Always keep a safe speed as per working conditions and state of the ground. While towing another piece of equipment, never proceed at high speeds.
10. When driving a shovel never carry your load above the heads to other people.
11. Follow traffic rules.
12. Always use proper tools and they should be free of dirt, grease and oil and properly maintained. Tools should never be dropped, tossed around the work area.
13. Never check for leaks in a pressurised system with your hands, as this may drive oil through pores and under the skin.
14. Never smoke when refueling and always stop the engine.
15. Never use a naked flame to inspect battery or any leakage.
16. A sufficient safety clearance should be kept from electrical aerial lines.
17. Before excavation, precise position of buried cables should be determined.
18. When not using, bucket, mold board, boom etc. is to be put on ground.
19. Equipments should be well maintained and kept in good working condition.
20. Guards and covers be opened when the power train does not run.
21. Maintenance work must not be performed during operation of the equipment.
22. Shovels and cranes must not be charged by loads exceeding the admissible loads.
23. Boom cranes be operated in such a way that their stability against tilting remains safeguarded, if required, they can be supported by stabilising equipment, using outriggers curves be negotiated at very low speed.
24. Equipments should be carefully inspected at regular intervals.
25. Operator should be aware of what other equipments are in operation at the work site.

26. Plant and equipment must be employed only for designated purpose and operated and maintained in accordance with the manufacturers instructions.
27. Always wear safety helmet when working in a quarry, tunnel or in similar environment.
28. Diesel or petrol engines must not be run in confined or poorly ventilated areas, since their exhaust gases are poisonous.
29. Never run machines above their recommended speeds.
30. Safety glasses or a face shield be used when drilling, grinding or hammering metals. Welder gloves, goggles, and an apron or other protective garments be used when welding or cutting. Safety shoes be used at all the times.
31. Tools should always be properly maintained. The pinned metal on such implements should always be ground off.
32. Always park or place the equipment or machine on a level area away from traffic. The vehicles should be securely supported on jack stands or rigid blocks at frame to ensure that it cannot roll forward, backward or fall.
33. While towing another equipment, never proceed at high speeds (say above 4 kms/hr).
34. While working with a crane, a related danger is shock loading. Sudden lifting or panic braking greatly increases the load on the boom. This is especially dangerous during capacity lifts.
35. If crane operator cannot see all parts of the load and its path clearly, a signal man should guide the load and ensure that it does not pass over any worker.
36. In a continuous operation, wire should be inspected everyday—check it for broken strands and excessive wear, and also check inside of the rope.
37. Always lower the load to the ground before leaving the crane for any reason. Never depend on the brake to hold a load suspended unless the operator is in the cab, at the control.
38. Even if the crane is equipped with one book on the jib and one on the main boom, never use both in lift loads at the same time. A loaded jib book puts stresses on the main boom that seriously affected its capacity to bear loads.
39. Develop safety consciousness through regular meetings, films, demonstrations etc.
40. Avoid short cut methods.
41. Always employ a skilled/trained worker for the job.
42. First-aid boxes with adequate supplies should be made available.
43. Fire fighting equipment be always kept in good condition.
44. Use proper tools in proper way.
45. Guards and railings be provided where necessary.
46. Park equipment on firm and level ground.
47. Servicing, adjustments or repairs be carried out only when machine is in stop condition.

48. Before working on hydraulic system, make sure that hydraulic pressure is released.
49. New employees should be deployed on job after completing the job-orientation programme.
50. Hold regular safety meetings of employees.
51. Job specific safety plans should be developed.
52. Investigate all accidents to find the cause to prevent future occurrences (not to blame).

5.11.2 Specific Precautions

1. For Dozers

1. Operator of every bulldozer before leaving the dozer shall take the following steps :
   (a) Apply brakes,
   (b) Lower the blade and ripper,
   (c) Put the shift lever into neutral,
   (d) Dozer left on level ground at the close of the work for which such bulldozer is used,
   (e) The bulldozer blades not used as brakes except in an emergency.
2. When working on slopes with a dozer, operate straight up and down. Side operation reduces stability which could cause the unit to roll over.
3. During transport of the load, speed of the dozer should be kept slow enough to enable the operator to keep full control over the dozer.
4. Ridger, curbs, logs or rail road tracks should be avoided while travelling.
5. Operator should keep the dozer away from the edges of the banks and pits, as they can cave-in or the machine can lose its footing and slide over the edges.

2. For Scrapers

1. The scraper should be joined to a tractor by a safety line when in operation.
2. Scraper moving down hill should be left in gear.
3. Scraper bowls should be blocked while blades are being replaced. Packing may be used while maintaining/altering the angle of the blade.
4. Ensure that the tractor driven scraper has brakes before putting it in operation.
5. The motorized scraper should move down the hill in low gear if fitted with hydraulic retarder.
6. During operation of the scraper, operator should lower the apron immediately after spreading and in preparation for transport.
7. The ejector should never be moved forward if the scraper is full and apron is closed.

3. For Loaders

1. During the loading stage, operator should keep the loaded bucket close to the ground for stability.
2. If an overload causes the loader to tip forward, lower the load.
3. During the transport of the load, keep the speed low so that operator is an complete control of the machine.

QUESTIONS

1. Justify the statement, "Tractor is a basic equipment for earth moving machinery'. Describe its construction in brief.
2. List out applications of a bulldozer.
3. Describe 'dozing' and 'ripping' action by bulldozers.
4. Describe construction and working of scrapers.
5. Describe construction and working of elevating scraper. Differentiate it with conventional scrapers.
6. Illustrate various applications of loaders. Mention merits and demerits of wheel loaders and crawler loaders.
7. Explain the relative advantages and disadvantages of a 'crawler tractor' and a 'wheel tractor'.
8. What are the operations that can be performed by bulldozers? Describe briefly the procedure for clearing of an area with bulldozers.
9. Discuss the factors which influence the output of earth moving machinery.
10. What is a tractor? For what purposes it is used?
11. What factors influence the selection of a tractor? Explain in brief.
12. How the power is supplied to the dozers?
13. Write a note on the blades of a dozer.
14. What is meant by rock ripping? How the rippability of rocks is determined?
15. What is a scraper? Discuss dozer pulled scrapers.
16. Give the classification of scrappers and discuss them in brief.
17. Explain different types of ripper attachments with sketch.
18. Write short notes on :

    (a) Types of dozer blades (b) Output of bulldozer
19. How would you calculate the output of rippers? How would you increase the ripping production from a dozer?
20. Suggest methods for increasing the scraper production.
21. Write short notes on the following :

    (a) Advantages of elevating scrapers.

(b) Cycle time for a scraper.

(c) Articulated type of loaders.

(d) Loader applications.

22. Explain different types of wheel loader attachments.

23. Explain different types of loader buckets and their applications.

24. How would you calculate loader output? Suggest methods for increasing the loader production.

25. Mention safety precautions to be taken in the use of following equipment :

(a) Dozer (b) Scrapers (c) Loaders

Chapter 6

Excavators

6.1 Introduction

Excavators also called diggers, mechanical shovel or 360-degree excavators, back-hoe. These are mainly used for following operations :

1. Digging of trenches, foundations.
2. Material handling.
3. Forestry work.
4. Demolition.
5. River dredging.
6. Snow removal with snow plough.

For all construction projects, excavation of earth is most important operation. Such projects may be roads, railways, dams, irrigation and other projects. The machines used for earth excavation are called excavators. Excavators include different category of excavating machines, which are broadly categorized as '*hydraulic excavators*' and '*shovels*'. The shovel family include dipper or power shovel, dragline, clamshell, hoes, dredgers. To convert one type of shovel into another, only the front end attachment is changed while the basic structure of the machine remains the same.

Hydraulic excavators are now becoming more and more popular and these enjoy various advantages. This can be fitted with various multipurpose attachments for various earthmoving jobs, like, laying pipes, removing trees, excavating drains, general earth moving jobs of cleaning areas, loading etc. The hydraulic system is very productive and efficient due to its mobility and lightness and lower maintenance costs, and hence contributing towards popularity. A most important advantage is the hydraulic wrist action of the excavator which directs the bucket teeth at their most efficient angle during digging operation. The hydraulic system also contributes for the smooth, shock-free operation during digging and traction. The hydraulic controls are easy to operate and respond quickly.

Mechanical or cable operated excavators are of either 'Hoe' type or 'Shovel' type. In 'Hoe' equipments the bucket opening faces towards the machine and the bucket is pulled towards the machine and are used for excavation below the standing level of the machine like, excavation of house and building foundations; trenches for irrigation, sewerage, cables, gas and oil pipe lines; maintenance and cleaning of rivers, canals and irrigation channels. Whereas in shovel the bucket opening faces away from the machine and the bucket is pushed away from the machine and is used for excavating or loading operations above or on the standing level of the machine, *i.e.*, for excavating of rock or earth; loading of material like earth, coal, aggregate etc. 'Hoe' and 'Shovel' are described separately in this book in the chapter on 'Shovels'.

6.2 Types of Excavators

Excavators are of following four types based on the type of carriers on which they are mounted :

(a) Crawler mounted excavator.
(b) Truck mounted excavator.
(c) Self propelled excavator.
(d) Excavators mounted on barge or rail.

(a) Crawler Mounted Excavator

These excavators are mounted on the crawler system and are very suitable for carrying out large works in rough terrain. Crawler excavators have following main characteristics :

(i) Can be used for work on soft or wet grounds.
(ii) Can be used on sharp rocks or other adverse conditions.
(iii) These can climb steep grades (even upto 40 per cent).
(iv) Requires very less turning space.
(v) Have very less speed for travelling.
(vi) Can be shifted from one site to another only on trailers.

(b) Truck Mounted Excavators

These excavators are mounted on truck chasis and has following main characteristics :

(i) High road speed and mobility is the main advantage.
(ii) Lower stability over sides and hence require counter-weight or outriggers.
(iii) Requires more operating space.
(iv) Tyres or outriggers give high ground pressure and hence it requires firm and smooth operating locations.
(v) Have two engines and two cabs, separately for truck chasis and excavator.

(c) Self Propelled Excavators

These excavators are self propelled and has rubber tyres. The main characteristics are :

(i) Medium travel speed generally between 10 to 30 km per hour.
(ii) Has one engine and one cab for control by one operator.

(d) Excavators on Barge or Rail

These excavators are mounted on barge or rail to carry out work of excavation in water or near railway line respectively.

Difference between an Excavator and a Back-hoe

Backhoes and excavators have a common purpose—digging—but the two machines have different designs that reflect their specific intended uses. Generally, attached to a front loader or tractor, a **backhoe** has a two limbed arm with a digging bucket on its end. The limbs are called the boom and the dipper, the dipper holds the bucket. An **excavator** also has a boom and a dipper with a bucket on the end, but is attached to a cab that sits on a vehicle with wheels or tracks.

An excavator can be a regular rubber tired backhoe or a trackhoe, which is also an excavator having tracks like a dozer.

6.3 Hydraulic Excavators

Hydraulic excavators are basically digging machines, having following three main components :

(a) An undercarriage to give mobility. This may be crawler track mounted or wheel mounted.

(b) A superstructure with operator's cabin mounted one either a slew ring to traverse through 360° or on a rigid frame.

(c) Hydraulically articulated boom and dipper arms with bucket.

Fig. 6.1 Hydraulic excavator (Courtesy : Liebherr).

Hydraulic actuated excavators have rotating superstructures which are somewhat different from those of the cable-actuated machines like back hoe, power-shovel, dragline and clamshell (explained in next chapter). However, attachments of backhoes, straight line telescopic hoes, and telescopic boom lift cranes are available for mounting on hydraulic actuated excavator. This increases the suitability, applicability and popularity of hydraulic excavators.

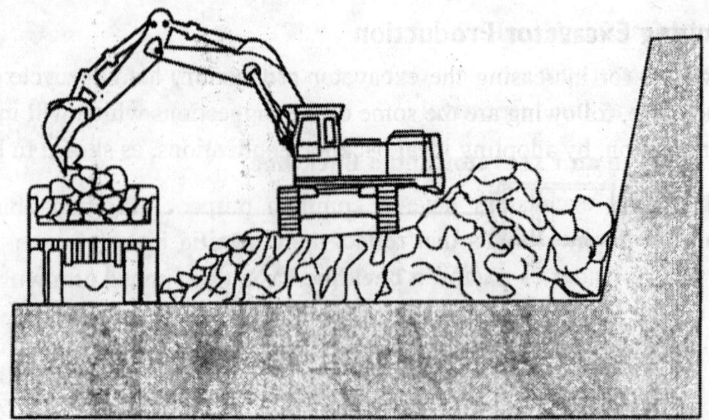

Fig. 6.2 Hydraulic excavator in loading operation (Courtesy : Liebherr).

The various digging actions are powered by hydraulic cylinders and motors and are controlled by hydraulic valves or variable-stroke pumps. The hydraulic excavator has the advantages that its digging forces do not tend to lift the bucket out of a deep trench, as does the cable pull on a cable-powered hoe. But hydraulic excavators need slightly larger engine as compared to that of cable operated, because hydraulic pumps are slightly less efficient than gear and chain drive, and also due to pressure deep in line and valve.

Hydraulic excavators are troubled by gradual errosion of pumps and valves from line dirt or by sudden failures due to large metal particles in the oil flow. Oil filteration is therefore very important. Care should also be taken that, foam or air must not be pulled into the pumps because air even in minute quantities can soon destroy a pump.

Now-a-days hydraulic excavators of various sizes upto 30 m^3 bucket capacity and 1730 kW engine output are available. These large sized, heavy hydraulic excavators are mostly used in exploitation of raw materials, open cast mining, for loosening and loading of large material quantities, and where transport vehicles of adequate size can be economically employed.

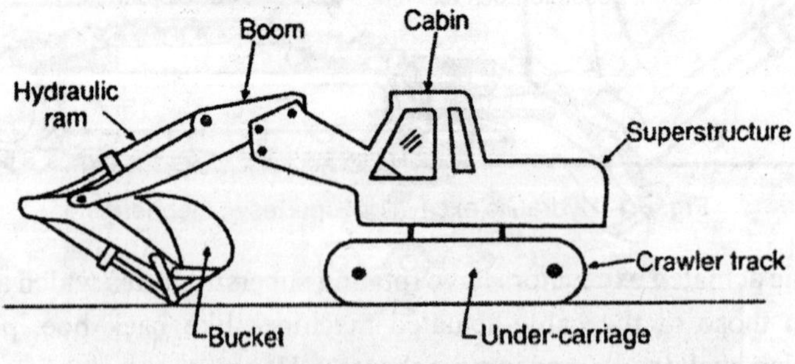

Fig. 6.3 Hydraulic excavator.

6.4 Optimizing Excavator Production

As we know that for increasing the excavator production, loading cycle should be reduced. Therefore, following are the some of the suggestions which will increase the excavator production, by adopting ideal backhoe applications, as shown in Fig. 6.4.

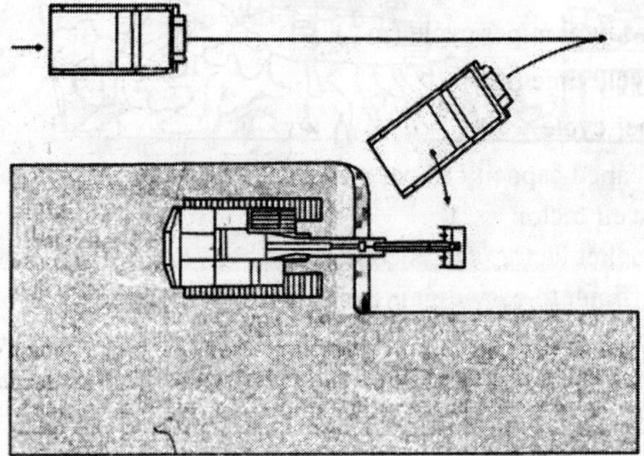

(a) Short swing angles and low material hoisting.

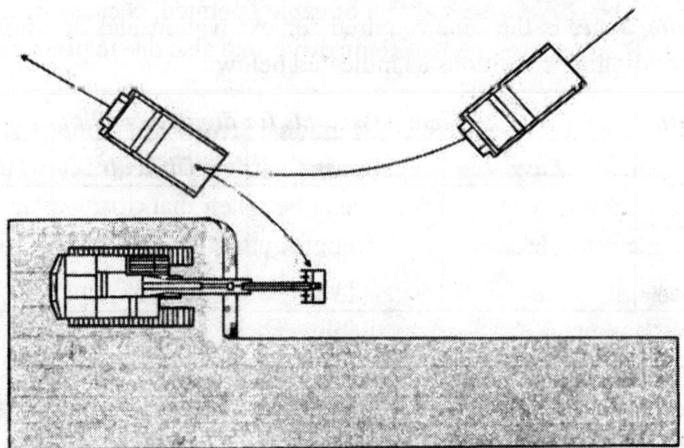

(b) Fastest possible truck exchange for high hourly production.

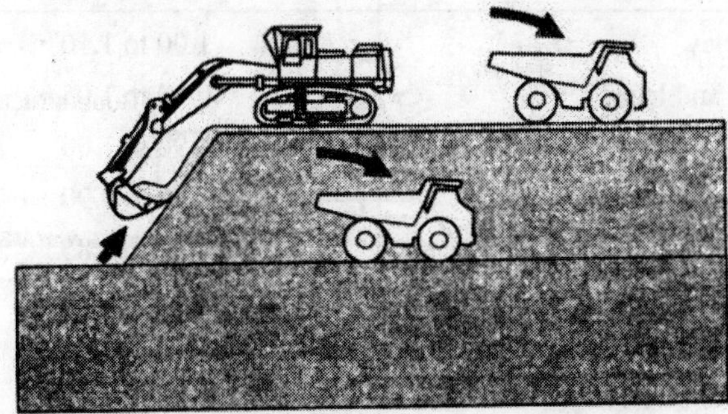

(c) Loading trucks "downstairs" and "upstairs" for highest possible production output.

Fig. 6.4

6.5 Output of Excavators

Hourly production in m^3/hr (Q)

$$= q \times \frac{3600}{C} \times \text{Efficiency}$$

where, q = Production per cycle (m^3)

C = Cycle time (sec)

Production per cycle $(q) = q_1 \times s \times k$

where, q_1 = Heaped capacity as per specifications of the excavator

s = Swell factor

k = Bucket factor, and is considered between 0.4 to 1.0 depending on difficult to easy digging and loading conditions.

Cycle time, is the time required for excavation, swing, dump and back swing. Where excavating time depends on digging depth and surface to be digged. Swing time depend on the degree and speed of swing and the skill of operator. Dumping time depends upon the proper spoting of transport vehicle and the skill of the operator.

Cycle time = Excavating time + 2 × Swing time + Dumping time

Excavating time, is the time required for excavation and depends on digging depth and other digging conditions as indicated below :

Digging depth	*Time in seconds,for digging conditions*			
	Easy	*Average*	*Difficult*	*Very difficult*
0–2 m	6	9	15	26
2–4 m	7	11	17	28
4 m and above	8	13	19	30

Bucket Fill Factors

Bucket fill factors depend on the material to be excavated. Following table indicates these factors for different materials :

Material	*Bucket fill factor*
(i) Soft clay	1.00 to 1.10
(ii) Earth and loam	0.90 to 1.05
(iii) Sank gravel and sand	0.90 to 1.00
(iv) Uniform aggregates	0.80 to 0.90
(v) Hard clay	0.75 to 0.85
(vi) Rock	
(a) Well blasted	0.60 to 0.75
(b) Coarsely blasted	0.40 to 0.60

6.6 Excavator Loaders

Excavator-loaders sometimes also known as backhoe-loaders, are basically digging and loading machines, and comprise following main components :

(a) A tractor with two- or four-wheel drive.

(b) A rear mounted digging arm and hydraulically operated excavator bucket, able to slew through a 180° arc.

(c) A front mounted loader arm assembly with loader bucket.

Excavator end is used for side tipping; excavating of house and building foundations, trenches or irrigation; sewerages, gas and oil pipe line work; and also for irrigation channel cleaning and maintenance. Whereas the loader end is used for loading and rehandling of materials such as excavated soil, aggregates, coal etc.

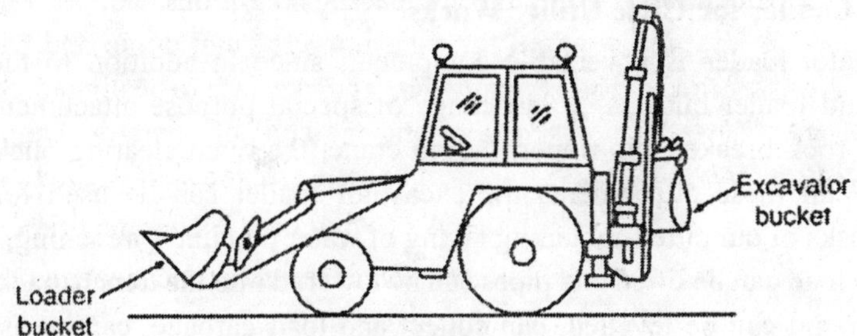

Fig. 6.5 Excavator-loader.

Fig. 6.6(a) Track loader cum excavator.

Excavator-loader can be made even more useful by using hydraulically operated attachments for road breakers, pumps, pole planters, winches, crane hook and boom etc.

Fig. 6.6(b) Wheeled backhoe-loader.

Excavator-Loader for Civie Utility Works

Excavator-loader is a versatile equipment, since in addition to the standard excavator and loader buckets, a vast range of special purpose attachments like the forklift, the rock breaker, the ripper, the jib crane, the ditch clearing bucket, can be provided. With these attachments the excavator loader can be used for handling numerous tasks of our cities, including laying of water pipelines, trenching, with crane attachments load can be lifted and pipes can be lowered into the trench, backfilling can be done, ground can be levelled, can collect and load garbage, can be used in road maintenance works, can be used on hot mix and crushing plants for loading of gravel and stone.

Fig. 6.7 Versatility of excavator-loader (Courtesy : JCB).

6.7 General Safety in Excavation

1. Before undertaking any activity, the soil should be tested and in case of availability of any explosive gas, the necessary arrangements must be made to remove/dilute such gases and in case they are found to be toxic or poisonous, the workplace must be purged and continuous ventilation maintaining the contamination below the permissible level ensured.

2. The position of underground installations such as sewers, water pipes and electrical cables should be verified and in case of their existence, they must be isolated.
3. If they cannot be isolated or removed or shutdown, they should be fenced, hung up or otherwise protected.
4. On every part likely to be visited by persons or where transport vehicles ply, the area should be suitably fenced, guarded or barricaded to prevent fall of persons, vehicles or live stock into the excavated area.
5. Warning signs should be erected and in the night hours the area should be illuminated to warn pedestrians and vehicular traffic.
6. Arrangements should be made to prevent external vibrations due to rail/road traffic.
7. Blasting should be carried out in accordance with the norms applicable in this regard. Special care should be taken to control the impact of vibrations/tremor caused by blasting to protect excavations to cave-ins.
8. Arrangements shall be made to save other structures in the affected zone or in the vicinity of the area of excavation, from collapse.
9. The sides of every excavation, where there is a danger of fall or dislodgement of earth, rock or other material forming the side or adjacent to any excavation shall be securely supported by adequately braced to any timber of suitable quality or other material unless the sides of the excavation are slopping to a safe angle.
10. In every excavation work along sloping ground, sides and slopes, excavation shall be maintained in a safe condition by sealing benching or barricading.
11. On steep slopes, workers shall not be permitted to work one above the other.
12. No excavation of earthwork below the level of any foundation of a building or structure shall be recommenced or continued unless adequate steps are taken to prevent danger to any person from collapse of the structure or fall of any part thereof.
13. Additional precautions be taken to prevent slides, slip or caveins when excavations are made in locations subject to vibrations from rail-road or highway traffic, etc.
14. In all trenches 1.5 m or more in depth, ladders should be provided.
15. Excavation areas should be adequate lighted for night work.
16. During hours of darkness all public sidewalks should be adequately illuminated and warning lights about the excavation should be provided.
17. A flagman should be posted to warn the public or approaching trucks and to direct the trucks in and out of the site of excavation.
18. Every accessible part of an excavation pit or opening in ground into which a person is liable to fall, suitable barrier should be

19. The side slopes and their stability should be carefully examined after every blasting operation.
20. Measures should be taken to prevent workers and spectators from approaching the dangerous areas.
21. All quarries shall be fenced and signs for warning people of the danger of blasting or otherwise shall be prominently pasted.
22. There should be no undercutting of banks at any time and any overhanging banks occurring as the result of slides or carvings should not be removed before beginning excavation operation beneath them.

6.7.1 Common Excavation Hazards

Following are the common hazards of excavation which should be considered for preventing accidents :

1. Hazardous atmosphere at the place of excavation.
2. Water accumulation.
3. Stability of adjacent structures.
4. Loose rock or soil.
5. Danger of fall of men, loads, objects and mobile equipment.
6. Cave-in.
7. Utilities located in the area to be excavated.
8. Access/Egress to the area where work is being carried out.
9. Vibrations.

6.8 Safety in Use of Hydraulic Excavators

1. Fire fighting equipment should always be provided on the hydraulic excavator.
2. Operator should be sure that the attachment of load does not catch on obstructions when lifting or swinging.
3. Operator should not swing, hoist or brake unnecessarily fast, as this can cause serious accidents.
4. Operator should never swing of position the attachment over ground crew or a truck cab.
5. Load trucks evenly to avoid overloading rear axles.
6. While working near gas, phone/electric cable/water or power lines extra precautions should be taken. If required, permission of concerned department should be taken.
7. Never exceed the lifting capacity.
8. If outriggers are available, utilize them after extending to fullest limit and support them on uniform surface.
9. The excavator should be kept away from the edge of excavation to avoid falling into the excavation.

10. Regularly check that bucket linkage or slings used to lift the load are of adequate strength.
11. Whenever a spark occurs over to the excavator despite precautions, do not leave the operator's cabin till the current is cut off; keep every one on the ground away from the machine; and if you have to leave the machine, jump, do not step off.

General safety precautions mentioned in the chapter on "earthmoving equipment" should also be referred.

QUESTIONS

1. What is an excavator? Describe working of a hydraulic excavator.
2. Mention different types of excavators.
3. How would you calculate output of excavators?
4. What is an excavator-loader? Explain various applications of excavator-loader.
5. Explain different types of excavating equipment. Explain the term shovel.
6. Write short notes on :
   (a) Shovel family (b) Back-hoe (c) Track-hoe
7. Explain construction, working and applications of hydraulic excavator.
8. Differentiate between excavator and back-hoe.
9. Explain as to how would you optimize the excavator production.
10. Discuss various applications (uses) of excavating equipments.
11. Discuss main components of a hydraulic excavator.
12. Discuss various safety precaution to be taken during the operation of excavators.

Chapter 7

Compaction Equipment

7.1 Introduction

Effective compaction of material is an essential part of construction engineering operations concerned with foundations, construction and maintenance of roads, airports, dams etc. The equipment required for these works range from the smallest vibrating rammers to the largest rollers of vibrating type. Quality characteristics such as strength, wearing resistance, evenness and impermeability of a pavement depends on the degree of compaction of various layers of the pavement and the subgrade supporting it.

The better the compaction, the better will be shear strength, density and bearing capacity of the individual layers and with that the lasting quality of the embankment or road, construction. For explaining this, we take an example of road, the complete road, from base to wearing course must be compacted to higher specifications than the compaction value of the axle weights of the vehicles using them. If this is not achieved, the vehicle will in a very short period break up the surface because of the further reduction of the voids as the heavier vehicles continue to compact the material.

Roller are used for compaction since long olden days. Over a thousand years ago the Chinese used huge cylindrical shaped stone rollers for road works, and the world famous builders of Rome used towed stone rollers. The self propelled road rollers, powered by steam engines were built in England in nineteenth century. As the time passed, road roller design continuously improved. Since the manufacture of the first diesel-engine-powered road roller in 1929, the development of compaction equipments has taken place rapidly.

Compaction

Compaction is the process whereby material particles are constrained to pack more closely together through a reductio of air void content, generally by mechanical means.

Compaction can also be defined as the process of densifying or increasing the unit weight of a soil mass through the application of static or dynamic force, with resulting expulsion of air and, in some cases, moisture. Static forces are produced by a roller or compactor which densifies soil primarily by its heavy weight, whereas dynamic forces utilise a combination of weight and energy to produce a vibratory or tamping effect on the soil. Compactors utilise both static and dynamic forces to achieve the required soil density.

Primary functions of compaction is to produce the reasonable surface finish in accordance to the layer position with in the whole road or embankment construction.

Compaction is measured in terms of dry density. The amount of compaction, applied can be controlled by the choice of compaction equipment, the thickness being compacted, the speed of the compaction equipment and the number of passes of compaction equipment.

Through soil is compacted itself naturally, but the process is very slow and may take several years. The compaction through artificial means reach the required density quickly. The main **objective** of compaction is not only to get the greater density (unit weight), but also to **improve the following properties of soil.**

(i) Prevention or reduction in settlement.

(ii) Increase in the strength of the soil.

(iii) Improvement in the bearing capacity of the soil, so that it can withstand permanent loads and traffic.

(iv) Controlling the changes in the volume of soil.

(v) Reduction in permeability of soil.

Though there are several methods for achieving desired properties of soil, but the most common method is the compaction of soil by compaction equipment at optimum water (moisture) content.

7.2 Soil and Rock

Soil and rock are used to support structures to support pavements for highways and airport runways; and in dams as impoundments to resist the passage of water. F"or project, appropriate soils are excavated from borrow areas are processed, and compacted to meet the engineering requirements. In addition, aggregates constitute approximately 95% by weight of asphalt concrete and 75% of cement concrete.

Design engineers and construction engineers are required to know about the properties, characteristics and behaviour of different soil types and aggregates. Sometimes soil and rock are suitable for required structural purposes in their natural state, but in many cases, the locally available material are not suitable for the purpose, and therefore it becomes necessary to modify them to meet the project demands in cost, effective manner. The modification is done by processing through adjusting moisture content or mixing and blending the other materials.

Some of the common terms related to soil and rock materials and compaction are discussed hereunder :

1. **Aggregate, coarse :** Crushed rock or gravel generally greater than 6 mm in size are known as coarse aggregate.

2. **Aggregate, fine :** These are the sand of fine-crushed stone used for filling voids in coarse aggregate. These are smaller than 6 mm and greater than a 200 number sieve in size.
3. **Borrow pit :** It is a pit from which fill material is mined.
4. **Cohesion :** It is the quality of some soil particles to be attracted to like particles, manifested in a tendency to stick together, as in clay.
5. **Optimum moisture content (OMC) :** The water content, for a given compactive effort, at which the greatest density of a soil can be obtained.
6. **Pavement :** A layer, above the base, of rigid surfacing material that provides with bending resistance and distributes loads to the base. There are usually constructed of asphalt or concrete.
7. **Rock :** It is the hard, mineral matter of the earth's crust, occurring in masses and often requiring blasting to cause breakage before excavation is done.
8. **Soil :** Soil is the loose surface material of the earth's crust created naturally from the disintegration of rocks or decay of vegetation. Soil can be excavated easily.
9. **Gradation of soils :** Materials gradation may be as under :
   (a) *Well graded soils* : In these the particle size distribution extends evenly over a wide range of particles, without excess or deficiency of one or more particle sizes.
   (b) *Poorly graded soils* : The particle size distribution contains an excess of some particle sizes and deficiency of others.
   (c) *Uniformly graded soils* : In these the size distribution extends over a very limited range of particle sizes.
10. **Soil, in-situ :** Soil in its original or undisturbed position is known as in-situ soil.
11. **Impervious soil :** A material that resists the flow of water through it is termed as impervious.

Road Structure

A road is usually built in several layers, each layer is having a special function. Following main structural elements in road or airfield construction are :

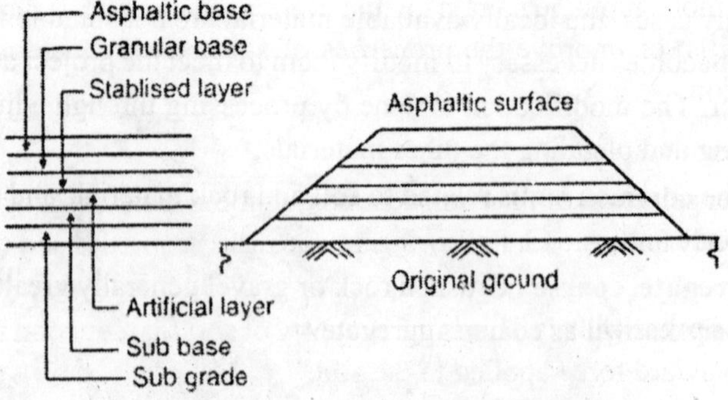

Fig. 7.1 Basic structural elements of a road.

(a) **Subgrade :** Native earth foundation of the embankment.

(b) **Subbase :** Selected material placed to furnish strength to the base.

(c) **Pavement :** Consisting of base, binder and surfacing courses.

Types of Soils

(i) **Gravel :** It is a rocklike material having particles of sizes larger than 6 mm. Pieces above 250 mm are generally called boulders.

(ii) **Sand :** Sand is a disintegrated rock whose particles vary in sizes from 6 mm down to 0.05 mm. Sand is further classified as coarse or fine sand depending upon the grain size. The sand is a granular, and non-cohesive material.

(iii) **Silt :** This is a very fine sand and is a granular material having particles of size smaller than 0.05 mm. It is a non-cohesive material and has little or no strength, and compacts very poorly.

(iv) **Clay :** Clay is a cohesive material having particles of microscopic size. Due to cohesiveness these have high strength when dry. These changes in volume considerably with the variation of moisture contents. The strength of these soils can be increased by blending with granular soils.

(v) **Organic matter :** These are partly decomposed vegetable matter. These makes soil unsuitable for construction purposes, and needs to be removed and replaced with suitable soil.

Most soils are made up of a mixture of these basic soil types and are classified according to the amount and type of each basic soil included, as a sandy clay, clayey sand; sandy silt etc. Study of the properties of these types of soil greatly help in selection of a proper compaction equipment. Like, gravel and sand are free draining; non-elastic and non-spongy coarse grained soils. Silts are non-plastic fines of particle size between 0.002 mm to 0.06 mm. Clays have plastic properties,and is hard and firm when water content is low. Above the optimum water content, it become more and more plastic when the water content is increased.

Compaction of clay or clayey soils with a high strength requires use of static or vibratory and or sheep foot rollers. Vibratory pad foot rollers (replaced sheep foot rollers) are able to compact thicker layers than static pad foot rollers. In order to achieve better result when wet clays are used either alternate layers of clay and gravel is used in get a more rapid reduction of the water content and a more stable fill as embankment fills; or improve the properties of silt and clay materials by means of lime-stabilization.

Soil Properties

For proper selection of the compaction equipment different properties of the soil should be properly understood. Following are the main properties and characteristics of the soil.

(i) **Compressibility :** This is the property of soil for reduction in volume due to downward force applied to the soil.

(ii) **Elasticity :** It is the ability of a soil to return to its original form after a compressive load is removed.

(iii) **Capillarity :** It is the ability of a fine-grain soil to absorb water and transmit it in all directions. In order to safeguard from capillary action, it is necessary to prevent it by placing an insulating course of sand or gravel between the soil and the source of water.

(iv) **Internal friction :** It is the soil's ability to resist slippage when a force is applied. Shearing resistance of a soil is determined by its internal friction and cohesion.

(v) **Internal friction :** It is a resistance of the soil particles to sliding over each other.

(vi) **Cohesion of soil grains :** It is the resistance to pulling away from one another. Thus a soil containing sand and gravel has high internal friction but to have cohesion it should have fine grain soil, such as clay.

(vii) **Shrinkage :** It occurs in fine grain soils when water in the soil is reduced by evaporation. The shrinkage property is responsible for poor foundation for a supporting surface.

(viii) **Consolidation :** If the soil mass is fully saturated, then expulsion of water takes place due to load acting continuously for a long time and thereby reduces volume of voids in the soil. This gradual compression of soil mass resulting from long term static load is termed as consolidation.

(ix) **Permeability :** It is the rate at which gravitational water flow through a soil. Sands and gravels are most permeable and clays are least permeable.

(x) **Settlement :** It is the decrease in surface elevation of the fill material within the embankment.

Swell and Shrinkage

Volume and density of earth undergo considerable changes when the earth in excavated, placed and compacted. It is therefore necessary to specify whether the volume is measured in its original position, in loose condition or in compacted condition. Bank-measure volume is measurement in original position before excavation, loose-measure volume is the measurement after it has been excavated from the natural position, compacted volume is the measurement after it has been placed in a fill and compacted.

The increase in volume due to loosening is defined as **SWELL** and is expressed as a percent of the original undisturbed volume.

The reduction in volume due to compaction under modern construction methods, from its volume under original condition is defined as **SHRINKAGE**, and is expressed as a percent of the original undisturbed volume.

If the earth removed from a borrow pit having a volume of 1 cu m is found to have a loose volume of 1.25 cu m. In this case the gain in volume is 25 per cent and hence the earth is said to have a swell of 25 percent. If the same earth when compacted has a volume (1 cu m volume of borrow pit). In this condition the earth is said to have a shrinkage of 10 percent. The percent of shrinkage, however, vary with the degree of compaction.

7.3 Soil Stabilization

Some soils undergo different amount of expansion and shrinkage with the change in moisture content. This reader pavements entirely failure. Such soils are essentially required to be stabilised to prevent or reduced the changes in volume in order to protect the pavement from excessive damages and also to improve the strength. Soils can be stabilised either in its natural position or during their replacement in a fill. In road construction, stabilisation may be carried out during subgrade,subbase or base formation. Soils can be stabilised by blending through disc horrow, rotavator, soil stabiliser etc. by adopting any one of the following methods :

(i) Blending and mixing heterogeneous soils to produced more homogeneous soils.

(ii) Mixing hydrated lime or lime-fly ash into soils having high clay content. Generally upper 15 cm layer is stabilised with 5 percent by weight of hydrated lime in the subgrade.

(iii) Blending asphalt with soil, granular soils are blended with 5 to 7 percent asphalts such as MC 30.

(iv) Mixing cement, cement-fly ash with the soil. Clay or silt can be stabilised (in the areas where gravel or rock are scarce) with 5 to 7 percent of cement by weight.

Stabilisation is carried out in addition to strengthen the soil and control the volume changes for decreasing plasticity, increase workability and reduce swell.

7.4 Influence of Soil on Compaction

Influence of various soils on compaction is described hereunder :

1. Cohesive Fine Grained Soils

Compaction of cohesive fine grained soils depends on (a) Moisture content (b) Plasticity; and (c) Particle size distribution.

The fine soil particles have a large surface area and therefore a high water absorption capability. With increasing moisture content the soil changes from a solid state to a liquid state, hence it is necessary to carefully control the moisture content of the cohesive fine graded soil.

Plasticity is due to the lubrication effect of the water film between the adjacent particles. The water absorption depends upon the "plasticity index".

A higher density and an increase of the mechanical cohesion, can be achieved through a shearing between the soil particles to overcome the existing cohesion. To accomplish this high compressive stresses are necessary, and which can be done by using compaction equipments with high specific pressure, such as,

- heavy rubber tyred compactors,
- heavy self-propelled vibratory compactors,
- heavy towed vibratory compactors,
- sheepfoot or padfoor vibratory compactors,
- tamping foot vibratory compactors.

2. Non-cohesive, Coarse Grained Soils

Compaction of non-cohesive coarse grained soils depends on : (a) Particle size distribution (b) Particle shape, and (c) Moisture content.

Shearing strength of non-cohesive coarse grained soils is determined by the friction between the particles and therefore compaction depends upon the soil grading. Well graded material can be compacted to a higher density than-uniformly graded soils.

Shear strength also depends upon the shape of the particles. Soils with smooth, and rounded particles are easier to compact than soils with rough and angular particles.

For the compaction of these soils, vibratory compactors are suitable since they vibrate each and every single particle, by dynamic effect. Depending on the application, size of construction work and thickness of the layer, following equipments can be used for the compaction of non-cohesive, coarse grained material :

- tandem vibratory compactors,
- double vibratory compactors,
- towed vibratory compactors,
- self-propelled vibratory compactors,
- rubber tyred compactors.

3. Fine and Coarse Grained Mixed Soils

Compaction of fine and coarse grained mixed soils depends on :

(a) Mix-proportions,

(b) Moisture content,

(c) Particles size distribution, and

(d) The plasticity of the fine content.

In mixed soils the shear strength is dependent on both, the mechanical cohesion and friction. Thus compaction depends on the moisture content and plasticity of the fine grained content and a function of the particles size distribution and particle shape of the coarse-grained content, as well as a function of the mix proportion.

Depending on the mix proportion, layer thickness and size of the construction site, the following equipments are recommended for the compaction of mixed soils :

- tandem vibratory compactors
- Double vibratory compactors
- light towed vibratory compactors
- light self-propelled vibratory compactors
- rubber tyred compactors

} For low fine grained contents

- heavy self-propelled vibratory compactors
- heavy towed vibratory compactors
- sheep foot vibratory compactors
- temping foot vibratory compactors.

} For high fine grained contents

The number of compaction passes and the compactable layer thickness are dependent on the type of soil and the type and size of he compaction equipment.

7.4.1 Influence of Moisture

Water together with the particle size and their distribution in a soil, determine physical qualities by improving :

(a) the cohesion of the particles (as binder),

(b) the placement of the particles (as lubricant).

When the water content is too low the material is stiff and it is difficult to compress. Low dry densities are obtained due to a high void content between the particles. By increasing the water content the material is soften and the voids are reduced, which increases the dry-density. If the water content becomes too high the particles are separated and dry density drops.

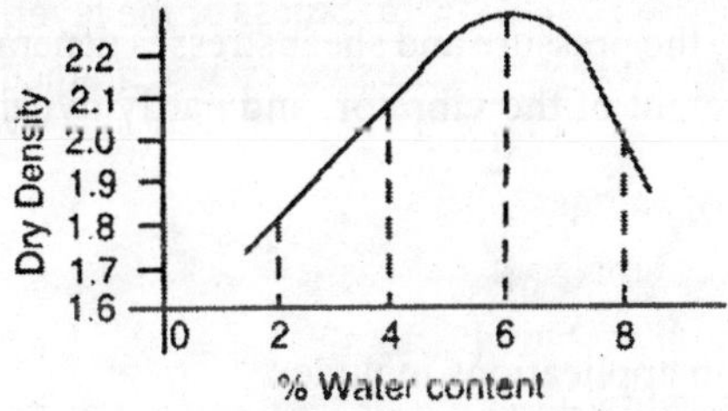

Fig. 7.2 Influence of water on compaction.

Compaction depends mainly on the moisture content and on the amount of compacting force applied. For each soil there exists an optimal moisture content (O.M.C.) at which a maximum compaction can be achieved. Further addition of water after achieving optimum moisture keeps the particles apart thereby reducing the density of the material. In bituminous materials the binder assumes the role of moisture in soil.

7.5 Soil Compaction Principles and Methods

Different principles for compaction can be described as static pressure, impact,and vibration. Static smooth wheel rollers,and static sheepfoot or padfoor rollers work with static pressures of different magnitude on the surface of the soil. Pneumatic-tyred rollers and sheapfoot or padfoot rollers work with static pressures with a kneading effect. Pneumatic-tyred rollers also have a closing of sealing on the surface. As long as a soil is in loose state, it is easy to compress and a elastic deformation occurs without any significant elastic response. When the degree of compaction increases,the soil becomes more dense and elastic.

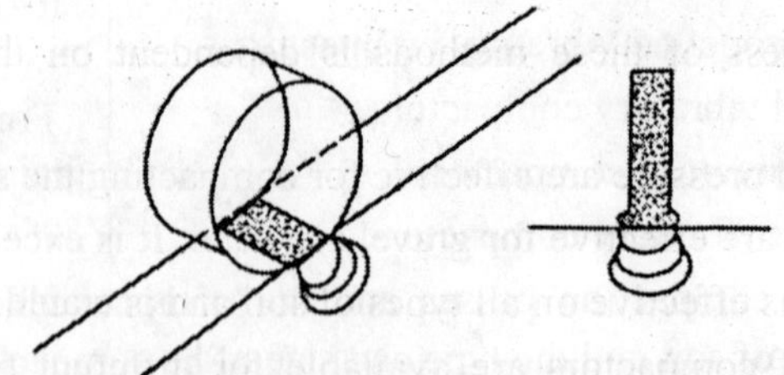

Fig. 7.3 Load applied with steel drum and pneumatic tyre.

Impact produces a greater force on the surface of the soil than a static load. A compression or pressure wave goes down into the soil generating high pressures also at large depths. This principle is used to compact soil and fill to large depths with heavy drop weights.

Vibratory compactors, produces rapid impacts and each impact produces a pressure wave in the soil. The soil particles are set in motion and the internal friction between the particles is virtually eliminated. During the state of motion, the particles find positions which make the volume as low as possible. In vibratory compactors, the compaction is achieved by two factors, (i) with the state of motion of the soil particles, the internal friction is eliminated and conditions are created for an effective compaction of the soil (ii) the pressure and shear stresses generated in the soil are partly static due to the static weight of the vibrator, and partly dynamic in form of pressure waves.

7.6 Applications

Important soil compaction applications include :

1. Highways, roads, streets and parking areas.
2. Airfields.
3. Industrial yards, storage areas, playgrounds, sport fields.
4. Railway embankments, ballast beds.
5. Earth and rockfill dams, reservoirs, and channel linings.
6. Fills used as foundations for buildings or residential and industrial sites.
7. Fills under floors and along foundation walls in buildings.
8. Fills at retaining walls, bridge abutments and around culverts.
9. Trench fills.

7.7 Selection of Compactors Based on Nature of Soil

For the purpose of compaction, energy is required to be supplied to a soil by one or more of the following methods :

1. Impact—sharp blow.
2. Pressure—static weight.
3. Vibrator—shaking.
4. Kneading—manipulation or rearranging.

The effectiveness of these methods is dependent on the type of soil to be compacted.

- Impact and pressure are effective for compacting the silt and clay.
- Vibrations are effective for gravel and sand. It is excellent for sand.
- Kneading is effective on all types of soil and is excellent for silt.

Many types of compactors are available for different types of soils and for different applications. The aim is to construct a quality embankment in the shortest time at least cost, which means that the compactor must be matched to the material. The appropriate compaction equipment can therefore be selected only after the soils are identified.

Appropriate compaction equipment are shown below based o the nature of material. The type of compactor, number of passes and thickness of soil layer etc. are shown in the table below :

S. No.	*Material*	*Thickness of layer (cms)*	*No. of passes*	*Types of compaction equipment*	*Remarks*
1.	Gravel	20-30	3-5	— Vibratory pad foot	— Foot pr. 10.5 to 14 kg/cm^2
				— Vibratory smooth	—
				— Pneumatic	— Tyre pr. 2.5 to 9 kg/cm^2
				— Sheep foot	— Foot pr. 10.5 to 14 kg/cm^2
2.	Sand	20-25	3-5	— Vibratory pad foot	—
				— Vibratory smooth	—
				— Pneumatic	— Tyre pr. 2.5 to 4.5 kg/cm^2
				— Smooth static	— Tandom 10 to 15 Ton
3.	Silt	15-20	4-8	— Vibratory pad foot	— Foot pr. 14 to 28 kg/cm^2
				— Tamping foot	—
				— Pneumatic	— Tyre pr. 2.5 to 3.5 kg/cm^2
				— Sheep foot	— Foot pr. 14 to 28 kg/cm^2
4.	Clay	10-15	4-6	— Vibratory pad foot	— Foot pr. 17.5 to 35 kg/cm^2
				— Tamping foot	—
				— Sheep foot	— Foot pr. 17.5 to 35 kg/cm^2

7.8 Types of Compactors

Today's compaction equipment are represented by many large, highly responsive, and versatile self-propelled units. These compactors and rollers can be divided into following major classes :

1. Static Smooth Wheeled Rollers

These are rollers used with or without ballast and may be 3 wheeled or tandem type (two rolls of equal width). These are the conventional rollers used for almost all types of rolling. It is not effective on uniformly graded sand, gravel or silt and on overmoist cohesive soil due to poor traction. Diesel powered rollers with modern technology of hydrostatic transmission rollers have replaced the traditional steam rollers which were first introduced some 100 years ago. The dead weight rollers (static rollers are some times called by this name) rely on weight alone to compact the material over which they pass. The units of 8 to 10 tonnes imparting pressure of 20 to 40 kg per linear cm are generally used. For light works, lighter rollers of weight upto 1 ton are also available. (Refer Fig. 7.4)

Fig. 7.4 Three wheel static roller (Courtesy : Aveling barford).

2. Sheepfoot or Padfoot Rollers

These may be self driven or tractor driven and are suitable on cohesive soils specially when water content is on the higher side. The inherent dynamic beat developed by these tamping pads or feet can in many cases produce a high degree of compaction at a faster rate.

3. Pneumatic-Tyred Rollers (P.T.R.)

These are used for compaction both in earthwork and bituminous road construction. Because of the oscillating axle layout, they produce more even compaction across the rolling width than wide steel wheel smooth rollers, which sometimes bridge the material leaving uncompacted areas of fill. On bituminous wear courses, it can eliminate surface cracking and material crushing caused by steel rolls : the tyres fold and knead the material to produce an almost total sealed finish. These rollers are available in weights ranging from 5 to 30 tonnes with 500 to 4000 kg per tyre and tyre pressure from 2 to 3 kg/sq. m.

4. Vibratory Rollers

Different types and sizes of vibratory rollers to suit specific conditions are available, like.

(i) Rollers with large vibrating drum infront with 2 steel or pneumatic tyred rear driving wheels. The pneumatic tyres offer better traction on gradients and in overmoist soil. These may be articulated or non-articulated type.

(ii) Roller with tandem smooth wheels, either one wheel vibrating and driven or both wheel vibrating and driven.

(iii) The small duplex roller with twin vibrating rolls weighing 1 to 1.5 tons for trench reinstatement.

(iv) Single roll pedestrian vibratory rollers weighing nearly 400 kg are used for compacting small areas such as foot or bicycle path, foundations etc.

(v) Towed vibrating rollers weighing 5000 to 11000 kg are used for mass earthworks, base constructions, embankments, rockfill dams etc.

Vibrations are produced by rotating eccentric weights within the rolls at high speed, the roll thus hitting the material to be compacted at high frequency. The vibration reduces the friction between the particles of material which are brought closer together as air voids are eliminated, thus binding the material into a denser state. Further compaction results from the dynamic forces applied by the vibrating roll onto the material being compacted.

Vibrating rollers are very effective on free draining type soil and granular base course. These are not effective on uniformly graded sand gravel or silt. Rollers with high amplitude are preferable for soil and granular base course. At high amplitude vibrations the effective pressure on the compacting material is around twice the static weight of the roller.

5. Tampers and Vibrating Plates

Tampers with small vibrating feed are used to tamp footings, trench bottoms, position posts, lay paving slabs or in any small area where high manoeuverability required. These can also be used on small road repair jobs, footpath construction and compacting trench bottoms or pipe laying. Operational weights fall in the range upto approximately 30 kg for tampers and as much as 300 kg for vibrating plates, although sizes larger than about 120 kg are seldom used. The tampers can deliver from 800 to 4500 blow per min and are generally powered by engines 2.5 to 12.5 H.P.

These static rollers are universal and can be used on any compaction jobs. For footpath lighter rollers of 3 tons approximately are used, whereas for road construction heavy rollers are used. Most popular range is 8 to 10 ton weight static three wheel self propelled compactor and is applicable for works ranging from earth work and sub base to bituminous road surfacing materials. Now-a-days self-propelled vibratory rollers and pneumatic rollers are used on bituminous material, but it is usual to have a steel wheeled dead weight (static) in attendance either to give initial precompaction to prevent sinkage and/or as a finishing roller to produce a reasonable surface finish to

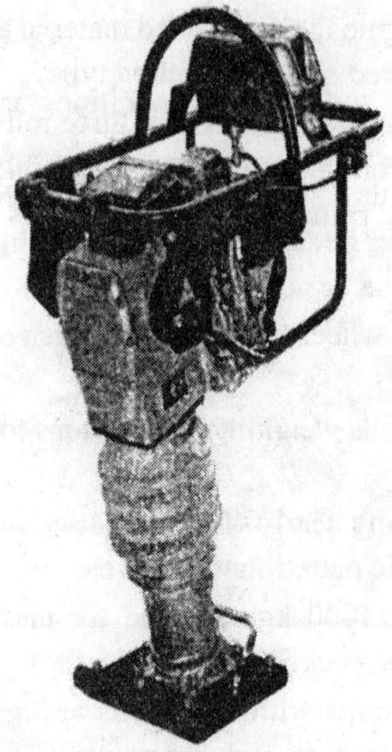

Fig. 7.5 Tampers with engine.

Fig. 7.6 Vibro plate compactor.

eliminate any rutting or surface marking which may occur. Tandem roller is preferred as a finishing roller on wearing course. Main advantage of tandem roller is that it gives a continuous rolling width with minimum of roll marking through the reduction of roll edges.

7.9 Static Compactors

Static compaction equipment can be divided into the following groups :

(a) Towed static smooth compactors.

(b) Static sheepfoot or padfoot compactors (towed or self propelled).

(c) Static three wheel self-propelled compactors.

(d) Static tandem compactors.

(e) Three axle static compactors.

(a) Towed Static Smooth Compactors : Smooth rolls were the first type of rolling compaction equipment used. These were pulled by men or horses and were first used by Roman to roll and smoothen their roads and paths.

(b) Static Sheepfoot or Padfoot Compactors : There are several types of feet or legs of different shapes available. When compacting earth fills, the feet penetrate deep into the loose material during the first passes and compact the soil from the bottom up. The kneading effect of the sheepfoot compactors is used to break up the earth lumps and reduce the air voids in cohesive granular soils. They are of little value for compacting non-cohesive granular soils. The design of the feet have been changed to cycloidal shaped feet in order to avoid ripping feet have been changed to cycloidal shaped feet in order to avoid ripping up the compacted material as the feet roll out of the soil. These may be towed or self propelled type.

(c) **Static Three Wheel Self-Propelled Compactors :** These have three rolls, a small usually 'split' steering roll in the front and two large drive rolls mounted on rear axle at both the ends. 'Split' principle in front provides a differential action during steering manoeuvers.

Fig. 7.7 Static three wheeled roller.

(d) **Static Tandem Compactors :** Tandem rollers have two equal sized rools and are centred in line-tandem. These are used for compaction of bituminous layers, as they leave a smooth surface. With the development of tandem vibratory compactors, the contractors prefer the larger size tandem vibratory compactors, which they can use either as static compactor or as a vibratory compactor as per the requirement.

7.10 Vibrating Compaction Equipment

Vibratory compactors can be divided into following groups :

(a) Tandem vibratory compactors,

(b) Towed vibratory compactors,

(c) Towed sheepfoot and tamping foot vibratory compactors,

(d) Self-propelled vibratory compactors,

(e) Handguided vibratory compactors.

(a) **Tandem Vibratory Compactors :** These are available with dual (all wheel) drive or single axle drive. They are available in two types, namely single drum vibrating or both drum vibrating. In double vibrating drum compactors, two tandem wheels are provided with separately controlled vibrators in the front and rear rolls. The double vibratory compactors have increased output by 80% as compared to tandem single drum vibratory compactor. These double drum vibrating compactors can be used, either with both vibrating drum operating or one vibratory drum operating.

(b) **Towed Vibratory Compactors :** These are mainly used for the compaction of cohesive soils, fine and coarse grained mixed soil, and rocky materials. The heavy towed vibratory compactors are used for the compaction of extremely thick layers (in dam or embankment construction). These have

Fig. 7.8 Tandem vibratory roller.

Fig. 7.9 Towed vibratory compactor (Courtesy : MARINI, Italy).

larger amplitude and therefore show 'tamping' motion (impact motion). Therefore, these are used with great success for the compaction of cohesive fine grained soils, and fine and coarse grained mixed soils.

(c) **Towed Sheepsfoot or Tamping Foot Vibratory Compactors :** These are mainly used for the compaction of highly cohesive soils, and soft rock. The kneading and crushing effect of the feet improves the compaction performance. Depending on the shape of the feet, the compactors can either be sheepsfoot or tempingfoot vibratory equipment. Sheepsfoot rolls are having cylindrically shaped feet with relatively small contact areas. Tampingfoot rolls have feet with larger contact areas and are designed so that the actual contact area increases with the penetration of the foot into the soil.

(d) **Self-propelled Vibratory Compactors :** Self-propelled vibratory compactors are available in large varieties mostly around 8 to 12 tons dead weight range, to suit the requirement of the job condition. Some of them are :

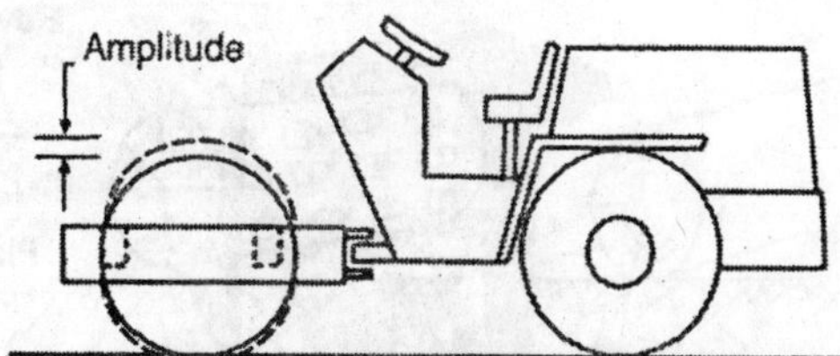

Fig. 7.10 Self propelled vibratory compactor.

Fig. 7.11 Self propelled padfoot vibrating compactor.

(i) Large vibratory steel roll in the front and two rubber tyres in the rear. The rubber tyres may either be smooth one for bituminous work or having treads for earth compaction work. Front roll (drum) may be smooth, padded, sheepfoot or rubber coated.

(ii) Vibratory steel roll in the front and two static steel rolls in the rear for multipurpose works.

(e) Handguided (walk behind) Vibratory Compactors : These may be either (i) single drum which vibrates with the operator guiding it from behind. These are generally designed with clear side so that it is possible to compact right upto a wall instead of leaving an uncompacted strip, or (ii) duplex (double drum) having either one or both drum vibrating.

These small compactors have usually less than a metre width and feature excellent gradability and cross-country mobility due to low centre of gravity. These are

Fig. 7.12 Walk behind duplex vibratory compactor.

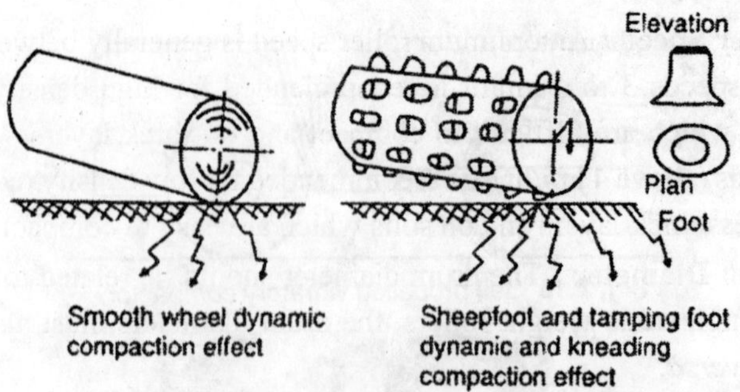

Fig. 7.13 Compaction effect of vibratory compactor.

used for compacting trenches, slopes, parking lots, small repair jobs, sport centres, inside buildings and other confined spaces, and preparing foot and bicycle paths. Some sort of leg or extra wheel arrangement helps to hold the machine in upright position (Fig. 7.12).

7.11 Compaction Speed and Number of Passes

The number of passes and compaction speed required when using vibratory compactor are determined by the necessary "compaction time". Tests indicate that, a limited increase in the compaction speed can be an advantage. Over 5 km/hr speed is not recommended. Since with more speed the number of vibration cycles per cm are not sufficient for achieving desired results. Generally a speed around 4 km/hr is preferred in a compactor for getting better compaction results.

The number of passes is an important criteria and to ensure economical compaction, number passes should not exceed 6. If 6 passes are not sufficient to attain desired compaction, than one should reduce the layer thickness or use another heavy compactor. Most productive compaction will be achieved with a smaller number of passes. If by reducing the layer thickness by few cms, the number of passes required for achieving desired compaction are reduced, so as to increase the hourly production of compaction, then it can be implemented to get better output.

7.12 Factors Influencing the Compaction

Following parameters influence the degree of compaction achieved by a vibratory roller :

(i) Static Weight : When the static weight of a vibratory roller is increased, keeping other factors unchanged, the static and dynamic pressures in the soil will increase more or less proportional to the weight. The depth effect of a vibratory roller is approximately proportional to the roller weight.

(ii) Number of Vibratory Drums : With two vibrating rolls, the number of passes can be decreased and the capacity is thereby increased.

(iii) **Roller Speed :** An optimum roller speed is generally between 3 to 6 km/h. The speeds 3 to 4 km/hr is recommended for high density requirements, soils which are difficult to compact and on thick layers. Whereas higher speeds (above 4 km/hr) are recommended for low density requirements, and for less thick layers and on soils which are easy to compact.

(iv) **Drum Diameter :** The drum diameter should be related to the static load. For high static weight rollers, the drum diameters must also be large and *vice-versa*.

(v) **Frequency and Amplitude :** Results have shown that the compaction effect has a maximum value at frequencies between 25 and 50 Hz (1500 and 3000 vibrations/min). An increase in amplitude gives a pronounced increase in a compaction and depth effect in the entire frequency range. For large volume soils and rock fill materials, large amplitude ranging 1.5 to 2.0 mm and frequency of 25 to 30 Hz (1500 to 1800 vibrations/min) are suitable. For granular base materials also the same vibration data are suitable. For asphalt compaction the optimum amplitude is 0.4 to 0.8 mm and frequency range is 33 to 50 Hz (2000 to 3000 vibrations/min).

(vi) **Relationship between Frame and Drum Weight :** A heavy frame is advantageous, as the drum thereby is pressed down against the soil and more regular vibrations are obtained. However, there exists an upper limit for the weight of the frame above which the frame begins to excessively dampen the vibrations.

(vii) **Driven or Non-driven Drum :** A driven drum on a vibratory roller has less tendency to push the surface layer of a full than a non-driven drum. Hence the driven drum also reduces the risk for surface cracks.

(viii) **Centrifugal Force :** Centrifugal force does not have relationship with vibrating force transmitted to the ground. Centrifugal force increases with the square of the frequency, while the vibrating force is mainly dependent of the amplitude. A centrifugal force gives, however, a general measure of the vibration intensity (acceleration) of the drum. A vibratory roller should not have a lower drum acceleration than 4 to 5 g. At equal static weights and frequencies, the centrifugal force can also be used for a direct comparison between two roller models, since it then shows the relative difference in amplitude.

(ix) **Total Applied Force :** The total applied force defined as the sum of the static weight and centrifugal force was commonly used earlier. Since the centrifugal force is not related to the compaction effect, the total applied force cannot give a correct measure of the compaction effect. Hence the term total applied force is not used now.

7.13 Rubber Tyred Compaction Equipment

The research discovered that a certain amount of compaction was performed by heavy commercial vehicles during the first few days of the opening of the road to traffic. It was for this reason that the pneumatic tyred roller (P.T.R.) came into being. The tyre configuration is of the odd number arrangement—five, seven, nine or more, with certain degree of overlap. Usually even number are provided on the rear axle. Rubber tyred or pneumatic compactors have been used more and more in the last few years for compaction in earth-works and in bituminous road construction. These are generally self-propelled and are built over a wide range of weights. They have proved to be very successful for the compaction of cohesive and non-cohesive soils and stabilised soils in airfield, embankment and road construction applications. These are very efficient on surface dressing owing to the fact that it causes negligible crushing of the stone chippings.

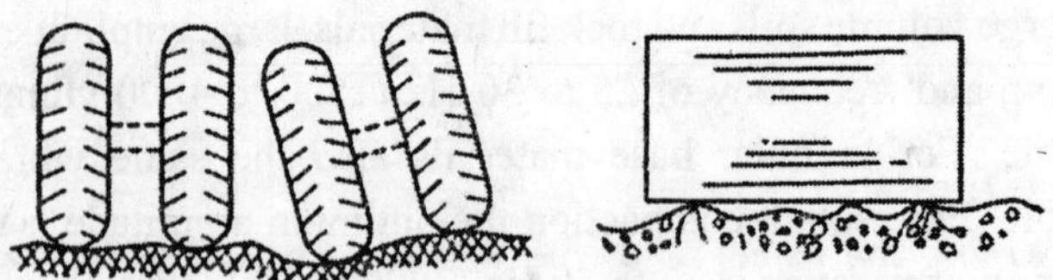

Fig. 7.14 (a) Oscillating wheels of rubber tyre roller,
(b) Bridging with steel wheel roll.

These provide a more uniform compaction effect than steel wheel compactors. Compaction with wide steel rolls sometimes produces a bridging of the material being compacted. Rubber tyred compactors with full oscillation of the front and rear tyres, and equal wheel load ensures that the compactor follows the cross-section of the ground contour. This assures uniform compaction throughout the layer.

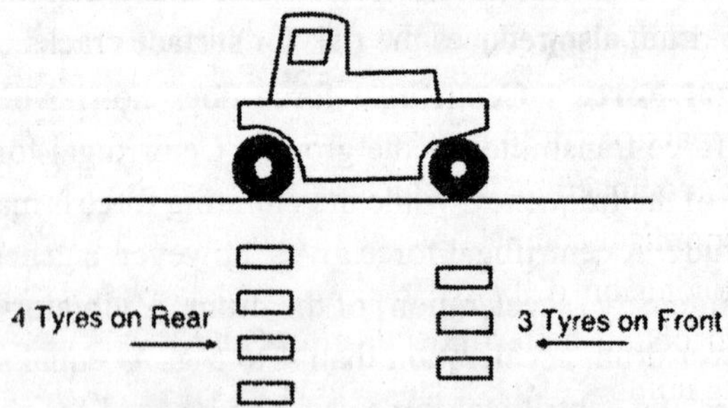

Fig. 7.15 Pneumatic tyred roller.

Main advantages of rubber tyred rollers over steel wheel rollers are :

(i) Surface of the layer is not bridged.

(ii) Bituminous layers which are compacted with a rubber-tyred roller are better sealed to keep out dirt and moisture.

(iii) When rubber-tyred rollers are used, post compaction by traffic will be negligible.

(iv) the compaction effect of the forces supplemented by the elasticity of the rubber tyres provide a 'Kneading effect' resulting in a better surface compaction and surface sealing, especially on bituminous layers.

(v) Unlike a steel wheel compactor, the rubber tyred compactor does not push the asphalt material ahead of it, the flexibility of the tyre actually fold over the initial contact point and impart a vertical force on the material. Therefore, the compaction cracks often produced by steel compactor's are eliminated by using the rubber tyred rollers.

Influence of Load, Inflation and Speed on Compaction

In a rubber tyred compactors, load, inflation pressure, and speed can be changed as per compaction requirement to get maximum productivity.

Surface pressure is generally used to indicate the compaction ability of rubber tyred compactor. It is calculated as follows :

$$\text{Surface pressure} = \frac{\text{Wheel load}}{\text{Contact area}} \frac{\text{kg}}{\text{cm}^2}$$

This surface pressure can be changed in following ways :

1. **Increasing the wheel load** with constant tyre inflation pressure, increases the contact area and the surface pressure.
2. **Increasing the tyre inflation pressure** w3ith constant wheel load, decreases the contact are and increases the surface pressure.

   Thus the compactive force is exerted on the area of the elliptical tyre 'footprint'. This 'footprint' or tyre contact area can be changed through increasing or decreasing either wheel load or tyre inflation pressure. Experiments have shown that increasing inflation pressure has a greater effect on the surface pressure than does increasing the wheel load.
3. **Influence of speed :** Experience have shown that :
   (i) For compaction of very thin layers and for surface compaction the best compaction speed is between 6 to 10 km/hr.
   (ii) For compaction of thick layers the most effective and most economical compaction speed is between 3 and 4 km/hr.

The logical conclusion o this is that, the first passes should be made at low compaction speed to obtain better indepth effect and then increase the compaction speed with increasing number of passes to achieve an optimum surface compaction and surface sealing.

7.14 Application of Rubber Tyred Compactors

1. In Soil Compaction

These can be used satisfactorily and economically to compact both cohesive and non-cohesive materials. It can also be applied equally well in soil stabilisation. The effective compaction depends on wheel load and the type of soil being compacted. Therefore, rubber tyred compactors should always be used at maximum wheel load.

The tyre inflation pressure is adjustable between 2 to 8 bar on all the rubber tyred compactors. Based on experience it can be adjusted as follows :

(a) For compaction of cohesive soils, well graded materials, dense graded aggregates and cohesive gravels at optimum moisture contents, it should be 5 bar or more.

(b) For non-cohesive materials, uniform sands and gravels, the tyre inflation pressure—depending upon the shear strength of the material—should be between 2 and 4 bar.

The compaction speed, as described earlier should be between 6 and 10 km/hr for thin layers, and between 3 to 4 km/hr for thick layers.

2. In Bituminous Material

For bituminous road construction, the bituminous material must be compacted to a specified density to achieve a sufficient deformation resistance. The pavement surface should also be sealed to keep-out dirt and water. Tests have shown that rubber tyred rollers compact and seal pavements better than the steel wheel compactors. The kneading action of the tyres ensures a better compaction. The rubber tyred rollers are thus efficient and productive for compacting all bituminous layers.

For the application on asphalt pavement, following guidelines are given :

(a) Wheel Load : Wheel load of 1500 to 2000 kg is desirable for less than 13 cm thick layers, while 2000 to 2500 kg for 13 to 18 cm thick layers, and 2500 to 3000 kg for 18 to 22 cm thick layers.

(b) Inflation Pressure : If the tyre pressure is too low, or the wheel load is too high, the tyre tread will camber to the inside (concave), whereas if the tyre inflation pressure is too high, or the wheel load is too low, the tyre will camber to the outside (convex). In both the cases correct compaction and surface smoothness can not be achieved. Correct adjustment o the inflation pressure can be checked by using a straight edge of the same length as that of the tyre tread width (as shown in the Fig. 7.16).

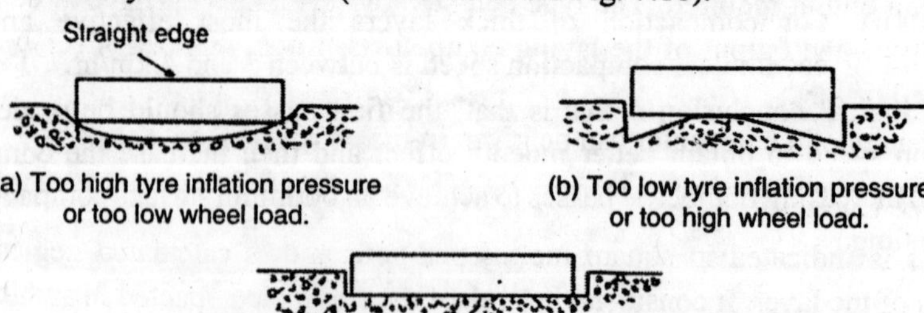

Fig. 7.16 Determination of the correct tyre inflation pressure.

Thus the inflation pressure should be at least 4 bar, higher limits of pressure is decided on the basis of wheel load so as to get straight edge of the tyre impression on the bituminous material, *i.e.*, the full tread width is in contact with the asphalt surface.

So as to get full depth effect of the rubber tyred compactor, it would always be ballasted (ballast container be filled with sand, water, gravel or iron scrap).

(c) **Compaction Speed :** As explained earlier, the best compaction speed is 6 to 10 km/hr for thin layers, whereas 3 to 4 km/hr for thick layers. Experiments have shown that the first compaction passes should be with low speed, and for successive passes the speed can be increased to achieve optimum output.

Fig. 7.17 Pneumatic tyred roller (Courtesy : VOLVO).

7.15 Capacity Calculations

Selection and application of a compactor depends upon the site conditions and the compaction output required. The type and size of the compactor have to be matched with the type and output of the laying equipments (truck, dumper or scraper, motor grader, and paver).

Capacity of a compactor can be given in two ways :

(i) Surface Capacity

This is indicated in square metres per hour and is calculated neglecting the thickness of the layer. It considers the area of the surface compacted in an hour.

$$Q = C\,.\,\frac{W \times S\,.1000}{P}\ \text{m}^2/\text{hr}$$

where, Q = Output, in m^2/hr

W = Drum width, in metres

S = Average compaction speed, in km/hr

P = Number of passes

C = Efficiency factor or site operating coefficient includes repair, inspections, breaks, overlaps and other factors affecting the efficiency. It is generally taken as,
0.8 under excellent conditions,
0.7 under good conditions,
0.6 under fair conditions.

Number of passes are calculated considering forward and return travel as two passes.

(ii) Volumetric Capacity

This gives a clear idea of the capacity of the roller, as it also includes the thickness of the layer, and is given in cubic metres/hr.

$$Q = C \cdot \frac{W \times S \times T \times 1000}{P} \text{ m}^3/\text{hr}$$

where,
Q = Output, in m^3/hr
W = Drum width, in metres
S = Average compaction speed, in km/hr
P = Number of passes
T = Layer thickness after compaction, metres
C = Efficiency factor or site operating coefficient.

7.16 Safety Precautions

1. No person, other than operator, should climb a moving compactor/road roller.
2. These should not move down the hill with the engine out of gear.
3. When the compactor (or road roller) is not in use, brake should be applied, engine should be put into gear and wheels be blocked.
4. As far as practicable, compactors should not be left on a highway or hauling roads after the close of work. Where this is not practicable, red lights should be provided at the two ends at night to clearly show their presence on the road.
5. Before a road roller/compactor is used on the ground such ground is examined for its bearing capacity and general safety, especially at the edges of slopes such as embankments on such ground.

General safety precautions mentioned in the chapter on "earth moving equipment" should also be followed.

QUESTIONS

1. What are the objectives of compaction of soil?
2. What is compaction? Discuss the compaction process for different types of soils.
3. How the moisture influences the compaction? Discuss.

4. Discuss soil compaction principles.
5. What is soil stabilization? How it should be done for different types of soils?
6. Discuss how compaction speeds and number of passes influence the compaction.
7. Explain the following in brief :
   (a) dry density
   (b) soil compaction applications
   (c) applications of vibratory compactors.
8. Discuss as to how load, speed and inflation pressure influence the compaction by rubber tyred compactors.
9. How would you achieve desired compaction in different types of soils during construction of highways?
10. How would you calculate the capacity of a compactor?
11. Describe (a) static smooth wheeled, and (b) sheep foot rollers. Indicate type of soil where they can be used.
12. Describe construction and working of pneumatic tyred rollers and type of work where they can be used.
13. Explain different types of vibratory rollers with their applications.
14. Discuss as to how will you select the compacting equipment for different purposes.
15. Discuss different types compactors.
16. Explain commonly used static compaction equipment.
17. Discuss various factors influencing the compaction.
18. Mention various safety precautions to be taken during the working of compaction equipment.

Chapter **8**

Finishing/Grading Equipment

8.1 Motor Graders and Its Construction

Motor graders, also known as 'finishing equipment', are used for levelling and smoothening the earthwork, spreading and levelling the base courses in the construction of roads and airfields. It can also be used for land reclamation, snow clearance, gravel road repairing, mixing of stabilizing materials such as tar, asphalt, cement and lime, maintaining quarry roads etc. A scarifier arrangement for raking hard material and sometimes a bulldozer attachment for dozing operations are also attached on this machine. Motor graders can also undertake large scale ditching and trenching work in irrigation schemes.

A grader may be either towed or motorised. Towed grader is drawn with a tractor and are of smaller sizes. Generally motor graders are self propulsive. The front of the grader frame is supported on a pair of front wheels and the rear over the heavier tandem

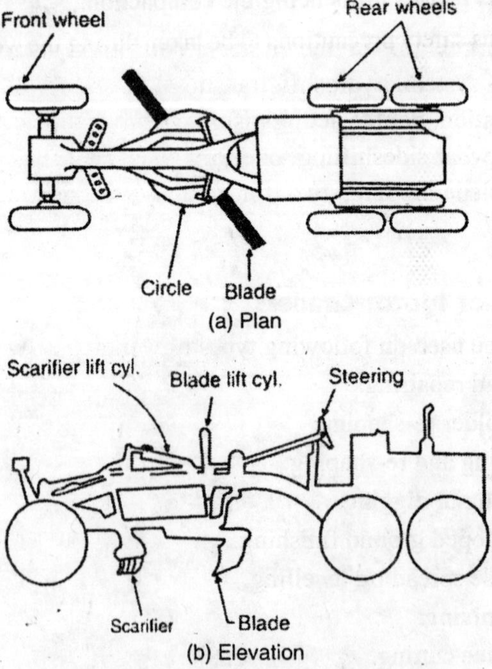

Fig. 8.1 An outline diagram of a motor grader.

wheels. A heavy and dozer like curved blade is supported on a circle and can be turned through an angle of 360°. This blade is fitted with replaceable edges on sides and bottoms, and can be angled and tilted to suit the soil conditions. The extended blade can be positioned vertically or at any angle for side bank sloping. An outline diagram of a motor grader is shown in Fig. 8.1.

Motor graders are self propelled and fast moving machines, travelling at a speed upto 40 km per hour at no load while moving on roads. The frame of the machine is arch shaped converging and raised at the front and low at the rear where the prime mover is mounted. The front of the frame is supported by a pair of front wheels and the rear on the heavier tandem wheels which are also the driving wheels. These frames are articulated by two hydraulic cylinders.

The blade is supported on a circle with inside gear teeth which can be turned through 360°. The circle is attached to a draw bar pivoted at the front on the main frame and supported at the rear by a pair of lift arms. Steering of the grader is done through front wheels. For projecting the blade out on any side a side toothed sector is provided.

The speed of the motor grader ranges from about 4 km per hour (at full load) to about 40 km per hour (at no load). Front axle may have oscillation angle and also assures stable machine travel. Hydraulic system allows front wheel to lean about 18° to each side. Full hydraulic steering control system with two steering cylinders are provided for actuating the knuckle arm.

Mold board of motor grader is a box-section constructed with a wear-resistant steal. Reversible overlay end bits and side edges are attached to the mold board. All blade movements and positions can be hydraulically controlled from the operator's seat.

Hydraulic control unit of the motor grader has hydraulic pumps (for work equipment, steering system, hydroshift transmission, and for differential), a hydraulic motor for blade rotation, double acting piston type hydraulic cylinders (two for blade lifting), one for drawbar sideshifting, one for blade side-shifting, one for front wheel leaning, one for blade tipping, two for front wheel steering and two for frame articulation.

8.2 Applications of Motor Graders

Motor graders can be used on following types of works :

1. Gravel road repairing.
2. Road shoulder re-shaping.
3. Bank cutting and re-shaping.
4. Ditch-filling or digging.
5. Level or sloped ground finishing.
6. Base course spreading levelling.
7. Material mixing.
8. Hard surface cutting.

9. Snow clearance.
10. Land clearance.
11. Frozen top soil and asphalt breaking.

Fig. 8.2 A motor grader with rippers.

For better efficiency a cutting depth of 2 to 4 cms are generally adopted. The speed of the motor grader is kept according to the job to be performed and nature and characteristics of the soil. In light duty operations the grading speeds are generally kept between 6 to 10 km/hr. Whereas in normal grading and heavy duty grading or fine finishing the speed preferred is 4 to 6 km/hr and 2 to 3 km/hr respectively.

8.3 Adjusting the Blade

The blade (sometimes called as Mold board) is the main tool of the grader. It is carried by a rotating circle and is easily manoeuverable to a wide range of cutting positions with the help of hydraulic controls. The blade and the circle are mounted on a fame and is supported at the front of the machine by a ball joint.

The blade can be adjusted to any position with the help of levers, as indicated below :

1. **Sideshift :** The blade has blade sideshift ram as shown in Fig. 8.3 which is operated by a lever provided in the operator's cabin. This lever when operated in one direction, shifts the blade to one side with the help of the blade sideshift, ram, whereas when this lever is operated in othe4r direction, shifts the blade to other side.

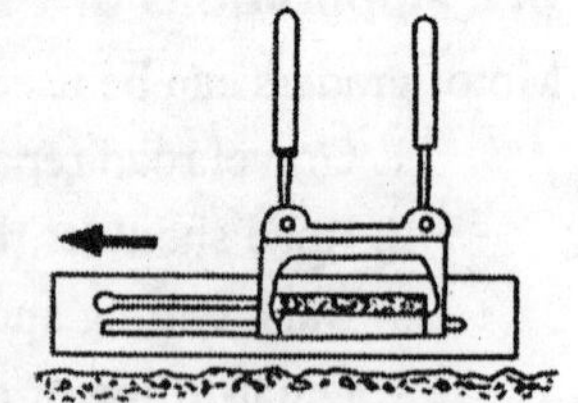

Fig. 8.3 Blade sideshift.

2. **Lifting the blade :** The blade can be lifted or lowered by levers operating the two rams fitted as shown in Fig. 8.4. With the help of these two rams operated separately the blade can be kept either horizontally, or raised or lowered towards left or right hand side to keep it inclined as shown in Fig. 8.4.

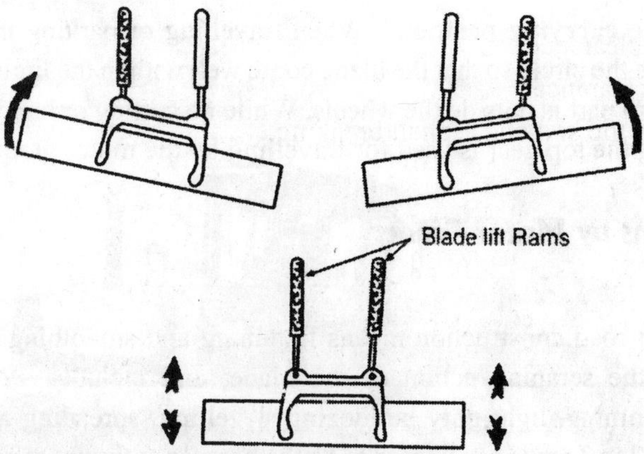

Fig. 8.4 Lifting the blade.

3. **Rotating the circle :** A hydraulic motor is provided to rotate the circle and blade. Blade can be rotated either in clockwise direction or in anticlockwise direction as shown in Fig. 8.5, by operating the lever. The blade may be rotated to any position and may even to completely reverse position. While reversing the blade by rotating care should be taken that it may not touch tyres etc.

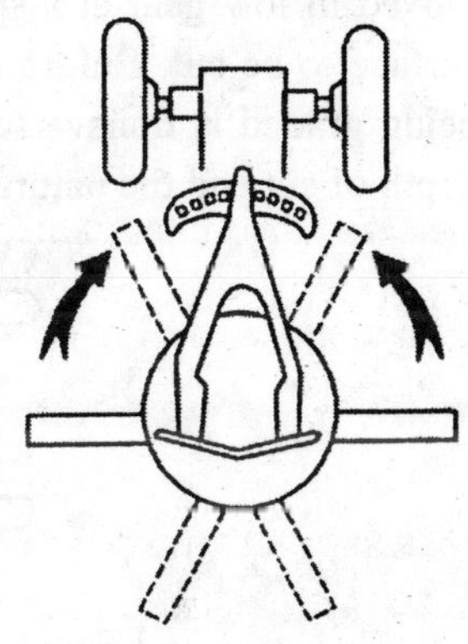
Fig. 8.5 Rotating the circle.

4. **Adjusting blade cutting angle (blade pitch) :** The vertical angle of the blade can be adjusted. For adjustments some motor graders provide a hydraulic tilt ram, whereas in some others the adjustments can be done manually. Both the adjustment mechanisms are shown in Fig. 8.6. The cutting angles are generally adjustable between 30° to 60°.

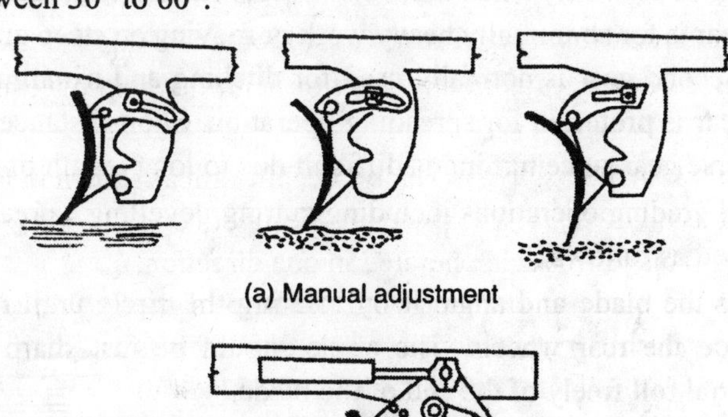
(a) Manual adjustment

(b) Hydraulic adjustment

Fig. 8.6 Blade cutting angle.

5. **Blade carrying position :** When travelling or parking the motor grader, rotate the circle so that the blade come well with in the limits of the machine and no part is outside the wheels. While no cutting or handling operation is done, the top gear is used for travelling by the motor grader.

8.4 Operations by Motor Grader

1. Grading

Grading in road construction means flattening and smoothing the road surface and others by the scraping action of the blade, and includes working operation like,surface skimming, light duty bulldozing, levelling, spreading and crowning. A cutting depth of 2 to 3 cm is considered to be the best for optimum efficiency. Under no circumstances it should be greater than 5 cm. For finishing cuts, the depth of cut is kept within 1 cm.

During the grading operation, motor grader is normally moved forward. It is moved in low gear at a speed allowed by the depth of cut and the condition of the surface to be cut. Before applying the second cut, entire portion of the road surface being graded is transversed. In subsequent cuts also the speed is determined by the depth of cut and the nature of the surface to be cut.

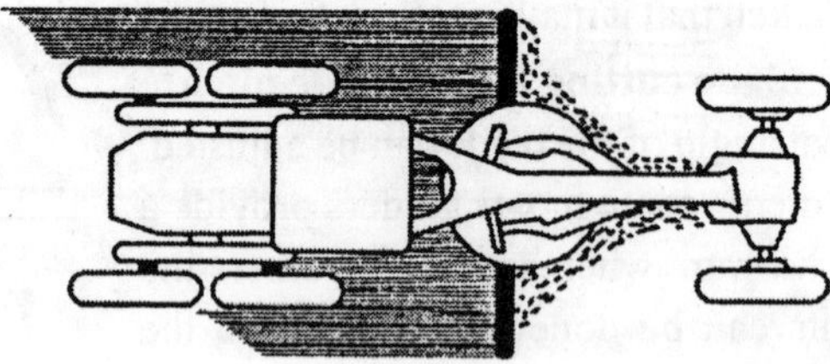

Fig. 8.7 Grading.

The top gear is used only when it travels without cutting or handling the material, while the first gear is for abnormally heavy work or moving on steep gradient or doing fine finishing. Second gear is normally used for ditching and trimming hank slopes, whereas third gear is preferred for spreading operation. Short distances are generally travelled in reverse gear since turning is difficult due to long length of the machine.

For normal grading operations including cutting, levelling, spreading etc. blade should be adjusted as follows :

(a) Move the blade and angle it by rotating the circle until rear end is just outside the rear wheels. The angle should be just sharp enough to let material roll freely of the end of the blade.

(b) At the start of a pass, rest the front and rear ends of the blade equally on the ground. As the grader begins to advance, increase the cutting depth by lowering the blade into the ground slowly to the extent limited by the resistance and the behaviour of the material ahead of the cutting edge. Try to match the gear and speed of the motor grader to the ground density.

(c) Note action of earth and try slight alterations of blade angle and speed until earth rolls along blade and forms a windrow. This helps in less power consumption and more output.

(d) To counteract the side draft, lean the front wheels to the right properly to keep the grade on its straight head course.

(e) Keep the scarifier lifted as far as possible, maintaining a proper clearance.

(f) Never allow the wheels to run into a windrow.

2. Spreading

Gravel together with binding material is spread by the motor grader. The *windrows* are spread in a set thickness by keeping, all the wheels straight. (Windrow is a row of loose material that spills of the trailing edge of a dozer or grader blade). The blade is kept in level and square to windrow. For spreading, the cutting angle is set at 60° nearly. Cutting edge of the blade is set above the ground at a distance equal to depth to which material is to be spread. As grader moves forward in low gear, the windrow is spread out by the blade in full length of the cutting edge as shown in Fig. 8.8.

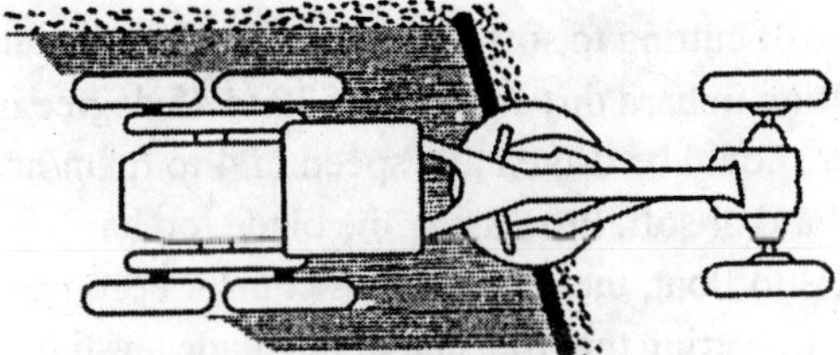

Fig. 8.8 Spreading a window.

3. Finishing and Levelling

In final finishing and levelling, surface have to be finished to fine limits. In such cases make the finishing pass with the blade only slightly angled and set to skim the surface. To avoid tyre marks, maximum circle and blade side shift is necessary to reach it well beyond the rear tyre, as shown in Fig. 8.9. In this operation always work in low gear and avoid sudden jerky movements on controls.

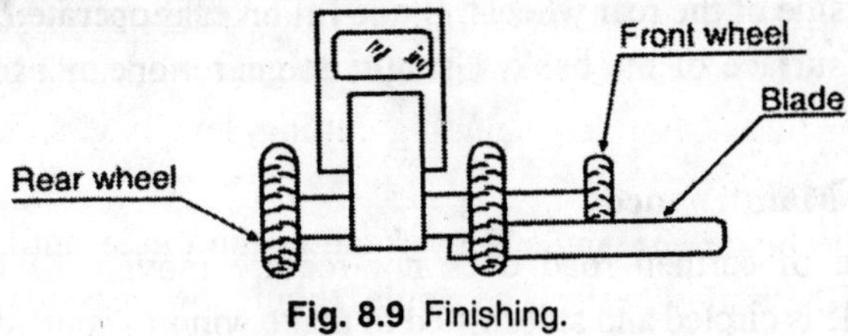

Fig. 8.9 Finishing.

4. Ditch Digging

The front end of the blade is tilted down and the rear end is tilted up above the road surface. The front end cuts into ground as shown in Fig. 8.10. This is used to dig drainage ditches and road side ditches. For this purpose angle the blade more sharply

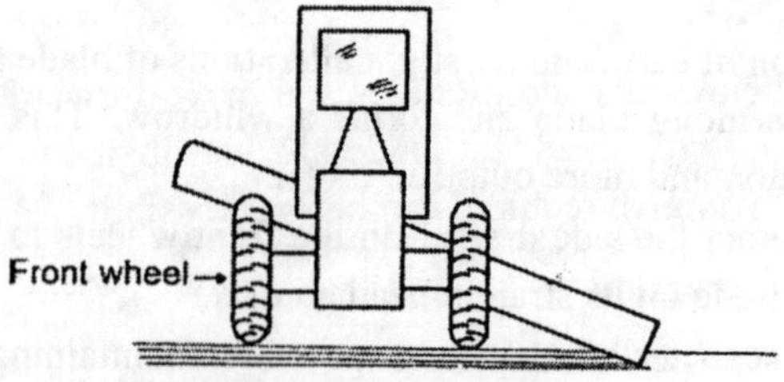

Fig. 8.10 Ditch digging.

than for the grading and move the front end of the blade out by rotating the circle and by side shifting. During the operation scarifiers are kept in lifted position.

The first cut is made for marking. Steer the grader to marking cut by driving the machine at about 4 km/hr and keeping the depth of cut between 10 to 15 cm, so that the windrow will line up on the inboard side of the rear wheels. After the marking cut, make further passes, each time digging as deep as possible without causing the rear wheels to slip. Repeat ditch cuts until required depth is reached.

5. Cutting

For one purpose of cutting to soft dirt, set the blade to an angle between 40 to 55 degree, while the cutting in hard dirt an angle of 30 to 45 degree is proper. To grade by cutting, motor grader should be driven at a speed of 4 to 6 km/hr, depending upon the type of surface, *i.e.*, hard or soft. Processing the blade too hard against the surface may cause the front wheels to float, thereby steering control becomes difficult and making the drive wheels slip. Lowering the front end of the blade an slightly raising the rear end will be helpful making the cutting edge dig into the hard surface.

For cutting of the material from the rutted surface, the depth of cut should be great enough to remove the ruts, and then the surface is levelled so that the compaction can be done uniformly.

6. Bank Cutting

In this operation, the position of the blade is for scraping or cutting the bank wall. Blade position is set by rotating the circle and tilt the blade forward with its rear end staying on the outside of the rear wheels. Blade lift lever is operated to align the blade along the sloped surface of the bank. Using first gear work of bank cutting can be proceeded.

7. Earthen Road Maintenance

Maintenance of earthen road does not require moving of large amounts of material. The blade is circled and sideshifted to make windrow outside or between rear wheels. The blade cuts high areas and fill low areas. First or second gear may be used depending on the nature of ground and depth of cut. If the earthen road is wide enough, first work along one side and then back along other side.

In repairing a rutted road, filling the hollows with loose material is not enough. The humps should be planed off and the loosened dirt be crowded into the hollows. Set the blade to cut just below ruts and pit holes and move forward to form a windrow. When an even surface is obtained, set blade at right angles to re-spread windrows angling blade vertically to give required camber or crossfall.

8. Earthen Road Construction

Earthen road is constructed as follows :

(a) Turf is striped off by setting blade square to motor grader with cutting edge level, and by lowering the blade just sufficient to roll up turf as grader moves forward in the first gear.

(b) Surface is then levelled by filling hollows and holes left by trees etc.

(c) Ditch is then made.

(d) If a camber to the earthen road is required, set the blade square to the machine and angled to give the required camber. Camber means centre portion of the road is slightly elevated above the shoulder portions to the cross-section. The object of 'crown' is to prevent forming of water puddles on the road.

9. Repairing Gravel Road

Motor grader should be used for repair of gravel road as follows :

(a) In first stage, side, ditches and road shoulders should be reshaped.

(b) Road surface should then be planned, keeping the crows as desired.

(c) Casting the loosened material towards the centre.

(d) Make a finishing pass as straight as possible. Straight forward grading results in better finish. Drive the grader as fast as the working conditions permit.

8.5 Special Attachments and their Operations

Following are the special operations, which can be performed with help of motor graders by using special attachments :

1. Scarifier Operation

A scarifier is a special tool attached with the motor grader for loosening the hard soil and has a set of teeth mounted on adjustable shanks. This attachment digs up hard ground like asphalt, old pavement, frozen surface and hard soil with vegetation and brushes which can not be removed by the blade. The teeth are replaceable, and the number of teeth can be varied to suit the ground hardness. High strength alloy steel tips can be mounted on the teeth to prevent teeth wear and extent their service for economical performance.

On very hard surfaces it is required to remove some teeth to get better penetration. It is better to remove alternate teeth from the scarifier block so that those remaining are evenly spaced. To remove heavy obstructions such as large stones, following procedure may be adopted :

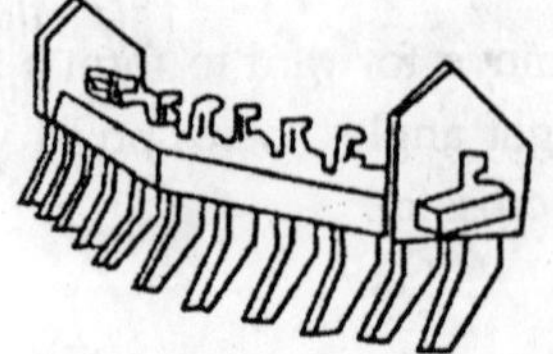

Fig. 8.11 Scarifier.

Fig. 8.12 Scarifier teeth with alloy steel tip.

(a) Lower the scarifier into the ground and move the motor grader very slowly until scarifier teeth are inserted underside the stone as shown in Fig. 8.12.

(b) Then lift the scarifier while continuing to move forward slowly (Fig. 8.13). When too strong resistance is experienced, further moving of the machine is stopped and operation as at (a) is repeated, until stone is loose enough to be rolled aside.

Fig. 8.13 Removing heavy stones using scarifier.

2. Bulldozing

The bulldozer blade is a front end attachment fitted to the grader for pushing the loads. This is used for volume push carry operations and facilitate difficult spreading jobs involving large heaps of slabby or rocky materials.

By providing a bulldozer blade in the front, the grader can efficiently be used as a bulldozer. The bulldozer blade can be hydraulically raised up enabling the grader to perform its regular job of grading, scarifying etc.

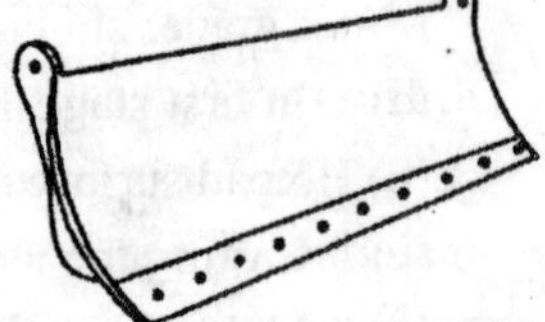

Fig. 8.14 Bulldozing blade.

3. Snow Clearing

The motor graders are also required to cast snow off the road surface in order to clear the road for traffic. For heavy snow clearance, fit the tyre chains, and keep inflating pressure to the specified value.

Deep snow is relatively soft immediately after a snowfall. All snow clearing should be done as soon as possible before it gets packed hard or turned to ice.

For road snow of less than 30 cm depth, the snow may be side cast with blade angled nearly to 40 deg. A good speed (15 to 25 km per hr) will help the wet snow to quickly pass off the blade (Refer Fig. 8.15).

When road snow is of more than 30 cm depth, use of plough is recommended. Make the first run with 'V' plough down the middle of the road at a good speed, as

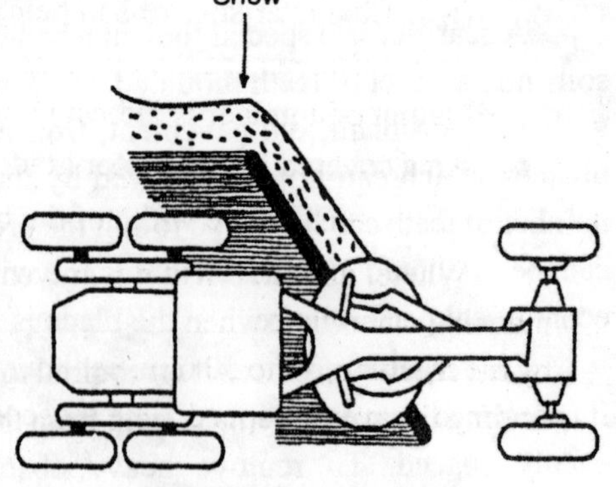

Fig. 8.15 Snow clearing.

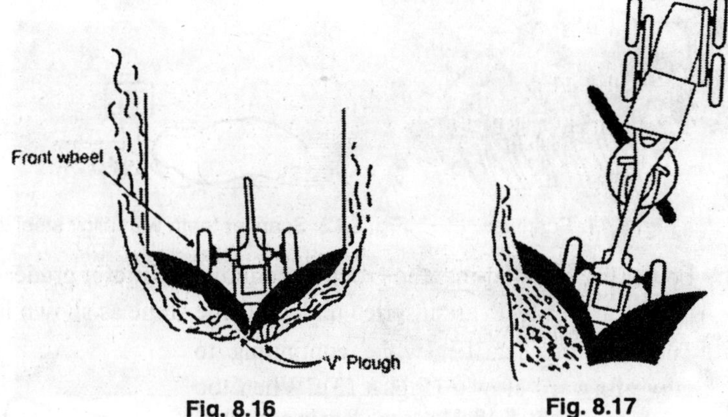

Fig. 8.16 Fig. 8.17

shown in Fig. 8.16. Afterwards push back the snow banks with one side of the plough, as shown in Fig. 8.17.

4. Ripper Operation

To ripper is used to break up materials too hard to cut with moldboard blade. The depth of cut is controlled by hydraulically operated ripper control level. Type of material to be ripped will determine position of the ripper shanks.

5. Horrow Operation

Horrow is mounted on the rear and is used to loosen, pulverize and blend materials. When horrow is used, blade or scarifier is freed. These with the help of scarifier are used to rip and pulverize old roads for easy blending, and with blade these are used for mixing base materials.

8.6 Output of Motor Graders

Output of a motor grader depends upon the following main factors :

(i) Size and mechanical condition of the motor grader.
(ii) Size of the blade.
(iii) Speed of travel.
(iv) Characteristics of soil being handled.
(v) Efficiency of the operator.

Output of a grader is indicated by the area covered by the grader per hour.

Area covered by the motor grader/hr.

= Effective width of the blade × Average speed × Efficiency

Where, effective width is the width of the blade when it is perpendicular to the machine otherwise, when the blade is at angle, it should be the width actually covered by the machine, 40 to 50 min. per hour is generally taken for working efficiency. While finding the average speed, time for acceleration and turning should also be considered.

Fig. 8.18 Motor graders in operation.

Time required for completing a particular job can be calculated using the formula given below :

Time to complete a job (in hrs.)

$$= \frac{\text{No. of passes} \times \text{Distance in kms}}{\text{Average speed in km/hr} \times \text{Efficiency factor}}$$

The number of passes depend on the nature of work and characteristics of the material. The efficiency factor in normal is taken as 0.7, which means the effective work which the motor grader done in about 42 min in an hour.

8.7 Safety Precautions

1. The pre-starting inspection should be performed by checking foot and hand brakes.
2. When operating near obstructions use low gear.
3. When operating on a public highway, the blade tips shall be flagged.
4. Keep a sharp look out at all times for other vehicles, cattle and pedestrians.
5. When parking the machine, the blade shall be turned inside the frame and lowered to the ground, set the hand brake, and block wheels if on incline. The transmission may be left in low gear after the engine has been shut off, if additional braking force is needed.
6. The motor grader should be kept away from the outer edge when working on a side hill road. The blade should be extended to move the material upon the outer edge.
7. The grader blades should be set in the offset position when ditching or grading with over hanging rock edges or trees. This will keep the operator away from obstructions.

QUESTIONS

1. List out different types of works where motor graders can effectively be used.
2. Giving an outline diagram, describe construction and working of motor grader.
3. Explain common operations which can be performed by motor graders.
4. What are the activities of land development where a "motor grader" can be used? Explain the procedure for doing those activities.
5. What is a grader? Discuss its working.
6. Name the attachments of a motor grader and explain the functions of its blade.
7. Explain the need for adjusting the motor grader. How the blades can be adjusted for different types of works?
8. How the motor grader is used for following functions :
   (a) Finishing and levelling the surfaces.
   (b) Ditch digging.
   (c) Bank cutting.
   (d) Snow clearing.
9. Explain as to how the output of motor graders is indicated?
10. Enumerate the safety precautions while using the motor graders.

Chapter 9

Hauling Equipment

9.1 Introduction

Hauling uits transport the earth, aggregate, rock, ore, coal and other materials. Hauling units may be road vehicles or rail-road locomotives. Haulage mainly consists of trailers pulled by tractors or trucks. Trucks have been mobility and can haul various types of materials. But their performance and output is greatly hampered on rough roads and in bad weather. For better performance, greater road maintenance with lesser grade is required. Whereas rubber tyred tractors with separate wagons have better mobility and haulage speeds on less maintained rough roads and can carry heavier loads than that of trucks. Crawler tractors with wagons are employed when roads are very rough and maintenance of roads is very costly. There are used for short hauls due to low speeds. Locomotives are suitable for long distance haulage on a fixed route, which is likely to be continued for a long period. These can be used in any weather and rail-road equipment require less maintenance.

The use of trucks provides a high degree of flexibility, as their number in service can usually be increased or decreased easily to permit modification in the total haulic capacity of a fleet.

9.2 Classification

Haulage trucks can be classified in many ways, including :

1. On-highway or off-highway.
2. The method of dumping the load—rear dump, bottom-dump, side-dump.
3. The type of frame—rigid frame or articulated frame.
4. The kind of drive—two-wheel, four-wheel or six-wheel.
5. The class of material hauled—earth, rock, coal or ore.
6. The capacity—gravimetric (tons) or volumetric (cubic meters).

On-highway vehicles are designed to be used on public highways, whereas off-highway vehicles are designed to be used on construction sites and are designed and manufactured to preclude their use on public roads and thus they may or may not comply with legal on highway limitations.

9.3 Dump Trucks

Dump trucks are open vehicles which are capable of carrying and dumping earth, aggregate or other loose material to construction sites on various projects such as dams, highways, ports etc. Generally heavy-duty machines of more than 10 tonnes payload are intended for on-site haulage of construction or mine materials. Dump trucks in many sizes with pay loads ranging upto more than 300 tonnes are available. These may have two axle or three axle, and may be 4×2 (2 wheels driven out of 4); 4×4 (all 4 wheels driven out of 4); 6×4 (4 wheels driven out of 6).

Special features of dump trucks usually include : heavy, all-welded chassis to sustain rough ground conditions, extra large wheel to support load and give good ground clearance,ultra heavy duty tipping bodies constructed by high tensile steel to withstand damage from high impact and highly abrasive materials.

As mentioned earlier the dump trucks are of two types, namely on-highway and off-highway.

9.3.1 Highway Dump Trucks

For a construction project dump truck is a very common and essential equipment and is available in various sizes and types. These on-highway dump trucks are generally classified by the volumetric or tonnage payload capacity. Generally dump trucks of capacities ranging between 3 to 25 cu m are commonly used with a speed upto 80 km per hour. However dump trucks of more than 200 cu m (300 tonnes) capacity have also been manufactured.

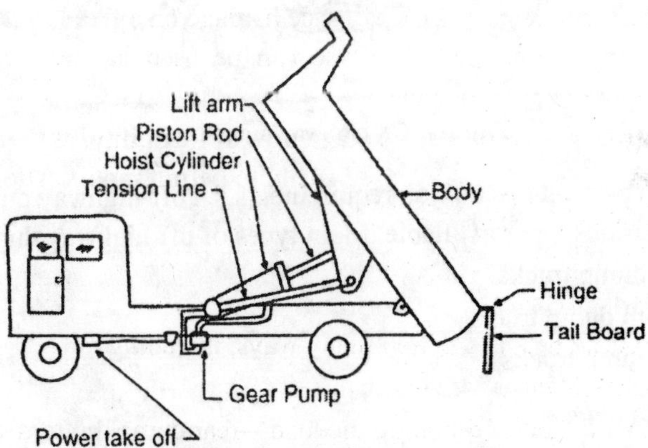

Fig. 9.1 On-highway dump truck.

On-highway dump trucks have chassis, prime mover and power transmission system similar to that of a truck, whereas the body of the dump truck is heavy duty type and is capable of tilting towards one side by means of hydraulic jacks and can be operated from the cabin. In on-highway dump trucks a tail gate is provided at the rear so that while moving on the highway the materials do not fell on the road. The tailgate opens when the body is doing the tipping operation for dumping the material. The speed with which on-highway dump truck travels is high and can be upto 80 km per hour or so depending upon the condition of the road.

9.3.2 Off-Highway Dump Trucks

Off-highway dump trucks do not have tail gates, therefore, the body floor slopes upward at a slight angle toward the rear. The floor shape perpendicular to the length of the body for some models is flat, while other models utilize a "V" bottom to reduce the shock of loading and to help center the load.

These are used off the highway specially in earth moving and mining applications. These are commonly known as dumpers. The body construction is specially designed to absorb high-impact loading. The floor of the body is of high-tensile steel to reduce abrasion damage. The ratio of gross vehicle weight to horsepower is generally lower than for an on-highway dump truck. Top speed of off-highway dump truck is also slow (30-40 km per hour). Since these are used on rough roads, oversize air cleaners and filters, shock proof mounting of all instruments, dust-proofing of electrical system, cushioned mounting for radiators etc. are provided.

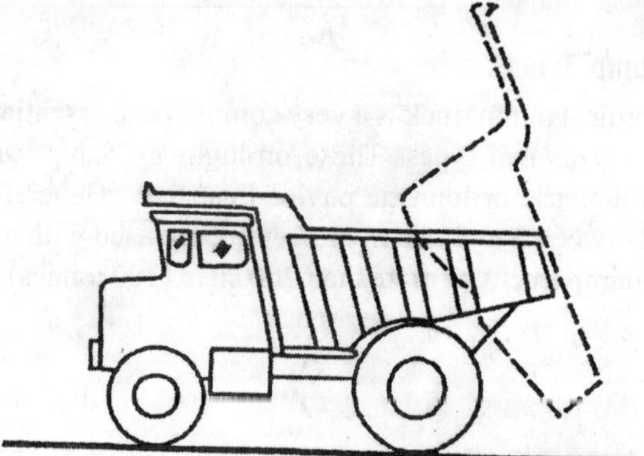

Fig. 9.2 Off-highway dump truck.

To satisfy a particular set of job requirements, an off-highway dump truck can be selected out of various types available. Main types of off-highway dump trucks are :

(i) Rear dump trucks.

(ii) Bottom dump trucks.

(iii) Side dump trucks.

1. Rear Dump Trucks

These are very common and heavy duty trucks and are capable of handling even quarry rocks. The body of these trucks is hinged at the back and fitted with a hydraulic ram (multi stage jack or a telescopic hoist) on the underside to lift the front of the body and tilt it to the dumping position. In on-highway dump trucks tailgates are provided at the rear whereas in off-highway dump trucks the shape of the body at the rear is such that it facilitate dumping. Top front of the body is extended to form a cap over the cabin to protect it from hitting while loading. The body rest on the main truck chassis frame provided with a number of rubber cushions to absorb shocks while loading and travelling.

These are suitable to handle many types of materials, but are most suitable for quarry rocks. These are also used when :

(a) Dumping is in restricted hoppers or fill.

(b) Loading under a large shovel or dragline is subjected to sever loading impact.

(c) Maximum flexibility is required for hauling a variety of materials such as earth, sand and gravel and more bulky material such as blasted rock, ore, coal etc.

(d) Maximum gradeability is required.

In colder climates, where there are chances for freezing the material being transported, the dumpers are available to prevent material from freezing. In these dump trucks, exhaust gases from the engine are carried through ducts in the front slope sheat, in the bottom of the body, and on a portion of the side walls. The heated body can also help when handling wet, adhesive clay soils, hauxite and other sticky materials.

Fig. 9.3 Dump truck in unloading operation (Courtesy : Ashok Layland)

2. Bottom Dump Trucks

These are suitable for long hauls of easy flowing materials like sand, gravel, dry earth and which are to be spread to layers as on a fill of a dam. The material is discharged through bottom while the vehicle is moving at a controlled rate by means of 2 longitudinal gates. These are unsuitable for big size material or wet or sticky materials due to limited openings.

In bottom dump trucks the material can be discharged while the vehicle is in motion and laid in a long windrow. This way of dumping will not hamper the passage of other vehicles and also reduce the levelling effects of the dumped material.

These sometimes known as bottom dump wagons, are the semi-trailers, front end of which is supported on the rear of the hauling tractor, and the rear end is resting on their own wheels. Wide top area facilitates quick loading under shovels. Due to low long bodies they have fast speeds on suitably maintained roads, but longer turning radius is required and manoeuvering becomes more difficult in restricted spaces. With these it is difficult to negotiable steep grades.

Therefore, bottom dump trucks should be used, when :

(a) The material to be hauled is relatively free-flowing.

(b) The road is suitably maintained, thus permitting high speed travel.

(c) Long and steep grades are not existing to the way.

(d) The load is to be spread in windrows.

3. Side Dump Trucks

These dump trucks are most suitable when dumping is required to be done in a long narrow length or on on one or both sides of a road (for dumping the material on road shoulders). These require very less time to dump its material, whereas the rear dump truck must stop, reverse and then dump is load which needs a considerably more time. Side dump trucks are available in self-propelled that is truck•type models or in a fully trailer type models (which is commonly known as side dump tractor-trailer).

9.3.3 Articulated Dump Trucks

Articulated dump trucks are made on two or more separate machine elements joined together to permit manoeuverability. It permits large machines to be separated into elements for transportation and increases operating efficiency. Now-a-days large dump trucks are gaining popularity because of their advantage in manoeuverability through articulation.

The articulated dump trucks are specially designed to operate in confined working locations where a rigid-frame trucks have problems. An articulated joint and oscillating ring between tractor and the dump body enable to turn the vehicle in limited

Fig. 9.4 Articulated dump-truck.

space. Articulated trucks can climb on steeper grades (upto about 35°) than right-frame trucks/dumpers.

9.4 Dump Truck Operations

For transportation of material by a dump truck, following operations are involved :

(i) Loading the dump truck.

(ii) Hauling.

(iii) Dumping the material at desired place.

Fig. 9.5(a) On-highway dump truck.

1. Loading

The dump trucks are loaded by draglines, shovels, or by wheel loaders. The dump truck or dumper driver, for best efficiency and more production, should keep it in most efficient working area of the shovel or dragline or wheel loader. Less the swing and distance moved by the shovel boom between the cut (from mine quarry) and the truck body the more amount of loading will be done by the shovels or a loader in a given amount of time.

After loading the truck, shovel operator signals the truck driver to move his vehicle from under the shovel. The driver then starts his vehicle for the haul road and reach the higher practicable gear range as soon as possible. The driver should take following precautions for his own and vehicles safety :

(a) Stay in the cabin during loading of the truck.

(b) Drive carefully in the working area and avoid hitting sharp rocks and shovel overflow.

(c) Do not move the truck until the shovel operators gives a signal.

2. Hauling

Drive the vehicle as per ground condition and the condition of the road, and use highest gear adjusting the road condition. Driver should ensure precautions for the safety of his own and for long life of the vehicle.

Fig. 9.5(b) Off-highway dumper.

3. Dumping

Dumping operation depends upon the type of work where dumping is required to be done. For instance, for dumping at exact point, a second person, known as 'spotter' is required to control the dumping work, who directs the rear dump to its dumping area. For dumping, the ore or limestone etc. into a hopper of crusher, marks should be made for the guidance of the driver so that he can dump the material into the hopper easily. In order to prevent any cut or abrasion in the tyres, he should prevent hitting the protecting rail at the hopper. When dumping is done to open area or in earth fill dam the load is usually dumped by the operator alone and picks his own dumping place. For earth fill dams the dumped loads are moved by the crawler tractors to the desired position. In order to save the tractor bulldozer efforts, load should be dumped as close as possible to the proceeding load.

9.5 Selection of Dump Trucks

Selection of type and size of a dump truck is very important task and should be carefully decided considering various factors. Some of the important factors are :

(a) **Nature of Work :** For earth hauling purposes rear, front or bottom dump trucks are generally used. The rear and front dump units are self-powered and are employed for loading by large shovels or draglines. The front dump units are used where space is restricted. The bottom dumps are generally semi-trailer type supported on rear wheels, the front of which is carried on the rear of the hauling tractor. For the transportation of rocks and other heavy materials under adverse road conditions, the rear dump trucks are most suitable. Bottom dump trucks are suitable only for free flowing materials and are used to spread the material on the fill.l The side dump units are suitable for transporting and dumping the large quantities of material on the one or both sides of the road.

(b) **Nature of Haul :** On steep grades, the self-propelled rear dump trucks are selected as the uniform load distribution causes greater weight to be placed. Whereas, in the bottom dump units, which are semi-trailer type, while moving upgrade causes concentration of load towards the rear. Thus these bottom dump units can be limited to the level ground.

(c) **Matching with other Equipments :** Capacities of the hauling should be decided after considering the size of excavator or loading unit. Generally, as a thumb rule size of the hauling unit is selected between 4 to 6 times the bucket capacity of the loading unit. The number of hauling units is decided by time required in one cycle, *i.e.*, loading, hauling, unloading and returning back. The care should be taken that the waiting time for a truck by a loading unit or by a truck for its turn for loading is kept minimum.

(d) **On-Highway or Off-Highway :** As explained earlier dump trucks are of two types, on-highway and off-highway. For the selection of a dump unit it is necessary to analyse the requirements. If an on-highway type unit is applied to a rugged off-highway situations or *vice-versa*, it will be too expensive and progress of work will be adversely affected. Generally, on-highway units are suitable for long, high speed hauls over roads with low rolling resistance. Loading in these vehicles be done by relatively small capacity power shovel or a loader. Whereas off-highway dump trucks also known as dumpers are used for short, low speed hauls over rough roads. They are capable of moving on steep grades, and has high power engines often fitted with turbocharger and torque converters. They can work in dusty atmosphere of quarries, crushers etc. as they are fitted with oversize air clearness and filters. These dumpers have body suitable for absorbing high impact leading and generally fitted with steel wear resistant plates to reduce abrasion damage.

The section of proper hauling unit should be decided on the basis of proper estimation, various proposals should be seen based on economical considerations. It has been seen on the basis of experience that, for short haul excavation upto 100 metres, crawler dozers are most economical. For longer haul where construction of haul roads are not practicable, crawler scrapers are economical. For still longer hauls, dump trucks on or off-highway types are economically employed.

From above discussions, it is clear that there is no straight formula to determine which equipment and which method is the best. In practice based on these considerations, an entire job economy has to be studied from various aspects for all possible alternatives. Most economical, feasible and efficient system under the required job conditions should then be adopted. Since this selected is most important decision which will effect overall cost efficiency and time requirement of the project, an utmost care and attention should be given to this decision.

9.6 Estimating Hauler Production

As discussed earlier, type, capacity and number of hauling units are decided after careful cost effective studies. For this purpose production of the hauler unit per hour is required to be estimated. Under optimum conditions the hauler production can be estimated using the formula :

Hauler production per hour

$$= \frac{60}{\text{Time required to complete one cycle in minutes}} \times \begin{bmatrix} \text{Hauler's payload per} \\ \text{cycle in tonnes or cu m} \end{bmatrix}$$

In order to assess the production we should first understand the term payload and cycle time.

1. Payload

The term 'rated payload' is the maximum recommended load for a hauling unit as prescribed by the manufacturer. Allowable load is limited by either volumetric capacity or the rated payload. While deciding the volumetric capacity, weight per cubic metre of the material (in place or loose) be kept in mind so that the payload is not exceeded than that of recommended.

Haulage vehicle payload is expressed in three ways : (i) rated capacity to kilograms of payload allowed (ii) struck capacity measure (level load) in cubic metres, and (iii) heaped capacity (2 : 1 slope) in cubic metres.

The trucks and wagons have these three methods of rating the capacities as defined hereunder :

(a) **Gravimetric capacity :** It is the load it will carry and expressed as a weight in kg or tons.

(b) **Struck volume :** It is the volumetric amount a truck will carry, if the load is water level in the body. It is expressed as cubic metres.

(c) **Heaped volume :** It is the volumetric amount a truck will carry, if the load is heaped on a 2 : 1 slope above the body. It is expressed as cubic metres.

In other words we can say that the struck capacity of a truck is the volume of material that it will haul when it is filled level to the top of the body sides. The heaped capacity is the volume of material that it will hauled when the load is heaped above the sides (with 2 : 1 slope).

Swell factor : Earthmoving is based on 'bank' or 'solid' cubic metres in undisturbed condition. In the shovel bucket or haulage vehicle, it is in loose or blasted condition.

$$\text{Swell factor} = \frac{100}{100 + \text{percentage of swell}}$$

$$\text{Loose m}^3\text{ weight} = \text{Bank m}^3\text{ weight} \times \text{swell factor}$$

$$\text{Bank m}^3\text{ weight} = \frac{\text{loose m}^3\text{ weight}}{\text{swell factor}}$$

A sample of material weights :

	Bank m³ weight (kg)	*Swell (%)*	*Swell factor*	*Loose m³ weight (kg)*
Sand and gravel	1405	18	0.85	1195
Rock, well blasted	1815	50	0.67	1215

2. Cycle Time

Each cycle of hauler's operation is consisting of :

(i) Loading time.
(ii) Hauling time.
(iii) Dumping and turn time.
(iv) Return time.
(v) Spotting and waiting time.

When all these times are added then it constitutes the cycle time, *i.e.*,

Cycle time = Time to complete one cycle
= Loading time + Hauling time + Dumping and turn time + Return time + Spotting and waiting time

(i) Loading Time : A hauling unit maybe loaded by a power shovel, dragline, clamshel, backhole, belt, hopper or by a front end loader. For various types of strata, loading units have different rate. Therefore, for calculating the loading time this factor should be kept in view. During loading, maximum efficiency can be obtained by placing the hauling unit as close to the loader as possible and at such an angle, so as to reduce travel distance between them. Loading time depends on size of vehicles, size and type of loading equipment, type and condition of material, and skill of operator.

(ii) Travelling Time : Hauling time (time taken by the loaded hauling unit from loading area to the dump area) and returning time (time taken by empty units from dump area to loading site) constitutes the travel time and is determined by using the following formula :

$$\text{Travel time (min)} = \frac{\text{Length of road section (km)}}{\text{Average speed over road section (km per hr)}} \times 60$$

The factor 60 is used to convert hours into minutes. It has been observed that the hauling time required for loading unit is more than that by empty unit while returning back to loading area from dump site, therefore, average speed is generally taken into consideration. Travelling time depends on road maintenance, rolling resistance, performance ability of hauler and safety.

(iii) **Dumping and Turn Time :** The time required to dump the payload and to manoeuver the hauling unit into position for return route is dependent on the destination of the material, the type and manoeuverability of the hauling unit, the type and condition of material and the condition of the dumping area.

(iv) **Spotting Time :** It is the time required for the hauling unit to be spotted at the loading unit in a position ready for loading.

(v) **Waiting Time :** This is the time required by the hauling unit for waiting its turn to come for loading.

(vi) **Job Efficiency :** During a cycle there may be certain hazards or obstructions in the haul road, which increases cycle time and reduces cycle efficiency.

Turning, dumping and spotting time : generally adopted timings for these elements are given hereunder :

Operating conditions	***Bottom-dump tractor-traffic***	***Rear-dump body***	***Side dump semi-trailer***	***Heavy duty scruper***
(A) Turning and dumping times (in minutes)				
Poor	1.5	1.5-2.0	1.5	1.5
Average	0.6	1.3	1.0	0.7
Favourable	0.3	1.0	0.7	0.4
(B) Spotting at loading machine (in minutes)				
Poor	1.00	0.50	1.00	0.90
Average	0.50	0.30	0.50	0.65
Favourbale	0.15	0.15	0.15	0.50

Factors affecting Cycle Time :

Cycle time depends on following factors :

(a) Size and specifications of loaders.

(b) Type and condition of materials loaded.

(c) Capacities of shovels and haulage vehicles.

(d) Skill level of operators.

(e) Efficiency of shovels and haulage vehicles.

(f) Hauling distance.

(g) Haul road condition.

(h) Grades and other conditions governing hauling speed.

(i) Manoeuverability of vehicles.

(j) Job efficiency : Idle time while loading, turning, dumping and spotting. 50 minutes working per hour is considered as an average efficiency, while 55 minutes per hour as outstanding and 40 minutes per hour as poor efficiency.

Fig. 9.6 A dumper being used for earth work on a hydel project. (Courtesy : Hindustan Motors).

Balancing of Hauling units with the Size of Excavator

The capacities of hauling units should balance with the output of the excavator; power shovels, draglines or loaders. If this is not done, either the hauling units or excavator will remain idle, and the combined cost of excavating, loading and hauling of the material shall be higher than when balanced units are used. For an excavator loading the earth or material into the truck, the size of the trucks must be carefully decided considering the following factors.

9.7 Comparison Between Various Types of Dump Trucks

Type	*Advantages*	*Disadvantages*
Articulated dump trucks	1. Can be used in most climates and terrains round the your.	More expensive
	2. Able to cope with extreme grades and difficult ground conditions.	Top speeds are generally lower.
	3. Due to lesser heights, use of variety of loading equipment is possible.	Not usually roadable.
	4. High manoeuverability.	
Rigid frame off-highway dump trucks	1. Less expensive than articulated dump trucks.	High axle load require good quality haul routes.
	2. Generally higher top speed especially on good quality haul roads.	Downtime increases in wet ground and difficult terrain.
	3. Long economic life under moderate condition.	Not usually roadable.
On-highway dump trucks	1. Lever purchase price.	Net suitable for continuous work in rugged off road conditions.
	2. Roadable.	Poor traction in wet grounds.
	3. High operating speeds.	Restricted payloads.

Factors in Favour of Large Size Trucks

(i) Lesser number of trucks required, which will result in less total investment in hauling units and lesser cost of maintenance and repairs.
(ii) Less number of drivers, thus reduction on operation cost.
(iii) More excavator output due to lesser time required in spotting the vehicle and ease in loading.

Factors in Favour of Small Size Trucks

(i) More flexible in manoeuvering, hence more advantageous on short hauls.
(ii) May have higher speeds.
(iii) Lesser loss of production when one truck in a fleer breaks down.
(iv) Easy is balance the number of trucks with the output of the excavator.
(v) Cost of maintenance of haul roads is less when small trucks are used, as heavier loads may cause more damages to the haul roads.
(vi) Easy to repair.

9.8 Haulage Tractors

From speed considerations, the wheeled tractors are the machine intermediate between the heavy trucks and the crawler tractor. As a haulage unit, the wheeled tractor has to depend entirely upon its own weight for its tractive reaction, whereas the trucks (including truck-trailers) derive its tractive reaction from the load it carries. A tractor for the better traction must have a high weight/H.P. ratio.

9.9 Trailers

The two types of trailer are used namely, full trailers and half (Semi-trailers). Full trailers, also known as wagons are self supported and are provided with a swivelling axle and a draw bar for connecting the prime-mover.

Semi-trailers are supported on their own wheels only at the rear, while front end is supported on the prime-mover. The semi-trailers have more manoeuverability as compared to full trailers. The front end of the semi-trailers has a goose neck resting on the rear of the prime mover (driving unit). The semi-trailers can be turned and operated to a more limited space than that needed for a truck or for a full trailers. This can turn upto 90° either to the right or to the left without moving forward. These are suitable on narrow-roads and where there are no steep grades.

Semi-trailers are usually attached to the hauling unit through an attachment which operates through an hitch. The hitch has two portions one mounted on the rear of

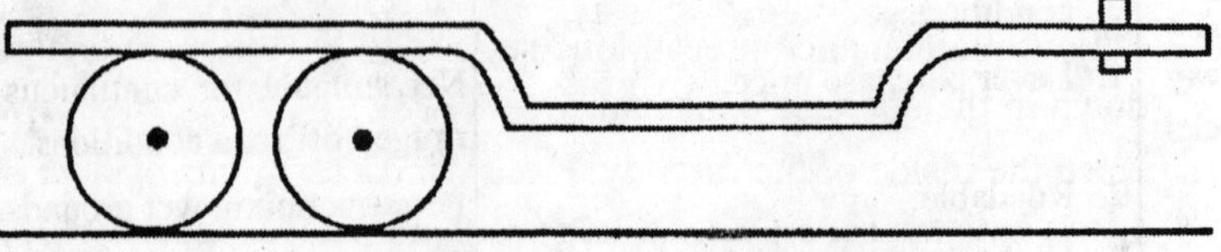

Fig. 9.7 Drop frame type semi-trailer.

the hauling unit, and the other under the goose neck of the trailers. On joining them together, a necessary coupling is provided. It provides a large surface area of contact between the pulling and the trailing units resulting in a good load distribution at the connecting end.

The braking system of a trailer or semi-trailer may be operated by either hydraulic or by vacuum or by air pressure. Trailer brakes are synchronised with that of hauling unit brakes. A provision is also made to apply trailer brakes automatically when its connection of brakes to from hauling unit.

Trailers for haulage of heavy equipment and machinery may have drop deck or level deck.

In drop deck (or drop frame) trailer loading and unloading is done from sides. These have lesser road clearance to allow more head clearance for tail machines. Level deck or flat bed trailers have abundant space on the deck, and it is easy to load and unload them from the rear. In order to keep the vehicle stable and safe during haulage, the height of the trailer should be such that centre of gravity of the loaded trailer remains near the ground.

Some times the machine mounted on the main frame work (girders) can transported directly without the deck to reduce the height of loaded trailers.

The platforms of the trailers can also be made tilting type with hydraulic system for easy loading and unloading. The trailers are tandem axle (two axle) arrangement with 8 wheels, and 3-axle arrangement with 12 wheels for haulage of heavy loads.

9.10 Safety Precautions

9.10.1 General Precautions

Following safety precautions should be strictly followed by the hauling equipment operator for preventing accidents :

1. Always remain alert and in proper physical and mental condition.
2. Always wear right cothing for the job, wear safety glasses, gloves, footwear,hard hat. Do not wear ties, rings or watches which can be caught by moving parts of the equipment.
3. Keep hands away from moving parts such as fan, V-belt, gears, drive shafts etc.
4. Before operation, make sure you know the equipment signal flags, sign and markings fully and also from where to get assistance and first-aid.
5. Give warning to nearby people that you are about to start up your equipment.
6. Follow maintenance precautions suggested by the manufacturer and laid down in the operator's manual.
7. Keep the inside of the cab tidy. Keep windscreen, mirrors and lights clean. Clean any grease, oil etc. off hand rails, footsteps, pedals etc.

8. Never allow unqualified people to operate your machine. Operator should be familiar with the capabilities and limitations of the equipment.
9. Always keep a safe speed as per working conditions and state of the ground. While towing another piece of equipment, never proceed at high speeds.
10. Only authorised person should drive a vehicle after familiarising himself with the traffic, relevant laws prevailing in the area, and equipments working in that area.
11. The driver/operator must carry out the specified "checks" of the machine before starting the day's work. Manuals supplied along with the vehicle give instructions regarding these "checks". The usual check points are listed below :
    - Horn, lights including brake and tail lights, wheel brakes, emergency brakes, wiper.
    - Steering, clutch.
    - Tie-rods, tyre pressure, stepney.
    - Fire extinguishers, first-aid kit, jacks and tools.
    - Diesel, lubricating oils, coolants, distilled water in the battery.

9.10.2 Precautions Regarding Transport Vehicles

1. All vehicles that are used on construction site must be in fit condition and should carry proper fitness papers.
2. A large number of accidents occur during the transportation of men and materials. Trucks, tippers, dumpers used on construction are normally loaded by shovels or loaders. Strong canopies should be built over the driver's cabin to protect them from injuries.
3. The cabin should have a system of sound and vibration suppression, back up alarm, rear view mirror, wiper, sun visor, seat belts etc. A foot board and handle should be provided for the driver's use.
4. Brakes and control should be designed so as to get locked when the vehicle is parked. While going down the gradient, the dynamic braking should be used instead of relying on brakes. Hydraulic retarders should be used for big size dumpers.
5. If the cabin is enclosed, it shall be provided with windows giving maximum possible view and shall be well ventilated. The driver shall be able to make on easy exit in case of any emergency.
6. Driver's seat shall have backrest and the seat shall be of such design, construction and dimensions as will absorb vibration sufficiently and provide reasonable comfort. The cabin should be so arranged that the driver can easily get off in case of emergency.
7. *Brakes and Controls* : Motor trucks, tractors and dumpers shall be equipped with brakes that will hold them under the heaviest load that may be hauled

in any operating conditions and shall enable the vehicle to be locked when stationary.

8. *Draw Gears* : Motor trucks, hauling trailers and tractors shall be equipped with draw gear such that during coupling no worker can come between the vehicles being coupled or the vehicles being coupled cannot run into each other.
9. Vehicle shall not move down the hill with the engine off or with the engine out of gear.

9.10.3 Safety Precautions by Drivers/Operators

Following safety precautions should be followed by drivers/operators of the construction equipment/vehicles :

1. Only competent and licensed person shall drive motor trucks and tractors.
2. Drivers shall be required to leave the cabins and stand in the clear while the motor trucks are being loaded.
3. Drivers of tripper trucks used for hot mix plants and batch mix concrete plants and similar operations shall wear the industrial safety helmets conforming to IS:2925 (Specifications for industrial safety helmet).
4. The log book of every vehicle should have a fly leaf containing the following instructions to the driver and the crew :
   (i) No person should be allowed to enter in the vehicle or travel in it except under written orders of the concerned Site Engineer or any other officer-in-charge or his subordinate duly authorized in this behalf. Any infringement of this rule shall render the driver and the cleaner liable for punishment.
   (ii) They should be prohibited from standing in the vehicle or sitting on the top of the side planks of the body.
   (iii) No person should be allowed to get down from or get into the vehicle while it is in motion.
5. In case of accident, the driver should :
   (i) Stop the vehicle immediately and offer/render assistance to human being affected by accident.
   (ii) Wait for the security persons/police to arrive at the place of accident or inform the police/security.
   (iii) Inform/give report of accident to his superior.
6. The driver/operator should follow the driving and company's rules. He should
   (i) Stop and proceed at unmanned or without signal road junctions.
   (ii) Stop vehicles at the unguarded railway level crossings, look right and left of the track and proceed further only when no train is coming rom either direction.

7. Constant attention, concentration and alertness shall be exercised by the driver while operating a motor vehicle. Driving will not be undertaken under fatigue, or drowsiness and drunkenness as they impair driving ability to a high degree until the condition causing the impairment has been relieved.

9.10.4 Safety During Parking

1. Park vehicle on firm and level ground, away from any unstable ground area or inadequately shored up excavation.
2. Apply the brakes.
3. Keep all control levers at dead center.
4. Shut down the engine.
5. Relieve pressure in the hydraulic system.
6. Lock the cab door.
7. Before driving, the driver should go round the vehicle to ensure that no man or cattle is resting under the vehicle or near by unde4r its shade.
8. Proper parking areas should be designated in the project area.
9. Although it is not a good practice to park a vehicle on a slope, if it becomes necessary, vehicles should be placed in gear preferably in reverse gear for down grade and first gear for upgrade. The wheels should be blocked as an added precaution.
10. Never park a vehicle in an aisle or doorway, nor to obstruct material or equipment to which another worker may need access. Accidents often happen when a vehicle is blocking a passageway, and an unauthorized person tries to move it.

9.10.5 Safe Operating Conditions

1. Every effort shall be made to avoid motor vehicles being loaded in a place where there may be danger from materials, such as rocks falling from-buckets passing overhead.
2. Motor trucks shall be stationed at such a distance from the power shovel (excavator) that there is a clearance of at least 0.6 m between the trucks and the superstructure of the power shovel (excavator) even when it pivots.
3. Where the driver does not have a clear field of vision the movement of motor trucks and tractors shall be controlled by a code of standard hand signals.
4. When uncoupling vehicles, both vehicles shall be blocked by brakes or chocks.
5. Vehicle being loaded or unloaded shall be effectively braked or blocks.
6. Motor trucks shall not be loaded beyond their capacity.
7. Before a loaded motor truck starts, the load shall be inspected to ensure that it is secure, evenly distributed and of safe height, length and width.

8. Sufficient stop blocks shall be provided at every tipping point and these shall be used on every occasion when material is dumped from the truck, dumper or other such vehicle.
9. Project management should ensure that workers, residents, motorists, pedestrians and equipment move on the site without danger or damage.
10. Specific hazardous areas should be identified after considering location, duration of site work, night time requirements, density of traffic, etc., and suitable warning devices installed.
11. Proper shoring is essential where traffic or machines cause ground vibrations.
12. If the travel path on the site cannot accommodate two-way traffic, flagmen or mechanical signals should be deployed for safe movement.
13. Many accidents at work places are caused by undue haste or short-cut methods in executing the work, particularly when workers are on piece rate method of payment. These accidents can be minimized by :
    (a) strict safety supervision.
    (b) erecting iron railings of suitable heights at corner where movement of vehicle is more frequent.
14. When trucks are being used on the site, traffic problems shall be taken care of. A reasonably smooth traffic surface shall be provided. If practicable, a loop road shall be provided to permit continuous operation of vehicles and to eliminate their hacking. If a continuous loop is not possible, a turnout shall be provided. Backing operations shall be controlled by a signalman positioned so as to have a clear view of the area behind the truck and to be clearly visible to the truck driver. Movement of workmen and plant shall be routed to avoid crossing, as much as possible, the truck lanes.
15. All the trucks shall be fitted with reverse horn, which shall automatically sounds when the vehicle is moving is reverse direction. The purpose of fitting this horn is to alert the people working while a vehicle is moving in reverse direction towards them.

9.10.6 Safe Loading

1. Side supports on power trucks and trailers for carrying heavy and long objects shall be
   (i) of sound construction and free from defects;
   (ii) provided with tie chains attached to the top across the loads for preventing such stanchions from spreading out; and
   (iii) kept in position while loading and unloading.
2. Safe gangways provided for to and fro movement of building workers engaged in loading and unloading of lorries, trailers and wagons.
3. Trucks and other equipment shall not be loaded beyond their safe capacity and carry workers engaged in loading and unloading of lorries, trucks, trailers and wagons in an unsafe condition.

4. Overloading causes more wear and tear of tyres, damages and surfaces and decreases efficiency of the moving components of the vehicle.
5. Overloading may cause anyone or all of the following mishaps resulting in an accident :
   (a) Loss of control on steering.
   (b) Inadequacy of brake power.
   (c) Failure of components due to fatigue.
   (d) Overturning while negotiating sharp bends.
6. Brakes should be applied when a vehicle is loaded or unloaded.
7. The loading in the vehicle should be uniform.
8. Stop logs should be used while tipping.
9. No person should be allowed to work near dumper while it is being loaded or unloaded.

QUESTIONS

1. Name different types of dump trucks indicating their applications.
2. What is a truck? Give the classification of hauling equipment, mentioning their applications.
3. Explain rigid frame type trucks.
4. What is a dump truck, where these are used?
5. Explain on-highway and off-highway rear dump trucks.
6. What is an articulated dump truck? Where are these used? Explain articulated rear dump trucks.
7. Explain in detail about bottom dump wagons.
8. Explain major activities involved in the dump truck operation.
9. Explain different criteria for selecting the dump trucks.
10. (a) How would you estimate the hauler production?
    (b) How will you estimate the cycle time for a dump truck?
11. Write short notes on :
    (a) Factors in favour of large trucks.
    (b) Balancing of hauling units with the size of excavator.
    (c) Haulage tractors.
12. How will you calculate the number of dump trucks required for a project?
13. Explain, what do you understand by full trailor and semi-trailor.
14. Enumerate safety precautions during the use of hauling equipment.

Part - III

CONCRETE AND ASPHALT PLANTS

Chapter 10

Aggregate Production

10.1 Introduction

Aggregates of various sizes are required for most of the construction activities, *e.g.*, construction of roads, buildings, bridges, canals, tunnels, dams, airfields and other concrete structures. Production of aggregate involves drilling, blasting, loading, transporting, crushing, screening, handling, ad storing. For the operation of crushing plant, production of drilling, blasting, and size of power shovel to load the stones should match with the capacity of the primary crusher. Size of the stone received from quarry should be able to pass through the opening of the crusher. Aggregates are produced from the rocks by crushing them in the crushing plants. The crushing plants may be 'mini crushers' with a production capacity from 3 tons to 10 tons per hour or 'Giant Plants' of size even upto 500 tons to 10 tons per hour. Mini plants are used very small work. Generally construction activities of modern nature employ plants of 50—150 tons per hour capacity. Here in this chapter we are discussing these types of crushing plants.

The crusher production is screened to give various sizes of aggregates. The range of these sizes may vary as per requirements. These aggregates of various sizes are mixed in a prescribed proportion to give a desired quality of aggregates mix. The plants used for mixing the aggregates are known as "aggregate mixing plants".

The amount of suitable aggregate material for construction purposes produced and processed depend on the nature of the raw materials available and the desired properties of end product. Following functions are required for accomplishing the desired results :

1. Quarry operation.
2. Crushing—particle size reduction.
3. Screening—grading the particles in different ranges.
4. Washing—elimination of undesirable materials.
5. Storage and transport—moving the material for further processing.

10.2 Quarry Operation

The aggregates can be quarried from the pits, or collected from sea-shore or river beds. The aggregate may be of naturally occurring (whether crushed or uncrushed) stones, river and shingle or pit gravel. It should be hard, strong, dense, durable, clear and the free from veins, and adherent coating. Good aggregates should be roughly cubical in shape. Flaky and alongated pieces should be avoided.

Quarry process involves the following activities :

1. Clearing
2. Treatment of overburden
3. Excavating
4. Loading and hauling
5. Maintenance of haul-road.

1. Clearing

Clearing means felling and removing timber and stumps so that the overburden can be stripped. Generally bulldozers are used for clearing operations.

2. Treatment of Overburden

In quarries, overburden generally refers not just to the soft layer of top soil, but also often includes the layer of weathered rock below this. The top soil can be stripped off and gathered together by the bulldozer, then loaded by a wheel loader or shovel onto drump trucks which carry if off for disposal. Backhoe type hydraulic excavations are used to remove the soil between the rocks. When excavating weathered rock, the rock can be broken up by blasting or ripping with a bulldozer.

3. Excavating

There are various methods available for quarrying, most common amongst them are : (a) drilling and blasting, (b) ripping by bulldozers, and (c) preliminary blasting to loosen the rock for ripping by bulldozers.

(a) Drilling and Blasting : The machines used for drilling include pneumatic crawler drills, hydraulic crawler drills, rotary drills and down-hole drills. Pneumatic crawler drills are driven by air motors which generally use portable air compressors as their power source. Hydraulic crawler drills are hydraulic operated drills powered by a diesel engine. Compared to the pneumatic crawler drill, these have lower fuel consumption and are quieter and have higher drilling efficiency.

The rotary drill is a large drill equipped with a diesel engine and air compressor. It has excellent drilling capacity in soft rock. The down-hole drill has a hammer at the tip of a rod. Its advantages are that the percussion force applied to the rod is transmitted directly to the bit, so there is little loss of percussion force when drilling long holes. The down-hole drill is suitable for drilling medium-hard and hard rock.

(b) Ripping : Another common method is breaking up the rock with a ripper attached to the rear of the bulldozer. Recently with the increase in size and capacity of bulldozers, it has become possible to break up even fairly hard rock economically by using the ripping method.

Rippers are of three types : (i) The ***fixed multiple shank ripper*** is used for comparatively simple ripping operations, (ii) ***Variable multiple-shank*** ripper can change the angle of its shanks and is used for ripping operations on job sites where there are many boulders, or where the quality of the rock is not constant, and (iii) The *variable giant ripper* has a single powerful shank, the angle of which can be changed so that it is suitable for use in ripping operations on job sites where there are boulders, or where the rock is hard.

(c) Preliminary Blasting : For quarrying operation, preliminary blasting is done to loosen the rock for ripping by bulldozer. Compared to normal drilling and blasting, the preliminary blasting method uses less than half the amount of explosive. It is only used to make cracks to the rock, thereafter bulldozers are used for breaking up the rock.

Blasting is done to loosen the rock for ease in excavation. Blasting is performed by discharging the explosive placed in the hole drilled for the purpose. Tremendous energy produced by blasting loosens the rock. Some of the terms used in blasting are defined below :

(i) **Blasting :** It is the discharging of an explosive to loosen the rock.

(ii) **Explosive :** Explosive is a chemical compound which when burnt under favourable conditions produce a high pressure.

(iii) **Blasting Powder :** It is a low explosive, made from sulphur, charcoal, and sodium or potassium nitrate. Since these are slow burning, hence are seldom used for rock blasting.

(iv) **Dynamite :** This is a high explosive with nitroglycerine or trinitrotoluene as the main constituents and are initiated by a detonator.

(v) **Gelatin Dynamite :** It is a water proof explosive obtained by dissolving nitro-cotton in nitroglycerin.

(vi) **Stemming :** It is the filling of an inert material.

(vii) **Primer :** It is the portion of a charge which is loaded with a firing device and initiates the explosion.

(d) Breaking Blasted Rock : The break up the large rocks produced by blasting, two methods are generally used : (i) Breaking up rock using hydraulic excavator with breaker attachment, and (ii) Drilling holes in rock, then carry blasting (small-scale blasting).

4. Loading and Hauling

If the blasted rock is in suitable condition for loading, it is immediately loaded and transported away. However, if it is difficult to load it must be made easy to load, by (i) using rippers of the dozer, (ii) breaking the blasted rock by any one of the methods explained earlier.

Generally, for hauling purposes 15 to 60 ton off-highway dump trucks arè used. The size of the loader should match the dump trucks. The loaders used for loading the quarry materials may be wheel loader, hydraulic excavator, electric mining shovel, or crawler shovel.

5. Maintenance of Haul Road

Maintenance of the haul road greatly influences production efficiency. Haul road maintenance includes operations such as using motor graders to keep the road surface flat, and using water sprinklers to keep the dust down. Advantages of such road maintenance are :

(a) Increased tyre life.
(b) Increased life of dump trucks and reduction in repair costs.
(c) Improvement in travel speed which means reduced cycle time and more production efficiency.
(d) Maintenance of good visibility.
(e) Maintenance of safety.

In an extreme case, where the road is full of patholes, the dump trucks will require excessive fuel, and shall have more wear and tear, and heavy repairs.

10.3 Stone Crushers

As mentioned earlier, crushing plants are used to produce aggregates. These crushing plants are fed with the stones broken from the rocks. The sizes of the stones fed, depend upon the capacity and the crushing system adopted. The main types of crushers are :

(i) Jaw crusher (ii) Impact crusher
(iii) Roller crusher (iv) Cone crusher

Crushers can also be classified according to the stage of crushing, such as primary and secondary. Primary crusher receives the stone directly from the quarry and produces the first reduction in size. The output of the primary crusher is fed to the secondary crusher which further reduces the size of the stone.

For getting fine particles, tertiary crushers are also used. The types of crushers used in primary, secondary and tertiary crushing are as follows :

1. **Primary Crushers :** Jaw, impact, and gyrating crushers.
2. **Secondary Crushers :** Cone crusher, impact crusher.
3. **Tertiary crushers :** Rod mill, roll crushers, and ball mill.

10.4 Jaw Crushers

Jaws crush the stones by compression. The jaw crushers are used as either primary or secondary crushers but are considered best for primary crushing. These are suitable where lesser fines are desired. These crushers have two jaws—one is 'fixed jaw' and another is 'swing jaw'. The swing jaws are made of either manganese chrome-steel or heavy duty cast steel, annealed and stress relieved to withstand the tough crushing operations. The fixed jaws are made up of high manganese chrome cast steel. Generally these fixed jaw plates are reversible for longer life. The capacity of the crushers is influenced by the size of the product, nature and type of rock or ore, *i.e.,* feeding material. Some rocks are brittle and shatter in one blow,while others are tough and break slowly. Greater production will be obtained when feeding mixed sizes of broken rock then when feeding all large pieces of one size. For maximum production, uniform controlled feed is essential.

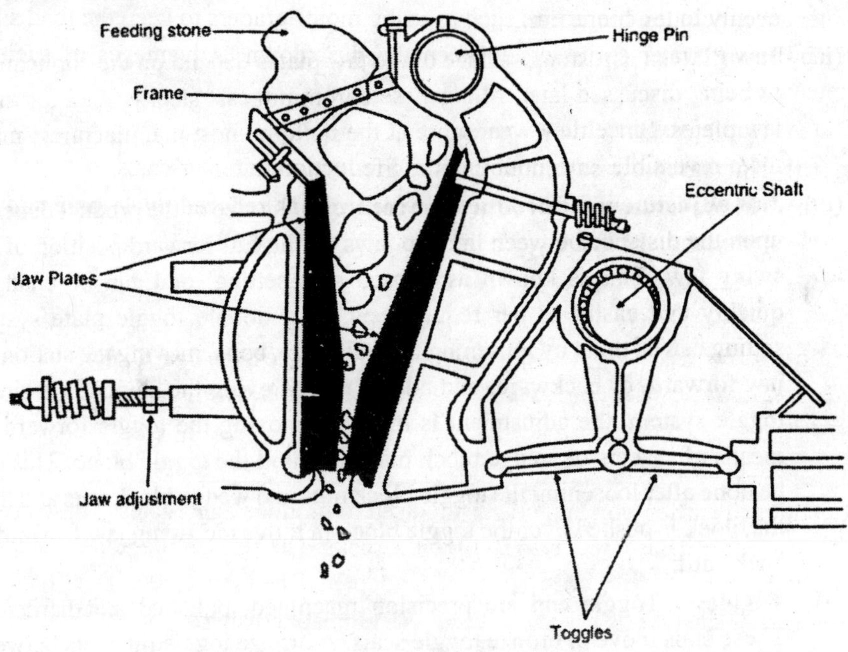

(a) Double toggle jaw crusher

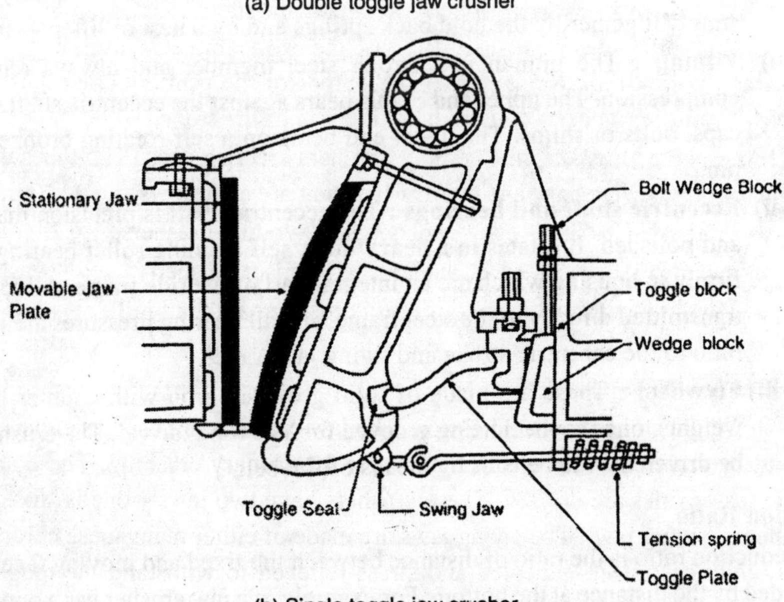

(b) Single toggle jaw crusher

Fig. 10.1

10.4.1 Main Components

Main components of a jaw crusher are described below :

(i) **Frame :** It is constructed with a heavy fabricated steel frame.

(ii) **Hinge Pin and Jaw :** A rigid steel hinge pin is clamped in the frame. The swing jaw assembly is fitted with long sleeve bearings to distribute the load evenly to the hinge pin.

(iii) **Jaw Plates :** Crushing surface of the jaw plates depend on the application, as being discussed later. Manganese chromium cast steel is used for these jaw plates. Since they wear more at the bottom, most manufacturers make them reversible, thus doubling the life.

(iv) **Jaw adjustment for product size control :** The size of the product depends upon the distance between the two jaws on the full forward position of the swing jaw. This is known as 'closed side setting' and can be changed quickly and easily as per requirement. In a double toggle plate system setting can be done by loosening the hold back bolts, moving the stationary jaw forward, or backward, and adding or removing the shims. In a single toggle system, the adjustment is made by moving the toggle forward by means of spacers or wedge block placed behind the toggle block. This can be done after loosening the toggle block nuts and wedge block nuts and then the block is pushed over the toggle block in move the swing jaw forward or backward.

(v) **Toggles :** Toggle end are precision machined, polished and hardened. These ends move in bronze toggle seats. A bronze toggle pin rests between the inner ends of the toggle and the pitman and the entire assembly is held snugly together by the hold back springs and by a nest of lifter springs.

(vi) **Pitman :** The pitman is a strong steel member and always remain in compression. The upper end of this bears against the eccentric shaft with no caps, bolts or shims. The lower end bears on a self-rotating bronze toggle pin.

(vii) **Eccentric shaft and bearings :** The eccentric shaft is precision machined and polished. It rotates in a heavy duty, self aligning roller bearings, held firmly in housing which are an integral part of the ride frame. All loads are transmitted directly to the steel frame, and all bearing pressures are indirect ratio to the eccentric stroke and swing jaw travel.

(viii) **Flywheel :** These are made of solid grey cast iron with counter balance weights, one flywheel being grooved for Vee rope 'drive'. The crusher may be driven by vee belts or by means of flat belt.

Reduction Ratio

Reduction ratio is the ratio of distance between the fixed and moving faces at the top divided by the distance at the bottom. For example, if a jaw crusher has a opening of 40 cms at the top and 10 cms at bottom, the reduction ratio is 4.

Similarly, for a roll crusher, it is the ratio of dimension of the largest stone that can be nipped by the rolls divided by the roll setting, which is the smallest distance between the rolls faces.

Single Toggle V/S Double Toggle

In a single toggle crusher, whole swing jaw is lifted, hence requires higher power. In these, heavier flywheels are provided. Due to elliptical motion, jaw plates of single toggle jaw crusher, wear out at faster rate. The single toggle crushers have lower initial cost and are used for non-abrasive and non-hard rocks.

Double toggle crushers give higher production for same energy consumption and hence are economical. Wear rate of the jaw plates in double toggle crusher is less and is economical for abrasive and hard rocks.

Jaws

1. **Jaw Setting and Jaw Opening :** Jaw setting also known as open-side setting, are measured at the bottom of the jaw plates with jaws in open position on the bottom side. The setting and opening is measured as shown in Fig. 10.2. The jaw opening at the top determine the size of the rock the crusher will receive (generally 5 cm smaller than the openings). The capacity of the crusher is dependent on the area of the opening at the bottom of the jaws.

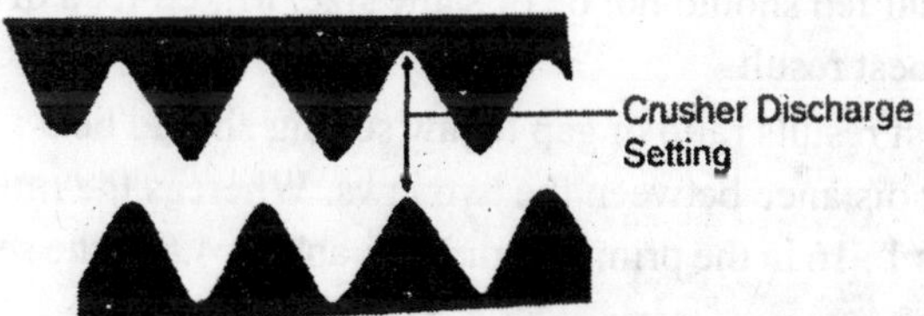

Fig. 10.2 Crusher jaw setting and jaw opening.

2. **Wear Limits :** With use,the teeth of the jaws are worn out. When the tooth plate gets worn out to about to 1/3 of the original corrugation height (as shown in Fig. 10.3), the jaw plates must be turned end-for-end. Wear limit dead line is when there remained no corrugation. When the entire crushing surface gets worn out, the teeth plate should be replaced with new one.

Fig. 10.3 Wear limit of tooth plate.

3. **Straight and Curved Jaws :** Straight jaws give a shallow crushing angle at the top of the jaws, in order to readily accept maximum size quarry-run rock or pit-run gravel. Straight jaws also ensure more even distribution of wear.

Most materials generally give satisfactory result with straight jaws, but some times,there are certain materials which are problematic, for instance :

(a) Soft rock tends to 'being back' in the jaws, thereby reducing throughout.

(b) Flaky rock tends to crush with a high percentage of 'slivers' in the product.

(c) A combination of 'soft' and 'flaky' rock, such as slate presents 'silver' problems, plus 'hanging back'.

Size of Jaw Crushers

Feed size is the basis for determining the size of the crusher. Mouth opening of the jaws denotes the crusher size. Thus a jaw crusher having a mouth opening of 1200 × 1000 mm is called a 1200 × 1000 mm crusher. Theoretically, a piece slightly smaller than 1200 × 1000 mm should go into the crusher mouth, but in normal practice it is just not possible, and size of piece is restricted to 70 to 80% of the gap size. Thus for this size of crusher regular feed size should be restricted to 700 to 800 mm (70 to 80% of 1000 mm).

10.4.2 Tips for Optimum Use of Jaw Crusher

(i) Do not allow bigger pieces going to the crusher mouth.

(ii) Material fed should not be of same size. Mixed feed of all sizes of material gives best result.

(iii) For best results ratio of gap to jaw setting should be 5 : 1 to 7 : 1. Gap is the longer distance between the two jaws. Whereas the ratio of gap to width of jaws is 1 : 16 in the primary crushers, and 1 : 4.5 in the secondary crushers.

10.5 Impact Crushers

These crushers are used where materials are too hard and abrasive and finished product requirement is for cubical shape well graded material. In this type of crusher, stones are broken by means of impact and not by compression as in jaw crusher. In the impact breaker, stone is normally fed into the top of a breaking chamber and struck by rotating hammers while it is in suspension. The hammers repeatedly throw the material against breaker bars forming the roof of the breaker chamber. Impact crushers are fitted with the one or two rotors and the hammers may be fixed or allowed to swing on pivots. These crushers are used for primary or secondary crushing.

Since impact is instantaneous, the breaking almost eliminates the possibility of the development of hidden cracks in the product. This quality is important for aggregate production. Instantaneous impact is derived from :

(a) the rotating impact hammers striking the material,

(b) the impact of the particles upon each other, and

(c) the impact of the materials against the breaker plates.

Crushing by impact gives good results *i.e.,* :

(a) high reduction ratio,

(b) effective production of a high percentage of fines,

(c) excellent shape, *i.e.*, free from flake,

(d) better mechanical strength, and

(e) high output per unit of energy.

These crushers have following advantages, in addition to the above mentioned results obtained due to crushing by impact :

(i) Lower initial cost.

(ii) Have fewer parts to maintain.

(iii) Wide range of product gradation can be selected.

(iv) These produce well graded cubical shaped product.

Types of Impact Crushers

Impact crushers are of following two types :

(i) Impact breakers (ii) Hammer mills

The main difference in these two is that, the breaker plates are rigidly fixed on the rotor in an impact breaker, but are swinging type in a hammer mill.

Impact breakers can crush even hard materials like basalt and granite. Impact breaker is a rugged and rigid machine, which is also provided with a safety device to prevent damage to the rotor etc. incase of accidental overload. To provide safety against stones flying out from the crushers, chain curtains are provided in the feed box to prevent rock dust and stones from flying out.

10.5.1 Construction and Working

While material is dropped by the centrally located chute in the path of rotating hammers, the hammers strike the material by dynamic impact and drive it against massive breaker blocks. The partially reduced material when rebounds it struck again by the hammers and the cycle continues until finished product finally drops through the bottom. Clearance between breaker blocks and hammers is progressively smaller from top to bottom so that oversize material tend to stay in their own size zone, until small enough, to continue through the crusher.

Rotor holds 4 to 6 rows of cast hammers, reversible and interchangeable to minimise wear. Regular systematic reversal balances wear between both faces of each hammer. Reversibility doubles the service life of hammers and breaker blocks and saves costs on maintenance. On each side of the crushers a large access door is provided to allow rapid adjustment and easy removal of uncrushable materials.

These are used for primary as well for secondary crushers. As a primary crusher it is used for soft, non-abrasive and easily crushable materials like phosphate, gypsum, asbestos rock etc. A a secondary crusher it can handle medium hard and slightly abrasive materials like, lime stone and brittle gravel.For a given setting of breaker

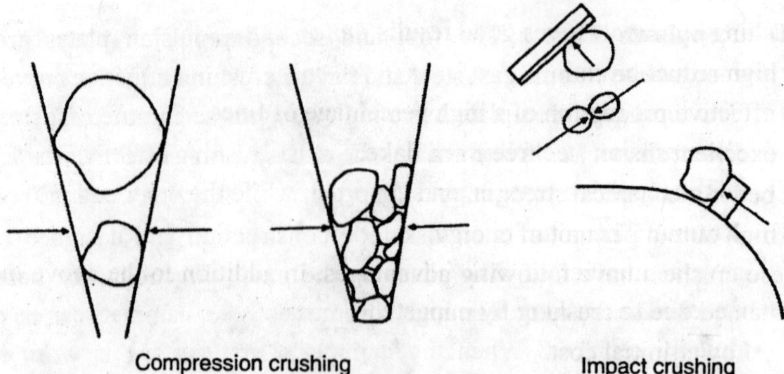

Fig. 10.4 Compression v/s impact crushing.

plates and grates,shape and size of the product depends upon the shape, weight and speed of the hammers.

The construction of an impact crusher is shown in Fig. 10.5.

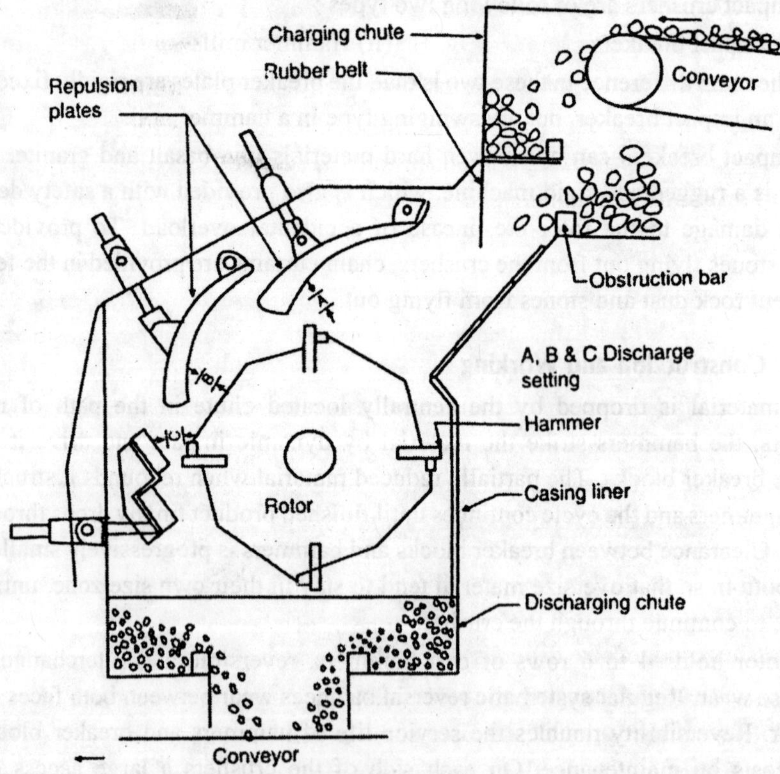

Fig. 10.5 Impact crushers.

(i) **Casing :** The casing is lined with a wear resistant cast steel liner which can be replaced when wears out. Upper portion of the casing has a wide opening door, which can be opened in order to facilitate a replacement of the consumable parts, and can be closed when the crusher is in operation.

(ii) **Repulsion Plate :** The first and second repulsion plates are of high manganese chrome cast steel and have a crushing effective curved surface. The third repulsion plate has a high manganese chrome cast steel liner on the repulsion steel plate and has the most crushing effective shape. One end of the repulsion plate is pin supported, while the other end moves freely.

(iii) **Rotor :** The rotor is of disk type construction and designed to arrange several number of disk plates in the axial direction. The hammers are attached to the rotor. The high chrome cast steel hammers can be easily and quickly replaced. When the hammer's first surface is worn away, the hammers are reversed so as to get same crushing effect as that of new one.

Points to Remember

Regarding hammer mills following important points should be remembered :

(i) Do not use very abrasive materials, as it will wear out hammers very fast.

(ii) Do not feed very wet and sticky materials, as it will stick to the hammers and clog the grates and stop the machine.

(iii) Do not feed material of size more than 70% of mouth size.

Hammer mills produce high percentage of fines, and has high reduction ratio. Since it has only one moving component and there is no vibration, whole system is simple in operation and maintenance, and has low installation cost.

Crushing Operation

Stones are charged into the casing through charging chute. These stones are then collision-crushed by the hammer attached to the highly rotating rotor, where the stones are struck in the tangential direction towards the moveable-type repulsion plates next collide against the plates and crushed. Also at the same time rebounded stones collide with each other into smaller sized-ones.

This cycle of operation is repeated and the crushed stones pass and fall down between the preadjusted repulsion plates and hammer, and then discharged from the outlet.

Product Size

Crusher product size depends on the following factors :

(i) **Effect of Charging Stone's Size :** The charging stone's size has an effect on crusher product size upto some extent, but out much.

(ii) **Effect of Amount of Charging Stone :** The greater the charging amount, the larger will be the size of crusher product.

(iii) **Effect of Rotor's Peripheral Speed (revolving speed) :** Since the crushing action depends on the impact given to the stones, the revolving speed greatly affects the grain-size of the products. The greater the speed, the finer will be the grain size of crushing.

(iv) **Effect of Gap Between Repulsion Plate and Hammer :** The greater the gap between repulsion plate and hammer, the larger the grain size of the crushing, and the smaller the gap, the finer the grain size. However, the excessive small gap will accelerate the wear of hammer and repulsion plate and also consume more power.

Replacement of Parts

Impact crusher has as provision for replacing the parts which wears out during the process of crushing. The main parts which are generally required to be replaced after a passage of time are :

(a) Hammer (b) Casing liner (c) Repulsion plate.

10.6 Roll Crushers

The roll crusher is a reduction crusher and follow a primary breaker in the crushing circuit. It is suitable for all types of materials, whether it is a gravel, rock, lime stone, or the toughest ore. In these crushers, the crushing members are two manganese steel shells mounted over two roll shafts which are further mounted on cast steel hubs. Both the rolls are positively driven, rotating towards each other. These are supported on the antifriction roller bearings.

The roller crushers can be adjusted to produce a wide range of sizes of material by changing the discharge opening. The material is fed into the crusher by means of a feeder discharging into the hopper.

Following are the few **advantages of roll crusher** :

(i) It produces more per hour of material or specified size considering weight of the crusher.
(ii) It can handle any material from hardest to softest, without clogging problem.
(iii) For a given capacity, it is cheaper in initial cost and installation.
(iv) A change of shells on the crusher rolls required lesser time.
(v) It consumes lesser power per ton of material crushed to specified size.
(vi) It produces uniform material.
(vii) Wide range of adjustment enables to conform strict specifications.
(viii) Since whole surface is used for crushing, uniform wear takes place.
(ix) It is economical for a given capacity and reduction ratio.
(x) Maintenance is simple.

Roller Dimensions

Minimum theoretical roll dia is calculated using the following formula :

Roll dia, $$D = \frac{d \cos \beta - S}{1 - \cos \beta}$$

where, d = Feed size
S = Roll setting (gap)
2β = nip angle = 2 × friction angle.

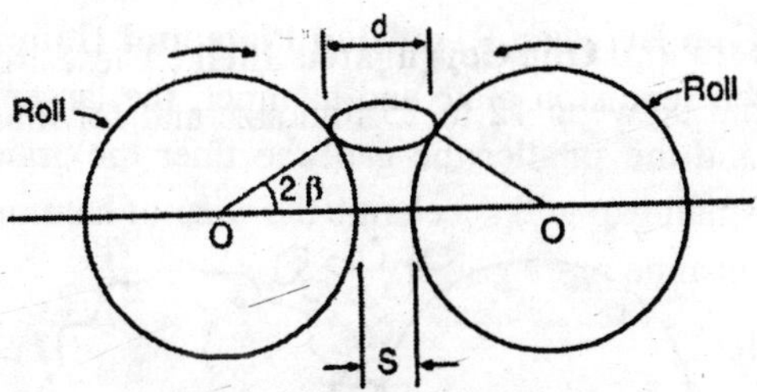

Fig. 10.6 Principle of roll crusher.

For a limiting condition of roll dia, the friction angle is half the nip angle. At nipping angle, the pieces may be just nipped or just slip.

For determining the width of the rolls, surface speed and the setting of the rolls is considered. The softer the material the higher the speed, and the biggest the material, the lower the speed.

Capacity, $$Q = B.S.V \times 3600 \times \eta$$

where, Q = Capacity in cu m/hr.
B = Roll width in meters.
S = Roll setting in meters.
V = Surface speed of roll in m/sec.
η = Efficiency.

Therefore, roll dia is selected to suit the feed size and output size, while the width of the roll is selected to suit the required output.

10.6.1 Types of Roll Crushers

The roll crushers can be classified according to the shape of roll shells, some times also called as tyres. These shells are casted from high grade manganese steel and then annealed to assure proper temper. These crushers may be with :

(a) **Both Roll Shells Smooth :** (Smooth roll crusher). These are used when producing material of 12 mm and under. These are widely used in quarrying industries, mining, chemical, ceramic and metallurgical industries. Throughput is determined by feed size, roll diameter, roll speed and gap width and also on method of feeding of the raw material. For better output, feeding must be across the entire width of the rolls. Out of the two rolls one roll is fixed while the other is floating. The floating roll can give way if uncrushable material falls into the feed opening. Each roll is individually driven by three phase squirrel cage electric motors via V-belt or transmission gearing. The gap can be adjusted to suit the size of the material.

(b) **Double Toothed Roll Crushers :** These are generally recommended for the production of material over 25 mm, and for reduction of coarse soft and medium hard, non-abrasive materials like coal, cokes slag, ore, lime stone etc. The principle of working is the same as that of smooth roll crusher.

(c) **One Smooth and One Corrugated Shell :** These are used when producing the material between 12 to 25 mm size and for material of medium hard qualities.

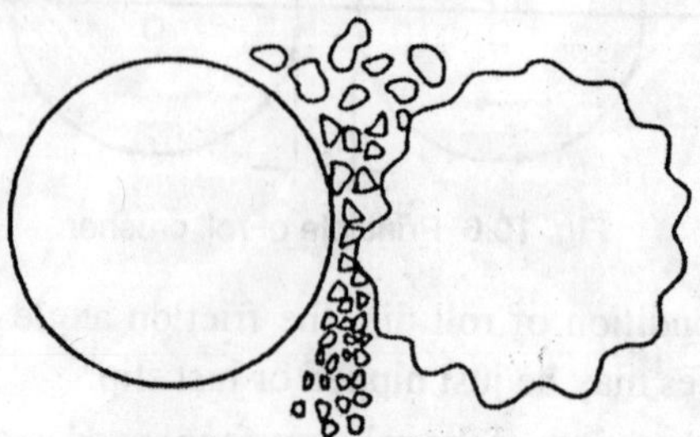

Fig. 10.7 Double roll crusher.

(d) **Corrugated Rolls :** These can take bigger feed size than plain rolls of the same diameter. The size of the corrugated (the pitch and the depth) is related to the product size, and hence, the smaller the product the finer is the corrugations.

(e) **Spiked Roll Crusher :** These are used for very high throughput capacity. These can take large feed sizes, even a slab of 1.2 m × 1.5 m × 0.3 m size. The life of spikes is longer due to the relatively slow speed. These have one spiked roll and one adjustable jaw, and are used for coarse crushing of materials like chemicals, coal, sinters etc.

Type of crusher to be selected, depends on feed size and type of material. Plain (smooth) rolls are normally employed for feed size upto 75 mm, while corrugated rolls are used for feed size upto 200 mm. Both the corrugated rolls are operated by one interconnected driving system to maintain the correct meshing of the corrugations. With both the rolls corrugated, the range of setting is limited because of limitations of interconnected drive. Considering this aspect, one corrugated roll and one plain roll makes a very suitable combination.

10.7 Cone Crushers

Cone crushers are used to produce the final product, since they can receive and crush smaller size of stones of ore and produce more fine aggregates. The stones are fed through feed chute, evenly into the crushing chamber where they are crushing quickly and uniformly. The stones from the feed chute first fall on a distributor plate which helps in distributing the feeding material in the cone-crusher. The crushing surface in the clearance between the concave and mantle is made of wear resistant high grade manganese steel for heavy duty operation and reduced wear. The crusher head has a gyratory, swinging motion so that the crushing is done by direct pressure. This results in a cubic product. The swinging motion is produced by an eccentric sleeve rotating in a bronze bushing.

Fig. 10.8 Cone crusher showing crushing cavity.

Adjustment of Cone Setting

Cone crusher setting is adjustable by rotating the crushing bowl (drum) in its thread. This is done by a hydraulic device. After the adjustment, the thread is locked in the crushing position.

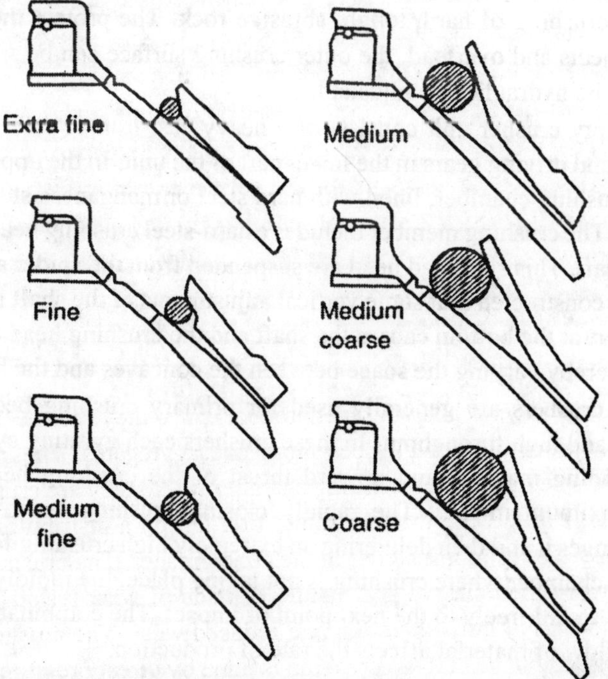

Fig. 10.9 Cone crusher mouth openings (Courtesy : Parker, England).

Lubrication

A hydraulic unit comprising of a large oil tank, gear type pump, filter and cooler ensures lubrication and heat dissipation. Heating element with thermostat for use in extreme cold climate for heating the oil to the required working temperature can be provided.

10.8 Gyratory Crushers

Like cone crushers, these also crush the rocks by applying pressure to the rock boulders between a stationary surface and a rotating curved surface. The crushed materials are discharged by gravity. Both gyratory and cone crushers belong to the same genus, but have some difference in constructional features. In both of them, both the crushing surfaces are conical and one one gyrates around vertical axis. These crushers have higher throughput capacity and are widely used where much production is required. In these crushers the annular opening (*i.e.*, outside diameter × gap) specifies the size of the crusher. Gyratory crusher, provides much larger crushing surface than that of jaw crusher and therefore has a much higher throughput capacity. It can have a reduction ratio 15 : 1, as compared to the 7 : 1 reduction ratio of a jaw crushers.

Gyratory crushers are the stone (or rock) crushers in which a steel center cone rotates eccentrically to crush the material against the outside cylindrical steel wall. The gyratory crushers provide continuous crushing action and are used for both primary and secondary crushing of hard, tough, abrasive rock. The protect the crusher from uncrushable objects and overload, the outer crushing surface can be spring-loaded or the mantle may be hydraulically adjustable.

The gyratory crusher unit consists of a heavy cast-iron or steel frame with an eccentric shaft and driving gears in the lower part of the unit. In the upper part thee is a cone-shaped crushing chamber, lined with hard steel or manganese steel plates called the 'concaves'. The crushing member includes a hard-steel crushing head mounted on a vertical steel shaft. This shaft and head are suspended from the spider at the top of the frame that is so constructed that some vertical adjustments of the shaft is possible. The eccentric support at the bottom causes the shaft and the crushing head to gyrate as the shaft rotates, thereby varying the space between the concaves and the heads.

Gyratory crushers are generally used for primary crushing because of larger reduction ratio and high throughput. In these crushers each gyrating cycle is timed so that the descending material and upward thrust of the crushing head meet at the moment of maximum impact. The rapidly closing crushing head catches falling material, rearranges it and then delivering an extremely high crushing force. In the part of the crushing chamber where crushing is not taking place, the rapidly receding head allows material to fall freely to the next point of impact. The combination of crushing force and free flow of material affects the rate of production.

The difference between the volume displaced by the crushing head when it is fully closed and fully open is termed the displacement volume. A larger displacement volume results in greater capacity, because :

(i) More material is crushed at each crushing cycle,
(ii) Allows more material to be fed,
(iii) More flow of material through the crushing chamber.

With hydraulic controls, setting/adjustments can be made quickly even when crusher is in operation.

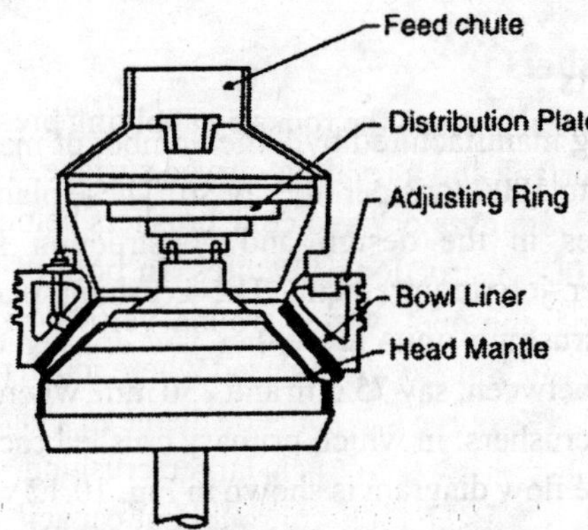

Fig. 10.10 Cone crusher.

Gyratory and cone crushers have some difference in constructional features. In a gyratory crusher, the apex of the gyratory cone is at the top and that of stationary cone is at the bottom, while in cone crusher, the apexes of both the cones are at the top gyratory crushers are best suited for primary crushing, while cone crushers are mainly used for intermediate or secondary crushing.

Salient Features for Gyratory and Cone Crushers

Salient features of gyratory crushers and cone crushers are :

(a) A small number of moving parts, hence less wear and tear and lesser maintenance.
(b) Dust has little effect.
(c) Long liner life.
(d). Wear is uniform and adjustment is simple.
(e) Hydraulic system enables finger tip control of the machine.
(f) Clearing by hydraulic system enables rapid restart after a blockage during operation. Jacks raise the assembly, thereby opening the crusher cavity and enabling the crusher to empty.
(g) These have devices to measure oil pressure, oil circulation and oil temperature, in case of abnormal situation their may be either (i) sound or visual alarm, (ii) stop the feed, or (iii) stop the crusher.

10.9 Selection of Crushing Equipment

Before selection of a particular equipment, it is essential to know following main informations along with other necessary informations :

1. The kind of stone to be crushed.
2. Needed production output to know the required capacity of the plant.
3. Maximum size of the feed stone, and size range of the feed.
4. Method of feeding the stones to the crushers.
5. Range of the product required.

10.10 Crushing Plants

Crushing plants are being manufactured by large number of manufactures all over the world with capacities upto 1000 tons per hour or so. These plants are either stationary or portable and changes in the design and construction from manufacturer to manufacturer and as per job requirement. The crushing plants employ 2 stages. Generally the primary crushing units are either jaw crusher or impact crusher and reduces the rocks to size between, say 75 mm and 250 mm, whereas the secondary units use jaw, impact or cone crushers, in which primary crushed rock is further reduced to sizes say 5 to 50 mm. One flow diagram is shown in Fig. 10.12 with jaw in primary and impact in secondary unit.

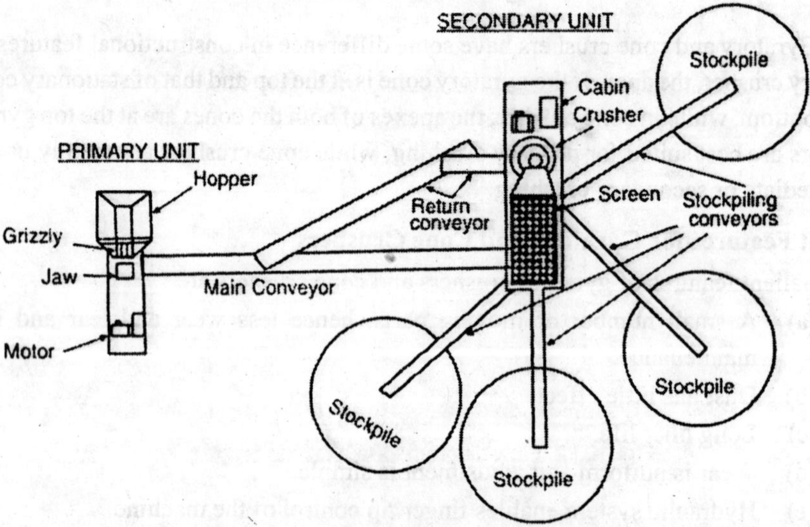

Fig. 10.11 General layout of crushing plant.

General layout of this crushing plant is shown in Fig. 10.11, which illustrates the relative position of various units constituting the crushing plant. This also indicates the cycle of operation starting from feeding stones, boulders, gravel etc. to the crusher products of tiny and uniform granules of sizes 0-40 mm (or 0-50 mm) staggered into 4 sizes viz. 0-5 mm, 5-10 mm, 10-20 mm and 20-40 mm (or 20-50 mm) or 0-5 mm, 5-13 mm, 13-20 mm, 20-40 mm (or 20-50 mm).

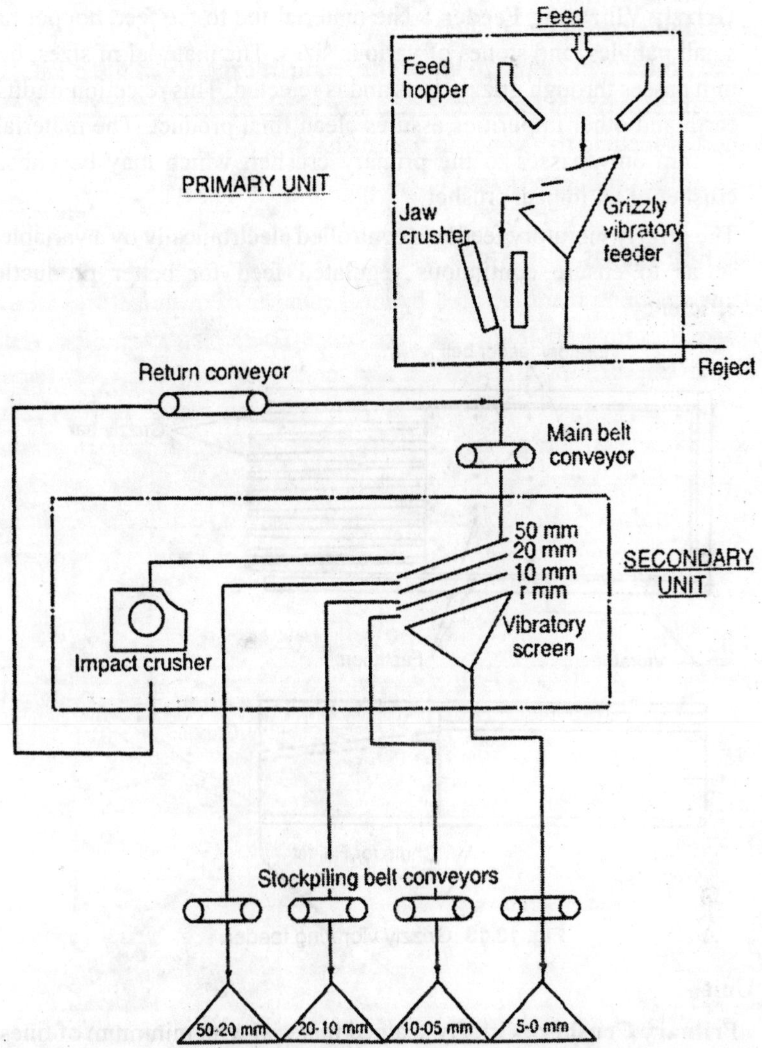

Fig. 10.12 Flow diagram for a crushing plant.

10.10.1 Construction and Working

Feeding Unit

The raw material (stones either from quarry, or river bed etc.) is dumped into feed hopper from a specially built platform and a ramp by means of a wheel loader or a dumper (in big size crushing plants).

(a) **Feed Hopper :** The feed hopper is a robust reinforced steel structure to withstand the sever impact and shock. Big hopper volume assures constant regulated feedby grizzly vibrating feeder into the primary crusher.

(b) Grizzly Vibrating Feeder : The material fed to the feed hopper has dust, small pabbles, and stones of various sizes. The material of sizes, below 50 mm passes through grizzly bars and is rejected. This rejection of dust, mud, earth and other impurities assures clean final product. The material above 50 mm only passes to the primary crusher, which may be either a jaw crusher or an impact crusher.

The grizzly vibratory feeder is controlled electronically by a variable motor, so as to ensure continuous regulated feed for better production and efficiency.

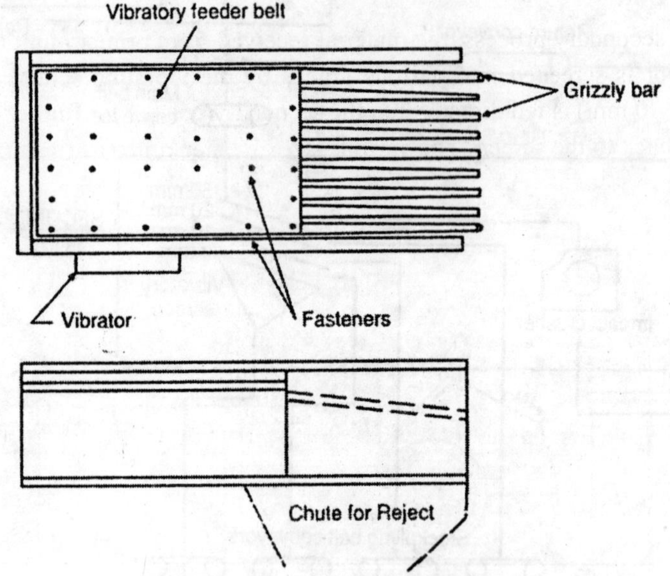

Fig. 10.13 Grizzly vibrating feeder.

Primary Unit

(a) Primary Crusher : Grizzly scalped material with minimum of fines passes into the jaw or impact crusher fitted in the primary unit. The jaw crusher

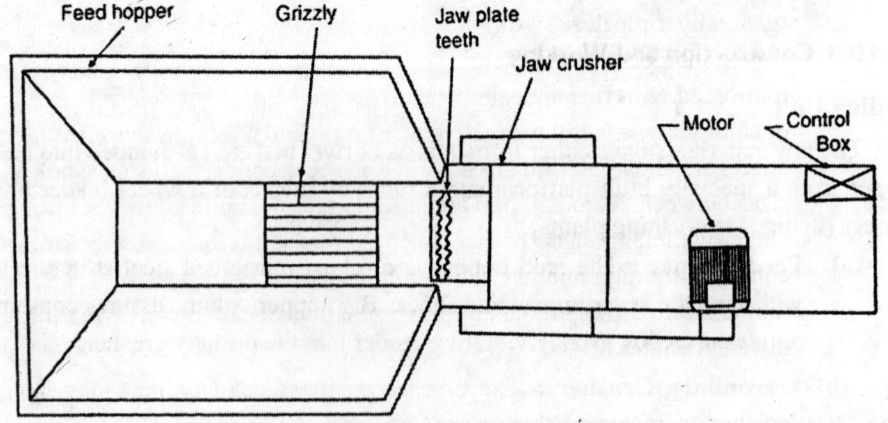

Fig. 10.14 Primary crushing unit.

may be either single toggle or double toggle jaw crusher. It is supported on a heavy duty steel plate, annealed and stress relieved frame to withstand tough crushing operations. The jaw or impact crushers have construction features as described earlier in this chapter.

(b) Main Belt Conveyor : Material crushed by primary crusher are carried to the secondary unit by the main belt conveyor, one end of this conveyor is installed just under the discharge chute of primary crusher. The other end of this conveyor is kept just above the feed end of the vibrating screen.

Secondary Unit

In the secondary process, the material received from primary unit through main belt conveyor is screened into various grades by the vibrating screen and oversize (+50 mm or 40 mm) is fed directly into the secondary crusher for further crushing and then return back to the screen. The various sizes are stockpiled as final products.

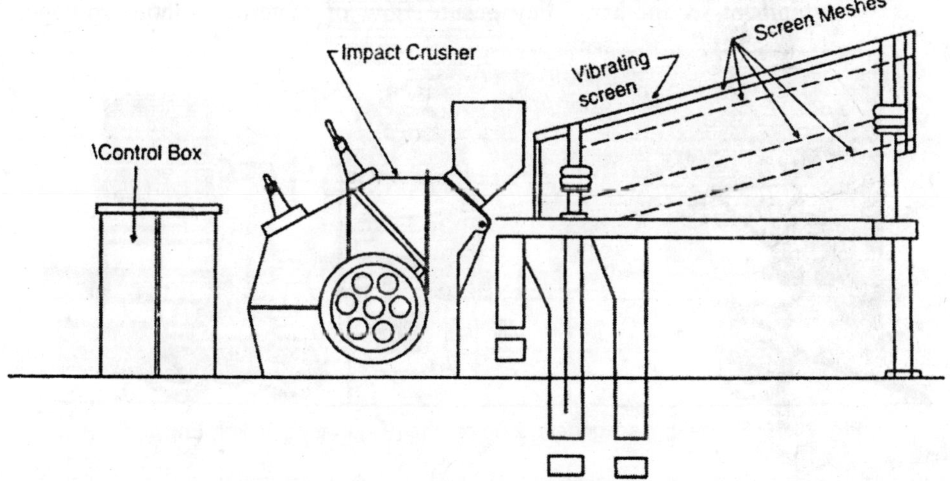

Fig. 10.15 Secondary unit.

(a) Vibrating Screen : This is an inclined vibrating screen of multideck (generally triple deck) with robust structure. The screen mesh is made of flat woven hardened steel wire. The frame of this screen is heavy duty, reinforced with ribs annealed and stress relieved. It has screens of desired openings say, *e.g.,* 50 mm; 20 mm; 10 mm; and 5 mm. In this example the aggregate above 50 mm sizes are fed to the secondary crusher whereas of sizes between 20 and 50 mm are taken to one stockpile conveyor through a chute, while aggregate of size 10 to 20 mm is taken to another stockpile conveyor through another chute. Similarly, the aggregates of size 5 to 10 mm and 0 to 5 mm are taken to two separate stockpile conveyors through different chutes.

(b) Secondary Crusher : The crusher on the secondary unit may be jaw crusher or impact crusher or cone crusher. The over size material received from the vibrating screen is crushed in this secondary crusher and then allowed to drop in the return belt conveyor through a chute.

(c) **Return Belt Conveyor :** Products crushed by the secondary crusher are carried back to the vibrating screen by return belt conveyor.

(d) **Stockpiling Belt Conveyors :** The final product delivered from the vibrating screen, are stockpiled by stockpiling belt conveyors. Each size of the product is carried by separate conveyors to separate stockpiles located at convenient places.

Speed of the conveyors ranges between 1 m/sec to 4 m/sec depending on size of material, characteristics of material (like density, abrasiveness, and friability), width and inclination of the belt etc. The inclination may go upto 22° depending upon angle of repose, size and shape of material, method of loading, speed of belt, moisture content etc.

(e) **Chutes :** These are required to transfer material from one piece of equipment to another. They ensure flow of material without spillage,

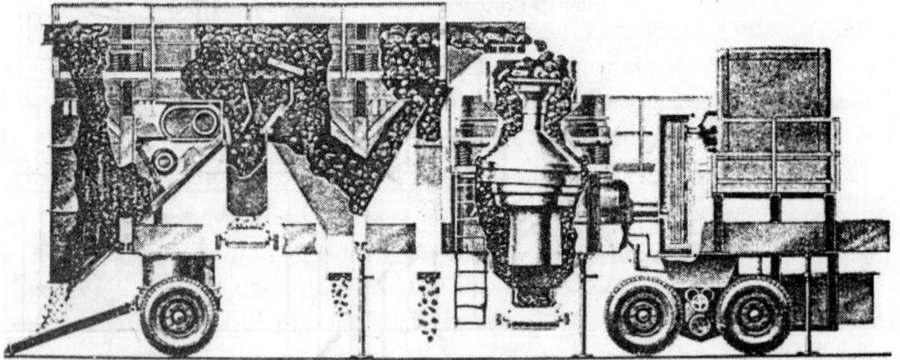

Fig. 10.16 Feeding of secondary cone crusher (Courtesy : Parker, England).

Fig. 10.17 Secondary cone crusher.

jamming, breakage or damage to the equipment. To increase the life of chute, lining suitable for the material is provided, so as to withstand the impact of the material. Inclination of the chute should be sufficient to ensure smooth flow of material, but it should not be unnecessary steep, otherwise, the material may break and lining may wear faster. Flow of material from the chute should be in the same direction as that of the belt conveyor receiving it as to avoid spillage of material and damage to the belt.

(f) Bucket Elevators : These are used only when restriction of space rule out the use of conveyors.

10.10.2 Screening

Screening is a device of grading material in different sizes. Screening efficiency is an indication of undersize material going into the oversize.

Types of Screens

Screens are of following two main types :

1. **Rotary Screens :** These are of cylindrical shape with circular openings. Capacity of the rotary screens is limited. The initial cost of these rotary screens is less than that of a vibrating screen. These have lesser screening efficiency and hence are less suitable for quality work.
2. **Vibrating Screens :** These are versatile and are suitable for most of the screening requirements. These are mounted either horizontally or inclined over a frame, which must withstand stress imposed by high gravity forces derived from the vibration. Structure of a vibrating screen comprises two side frames held rigidly by the shaft housing and screen mesh support frame. The feed end is enclosed by rubber covers which prevent spillage and permit ease of access for screen mesh replacement.

Fig. 10.18 Vibrating screen.

A feed box distributes the feed material evenly across the width of the screen without any reduction in the screening area. The whole assembly is supported on springs, to eliminate the vibrations to supporting structure. Rubber shock absorbers or a friction block reduce the tendency for excessive throw to occur during start-up and about-down.

Vibrating Mechanism

Vibrations are created by weights which rotate on shafts held on the screen frame. Different models of vibrating screens have their own method of generating the vibration, differentiated by shaft and weight configuration.

(a) **Vibrating Single Shaft Mechanism :** Screens using this mechanism are of various sizes with 2, 3 or 4 decks so as to give upto 5 products (including oversize). In this mechanism, the shaft motion is circular, enabling rapid separation resulting in higher efficiency. The inclined screen (generally between 15 to 20°) is advantageous due to assistance of gravity in screening.

The vibration is generated by a single eccentric shafts, supported by roller bearings located at the centre of gravity of the screen. Counterweights are fixed to the shaft, and the addition of extra weights enables adjustment of the amplitude. The whole assembly is encased in a protective housing, sealed against dust entry. Screen pulley design compensating for vibration in belt tension. The drive assembly can be mounted on either side of the screen.

(b) **Vibrating Double Shaft Mechanism :** These have a linear action, the motion deriving rom contra-rotating shafts onto which counter weights are fixed. The linear action conveys the material across the screen without gravity assistance.

Linear motion is obtained by the shafts contra-rotating at the synchronous speed. The shafts are supported by bearings in housings which are bolted to the screen frame. Counterweights are identical, and adjustable for different applications. The weights are keyed onto the shafts and separate drive motors are provided for each shaft.

The screens adopting this mechanism, has 2 or 3 decks to provide 3 or 4 products (including oversize).

Screening Applications

Screening is done for following purposes :

(i) Grading (ii) Scalping (iii) Dust removal

(iv) Dewatering (v) Deslurrying

1. Grading

Mesh opening is kept fairly close to the required grading depending upon the feed material (*i.e.*, its sieve analysis, shape, moisture content etc.). Water content in the feed material is the feed material is most important factor. The screenings are therefore classified as dry, moist or wet.

(a) **Dry Grading :** When water content is less than 2%, it hardly affects the screening characteristics. With dry material, large throughputs per square metre are obtained and screening is possible on small mesh openings down to about 0.5 mm.

(b) **Moist Grading :** The higher the water content in feed material the higher the cohesion between the particles and lower their free movements and the screening efficiency. If water content further increases, after a certain limit, the cohesion decreases and screening is than again possible. The smaller the mesh openings, the higher the adverse effect of the water content.

(c) **Wet Grading :** In this process water content is increased to a limit when cohesion is reduced to a minimum. The fines are rinsed with the water and then dewatered.

2. Scalping

Scalping is done on relatively large sieve openings. These are used to remove unwanted size of material, may be either ton small or too big.

Relief screening is required before crushing to prevent smaller pieces going into the crusher. For example a crusher is operating at 150 mm setting and is being fed with 500 mm size boulders along with small piece. If a scalper having 150 mm openings is employed, then material below 150 mm will bypass the crusher and only boulder will pass through the crusher. This will avoid unnecessary overload on the crusher.

Control screenings are used for the removal of coarse lumps and larger size material then required. For example, in drum mix asphalt plants, where oversize lumps or stone metals are required to be removed and rejected, these scalping screens are used. The sieve opening is larger by many times, than that of the maximum allowable particle size, the facilitates large throughput.

3. Dust Removal

It is the screening of granular products with a view to remove unwanted very fine particles were formed during the process (by size reduction or abrasion).

4. Dewatering

It is like straining unwanted water from the feed material. This water was added during wet gradation, wet sorting floatation etc. The dewatered material is then dried further either, mechanically, or thermically or both.

5. Deslurrying

It aims at removing certain particles range along with the water, *e.g.*, in order to reduce ash content in coal or to remove dissolved clay from sand and gravel.

10.11 Screening Plants

When different sizes of gravels, pabbles or boulders are available in large quantities, there is no need of sending whole material to the crushing plant. In such cases screening plants are installed, generally near the place where the raw material is available. The screening plants has a multideck screen with stockpile conveyors to saggregate various sizes of material, *e.g.*, +50 mm; 20-50 mm; 10-20 mm; 5-10 mm and 0-5 mm. The material above 50 mm can be taken to the crushing plant and material of other sizes can be utilised in construction activities. In case these 0-50 mm sizes aggregates fulfill the requirement than only screening plant is sufficient and there is no need for crushing plant. Thus these screening plants are suitable where nature has given material of various sizes between 0 to 50 mm in one location only. (Refer Fig. 10.19 and 10.20).

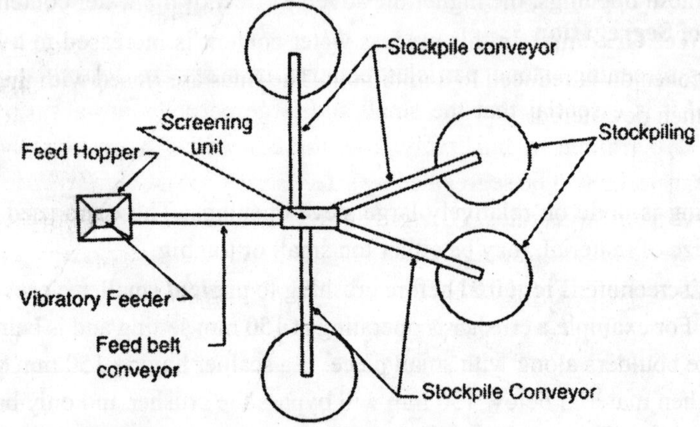

Fig. 10.19 General layout of a screening plant.

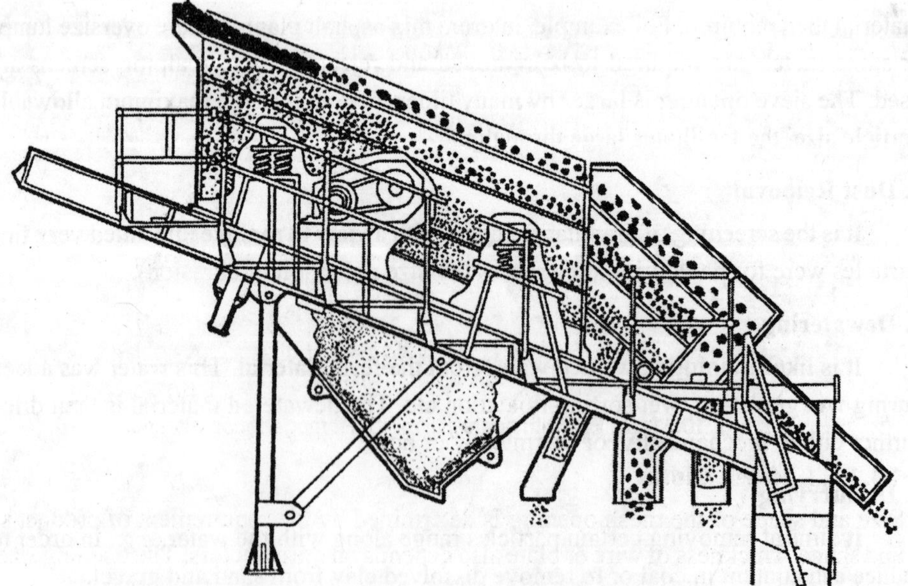

Fig. 10.20 4-deck screening unit—sectional view (Courtesy : Parker, England).

A screening plant consists of following units :

(a) **Screening Unit :** Screening unit has an inclined vibrating screen with screening meshes of different sizes on a triple deck and driven by a motor. The details have already been explained earlier.

(b) **Feed Hopper :** It is a hopper in which material is fed by wheel loaders from a ramp. The material passes from hopper to the screening unit through vibrating feeder to saggregate the material as per the sizes.

(c) **Vibrating Feeder :** The vibrating feeder passes the material from hopper to the screening unit by means of vibrations.

(d) **Stockpilling Belt Conveyors :** These conveyors carry products of different sizes from screen to the stockpiles.

Problem of Segregation

After screening, stone particles blended in sizes are conveyed through belt onveyors. It is essential that the small and large particles are not separated. I the aggregate is permitted to fall freely from the belt conveyor, especially from some height, the material will be segregated by sizes. Strong cross-wind tends to separate the smaller sizes from larger ones. To avoid this problem, the end of the belt should be kept as low as possible, and the aggregate should be discharged through a rock ladder, having baffles (Refer Fig. 10.21).

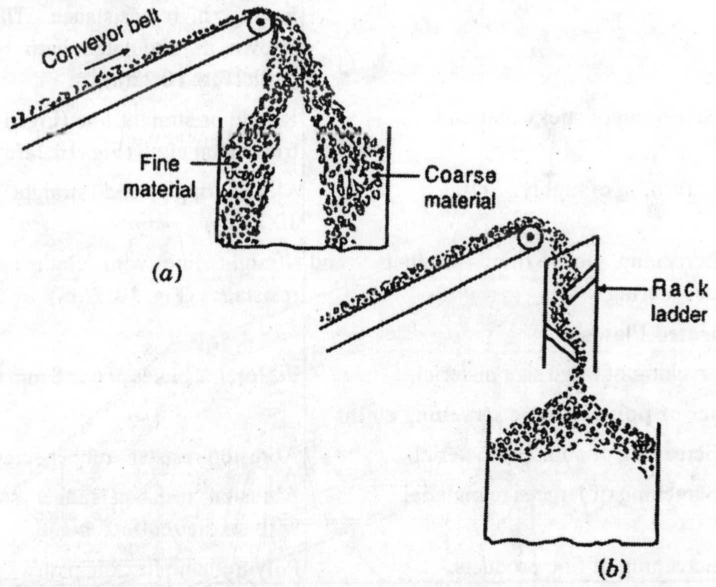

Fig. 10.21 (a) Fall with segregation, (b) Homogeneous material.

10.11.1 Screen Cloths

Size and shape of the mesh opening is determined by the requirement of product size and shape. Thickness of wire or plate also depends on these factors. The opening size of mesh means the inside measurements, *i.e.*, diameter or length and width.

Screen cloths are of different types, some of them are indicated hereunder showing their application :

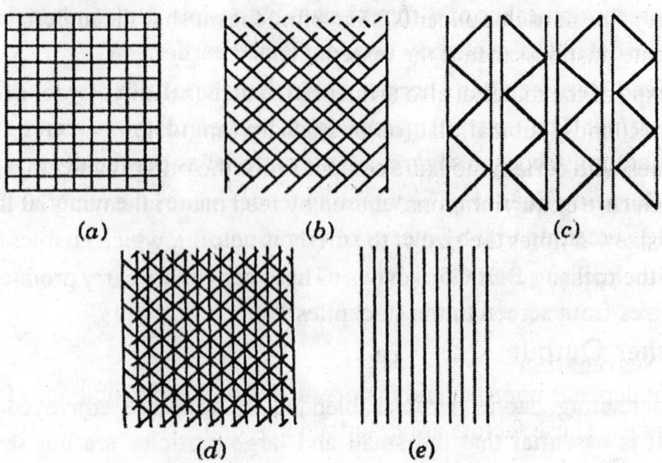

Fig. 10.22 Types of screen cloths.

	Application	Type of screen cloth
1.	**Wooven Wires**	
	(a) General screening.	Conventional woven wire screen cloth having high resistance. This is also known as undulated harp type screen cloth (Fig. 10.22(a)).
	(b) Screening of sticky material.	Ripple or straight line (Fig. 10.22(b)) or tria screen cloth (Fig. 10.22(c)).
	(c) Screening of highly.	Mixed ripple and straight line (Fig. 10.22(d)).
	(d) Screening of fine products and dewatering.	Straight line wire cloth having high resistance (Fig. 10.22(e)).
2.	**Perforated Plates**	
	For screening of large size material.	Perforated plates of 6 to 8 mm thickness.
3.	**Rubber or polyurethane screening cloths**	
	(a) Screening of abrasive material.	Abrasion resistant rubber screen.
	(b) Screening of large size material.	Abrasion resistant rubber screen cloth with textile reinforcement.
	(c) Screening of fine products.	Polyurethane flexible plate.

10.11.2 Points to be Remembered During Screening

Following points should be remembered for screening :

(i) The more the marginal particles (near mesh size), the more difficult is the screening because marginal particles cause pegging.

(ii) Higher proportion of particles smaller than half the mesh opening, faster the screening.

(iii) Very fine particles under 0.5 mm blind the mesh if the material is moist, and create dust nuisance if the material is dry.

(iv) Shape of the material also influence the screenability. Order of screenabilty is : Rounds, cubical, flat (oblong), sharp (angular).

(v) Fines with certain moisture content forms the bridges and clogs the mesh. In such case extra vibrations, caused by feed material having 20-25% material of size 4-5 times the size of the mesh, is helpful, which enables self cleaning of the mesh.

10.12 Crusher Output

Crusher output depends upon several factors, which are responsible for variation in the crusher capacities. These factors are described hereunder :

1. **Jaw Opening :** Lesser the opening, lesser will be the output and more the opening, more will be the output of the crusher.
2. **End Product :** If the maximum size of the end product (*i.e.*, crushed material) is in lesser quantity, the output will be less and if the end product needed has larger quantity of bigger size aggregate, the crusher will give more output.
3. **Nature of the Rocks :** If the rock is soft, and has less quantity of dust, earth etc. the output will be more and *vice-versa.*
4. **Feedline Efficiency :** If the feeding is continuous and the crusher runs full, the output will be more and *vice-versa.*
5. **Working Efficiency :** If working efficiency is higher, means no down time for inspection, maintenance, repair etc. the output shall also be more.
6. **Bulk Density :** If the density of the stone is more, crusher output shall be more and *vice-versa.*
7. **Water Absorption :** With lesser water contents, output shall be higher and *vice-versa.*
8. **Specific Gravity :** Crusher output is inversely proportional to the specific gravity of the stone fed.
9. **Crushing Strength :** Higher the crushing strength of the stone, lesser will be the output.
10. **Size of Aggregate in Raw Material :** When percentage of smaller size of stone in the feed material is more than the production will also be more. Experiments have shown that,
    (a) with 25% undersize material in feed, increase in output is 7% to 15%.
    (b) with 50% undersize material in feed, increase in output is 35 to 45%.
    (c) with 75% undersize material in feed, increase in output is 50 to 60%.

10.13 Screening Capacity

$$\text{Screening efficiency} = \frac{w-a}{w} \times 100 \text{ (percent)}$$

where, w = Total undersize in the one feed.

a = Actual undersize passed with oversize.

Actual capacity of the screen can be determined by using the following equation :

$$Q = A.C.E.D.G.$$

where, Q = Capacity of screen, tons per hour.

A = Area of screen, square meter.

C = Theoretical capacity of screen in tons per hour per square meter. For knowing the theoretical capacity, screen manufacturers chart should be referred.

E = Efficiency factors. It generally varies rom 1.00 to 2.00.

D = Deck factor. For 1 deck it is 1.00, while for 2, 3 and 4 decks, deck factor is 0.90, 0.75 and 0.60 respectively.

G = Aggregate size factor. If the material to be screened contains a surplus of small sizes, the capacity of the screen is increased, whereas if the material contains a surplus of large sizes, the capacity of the screen will be reduced. If the 40% of the aggregate is less than half the size of screen openings the aggregate size factor is 1.00. Similarly for 10% smaller aggregate factor is 0.55, and the factor increases to 3.00 when 90% aggregate is less than half the size of screen opening.

In order to determine the minimum area of screen to provide a given capacity, the value of

$$A = \frac{Q}{CEDG}$$

10.14 Fine Crushing

If no natural material is available, fine fractions are often produced in impact breakers, rod mills and ball mills or cone crushers.

Grinding Mills

These are used to produce fine materials to be used as sand. Since ball mills are not common, other two type of mills are described here.

(a) **Rod Mills :** These grinds aggregates of about 12 mm size to produce graded sand. Grinding media being long rods, they allow less voids as compared to the balls in ball mill. As a result, grinding is faster and naturally, the capacity of a rodmill is higher. The rods gives heavier impact due to line contacts of the rods.

(b) **Twin Tube Vibrating Mills :** A vibrating mill is a grinding equipment like a ballmill, in which the material is ground by means of grinding balls. Twin tube vibrating mills are of continuous type and are most suited for grinding all type of materials from medium feed size to the finest finished product. Different types of flow arrangements are available, as shown in the figure below, to obtain a high rate of throughput with higher degree of fineness of product. These give better result as compared to ball mills. In ball mill,the impact of the grinding balls on the material is affected by the force of gravity only (1 G). But in a tube mill, the impulses of the vibrating tubes are imparted to both the grinding balls and the material at such a high acceleration, that the force of impact can be as high as 15 G. Because of high impact force, this process of grinding is faster than that to a ball mill.

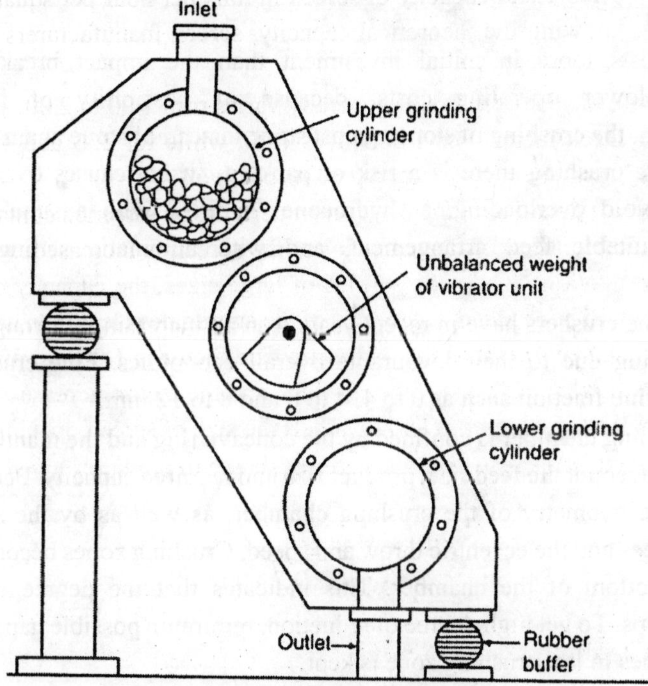

Fig. 10.23 Twin tube vibrating mill.

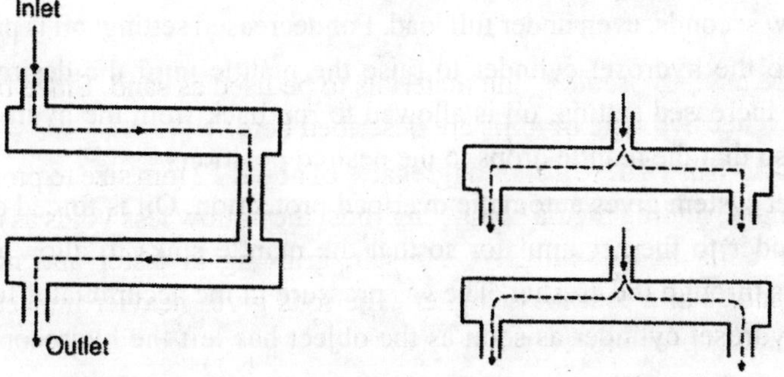

Fig. 10.24 Flow arrangement in twin tube vibrating mill.

The crushers are normally not used to produce finer than 0 to 3 mm. For materials finer than 0-3 mm rod mills and ball mills are used. Generally these are used in cement industries and are not common in stone crushing.

Impact Breakers

In these, crushing force is dependent on both rotor speed and feed size, a high rotor speed is therefore, necessary to give sufficient crushing force for the fine crushing. Feed smaller than 10 mm are difficult to crush in impact breaker due to the low mass of the individual feed particles. Although it gives good cubicity, its main draw back is high operating cost when abrasive material is crushed.

Cone Crusher

These costs more in initial investment than the impact breaker, but has considerably lower operating costs, because of possibility of inter-particle communication, the crushing of stone against stone instead of stone against a crushing surface. In fine crushing there is a risk of packing, which causes overloading the crusher. To avoid overloading, a 'hydrocone' is fitted with a suitable crushing chamber, a suitable feed arrangement, and with automatic setting regulation equipment.

Hydrocone crushers have in recent years won an increasingly strong position in the fine crushing due to their favourable overall economics. Fine crushing is the production of fine fraction such as 0 to 4, 4 to 8 and 8 to 12 mm.

The crushing chamber is confined by the concave ring and the mantle. Its design must take into account the feed size, product size and required capacity. Performance is affected by the geometry of the crushing chamber, as well as by the slope of the crushing surfaces and the eccentric throw and speed. Crushing zones become narrower towards the bottom of the chamber. This indicates that the degree of reduction increases in steps. To get high degree of reduction, minimum possible gap between the crushing surfaces in last crushing zone is kept.

Hydrocone has a hydroset system, which consists essentially of a robust hydraulic jack which supports and adjust the crusher's main shaft. Setting adjustment takes just a few seconds, even under full load. For decreased setting, oil is pumped form the oil tank to the hydroset cylinder to raise the mantle until the desired setting is obtained. For increased setting, oil is allowed to run back from the hydroset cylinder tothe oil tankso that the mantle drops to the desired position.

Hydroset system gives automatic overload protection. Oil is forced out from the hydroset cylinder to the accumulator so that the mantle sinks to allow uncrushable objects to pass through the crusher. The gas pressure in the accumulator forces the oil back to the hydroset cylinder as soon as the object has left the hydrocones crushing chamber.

10.15 Aggregate Processing Plant

Aggregate processing consists of crushing, grading, washing and stock piling of aggregate and sand. Large processing plants comprises of primary crusher, scalping (primary) screen, washing system, secondary crusher, grading screens, belt conveyors, sand mills, sand screens, storage piles and reclaiming system.

Quarry material as recovered is delivered to the scalping screen where acceptable sizes of aggregate are separated, fines are removed, and oversize is passed on the primary crusher. The crushed aggregate received from primary crusher is conveyed to the screens for grading the aggregates as required for concrete mix. Jets of water are directed over the screens, to produce clean aggregate which when moves to the grading screen. Water requirement is about 60 to 90 lits per min per TPH capacity of the plant. Aggregate from stock piles is reclaimed through belt conveyors running under the stock piles in reclamation tunnel. It may also be reclaimed through skip buckets operated by hoist cable or by a grab.

Sand producing plants (some times known as sand crushers), consists of sand mills or crushers, dry screens, washers, conveyors and storage bins. Arrangements for removal of waste products from aggregate producing plants are also made.

10.16 Washing Barrels

Cleanliness of aggregates is becoming vital aspect as specification require more stringent quality control. Whether from quarries or gravel pits, the deposits are often contaminated with mud, silt, earth, clay etc. For high quality products removal of contaminants and recovery of the maximum quantity of usable products is necessary. For this purpose washing barrels are used.

Working Procedure

Process of washing is carried out in following steps as shown in the Fig. 10.25.

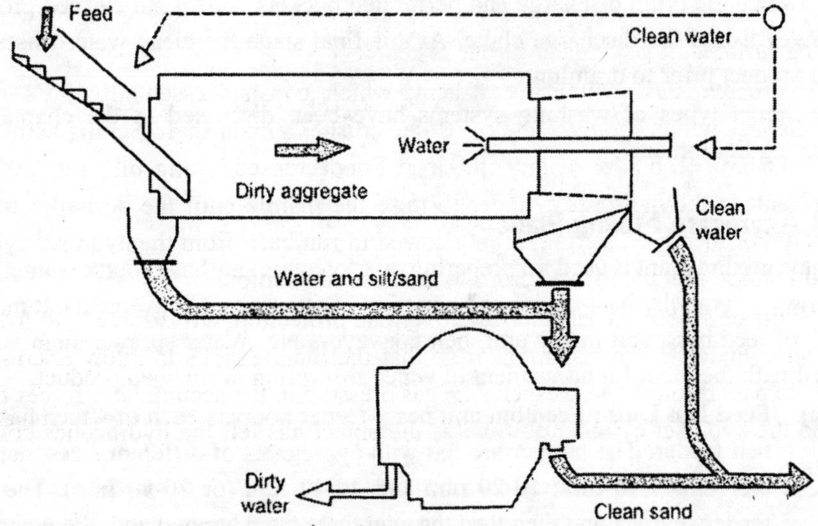

Fig. 10.25 Working of a washing barrel.

(a) **Pre Washing :** For feeding dirty material, a chute is provided which has a stepped arrangement to tumble the feed through water sprays. This enables a partial cleansing action prior to introduction into the drum itself.

(b) **Washing :** Inside the drum the material is subjected to an intense mixing action through a flow of water passing in opposite direction. Thus the agitation takes place which cleans the material as it passes along the drum—the clots being broken up and the mud, silt etc. being carried to discharge within the water.

(c) **Rinsing :** The barrels where water and dirty feed travel in opposite direction gives better results, as compared to those where both travels in the same direction. Where clean water and dirty feed travels in opposite direction, material continuously passes into progressively cleaner water, which ensures that a rinsing in clean water takes place immediately prior to the product being discharged from the drum. During cleansing material progresses through the drum due to the pushing action of the blades.

(d) **Sand Recovery :** Sand contained in the dirty water (including that received from the prewashing chute) is conveyed to a sand reclaiming/dewatering wheel which separates the sand from the water and silt, and removes excess water from the washed sand.

Construction Principle

Dirty aggregates after being pre-washed, are stirred and lifted by a series of blades and ploughs within the washing drum. Constant flow of water passes in the opposite direction to the material through this revolving assembly. Repeated lifting and dropping of the material by the ploughs and continual agitation within the water dislodges and removes the particles of clay and earth, and which are then carried away by the water and discharged at the drum feed end.

Towards the drum discharge and perforated buckets collect the cleaned product and convey it into the discharge chute. At this final stage the clean water rinses the washed product prior to draining.

Different types of washing systems have been discussed in the chapter on "Concreting Equipment".

10.17 Aggregate Mixing Plant

Aggregate mixing plant is used for preparing mix for aggregate base course, sometimes also known as granular base course to be used in construction of pavements. It mainly consists of feed bins, soil mixer unit, belt conveyors etc. Water spray system is also provided with the plant for adjustment of water absorption in finished product.

(a) **Feed Bin Unit :** Feed bin unit has 4 feeder hoppers each of which has one belt feeder. The hopper are fed with aggregates of different sizes, namely 0-5 mm; 5-10 mm; 10-20 mm and 20-40 mm (or 20-50 mm). The belt feeders extract and then feed the aggregate from hoppers into the inner belt conveyor. This inner belt conveyor carries all the 4 sizes of aggregate to the mixture unit through feed belt conveyor. The feed bin is made of heavy-duty reinforced steel structure.

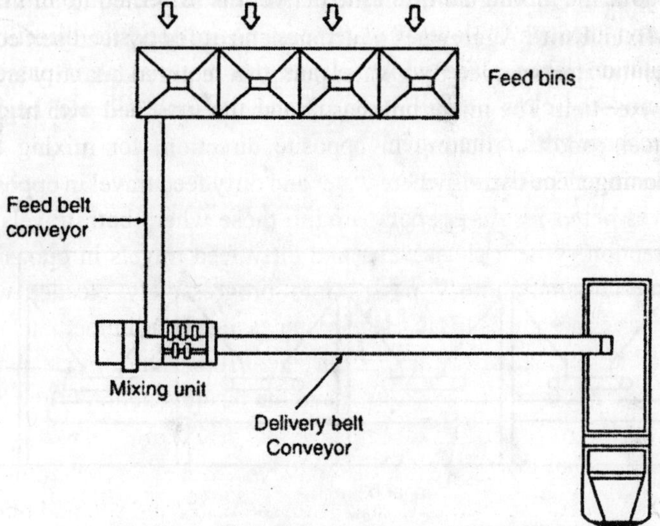

Fig. 10.26 Layout plan of aggregate mixing plant.

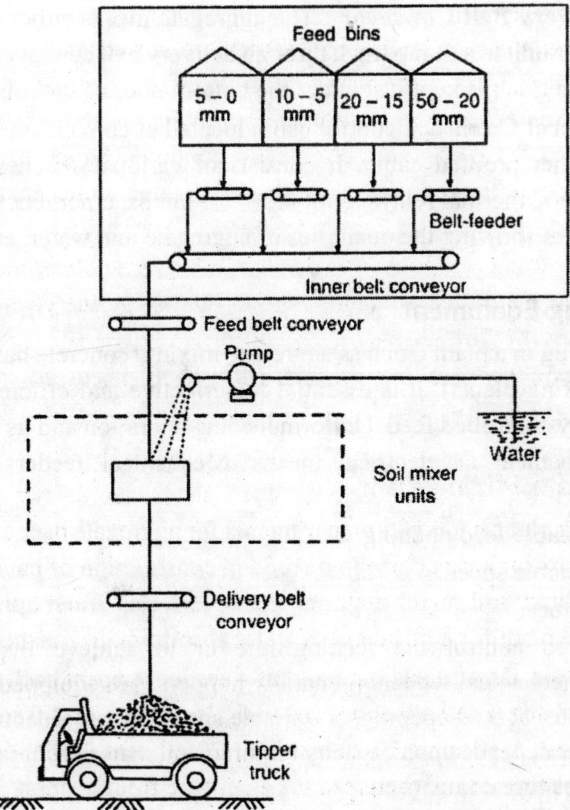

Fig. 10.27 Flow diagram for aggregate mixing plant.

(b) **Feed Belt Conveyor :** Feed belt conveyor carries the aggregate from inner belt conveyor to the mixing unit. One end of the feed belt conveyor is located just below the inner belt conveyor's chute, while the other end is above the mixing unit, so as to deliver the material into this mixing unit.

(c) **Mixer Unit :** Aggregates of different sizes fed by feed belt conveyor along with water, sprayed by a water pump, in required quantity are mixed in the mixer unit. The mixer unit has two shafts, attached with high chrome cast steel paddles, rotating in opposite direction, for mixing the aggregate homogeneously.

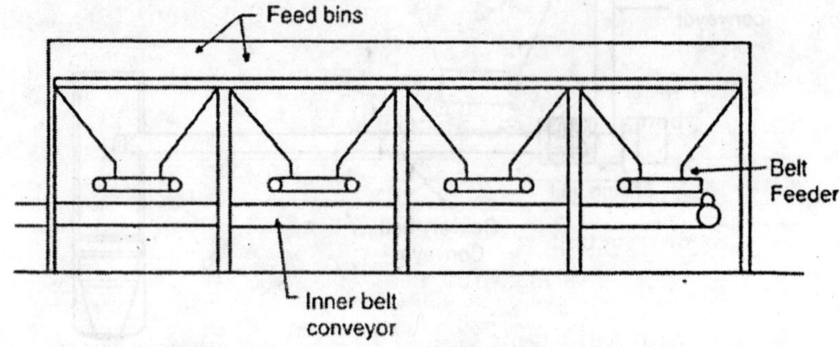

Fig. 10.28 Feed bin unit of aggregate mixing plant.

(d) **Delivery Belt Conveyor :** The aggregate mix is either delivered from the mixer unit to a dump truck through delivery belt conveyor or some times the dump truck is kept just under the bottom door of the mixer unit.

(e) **Control Cabin :** A control cabin located at convenient place is a dust and weather proofed cabin. It consists of various switches, circuit-breakers, starters, thermal relays, pilot indicator lamps, emergency stop buttons, dial gauges showing the quantities of aggregate and water, etc.

10.18 Feeding Equipment

During processing in a plant (such as aggregate mixing, concrete batching and mixing, and asphalt mixing plants), it is essential for effective and efficient performance to have a uniformly controlled feed. Uniform feeding operation and its control is obtained either by mechanical or electrical means. Mechanical feeders are generally of following types :

- Adjustable feed opening.
- Adjustable speed.
- Vibratory.

In order to control the feeding rate or to achieve the varying feeding requirements, mechanical feeders (generally hoppers) are equipped with provision of adjusting the gates at feed opening, or variable speed drives. Selection of the type and size of the feeder depends upon capacity requirement, material characteristics and size, flow-ability, moisture contents etc.

Commonly used feeding arrangements are :

(a) **Belt Feeders :** These are the short belts and feeds the material at a uniform rates. These are provided at the bottom of the hopper and extracts the material from it. For varying the rate of discharge the speed of feed belt is varied as per requirement.

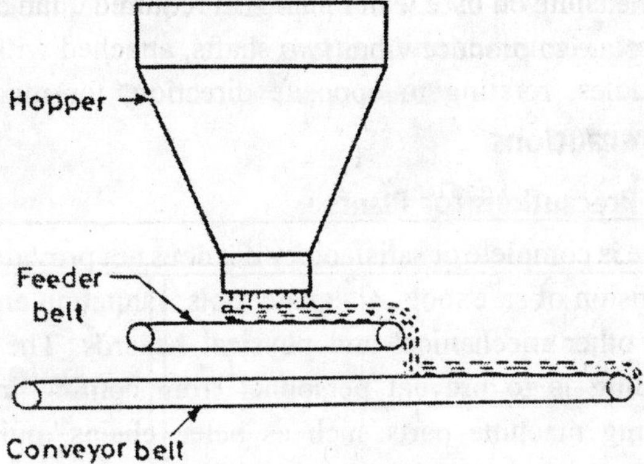

Fig. 10.29 Belt feeder.

(b) **Hoppers with Adjustable Gates and Chutes :** These are used for feeding the material to the belt conveyors. These are used for uniform loading the running belt through a chute and rate of material flow is controlled through gates at the mouth of the chutes. These gates can be controlled either manually, or hydraulically or electrically or by means of compressed air chute is used to discharge the material on the conveyor belt in its direction of movement, so as-to reduce the impact of material on belt. The size of the chute opening should be designed in such a way so as to avoid spillage of material from belt, and also avoid blockage of opening by lumpy material, if any. The inner walls of the chute should be lined with the anti abrasive material. To avoid the spillage of material and guiding the material on belt, two rubber pads are also provided on the sides at the loading point.

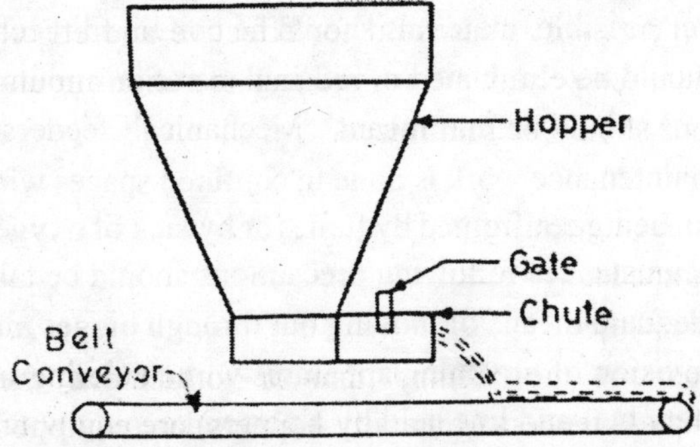

Fig. 10.30 Hopper with adjustable gate and chute.

(c) **Vibrating Feeders :** When loading non-free flow materials, vibrating feeders are used. Vibrations are produced by electromagnetic means or mechanical means. This feeding system is most suitable for almost all types of bulk materials : may it be dry or damp, hot or cold, or fine or coarse size grains. The vibrating mechanism is fitted either on the wall of the hopper above the chute on in case of rectangular container the device is fitted at the bottom plate to produce vibrations.

10.19 Safety Precautions

10.19.1 General Precautions for Plants

No safety procedure is complete or satisfactory if it does not provide for the guarding of machines, the provision of safe tools, adequate tools, sanitation and for the correction on elimination of other mechanical and physical hazards. The basic objective of machine safeguarding is to prevent personnel from coming in contact with any revolving or moving machine parts such as belts, chains, pulleys, gears, shafts, couplings and any working part of the plant which creates a shearing or crushing action or may entangle the worker.

Safety at the point of operation may be accomplished by following principles :

1. Providing enclosures, covers and barricades.
2. Providing mechanical feeding devices.
3. Providing remote-control operating mechanism, which include push-buttons, switches, levers or handles.
4. Design to tools for the purpose of eliminating or at least, minimizing the danger of injury.
5. Photoelectric cells can be applied to the operating mechanism of power tools, by placing them such that the interruption of the beam will prevent further movement.
6. Lubrication, wherever possible, should be automatic and continuous when machine is in operation.
7. Wherever possible, materials should be conveyed mechanically.
8. Noise should be eliminated or reduced to the minimum.
9. Vibrations should be minimized.
10. When maintenance work is done in confined spaces where there is a risk of workmen being confronted by fumes or by lack of oxygen for respiration. In such circumstances following precautions should be taken :
    (a) Adequate means of moving out through bigger manholes.
    (b) Provision of breathing apparatus while entering unsafe spaces with a safety belt and line held by a person keeping witch outside.
    (c) Deposits likely to give off fume should be removed.
    (d) No work in the furnace or flues be allowed until the space is sufficiently cool to work safely.

11. No welding should be allowed on tanks that have carried inflammable liquid or gas until all substance and fumes are removed to make it non-explosive.
12. Only 24 V hand lamps with isolation transformer should be used in confined spaces.
13. Persons working on the construction plants should use safety apparel such as safety shoes, helmet, safety goggles,hand groves, ear plugs, etc.
14. Ensure adequate lighting in area of operation and its vicinity.
15. Communication source should be available near the area of operation.
16. Take care of all hazards due to electricity.
17. *Safe Access* : Safe and adequate means of access including handholds and footholds shall be provided to all parts where a person may have to walk, climb or work.
18. Maintenance :
    (i) No part of machinery, while in motion or in operation shall be examined, lubricated, adjusted or repaired except by a duly authorized person. Any repairs to machinery while in motion or in operation shall be carried out only when unavoidable.
    (ii) Parts of machinery shall be cleaned when the machinery is stopped. If the cleaning is unavoidable when the machinery is working, this shall be done by a duly authorized person in conformity with accepted standards of safety.
    (iii) Electric power shall be shut off and relevant fuses removed when repairs are carried out to any electric machinery.
    (iv) Any machinery, equipment or part thereof which is suspended or held apart by use of slings,hoist or jacks shall be substantially blocked or cribbed before men are permitted to work underneath or between such machinery, equipment or part thereof.
19. First aid and fire fighting :
    (i) A first aid box or kit shall be provided at the site.
    (ii) When operation of the construction machinery is confined to one place or is with in a restricted area of about 30 m radius, a fire point shall be established at a suitable and easily accessible location within the area. The fire point shall be provided with the following equipment, which shall always be kept in serviceable condition :

    5 kg dry powder extinguisher conforming to relevant IS   2 Nos.

    Sand buckets   2 Nos.

    (iii) Where the construction machinery in use is a mobile type and during the course of operation has to shift its location frequently, one 5 kg DCP extinguisher shall be carried on the machine itself at a suitable position on the machinery so as to ensure its easy availability. It shall also be ensured that these extinguishers are inspected and maintained properly according to relevant IS and that all persons employed on construction work are well conversant with the method of operation of the equipment.

(iv) When sand is used for extinguishing a machine fire it involves through cleaning immediately after the fire is extinguished. However, this work be undertaken only under the supervision of a competent person.

10.19.2 Screening and Processing (Aggregate Mixing) Plant

1. Screening and processing plants should be adequately designed to carry all loads and withstand all stresses placed on them. All gears, belts, chains, and exposed shafts should be equipped with guards.
2. All vibrating or rocker screens should be equipped with sides and baffles to prevent cobbles from falling off the screen to the operating floor.
3. Where materials are processed dry, an exhaust system should be installed to remove the dust, or respirators made available for the workmen.
4. All oil or grease cups should be so located or extended that they can be serviced without the oiler exposing any part of the body to possible accident. Where this is not practicable, the machine should be but down while being oiled.
5. All walkways not permanently enclosed shall have guard rails with toe boards installed. All working platforms should be thoroughly guarded. Access stairways and ramps should have adequate guards.
6. Washing equipment, clarifiers, screw classifiers, etc., should have substantial guard-rails.
7. All discharge chutes and all conveyor belts operating on steep slopes should be equipped with sides of sufficient height, and baffles, to prevent the spilling of material.
8. Suitable change house should be provided for the use of men, who work with cement or other substances which might be harmful to the skin, or who work in excessively dusty, not or humid places. The change houses should be equipped with showers, and with dry ventilated lockers for clothing.
9. Storage bins and hoppers for sand, gravel, etc., should be adequately designed so as to withstand any load to which they may be subjected. When the discharge is by gravity through and opening in the bottom of the bin, the slopes of the sides shall be such that it will not be necessary of workmen to loosen the material or to force it through the outlet.
10. All the general precautions as explained in the previous section.

10.19.3 Aggregate Production Equipment (Crushing Plants)

1. Enough space should be provided around all units for personnel movement and the use of tools.

2. All aggregate production equipment are provided by the manufactures with moving parts. These should not be modified or changed in any manner that eliminates the accident prevention characteristics.
3. Always follow the basic safety practices even with safety devices.
4. Do not remove guards, covers or shields when the equipment is running.
5. Never lubricate or maintain the equipment when it is in motion.
6. Place all guards, covers or shields at proper positions after maintenance.
7. Always establish a positive lockout of the involved power source before starting the maintenance.
8. Block parts as necessary to prevent unexpected motion while performing maintenance or repair. For example, an accident may occur due to failure to shut off and block the jaw crusher before attempting to dislodge rocks.
9. Do not attempt to remove jammed product or other blockage when the equipment is running.

10.19.4 Safety in Quarries, Borrow Areas etc.

1. All quarries,borrow areas, etc. should be fenced and signs for warning people of the danger of blasting should be prominently posted.
2. The rock face of the quarry should be scaled frequently to maintain safe working conditions. Scalers should be wear hard hats and safety belts and be securely tied off while at work.
3. So far as practicable, a minimum distance of 3 m shall be maintained between workmen unless two or more are required to accomplish the same task.
4. Drillers and other workmen should wear respirators if dry-air drilling methods are used.
5. Visitors should not be allowed to enter quarries in operation unless accompanied by a project official or his designated representative.
6. Excavating and loading operations on frozen materials (quarrying other than rock) are hazardous and require continuous care and alertness to avoid the possibility of being injured or buried by sliding of falling masses of the material.
7. There should be no undercutting of banks at any time, and any overhanging banks occurring as the result of slides or cavings shall be removed before beginning excavation operations beneath them. Extreme care, should be exercised in the use of trucks and other equipment on or near the rim of the gravel pit, or on terrace or beams.

10.19.5 Safety During Excavation in Underground

Because of the many services such as electric power cables, telegraph cables, gas pipes, water pipes, oil pipes and sewer reticulation that are located underground, employers must, before starting work, ascertain the location of all services that are likely to be affected by the excavation. The owner of these service must be advised and their assistance sought.

When the existing services are uncovered during excavation, proper supports must be provided and all practicable steps must taken to prevent danger to employees or unnecessary interruption to these services. Suitable waning devices must be erected to warn employees and persons in the vicinity.

QUESTIONS

1. Why crushing of rock is required?
2. Give the classification of rock crushers. Also mention the field of application of each type.
3. Discuss various activities involved for aggregate production, and procedure for producing the aggregates.
4. Explain the construction and working of different types of crushers with the help of line diagrams.
5. Describe various activities involved in quarry operation.
6. Discuss construction and working of screening plant for grading of aggregates required for different construction activities. Also draw a general layout.
7. How aggregate mixing is done for a granular base course, with the help of an aggregate mixing plant?
8. Explain the construction and working of an impact crusher. Differentiate it with a jaw crusher.
9. Explain different types of roller crushers.
10. Explain the gyratory crusher. How it differs with cone crusher?
11. Explain the construction and working of a jaw crusher.
12. Write short notes on :
    (a) Reduction ratio in a jaw crusher.
    (b) Optimizing the jaw crusher production.
13. Explain the construction and working of a crushing plant. Draw its general layout.
14. Explain different types of screens used in aggregate production.
15. Write short notes on :
    (a) Scalping screen.
    (b) Vibrating mechanism for screens used for grading the aggregates.
    (c) Problem of segregation of aggregates.
16. Explain different factors governing the crusher output.
17. Explain the methods of producing the fines.

18. Explain the constructed and working of a washing-barrel.

19. Write short notes on :

(a) Screen capacity.

(b) Selection of crushing output.

(c) Toggles for jaw crushers.

20. Explain the different components of a "Crushing and screening" plant.

21. Explain the construction and working of a screening plant. Also draw a general layout of a screening plant.

22. Explain different types of screen clothes. Also mention their applications.

23. Explain different safety precautions for crushing plants.

24. Mention safety measures which should be adopted in the use of screening and processing plants.

25. List out the safety precautions in the operation of crushing plants.

26. How will you calculate the capacity of :

(a) Screening plant (b) Roll crusher

27. How will you enhance the production capacity of :

(a) Jaw crushers (b) Hammer mills

(c) Screening plants (d) Crushing plants

□□□

Chapter **11**

Concreting Equipment

11.1 Introduction

Concrete is basically cement, aggregate, and water mixed together and then deposited and permitted to solidify. Sometimes admixtures are used for various purposes such as to improve workability, accelerate setting, to produce desired colour. Operation involved in concrete production vary with the type of work, but generally involves; batching and mixing, handling and transportation, placing, compacting, finishing and curing.

Various types of concrete batching and mixing plants are available to suit various requirement. These may be operated manually semi or fully automatic. These are either static, fully mobile or transportable and are available upto 300 cu m per hour capacity.

The concrete plants consist of all arrangements for :

(a) receiving all ingredients of concrete, *viz.* : aggregates and sand from storage bins, cement from soils and water from tank;

(b) weighing each ingredient for each batch of the mix; and

(c) mixing these ingredient thoroughly to form a concrete of required specification.

For small jobs, portable concrete mixers are used which are fed with measured quantities of each ingredient either manually or through hoppers attached to the mixers. For large jobs, automatic arrangements are available for feeding the raw material of concrete and then mixing, and mixed product is then handled by mechanical means. For carrying out the works at certain distance, dry mix batching plants are used, which supply dry batch to the truck mixers; the mixing is then done in these truck mixers while travelling to the site of works.

11.2 Concrete Mixers

Concrete mixers are used to mix the ingredients of concrete. Efficiency and quality of concrete depends largely on duration of mixing, speed of the mixing drum, timely supply of water, correct setting of the machine, proper cleaning of the mixing blades and of inner surface of the drum. These mixers are available in various sizes and are specified by the volume of mixed concrete produced after mixing of each batch.

Sometimes the mixers are specified by two quantities. Total volume of unmixed ingredients is given first in cu ft, cu m or lit, whereas volume of mixed concrete is given afterwards in the same units, *e.g.*, 10/7 mixed takes 10 cu ft of unmixed material and gives 7 cu ft of mixed concrete in each batch; 285/200 litres mixer takes 285 litres unmixed material and gives 200 litres of mixed concrete in a batch.

The concrete mixers are made either stationary or portable. Portable mixers are common in construction industry and are mounted on either metal or tubber tyred wheeled trollies and has one drawbar for towing. The power to drive the concrete mixer is obtained from a diesel engine or from an electric motor. Diesel engines are generally used due to its reliability and problem of availability of electric power supply.

Following types of concrete mixers are generally used for construction works :

1. Hand Fed Tilting Drum Mixers

These are the smaller capacity mixers. Aggregate, cement and water are fed into the drum by hand. The revolving drum with its mixing blades gives a lifting, combing and agitation to mix the concrete.

Fig. 11.1 Hand fed tilting drum concrete mixer.

The drum with cast base and steel plate body rotates on bearings through gear mechanism. The inside of the drum is generally fitted with renewable liners. A set of blades provided in the drum gives continuous agitation of the material while mixing. It is fed by hand through buckets directly into the drum.

2. Loader Fed Tilting Drum Mixers

These mixers are of larger capacity as compared to the hand fed tilting drum mixers and are fitted with a loading hopper operated by a wire rope for feeding the aggregate and cement into the drum. The hoppers are provided with brake to stop and

Fig. 11.2 Loader fed tilting drum 10/7 concrete mixer.

hold skip automatically. Water is supplied to the drum from a measuring tank operated by hand lever provided above to discharge water directly into the drum. The principle of mixing is same as that of hand fed mixer. The mixing drum is supported on solid cast iron yoke and can be tilted on either side. Mixers are mounted on study chassis with either 3 pneumatic or metallic wheels. A draw bar with turn table is provided on front axle.

3. Reversing Drum Mixers

This type of mixer is used on comparatively larger works. The mixing drum is in horizontal position and is non-tilting type. It has two sets of blades, one blade mixes the mix while drum is rotated in one direction, the other set of blades discharges the mix when the drum rotation is reversed. The drum is fed by a loading hopper. The hopper commonly mounted on four rollers moves on channel run-ways. The hopper is lifted upward by wire-rope winding and unwinding on power operated drum. Discharge gate of hopper opens through a lever when it reaches its discharge position. Safety arrangement is provided to prevent over running of hopper. Water storage tanks, measuring tanks and pumps etc. are provided to supply desired quantity of water at desired time. These mixers are driven either by diesel engines or electric motors through reduction gears and reversing gears. Like other mixers these are also mounted on a chassis with 2 axle having 4 pneumatic wheels with draw bar and turn table arrangements.

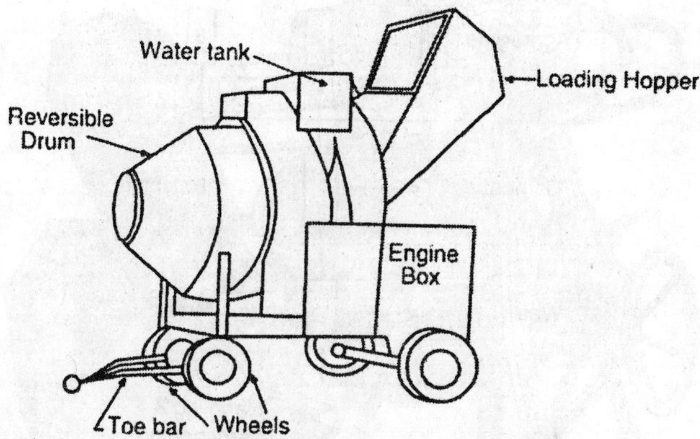

Fig. 11.3 Reversing drum mixer.

4. Roller-Pan Mixers

These mixers are primarily used fo mortar. The rollers and mixing blades rotates in a pan and not only mix the material but also produce a kneading and crushing action. The mix is discharged through a gate in the floor of the pan. The drive to the rollers and mixing blades provided by either diesel engine or electric motor (generally diesel engine) through the bevel gears.

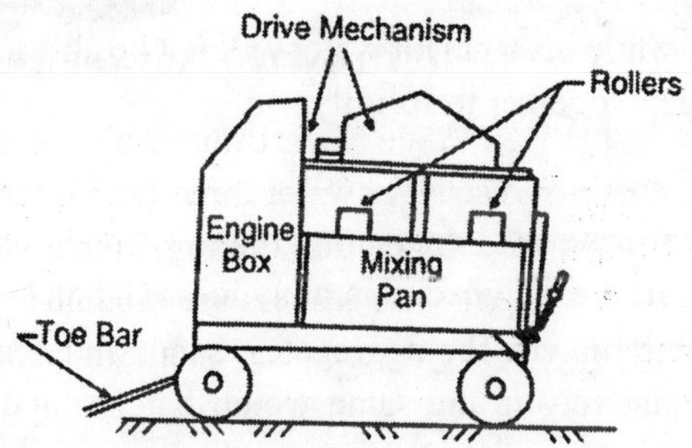

Fig. 11.4 Roller pan mixer.

11.3 Concreting

Concreting consist of the following activities :

(i) Proportioning and Batching	(iv) Placing
(ii) Mixing	(v) Compacting
(iii) Transporting	(vi) Curing

A flow diagram for concreting operation is shown in Fig. 11.5.

Concreting Design

Aggregate, cement, and water plus desired admixtures are mixed in proper proportion to produce as concrete having desired properties. Determination of this proportion is known as design of concrete mixture. The aggregates are joined together into a solid body by the solidification of a paste made of cement and water. The function of water is to hydrate the cement into solid mass and give sufficient plasticity to permit it to be formed into the desired shape. Excess water dilutes the paste and

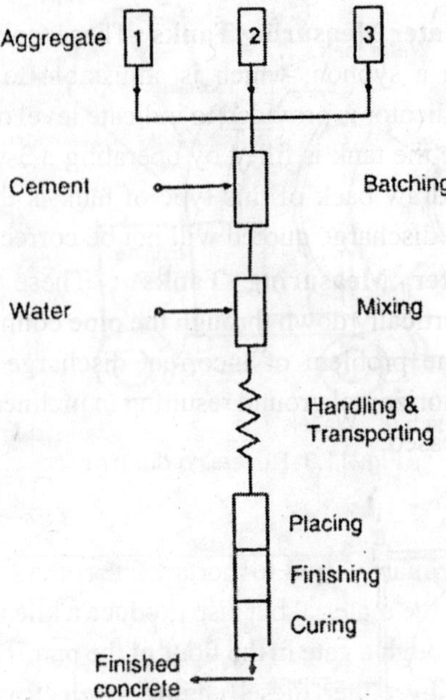

Fig. 11.5 Flow diagram for concreting.

weakens the concrete, while insufficient water will not be able to make paste to join all the particles of aggregate together to solidify.

Weigh Batchers

Ingredients of concrete *viz.,* coarse aggregates, sand, cement and water for a particular mix of concrete are weighed separately for each batch in the weight batcher.

For small concrete mixers, the aggregates, sand, and cement are weighed one after the other commulatively in the same weigh batcher and are dumped into the feeding hopper of the mixer.

For large batching plants, individual batchers are used for each ingredient. In such plants the weigh buckets are provided under the feeding hoppers of storage bins. Discharge gates, generally operated pneumatically or electrically, are at the bottom of the buckets.

Measurement of Water

Accurately measured water is required to be supplied to the mixing drum for each batch of concrete. A water tank with measuring arrangement, which can hold a required quantity of water for a batch and arrangement to deliver it at required time is provided to the concrete mixers. After each discharge this water is required to be filled again for the supply to the next batch. The filling of water in the tank should take place by the time the concrete is mixed.

Water measuring tanks are mainly of following two types :

(a) Horizontal type (b) Vertical type

(a) **Horizontal Water Measuring Tanks :** These tanks deliver the water to the mixer through a syphon, which is adjustable to regulate the discharge. Water level indicator is provided to indicate level of water in the tank. After each discharge the tank is filled by operating a 3-way valve by means of a handle. Main draw back of this type of tank is that when the tank is not horizontal, the discharge quoted will not be correct.

(b) **Vertical Water Measuring Tanks :** These has a central syphon discharging vertically down through the pipe connected to the mixer drum. This avoids the problem of incorrect discharge when the mixer is not standing on a horizontal ground resulting in inclined water discharged when the lever is pressed.

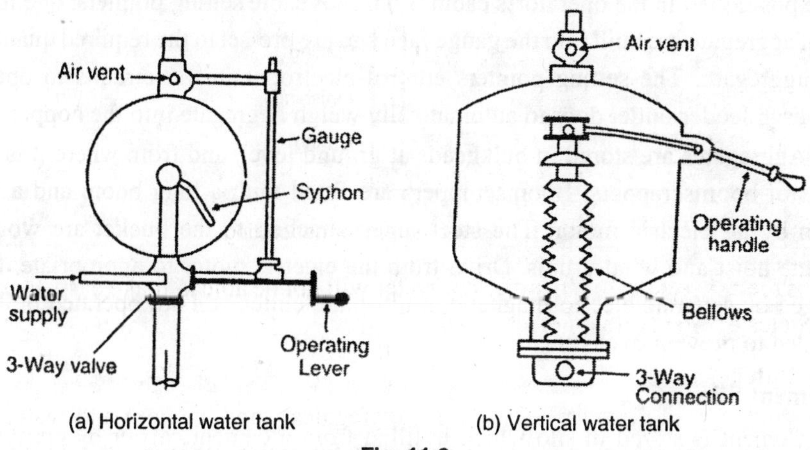

(a) Horizontal water tank (b) Vertical water tank

Fig. 11.6

11.4 Concrete Batching and Mixing Plant

As its name suggests the plant has main function of 'Batching' and then 'Mixing'. Batching means proportioning of ingredients of concrete, *viz.* : aggregates, sand, cement and water separately for each batch. Batching and mixing plants used in construction field generally consists of the following main constituents :

1. Aggregate Feeders

Separate aggregate feed bins are used for each size of the aggregate and sand, and controls their quantity. Weighing system is used for important jobs, since control by volume is not perfect as it varies due to closeness of packing of the material.

The aggregate feed bins are loaded by any of the following methods :

(a) By shovels directly into the bins.

(b) By lorries tipping directly into the bins.

Each of these aggregate feed bins are fitted with pneumatically operated outlet door. The bin for sand is provided with an electric vibrator to ensure free flow through the outlet door. Aggregate weighing is done by means of a hydraulic capsule located in

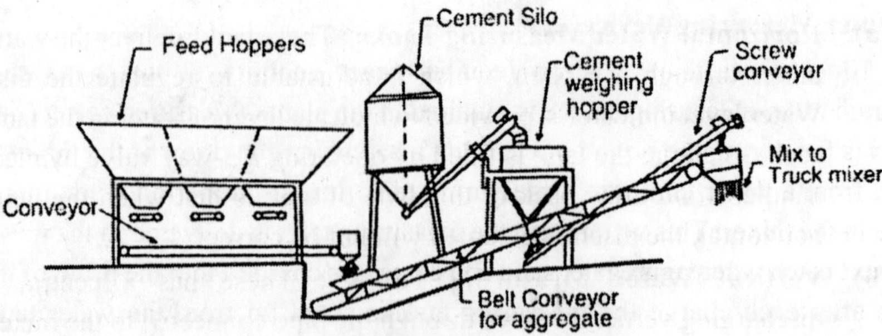

Fig. 11.7 Concrete batching and mixing plant.

the weigh frame which sense the weight of aggregate and registers on a measuring dial gauge positioned in the operator's cabin. Four moveable setting pointers, one for each size of aggregate are built into the gauge face and are pre-set to the required quantity for each aggregate. The setting pointers control electropneumatic circuits to open and close each feeder outlet door to automatically weigh aggregate into the hopper.

Aggregates are stored in bulkheads at ground level, and from where it is fed by means of boomscrappers. Boomscrappers are fitted with a long boom and a bucket driven by an electric motor. The steel ropes attached to the bucket are wound on separate hoist and wind drums. Drive from the electric motor to appropriate drum is engaged by separate electro-magnetic, multi-plate clutches. Foot operated brakes are provided to prevent over-run.

2. Cement Silo

Cement is stored in silo which is filled from a cement carrier by pumping the cement into the silo under pressure. Weigh batching is provided for measuring the quantity of cement to be fed for each batch mix. This weighed cement is carried to the mixing unit through the conveyor belts which are totally enclosed to avoid any loss.

During filling under pressure by bulk tanker, cement laden air is vented to atmosphere through a filter. Cement/air filters are generally, 'multi sock' type having number of easy-to-renew nylon socks giving mixing filteration area. These nylon socks trap cement. Access door allows inspection and cleaning when necessary. Dust from the filters falls back into the silo when the shaker device is operated from ground level controls.

Cement enters the silo through a valve provided on an inlet pipe connected either to a screw conveyor or rotary blower pressurising the pipe line, carrying cement, at about 0.4 bar. These are used to inject the cement received from either of the two sources from a bag splitting hopper, or from standing bulk cement carrier. The bag splitting hopper is of steel construction and is fitted with a bag splitting knife to cut the bag and a grill which allows cement to fall through into the hopper whilst trapping the bag and any other destruction.

3. Water Measuring Device

Since concrete production requires exact quantity of water, a reliable and accurate water measuring device is required in the plants. Measured correct quantity of water is fed during the period of charging a batch into the drum of the mixer. Water is filled from a water tank into a measuring tank during the period when mixing takes place in the mixer. This water from the measuring tank is delivered to the mixer during the next batch when aggregate, sand and cement is charged into the drum of the mixer. Thus after each charge the measuring tank is filled up from the water tank by the quantity needed for a batch for the supply to the next batch. This water from the measuring tank is supplied to the mixer, through the adjustable spray bar so as to achieve homogeneous mix within a shortest time.

4. Mixing Unit

Mixing unit consists of two parallel shafts made of cast steel provided with adjustable paddle mounted to external supports provided with bearings. The mixer discharges the mix into a hopper for delivering it to the concrete dumpers directly or into bin where the mix is stored temporarily. The mixer is then taken to the construction site. The walls of mixing units are made of wear resistant steel.

Some times pan-mixers are used in place of paddle mixers, which uses mixing blades for uniform mixing. Split drum mixers are also becoming common in batching plants.

5. Batching and Mixing Controls

Central console housed in operator's cabin has necessary electrical equipment to allow the following three methods of operation :

(a) Manual operation of the individual pushbutton enables production of single batch or test mixes.

(b) Automatic weighing, loading, mixing and discharging into the storage hopper of a single batch using only one pushbutton.

(c) Fully automatic operation producing successive or any predetermined number of batches unassisted by the operator.

11.5 Washers

We have already discussed about washing of aggregates in a barrel in the chapter on "aggregate production" here we are discussing other methods of washing the aggregates and sand.

Washing of aggregate or sand can be done in following 3 ways :

1. Screw washers
2. Spray washers
3. Rotary washers or scrubbers.

1. **Screw Washers :** Rotation of a screw washes the fine material like sand and conveys it up an inclined rectangular tub out of water. Thus these washers are used for washing, classifying and dewatering of fine aggregate or sand.

2. **Spray Washers :** In these washers, spray bars are provided over the vibrating screen. Water is sprayed at pressure over the aggregate as it passes over the screen and shakes off large portion of loose water and impurities due to vibrating action of screen.
3. **Rotary Washers or Scrubbers :** These are most effective when impurities are such which cannot be easily removed by above two methods. Vigorous scrubbing in water is an efficient and economical method of cleaning sand and gravel. Processing takes place in a rotating horizontal drum fitted internally with lifting flights. The deep bed of material in water becomes a churning mass inside the rotating drum, creating an intense grind which scrubs away dirt, clay and other adhesive from the aggregate. Caked deposits are broken down by impact as material cascades from lifters high in the drum. A constant level of material maintained in the drum maximises scrubbing action.

This system of washing have been discussed in detail in the chapter on "Aggregate Production".

The drum is lined with wear resisting rubber or steel plates. Rubber lining is highly resistant to abrasion, corrosion and noise. Scrubber drum is driven by an electric motor through a reduction gear box. Relatively low speed of the dump develops maximum scrubbing action. Scrubbed material passed from the drum for screening is simultaneously rinsed by high pressure water sprays, giving exceptionally clean product. Time spent in the drum is dependent on the feed rate. Very dirty material requiring longer treatment is fed at a slower rate compatible with condition. When the material is very dirty, a vibrating screen with water sprays removes a proportion of dirt from the feed prior to scrubbing.

11.6 Transporting the Concrete

Concrete may be handled and transported by several methods, such as truck mixers, concrete dumpers, concrete pumps, buckets handled by cranes, hoisting towers or cables, chutes, and belt conveyors. The method to be adopted is selected depending upon the conditions of work.

Selection of the method of transportation of concrete should be done in such a way that the properties of the concrete are maintained and following objections are achieved :

(a) Economy in transport.

(b) Segregation of materials of concrete is prevented.

(c) Concrete should be finally placed at the site before it starts setting.

Transfer of Concrete

Concrete can be transferred from central batching and mixing plant to the work site of mass concreting by following ways. The method can be selected considering the size of job, height and other conditions of the worksite.

1. **By Buckets :** Concrete is discharged by mixers directly into the buckets which are then either (i) hoisted to the place of dumping by cranes, or (ii) hauled over flat bed carriers to a place of work, or (iii) combination of these two, or (iv) by cableways.
2. **By Dump Trucks :** In this method, concrete is discharged directly into the dump truck body, which is then taken to the site of work. The trucks either discharge the concrete directly to the work place or into the buckets handled by cranes or cable ways.
3. **By Belt Conveyors :** In this system, belt conveyors are employed for dry mixes. Deep troughing idlers are used to prevent spillage and segregation. Concrete is first poured into buckets from conveyors and then taken to the place of work as explained in previous paragraphs.
4. **By Monorail :** Transportation of concrete for a moderate distance in large quantities can be handled by a especially constructed single track rail.
5. **Chutes :** These are made of metal with sound bottoms. These are given a slope so as to have a uniform speed of flow of all materials of concrete in order to prevent segregation. This method is used only for limited distances.
6. **Truck-Mixers :** Concrete mixed batch is transported from the batching and mixing plant to the construction site. Fully or partly mixed concrete is transported through the truck mixers. Where the construction site is far from the batching plant, entire mixing operation is carried out in a transit truck mixer during the journey.

   For a transporting the concrete mix following means are adopted :

   (a) Transit truck mixer (b) Truck agitators

   (a) Transit Truck Mixers : Dry mix material are fed into the truck mixers from a dry batching plant, after measuring the quantities of various constituents other than water, *i.e.*, aggregate, sand and cement. The transit mixers then transport it to the work site and mixes during the journey using its own water supply. These transit mixers are provided with a suitable water system having a sufficiently large water tank, a meter and a pump for supplying water for mixing and for cleaning the drum.

Fig. 11.8 Concrete truck mixer.

The mixing drum is supported on a truck chassis in such a way that it can revolve and also can be raised or lowered at one end. The size and capacity of the truck chassis is selected depending upon the capacity of the mixing drum, which is varying from 4.0 cu m to 12 cu m. For smaller capacity 2 axle chassis and for larger capacity 3 axle (1 front and 2 rear) chassis are preferred.

The mixers have mixing drum with mixing blades made of abrasion resistant and corrosion proof steel. Whereas feed chute and discharge chute are lined with wearing plates.

The drive for mixing blades is taken from the truck power take off (PTO). The mixing blades mix the material when it is rotating in one direction and discharge the material while rotating in other direction.

Fig. 11.9 Concrete truck mixer.

(b) **Truck Agitators :** Truck agitators are used solely to transport ready mixed concrete prepared by batching and mixing plants. The fully mixed concrete is kept in plastic state and saved from segregation or drying out or setting through continuous agitation of the drum of the mixer.

The main difference between the transit and agitator mixer is that the large volume of water is carried by the transit mixer which should be sufficient to mix the concrete during the transportation and also no subsequent wash-down the mixer. The agitator simply transport the ready mix to the work site and agitates the mix in order to prevent segregation or setting. Results have shown that the concrete must be delivered and discharged from the mixer within $1\frac{1}{2}$ hours from the introduction of water to the cement and aggregate.

7. **Concrete Dumpers :** Concrete dumpers are used to carry concrete mix from concrete mixer to the site of works. Concrete mixer is kept near the site at convenient place and from this place the concrete dumpers take the mix to

the exact place of work. Thus these are used for short leads only. These dumpers may be two wheel or four-wheel drive propelled by a diesel engine and has a low centre of gravity for stability even in adverse site conditions. It has a skip of various capacities generally between 750 kg to 2000 kg capable of unloading the mix either in the front or in the sides.

11.7 Concrete Pumps

Concrete is either mixed at the site itself or transported into truck mixer for placing into required position. This placing of concrete is traditionally done by the cranes, skips, dumpers or wheel barrows. Now-a-days concrete pumps (also known as pumpcrete) are used for placing the concrete accurately and in continuous flow directly from the truck mixer on the column or section of the building, tunnels, subways, underwater works etc.

The concrete pump have a boom for placing the concrete in position. The booms of various sizes are available as per requirements. The pumps capable of handling volumes upto 45 cubic metres per hour and giving vertical lifts upto 50 m and for horizontal distances upto 300 m are generally available. Concrete pumps require a good grading or materials in the concrete mix. Pumps with a maximum output of 150 m^3/hr and with maximum pressure of 200 bar are available in the market.

In the concrete pump, pumping is done by means of 2 parallel long stroke cylinder system. These pumps are basically reciprocating pumps having two cylinders so as to maintain continuity. Pumping cylinder dia go from 150 upto 230 mm and strokes from 500 upto 2000 mm. Each cylinder is hardened and connected to

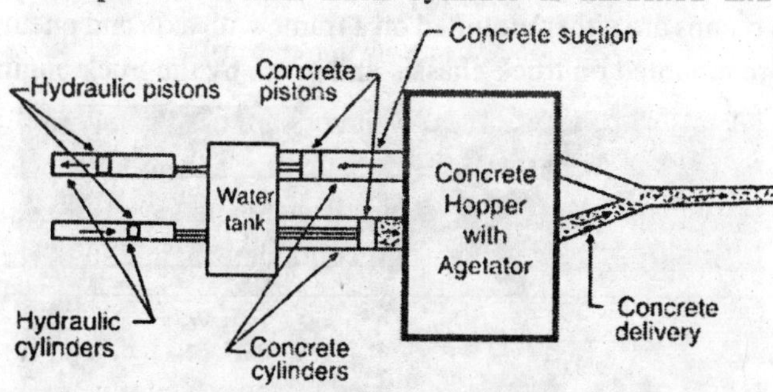

(a) Concrete pump with dual cylinders

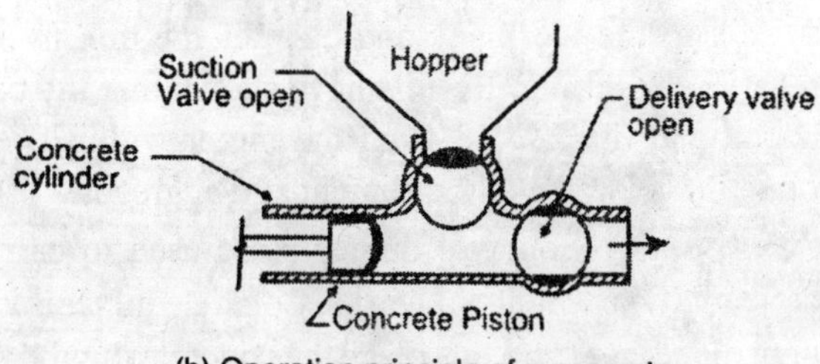

(b) Operation principle of pumpcrete

Fig. 11.10

distribution pipe. Each cylinder system has two valves one on the suction side located at the bottom of the hopper and the other on the discharge side, controlling the concrete entering to the distribution pipe. The opening and closing of the valve is timed with respect to the movement of the piston, *i.e.*, in suction stroke when piston is moving away from the hopper side the concrete enters by gravity, suction valve is opened and discharge valve is closed; and while piston is coming closer to the hopper side, suction valve closes and discharge valve opens and the piston forces concrete into distribution pipe. The two cylinders are timed in such a way so that when one cylinder has suction another has discharge stroke. Thus the flow of concrete from pump to work place remain continuous. An overhead hopper is provided with agitator blade so as to enable feed of homogeneous mix of concrete into pump suction.

During pumping care should be taken that :

(i) all joints should be tightened.

(ii) concrete level in the hopper is never allowed to fall below the neck level.

(iii) at the time of starting nearly 0.5 cu m of grout should be fed to the pump, as cement mortar works as a lubricant in the pump.

(iv) at the end of day's work, inside of the pump and the pipe line should be cleaned.

Concrete pumps are either powered by the engine of the trucks on which they are mounted or by a separate diesel engine or electric motors. The drive to the piston is hydraulically controlled.

Largest manufactured concrete pump powered by a 400 kW engine was used for pumping concrete upto 432 m vertically.

Concrete pumps are either mounted on a frame with axle and pneumatic tyres and are towed, or are mounted on truck chassis and given by the truck engine.

Fig. 11.11 ELBA truck mixer combined with concrete pump and concrete distributor boom.

For selecting a pump, engineer should know the maximum output, Q_{max} and also the maximum pressure, p_{max}. Q_{max} and p_{max} can not be achieved simultaneously, as in this case required power would be just too much. At a certain power P the production is Q depending on the displacing pressure p which again depends on the resistance.

$$Q = \frac{P}{p}$$

or $$P = Q \times p = \text{Constant.}$$

Therefore at a certain and fully utilised power, the production of a pump will decrease when the pressure increases.

As stated earlier pressure p, depends on the resistance, which ultimately is dependent on following :

(a) Length of pipe line and vertical head.

(b) Stiffness and richness of a mix.

11.7.1 Pumping the Concrete

By using the different types of pumps, concreting can be placed in different circumstances. The pump configurations suitable in different circumstances are discussed hereunder :

1. **Pump with a Pipe :** In this configuration pipe line is assembled and connected to the pump before the pumping operation begins. The pipeline is laid from the pump location to the concrete casting area, where the pump is located such that the ready-mixed concrete trucks have the easy access to it. Where the concrete is placed in more than one locations, several pipelines can be stretched from the pump, thus saving the relocation of the pipeline has a flexible rubber pipe of about 3 to 10 m length connected to it for better control of the concrete discharge location and for earlier handling.
2. **Pump with Boom :** In this configuration the pump is mounted on a truck and equipment with a evolving boom to which a fixed-length delivery line is connected. Similar to the earlier configuration, here too the free end of the line has a flexible pipe (hose) of about 3 m length is connected to it. In these, hydraulically operated and articulated booms of 25 to 40 m length are commonly used. In the truck-mounted pumps these are generally available in three to five sections.
3. **Pump with Pipeline and Tower-Mounted Boom :** This configuration combines the elements of both the earlier systems. In this system, the stationary/trailer pump is at the concrete-loading end, a separate boom at the concrete-placing end, and a pipeline running from the pump to the boom. The high rise structures which are beyond the reach of a boom pump, are provided with this type of configuration. The boom, similar to that used in hydraulic articulated placing boom in the boom pump, is mounted on a tower (mast).

Concrete transportation and placement, through concrete pumping should be considered mainly in construction projects requiring heavy concreting like; bridges, retaining walls, dams, raft foundation, high-rise buildings, etc. These are also used at sites with accessibility limitations such as :

(a) difficult site conditions, rough terrain, or muddy ground,

(b) physical obstructions like ponds,

(c) no vehicular access is possible etc.

11.7.2 Concreting Pump Applications

As concrete pumps have high placing rates, work convenience and the ability to deliver the concrete while bypassing project site obstructions. The concrete pumping should be considered for on site concrete transportation and placing mainly in the following cases and types of projects :

1. Projects where concrete is main material to be transported like bridges, retaining walls, and other concrete structures.
2. Large concrete structural elements like dam and raft foundation construction. In exceptionally large concrete volume placements, more than one pumps are used simultaneously.
3. Sites having accessibility limitations *e.g.*,
   (a) difficult on-site conditions, rough terrain, muddy ground and obstruction by water bodies.
   (b) sites where vehicular access is not possible, and
   (c) any other obstruction.
4. Projects where large productivity is required which is not possible with other means.

11.8 Placing of Concrete

Concrete should be placed as near as possible to its final position, which may be any building, underground or overground or any other construction site. While placing the concrete care should be taken to prevent separation of coarse aggregate from the concrete. During placing operation the heavier materials tend to settle and the lighter materials tend to rise towards the top. The separation of the aggregate from the concrete generally occurs at the ends of chutes and conveyor belts, at hopper gates, and during transportation.

It is also necessary to avoid the entrapment of air in the concrete. The placing work should proceed from the corners and ends towards the centre. The batching, mixing, transporting and placing must be done in such a way that work of concrete placing is continued without interruptions.

The placing can be done by using chutes, buckets, pumps or belt conveyors. It large scale concreting, placing is generally done by means of concrete distributor booms. The booms of different reaches between 10 to 40 metres and dia 125 or 250 mm are generally available. The booms of large reaches are mounted onto the turntable of tower cranes by means of a special frame.

Placing Boom Sections

Increasing the number of boom sections, reduces the length of the vehicle (on which it is mounted) movement on the road and makes it easier to unfold the boom around site obstructions and reach into inaccesible corners. It is also capable to eliminate dead areas where the boom can not reach, or can not safely operate.

Placing of Concrete in Cold or Hot Weather

Concrete should be placed between 5°C to 28°C. Lower temperature reduces the rate of setting, while higher temperature reduces the ultimate strength. For placing the concrete in cold weather, water is preheated for providing the required temperature as it will ensure an early setting and gain in strength. Freshly laid concrete shall be maintained at a temperature of not loss than 20˜C for 3 days or 10°C for 5 days after it is placed.

For placing the concrete in hot weather, the concrete is required to be precooled to keep it within prescribed range. This can be achieved by installing an ice-manufacturing plant near the concrete-mixing plant. Flacked ice is added to the concrete as part of the water.

Placing the Concrete in Water

For placing the concrete in the water, pipe long enough to reach the bottom of the water should be used. The bottom of this pipe should be kept continuously below the surface of the concrete so that the fresh concrete do not come in direct contact with water.

For the construction of deep foundations, dams, bridges etc. concrete can be placed under water either by Tremie or by Buckets.

(a) Placing of Concrete by Tremie : A water tight pipe of 25 cm to 40 cm diameter is extended from the level of working platform to the lowest point where concrete is to be laid. Concrete is poured through a hopper fixed at the top of this pipe. The tremie is raised gradually while concreting proceeds. The bottom end of the trimie is to be kept inside the freshly laid concrete to prevent the entry of water into the trimie pipe.

(b) Placing of Concrete by Buckets : A bucket with open top and collapsible bottom shutter is used for concreting at a considerable depth. Fresh concrete is filled up in the bucket and the top of the bucket is covered with canvas to protect from water. The bucket is then lowered to the desired depth and the bottom shutter is removed to deposit the concrete. The bucket is then withdrawn. Lowering and lifting of bucket is carried out by crane.

11.9 Consolidation by Concrete Vibrators

Concrete normally contain large quantity of voids when placed. The purpose of consolidation is to remove these entrapped air voids, as entrapped air can render the concrete totally unsatisfactory. Consolidation is normally achieved through the use of mechanical vibrators. Only in case of very small/thin wet concrete mixtures is consolidated by hand tools. Properly vibrated concrete is higher-quality concrete, mainly in terms of strength, but also in terms of reinforcement protection, resistance to aggressive agents, and overall appearance. Consolidation is sometimes also known as compaction.

For compacting the concrete after its placement, concrete vibrators are used. With the help of these vibrators it has become possible to place large volume of concrete quickly and easily particularly in intricate positions. The vibrators help in producing concrete of higher density by reducing air voids in the concrete. The concrete thus produced has better resistance to the seepage and gives better strength.

Concrete vibrators of following two types are generally used for construction purposes :

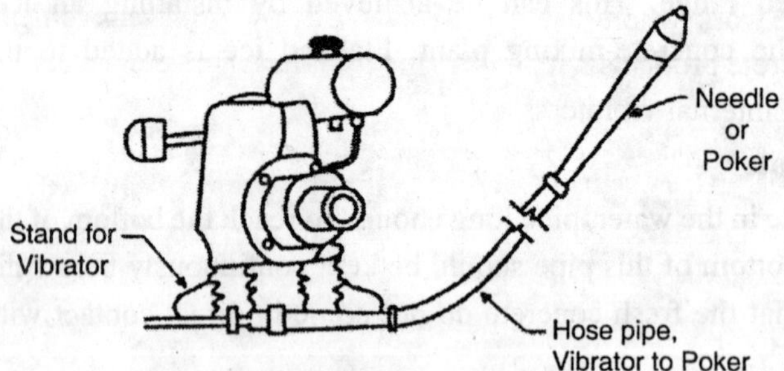

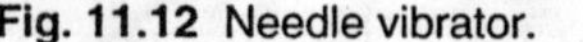
Fig. 11.12 Needle vibrator.

Fig. 11.13 Surface vibrator.

(i) Internal Vibrators

These are also known as immersion, needle or poker vibrators. These are immersed in the freshly placed concrete and it vibrates the concrete while in immersed position. Generally vibrators with 10,000 to 15,000 vibrations per min. at amplitudes between 0.8 mm to 1.6 mm are available for providing rapid and reliable compaction. The pokes of size 25 mm to 60 mm in dia are commonly used. These vibrators can be lifted and can be placed manually near the work place.

The vibrators are driven by diesel engine, compressed air or electric motors. Pneumatic vibrators are lighter and easy to handle, when compressed air or electricity is not available at work site diesel engine driven vibrators are used.

These vibrators have a flexible shaft, which gets its drive from the engine, and is enclosed in a hose. The shaft produces vibrations in the needle through an eccentric. Care should be taken that while using it, avoid bending of the flexible hose through small radii.

Fig. 11.14 Pocker vibrator.

(ii) External Vibrators

These are also known as surface or platform vibrators. External vibrators are placed on the surface of the concrete through which vibrations are conveyed to the interior. These are generally used in construction of pavements, canal linings and various types of precast work where use of internal vibrator is not convenient, for example, long post, concrete products with mesh type reinforcement etc. where lack of space restricts the use of internal vibrators.

Fig. 11.15 Surface (platform) vibrator.

The surface vibrators consist of a rectangular pan, which is placed on the surface of concrete to be compacted. The driving unit which may be either an engine or an electric motor, is mounted above the vibrator and is carried on antivibration springs. The power is supplied to the vibrator, securely fixed to the pan. The effective depth of compaction by these vibrators vary from 20 cm to 30 cm. These vibrators have frequency generally from 3000 to 4000 vibrations per min at an amplitude of 0.4 mm to 0.5 mm.

11.10 Curing of Concrete

To attain its maximum strength and other desirable properties, concrete should be cured with adequate moisture and at a favourable temperature between 5°C to 28°C. The loss of moisture due to evaporation is accomplished by keeping the surface wet. Placing of concrete at lower temperature reduces the rate of setting while higher temperature reduces the ultimate strength.

If efficient curing is done, either by preventing evaporation or by keeping the surface of the concrete continuously wet, the strength of the concrete increases with the passage of time. This increase in strength is rapid in initial stages. Curing also increases the impermeability, durability of concrete, and resistance to abrasion. This also helps in achieving a hard dense surface and prevent cracking.

Heat is generated by concrete during its setting and curing is done to extract heat. Amount of heat generation per cu m depends on quality and quantity of cement used in the concrete. In small works since placement is at a slow rate the heat is lost mainly through convection and radiation. Now-a-days with the latest developments since high rate of placement is possible, therefore cooling of concrete becomes essential specially where mass concreting is done.

In order to place the concrete within its most effective temperature range, cooling of various ingredient like cement, sand, aggregate and water becomes essential. Use of flaked ice has become popular in lowering down the concrete temperature. Some of the methods for cooling in mass concreting are :

(a) **Coarse Aggregate Cooling :** Coarse aggregate can be cooled either at the stockpile or on the conveyor by evaporation of controlled amount of water sprayed on it. The aggregate can be cooled by the blast of cold air injected near the bottom of bins and passed upwards through the aggregate.

(b) **Cement Cooling :** Cement is cooled by chilled water by circulating it through the flies. The temperature of cement leaving the cooler is maintained at required level.

(c) **Sand Cooling :** Cool brine of about minus 7°C is circulated through the sand cooler in sufficient quality to cool the sand leaving the cooler before it is fed to the batching plant.

(d) **Water Chilling :** Water used for making concrete mix is cooled to temperature between 1°C to 5°C.

(e) **Ice Making and Storage :** Ice for this purpose is manufactured in a crystalline form with a consistency very similar to snow. Ice is manufactured at ground lever and then elevated to a refrigerated storage bin. This ice is fed to the weigh batcher by means of a screw conveyors.

The aggregates, sand and cement are pre-cooled and chilled water is used during mixing at the mixers in the concrete batching and mixing plant supplement with ice, during hot weather. Some times cooling is done for aggregates only, while cement and sand are not cooled.

11.11 Shotcreting (Guniting)

Shotcreting is concrete (or mortar) conveyed pneumatically through a hose and projected at high velocity on to a surface. The force of the concrete impacting on the surface compacts the mixture. It, being relatively dry mixture, support itself without sagging or sloughing, even for vertical and overhead applications. It is commonly used for repair work, thin layers or fiber-reinforced concrete layers.

Shotcreting is also commonly known as Guniting.

Guniting is the process of conveying desired mixture of dry cement and sand through a hole and depositing the same on the surface to be treated under pressure with just sufficient quantity of water for hydration.

The material deposited by this process is called GUNITEE. In this process, the mixture of cement and sand is conveyed by compressed air at high velocity ranging from about 30 metres/sec at hose entrance to about 100 metres/sec at the nozzle tip. Before leaving the nozzle, the mix instantaneously hydrated in the central chamber where water is supplied under pressure from a pressurised water tank. The hydrated mix is then shot on the surface to be treated.

Application

Guniting is used in various places, some of them are :

(i) Renovation of plain or RCC structures deteriorated due to weather, bad workmanship etc.

(ii) Strengthening of old structures.

(iii) Lining of water reservoir, canals, etc.

(iv) Water-proofing on the surface which directly comes in contact with water.

(v) Removal of leakage with rich cement mix after Guniting is done in leaking surfaces.

(vi) For protection of exposed pre-stressed wires in structures like water towers, chimneys, concrete pipes etc.

Guniting Equipment

Guniting equipment consists of three items namely, Gun; twin water tanks; and placing nozzle with accessories.

The Gun consists of two conical shaped buckets connected one above the other and each having a compressed air inlet. One cone valve is provided at the junction of these two to connect or disconnect both these vessels (buckets) with each other. At the top of the upper vessel a hopper is provided for feeding sand cement mix. A valve is also provided between this hopper and the upper vessel. The material is continuously fed to the material outlets to carry further to the nozzle via a pressure hose pipe from air compressor. An air compressor of required size is required for this purpose (generally 260 c.f.m. at 7 kg/cm^2).

Two tanks of water connected with each other through pipes having valves are mounted to a trolly. These can be pressurised by compressed air, alternately, *i.e.*, when one is being filled with water other is pressurised. Water under pressure is thus supplied to the nozzle through a hose pipe. When this water tank is emptied the first tank supplies water and this one is filled so that the process is not interrupted.

Placing nozzle is made of gun metal. The water hose pipe from pressurised tank is connected to a nipple, which is further connected to a nozzle body through a regulating valve. Water goes into central chamber, where it hydrates the sand-cement mix coming through material hose pipe and instantaneously forced out through the nozzle, and is deposited on the surfaces to be treated.

Working Procedure

The surface to be Gunited should be cleaned off all loose and foreign materials. If required, the surface should be chiselled or sand blasted to make it rough to receive Gunit. Rust or scale on reinforcing steel must also be cleared off.

Cement and sand is mixed in required proportion. About 5% of water is also added to make the mixture damp to avoid segregation of cement and sand during pneumatic conveying. When quick setting action is desired additives are added for fast setting. Powdered iron, *i.e.*, 'Ironite' can be added to the mix for water-proofing purposes.

The hopper is filled with cement-sand mix keeping the bottom valve closed. Keeping the bottom cone valve closed, air is supplied in the lower vessel. Top cone is opened and mix is then allowed to fall in upper bucket. Now top cone valve is closed and air pressure in both the vessels become same. The bottom cone valve is opened and material slides down in the lower vessel. The air from upper vessel is exhausted out and air exhaust valve is closed.

The feed wheel now feed the material to the material hose pipe which is connected to the nozzle end. Air is supplied to the material hose pipe at gun end by opening the concerned valve, at the signal of the nozzle man. The material then instantaneuosly mixes with water in the nozzle and is sprayed out on the surface to be treated.

Basically Gunites are of two types : high velocity and low velocity Gunites, (i) high velocity gunite is produced by using a small nozzle and high pressure air, resulting in impact velocities of 90 to 120 m/sec. This results in high compaction but low placement, (ii) for low velocity gunite, a wide nozzle with large output machine is used. Though such a gunite is not as well compacted as high velocity gunite, still with low water cement ratio and high cement content, adequate in-situ compaction can be achieved.

It has been observed that for a mix of 1 : 4 about 10% rebound occurs, leaving in-situ mix of 1 : 3.7. Thus the in-situ mix will always be richer than the mix adopted for guniting work. Charts must therefore be developed by the users, for co-relating the initial mix with the resultant in-situ mix and expected 28 days strength.

Care in Guniting

(i) All surfaces must be cleaned before guniting.

(ii) Air operating pressure at gun outlet should be more than 240 kN/m^2.

(iii) Nozzle should be held at right angle and at 0.6 m to 1.2 m from the receiving surface.

(iv) Vertical surface should be worked from bottom up.

(v) Rebound material should not be used.

(vi) Mix should not be used after more than one hour of mixing.

(vii) Adequate curing is necessary.

(viii) All rebound and sand pockets should be cut out and made good during course of work.

Advantages

The Guniting offers following advantage over ordinary concretes :

(i) Specific gravity of gunited concrete is about 2.16 to 2.18, which is much higher than any concrete done by any other method. It is very near to the theoretically perfect dense concrete.

(ii) Gunited concrete makes a perfect bond between the concrete and masonry surfaces.

(iii) Gunited concrete is more resistant to weather and chemical action than ordinary concrete.

11.12 Grouting and Grouting Equipment

Grouting is an engineering and art combined to fill up to the voids or cavities in rock or soil masses with a fluid that will increase the overall strength and/or impermeability of the mass. The type of grout to be used and general conditions of work are decided on the basis of type of work involved. The success of grouting greatly depend on the experience and skill of workmen. Cement, water, sand, pozzolana, clay, bentonlite and other special purpose materials are used to different proportions based on the type and place of work where grouting is required to be done.

Grouts are proportioned, so that they may be pumpable and be able to penetrate the material into which it is pumped. After it is in place, it must harden to a stable condition and provide strength and/or impermeability. Therefore, proportioning must be depending upon the type of void to be filled, *e.g.*, fine seams or cracks in rock under dam or associated structures; precision grouting like grouting under machinery where precise alignment is required etc.

In many cases rock deposits contain cavities, slips, seams, breaks etc., which make then unsuitable for dams, reservoirs, buildings, bridge piers, tunnels etc. In such cases it becomes necessary to adopt corrective steps to make the foundation suitable for the intended use. If correction is impossible or too expensive, then it is necessary to abandon the site. The operation to correct the foundation conditions is known as pressure grouting. The foundation under or adjacent to a structure is grouted with the object,

(i) to solidify and strengthen the formation in order to increase its capacity to support a load.

(ii) to reduce or eliminate the flow of water under a dam or into a tunnel.

(iii) to reduce the hydrostatic uplift under a dam.

Grout Mixing

For volume work, weight batching with conventional equipment is adopted, but for general purpose ordinary works, hand handling or whole sacks of cement and cubic foot boxes of sand is generally accepted for proportioning.

Mixing for large-volume work is generally done in horizontal drum mixers with paddles of rubber tips to sweep the walls of the drum. The drums are available in sizes of the 1 to 5 cubic-metre depending upon the requirement of work. The materials in desired quantities are added and mixed for some time depending upon the properties of the ingredients. The mixed grout is then delivered to the funnel of the pump.

The grouts should be screened as they leave the mixer to protect the pump from stones, pieces of wood etc. and to safeguard against premature choking of the seems or cracks in the rock or voids in the granular materials. For thin grouts containing only cement and/or clays a 5 mm screen resisting on a funnel attached to the pump intake is sufficient, while for thicker grouts including those containing sand, a 10 mm or 12 mm heavy wire screen is suitable. It is necessary to clear of the screening regularly. For volume work these screens,should be mounted on an agitator.

Grout Pumping

The grout pumps are generally piston-displacement type. These pumps are provided with case hardened steel cylinders, rubber piston heads, and rubber valves and/or valve seats. The pump can easily be disassembled for thorough and frequent cleaning purposes.

Application

Grouting is essential for making foundations, mine shafts, tunnels etc. compact and strong enough to prevent settlement and seepage and to reduce hydrostatic uplift to avoid possibilities of damages in future. The grouting precedes construction works like dams, bridges etc. as well as it is also carried out during their construction and post-construction periods.

Materials used for Grout :

Commonly used materials for grouting are :

(i) Cement and water.

(ii) Cement, rock flour and water.

(iii) Cement, clay and water.

(iv) Cement, clay, sand and water.

(v) Asphalt.

(vi) Clay and water.

(vii) Chemicals.

Cement and water is injected into fine seams. Rock flour and clay is added to the cement grout to achieve economy if the seams are small, while the sand is added if the seams are large enough to permit the sand to penetrate.

If a formation contains fissures with water flowing through them, the velocity of water tends to sweep the grout through the openings, with solidifications, the injection of asphalt grout in such cases seals the fissures and stops or reduces the flow of water. When the flow of water is stopped, cement grout is injected.

Clay grouting produces high resistances to the flow of water and makes it an excellent barrier to water seepage. Chemical grouting, being a liquid, can be pumped into through very small openings and requires less setting time. Sodium silicate and cacium chloride are more popular chemicals used for purpose.

Admixtures

Following are the common admixtures used with cement grout :

1. Calcium chloride 2. Sodium hydroxide 3. Sodium silicate	— For accelerating setting time
4. Gypsum 5. Lime sugar 6. Sodium tannate	— For retarding setting time
7. Fine bentonite 8. Clay	— For increasing plasticity and reducing grout shrinkage
9. Grout shale 10. Rock flour	— For reducing cost of grout and reduces strength of grout

Cement Grouting Equipment

Cement grouting equipment includes :

1. Air compressor.
2. Grout mixers.
3. Agitator type reservoir tank.
4. Grout pumps.
5. Grout discharge pipe or hose, valves, pressure gauges etc.

The grout mixer is having a shaft with paddles, mixes the grout and discharges into a tank having an agitator to prevent separation of solids from the agitator tank and discharges into the grout hole through a pipe, a rubber hose having valves.

Cement grout is injected by piston type pumps to produce necessary pressure. These pumps are generally air driven duplex double-acting type. The number of strokes per minute and the pressure of the grout can be varied by regulating the quantity of compressed air supplied by the air compressor to the pumps.

Drilling Injection Holes

Holes for the injection of grout are drilled with jackhammers, wagon drills or diamond drills, depending on the terrain, class of foundation material, and size and depth of holes. Diamond drills usually give holes of uniform shape, while wagon drills are satisfactory for holes upto about 10 meters depth.

Washing and Grouting the Seams

Preparations for washing or grouting seams, consists of installing a section of pipe of about 35 to 50 mm dia and 0.50 to 1.0 meters long in the grout hole with the top end projecting out a short distance for connection to an air line or a pump. For grouting the seams with neat cement for consolidation purposes, it is desirable to deposit the cement in clean seams by removing any clay or any other unwanted materials. For this cleaning effective method is to force a mixture of air and water through the seams.

For deciding the pressure for grouting operation, most common practice is to use a pressure 0.2 kg/cm^2 for each meter of depth of hole.

11.13 Safety Precautions

11.13.1 Concrete Mixing (Batching) Plants

1. All gears, chains and rollers of mixers shall be properly guarded.
2. If the mixer has a charging skip the operator shall ensure that the workmen are out of danger before the skip is lowered. Railings shall be provided on the ground to prevent anyone walking under the skip while it is being lowered.
3. All cables, clamps, hooks, wire ropes, gears and clutches, etc., of the mixer, shall be checked and shall be cleaned, oiled and greased and serviced once a week. A trail run of the mixer shall be made and defects shall be removed before operating a mixer.
4. When workmen are cleaning the inside of the drums, the operating power of the mixer shall be locked in the off position and all fuses shall be removed and suitable notice hung at the place.
5. Hoppers into which a person could fall and revolving plates of through or batch type mixers should be adequately guarded by grating.
6. When dry ingredients of concrete are being mixed in confined spaces : (i) the dust shall be exhausted at the time of such mixing; and (ii) in case the dust can not be exhausted, the workers should wear respirators at the time of such mixing.
7. All the precautions as mentioned in Section 11.2.

11.13.2 Concrete Vibrators

1. Vibrating unit shall be completely enclosed and belt transmitting the power to the unit adequately guarded.

2. Vibrating needles of poker type vibrator shall be completely sealed against concrete.
3. Electrically operated compactor vibrator shall be totally enclosed units.
4. Air-operated type vibrators shall have arrangements to change the speed of rotating shaft and air motor to rotate the vibrating needle, which shall be completely sealed against concrete.
5. Power operated vibrators shall be provided with effective means of stopping the vibrator (if possible by disengaging the vibrator from the engine/motor drive).
6. Where possible, the vibrators shall be fitted with shock absorbing handles with rubber or other suitable grips for ease in handling.
7. Electrically operated vibrators shall be protected against overloads by suitable overload relays and shall be effectively earthed and where the operator has to be in direct contact with the vibrator during its operations, low voltage drive with suitable transformer is recommended.
8. While starting the poker vibrators, the needle shall not be resting on a hard surface to avoid bouncing. The poker should be completely inside the concrete when the vibrator is started.
9. Excessive bending of the flexible shafts of the poker vibrators while in operation shall be avoided.

11.13.3 Concrete Pumps

1. No pipe coupling should be removed until the pressure has been released by reverse pumping.
2. Compressed-air cleaning of pumping lines is more hazardous than high-pressure water cleaning. It should only the carried out under the supervision of an experienced person, with all instructions and precautions followed.
3. The rubber hose lines should be handled firmly with more care, as due to heavy weight combined with flexibility their control may be lost and it can whiplash.
4. On restricted sites, boom pumps must be positioned such that the boom does not hit nearby structures and other obstructions when slewed and it should also be ensured that no people is trapped by the boom.
5. Outrigger-stabilized boom pumps should be positioned on firm and horizontal ground and not too close to excavations or man holes.

QUESTIONS

1. Explain the methods usually adopted to compact concrete at site and discuss their merits.
2. Discuss the methods of transporting the cement concrete from the site of mixing to the site of placement.

3. Describe different methods of placing the concretes.
4. Discuss methods of curing the concrete.
5. What is under water concreting? Explain in detail.
6. What is transit mixer? Where will you recommend its use?
7. Write a note on concrete batching equipment (plant).
8. Explain the need of 'compaction of concrete', and describe various methods commonly used for the same.
9. Give a brief account of equipment used for handling and transporting concrete. State their merits and demerits.
10. What is 'Guniting'? Discuss its procedure, application, and equipment.
11. Write an essay an 'shotcrete'.
12. Compare the tilting and non-tilting type concrete mixers.
13. Describe construction and working of concrete pumps.
14. Give the characteristics of the pumpable concrete.
15. Describe different types of concrete vibrators.
16. Describe construction and working of truck mixers.
17. Discuss the advantages of pump transportation of concrete.
18. Describe the procedure for concreting.
19. Write short notes on :
    (a) truck agitators,
    (b) washing of aggregate and sand,
    (c) reversing drum type concrete mixer,
    (d) concrete placing boom.
20. Explain the procedure for placing of concrete in cold, and hot weather.

Chapter **12**

Asphalt Mixing and Laying Equipment

12.1 Introduction

The asphalt plants are used to prepare asphalt. Asphalt is a mixture of bitumen and inert mineral matter and is utilised in the construction of

(i) bitumen macadam or bitumen base course, and

(ii) surface courses including binder course and wearing course.

1. **Bitumen macadam** is an open graded asphalt mix using coarse aggregate bound together with bitumen. Bitumen may be incorporated in macadam construction either by penetration or by mixing. Now a days bitumen bound bases are becoming more popular over other types of base courses. Experience has proved that bitumen bound bases are stronger and more economical than conventional bases due to more life. **Bitumen bound bases** are found to be useful, where;
   (a) the saving in thickness in the construction of new roads such as National Highways, Express Highways etc., to carry heavy traffic, where large base thickness are specified;
   (b) overlays to upgrade existing bitumen and cement concrete roads to carry heavy traffic;
   (c) high quality final riding surface is required; and
   (d) speed of construction is required to be fast due to traffic hold ups.

2. **Surface course** is subjected to the heaviest stresses caused by traffic loads, and is usually the most expensive. Main ***functions of the surface course*** are :
   (a) to provide a water proof, anti skid and smooth riding surface over the base course;
   (b) to provide a surface resistant to weathering, and abrasion caused by traffic; and
   (c) to provide a resilient and flexible structural layer resistant to traffic stresses which it further distributes over the base course.

Following are the main *types of bituminous surface courses* :

(i) Surface dressing

(ii) Penetration methods

(iii) Cold mix } Also known as pre-mix

(iv) Hot mix }

(a) **Surface dressing** is the application on pavement of a thin layer of bitumen followed by a covering of stone chippings or course sand, which is then lightly rolled. This is suitable for light traffic.

(b) **Penetration method** consists of applying bitumen to a compacted layer of coarse aggregate to bind the stones together. This is suitable for medium traffic.

(c) **Pre-mix :** Cold mix and hot mix are also known as pre-mix and includes bitumen macadam.

Advantages of pre-mix : Following are the main advantages of pre-mix :

(i) Uniform coating of aggregate with bitumen, thereby ensuring an efficient use of bitumen and aggregate.

(ii) Easier quality control.

(iii) Controlled dimensions of bitumen/aggregate.

(iv) Better compaction.

(v) Suitable for mass production.

Technical Terms

Some of the important terms related to asphalt equipment and construction processes are :

1. **Asphalt Concrete :** It is an asphalt paving material prepared in a hot mix plant and used for construction of highway, parking lot, or airfield pavements.
2. **Binder :** Binder is an asphalt cement material in a paving mix used to bind the aggregate particles together, to prevent the entrance of moisture, and to act as a cushioning agent.
3. **Leveling Course :** It is a new layer of asphalt mix placed over a distressed roadway to improve its geometry prior to resurfacing.
4. **Subgrade Course :** It means prepared and compacted soil immediately below the pavement system and extending by such depths as will affect the structural design.
5. **Pavement :** Pavement means the combined wearing, levelling course (if any), binder course (if any), base course and sub-base course (if any) considered as a single unit of pavement.
6. **Sub-Base :** It means one layer or more of specified or selected material of designed thickness, placed over the subgrade.

7. **Granular Base :** Granular or aggregate base course means one layer or more of selected granular material used in the pavement system as foundation of the asphalt concrete courses.
8. **Base Course :** Base course means the lower asphalt concrete course of variable thickness used in the pavement system.
9. **Binder Course :** It means the asphalt concrete course used in the pavement system between the base and wearing course.
10. **Wearing Course :** It means that asphalt concrete course used in the pavement system which will constitute the finished road surface.
11. **Prime Cost :** The bituminous material which is applied to the existing surface of granular base course.
12. **Tack Cost :** The bituminous material which is applied to the prepared course to provide bond for the superimposed asphalt concrete course.

12.2 Flexible Pavements

Asphalt binders offer great flexibility co construct pavements according to the requirements of the local situation. Material selection and construction process vary depending upon the type of pavement. The pavements are constructed in layers as shown in Fig. 12.1. The structure consists of a prepared subgrade, an aggregate sub-base, an aggregate base, and as asphalt-bound surface layer. The asphalt surface layer consists of two courses, the binder course and the surface wearing course.

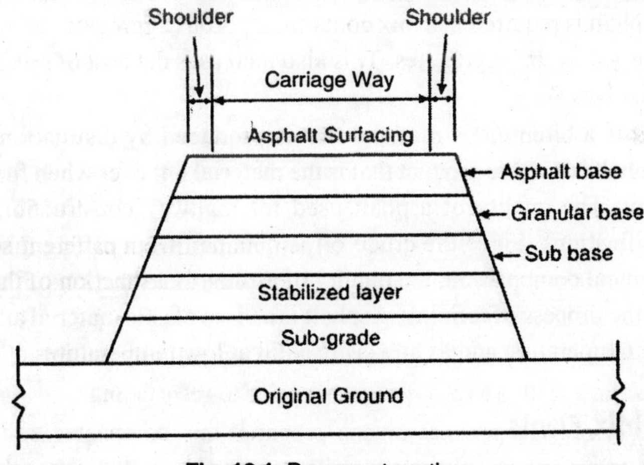

Fig. 12.1 Pavement section.

The aggregate characteristics and amount of asphalt are designed specifically to match the needs of the binder and surfacing courses. The aggregates and binder are heated and mixed to produce the hot mix asphalt concrete. The mix is placed at high temperature.

The pavement structures are used in many traffic situations and the method of their construction is discussed in subsequent sections of the chapter. To meet the needs of increased traffic demands (higher wheel loadings), there is a practice to replace the base and sub-base layers with asphalt-bound materials. The two base materials can be proportioned and mixed in many ways to produce a pavement surface suitable to the desired conditions.

Objectives of Pavements

Pavements are designed to meet the following objectives :

1. Support the axle loads imposed by the traffic and resist the kneading action of wheel rotation.
2. Protect the base and sub-base from moisture.
3. Provide a stable, smooth and skid resistant riding surface.
4. Resist weathering effects, *i.e.*, effects of moisture, heat and cold.
5. Provide economy including fuel efficiency of the vehicles.

The aggregates and asphalt binder is blended so as to achieve a final product that satisfies all these objectives.

The load imposed by the traffic to an asphalt pavement is primarily carried by the aggregates in the mix, which accounts for 90 to 95% of the material by weight. Good quality of aggregates and their proper gradation is important to the performance of the mix. Besides gradation, the aggregate properties of cleanliness, resistance to wear and abrasion, texture and porosity are also important. Here cleanliness means absence of foreign matter, whether soil or organic matter as it reduces the load-carrying capacity of the pavement. Porosity of an aggregate affects the amount of asphalt required in a mix. More asphalt is required in a mix containing porous aggregates to make up for that which is absorbed by the aggregates. This also increases the cost of mix and reduce the ability of resist wear.

Asphalt is a bituminous material that is produced by distillation of petroleum crude oil. Asphalt is a waste product that is the material left over when fuels is extracted from crude oil. The quality of asphalt used for highway construction is controlled through specifications. Since the crude oil is obtained from different sources having different chemical composition, the quality of asphalt is a function of the origin of the crude oil and the process of refining. Asphalt is a visco elastic material and behaves as a liquid at high temperature and as an elastic solid at low temperatures.

12.3 Cold-Mix Plants

These consist of an engine driven pug mill type of mixer. The mixer is fitted with 2 shafts rotating in opposite directions. On each shaft paddles with interchangeable tips are attached. The mixer is lined on the inside with a renewable manganese steel plate. There is a trap door at the bottom of the mixer box controlled by a lever operated from the loading platform, to permit discharge of the mix into a wheel barrow placed below the trap door. The mixer capacity generally ranges from 5 cu ft (0.15 m^3) to 10 cu ft (0.30 m^3) per batch.

Paddle mixers are generally termed as cold mixing plants. Its construction is described here under :

Following are the main components of a paddle mixer :

(i) Chassis	(ii) Prime mover
(iii) Drive	(iv) Loading skip
(v) Mixer	(vi) Bitumen measuring bucket and the pump.

(i) Chassis : The whole plant is mounted on the strong steel chassis with four heavy duty pneumatic road wheels. It also has a draw bar with a turn table. Complete plant can be towed and moved while working. For moving the plant to a long distance, it is advisable to move it after loading on the trailer, while for short distances it can be towed with a road roller or a tractor.

(ii) Prime-Mover : Cold mix plants have a diesel engine, which is operated by a battery. The size of the engine depends upon the quantity of mix per batch. The engine is enclosed in a sheet steel housing so to safeguard from dust etc.

(iii) Drive : The power from the prime-mover is transmitted through a centrifugal clutch, reduction gear and chain driving sprocket fitted to the take-off shaft. The chain transmits the power to the driven sprockets on the shafts of the mixer.

(iv) Loading Skip : Loading skip of full batch capacity feeds the batches for unmixed materials to the paddle mixer. The loading skip is mounted on a carriage equipped with roller for running in the steel channel track. The skip is elevated by wire rope, winding on large diameter drums mounted on the hoisting shaft, which is driven through conical friction clutch and a roller chain. A break is fitted to the hoisting shaft to hold the loading skip in its discharging position. The break is automatic. Once the clutch is engaged, the loading skip moves up the track, and stop automatically, disengage the clutch and apply the brake and discharge its contents. In smaller size plants, the material is fed by basket and bucket into fixed hopper mounted over the top of the mixer body.

(v) Mixer : The mixer has twin paddle shafts, and are rotated in harmony by means of spur gears. The mixer body is constructed of heavy cast iron plates. The lower sides and bottom plates are made up of abrasion resistant material and is removable. The paddles have cast steel bases with renewable manganese steel tips. These paddle are fixed on shafts of square mild steel with round (turned) ends, rotating in heavy cast iron bearings with adjustable caps and brasses. Trap door at the bottom of mixer box is controlled by a lever operated from the loading platform, to discharge the mixer batch into a wheel barrow placed below the trap door.

(vi) Bitumen Measuring Bucket : Bitumen measuring bucket of mild steel construction is suspended on brackets attached to the mixer body. A rotary gear pump is also provided to deliver the bitumen to this measuring bucket or when connected to the piping from kettles, to form a continuous circulation from and to the kettle when the delivery cock to the mixer is closed.

12.4 Hot-Mix Plants (H.M.P.)

Capacity of the H.M.P. is indicated by two capacities, *viz.* : 60/90 T.P.H. This means the plant has a minimum capacity of 60 tons per hour when dry aggregates having an initial surface moisture content of 6% by weight and a terminal temperature 350°F (180°C) and whereas it has a maximum capacity of 90 tones per hour at 2% moisture content.

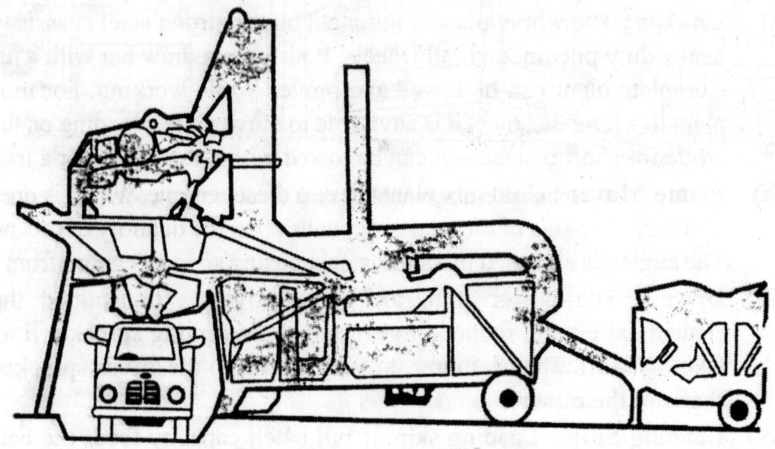

Fig. 12.2 Hot mix asphalt plant.

The capacity is generally based on the material weighing not less than 60 kgs per cu ft (or 2160 kgs per m^3). In order to maintain optimum operations and output, the feed to the plant should be in the proportion of the required end product.

A high proportion of graded stone will slightly increase the output of the dryer for a given moisture content and terminal temperature, whilst a high proportion of fines will slightly reduce the output.

Functions :

(i) Heating and drying the aggregates.

(ii) Screening the aggregates into required sizes and measuring the required quantity of the aggregate, the filler and bitumen.

(iii) Mixing the aggregate, the filler and the bitumen in required proportion and to produce homogeneous mix.

Types :

Asphalt hot-mix plants are of mainly following 2 types :

(i) Batch type (ii) Continuous mixing type.

12.5 Asphalt Batch Hot-Mix Plants

These hot-mix plants consist of the following :

(i) The cold **aggregate feeding bins**, to feed the aggregate to the drier drum.

(ii) **The drier**, a revolving cylindrical drum where the aggregates are heated. The drum is also provided with a burner. A dust collector is also usually provided.

(iii) **The screens,** which are provided in deck form, separates the aggregate into the required sizes, throwing out the oversized stones.

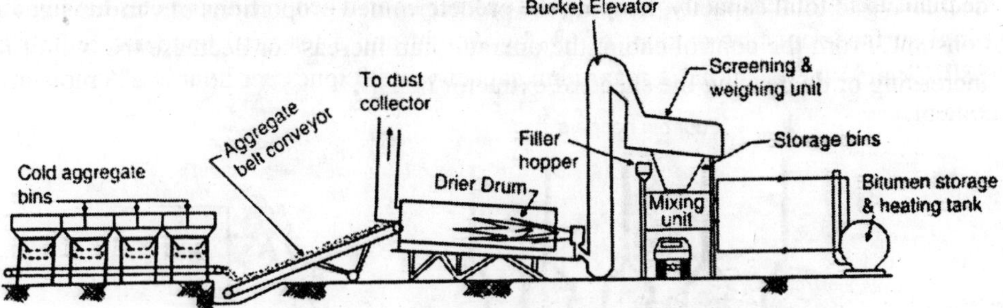

Fig. 12.3 Schematic diagram of asphalt batch hot-mix plant.

(iv) **Aggregate weighing system,** weighs various sizes of aggregates and allow them for mixing in a desired proportion. In some hot-mix plants, aggregate proportioning is done by volume.

(v) **Bitumen storage tanks,** have heating system with a thermostat to keep the bitumen at a constant temperature. These tanks are provided with the heat insulators.

(vi) **The mixing unit,** which consists of a box with 2 horizontal shafts rotating in opposite directions. These shafts are fitted with removable mixing paddles. These mixing boxes have an opening gate the bottom at a sufficient height to discharge into the waiting pump trucks.

12.5.1 Construction and Working

Constructional aspects of each of the major units provided with asphalt batch hot-mix plants are described hereunder :

1. Bin Feeder

Generally 4 hoppers are provided which feed the coarse as well as fine aggregates. The capacity of these hoppers depend upon the capacity of the hot-mix plant. The sides of the hoppers are kept very steep so as to ensure uniform flow without forming bridges. The hoppers used for fine aggregates and sand are fitted with intermittent vibrators, so that flow remains continuous and uniform. The feed hoppers are loaded through wheel loader or directly by the dump trucks.

Each hopper has a gate, the opening of which is graduated, so that the gate opening can be set according to proportion required of the particular size of the aggregate. This helps in volumetric proportioning the various sizes of the aggregate from these hoppers as per mix design approved by a

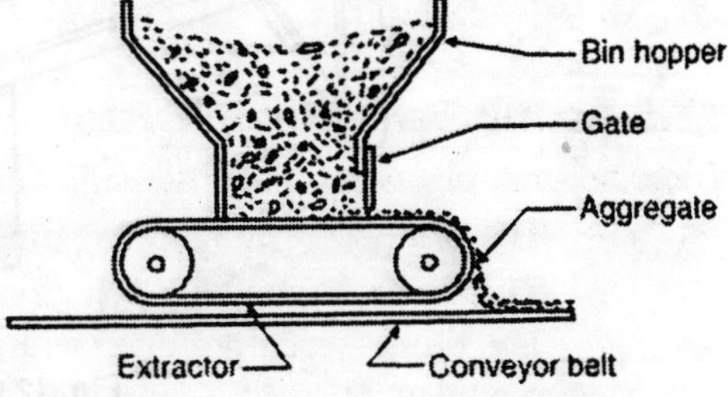

Fig. 12.4 Bin feed hoper with extractor belt.

quality control laboratory. The material is extracted from each hopper by means of an extractor belt. A speed variator, operating these extractor belts, permits increasing or decreasing to total capacity, keeping the predetermined proportions of various sizes as constant. From the control cabin, the operator can increase or decrease the output by increasing or decreasing the speed of extractor belts.

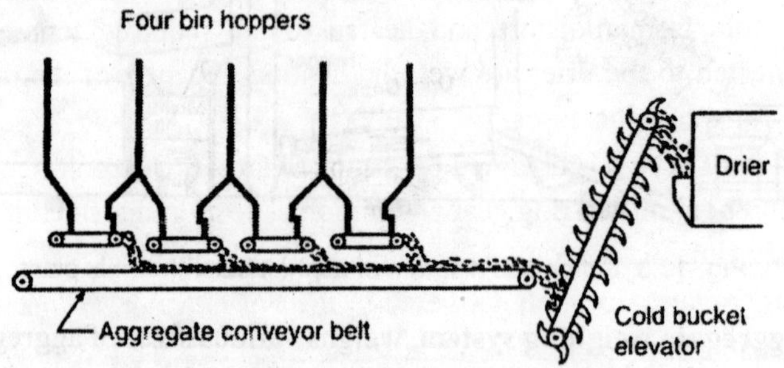

Fig. 12.5 Bin feed to cold elevator.

All discharges of various hoppers fall on a conveyor belt, driven by its own motor. This conveyor belt carries this proportioned aggregate to the cold elevator.

The cold elevators consists of buckets attached to a chain resting on wheels at the top and bottom. Sometimes conveyor belts are also used to carry the aggregate from bin feed hoppers to the drier drums.

2. Drier

Drier consists of a long hollow steel cylinder with firebricks lining and containing projecting radial fins. The inlet end is kept slightly higher than the outlet, at the time of the installation of the plant. Heat is supplied by a jet of flame, fed by air

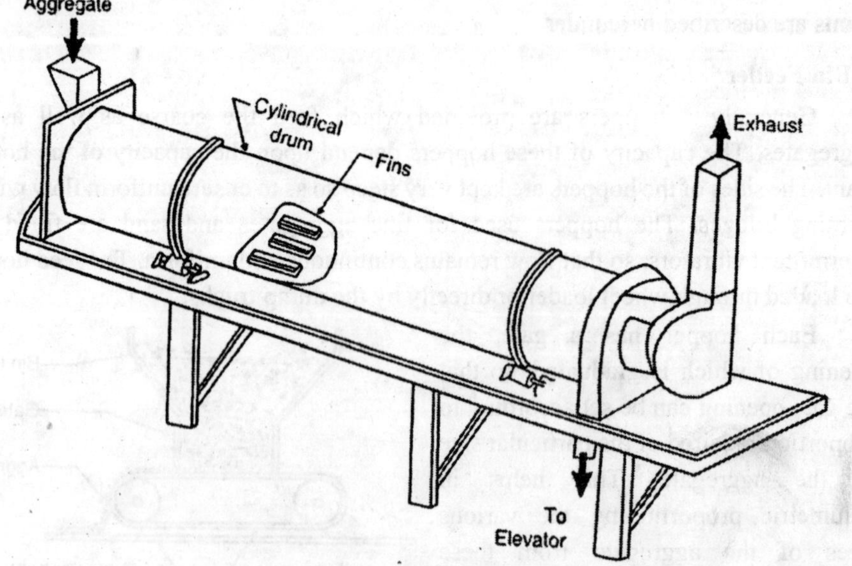

Fig. 12.6 Drier.

vapourised oil. The low pressure, air ventilated burner, using diesel as fuel oil is provided at the lower end. The burner flame can be adjusted from the control cabin as per heat requirement to get a proper temperature.

As the cylinder rotates, the aggregate is carried to the top by the fins, from where it falls downward and a little towards the outlet due to inclination. This way the aggregate proceeds further. By the time the aggregates have travelled the length of the drier, they are free from moisture and heated to the required temperature. If the aggregates being fed to the drier are wet, the heating capacity of the drier is greatly reduced and heating cost increases.

The rotation of dryers is obtained by means of an electric motor connected to an oil bath reduction box, milled ring gear and pinion. The cylinder fixed to the ring gear and to two sturdy rings rotates on 4 C.I. rollers.

The hot aggregates are then delivered to the hot elevator, whose function is to carry hot aggregate from the dryer to the vibrating screen in the gradation control unit. The hot elevator is similar to the cold elevator, except that hot elevator is totally enclosed to prevent the heat loss.

3. Dust Collector

To get a proper combustion and heating effect, a draft is created by providing an exhaust fan and a chimney. But this draft carried with it much of the fine dust introduced with the aggregate, which not only wasted the dust but also created a public nuisance in the habitate areas. These lost fines are generally replaced by expensive mineral filler. The dust collectors are therefore provided which traps the fine particles and returns them to the heated aggregates below the drier. The dust collectors may be either :

(i) cyclone type dry dust collectors, which returns the fines to the aggregates, or

(ii) wet dust collectors, which collects the dust by means of atomised water, or

(iii) dust lag filters.

4. Filler Storage Bins

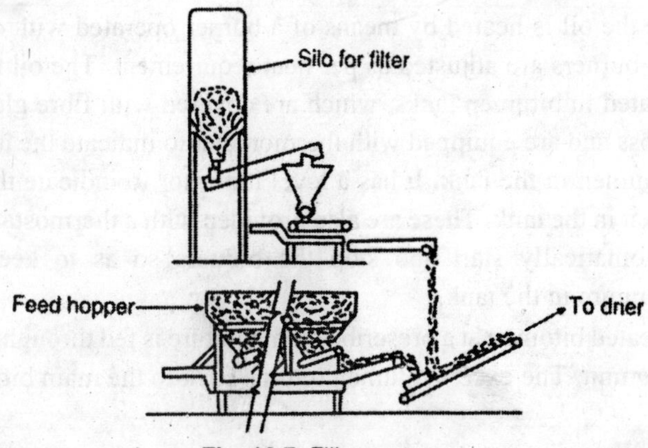

Fig. 12.7 Filler system.

Hot recovered fines are stored in these storage bins and additional filler materials are also stored in these filler storage bins. These are also provided with metering systems so as to feed the filler material in required proportion.

5. Screening, Weighing and Mixing Units

The vibrating screen of 4 sizes separates the aggregate into the required size throwing out the oversized stones. The 4 sizes of aggregates are collected in four aggregate storage bins. Each size of the aggregates are weighed accurately in a weighing hopper. The weights are indicated on a dial provided in the operator's cabin. The hot aggregate is then fed directly to the mixing unit also known as pugmill.

Filler bucket elevator, brings the filler material to the filler storage hopper. This hopper is connected to a separate weight-dial. The weighing hopper of the filler has a discharge door of width equal to that of mixer, so that the filler distribution is immediate the uniform.

Predetermined percentage of bitumen, as analysed by the quality control laboratory is fed through a bitumen metering device. This weighed bitumen is sprayed over the whole mixer area for uniform and quick coating.

The mixer pug mill with 2 steel shafts has cast steel double arms. The paddles which are fixed with bolts can be adjusted to turned around or replaced. Thus the aggregates and filler dropped in weighed quantity into the mixing unit, is then mixed with the bitumen sprayed along the full width of the mixer.

The gates for discharging the hot mix open at pre-set timing to allow the mis to fall directly into the truck standing below it. These twin discharge gates are controlled pneumatically.

6. Bitumen Heating System

Bitumen heating can be done in following two ways :

(a) Bitumen storage and heating tanks. These are used where the bitumen is transported in bulk from refinery to hot-mix plant in bitumen carriers.

(b) Melting furnace for bitumen in drums.

(a) Bitumen Storage and Heating Tanks : These consist of thermic boilers where the oil is heated by means of a burner operated with diesel as fuel. These burners are adjusted as per heat requirement. The oil thus heated is circulated in bitumen tanks, which are covered with fibre glass to prevent heat loss and are equipped with thermometer to indicate the temperature of the bitumen in the tank. It has a level indicator to indicate the quantity of bitumen in the tank. These are also provided with a thermostat arrangement to automatically start and stop the burners so as to keep a constant temperature in the tank.

The heated bitumen at a prescribed temperature is fed through a pump to the mixing unit. The excess bitumen returns back to the main bitumen tank.

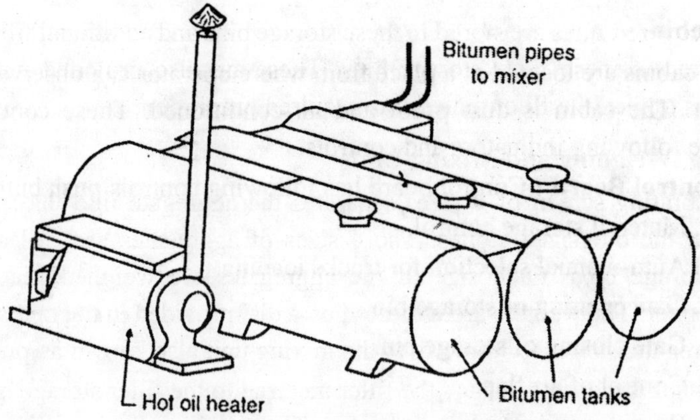

Fig. 12.8 Bitumen heating and storage tank.

(b) Melting Furnace for Bitumen in Drums : The hot chamber for drum decantation holds number of drums. The lifting and positioning of the drum is affected by an hoist and hydraulic pusher for positioning and causing the exit of the empty drum. The melting tank is insulated and has a burner which uses diesel as fuel. It also has a thermometer. It also feeds the bitumen into the mixing unit through a pump.

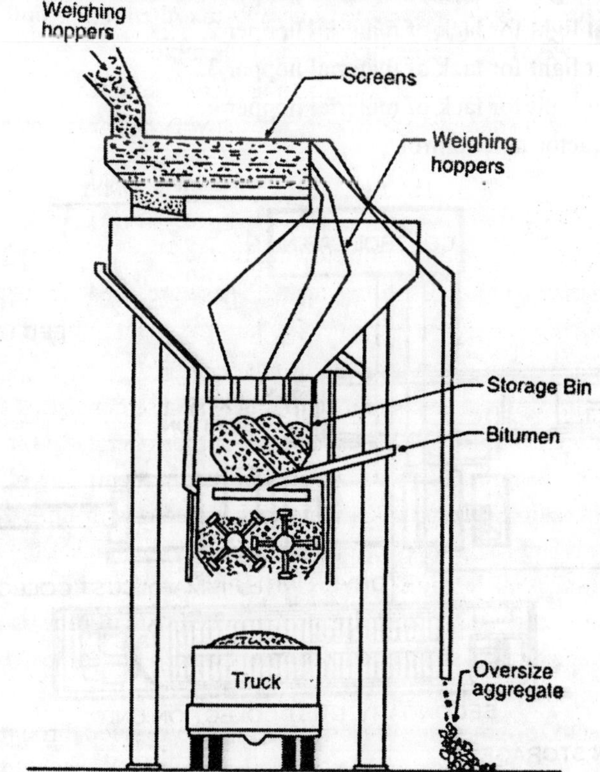

Fig. 12.9 Section of screening and mixing unit.

7. Control Cabin

Control cabins are located at a place from where operator can observe complete hot mix plant. The cabin is dust proof and air-conditioned. These control cabins generally have following indicators and controls.

(a) Control Board : Control board has following controls/push buttons :

1. Material storage control.
2. Auto-manual selection for trucks loading.
3. Gate opening of storage bin.
4. Gate closing of storage bin.
5. Control of air flap.
6. Burner rate control.
7. Fuel valve control.
8. Burner ignition control.
9. Flame defect pilot light.
10. Exhauster damper control.
11. Emergency siren.
12. Bitumen pump control.
13. Pilot light for lack of material hopper 1.
14. Pilot light for lack of material hopper 2.
15. Pilot light for lack of material hopper 3.
16. Pilot light for lack of material hopper 4.
17. Extractor-belt control.

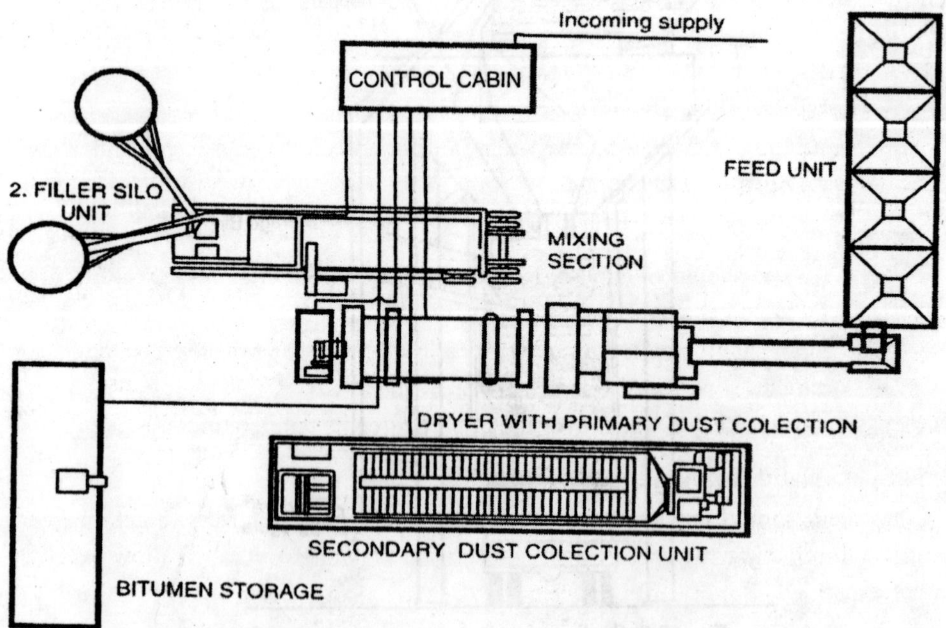

Fig. 12.10 A typical plant layout for a batch mix asphalt plant (Courtesy : Parker, England).

18. Feeder-belt control.
19. Wall vibrator control.
20. Switches for various motors.

(b) Inspection Board : Inspection board has following indicator/dials :

1. Number of batches for truck loading.
2. Bituminous mix temperature indicator.
3. Air flap position indicator.
4. Fuel valve position indicator.
5. Binder temperature indicator.
6. Hot aggregate temperature indicator.
7. Bitumen pump speed indicator.
8. Indicator for flow of aggregate.
9. Indicator for speed of extractor belt.
10. Material flow indicator.

12.5.2 Good Quality Mixing

To ensure asphalt hot mix of good quality following precautions should be adopted :

1. Aggregate Feeding

(i) Feed hoppers should be fed with correct sizes of aggregate and should always be kept sufficiently full so as to get an even flow of the material.

(ii) Feeder gate opening should be carefully calibrated in volumetric proportions depending on the job mix formula.

(iii) Fine aggregate should be fed first on the belt conveyor, therefore fine aggregates should always be loaded in the first of the 4 hoppers.

(iv) Mineral filler should be dry.

(v) Arching of fine aggregate should be prevented by providing a vibrator on the outside of the hopper.

2. Drying

(i) Burner should be adjusted for correct operation so as to get trouble free flame to get a constant temperature.

(ii) Drier should not be overloaded by allowing more aggregates than that it can handle.

(iii) Always keep a watch over the dried aggregate temperature.

3. Screening and Hot Aggregate Storage

Screens should be checked periodically for clogging and wear. Since clogged screen will reject the correct size aggregates, whereas worn screen will allow oversize aggregates.

4. Bitumen

(i) Bitumen should be maintained at the correct temperature.

(ii) Add bitumen from the bitumen carrier into the tank at the correct temperature, specially when the plant is in operation.

5. Material Proportioning

(i) The aggregate, filler and bitumen weighing scale should be correctly calibrated and checked from time to time.

(ii) The temperature of the aggregate should always be correct.

6. Mixing

(i) The clearance between the paddle tips and the inside lining of the mixing box should be checked periodically. Normally this clearance should not be more than 2 cm.

(ii) To get a homogeneous mix each batch should have correct quantity of material.

12.6 Drum-Mix Asphalt Plants

Drum-mix asphalt plants are becoming more and more popular because, initial capital investment cost of these plants is less than that of conventional batch type asphalt mix plants, and running costs are also greatly reduced due to fewer moving and wearing parts.

These plants consist of following main components :

(a) Cold aggregate feeder with mineral filler supply system.

(b) Dryer and mixing unit with dust collection system.

(c) Bitumen storage, heating and delivery system.

(d) Mix storage unit.

(e) Operator cabin and controls.

1. Cold Aggregate Feed System

It is essential to feed these mixers with accurate proportions of aggregate sizes. Multi compartment bin feeder system ensures this accuracy. Number of bin hoppers vary on the requirement of asphalt mix specifications, however 3 to 5 bin systems are common. Each bin hopper is loaded with a specific size of aggregate which is discharged on the collecting conveyor. These bin hoppers are mounted on a rigid frame. In a mobile plant these are mounted on a robust chassis and are fitted with pneumatic tyres.

Each bin has independent belt feeder under it driven by independent and mutually synchronised variable speed electric motors. Each bin hopper is fitted with precision adjustable quadrant gates. With the variable speed electric motors fitted with technogenerator, belt speed can be accurately varied to regulate the rate of aggregate flow from the bin. When discharge rate of each aggregate is required to be controlled by weight, weighing system is provided on each belt conveyor to indicate the weight in T.P.H. (tons per hour) on gauges in the operator's cabin. Synchronised variable speed motor is provided to increase or decrease the aggregate flow in same proportion from each bin in order to increase or decrease the production of mix. Smallest size aggregate hopper is fitted with anti-logging electromechanical vibrator on one of the side plates to maintain continuous flow of material.

Filler is accurately proportioned by screw conveyor with variable speed motor, from a bulk storage silo or bag filled arrangements. Filler is fed on to the collecting (or some times called gathering) conveyor (described in the following paragraph) after the sand but before the stone aggregate, thereby securing filler within a feed 'sandwich'. Filler may be mineral dust, lime or cement. Sometimes these are directly fed into the mixing zone of the dryer drum.

Gathering conveyor collects the discharges from each of the independent belt conveyors and is equipped with electronic weigh bridge and a suitable size electric motor. The weight of the aggregate in T.P.H. is indicated in the cabin.

Belt weigher is fitted with each of the conveyor belt to record the weight of the aggregate in T.P.H. passing over it. In volume control system, belt weigher is provided with gathering conveyor to know the production rate of mix from the plant. Wherever control of aggregate is by weight, belt weighers are provided with each of the belt feeder and also with gathering conveyor. The belt weight constantly monitors the material feed rate. A signal from the belt weigher is transmitted to the plant control system so that adjustments can be automatically effected.

Scalping Screen : Feed material entering the drum mixer is required to be accurately sizes, so that where there is a possibility of oversize material or unwanted elements contaminating the feed aggregate, a scalping screen is installed between the cold feed gathering conveyor and the weigh conveyor which is discharging into the drum mixer.

2. Dryer and Mixing Unit

A drum mixer is basically a long rotating cylinder fitted with a burner in which aggregate is mixed, dried and coated with binder. Inside the drum, aggregates are first thoroughly mixed in cold state and then dried and heated. In the latter half of the drum, binder is added and final mixing takes place.

The drum is fitted internally with removable curved and angle flights. The drum rotates in machined rings generally two, supported from barrels on brackets. Drum is driven by steel chain sprocket ring bolted to drum. Driver is by a sufficiently strong electrical motor. The drum is mounted on a frame. In case of mobile plants, the frame is mounted on pneumatic tyres.

At first sight a drum-mixer could be mistaken for a conventional aggregate dryer (as in Batch type plants), but these have following important differences :

(i) **Longer Length :** Since these have three processing zones, *i.e.,* cold mixing, heating and bitumen coating, against only heating in conventional dryers, and hence are longer in length for the same diameter.

(ii) Material Flow : Drum mixers employ parallel flow principle of operation which means that material enters the drum at the burner end, so that aggregates, flame, exhaust gases and steam move in the same direction. Conventional dryers operate in counter-flow with the burner situated at the discharge and firing against the flow of aggregates, as shown in Fig. 12.11.

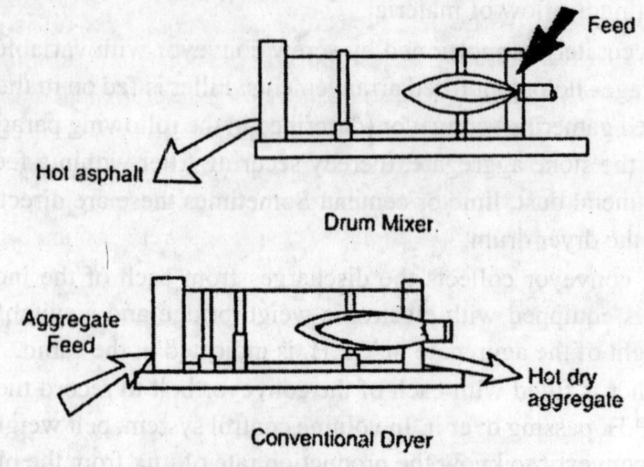

Fig. 12.11(a) Material flow system.

(iii) Burner Flame : In drum mixers,the burner flame stops short of the bitumen mixing zone and is wide and flat, whilst in conventional dryers, the flame reaches the full length of the cylinder and is long and penetrating.

(iv) Internal Construction : Drum mixer internal flights are designed and arranged to perform specific duties in their respective zones during operation. Specific functions performed in each zone in the cylinder are : In **zone 1,** cold wet aggregate with filler, water or additive are mixed together before being subjected to the heat from the burner flame. In **zone 2,** the moisture is evaporated and the aggregates heated in an area where the radiated heat from the burner and the conducted heat from the drum is at its maximum. In **zone 3,** the binder is added to the partially dried and heated

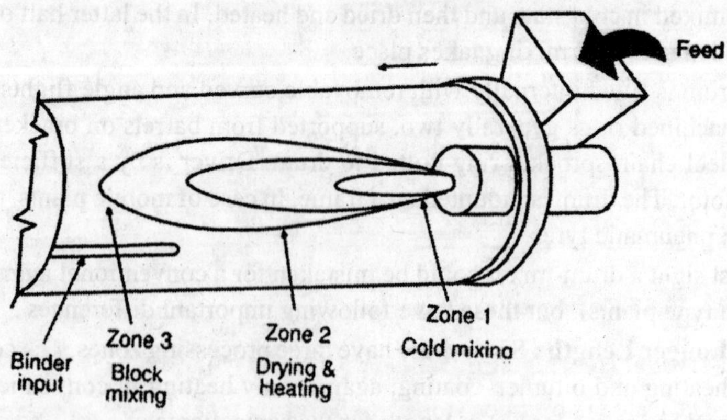

Fig. 12.11(b) Zones in dryer.

aggregate, mixing in this zone produces a homogeneously mixed material. Number and functions of zones vary from manufacturer to manufacturer. Some has 2 zone : Heating and mixing, some has 3 zones for heating, bitumen spray and mixing respectively.

Burner : Multi nozzle single flame burner is fitted in the dryer drum. In advanced dryer drums burners are 'Turbo Jet' type fully automatic. Fuel oil is pumped at the required pressure to the burner nozzles and combustion air is supplied by an axial blower. The burner is infinitely variable between maximum and minimum setting. After initial setting up, the actuating motor adjust the fuel oil control valve and air valves proportionately. The fuel pump is linked with the drum drive to prevent the use of the burner when the drum is stationary. In latest drum mixers, burner works automatically as well as manually and have remote/automatic control of burner flame to maintain specific temperature aggregate.

Dust Collection : Dust collection system is given in detail under separate heading in this chapter.

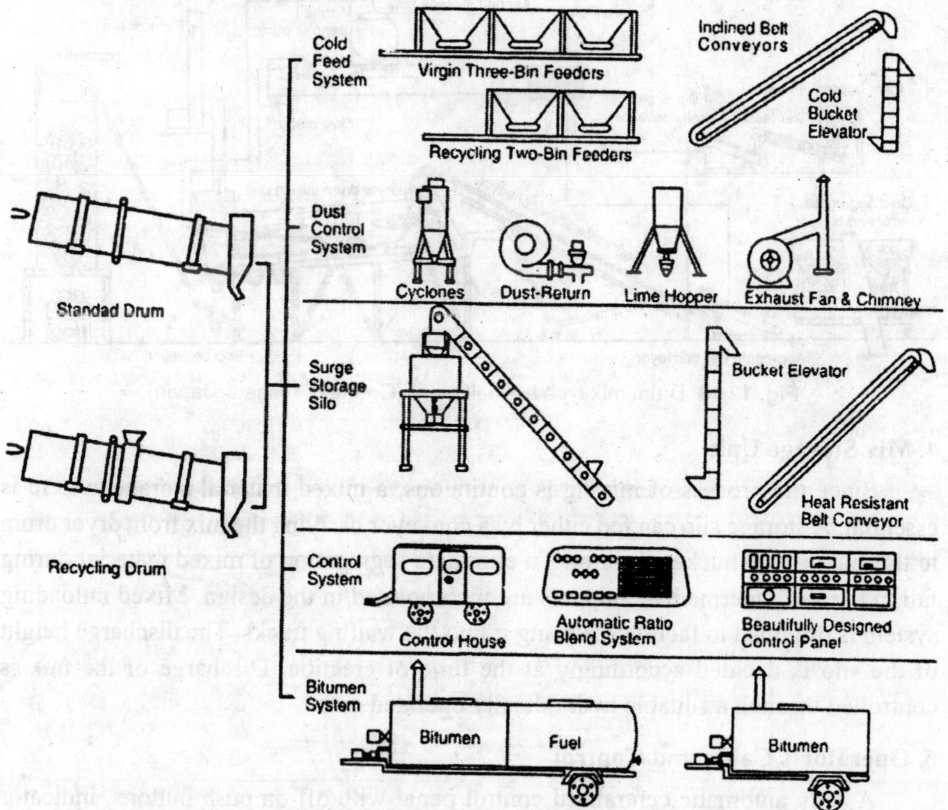

Fig. 12.12 Components of drum-mix asphalt plant (Courtesy : Apollo).

3. Bitumen Storage, Heating and Delivery System

Bitumen is heated in bitumen storage and heating tanks by any of the means, like, hot oil circulation, direct oil fired or electrically heated. Hot oil heaters are more common. In these, oil is heated up by means of fully automatic burner to a pre-set temperature (normally 120° to 210°). The heated oil is circulated by the hot oil circulating pump to keep the asphalt tank and pipe lines at a pre-set temperature.

These tanks are insulated having level indicator, thermostat, temperature indicator, pumps for sucking bitumen from bitumen carriers, feeding to the bitumen distributors or carriers, and transferring the bitumen from one tank to another. All pipe lines and fittings are either steam or oil jacketed and properly insulated to prevent loss of heat.

Heated binder is delivered to the plant by a positive displacement pump *via* the ganged flow control valves operated by an electric actuator, rotary piston type meter, and pneumatically operated ring main valve. The binder percentage required is pre-set at the control console and signals received by the ratio controller from the belt weigher will automatically adjust the binder feed rate to meet the mix specifications. Delivery rate of bitumen is also indicated in T.P.H. (Tones Per Hour) on the control console.

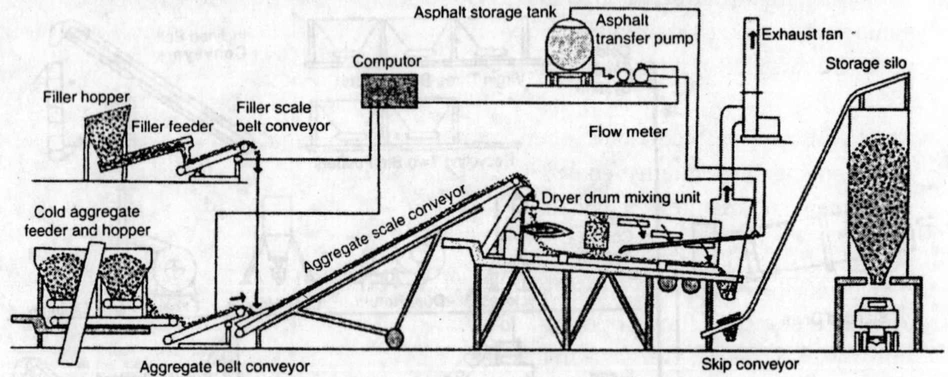

Fig. 12.13 Drum mix type asphalt plant (Courtesy : Nigata, Japan).

4. Mix Storage Unit

Since the process of mixing is continuous, a mixed material storage system is essential. A storage silo can fed either by a conveyor carrying the mix from dryer drum to the silo or by a bucket elevator. To eliminate segregation of mixed material during fall in the silo, intermediate hoppers are incorporated in the design. Mixed unloading system is provided to facilitate placing it into the waiting trucks. The discharge height of the silo is decided accordingly at the time of erection. Discharge of the mix is controlled through a suitable hydraulically operated gate.

5. Operator's Cabin and Control

A fully automatic centralised control penal with off-on push buttons, indicator flights, gauges etc. is provided inside a cabin, like that for batch type asphalt plant. Operator from this cabin can operate all motors, burners, blower, conveyor belts etc. and control the temperature and flow of aggregate, bitumen, and filler etc. and controls the mix storage gates etc.

Advantages of Drum-Mix Plant Over Conventional Plant

Like conventional plant, these do not have the hot stone elevator screen, hot stone bins, weigh hoppers for gradation control, and pedal mixers and their associated wearing parts. This feature results in following main advantages :

(a) Expenditure on spare parts reduces considerably.

(b) Expenditure on men-hour for maintenance is also reduced.

(c) This reduces the requirement of power.

(d) Initial cost of the plant is less than that of a similar capacity conventional plant.

In addition to above advantages, with these plants it is possible to achieve good quality of coating even at a lower temperature, hence it saves the cost of fuel per unit quantity of mix.

These plants are simple and easy to operate. Easy to transport from one site to another.

Most important advantage of this type of plant is that, the chimney of this type of plant emits less dust than a traditional plant. This is because the heating and mixing process is carried out in the same drum which renders this type of plant self-dust collecting.

Thus, these plants are economical, saves energy, highly mobile, protects environment, high quality coated material production besides having lower capital investment and maintenance coats.

12.7 Pollution Control Equipment (Dust Collectors)

The main purpose of an air pollution control system is to remove suspended particles (mostly dust) from the gas stream that leaves the dryer drum through the stack (chimney). If the initial aggregate material contains a high percentage of fine dust, or fine dust that could be dragged easily along by the gaseous current, or if hourly production of asphalt plant is high, the personnel engaged on the plant are badly affected by the pollution (dust nuisance). This also affects the nearby residential areas, and cultivated farm and adversely.

Types of Air Pollution Control Equipment :

Based on the process involved for removal of the particles from the gas stream, these equipments are classified in following two categories :

1. Dry Dust collectors 2. Wet washers

Each of these has its own functions and application in the air pollution control system. Some of the types of these are briefly described hereunder. De-dusting units can be either the wet type, or dry type, or a combination of both.

1. Dry Dust Collectors

This type of equipment collects particles from the air stream and allows these fines to be introduced into asphalt concrete manufacturing process. Main type of dry dust collectors are :

(a) Expansion chamber type (b) Centrifugal type

(c) Bag house type.

(a) Expansion Chamber Type Dry Dust Collectors : These are very simple type of dust collectors with less efficiency and are used for small plants located at places where residential colony or cultivated lands are not in the nearby areas. These are based on the principle of decreasing the velocity and settle out by gravity. Dust collection efficiency can be increased by installing the baffles or shelves. The particles fall to the bottom of the chamber and the discharged through a valve.

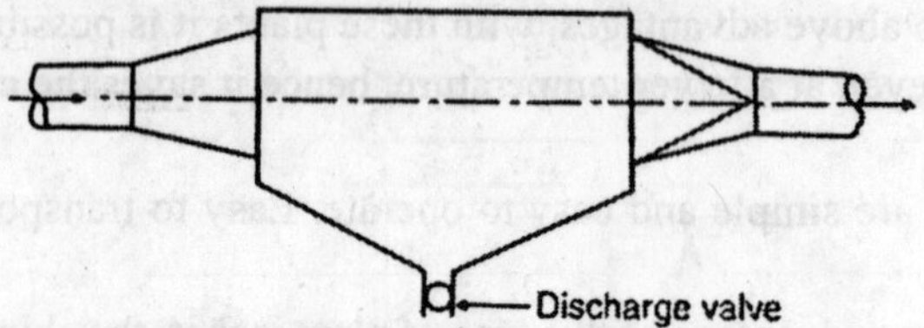

Fig. 12.14 Expansion chamber type dry dust collector.

(b) Centrifugal (Cyclone) Dry Dust Collectors : Centrifugal type (also known as cyclone type) by dust collectors separate the dust particles from the gas by using centrifugal and gravitational forces. Particles of dust (being of higher density than the gas) are forced against the wall of the cone in a spinning motion. The particles become increasingly heavy enough, as the dia of the cone becomes smaller, through centrifugal force as they travel downward towards the bottom of the collector cone. All large particles present in the gas are collected and discharged through the bottom opening of the collector cone.

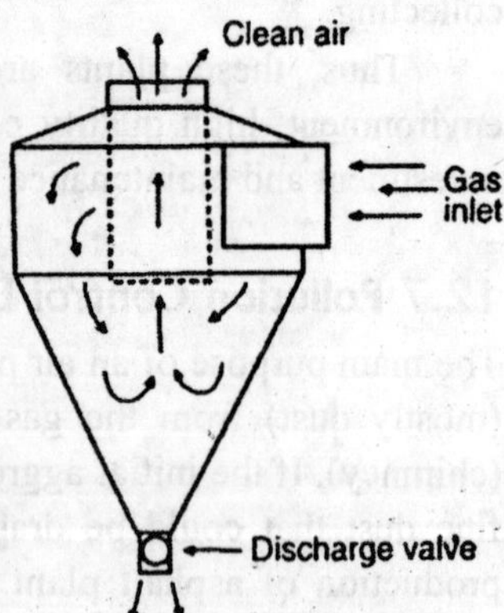

Fig. 12.15 Centrifugal (cyclone) dust collector.

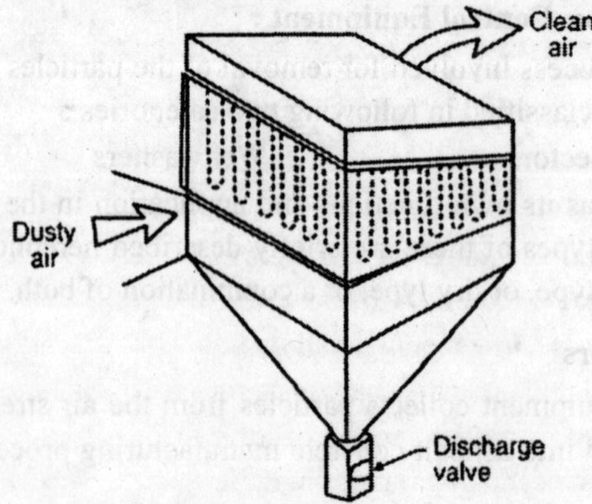

Fig. 12.16 Multiple centrifugal dry dust collector.

Some times in place of above mentioned type 'large diameter single collector' or 'small diameter multiple collectors' are used. These function on the same principle as described above, except that these have common intake and one common discharge valve as shown in the Fig. 12.16.

(c) Bag House (Fabric-Filter) Dust Collectors : Dust laiden air enters the collector, and passed through the large number of bags either from inside to outside or from outside to inside, as it rises in upward direction. Dust is thus collected on the surface of bag and clean gas passes upward. The bags are made up of fabric and fibre. Fabric used are either Glass, Polyesters, Dacron, or Nomex type nylon. To prevent collapsing, the bags are required to be supported by some means (wire cages are more popular).

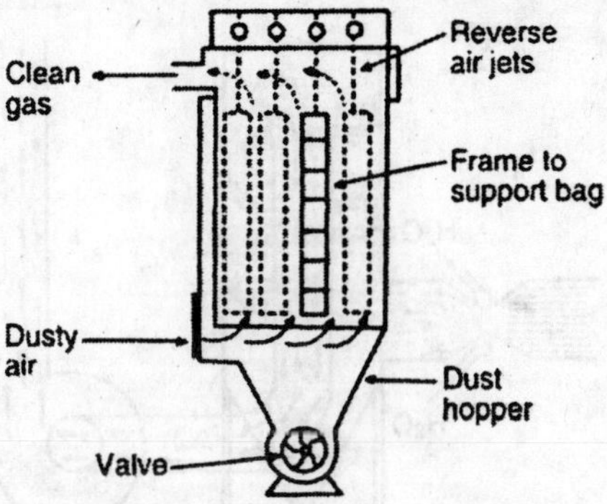

Fig. 12.17 Bag house dry dust collector.

Cleaning of the bags is done either by (i) Compressed reverse air flw, or by (ii) shaker type bag cleaning.

2. Wet Washers (Wet Collectors)

Wet collectors work on the principle of wetting dust particles present in the gases and trapping them in water droplets which are drained from the system in the form of water sludge. Wet washers (collectors) are of following types :

(a) Spray chamber type.

(b) Centrifugal or cyclonic wet collectors.

(c) Venturi type wet collectors.

(a) Spray chamber type washers : Simplest type of washer is a chamber having baffles with water spray nozzles.

(b) Centrifugal or cyclonic wet collectors (Fig. 12.18) : In these collectors, the dust laden gas enters tangentially and takes a spiral path, and the spray nozzles are mounted on the wall of the collectors. The centrifugal motion of the

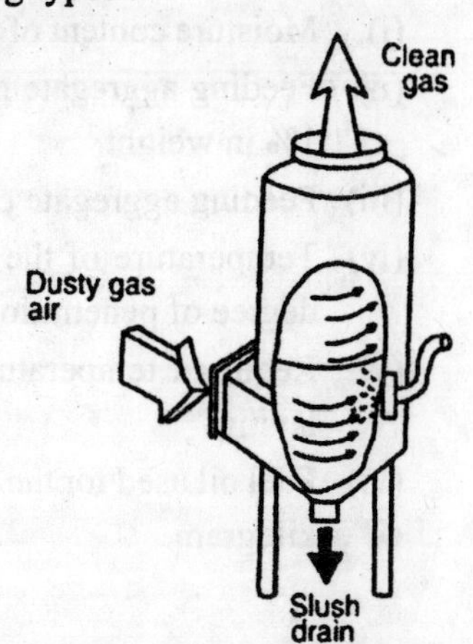

Fig. 12.18 Centrifugal wet collector.

spray imparted by the rotating gas causes the droplets to impinge against the collector walls and then drain to the bottom by gravitation.

(c) **Venturi type wet collectors :** This is based on the principle of throat and a divergent section. The dust laden gas enters the convergent section and is accelerated to high velocity as it approaches the throat. Water is injected either directly into the throat section, or at the top of the venturi. The high velocity gas (dust laden air) atomizes the water into a fine mist. Gas and dust laden liquid enter the separator in a cyclone, as shown in the Fig. 12.19, where the liquid is thrown to the wall of collector by centrifugal forces, and drains to the bottom by gravity. The clean air then exits through the upper portion of the separator.

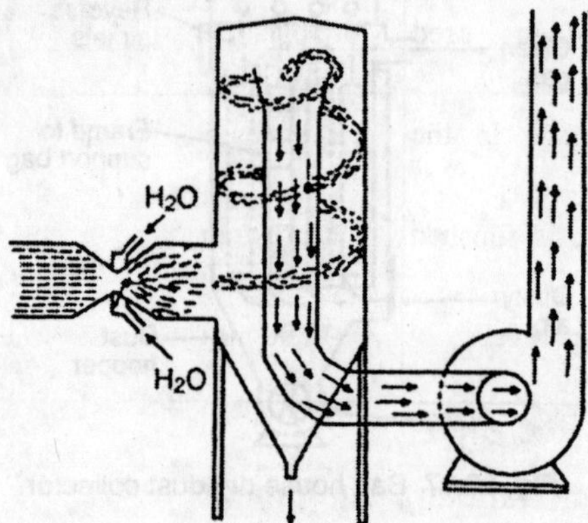

Fig. 12.19 Venturi type wet dust collector.

12.8 Maximum Production of Asphalt Concrete

Asphalt mixing plant gives maximum production when overall conditions are good, that is the quality of aggregate, climatic and weather conditions, state of mixing plant, and following other factors :

(i) Moisture content of the aggregate material fed to the plant is less than 3%.

(ii) Feeding aggregate material, passing through 200 ASTM sieve is less than 1% in weight.

(iii) Feeding aggregate contain a minimum quantity of chips and flakes.

(iv) Temperature of the bitumen is not less than 180-200°C according to the degree of penetration of the bitumen used.

(v) Required temperature of the mix is not more than 110°C at the time of laying.

(vi) Fuel oil used for the burner has a heat value not less than 10,500 calories per kilogram.

Factors Affecting Asphalt Production

S. No.	*Factors*	*Excellent Conditions*	*Normal Conditions*	*Poor Conditions*
1.	Surrounding temp.	More than 30°C	From 20 to 30°C	Less than 20°C
2.	Content passing through 200 ASTM sieve in the aggregate feed	Up to 1%	Up to 3%	More than 3%
3.	Temperature of finished product minus surrounding temperature, *i.e.*, temperature rise	Less than 70°C	70 to 120	Over 120°C
4.	Kind of bitumen used penetration	More plastic than 80-100	80-100	40-60
5.	Bitumen percentage in the mix	More than 5%	4 to 5%	Less than 4%
6.	Specific gravity of finished product	More than 1.7 kg/cu m	1.5 to 1.7 kg/cu m	
7.	Altitude above sea level	0-200 mtr.	200-600 mtr.	More than 600 mtr.

12.9 Bulk Bitumen Handling Equipment

Present system of handling bitumen involves the use of non-reusable drums filled and sealed at the refinery and transported to worksite where they are emptied into bitumen boilers. Since one drum carries only 155 to 162 kg of bitumen, a large number of drums are required to be handled.

Bulk bitumen transportation in tankers of large capacities has following main advantages over transportation in drums :

(i) Saves cost of drums which are made of steel.

(ii) Saves fuel consumption.

(iii) Control of temperature of bitumen is accurate and easy.

(iv) Avoids contamination and leakage during transport and storage.

Equipment Required for Bulk Bitumen Handling

Following equipments are basically required for handling bitumen in bulk :

(a) Transportation tankers.

(b) Storage tanks.

(c) Ancillary equipment for handling bitumen.

Equipments mentioned at (b) and (c) have been discussed alongwith hot-mix plants.

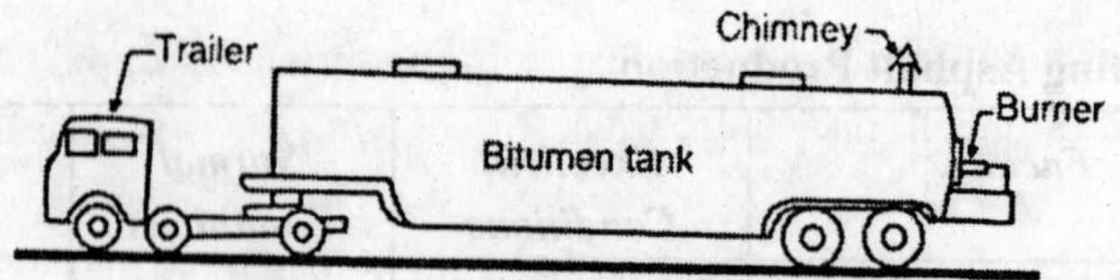

Fig. 12.20 Bitumen transport tank.

Bitumen Transportation Tanker : Bulk bitumen is delivered by the refinery into the bitumen transportation tankers at a temperature of about 150°C. After transporting the bulk bitumen, it is filled in the site (i) storage tanks located near the hot mix asphalt plant, or (ii) bitumen distributors.

These are used for transporting bitumen or tar in bulk, and are kept in hot condition and can be further heated as per requirement. They are containers that are fully insulated to prevent excessive heat loss and are provided with burners to boost the temperature, if required. Gear pumps are installed for loading and unloading the tank as rapidly as possible.

Now-a-days binder is transported from the refinery to storage tanks in bulk by trucks or trailers. Tank volumes range from 10,000 to 65,000 iitres, and are mounted on suitable truck chassis or draw trailers or semi-trailers. The pump and the air compressor for the burner operation are driven by a separate diesel engine provided with the tank. Two gauges indicating the bitumen temperature and its quantity in the tank are also mounted on the tank.

12.10 Asphalt Laying (Paving) Equipment

As discussed earlier asphalt plants uniformly blend, heat and mixes the aggregates and asphalt in the required proportion to produce asphalt concrete to be laid in layers on the prepared subgrade, an aggregate sub-base and an aggregate base to construct the pavements. The laying of asphalt layers is done through the **asphalt pavers**. Asphalt pavers consist of a tractor either track or rubber-tired, and a screed. Screed is that part of an asphalt paver that smooths and compacts the asphalt mix. Mat thickness, which is controlled by the screed, can be maintained by using grade sensors or by tracting an external reference.

A modern paver finisher, in addition to asphalt mixes can also lay all kinds of base material with a high degree of accuracy in longitudinal and transverse gradients. The pavers also pre-compact these mixes to "near final" densities so that rolling work is substantially reduced and an excellent surface evenness is reached. This pre-compaction virtually eliminates the surface irregularities resulting from rolling work thus ensure uniform density and an excellent surface evenness.

Before laying the asphalt concrete the surface is required to be prepared by cleaning and then applying the tack or seal coats. The asphalt concrete after laying is compacted by compaction equipments so that the pavement can take load of traffic. The complete asphalt laying process requires a number of different pieces of equipment. These include :

1. Sweeper/broom for removing dust from the surface to be paved.
2. Asphalt (bitumen) distributor truck for applying the tack or seal coats.
3. Paver.
4. Trucks for transportation of the asphalt mix from plant to the construction site.
5. Rollers.
6. Road marking machines.

12.10.1 Paver Finishers

A paver finisher is a machine for laying and spreading sub-base, base courses or asphalt for road construction to give accurate depth, even levelling and good surface finish before rolling. Pavers are also used in various construction activities like construction of footpaths, parking areas, sports grounds, highways, airport runways and railways (for laying track ballast).

Earlier paver finishers were used only a asphalt works, but during last about thirty years the use of pavers for sub-base and base courses has gained popularity. Use of paver finisher, compared to the traditional Motor-Grader method is found more suitable, because,

(a) Better and easier control of levels, both longitudinal and transverse.
(b) Improved homogenity of the plant prepared mix.
(c) Uniform pre-compactin.
(d) Complete elimination of final levelling, reduces the efforts and thus costs.
(e) Improved adherence of asphaltic courses.

The pavers can easily handle asphalt and all asphalt mixes, coated and uncoated materials, crushed stones and dry lean concrete, in fact all road making materials other than wet concrete.

A paver finisher, during constructing bituminous pavements, ir fed by the mix transporting vehicles into the hoppers at the front. Two conveyor belts take up the mix which has been fed into the hopper, to an auger which distributes it in the prescribed thickness over the operating width. The mix is then laid in required width and depth and levelled and compacted partially by the screed. The screed is heated either by propane gas burners or diesel oil burners, evently distributed over the entire operating width. Although the degree of compaction achieved by the screed has, in course of time, been steadily increased, final compaction by rollers is still necessary. Compactibility of a bituminous mix is considerably reduced as the mix cools and then requires more compacting energy to achieve a degree of compaction at a lower temperature.

To enable pavers to deal with changes in road width, without interruption operation, hydraulically extendible screeds for both sides of the finishers were developed during last few years. With such units it is possible to infinitely vary the basic operating width of the paver finishers. With these screeds, the width can be increased to 6.0 m. For pavers with rigid extensions widths upto 12.0 m can be reached.

Single layer upto 30 cm thickness can be placed. The operating speeds which depend upon the size of the object and the type of work ranges from 1 to 60 m/min and can be infinitely selected. Maximum extendable width of the screed, may be hydraulically or mechanically, determines the size of the paver.

The screeds used in paves are of three types :

(i) having only tamping.

(ii) having only vibrating, and

(iii) having a combined tamping and vibrating.

The pavers are either mounted on tyres or on crawler tracks. The power is provided by a suitable diesel engine.

12.10.2 Construction of Paver Finishers

Main constructional features of the paver finishers are described hereunder :

1. Chassis

Chassis is robust and composed of the under carriage and super structure. The under carriage carries the material conveyor system and front hopper, crawler system or pneumatic wheels and rubber tyres duly fitted. It also accommodates the power unit, transmission system and augers. The hydraulic system and various control units are also mounted on the undercarriage. Push roller bar is provided at the correct height for standard material transport vehicles. Driver's seat is located at a place so that the sits directly above the auger and can see the overall distribution of material in front of the screed, and thus he can observe and control all the function of the paver finishers.

2. Transmission

The prime mover for the paver finishers are diesel engines. The power generated by the diesel engine is supplied to the gear box, traction conveyor drives, auger and screed vibrations. The gear box has a very wide range of speeds. The speed selected depends upon various factors such as :

(i) If the paver is shifted, high speed is required.

(ii) ?When the supply of material is high the speed is also high and *vice-versa*.

(iii) "When laying material for lesser width and lesser thickness the speed should be more whereas, while laying more width and higher thickness the speed of paver should be less. Thus the operator choses the working speed according to the paving material, the relevant mixing capacity, the feeding capacity, the thickness and width of layer to be placed. Speed of the paver while working is generally kept upto 3 km/hr (or 50 meters per min).

3. Hopper

Self-dumping hopper consists of two wings and an apron, all independently operated with the aid of hydraulic rams. This operation is carried out by the driver from his seat by activating the control valve with the help of a connecting rod. It can be held in any position.

The material is fed into the hopper by the trucks which back up against the guide rollers of the paver finisher. During this dumping process, the truck is pushed forward by the self propelled paver finisher. Generally the capacity of the hoppers are from 12 tons to 14 tons.

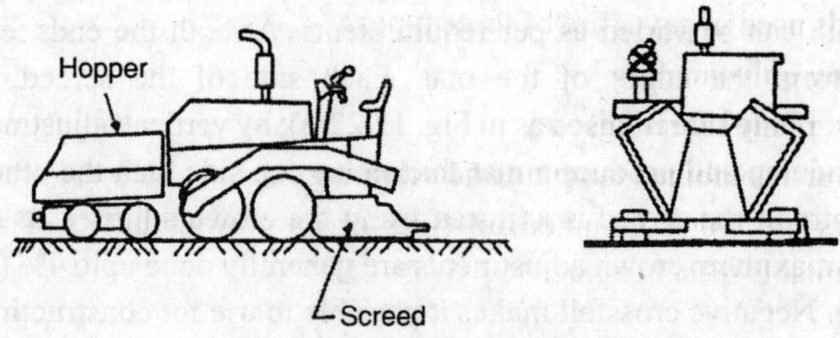

Fig. 12.21 Paver finisher.

4. Conveyors

Conveyors, two in numbers are driven independently from the engine power generally by roller chains and sprockets. Speed of the conveyors can be controlled by the driver as per requirements. The conveyors are self cleaning, *i.e.*, they are designed in such a way that material does not settle on them. The material poured into the hopper by the tipping trucks is conveyed to the augers by these two conveyor belts. Each belt with its corresponding auger has its own drive (mechanical or hydraulic) so that the material is independently conveyed on either side. This helps to suit the varying material requirements of each side.

5. Auger

The auger can rotate to both left and right, therefore they can convey material both inwards and outwards. Thus it spreads the material uniformly in the auger box so that the material can be layered by the screed in the desired thickness throughout the width. The augers have super hardened cast faces bolted to the flights to give long life.

The amount of material delivered to the auger box is maintained at a level which wi'l ensure a steady supply by the augers across the leading edge of the screed. To achieve this flow control gates situated on the rear wall of the hopper are set, so as to get the material as per requirement only. As excessive build-up of material will create a bulldozing effect by the screed and also material will becomes cold and the quality of mat will result in loss of level and holes will appear in the mat.

The height of the auger is required to be adjusted depending upon the thickness of the material to be laid. Although, no hard and fast rules can be laid down for auger height settings, but since the augers are used to gauge the level of the material, an incorrect auger height setting could result in an over or underfilled auger box. As a general rule, for bituminous materials, the lowest point of the auger should be not more than 50 to 75 mm above the level of the finished mat.

Auger extensions are available with each paver finisher so as to extend or reduce the paving widths and contain the material within the required width limits.

6. Screeds

Each of the screeds is of box section construction and has a basic width, and to this extension parts of widths of 500, 250 and 125 mm each can be added on each side. Pavers with screeds which can be extended up to 12.5 m are now available. Thus the operating width can be varied as per requirements. At both the ends, end plates are provided to form the edges of the mat. Each side of the screed is controlled independently. If one side is raised as in Fig. 12.22(a); by vertical adjustment of the two point, it will ride up and produce a mat thicker on one side then the other. To form a crown the centre of the screed is adjusted using the crown adjuster, as shown in Fig 12.22(b). The maximum crown adjustments are generally done upto 4% (positive) and 2% (negative). Negative crossfall makes it possible to use for constructing farm roads with centre drainage, or for removing rutting in the wheel paths of the pavements.

Fig. 12.22 Screed adjustments.

The material received from conveyors is distributed by the auger in front of the screed upto the screed end plates. As soon as enough material is accumulated the paver finisher can start paving.l

Both screed halves are connected at the bottom centre by union bearings and spring loaded tie bolts and at the top by 2 turn buckles. These turnbuckles constitute the crown control for both screed halves.

As mentioned earlier the screeds are of 3 types having tamping only; having vibrations only; and tamping and vibrating combined. Now-a-days screeds with tamping and vibrating combined are preferred since it gives better initial compaction and good mat surface.

(a) ***Tamping System*** : Generally good screeds are composed of two tampers driven by same eccentric shaft which are arranged in front of the vibrating screed plate, *i.e.*, in the material flow area of the spreading augers. Due to its chamfered surface the first tamper has a proportioning, pre-compacting effect whereas the main tamper with its differently shaped bar reaches the

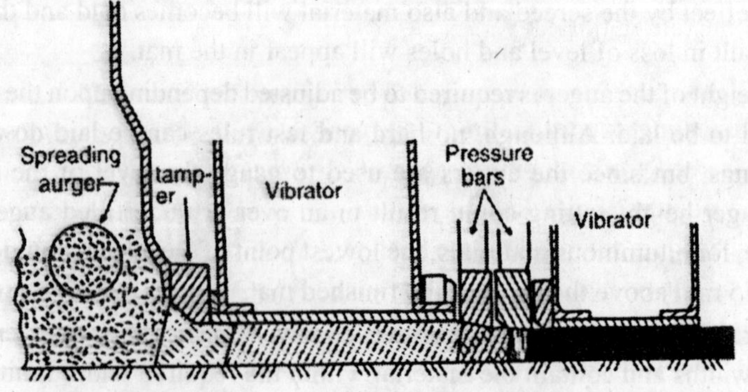

Fig. 12.23 Tamping and vibrating arrangement of screed.

final compaction. The amplitude of the first tamper is adjustable between 0-12 mm and that of the main tamper between 3-9 mm independent of each other. These adjustments of tamper amplitudes together with the variation of tamper speed and vibration frequency controls the compaction requirements of different types of mixes and mat thicknesses.

The speed of tamper shaft is controlled from the control panel where tamper blows per min are indicated. The speed of the shaft can be varied as per requirement varying from 0 to nearly 1500 r.p.m. (25 Hz).

(b) ***Vibrating System*** **:** Vibrating screed plate behind the tamper plate portion provides additional compaction and also improves the surface texture, especially when laying asphalt wearing courses. The vibration shaft speed is variable between 0 and maximum 4200 r.p.m. (70 Hz).

(c) ***Tamping and Vibrations Combined*** **:** The amplitude adjustment of both tampers, independently of each other, and the infinite variation of the tamper speeds and vibration frequency make it possible to adapt the screeds compacting effect to different types of mix and varying layer thicknesses.

Experience shows that Marshall and Procter densities reached with paver finishers equipped with high density screeds having duel tamper and vibrating arrangements, are about 7-10% higher than those obtained with single tamper/vibrating speeds :

(a) vibrating screed	approx. 80-82% mod. Proctor
(b) tamping and vibrating screed	approx. 88-92% mod. Proctor
(c) double tamping and vibrating screed	approx. 95-100% mod. Proctor

Economic Advantages of High Density Screeds :

1. A substantial reduction of rolling work. In many cases elimination of one or even more rollers, lower labour cost.
2. Uniform densities and excellent surface evenness, surface irregularities caused by rolling work are virtually eliminated.
3. Considerable lower risk of disputes over penalty/payment deduction for not meeting specification requirements.
4. Further extension of the pavers' field of use, *e.g.*, laying roller compacted concrete in thick layers.

Screed Heating

Screed heating is used mainly to prevent material adhering to the screed and to prevent the screed from making drag marks to the surface. Normally the screed is heated to few degrees above the temperature of the material being laid and the flame is extinguished and it is not necessary to heat the screed through out the paving operation. The heaters can be re-lit as necessary to maintain the temperature difference.

Two systems are in use for heating the screed, using diesel oil as a fuel and using propane gas, later is more common.

(a) **Diesel Oil Burner System :** In this system diesel oil is fed from fuel tank by a burner pump through the filter to the burner for heating the screed.

(b) **Propane Gas Burner System :** Propane gas for the burner system is supplied from a bottle. As propane gas burns very cleanly no carbon deposits will be found on the burners.

Screed Maintenance

After the use, all traces of paving material are removed using the diesel spray hose for bituminous materials and water for dry materials, special attention should be paid to the tamping machines, to the tampers and tamper shields cleaning. Keep all nuts and bolts tight.

Requisites for a Good Paver

A good paver finisher must fulfill following requirements :

(i) Must be able to handle all types of mixes.

(ii) Must evenly spread and initially compact, leaving a finished surface ready for final compaction by the steel and pneumatic tyred rollers.

(iii) Must be able to compensate for minor grade irregularities.

(iv) Must be able to form proper crowns and super-elevations.

(v) Must be able to push the large trucks while unloading the bituminous mix into the hopper of the paver.

12.10.3 Tracked V/s Wheeled Pavers

Earlier, tracked pavers were associated with new construction paving, while rubber tired with resurfacing. Rubber tired pavers are now-a-days predominate, and are used on laying of all kinds of sub-base and base materials, mixes as well as wet-mix aggregate and lean concrete. This eliminate the need for a motor grader for spreading base courses, and also reduces the number of compactor passes required, as paver screed itself does some work of pre-compaction due to its tamping and vibrating actions.

The wheeled paver has greater mobility. It can travel on its own. With the textendable screed, the latest pavers can travel narrow and lay wide.

Wheeled pavers have following **advantages** over tracked pavers :

(i) Wheeled pavers can be transported under their own power easily and quickly on site either from one end of the site to another or even from the end of a laid mat to commence a matching joint on its adjacent run.

(ii) Wheeled paver lay a truer mat,due to its free rolling movement which does not inherently place into the mat a series of ripples produced by its tracked counter part.

(iii) A paving machine, because of its duties, has an inherent vibration from its operating machinery, its tampers and/or vibrators. On wheeled pavers, this inherent vibration is, toa large extent, absorbed due to pneumatic tyres and, therefore, the amount of vibrations affecting the operator is cut to the minimum leading to less fatigue. In tracked pavers the absorption of vibration is very less.

Tracked pavers have following **advantages** :

(i) These have advantages when the ground conditions are very soft or loose, as the greater pressure area over the tracks as against the foot print of the rubber tyres, assist it in travelling over these conditions on which the wheel version could quite easily develop wheel spin.

(ii) It has an advantage in paving oddly shaped intersections as it can manoeuver faster than the wheel paver.

12.10.4 Electric Sensing Device

This instrument has two main parts. One to take a reference signal from the reference line and the second one to stimulate the movement, parallel to the reference line.

For this purpose it is essential to pull a wire all along the length of the track to be laid. This wire is set at the exact level and curve, so that the electronic levelling instrument takes reference from the line. A mechanical arm, loosely touches the wire as the machine travels, gives signals to the main electromagnetic hydraulic system.

If the position of the screed with reference to the 'reference line' is correct, the machine maintains the same setting and keeps on laying the same thickness. The moment there is a variation of any kind, *i.e.,* dent or a bump on the road, the wheels of the machine sinkdown or rise up with respect to the reference line and then the mechanical arm changes its position with respect to the reference line. This sends an impulse to the main control unit which actuates the hydraulic cylinders on the auxiliary arms. This concretes the screed suspension in such a way that the laid track maintains the same level difference all the time.

Automatic Level and Crossfall Sensor

Automatic level and crossfall in an electro-hydraulic system that enables the paver to lay a mat to a predetermined level and crossfall, regardless or undulations in the road base. The system when fitted to the pavers level automatically and when once set for proper thickness and left undisturbed, it will produce a better surface then when manually controlled. If it is necessary to adjust the controls do not move them too much at one time without giving the machine time to react, otherwise this will cause over adjustment. Automatic levelling systems is applied in two ways, either to have one grade controller mounted on any one side of the paver plus slope controller or to have two grade controllers, one on each side. The use of grade controllers requires stretched guide wires as corresponding reference lines.

12.11 Paver Output (Laying Rate)

The higher the paving speed, the greater the thickness and more the width, the greater will be the quantity of material passing through the paver during a given time, and *vice-versa*. The following formulae will enable quick calculations to be made of the quantity of material required per hour for a given width and thickness of mat :

$$Q = W \times \frac{T}{100} \times S \times D \times 60 \times \eta$$

where, Q = Quantity of material required in kg/hr
W = Mat width in meters
T = Mat thickness in centimetres
S = Working speed in metres/min
D = Material weight in kg/cum
η = Efficiency of operation.

Using the same formulae, the working speed to suit the given rate of material supply can be calculated as follows :

$$S = \frac{Q \times 100}{W \times T \times D \times 60 \times \eta}$$

Here efficiency depends upon the time loss caused by the feeding cycle, number and haulage capacity of the feeding trucks. For planning purposes it is generally considered as 0.7.

12.12 Compacting Equipment for Asphalt Works

Compaction methods, rolling procedures and different types of compactors used for the purpose have been discussed in detail in the chapter on "Compaction Equipment".

The compaction capability of pneumatic and steel wheel vibratory rollers can be altered to match the construction conditions. In pneumatic rollers, changing the ballast and tire pressure alters the compaction effort. In vibratory steel wheel rollers, adjusting the vibratory frequency and amplitude alters the compaction effort. These capabilities help in enhancing the operational flexibility of both these types of rollers.

The maximum amount of compaction per pass will be achieved by selecting the highest possible frequency as this means more impacts per unit distance travelled. Care should be taken that higher amplitude be considered only in the case of mat thickness greater than 7.5 cm. A high amplitude setting on a thin mat causes the roller to bounce, making effective and uniform compaction to be difficult. For mats having a thickness of 2.5 cm or less, rollers should be operated without vibrations.

The traditional system of three rollers, *i.e.,* smooth wheeled vibratory asphalt rollers, conventional pneumatic-tired rollers, and 3 wheel static rollers is presently replaced by high density screed paver followed by combination roller. Combination roller has 4 smooth rubber tyres, vibratory type 'compactor', combining in itself the high compacting effect of vibratory-type rollers with sealing effect of rubber-tired rollers. Complete overlap of tyre marks due to narrow spacing in relation to tyre width and wide front steel drum which also prevents lateral displacement of finished pavement.

Fig. 12.24 Rubber tyred vibratory roller (combination roller).

Combination roller which is now becoming popular for asphalt mix compaction and paving work in general combine in itself the high compacting effect of a vibratory roller (from front steel roll) with the sealing and "tightening" effect of a smooth pneumatic tired roller (from rear mounted tyres). This combination roller replaces the requirement of separate static or vibratory tandem-type or three wheeled roller.

To make these versatile, these can be quickly converted to soil compactors in the field by interchanging their 4 smooth tyres on the rear axle with 2 earthmover "grip" tyres and *vice-versa*.

The 2-stage vibration system with combined frequency and amplitude adjustment ($33\frac{1}{3}$ Hz with high amplitude for depth compaction or 50 Hz with low amplitude for surface compaction) makes it possible to adapt the compacting effect to different types of materials and varying layer thicknesses.

Important Features and Advantages of Combination Rollers

1. It is a versatile roller and can be used for all types of asphalt as well as soil compaction works.
2. Good kneeding effect of the multi-wheeled axle due to high contact pressure.
3. High compacting effect and excellent surface finish due to the well balanced relationship between static linear load, vibration frequency, amplitude and centrifugal force.
4. Automatic and instantaneous hydrostatic braking of the vibrator before the roller reverses of comes to a halt.

12.13 Bitumen Distributors

It is mounted on a truck chassis and have a tank with pump, valve system, and spray bar. Usual size of bitumen distributor tanks range between 5000 and 12000 litres.

Bitumen distributor must satisfy following minimum requirements for economic distribution of material :

(i) It must spread the binder evenly both longitudinally and transversely.

(ii) It must be able to vary the amount of binder per surface unit from 0.2 to 10 kg/m^2.

(iii) It must heat up the binder and maintain it at the correct temperature.

(iv) It must be able to distribute all existing types of binders.

Construction

The tank mounted on the truck chassis is an insulated tank with a heating system usually oil fired burners with the direct heat from the flues passing through the tank. The heating flues are along the whole length of the distributor tank and are supported in sleeves by the surge plates and have liners of heat resistant steel. These liners are removable for inspection and replacement. The tank has two gauges, one for indicating bitumen temperature and another for indicating bitumen contents in the tank.

It is equipped with a compressor and/or a gear type rotary pump for feeding the bitumen to the spraybar mounted across the rear of the machine. The spraybar is fitted with nozzles spaced equally across and so arranged that they give an application of binder by spraying the bitumen under pressure and that is constant across the width. The speed of the distributor and in some cases speed of the bitumen pump can be determined for the given application rate. The spraybar can easily be adjusted vertically. The each nozzle spray is overlapped as shown in Fig. 12.25 so as to give uniform application along whole length. The spray bar is full circulating type, *i.e.,* when bar is not spraying, the bitumen circulates from tank to spraybar and again to the tank. A thermometer is mounted on the tank to indicate bitumen temperature.

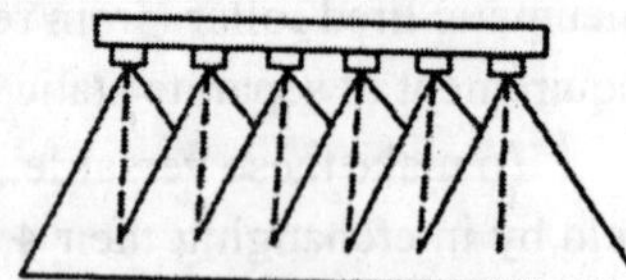

Fig. 12.25 Overlapped nozzle spray.

A great attention is given to safety and reliability of operation because of fire hazard and importance of work. It provides pressure relieving manhole cover, safety relief valve provided on the bitumen pump, replaceable heat resistant liner at burner end of the heatflue, non-skid catwalk and a hand rail folding sideways with a ladder.

The various units requiring power like blower, bitumen pump etc. get power from a diesel power unit with clutch and transmission mounted on rear operator's platform.

Functions

Bitumen distributors are designed to perform the following functions :

(i) Bitumen is easily fed into the tank from an outside source such as tank, vehicle carrying bitumen, drums etc.

(ii) Bitumen is sprayed through spraybar or hand spraybar, uniformly and at a desired rate.

(iii) Bitumen can be transferred from one outside source to an other outside source by using loading hose and discharge hose.
(iv) Bitumen can be discharged to the tank by using the bitumen pump.

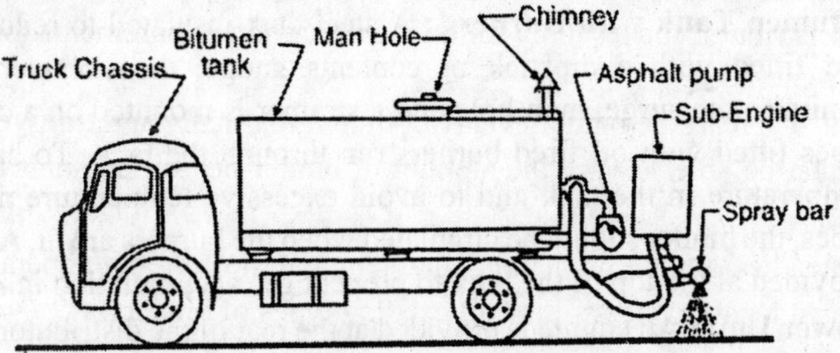

Fig. 12.26 Bitumen distributor.

(v) Cleaning of pump, all pippings, spraybar and hand spray attachment can be done easily by flushing oil sent from the flushing oil tank.
(vi) Bitumen distributor must have a heating system.
(vii) It must operate by means of a pressure system.
(viii) It must have a binder circulating pump to circulate the bitumen in the tank to prevent overheating near the flue pipes and to prevent the clogging of the nozzles when the distributor is in standing position.
(ix) Spraybar width must be adjustable, so as to obtain the desired application width.
(x) Distributor must have a tachometer located infront of the driver to show the travelling speed of the distributor in meters per minute.
(xi) It should have a chart for determining the discharge in litres per min for each size of nozzles and truck speeds to obtain correct binder application rate.

Care in Operation

(i) The bitumen should be at its correct viscosity, *i.e.*, temperature.
(ii) Correct and constant pressure should be maintained throughout the length of the spraybar and throughout the spraying operatin.
(iii) The distributor should be driven at a constant speed.
(iv) Nozzles should be set at correct angle and at correct height with the spraybar, and checked for uniform and correct amount of delivery.
(v) To avoid blocked jets, stainers and in-line filters in the binder feed system must be regularly cleaned.
(vi) Before commencing spraying the spraybar and jets should be preheated by circulating hot binder, and thin jets should be operated for a few seconds discharging on to waste ground to ensure their free operation.
(vii) During brief interruption, spray bar should be kept hot by circulating hot binder.
(viii) Do not operate burners when distributor is spraying or moving.
(ix) A fire extinguisher should be located in convenient position.

Components of Bitumen Distributors

Brief description of the main components of a bitumen distributor is given here under :

1. **Bitumen Tank with Burners :** A steel tank insulated to reduce heat loss and fitted with a dipstick or contents gauge, thermometer, baffles to minimise the surge, man-hole and a strainer is mounted on a chassis. Flue pipes fitted with oil fired burners run through the tank. To have uniform temperature in the tank and to avoid excessive temperature near the flue pipes, the binder should be circulated when the burners are lit. A vent pipe is provided at the top of the tank to prevent gas accumulation in the tank.
2. **Power Unit :** An engine is provided at the rear of the distributor to drive the binder pump, and a small air compressor to supply air for burners. The power is supplied through a clutch and a reduction gear.
3. **Binder Pump :** Generally rotary gear type pumps are used for this purpose. Those pumps are fitted inside the tank into a pocket so as to ensure to flooded suction during the entire spraying period and also to keep it hot by the surrounding binder.
4. **Pressure Relief and Regulating Valve :** A spring loaded pressure relief valve is fitted in the delivery line, and controls and maintains the pressure in the spray bar during circulating and spraying to ensure constant output at the nozzle.
5. **Spray Bars and Jets :** Combined nozzles and shut off valves are built into spraybar and ganged together for simultaneous operation by main lever, or they can shut off individually to reduce or increase width of spray when desired, the remaining nozzles being ganged to give instantaneous cut off. Every spraybar is fitted with a height with a height adjuster which raises or lowers the spraybar hydraulically. A hand spray take off is provided with flexible hose with hand lance, jet and a control valve.

   Spray bars are also provided with folding extensions to enable these to be retracted within the width of the vehicle for travelling. When the spray bar extensions are in the spraying position, the valve allows the binder to be circulated or sprayed through the extension(s) and main spray bar.

Fig. 12.27 Bitumen distributor in operation.

12.14 Safety Precautions in Asphalt Mixing Plants

1. Piping for hot oil and asphalt shall be adequately insulated to protect workers from injury by burns and flexible piping shall be metal encased. The flexible pipe, when not in use, shall be left in the ground.
2. Operation of asphalt plant shall be under the supervision of a competent person and the plant shall be inspected by a competent person at periodical intervals.
3. Workers handling hot asphalt shall wear gloves, rubber boots, goggles and if necessary, to prevent danger, suitable protective clothing.
4. No open light shall be used for ascertaining the level of asphalt and thinners shall not be heated over an open flame.
5. If burner goes out, the fuel supply shall be cut off and hot tube shall be thoroughly blown out by the fan so as to prevent back fire.
6. Spilled asphalt shall be promptly cleaned up0.
7. A chimney or other suitable exhaust arrangements shall be provided to remove the combustion gases and dust.
8. A mixture elevator should be within an enclosure with a window for observation, lubrication and maintenance.
9. Bitumen scoops should have adequate covers.
10. When asphalt plants are working on a public road, adequate traffic control is established on such road and the workers working with such plant are provided with reflecting jackets.
11. A sufficient number of fire extinguishers are kept in readiness on such workplace where fire hazards may exist.
12. Inspection opening is not opened till there is a pressure in the boiler which may cause injury to the worker.
13. Molten asphalt generates fumes that can cause skin diseases and eye and respiratory tract irritation, therefore personnel working around the plant must be safety conscious.
14. Maintenance should only be performed when the plant has been completely shut down.
15. All fuel, asphalt and oil lines should have control valves that can be activated from a safe distance.
16. All the precautions as mentioned in section 16.2 above.

QUESTIONS

1. Indicate various structural elements on the sectional diagram of a highway or airfield. Explain these elements.
2. Write short notes on :
   (a) Bituminous macadam (b) Surface course
   (c) Granular (aggregate) base courses.
3. Discuss 'hot-mixing' of asphaltic concrete. What are the requisites, properties and materials of the asphalt concrete mix.

4. Discuss the procedure for preparing hot mix asphalt in a continuous type hot mix asphalt plant.
5. Discuss the construction and working of batch type hot mix asphalt plant.
6. Discuss the procedure for preparing hot mix asphalt in a batch type hot mix asphalt plant.
7. (a) Discuss ideal conditions for maximum production of asphalt mixes by a hot mix plant.
   (b) Discuss different factors affecting asphalt concrete production.
8. Precautions to be taken for good quality asphalt mixing.
9. Differentiate between (a) Batch type, and (b) Continuous type hot mix asphalt plants with regards to their construction and working.
10. What is the necessity of producing asphaltic concrete?
11. Explain the construction and working of 'paddle mixer' type of cold asphalt mix plant.
12. Explain different materials used in hot asphaltic concrete mix.
13. Name different components of an asphalt batch type hot mix plant on a neat line diagram.
14. Explain the construction and working of a drier drum of a continuous type of hot mix asphalt plant. Draw a neat sketch of the construction of drier drum.
15. Explain any two types of air pollution control equipment used in hot mix asphalt plants.
16. (a) What is flexible pavement? Why is it necessary?
    (b) Explain the term asphalt, and asphalt concrete.
17. Discuss the method of asphalt laying by a paver.
18. Describe the procedure for 'laying the mat' by a paver.
19. (a) How mat thickness is controlled in a paver?
    (b) Discuss automatic level and crossfall censor used in paver.
20. Discuss common troubles felt during paving with their causes and remedies.
21. Explain the construction and working of paver finisher.
22. What are the functions of screeds provided in paver finishers?
23. How would you specify a paver finisher for the construction of bituminous road for 'express highway'?
24. Describe different types of rollers used in asphaltic works. How an asphalt layer should be compacted?
25. (a) List out the equipments used in asphalt laying.
    (b) Mention the main specifications of equipments, you would like to use in asphalt laying of 3 lane expressway.
26. Give advantages and disadvantages of laying the asphalt by motor grader method, and by using the paver.
27. Explain the method of compaction by the screed of paver finisher.
28. Write short notes on :
    (a) Requisites of a good paver (b) Paver output
29. Compare tracked and wheeled paver finishers.
30. Explain the construction and working of bitumen distributors.

Part - IV

OTHER CONSTRUCTION EQUIPMENT

Chapter 13

Shovels (Cable Operated Equipment)

13.1 Introduction

The earth excavating equipment may be hydraulically operated (already discussed in previous chapter) or rope-operated. These may be divided into four categories, *viz.* face shovels, backhoes (also called simply as hoes), draglines, and clamshell or grab. The type and size of the equipment depends upon the nature of the task, the type of soil, digging depth and the desired level of production.

The excavating equipment operate in a stationary mode and dump the excavated materials on the sides, or directly into waiting tippers/dump trucks. These excavating equipment gradually shift their position as the excavation progresses.

Shovel family represents rope-operated excavators and uses different types of front end attachments. Following are the four types of front end attachments, by changing them only, one type of machine is converted into another type,k basic structure remains unchanged.

(i) The Dipper or Power Shovel

(ii) The Dragline

(iii) The Clamshell

(iv) The Backhoe or Hoe

Sometimes the first type is called by the name 'shovel' only, which is used for excavating and is fitted with a short-length boom working in forward strokes. The distance the material must be moved by the machine from the digging point to the dumping point will determine which type of front and machine is most advisable. The type of material to be excavated also determines the actual type of machine employed. Shovel and Hoe booms are some what short as compared with the longer booms on a dragline or clamshell. Shovels and Hoes can dig tougher material than lies within the possibilities of the longer boom machines.

The shovels are available in various sizes varying from a fraction of cu. m. to over hundred cu. m. in bucket size and can handle the material weighing from a few tonnes to hundreds of tonnes. The basic structure of all types of shovels, namely, Dipper, Dragline, Clamshell, Back Hoe and Mobile Shovels may be either crawler mounted or truck mounted. If the work is concentrated in one area and has a large job, mobility is of less importance, then crawler-mounted shovel are more useful. Where the jobs are scattered at various places truck-mounted shovels are preferred. The crawler mounted shovel can operate on ground surfaces which are not strong enough to support the truck-mounted shovels.

Structure of the basic shovel provides basic operations, namely,

(a) movement of the machine, known as 'walking'.

(b) revolving action of the superstructure for handling loads, known as 'Swinging', and

(c) actual working of the attachment like digging, hoisting etc.

The power for all these operations is provided by the prime-mover.

13.2 Dipper (Front or Power) Shovel

These are used for digging hard rock to quarries or ore in mines. These are used for digging above the machine base level, and have faster and more accurate digging and dumping cycle as compared to that of draglines, hoes and clamshells.

Fig. 13.1 Photoview of a dipper shovel.

These are also known as face shovel and operates from a flat surface, producing upward digging action, excavating and filling the bucket as it climbs. After the bucket is filled, its upper part swings to the dumping position where the bucket is emptied in a waiting truck or on to a stockpile. It then returns to its original position and starts the next cycle of excavation. It is capable of working in all types of dry soils. These shovels are mainly used for digging hard earth above the track level and for loading haul units. Loading of big boulders or shot rock is also possible, as these are capable of developing high break-out force with their buckets, but the material excavated should be such that it can stand perpendicular to the ground.

The power shovel consists of boom, dipper stick, the bucket and the mechanism of operation. The boom and stick are connected as shown in Fig. 13.2. The lower end of the boom is hinged to the support bracket of the revolving deck and the upper and (also

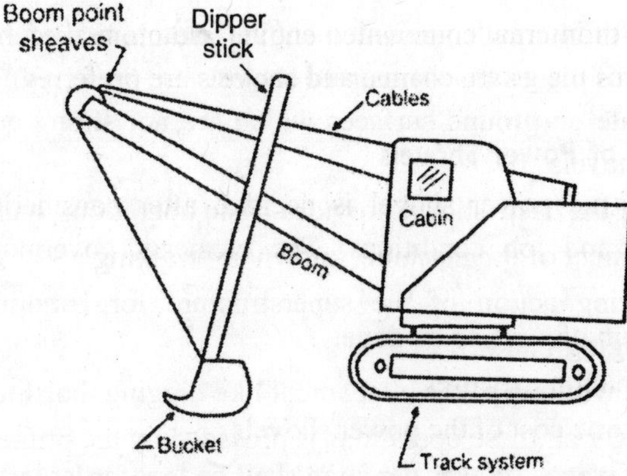

Fig. 13.2 Dipper shovel.

known as point), carries the bucket hoist sheaves. The dipper stick moves back and forth on a shipper drum through a guide formed by a saddle block attached to the boom. The shipper drum is mounted on a shipper shaft which is passing through the boom and supported on it at the ends. The shipper drum is rotated by pulling the cable and causing the stick to slide back and forth. The bucket is provided at the end of the dipper stick.

The buckets of the power shovels are strong built steel box which are open at the top and provided with a hinged door at the bottom. The buckets are made in the sizes varying from 1/2 cu m to hundred cu m or more depending upon the size and capacity of the power shovel. The design and shape of the bucket is such that, it can easily handle the material to be excavated. Front edge is given a lip formation so as to make cuts conveniently. Lip has tapered sockets to receive similar shanks made into the teeth. The teeth are made of manganese steel and are replaceable. Depending upon the job conditions the teeth designs are of sharp, rock and general purpose types.

So as to ensure optimum production, rebuilding of the bucket tooth points is necessary. The bucket teeth material austenitic manganese steel is characterised for high strength, high ductility and extreme toughness. Due to severe impact the surface becomes work hardened, while the interior remains soft and tough. This prevents the teeth from breaking into pieces. Repointer bars of austenitic manganese steel are available for reclaiming worn dipper teeth. The exterior surface of the worn tooth is cut and removed by oxy-acetylene flame. The size of the repointer bar is selected depending upon the extent of damage of the tooth. The bar is cut to the required size and then welded with a medium heavy coated, all-position, low-hydrogen type austenitic stainless electrodes. In case austenitic manganese steel pointer bars are not available, carbon steel pointer bars may be used but they shall give a lesser life.

13.2.1 Electrical Shovels

Electrical shovels and draglines normally operating on three-phase alternating current (AC) furnished between 2000 and 6000 volts. Electric shovels can also be operated by the electricity generated by generating sets or a diesel engine and a generator installed in the shovel itself. Such shovels are called diesel-electric shovel. Use of electricity eliminates the use of internal combustion engine, clutch, brakes, mechanical controls, to eliminate some of the gears, chains, and cables.

13.2.2 Selection of Power Shovels

Type and size of the power shovel is decided after considering various techno-economic factors and job conditions. The elements governing the rate of unit production are :

1. Quantum of work to be done.
2. Depreciation expenses.
3. Down time cost of the power shovels.
4. Cost of wages. Wages per cu m shall be less for larger size shovel.
5. Ownership and operational expenses.
6. The cost of drilling, blasting and excavating the rock should also be considered, as bigger size shovel need less expenditure on these as they themselves can handle bigger rocks, and thus saves expenses of drilling and blasting.
7. To lift excavated earth from a basement or trench into trucks at ground level will need long reach of a large shovel.
8. Large size of dipper is needed when bigger rocks are to be handled.
9. Size of hauling units in which the excavated materials is to be loaded.
10. Large size of shovels are required for hard and tough materials.

Operation of Power Shovels

Before actual operation, the power shovel faces the job with stick projecting forward horizontally. For operation, first step is to release hoist to bring the bucket down and move the stick in vertical plane and hoist brake is applied again before it hits the ground down on the shipper drum till the bucket teeth rest on the ground. Now the bucket is moved forward and downward,by lifting the hoist brake and engaging the clutch. The depth of cut and angle of digging is controlled as per requirement of the job considering the ground conditions. When bucket is filled, the next step is to retract the stick to pull out the bucket and also to hoist it till the machine can be swung around for dumping. During swinging the position of the bucket is so adjusted that it comes in most suitable dumping position considering the position and height of the carrier used for transporting the excavated earth. To empty the bucket, the door is opened by unlatching it through the trip arrangement. The cycle is thus repeated again and again.

Power Shovel Applications

As mentioned earlier Power or Dipper Shovel is most suitable for close range works. These are used for digging very hard material and can remove big boulders. For working, it need to be kept on fairly solid footing on the ground. These can be used on various jobs of digging in rock, gravel, clay etc. Therefore, they find application in road works for trimming and dressing slopes and banks, mining work (open cut) etc.

13.2.3 Types of Shovel-Buckets

Shovel-Buckets are of following types :

(a) Front dump bucket

(b) Bottom dump bucket

(a) Front Dump Bucket

These buckets are used for special applications, like hot slag or extremely abrasive material etc. These have following advantages and disadvantages over bottom dump buckets.

Advantages : Greater capacity, less weight, lower maintenance cost.

Disadvantages :

(i) Bucket has to be hoisted higher for dumping.

(ii) More wear on truck bodies.

(iii) More shovel rotation required.

(iv) More wear of parts.

(v) No partial dumping possible.

(b) Bottom Dump Bucket

This type of bucket has a much wider scope of applications and has many advantages over front dump bucket. Since these buckets are heavy and hence offers less capacity. Some of the advantages of these buckets are :

1. Controlled Loading

This has following advantages :

(i) The bucket usually dump material much closer to the body floor, thereby decreases the drop height of the material, and since the bucket opens from the bottom, finer material will run out first and form a cushion in the truck body which will increase body life.

(ii) The last bucket can be spread over the truck body to more completely fill it to capacity.

(iii) Easier placing especially when loading small size truck.

(iv) Less material is lost from the sidewall of the truck body.

2. Faster Cycle Times

(i) Because of faster positioning and quicker dumping, cycle times will be 10 to 15% shorter.

(ii) Sticky and wet material will clear out much more completely and easily.

(iii) Required hoist height is lower, since material is being dumped out from the bottom. This shortens the cycle time further.

3. Versatility

Other advantages of bottom dump buckets are :

(i) If required the bucket can be used to sort rock with clamshell bucket. This allows sorting of oversize boulders which can help avoiding bridging in crusher mouth and thus increases the crusher production.

(ii) The bucket is also suitable to clean the truck parking spot between truck exchanges.

13.2.4 Production of Power Shovels

The production capacity or output of a shovel is expressed in cubic meter per hour. The output varies for various types of materials to be digged. Following are the main factors which effect the output of a power shovel :

1. Nature of soil.
2. Height or depth of cut.
3. Type of material.
4. Angle of swing.
5. Capacity of hauling unit and continuity of work, *i.e.*, waiting time.
6. Mechanical condition of shovel.
7. Efficiency of the operator.
8. Relative positions of the shovel and hauling unit.
9. Size of bucket.
10. Type of machine (such as crawler or wheeled).
11. Total cycle time.

Following factors should be kept in view to **get better output** from a shovel :

1. Working cycle should be smooth, well balanced and well managed.
2. Have a clear swing.
3. Have sufficient number of hauling units to keep the shovel busy. Avoid waiting time for the hauling units as well as for the shovel. Also see that the hauling units rolling is evenly distributed.
4. Load the hauling units uniformly, avoid overloading.
5. Position the shovel at a place so as to get proper rake, swing and position with respect to type of material handled and position of the hauling units.
6. Dig the top half of the high bank first to avoid lowering of the boom in each cycle. Then digging o the next half should be taken up. This helps in reducing the cycle time.
7. While waiting for the hauling units, do not keep shovel idle. This time should be utilised in cleaning the pit area, loosening the bank, cleaning-up the corners, levelling the grade etc. so that, these operations may not consume time once the hauling unit arrives.

8. Keep dipper teeth well sharpen and have the dipper adjusted for proper digging angle.
9. Fill the dipper each time, generally when even cut is not made the bank corner are not filled up. Avoid this by making even cut.

Size of Power Shovel

The size of the power shovel is me3asuredby strucking the dipper into the earth even with the contour of the dipper. This is known as struck volume. Another method of measuring the size is by picking up of loose soil from the heap, and is known as heaped volume. Due to swelling of the soil when loosened, the loose volume will be more than the bank-measure volume. Thus for a dipper of 2 cu m when excavating a soil whose swell is 25 percent, the bank-measure volume will be $2 \div 1.25 = 1.6$ cu m.

13.2.5 Output of Shovels

Output of a shovel can be calculated using the following formula :

Hourly production (cu m/hr) = Q

$$= q \times \frac{3600}{C} \times \text{Efficiency}$$

where, q = Production in cu m per cycle

= Heaped capacity × Swell factor × Bucket factor.

C = Theoretical cycles/hr

Following are the elements of the production cycle of a shovel :

1. Load bucket, 2. Swing with load,
3. Dump bucket, 4. Return swing.

Output of a tractor shovel depends upon the size of a bucket, soil characteristics, type of working surface and type of shovel, *i.e.*, whether crawler or wheel mounted. Manufacturer of the equipment used to provide a graph between bucket size v/s production/hr. Since this gives production in ideal conditions, the figures thus obtained should be scaled down to expected production by using efficiency factor and bucket fill factor. These factors are generally taken as follows :

(a) *Excavation efficiency factor* :

(i)	Sand, gravel, common earth	60%
(ii)	Clay	50%
(iii)	Blasted rock	40%

(b) *Bucket factor* :

(i)	Sand, gravel, common earth	90%
(ii)	Well blasted rock	70%
(iii)	Poorly blasted rock	50%

Above figures are for crawler type of tractor shovel, however for wheeled shovels, bucket factor is about 10% lesser than those mentioned above.

Matching of Truck and Loading Machine

The correct sizing of the loading machine is determined partially by the size of the available trucks and *vice-versa*. Experience has shown that the most advantageous to load a truck in 2 to 3 minutes to utilize trucks to their best. This has now become an accepted rules. Considering the workcycles for different reach between 22 to 32 seconds, which results in 5 to 7 buckets per truck.

Performance Capacity of Shovels

Performance capacity of earth excavating machines depends on :

(a) **Bucket capacity :** For best performance the bucket has to be chosen to best fit the material. It is important to consider the kind of material, its specific weight, the condition of the material, its abrasiveness and the size of its particles.

(b) **Degree of fill :** The fill degree of the bucket depends on the bucket shape, attachment geometry, and sizing.

(c) **Work cycle time :** This time has following components :

(i) fill bucket,

(ii) hoisting and swinging of full bucket over receiving container,

(iii) dumping, and

(iv) lowering and swinging towards material.

The cycle time further depends on many other factors such as size of loading machine, kind of material and its preparation, positioning of truck and experience of the operator.

(d) **Real work time per hour :** The length of real work time per 60 minute hour depends on the application and organization of the job itself. This factor includes all not preplanned interruptions which exist in any job. Interruptions due to weather, traffic, blasting, change of buckets, management of job, reduce the available work time, known as "average real work time".

Considering normal conditions production are calculated per 50 minute hour (83% efficiency). Under bad conditions, the real available work time might drop to 45 minutes per hour (75% efficiency) or less. Under varying real work time per hour, job efficiency is mentioned hereunder :

Real worktime per hour	*Job efficiency (in %)*
60 minutes	100
55 minutes	91
50 minutes	83
45 minutes	75
40 minutes	67

Bucket Capacities of Shovel (Size of Shovel)

The size of a shovel is indicated by the size of the bucket expressed in cubic meter. In measuring the size of the bucket the earth is struck even with the contour of the bucket. This is called the **struck volume.**

Struck Capacity : The volume actually enclosed by the bucket with no allowance for bucket teeth is called struck capacity.

Heaped Capacity : The rated heaped capacity represent a net section of bucket volume. The angle of repose of the fill material may be taken as 45° or 1 : 1.

Fill Factor : The amount of material actually in a bucket compared to its volume is called fill factor. This factor is used for determining the shovel production. Fill factor is the percentage that, when multiplied by the rated heaped capacity, represents the volume of material loaded into the bucket.

Factors Affecting Output of a Power Shovel

There are so many factors which affect the output of the power shovels. In order to achieve maximum output following points must be considered :

(a) **Effect of the depth of cut :** If the excavating material is too shallow, it will be difficult to fill the dipper completely in one pass, and hence reduces the output of the unit. Similarly the output will be less if the depth of the face is greater than optimum depth.

(b) **Effect of angle of swing :** The angle of swing of a power shovel is the horizontal angle, between the position of the dipper when it is excavating and the position when it is discharging the load. If the angle of swing is increased, the time for a cycle will be increased and *vice-versa*. It has been observed that if the angle of swing is reduced from 90 to 60°, keeping other conditions same, the output will be increased by 16 percent.

(c) **Effect of job conditions :** Output of a shovel is maximum under excellent job conditions. The conditions are excellent when it is operating in a large open pit, with a firm, well drained floor, and where the tippers/dumpers are spotted on either side of the shovel to avoid waiting time, the ground is uniformly level to always have optimum depth of cut. The conditions are poor when material is excavated for a highway cut through a hill, for a depth of cut varying from zero to more than optimum depth, sides of the slope are too sloped, cut is narrow so that a loaded tipper si to be taken out before empty truck can back into loading position, tipper is spotted behind the shovel to have the angle of swing of about 180°, muddy floor of cut.

The conditions in reality are in between excellent to poor and are classified as excellent, good, fair and poor.

(d) **Effect of management conditions :** Management conditions also effect the output considerably. Some of these conditions are :

(i) Maintenance and inspection of the shovel.

(ii) Timely change of dull dipper teeth.

(iii) Storage of fast moving spares.

(iv) Keeping the pit floor clean for smooth spotting of tippers and to reduce angle of swing.

(v) Proper management of hauling trucks to reduce waiting time.

13.3 Hoe (Back-Hoe) or Drag-Shovel

This equipment is also known as Drag-shovel or Pull-shovel. Since the digging mechanism resembles to an ordinary garden hoe, this equipment is named as Hoe. The equipment has an ability to penetrate even the toughest of materials. Due to this ability these are commonly used in quarries which have tough digging conditions and are prone to flooding, rendering the use of conventional shovel operations impractical.

The drag shovels are extensively used in trench digging applications, and can dig easily to greater depth below the level of the equipment. Like power shovels, hoe also has accurate spotting of the digging bucket. The dumping into the carrier units is difficult and not as efficient as a power shovel, and also has a slow working speed.

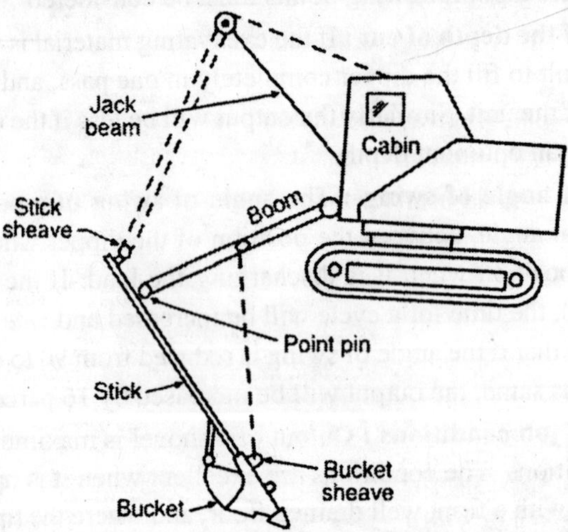

Fig. 13.3 Drag shovel or hoe.

As the name Drag or Pull shovel suggests, digging is done by dragging or pulling of the bucket towards the machine, whereas power shovel makes outward strokes while digging. This shovel consists of a boom and stick; a jack boom and the bucket attached at the end of the stick. The stick in Hoe is hinged by a pin with a boom as shown in Fig. 13.3 and thus enables to turn over the pin to take any desired direction best suited for digging or dumping operations. The lower end of the stick carries the bucket, while the upper end carries a sheave having the hoist cable supported on a jack boom at the other end and passes on to the hoist drum. Therefore, when a pull is applied to the hoist cable, the reaction at the stick hinge enable to move the boom with stick, up or down. Thus the boom can take any position in vertical plane.

Applications : Hoes or drag shovels are used mainly for following types of jobs :

(i) For digging trenches, footings or basements.

(ii) To dug materials which are hard.

(iii) Where close trimming is required during excavation.

(iv) Where excavation is required below the ground level and then dumping is done at a short range.

Booms for Dipper or Drag Shovels (Hoe)

Each boom and dipper stick is a matched assemble, designed to provide maximum productivity for specific attachments and job requirements. Since these excavators (dipper or hoe shovels) can perform several jobs, it is important to select right boom and dipper stick combination. Three types of booms are generally available, namely : adjustable, monoblock and multipurpose.

(a) Adjustable Boom : These are most versatile boom, and can be adjusted in several ways. High angulation setting is helpful maximum reach or dump height, whereas low angulation is helpful for greater digging depth. Retracted position of the boom allows the least amount of reach and digging depth with greatest amount of lift capacity with stability, while extended position of the boom allows maximum depth or reach with less favourable lift capacity, whereas intermediate position is a general purpose setting for satisfactory operation on most applications.

For use with adjustable boom, three types of dipper sticks are available : standard, short, and long.

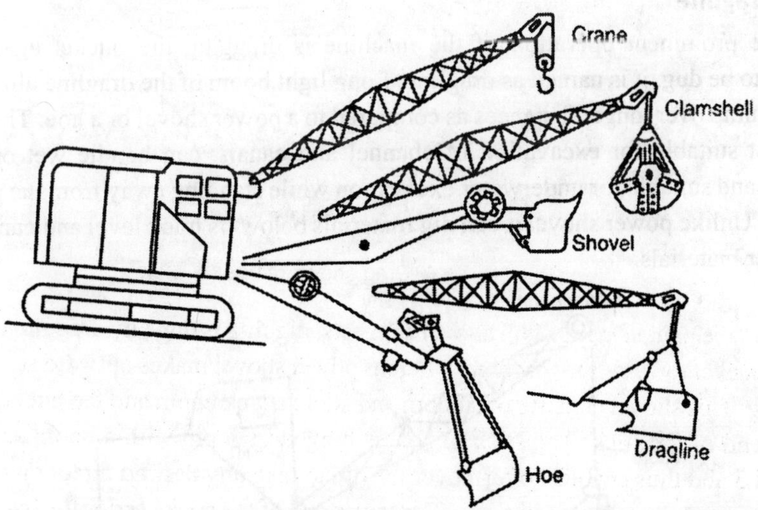

Fig. 13.4 Boom attachments.

(b) Monoblock Boom : Monoblock boom are designed basically for back hoe excavating operations. It is built on the principle that less weight in the assembly means more payload per lift. Because of the one piece construction, these have high strength with less weight. The monoblock booms are used with either standard or long dipper sticks.

(c) **Multipurpose Boom :** This boom is comparatively short boom with the driving cylinder mounted on the underside, rather than on top of the boom, this will utilize maximum driving cylinder power for extending and lifting the dipper stick, rather than pressing in. This configuration is advantageous for ditch cleaning attachments and for heavy lifting power. An adjustable dipper stick is used with the multipurpose boom, which can be set at two positions, *i.e.*, retracted or extended.

13.3.1 Production of Pull Shovel

For better efficiency of pull shovel, following suggestions are made :

1. Keep bucket teetch sharp, built upto proper size.
2. Try to keep the shovel higher than trucks or dumpers when loading.
3. Line shovel up to cut outer edges of excavation in a straight line.
4. Optimum depth of cut for a hoe depends upon the type of material to be excavated, size and type of bucket.
5. The most effective digging action takes place when the dipper stick and boom are at right angles.
6. Maximum output can be obtained when the digging is done near the machine.

13.4 Dragline

Since the prominent operation of the machine is dragging the bucket against the material to be dug, it is named as dragline. Long light boom of the dragline allows it to dig and dump over longer distances as compared to a power shovel or a hoe. Therefore, it is most suitable for excavation of channel and canals, can handle wet or foggy material, and suitable for underwater excavation while standing away from the pit, on a firm soil. Unlike power shovel it can dig materials below its track level and can handle only other materials.

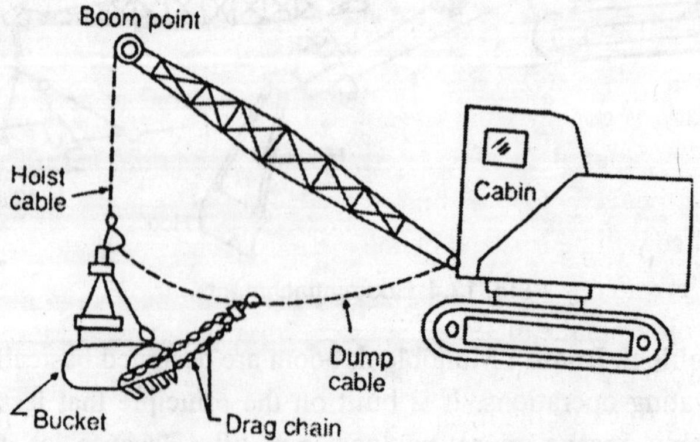

Fig. 13.5(a) Dragline-Line diagram.

Capacity of a dragline is indicated by the bucket capacity measured in cubic meters and generally available in 1 to 5 cu m capacities. Front end of a dragline consists of the boom, a bucket, a failead, and hoist, dump and drag cables as shown in Fig. 13.5(a). The boom is like a crane boom, the top and bottom ends of which are known as the 'point' and the 'foot' respectively. To make the boom lighter the section can be made up of tubes. The boom is attached to the deck with pins at foot and supported at the point through the boom hoist cable passing over a pair of sheaves placed one on each side.

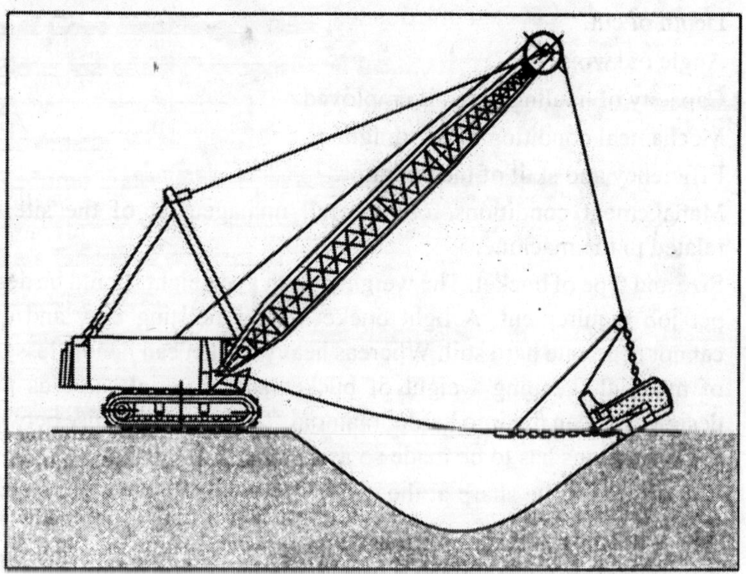

Fig. 13.5(b) Dragline.

Buckets

Draglines have following types of buckets :

(a) **Light :** These are suitable for loose, dry soils, sand and gravel.

(b) **Medium :** These are used for clays and compacted gravel etc. where bucket teeth penetrates with difficulty.

(c) **Heavy :** These buckets are used for handling hard materials and broken rocks.

It is necessary to consider the weight of the bucket, since weight of the bucket with weight of the material in it is determined by the boom strength. Hence for a particular boom if the weight of the bucket itself is more than the necessary, it means the material handled will be less and hence the output shall be low.

For the underwater works, the buckets with perforations and geneally used to permit water to drain from the material. For a common dragline operation, the bucket is a steel box open from the top as well as in the front and has cutting teeth fitted to lower front edge, pointing towards the machine. A drag chain is provided in the front of the bucket and is connected with a drag yoke, to which a drag cable is anchored. A hoist is attached to the rear of the bucket. A dump cable is stretched between the drag yoke and the dump sheave. It is used for turning the bucket upside down, teeth pointing downward. Thus the bucket is controlled by three ways, namely, the drag, the hoist and the dump.

13.4.1 Output of Dragline

Output or the performance of the dragline depends on the following factors :

1. Nature of soil.
2. Depth of cut.
3. Angle of swing.
4. Capacity of hauling units, if employed.
5. Mechanical condition of the dragline.
6. Efficiency and skill of the operator.
7. Management conditions, *i.e.*, overall management of the site of work related to the machine.
8. Size and type of bucket. The weight, width and height should be designed as per job requirement. A light bucket makes hoisting easy and quick but cannot penetrate hard soil. Whereas heavy bucket can handle lesser amount of material (keeping weight of bucket and material same as per boom design), but can dig into harder material. Thus a compromise between these two conditions has to be made so as to get economical output.
9. The teeth must be sharp at the cutting edge and tight on their bases to get best results.
10. Working cycle. It should be kept low by avoiding dragging of the bucket unnecessary. As after the bucket is full no material can be loaded by further dragging it.

Suggestions for dragline operation :

1. Keep bucket teeth sharp and built upto the proper size.
2. Dig in layers, not in ditches.
3. Keep digging surface sloped up towards shovel.
4. Pick up bucket as soon as it is full.
5. Do not swing until bucket or load is clear of the ground as boom may get twisted.
6. As far as possible keep the trucks in the pit for loading, as this increases the production by about ten percent, compared to that when it is being loaded on the same level.

Dragline Production

$$\text{Dragline prodution} = \text{Dragline capacity } (\text{m}^3) \times C \times f$$

where, C = Theoretical cycles/hr = 120 cycles/hr.

f = Correcting factor

$= f_1 \times f_2 \times f_3 \times f_4 \times f_5 \times f_6 \times f_7$

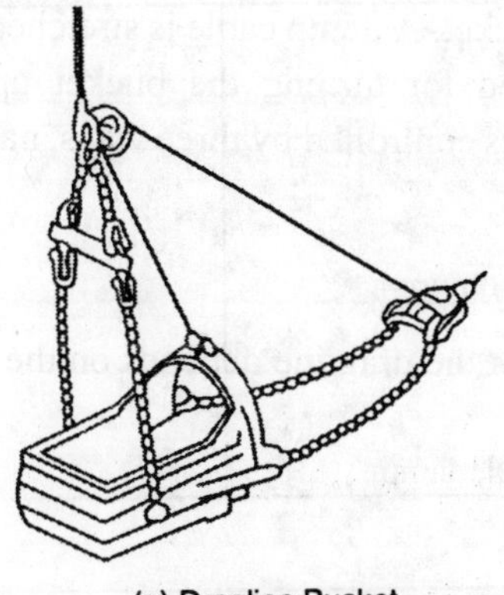

(a) Dragline Bucket

(b) Dragline in operation

Fig. 13.6

Data are taken from 'Liebherr's Technical Handbook Earthmoving Product line, Edn. 1986/87'.

f-Correction Factors

1. f_1—*Fill factor* :

	Class	*Fill factor*
1.	Sand or fine gravel	
	(a) dry	1.1 to 1.2
	(b) damp	1.0 to 1.1
	(c) wet	0.9 to 0.8
2.	Clay	
	(a) sandy clay, dry	0.95 to 1.0
	(b) cohesive, dry	0.90 to 0.95
	(c) very cohesive, hard	0.88 to 0.90

3.	Earth with sand or gravel, dry		0.85 to 0.88
4.	Top soil		
	(a) sandy clay		0.82 to 0.85
	(b) clay, damp		0.80 to 0.82
5.	Clay with sand or gravel, dump		0.75 to 0.80
6.	Slate like rock, gravel		0.72 to 0.75
7.	Gravel with clay, hard		0.70 to 0.72
8.	Clay with large size gravel, damp		0.68 to 0.70

2. f_2—*Digging factor* :

Boom length (m)	12	18	24	30
Digging factor, f_2 =	0.86	0.79	0.72	0.65

3. f_3—*Hoist factor* : (simultaneous swing and hoist)

Boom length (m)	12	18	24	30
Hoisting factor, f_3 =	0.95	0.92	0.90	0.87

4. f_4—*Swing factor* : (simultaneous dumping and swing)

Angle of swing (deg)	90°	120°	180°
Swing factor, f_4 =	0.98	0.95	0.91

5. f_5—*Loading factor* :

Method of dumping	Truck	Hopper	Stockpile
Loading factor, f_5 =	0.98	0.96	1.0

6. f_6—*Job efficiency factor* :

Actual working time	60 min/hr	50 min/hr	40 min/hr
Job efficiency factor, f_6 =	1.0	0.83	0.67

7. f_7—*Operator factor* :

Operator	Experienced	Average	Beginner
Operator factor, f_7 =	1.0	0.95	0.85

■ EXAMPLE 13.1

An experienced operator has to excavate 'wet gravel' with a dragline bucket of 2.3 m^3. The boom length is 18 m and the swing angle will be 120 degrees. The material is dumped on a stockpile. Actual working time is 50 min per hour. Estimate the likely production per hour.

SOLUTION : Dragline production = Bucket capacity $\times c \times f$.

(where c = theoretical cycles/hr generally taken as 120)

$$= 2.3 \times 120 \times f$$

where, $f = f_1 \times f_2 \times f_3 \times f_4 \times f_5 \times f_6 \times f_7$

$= 0.8 \times 0.79 \times 0.92 \times 0.95 \times 1.0 \times 0.83 \times 1.0 = 0.4588$

Therefore, using the data given in the tables,

$$\text{Dragline production} = 2.3 \times 120 \times 0.4588 = 126.4 \text{ m}^3/\text{hr}$$

13.5 Clamshell

Clamshell is a machine having most of the characteristics of dragline and crane in common. Digging is done like a dragline and once the bucket is filled,it works like a crane. It is very useful for accurate spot dumping of material in a confined space is a vertical plane. It can be used for handling of loose or soft and medium hard materials only. Although it can be used for all the job expected from a shovel family but it not very efficient due to its slow operation.

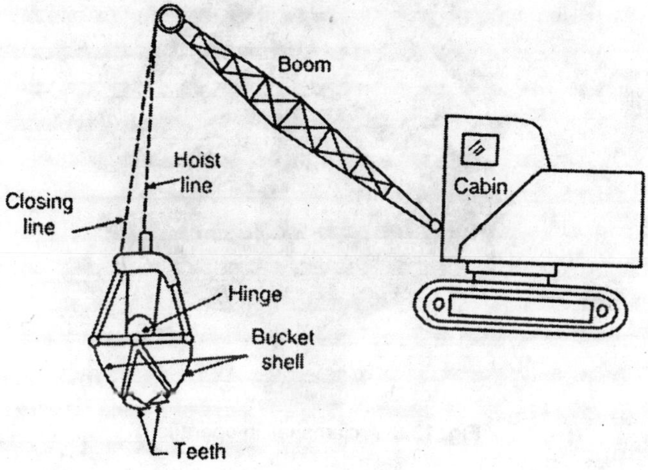

Fig. 13.7 Clamshell.

Clamshell can be used in following types of **applications** :

(a) Where digging or dumping in a vertical plane, *i.e.*, below, at or above ground level is required.

(b) Where material is relatively soft or medium hard.

(c) For digging trenches.

(d) For charging the materials in a bin or a stock pile.

(e) Where accurate dumping is required.

Since the shape of the bucket is like a clam fish and has hinged double shell, it is named as 'clamshell'. The clamshell has a crane boom like a dragline with a specially designed bucket attached to it at the upper end through cables. The bucket is in two halves (known as shells) hinged at the top and has either sharp edge or the teeth at the bottom.

For the purpose of digging, bucket is lowered with shells open over the surface to be dugged till it makes a good contact with it and than it is closed. While closing, the

Fig. 13.8 A clamshell in operation.

weight of the bucket helps the sharp-edge or the teeth at the bottom to dig into the surface or material, thereby filling the bucket. The bucket after being filled is hoisted and swing to the position where dumping is done and then the contents are dropped. Clamshell and its bucket is shown in Fig. 13.7 and 13.8.

Like dragline, it is a rope-operated boom fitted crane type machine having a grab or clamshell bucket. The grab bucket has interlocking teeth penetrate loose soil, whereas the clamshell bucket has no teeth. These machines are generally used for deep confined excavations, such as shafts, wells and spoil heaps removal.

Like buckets of a dragline, the buckets of clamshell are also classified as (a) Light buckets and (b) heavy buckets.

(a) Light buckets : These are used for handling stockpiles of loose materials, like, sand, gravel, etc. and are generally without teeth.

(b) Heavy buckets : These are used for digging purposes and has long and sharp teeth. But due to its heavy weight and more force required for closing operation, working with such buckets become slow. Due to effective grip these are also used for lifting heavy rock pieces.

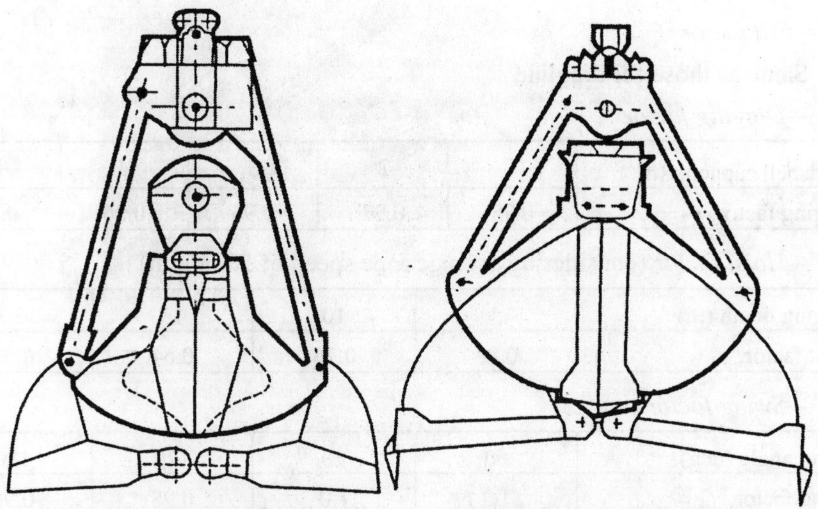

(a) Clamshell bucket for Bulk Material (b) Clamshell bucket for Excavation

Fig. 13.9 Clamshell buckets (Courtesy : Liebherr).

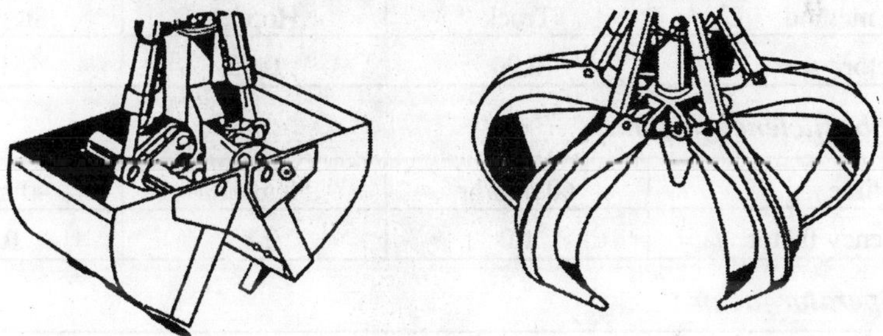

Fig. 13.10 Clamshell and grapple attachments (Courtesy : Liebherr).

13.5.1 Clamshell Production

For optimum production by a clamshell following points should be observed :

1. The machine should be placed on level ground.
2. The distance of the machine from digging and dumping places should be equal.
3. While working in soft materials the teeth of bucket should be removed.

Clamshell production (m^3/hr) = Clamshell capacity × $C \times f$

C = Theoretical cycles/hr = 120 cycles/hr

f = Correcting factor

$$f = f_1 \times f_2 \times f_3 \times f_4 \times f_5 \times f_6 \times f_7$$

Correction Factors

Data are taken from "Liebherr's Technical Handbook Earthmoving Product line, Edn. 1986/87".

1. f_1—*Fill factor* :

Same as those for dragline.

2. f_2—*Digging factor* :

Clamshell capacity (m^3)	1	2	3	4	5
Digging factor, f_2 =	0.98	0.97	0.96	0.96	0.95

3. f_3—*Hoist factor* (considering average rope speed of 50 m/min) :

Digging depth (m)	5	10	15	20
Hoist factor, f_3 =	0.88	0.76	0.64	0.52

4. f_4—*Swing factor* :

Swing angle (deg)	60	90	120	180
Swing factor, f_4 =	1.2	1.0	0.98	0.90

5. f_5—*Dump factor* :

Dumping method	Truck	Hopper	Stockpile
Dump factor, f_5 =	0.90	0.95	1.0

6. f_6—*Job efficiency factor* :

Working time	60 min/hr	50 min/hr	40 min/hr
Job efficiency factor, f_6 =	1.0	0.83	0.67

7. f_7—*Operator factor* :

Operator	Experienced	Average	Beginner
Operator factor, f_7 =	1.0	0.95	0.85

■ EXAMPLE 13.2

An average operator has a excavate 'damp sand' with a clamshell of 2 cu m. The digging depth is 10 m and the swing angle will be 120 degrees. The sand is loaded into trucks and actual working time is 50 min/hr. Estimate the production per hour.

SOLUTION :

$$\text{Clamshell production } (m^3/\text{hr}) = \text{Clamshell capacity} \times C \times f$$

$$= 2 \times 120 \times f$$

Correction factor,

$$f = f_1 \times f_2 \times f_3 \times f_4 \times f_5 \times f_6 \times f_7$$

$$= 1.0 \times 0.97 \times 0.76 \times 0.98 \times 0.9 \times 0.83 \times 0.95 = 0.5127$$

$$\therefore \text{ Clamshell production} = 2.0 \times 120 \times 0.5127$$

$$= 123.0 \text{ m}^3/\text{hr}.$$

13.6 Comparison between Different Shovels

Table given below shows the comparison between different types of shovels depending upon their application.

S. No.	*Points of Consideration*	*Dipper Shovel*	*Dragline*	*Backhoe*	*Clamshell*
1.	Operation in hard soil or rock.	good	poor	good	good
2.	Operation in wet soil or mud.	poor	fair	poor	fair
3.	Distance between footing and digging.	small	long	small	long
4.	Loading efficiency into the vehicles.	very good	fair	good	precise but slow
5.	Digging level.	At or above footing level	below footing level	below footing level	At, above or below footing level
6.	Cycle time as compared to dipper shovel.	—	more	slightly more	high

When excavating a trench having a rock which requires blasting,hoe is most suitable, dragline is less desirable substitute. If the soil is unstable, water saturated material, dragline, hoe or clamshell may be used and walls be allowed toform a stable slope. If it is necessary to install solid sheeting to hold the walls in place, a clamshell is suitable, which can excavate between the trench braces that hold the sheeting in place.

13.7 Dredging Equipment (Dredgers)

Dredgers are used for excavation from river bed, lake or sea for the purpose of deepening them. Dredging is an important operation in navigation canals, harbours, dams etc. Since clamshells and draglines can not perform excavation standing on one back, dredgers are very effective for this purpose.

Dredgers are of following types :

(a) Dipper dredger (b) Ladder dredger (c) Suction dredger

(a) **Dipper dredger** is mounted on a floating platform. It is stabilised by means of pair of spuds held firm into the water during the operation of digging. The boom of the dredger can swing through an angle of 180° to deposit the excavated material either on the bank or on a floating barge. The dredgers generally have production rate of 50 cu m/hr/cu m bucket capacity. Dredgers upto 12.5 m^3 bucket size and 30 m dumping range and capable of digging to a depth of about 15 to 18 m under water are available.

(b) **Ladder dredger** equipped with bucket elevator is mounted on a barge. This bucket elevator, used for digging and lifting, is supported on a steel ladder which can be extended to the river bed. Bucket while moving dig into the bottom of the river bed, loads, travel up, and dump into a hopper on the top of the elevator. From the hopper, this excavated material is conveyed to the bank or to another barge through a conveyor. This type of dredger is suitable for excavating soft ground, sand or gravel.

(c) **A suction dredger**, some times known as pump excavator, consists of a heavy duty pump mounted on a barge with suction line supported on a ladder and extended down up to the river bed, with the help of winches. During suction from the bottom, rapid flow of water loosen the soft material and suck along with water discharged through a pipe line extended from the pump to the bank. For hard bed, a cutter head is mounted close to the suction pipe mouth, which is rotated by a separate motor and its motion soften the material to allow it to be sucked into the suction pipe and discharged out. Some times extra high pressure water jet is employed to loosen the bed to enable it to be sucked by the pump. Suction dredgers are specified by the diameter of the discharge pipe.

Digging Deep—Selecting and Using Dredgers

Dredging is, simply, removing material from beneath the surface of water either to get rid of it, *i.e.*, when opening a channel during canal or waterway construction, or to recover it for the reclamation of new land for mining or the production of concrete aggregate.

The equipment employed for moving wet earth can be divided into following groups :

- Mechanical dredgers.
- Hydraulic and pneumatic dredgers.

1. Mechanical Dredgers

These dredgers dislodge, raise and transport material mechanically. They may be bucket dredgers, dipper and backhoe dredgers, grab dredgers and rockbreakers.

2. Hydraulic and Pneumatic Dredgers

Hydraulic dredgers utilize the principle of the centrifugal pump. This implied that water is always used as a carrier of the solids. Various equipment are employed to dislodge the soil including cutters, wheel excavators, dragheads and water jets.

(a) **The profile dredger :** A suction pipe is connected to the dredger pump and is suspended in a well by means of a simple gantry. The sand is drawn by the pump and is either discharged into barges or pumped ashore. The size of a profile dredger is measured by the dia. of the suction pipe varying between 250 mm and 800 mm. These are used only to recover sand for reclamation purposes or in the production of concrete aggregate.

(b) **Cutter-suction dredger :** Here, a ladder is suspended from a well inside the pontoon and the suction pipe, connected to the dredge pump, passes through the ladder. At the ladder's lower end, beyond the suction inlet, is a cutting tool, which is used to dislodge the soil. The mixture then passes via pump and a delivery pipeline to the point of reclamation.

13.8 Trenching Equipments

These machines are used for digging trenches at a faster rate and with proper control of depths and widths, and are capable of digging any type of soil except rock. They are available in various sizes for digging trenches of various depths and widths. These are generally crawler mounted having large range of speeds to permit the selection of the most suitable speed for any job conditions, ranging from canal excavation to laying cables.

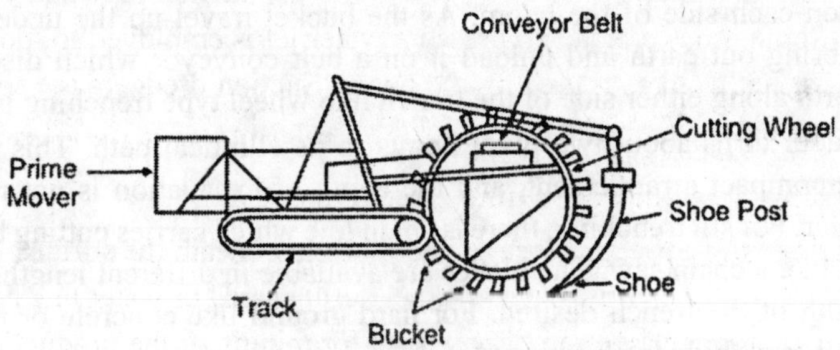

Fig. 13.11 Trencher.

Trenching machines are of two types, namely wheel trenchers and ladder trenchers and are described hereunder :

(A) Wheel-Trenchers

Trenchers are the equipments used for excavating trenches or ditches of variable width and depth. The trenches of width upto 12 metres and depth upto 3 metres can be excavated in one pass with the trenchers available now-a-days. A trencher consists of : (a) self-propelled tractor or carrier fitted with either crawler type or wheel-type running rear; (b) an excavating device consisting of several buckets on the periphery of a wheel or several cutters attached to a chain for digging and discharging continuously; (c) a means of conveying the excavated material to either side of the excavated trench and depositing it in windrows.

Wheel trenchers are most common type of excavators. Excavating member of these wheel trenchers consist of a pair of circular rims whose outside diameters are connected by U-shaped buckets or cutters. The wheel is turned by a chain drive which connects to the power source. The wheel turns in a direction with the buckets travelling away from the carrier in the top position when discharging material, and toward the carrier at the bottom of their travel while digging. The buckets or cutters on the wheel perform the work of excavation while travelling upward. When the wheel reaches the top position, the excavated material drops from the buckets on the conveyor and discharges alongside the trench to form windrow, keeping some clearance between the windrow and the edge of the trench. The wheel trenchers are very suitable equipment for digging canals and other trenches.

The trenches may be for water, gas and oil pipe lines, telephone cables, drainage and sewers. These provide for digging with positive control over depths and widths of trenches and needs minimum efforts for finishing. These can dig any type of soil except rock, and are available in various sizes for digging trenches of varying depths and widths.

(B) Ladder-type Trenching Machines

In these machines buckets are provided with chain links on ladder type frame or boom. By providing extensions to these ladders and by adding more buckets, it can dig trenches upto 10 meter depth. These machines are used where depth of trench required is more than 3 metres. Width of the trench can be increased by installing shaft mounted side cutters on each side of the boom. As the bucket travel up the underside of the boom, they bring out earth and unload it on a belt conveyor which discharges this excavated earth along either side of the trench like wheel type trenching machines.

The ladder turns about two pivot points in its elliptical path. This makes for a flatter, more compact arrangement, and the depth of excavation is not restricted by wheel diameter. For slit trenching, there is chain line which carries cutting blades along its periphery like a chain saw. The blades are available in different lengths depending upon the width of the trench desired. For hard ground like concrete or rock-studied ground, tungsten carbide teeth are used.

Advantages in Using a Trencher

By using a trencher following advantages can be achieved :

(a) It is faster and cheaper method of trenching.

(b) It digs only as much as is necessary. A 10 cm pipe cn be installed in a 15 cm wide slot cut by a trencher.

(c) It is a continuous process and is not like that of back-hoe excavator, *i.e.*, dug-lift-dump.

Selection of Trenchers

The selection of a trenching equipment depend on the job conditions, depth and width of the trench, type of soil, disposal of excavated earth, availability of ground water.

Factors influencing the selection of trenching equipment for excavating the trenches are :

1. Job condition.
2. Soil condition.
3. Depth and width of trench.
4. The extent to which the ground water is present.
5. The width of the right of way for disposal of excavated material.
6. Topography.

For relatively shallow and narrow trench in a firm soil, the wheel type trenching machine is suitable.

In case the soil is water saturated and unstable, a hoe or clamshell may be used. If necessary, solid sheeting is installed to hold the walls in place, then either a hoe or clamshell is preferred, which can excavate in between the trench braces that hold the sheeting in place.

13.9 Safety Aspects

The major safety aspects of shovels (both mechanical, *i.e.*, cable operated or hydraulic) including power shovel, hoe, dragline and clamshell are as under :

1. **Stability :** Power shovels (excavators) shall be so operated as not to lose their stability.
2. Power shovels (excavators) that are equipped with unit for deep digging shall either be so designed that the bucket teeth cannot come nearer the boom than 40 cm or be provided with a reliable stop that prevent the bucket to come nearer than the specified distance.
3. **Boom :**
   - The boom of power shovel (excavator) shall be prevented from accidentally swinging during operation or transport.
   - The boom shall not be pulled tight against the emergency stops while supporting a load.
   - The maximum boom length stipulated by the manufacturer shall not be exceeded. The wire ropes used for the boom suspension as well as for the shovel/bucket shall be of the specified diameter and construction.
   - Due attention shall be paid to the length and condition of the pendant ropes and the end connection. The safe operating radius for the load under consideration shall not be exceeded.
   - History sheet and schedule for replacement of ropes shall be maintained.
4. **Bucket or grab :**
   - The bucket or grab shall be of the right size taking into account the power to the machine or motor, length of the boom, the operating radius contemplated and total weight including the self-weight of the bucket or grab and other lifting accessories.
   - While operating power shovels (excavators) the driver shall ensure that no person is working, passing or standing under the raised bucket or grab.
   - The bucket or grab of a power shovel (excavators) shall be prevented from accidental dipping, tipping or swinging in operation. The bucket or grab of the shovel shall be pulled out of the bank as soon as it is full.

When not in use, the bucket shall be kept resting on stable ground and shall not be hanging.

- The bucket or grab of a power shovel (excavator) shall be fixed to restrict movement while it is being repaired.

5. When power shovel (excavator) is operated near edges of excavations or embankments substantial space shall be provided to prevent it form approaching a dangerous position and the side of the excavation shall be adequately shored. Heavy equipment, such as excavating machinery and road traffic shall be kept back from as excavated sides at a distance not less than the depth of trench or at least 6 m from trench deeper than 6 m.
6. Power shovels (excavator) shall not be left on a slope with the engine or motor running.
7. The height of the benches in over burden shall not be more than the height of the boom of the machines used for digging excavation or removal.
8. Load charts for various boom lengths (provided by the manufacturers) should be adhered to while operating the shovel.
9. In case of mechanical shovel, the wire ropes should be changed after inspection as specified in the manual.
10. For hydraulic hoses, the connections should be tight and leak-proof.
11. In case of trenching, the estimated location of utility installation such as sewer, telephone, T.V. cable, fuel, electric, water lines, or other similar underground installations that reasonably may be expected to be encountered during excavation work, should be determined prior to opening an excavation.
12. Any trench measuring 1.5 meters or more in depth must be sloped, benched, shored or shielded.

QUESTIONS

1. Describe different types of shovels in brief with the help of sketches, indicating their applications.
2. Explain the components and operation of shovel and a dragline. Where will you recommend the use of each of them?
3. Explain the working of a shovel and discuss how it differs from a dragline.
4. Draw a neat sketch of a power shovel and name the parts of it.
5. Show with a neat sketch the basis parts of a dragline and also explain its operation.
6. What is a shovel? Discuss the basis parts of a power shovel.
7. Discuss the advantages of hydraulically operated power shovel.
8. What are the factors which govern the size of a power shovel?

9. Mention the factors which affect he production of a shovel.
10. What is a dragline? Discuss its operation.
11. Draw a neat sketch of the dragline, and mention important parts on it.
12. What is a clamshell? Discuss its characteristics.
13. Discuss the construction and working of a clamshell bucket.
14. Give the comparative advantages and disadvantages of various excavating machines.
15. Explain the different types of trenching equipment.
16. Discuss the advantages of using a trencher.
17. What are the different factors considered for the selection of a trencher?
18. List out different safety aspects considered while using the shovels.

Chapter 14

Drilling and Blasting Equipment

DRILLING

14.1 Introduction

Drilling and blasting is done before taking up the excavation work. This is commonly carried out for aggregate production, excavating in tunnels, breaking pavements or rocks etc. Selection of suitable drilling equipment, designing of drilling pattern, and proper loading leads to economic production. Suitable type of drilling equipment is selected on the basis of nature of rock, size of project depth and size of holes, type of and size of aggregate production required. Good drilling and blasting lead to a uniform fragmentation and this ensures efficient mucking operation in open excavation or tunnels or shafts.

The machines used for drilling include pneumatic crawler drills, hydraulic crawler drills, rotary drills and down-hole drills. Pneumatic crawler drills are driven by air motors which generally use portable air compressors as their power source. Hydraulically crawler drills are hydraulic operated drills powered by diesel engine. Compared to the pneumatic crawler-drill, these have lower fuel consumption and are quieter and have higher drilling efficiency.

The rotary drills are large drills equipped with diesel engine and air compressor. These have excellent drilling capacity in soft rock. The down-hole drill has a hammer at the tip of a rod. Its advantages are that the percussion force applied to the rod is transmitted directly to the bit, so there is little loss of percussion force when drilling long holes. The down-hole drill is suitable for drilling medium-hard and rock.

For quarrying operation, preliminary blasting is done to loosen the rock for ripping by bulldozer. Compared to normal drilling and blasting, the preliminary blasting method uses less then half the amount of explosive. It is used to make cracks in the rock, thereafter bulldozer is used for breaking up the rock.

Blasting is performed by discharging the explosive placed in the hole drilled for the purpose. Tremendous energy produced by blasting loosens the rock.

The drilling may be performed to explore the types of materials to be encountered in the project, or it may involve production work such as drilling holes for loading explosive charges to blast rock. It is necessary to select the drilling equipment and drilling method best suited to the specific service. For example in highway construction must usually drill rock under varying conditions, therefore, the equipment that is suitable for variable application should be selected. However, when equipment required for drill rock in a quarry where the material and conditions will not change, specialized equipment should be considered.

Drills in construction are operated either by air or hydraulics, and are explained in this chapter.

14.2 Types of Drilling Equipment

Drilling equipment are grouped into following broad categories :

1. Percussion drills
2. Rotary drills : (a) Pressure drilling (b) Abrasion drilling.

1. Percussion Drills

These can economically drills rocks of wide range of hardness. Percussion drills employ a reciprocating air operated hammer (piston) which strikes a rotating bit or a string of rotating drill with a bit on its bottom. An air or water system is used to remove stone cuttings from the drill hole. Jack hammers, drifters, feed leg drills, wagon drills are the examples of percussion drills, and have been discussed in detail in this chapter.

2. Rotary Drills

In rotary drills the movement of the bit is due to the rotation of the drill bit.

(a) **Pressure Drilling :** In this system, drilling action is provided by applying the down pressure on the bit. The pull down pressure and the drill rotation is created by the hydraulic or electric variable speed motors. These drills are powered either by diesel engine or electric motor. Air compressors remove the cuttings, from the hole as drilling progresses. The bit pressure and quantity of air are controlled as per requirement.

(b) **Abrasion Drills :** Diamond-core drills and shot-core drills are common drills of this category. Diamond core drills are more common and popular amongst these two and are described in detail in this chapter. Shot-core drills are used for large dia drilling and are slow in drilling. Shot-core drills are suitable for dia upto 1.8 meters and depths upto 300 metres.

14.3 Pneumatic Rock Drills

Rock drills may be *either percussion type or rotary types*. The movement of the bit in percussion drill is mainly due to reciprocating action of a piston inside the cylinder, whereas in rotary drill, the rotation of the drill is due to the air motor. Percussion tools may be plug drills, sinkers, drifters, wagon drills or pavement breakers. Rotary tools may be abrasion drills, diamond drills etc.

Pneumatic drills provide a hammering action together with rotational movement of the steel. The steel is tipped with chisel or cross bit to make holes in rock, concrete and other hard surfaces.

Jack hammer is a basic tool of the percussion type of rock drills. Jack hammers are hand held, air-operated percussion-type drills. A complete jack hammer consists of a hammer, drill steel, and bit. The jack hammers are generally used for holes upto 3 in depth, though they can be used to drill holes upto 6 m deep. The heavier hammers may drill holes upto 6 mm in diameter. Drill steels are usually available in lengths of 60 cm, 120 cm, 180 cm and 240 cm lengths.

The jack hammers are generally classified according to their weight as follows :

1. Sinkers

These are hand held unmounted drills generally ranging in weight between 7 kg to 40 kg. Small sinkers between7 to 9 kg weight are sometimes called as *plug drills*. Sinkers are used for drilling blast holes downwards.

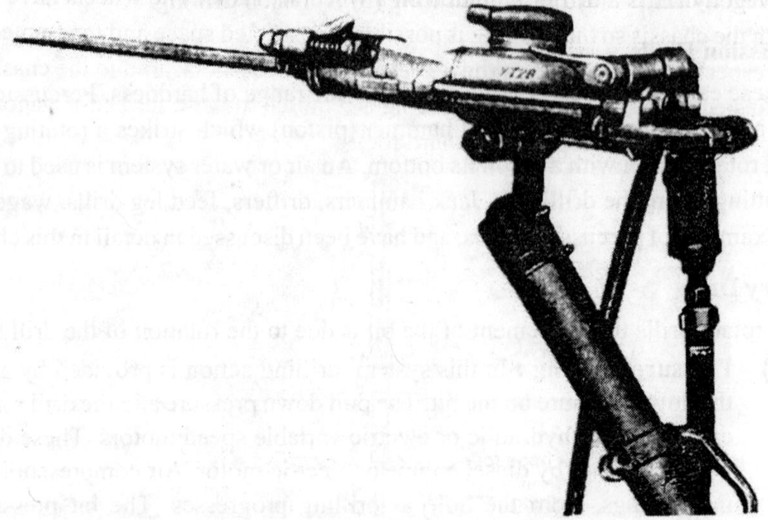

Fig. 14.1 Leg drill in operation (By Courtesy : Consolidated Pneumatic Tool Co. (India) Ltd.).

2. Leg Drill

Similar to sinker but mounted on a pneumatic ram, or leg, which can be jammed against a rock on the floor to drill a hole horizontally. These are used for drilling blast holes in tunnels.

3. Stopper

Similar to a leg drill but with the air leg made as part of the drill's construction, fixed inline with the drill steel (drill rod). With the foot of the leg on the floor, the steel points vertically up to the roof. These are used for roof bolting or raise blasting.

All jack hammers whether sinkers, leg drills or stoppers either work dry or wet depending upon the use of air or water to perform the work of cleaning of the bit and of the inside of the hole. In the dry system air is blasted from the working cylinder during each cycle through the steel into the bit in order to keep the bored hole clear of rock dust. In the wet system water is carried through the steel into the bit in order to keep dust down. Wet system is very useful specially where closed spaces or in underground work creates difficult working conditions due to dust.

4. Drifters

These are also rock drills of jack hammer type but are heavy in weight, *i.e.*, between 45 kg to 70 kg or more. These are used for drilling bigger size holes usually 7.5 to 10 cm in diameter. These can be used for drilling in harder rocks at greater speeds and are normally employed for excavation work in mines and tunnels. These can be employed for drilling holes in horizontal, vertical or inclined directions by mounting on suitable frames. To provide mobility these are mounted on track carriages.

5. Wagon Drills

A wagon drill is a drifter mounted on a wheeled frame. The wheels have swivel joints with the chassis so that turning is possible in restricted space and the frame can be turned irrespective of direction of the wheels. A guideway is secured to the chassis and can be adjusted at any angle at which drilling is required to be done. These wagon drills are suitable for drilling deep holes in hard rocks.

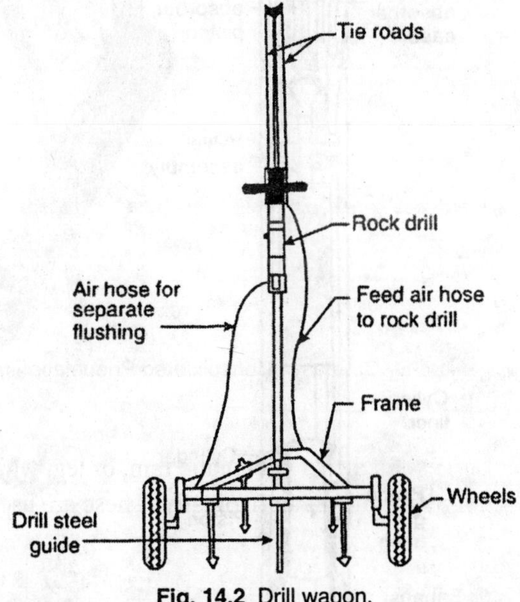

Fig. 14.2 Drill wagon.

Construction of Jack Hammers (Fig. 14.4)

Jack hammer is a main and widely used pneumatic rock drill. One end of the jack hammer holds the tool (drill rod with bit) while the other end houses the air blower arrangement. The middle portion has a cylinder in which pawl and ratchet arrangement is provided which permits one way rotation of the steel (Drill rod) through rifle bar. Drilling operation includes the hammering action on the steel as well as its turning in the hole. Air enters from the top potion, known as backhead, and then into a regulating valve which allows the air alternately to top and bottom of the cylinder. When air enters from the bottom of the cylinder the piston is pushed upward of pawl and ratchet arrangement with the help of splined rifle bar and gives a turning motion to the steel through the chuck. In the downward stroke (*i.e.*, when the air enters from the top) the piston is allowed to come straight down, without rotation, and strike the head of the steel, giving a hammering blow. This air then leaves and passes to the drill bit through the central hole in the steel. This helps in cleaning of the cutting edge of the drill bit and clean the hole by blowing the drilled rock out.

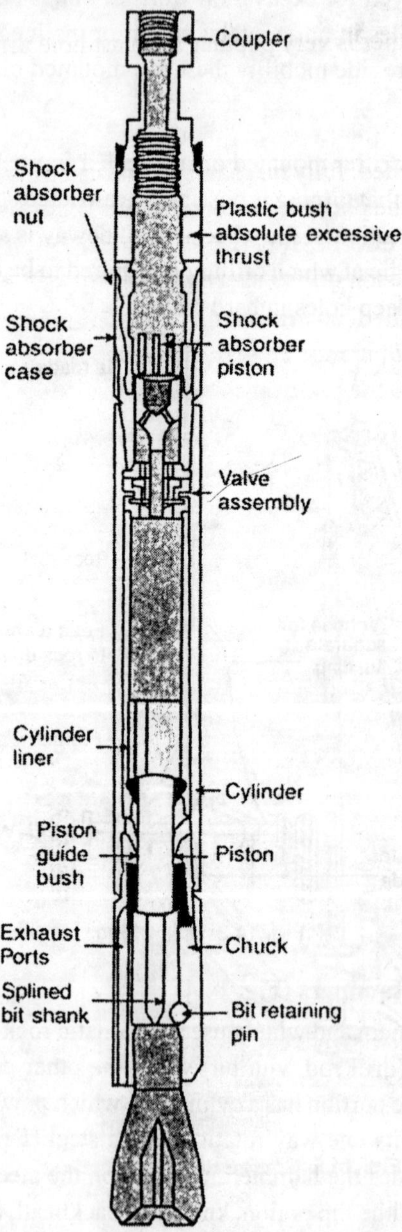

Fig. 14.3 'Down the Hole' drills (Courtesy : Killick Nixon Limited).

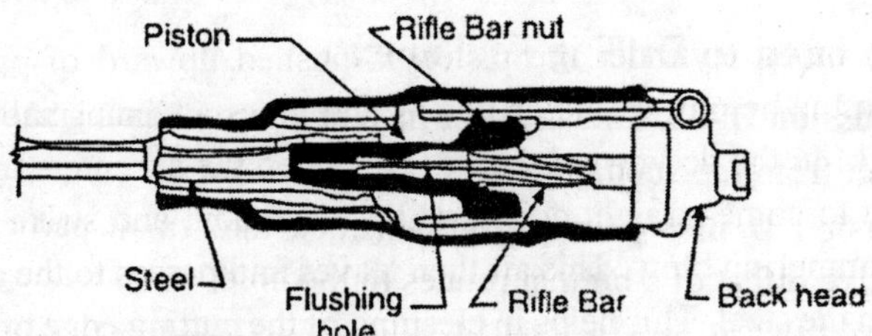

Fig. 14.4 Construction of jack hammer.

The use of jackhammer is very popular for blast hole drilling in quarries, mines, rock excavation etc.

Crawler Drills

These are self-propelled, fully mechanised, and can travel easily from one hole to another hole and can two the portable air compressor. These have drill tower which can be quickly positioned by effortless hydraulic cylinder operation. These are used by rugged, heavy duty percussion drills attached to the drill rod.

The complete installed power output of the diesel engine can be used for propelling the drilling equipments. Power to operate the drill, drill advance and other adjustments in supplied by the basic machine's hydraulic circuit (Refer Fig. 14.5).

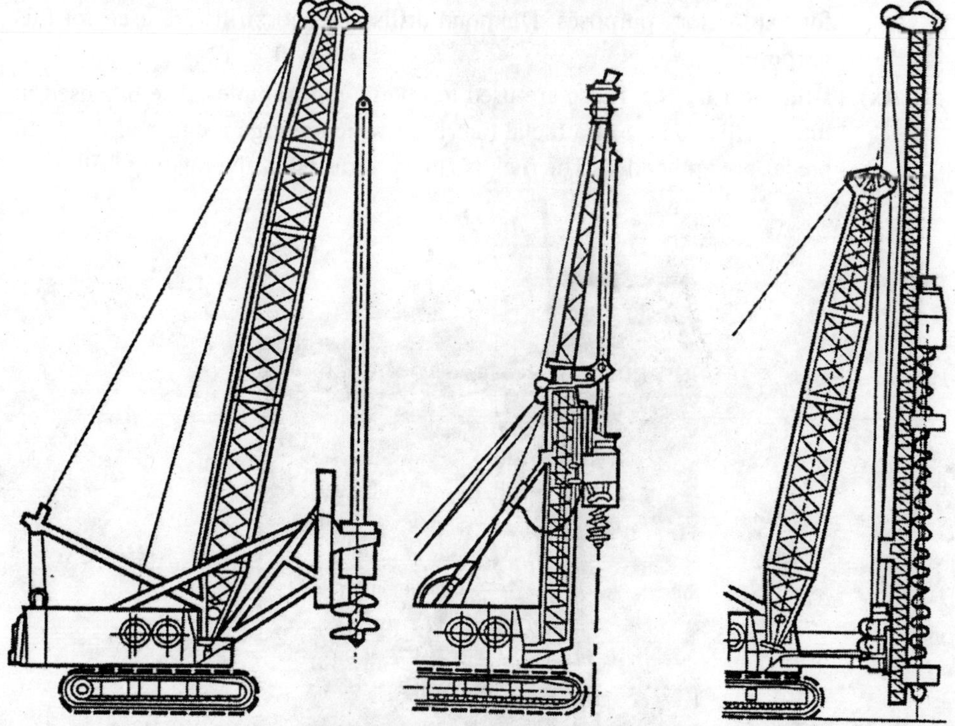

Fig. 14.5 Crawler drilling equipment.

14.4 Terms Related to Drilling Equipment

(i) **Percussion Drill :** This is drill which breaks rock into small particles by the impact from repeated blows.

(ii) **Abrasion Drill :** This drill grinds rock into small particles through the abrasive effect of a bit that rotates in the hole.

(iii) **Dry Drill :** This is a drill which uses compressed air to remove the cuttings from a hole.

(iv) **Wet Drill :** This is drill which uses water to remove the cuttings from a hole.

(v) **Drilling Rate :** Drilling rate is the number of meters of hole drilled per hour per drill.

(vi) **Face :** It is the approximately vertical surface extending upward from the floor of a pit to the level of drilling.

(vii) **Burden :** This is the horizontal distance from a face back to the first row of drill holes.

(viii) **Drilling Pattern :** Drilling pattern is adopted for drilling holes in surface or underground works by fixing proper depth, spacing and location of holes.

(ix) **Core Drilling :** Core drilling is adopted to obtain the core sample of rock for exploratory purposes. Diamond drills and shot drills are used for this purpose.

(x) **Diamond Drill :** These are used to obtain core samples. The bits used in these drills consist of a metal matrix in which a large number of diamond pieces are embedded. The rock is cut by abrasion of the rotating drill.

Fig. 14.6 Crawler pneumatic drill (Courtesy : Ingersoll-Rand (India) Limited).

(xi) **Shot Drill :** In these drills while bit is rotated under pressure, chilled steel shot is supplied under the bit to disintegrate the rock. The water is used to remove the cuttings. The bit is made of a section of steel pipe with a roughened surface at the bottom.

(xii) **Bit :** Bit is a bottom portion of drill which is indirect contact of the rock and disintegrate it.

(xiii) **Burden Distance :** It is the distance between the rock face and a row of holes or between adjacent rows of holes.

(xiv) **Core Drill :** It is drill designed for obtaining samples of rock from a hole for explanatory purposes. Diamond and shot drill are used for core drilling.

Fig. 14.7 Pavement breakers in operation.

(xv) **Shank or Striker Bar :** It is a short piece of steel that attaches to the percussion drill piston for receiving the blow and transferring to the drill steel.

(xvi) **Spacing :** It is the distance between adjacent holes in the same row.

14.5 Quantity of Compressed Air Required

	Equipment or tool	*Capacity or size*	*Air consumption in cu m*
1.	Drills or borers	(a) 2.1 cm dia	5.7-6.6
		(b) 5.2 cm dia	8.2-13.9
		(c) 10.4 cm dia	15.2-18.9
2.	Pavement breakers	(a) 15.7 kg	4.9-5.7
		(b) 27.3 kg	6.6-7.4
		(c) 36.3 kg	8.2

3.	Wagon drills drifters	(a) 7.5 cm piston	24.6-28.7
		(b) 8.8 cm piston	30.0-34.0
		(c) 10.0 cm piston	37.0-44.0
4.	Jack hammers	4.5 kg 60 cm depth	2.5-4.1
		6.8 kg 60 cm depth	3.3-5.7
		11.34 kg, 60-244 cm depth	4.9-8.2
		15.9 kg, 244-365 cm depth	9.0-12.3
		20.4 kg, 365-487 cm depth	13.1-16.4
		25.0 kg, 487-731 cm depth	14.7-18.6
		34.0 kg, 244-731 cm depth	24.6-28.7

14.6 Hydraulic Drills

Due to certain advantages, hydraulic drilling is becoming more popular than the pneumatic drilling. A hydraulic drifter is more efficient because of its higher operating pressure ranging between 100 to 250 bar, and provides a higher percussion output and a 50 to 100% higher penetration rate than pneumatic drifter. The use of hydraulics allow greater saving in energy costs. It consumes nearly one-third of the energy consumed in pneumatic drilling. The life time of the drilling equipment in hydraulic drilling is 20 to 30% longer than in pneumatic drilling.

(a) Hydraulic Breaker (Fig. 14.8)

These are relatively quiet, easy and safe to operate. These are used for quarrying, demolition, trenching, foundation digging and pavement breaking etc. These are generally used as an attachment to hydraulic excavators.

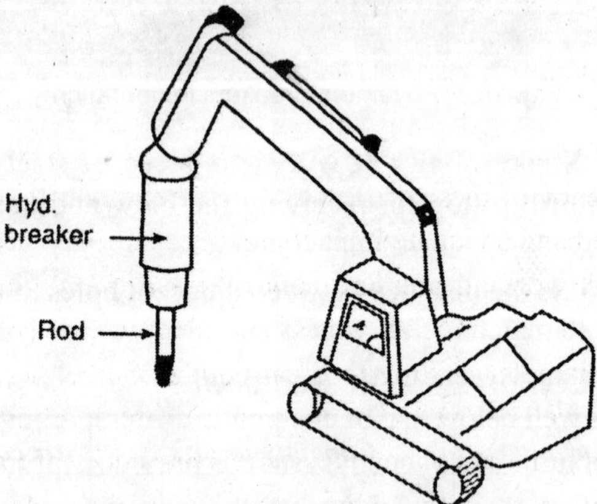

Fig. 14.8 Hydraulic breaker fitted on excavator.

(b) Mobile Hydraulic Drilling Machines

These machines are mounted on pneumatic tyred wheels and can be taken to the site by toeing and is suitable for drilling in rock and over burden in uneven terrain and hill slopes. Hydraulic operation and controls allow faster drilling and closer monitoring down the hole. Hydraulically operated feed with least vibrations enable it to give better core recovery and faster penetration at uniform rate both in soil and rock strata.

(c) Hydraulic Jumbo (Fig. 14.9)

These are extremely suitable for use in tunnel and other underground works. These have booms which can be hydraulically extended and work smoothly with higher efficiency and less noise. These are either tyre or track mounted and moves forward and backward with electrical or hydraulic system. The drifters are used in the jumbo. Twin boom or tripple-boom jumbo with 2 to 3 drifters respectively are commonly used. Air and waterline manifolds are also mounted on the jumbo, which had to be specially designed so that the mucking equipment could be used around the machine. For better efficiency in underground excavation, sliding and elevating deck is provided for ancillary operations like, dynamite loading, rock bolting, rock removal etc. Drilling jumbo have been discussed in detail in chapter on "Tunneling Equipment".

Fig. 14.9 Drilling jumbo operating in a tunnel.

(d) Hydraulic Drifters

Operating efficiency of these drifters is about two times than that of pneumatic drifters. The high speed and adequate impact punch capabilities combine to extend bit and rod service life. A working pressure control valve is provided to automatically adjust impact pressure to match rock hardness and bit diameter. High torque hydraulic motor helps in large diameter drilling to great depths. Since there is no air exhaust, operating noise level is well below that of pneumatic drifters. A dust collector, having a hydraulic motor driven turbo fan vacuum system is provided for trapping coarse stone particles produced before their secondary crushing in the hole. This assures easy maintenance and enhance drilling efficiency.

14.7 Rotary Drills

With these drills the rock is ground away by applying a down pressure on the drill steel and bit and at the same time continuously rotating the bit in the hole. Compressed air is constantly forced down the drill steel and through the bit to remove the rock cuttings and cool the bit.

These drills are self-propelled drills that can be mounted on a truck or crawler tracks.

14.7.1 Drill Bits and Steels

Drills steels are of two kinds,

(a) With formed bits (b) With detachable bits

In the formed bit steel, the lower end of the steel itself is forged into a cutting bit or is tipped with tungsten carbide to make it more durable, impact and wear resistance, whereas in the detachable bit steel, this end of steel is threaded and the bit is screwed over it. Detachable bit steels are commonly used these days.

The drill rod is generally constructed from high manganese alloy steel and is made in hexagonal or square shape sections. For drilling long holes, complete set of rods in graded lengths are available. As shown in Fig. 14.10 the top end is called the shank and usually of 8 to 10 cm long and its of same diameter as the rod and provided with a collar to prevent upward penetration of steel into the chuck. The rod has a hole in the centre along its length.

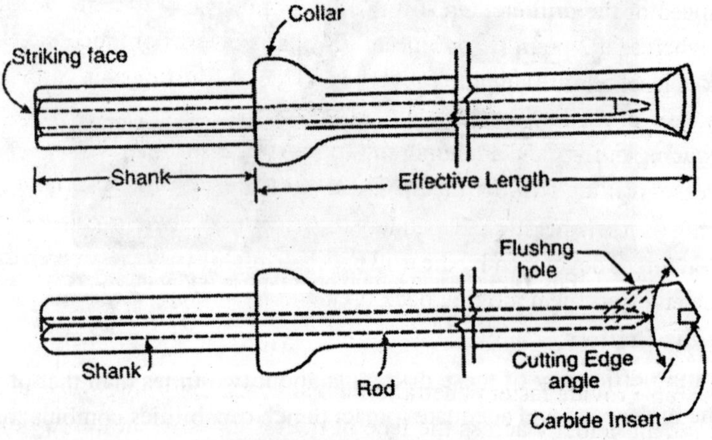

Fig. 14.10 Rock drill steel.

The compressive stresses are introduced into the surface layer of the drill steel in order to resist fatigue which might caused due to blow setting off the shock waves in the rod put through a large number of load cycles due to hitting the steel hard and fast by the drills (hammering action in the jack hammer).

Drilling Bits may be either throw-away type or multi-use type. The throw-away type bit is discarded when worn out and a new one is used. Multi-use type of bit is preferred on large jobs. When these bits are worn out along the cutting edge or on the sides, they are reconditioned and then again used.

Fig. 14.11 Drilling button bits (Courtesy : Ingersoll Rand USA).

Shape of the cutting edge of the bit depends upon (i) nature of rock (ii) size of the hole (iii) speed of the drill etc. On soft rocks 6 point rose or 4 point 'X' design bit is preferred, whereas a 2 point 'I' or 3 point 'T' shape bit will produce large chips with brittle rock. Chisel bits are suitable for very hard rocks. The tungsten carbide insert bits give many feet of drilling in very hard rocks and many metres of drilling is done without reducing in size, and are hundred times long lasting than that of steel bits. This results in lesser drilling cost per meter. These can be re-used after grinding.

Drilling is the operation dependent on drill and bit. Bit utilises impact and compression forces developed by the drill to break out the rock chips, clear them for the cutting face and start them moving back up the hole.

Button Bits

These bits provide faster penetration in hard rock. Finishing slots are designed to maintain high air velocity across the face of the bit for efficient removal of hard rock chips and dust.

Extending the Life of Drill Steels

Life of drill steels can be extended by adopting following steps :

(a) **Proper Feeding :** During drilling, excessive feeding shortens the life of the drill steels, whereas insufficient feeding causes rapid abrasion on the tungsten carbide inserts.

(b) **Adequate Flushing :** Tungsten carbide inserts will wear out faster if the cuttings are not discharged by sufficient flushing. Poor discharge of the cuttings also causes jamming of drill steel.

(c) **Centre-Aligned Drilling :** The drill steel will be stressed and bended if the drilling is done by non-alignment of the centre of drill steel. This may cause accidental breakage of the shank of drill steel.

(d) **Careful Treatment :** When the drill steel jams in the hole, do not hammer it, but rotate with a spanner.

(e) **Regrinding in Time :** Regrinding is necessary when the width of cutting edge has worn about 3 mm. Grinding wheels specified with Grain size 45-60, Grade J and Abrasive C or GC in I.S.O. are the most suitable for grinding drill bits.

Purposes of Drilling Holes

Holes are drilled in the earth for several purposes, some of them are :

(i) For blasting.
(ii) For grout injection.
(iii) For exploration and obtaining samples of soil for test purposes.
(iv) To locate and evaluate deposits of aggregate.
(v) For providing wells for supply of water.
(vi) For providing cast-in-situ piles or shafts to support structures.
(vii) For providing shafts in mines and tunnels.

14.8 Selecting a Drilling Equipment

Best equipment is the one which performs its job effectively and economically. Major factors affecting the selection of drilling equipment are mentioned hereunder :

(i) Nature of terrain.
(ii) Required depth of holes.
(iii) Rock hardness.
(iv) The purpose for which holes are required to be drilled, *i.e.*, for blasting or grouting or for exploration purposes.
(v) The size of the project.
(vi) Extent to which the formation is fractured or broken.
(vii) The availability of water for drilling purposes. Lack of water favours dry drilling.
(viii) The extent to which the rock is to be broken for handling or crushing.
(ix) The core size required for exploration purposes.

Jack hammers are used for small-diameter shallow blast holes, and can be used on rough terrains also. Crawler mounted drilling equipment are used for drilling blast-holes upto about 15 cms in diameter and upto about 15 meters deep. Rotary drills are suitable for drilling holes from 15 to 30 cms diameter and from 15 to 100 meters deep. Diamond core drilling machines are most suitable for taking cores upto about

20 cms diameter and can drill holes in any direction. Shot drills can be used for taking cores of diameter more than 8 cms through vertical drilling.

14.9 Optimum Use of Drilling Equipment

The drilling tools though made from top quality materials, having great resistance to wear and capable of withstanding considerable stress, it still required to be handled and maintained in the correct way, in order to achieve optimum total economy. This means that drill should be able to produce more drill meters in less time. In order to achieve this object following actions are necessary :

(i) The feed must be *braced firmly against the rock*, so that it does not move during drilling. If the feed changes alignment during drilling, bending stresses will be developed in the dril! steels, and may lead even the breakage. Therefore, the drilling should not be started, until it has been given stable set-up.

(ii) The *percussion mechanism should not be started until the drill bit has been pressed against the rock face.* Percussion can damage the drill bit and loosen the threads in the drill string.

(iii) *Flushing should be switched on immediately*, to keep the drill bit at a steady temperature. If flushing is switched on too late, the sudden cooling effects will damage the cemented carbide inserts.

(iv) *In soft and fragmented rock, the percussion energy should be reduced.*

(v) The *right feed pressure* always give the best drilling economy. Feed pressure when too low gives low penetration rates and causes the coupling sleeves to rattle loose. If the feed force is too high, the rotation speed of the drill bit diminishes. The risk of jamming increases, and the penetration rate drops. It also increases bending stresses in the drill rods.

(vi) The *larger is the drill bit, slower should be the rotation*. Rotation that is too fast will wear-out the cemented carbide inserts. Wear will be worst around the periphery of the drill bit, where the speed of rotation is highest.

(vii) The bottom of the drill *hole must be kept free of cutting*. Good flushing washes out the drill cuttings and keeps the hole open. Poor flushings reduces the rate of penetration and increases the risk of jamming.

(viii) *Timely grinding of inserts is necessary.* If wear is allowed to go unchecked, both the steel and the cemented carbide will be subjected to abnormally high stresses. This results in reduced penetration rate, the risk of damage, and often, tendency towards increased hole deviation.

(ix) To achieve economy, and for easy and quick grinding, it is desirable to redress bottoms when the wear flat is about a third of the diameter of the bottom.

BLASTING

14.10 Introduction to Blasting

Drilling and blasting is the most frequently used rock excavation technique. It is performed to break rock so that it may be quarried for processing in an aggregate production operation, or to excavate. Whenever there is a requirement to remove rock, blasting should be considered as it is generally more economical than mechanical excavation.

Blasting is done to loosen the rock for ease in excavation. Blasting is performed by discharging the explosive placed in the hole drilled for the purpose. Tremendous energy produced by blasting loosens the rock. Explosives, confined within a relatively small space (the shot hole) induce chemical reactions in the course of which gases and heat will develop in such quantities that the stresses produced in the surrounding rock by developing gas pressure will exceed the strength of rock in certain zone.

Some of the **terms used in blasting** are defined below :

(i) **Blasting :** It is the discharging of an explosive to loosen the rock.

(ii) **Explosive :** Explosive is a chemical compound which when burnt under favourable conditions produce a high pressure.

(iii) **Blasting Powder :** It is a low explosive, made from sulphur, charcoal, and sodium or potassium nitrate. Since these are slow burning, hence are seldom used for rock blasting.

(iv) **Dynamite :** This is a high explosive with nitroglycerine or trinitrotoluene as the main constituents and are initiated by a detonator.

(v) **Gelatin Dynamite :** It is a water proof explosive obtained by dissolving nitro-cotton in nitroglycerin.

(vi) **Stemming :** It is the filling of an inert material.

(vii) **Primer :** It is the portion of a charge which is loaded with a firing device and initiates the explosion.

(viii) **Bench :** It is an horizontal ledge of an excavation face along which holes are drilled for blasting.

(ix) **Benching :** It is the process of excavating using ledges in a stepped pattern.

(x) **Bench Height :** It is the vertical distance between the base of an excavation and the ledge above where the blast holes are drilled and blasted.

(xi) **Blast Hole :** It is a hole drilled into rock to enable the placing of an explosive.

(xii) **Burden :** It is the distance from the explosive charge to the nearest free or open rock face.

(xiii) **Rounds :** Round is a term which includes all the blast holes that are drilled, loaded, and fired at one time.,

(xiv) **Tamping :** It is the process of compacting the stemming material placed in a blast hole.

Economy in Drilling and Blasting

Economy of excavation mainly depends on how methodically the drilling and loading of the holes have been done. The cost of drilling the holes, includes : (i) direct labour cost; (ii) cost of drilling equipment and its accessories, whereas cost of loading includes : (i) cost of explosives; (ii) cost of detonators; and (iii) cost of its accessories.

The construction engineer is therefore required to pay due attention for good drilling and loading as it leads to a good blast of desired uniform fragmentation. He should be well-versed with nature of rock strata and suitability of explosives for the strata. Construction engineer should select proper drilling equipment and the drilling pattern depending upon job requirement.

14.11 Explosives

Explosives have much importance as they enable for quarrying large quantities of coal, limestone, iron ore and other materials required for various industries. The explosives are extensively used in rock excavation, in tunneling, in mining, for demolishing, for making roadways, in hydroelectric and multipurpose irrigation and power construction projects.

Explosives are compounds that detonate on introduction of a suitable initiation (an act of detonation) stimulus. The detonation results into reaction of an explosive compound at high speed, liberating heat and gas, causing very high-pressure, high temperature gases.

Explosives have following **characteristics :**

1. **Strength :** It refers to the energy content of an explosive, which is a measure of the force it can develop and its ability to do work.
2. **Sensitivity :** The sensitivity of an explosive product is defined by the amount of input energy necessary to cause the product to detonate reliably. To detonate explosives, a primer or booster is required to be used in conjunction with the electric detonator or the cap.
3. **Detonation Velocity :** It is the speed at which the detonation wave moves through the column of explosive. Commercially available explosives have velocity in the range of 1600 to 8000 m/sec. High velocity explosives are used in hard rock, while lower velocity explosives should be used in softer rocks for better results.
4. **Water Resistance :** Water resistance of an explosive is expressed as the number of hours a product can be submerged in static water and still be detonated reliably.
5. **Flammability :** It is the characteristics of an explosive that describes its ease of initiation from spark, fire or flame.
6. **Generation of Toxic Fumes :** It is the characteristic of an explosive which indicate the amount of toxic gases produced by it during the detonation process.

Explosives are mainly of following **types** :

(a) Low explosives (b) High explosives.

(a) Low Explosives : These are oldest known blasting explosives of black powder (known as gun powder) form. These burn without the production of intense shock wage and therefore the gases are released at lower pressures. These are mixtures of sulphur, charcoal and sodium or potassium nitrate. These are used where a slow heaving action is required. It does not shutter the rock as much as by high explosives, and therefore are used in the production of building and monumental stones.

(b) High Explosives : These usually contain either nitroglycerine (NGL) or trinitrotoluene (TNT) as the main constituents and are initiated by a detonator. The detonator initiates an intense shock wave in the explosive followed by the production of large volume of gases at exceptionally high pressure, which causes better destruction. Thus the action of high explosives is very fast and gives better production as compared to that of low explosives.

Care in the Use, Transport and Storage of Explosives

(i) All laws in this respect should rigidly be followed.

(ii) Do not leave an explosive in any location.

(iii) Do not smoke, permit smoking or have any source of fire or flame near the explosives.

(iv) Do not keep explosives where they are exposed to excessive heat, spark or impact.

(v) Do not allow any unauthorised or unrequired person to be present where explosives are handled, used or stored.

(vi) Detonators should not be stored with other explosives.

(vii) Vehicles transporting explosives should be marked with the word "explosives".

(viii) Vehicles transporting it should not be overloaded, and should be in perfect working condition.

14.12 Principles of Blasting

Drilling pattern is first designed considering various parameters of blasting. For deciding optimum drilling pattern few plans are designed and best is selected after few experiments. For this, position of holes to be drilled is marked on the ground and proper record of drilling and loading of holes is maintained to carefully relate the 'hole spacing' and 'burden' kicked out at the toe with the drilled hole diameter and their depth. The drilling pattern which gives best result for the particular strata is than selected and followed.

Principle for Producing Good Blast

(i) For a given diameter hole, more toe burden can be kicked out by drilling deeper holes.

(ii) Burden depends upon the nature of strata and degree of fragmentation required so as to suit available earthmoving equipment.

(iii) In a bigger diameter hole, more explosives can be loaded to kickout more burden at increased 'spacing of holes'.

(iv) If due to topography of the pit area the burden is more spacing of holes should be reduced.

(v) As a thumb rule (a) spacing is generally kept equal to burden, (b) depth of hole be not less than twice the burden, (c) burden is kept about 30 times the diameter of holes, and (d) stemming should be about 0.75 times the burden.

(vi) Packages or containers of explosives should not be thrown or dropped while loading or unloading.

(vii) Explosives and detonators should be stored separately in detached, dry, ventilated and fire resistant magazines, away from other buildings, railroads, and highways.

14.13 Commercial Explosives

The principal commercial high explosives used for blast hole charges are of three categories : 1. dynamite, 2. slurries, and 3. ANFO. To be a high explosive, the material must react at a speed faster than the speed of sound, and the reaction must be accompanied by a shock wave.

1. **Dynamite :** Dynamite is a nitroglycerin-based product and is the most sensitive of all the generic classes of explosive being used. It is available in the market in many grades and sizes to meet the requirements of different jobs of mining, quarries and construction. For firing the dynamite, a detonator is used. If a detonator is used, one of the cartridges serves as a primer. The detonator is placed within a hole made in this cartridge.
2. **Slurries :** A slurry explosive is made of oxidizing salts (ammonium, calcium, or sodium nitrate) and a fuel sensitizer mixed with water gel or emulsifying agent along with varying amounts of water. These are suitable in wet conditions.
3. **ANFO :** The "ANFO" (ammonium nitrate and fuel oil mixture) is used extensively for construction blasting. It is the cheapest source of energy and is much safer than dynamite because it can be detonated by special primers.

Primers and Boosters

Primers are the cartridges of dynamites, highly sensitized slurries, or emulsions together with detonators or a detonating cord. The obtain optimum performance of ANFO, the size of primer should match the borehole diameter. The primer, which is the point of initiation of an explosive column, should always be at the bottom of the blasthole.

Boosters are the highly sensitized explosives or blasting agents, used either in bulk form on in packages of weights greater than those used for primers. Boosters are placed within the explosive column, where additional breaking energy is required.

14.14 Initiation System

Initiation is an act of detonating a high explosive. The term initiator used in the explosive industry describe it as any device that can be used to start a detonation. An "initiation system" is a combination of explosives and component accessories designed to convey a signal and initiate an explosive charge from a safe distance. The signal function may be electric or non-electric. The order and timing of the detonation of individual holes is regulated by the initiation system. Fragmentation, vibration, and violence of a blast are all controlled by the firing sequence of the individual blastholes.

14.15 Electric Detonators

Electric detonators contain a base charge of Pentaerythritol Tetranitrate (PETN) with a priming charge of lead Azide, lead Styphnate and Aluminium powder (ASA) composition in an aluminium or copper tube. The electric firing portion (called as fuse head) consists of a small diameter corrosion resistant bridge wire attached to two insulated leg wire, as shown in Fig. 14.12. When the electric current is supplied (either from battery or the mains), the bridge heats to incandescence and the fuse head explodes and the ignition charge is ejected from a burning dust cloud which heats up the explosive charge and explodes causing the blasting cap to detonate.

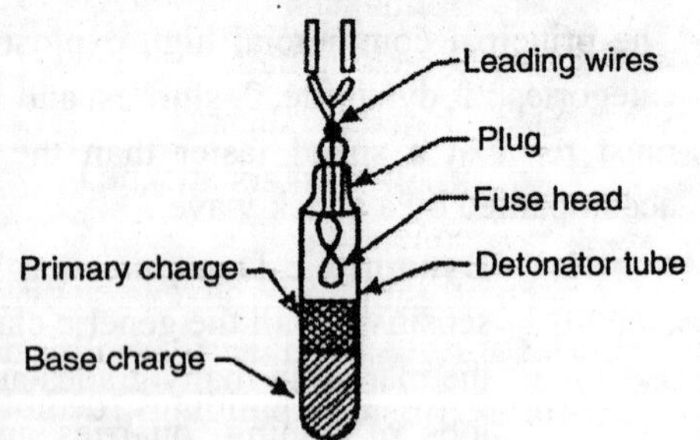

Fig. 14.12 Electric detonator.

14.16 Blasting for Quarrying/Excavation

While blasting for quarrying or excavation purposes following parameters and their co-relation should be examined :

(a) Spacing of the drill holes.
(b) Diameter of the drill holes.
(c) Depth of the drill holes.
(d) Burden of the rock at the toe.
(e) Burden of the rock at the crest.
(f) Degree of fragmentation desired.
(g) Strength of the explosives to be used.

Loading of Holes

While loading the hole, one gelatine cartridge is first inserted and pushed to the bottom of the hole and thereafter the primer is lowered, such that the detonator points outwards. More explosive cartridges are then inserted and tamped with wooden tamping rod to compact the column of explosives in the hole. When sufficient explosive charge has been loaded, the top portion of the hole is stemmed with either sand or clay or mixture of both.

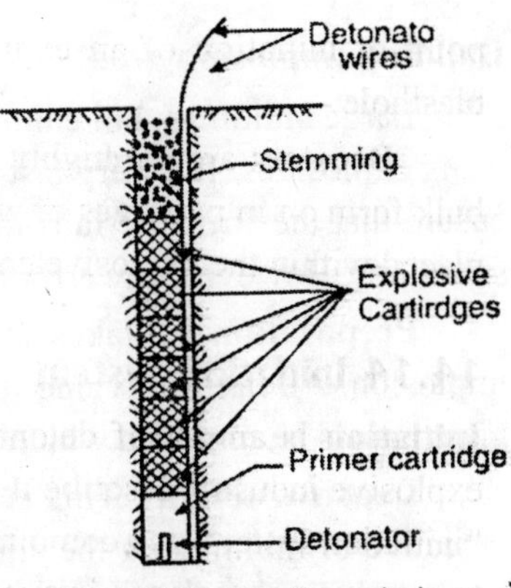

Fig. 14.13 Loading a hole.

14.17 Demolition Equipment

Commonly used equipment for demolition of buildings and other structures such as chimneys, bridges etc. are :

- Large hydraulic breakers,
- Elevated work platforms,
- Cranes,
- Excavators,
- Bulldozers,
- Wrecking ball,
- Hydraulic shears,
- Rock breakers attached to excavators to cut or break through wood, steel or concrete.

These equipment have been discussed at relevant places in the book.

As we know that **'demolition'** is the tearing down of buildings and other structures. In small buildings, demolition is a simple process as they can be pulled down either manually or by mechanical means that is by hydraulic equipment elevated work platforms, cranes, excavators or bulldozers.

Large buildings may require the use of a wrecking ball, a heavy weight on a cable that is swing by a crane into the sides of the buildings. This method is effective but is difficult to control and less efficient.

Hydraulic excavators may be used to topple one or two storey buildings by an undermining process. After determining where undermining is necessary, the building is pulled in the desired manner and direction. The walls are typically undermined at a building's base. Safety aspects are also required to be considered. Hoe rams are used for removing the concrete road deck and piers during bridge demolition, while hydraulic shears are used to remove the bridge's structural steel.

High reach demolition excavators are commonly used for tall buildings. Excavators with shear attachments are used to dismantle steel structural elements.

Hydraulic hammers are used to crush concrete to a manageable size and to remove reinforcement steel.

Building Implosion

Large buildings, tall chimneys, bridges may be destroyed by building imposition using explosives. It is very fast—the collapse itself only takes seconds. An expert can ensure that the structure falls into its own footprint, so as not to damage neighboring structures. However, any error can be disastrous.

Preparation : It takes several weeks or even months to prepare a building for implosion. All items of value such as copper wiring are stripped. Some materials like glass panels be removed which can form deadly projectiles.

Deconstruction : This is a new approach to demolition. This is done with the objective of minimizing the amount of materials going as waste to landfill. This is a 'green' approach and is applied by removing the materials by segregating them as per their category for reuse or recycling. On site, crushers allow the demolished concrete to be reused as crushed aggregate. Timber waste can be shredded to form manufactured timber boards.

14.18 Safety Aspects

1. All operations involved in transportation, handling, storage and use of explosives should be as per Indian Explosive Act.
2. Explosive shall be handled by or under the supervision of competent and experience persons.
3. **Transport and handling :**

(i) Explosives should not be transported to the site of operation except in suitable cases or containers which are so made as to prevent any spillage of explosives and any danger of sparks or other sources of ignition during conveyance.

(ii) Following should be observed regarding vehicles used for transport :

(a) Vehicles must have springs under the body.

(b) Detonators and ignitors must not be carried in the same very with explosives.

(c) The vehicle carrying the explosives must not be used to transport workmen or other materials.

(d) Drivers should not leave the vehicle unattended.

(e) All vehicles transporting explosives shall be marked or playcarded on both sides and ends with the word "EXPLOSIVES" in white letters not less than 75 mm tall on a red background.

(f) A motor vehicle carrying explosives should not be refueled except in emergencies and even then only, when motor is stopped and other precautions taken to prevent accidents. Such vehicles should invariably have atleast two fire extinguishers placed at convenient points.

(g) Vehicles transporting explosives should never be taken to repair shop, or parked in congested areas, or stored overnight.

(h) Explosives should not be transported on a public highway during hours of darkness.

(i) Persons employed in the transport or handling of explosives should not carry with them or in the vehicles, matches, loaded fire arms, petrol etc.

(j) Smoking should be prohibited during handling and transport of explosives.

(k) Explosives should be protected against them.

(iii) Vehicles used for transporting explosives should be carefully inspected daily to ensure that :

(a) Filled and serviceable fire extinguishers are in position.

(b) Electric wiring is well insulated and firmly secured.

(c) Chassis, engine and body are clean and free from surplus oil and grease.

(d) Fuel tank and feed lines are not leaking.

(e) Lights, breakes and stearing mechanism are in good working order.

(iv) Boxes of explosives should be handled carefully and not to be allowed to fall.

4. **Storage :**

(i) The magazine should be kept clean. High explosives like dynamite should be stored in a dry, clean, well-ventilated, bullet-proof and fire-proof building constructed in accordance with Indian Explosives Act, on an isolated well guarded place.

(ii) Sufficient number of lightning conductors should be provided on top of the magazine.

(iii) Separate magazine shoes, without mails, should be kept in the magazine and persons entering the magazine must put on these magazine shoes.

(iv) Light should be obtained from an electric storage battery lantern.

(v) No person having articles of steel or iron be allowed to enter a magazine.

(vi) Oily cotton rags, cotton waste and other articles liable to spontaneous ignition, should not be taken into a magazine.

(vii) Packages containing explosives should not be allowed to remain in the sun.

(viii) Adequate fire fighting equipment shall be provided in the magazine.

5. **Drilling :**
   (i) Holes should be of greater diameter than the diameter of the cartridges of explosives used.
   (ii) Loading and drilling should not be carried out at the same time in the same area.
   (iii) Drilling should not be resumed after blasts have been fired until and through examination has been made to make sure that there are no exploded charges which the drills may strike.

6. **Loading :**
   (i) Bore holes must be cleared of all debris before a cartridge is inserted.
   (ii) All loaded holes or charges shall be checked and definitely located before firing.
   (iii) Holes in the cartridges shall be made with a sharpened wooden. Detonators shall be inserted only in a hole in the end a cartridge prepared specially for that purpose.
   (iv) No welding shall be done inside the tunnel at the time of loading of the face, till the blast has been taken.
   (v) After the loading of a blast in completed, all excess explosives and detonators should be removed to a safe location.

7. **Blasting :**
   (i) The charge should fired successively and not simultaneously.
   (ii) Prior to the firing, all persons in the area should be warned of the blast and sent to a safe distance.
   (iii) Flagmen with whistles should be posted to stop traffic at access points on each possible route of travel. Blasting should be done at fixed hours and displaced on a Notice Board.
   (iv) A loud, warning signal shall be given at a proper time before firing a blast, and all clear signal shall be given when the blasting is over.
   (v) After a blast has been fired and firing line is disconnected, a careful inspection should be made by the blaster to determine if all charges have been exploded.

QUESTIONS

1. What is the necessity of drilling a rock? Discuss.
2. Name different types of drills used for drilling rocks. Discuss different types of jackhammers.
3. What factors affect the selection of drilling equipment?
4. What factors affect the rate of rock drilling? Discuss.

5. Write short notes on :
   (a) Percussion drill (b) Rotary drill
   (c) Wagon drill
6. Explain construction and working of jackhammers.
7. Discuss the following in brief :
   (a) Hydraulic drills (b) Drill steels
   (c) Drilling bits
8. What is a "drill penetration rate"? Discuss characteristics of rock.
9. Discuss different types of drilling equipment.
10. Write short notes on :
    (a) Hydraulic jumbo (b) Abrasion drilling
    (c) Crawler drills (d) Diamond bits
11. Discuss various factors for estimating drilling production.
12. What is blasting? Why it is required in construction projects?
13. What is an explosive? Discuss various characteristics of explosives.
14. Explain in brief :
    (a) High and low explosives.
    (b) Care in the use, transport and storage of explosives.
    (c) Principle of blasting.
15. Discuss different types of commercial explosives. What is the role of primers and boosters in blasting?
16. (a) What is an "initiation system" in blasting?
    (b) Discuss the construction and working of electric detonator.
    (c) Explain the procedure for loading a hole for blasting.

□□□

Chapter **15**

Tunnelling Equipment

15.1 Introduction

Due to increasing needs of men, tunnelling in recent years has gained importance in construction industry. These are required generally for following purposes :

1. For underground traffic, *i.e.,* passageways for railroads and for automotive vehicles.
2. Conduit for water, *i.e.,* for diversion of rivers while constructing hydroelectric plants,and also for providing water supply or drainage system.
3. Vertical/inclined shafts.
4. Caverns.
5. Accesses to mines.
6. Conduit for utility services, like laying electric, and telephone cables. etc.
7. Subways, underpasses, underground parkings etc.

In order to utilise huge potential of hydropower, and minerals, tunnel construction has gained momentum and lot of such construction activities are likely to come in near future. Metro rails are also required in many cities, as these are the only solution to solve the traffic problems in highly populated areas. Since the excavation, supporting, and lining are concentrated in small space provided by the tunnel bore, a thorough planning and application of mechanised system is essential to work with speed, economy, and safety.

Modern methods of drilling, blasting and mucking have made the operation of tunnelling much more rapid and economical than it was before. Tunnelling, however, remains an expensive operation and may well account for considerable proportion of the total cost of the project. Economic considerations therefore plays an important role in planning and selection of equipment. The tunnelling works in a hydro-electric scheme frequently include the excavation of surge chambers and of other shafts or edits for access or for the intake of water. Now-a-days there has been an increasing trend to locate power stations underground, which involves the excavation of underground chambers/caverns of considerable size, both for the turbine hall and transformer hall.

Since tunnelling is most expensive, a great emphasis is given to geological survey, detailed investigation, and planning. Rock characteristics, rock pressure, geological profile along the tunnel axis, hydrological data and other factors are considered for deciding the tunnel axis, methodology for constructing the tunnel, and also the type of equipment to be deployed for the work.

For a tunnel driven through the solid rock, little or no roof support is required, whereas for a badly broken rock, extensive wall and roof supports are required. If high quantities of ground water is noticed during exploration, change of locations desirable and if this is not possible pressure-grouting of the formation ahead of excavation is carried out for reducing the flow of water, however higher capacity pumps in large number shall be required for removing the water in such cases.

Intermediate Tunnel Entrances

Tunnels of short length upto few hundred meters are driven from one entrance only, while longer tunnels are driven from both ends to avoid problems related to general congestion, long time required for completing the tunnel, excessive haulage distance, high haulage costs, ventilation etc. For still longer tunnels it is desirable to provide intermediate openings for facilitating removal of much and water, and supply of materials, utilities, air for ventilation etc. The intermediate openings provide two working fronts for each such opening and therefore reduces the construction time.

15.2 Tunnel Shapes

Shape of a tunnel depends on the purpose for which it is constructed and on the ground pressure. In solid rock, any shape of the tunnel can be selected depending upon the purposes, *i.e.,* circular or elliptical for water and sewerage conduits, while semi-circular arch with vertical sidewalls for vehicular traffic tunnels. Tunnels in soft ground are generally made circular in order to resist the pressure on exposed surfaces, as circular cross-section is best section to resist external and internal stresses. When tunnel is required for rail-road or for automotive vehicles circular section will not serve the purpose, whereas driving tunnel of semi-circular arch with vertical walls will not be

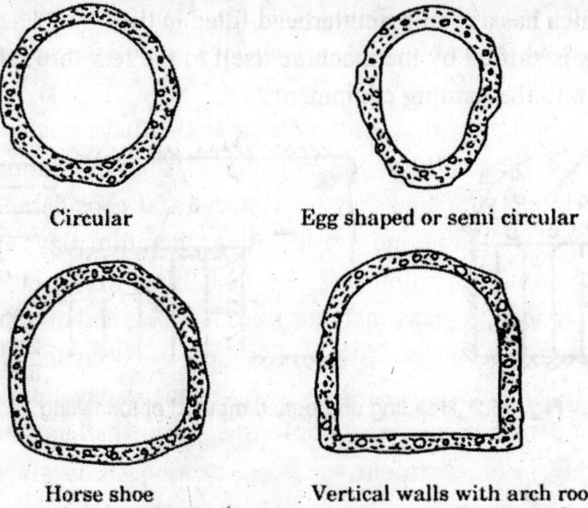

Fig. 15.1 Shapes of tunnels.

possible due to soft soils. Hence in such soils a horse shoe shaped tunnel is provided, which is a compromise between the two. These tunnels have a semi-circular roof together with arched sides and inverts. Such tunnels are most commonly used in hydraulic structures. When these tunnels are lined, they are strong in its resistance to the external pressure.

15.3 Methods of Tunnel Driving

Following methods are generally used for driving a tunnel :

1. Full face heading
2. Heading and bench method
3. Drifts method
4. Pilot tunnel method

1. Full Face Heading

In this method, the entire face of the tunnel is attacked at the same time. For this purpose following techniques are adopted :

(i) Conventional method of "drill and shoot".

(ii) 'Mole' tunnelling, *i.e.,* tunnelling by machine.

Conventional method of 'drill and shoot' involves the drilling by pneumatic rockdrills on entire face and then the holes so drilled are loaded and blasted. For large tunnels, drilling jumbo, on which large number of drills are mounted in the front and operated simultaneously, are used for greater efficiency and fast speed. After blasting is over and ventilation is complete, operation of removal of excavated material, known as mucking is started. If collapse of the roof is anticipated while tunnelling in poor fornation, temporary supports are provided before starting the mucking. Tunnel concreting is done after the mucking is over. By adopting efficient loading patterns, fast drilling equipment, *i.e.,* use of drifters and drilling jumbo, better drills for along holes and using efficient mucking and hauling equipment, very fast rate of tunnel driving is possible.

Tunnelling machines, also known as moles are also now-a-days used for full face tunnel driving, which has a rotating cutterhead fitted in the front. The much formed by cutting of the rock is shifted by the machine itself to the rear through a conveyor belt and is discharged into the hauling equipment.

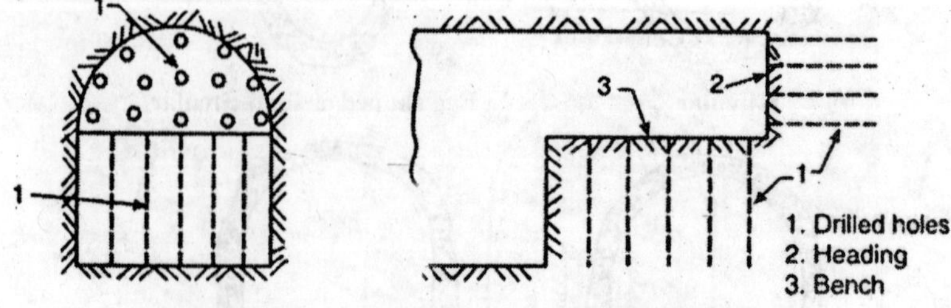

Fig. 15.2 Heading and bench method of tunnelling.

2. Heading and Bench Method

In this method, top portion is drilled first and blasted ahead of the bottom portion. The upper portion is known as heading and lower as bench. The lower portion is removed in one or more benches by drilling and blasting vertical and/or horizontal holes after certain length of heading is driven. In good rock where supports are not required, top heading is advanced one round ahead of the bottom, but in case of badly broken or weak rock the top heading is driven well ahead of the bench and the bench is used for providing support to the roof for initial concreting of top arch so as to provide full safety during bench excavation.

3. Drifts Method

As explained earlier, in week rock it is not possible to drive the full face of the tunnel, a small tunnel, known as drift is driven for a portion of tunnel length or sometimes for full length before taking up the excavation of full cross-section of the tunnel. The drift is driven at centre or bottom or side or at the top. According to the position with respect to the main cross-reaction these drifts are known as centre drift, bottom drift, side drift or top drift. Drift method of tunnel excavation has the following advantages :

(i) It helps to determine the region of bad rock or excessive ground water before actually taking up the full excavation, so as to enable to take up the corrective measures.

(ii) The drift provides ventilation while driving the main tunnel.

(iii) It reduces the consumption of explosives.

However the drift requires more mucking and drilling costs.

Drifting method, and heading and bench methods can be combined in very weak rocks, in that case top or side drifts are used before head driving.

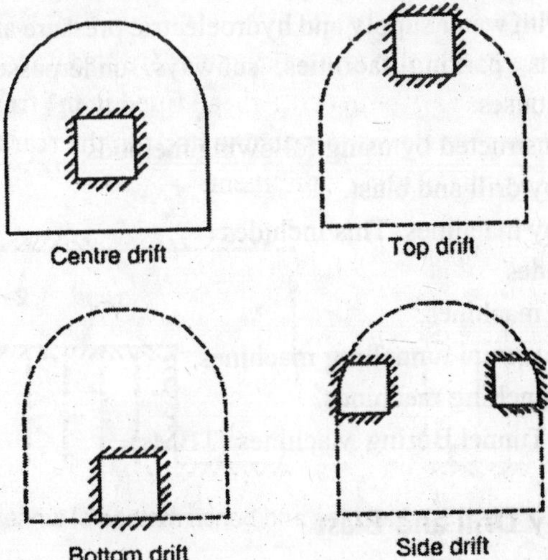

Fig. 15.3 Positions of drifts in tunnelling excavation.

4. Pilots Tunnelling

A small rectangular tunnel, known as pilot tunnel is driven at the centre of the proposed tunnel. For enlarging the section the holes are drilled readily along a ring, each such ring is spaced about 1 to 1.2 m apart. About 4 such rings, *i.e.,* 4 to 5 meters length of the tunnel, is blasted in one blasting in one blasting operation. While mucking is carried out in this portion, another set of 4 rings are drilled and loaded. As soon as the mucking is over, four more rings are blasted and thus the cycle of mucking is continuous. This method helps in achieving very high rate of progress.

Method of pilot tunnelling can also be used for inclined portions of the penstock tunnels, since in this case full face drilling is not possible.

15.4 Selection of Equipment for Tunnelling

Selection of equipment for tunnelling depends upon mainly on quantum of work involved, so that tunnelling work is carried out economically, speedily and safely. For short tunnels minimum tunnelling equipment consisting of air drills mounted on wagon drills or on jumbo, and loaders and dumpers for mucking are adopted. For long tunnels, larger capacity excavating and hauling equipment are used. The size and type of these equipment depends upon type of rock and size of the tunnel. Tunnel boring machines can be used for long continuous jobs. Steel lines or precast concrete liners can be used as tunnel supports. The bench canbe ripped with the help of a heavy duty ripper in very soft or week rock and the much can be loaded into the dumpers by using front end loaders. For a long tunnel works railroad equipment, like battery locomotives with mine cars and muckers for loading the mucks, are economical.

15.5 Methods of Tunnelling

Today, the tunnel construction is mainly concerned with highways and underground railways as well as with water supply and hydroelectric pressure and diversion tunnels, public utility tunnels, parking facilities, subways, underpasses, water conductor tunnels, and power houses.

Tunnels are constructed by using following methods :

1. Tunnelling by drill and blast.
2. Tunnelling by machines. This includes :
   (a) Road heades.
   (b) Reaming machines.
   (c) Partial face/mini tunnelling machines.
   (d) Shield tunnelling machines.
   (e) Full face Tunnel Boring Machines (TBMs).

15.6 Tunnelling by Drill and Blast

Method of tunnelling by drilling and blasting is common in mining or underground excavation since long. It has been experienced that only about 25% of explosive energy is utilised in actual rock breaking process and the rest is dissipated through surrounding medium.

If the pattern of blasting is not properly designed, even this 25% of explosive energy may lead to :

(i) poor fragmentation requiring secondary blasting,

(ii) severe over-break or back-break causing damage to excavation lines, and

(iii) damage to men and material due to fly rock in neighbouring area.

This method result in unequilibrium of the in-situ rock mass which leads to rough uneven contours with cracks penetrating for into the rock thus creating large over-breaks and generating more ground vibrations endangering the stability of nearby structures.

With the adoption of controlled blasting it is possible to get a smooth wall or contour free from over-breaks and ground vibration within tolerable limits. This method of drilling and blasting is more versatile and can be adopted in any type of strata but the tunnelling rates are comparatively low. The excess amount of over-break increases the cost of lining. In this system the tunnelling can progress in all types of hard and soft rocks, river-borne material, shear-zones, thrust zones, and there may be continuous ingress of water with chimney formations or squeezing ground conditions since, it does not require special technique for different media and moreover the problems encountered can be tackled simultaneously, *e.g.*, grouting, shotcreting, progressing by heading and benching method etc. The system can be used for any shape and size of the tunnel.

Following sequence of operations are generally adopted for **driving the tunnel through rocks** :

1. Setting up and drilling.
2. Loading the holes with explosives and firing.
3. Ventilating and removing the dust resulted by explosion.
4. Loading and hauling the muck.
5. Removing groundwater from the tunnel, if necessary.
6. Erection of supports for the roof and sides, if necessary. This includes rock-bolting or steel supports.
7. Placing reinforcement.
8. Placing the concrete lining.
9. Curing and shuttering removal.

Drilling

Various drilling equipment and their bits have already been described in previous chapter in the book. Here we shall restrict our discussions on their applications in tunnelling. For driving a tunnel, number of holes are drilled as per drilling pattern in size and depth as decided depending upon the size of the tunnel and its formation. Drifters are generally used for drilling in the tunnels where in water is used to remove the cuttings from the holes instead of compressed air to reduce the amount of dust in the air. The modern equipment used for drilling blast holes in tunnels is 'drill jumbo' and is being discussed in following paragraph. Holes are drilled slightly deeper than the advance per round to take care of loss in depth during blasting. Depth advance due to drilling and blasting operation is called as 'one round' or 'pull' and depends upon length of holes, type of explosive, number of holes charged and pattern of holes.

Drill Jumbo

Drill jumbos used in tunnels are also known as tunnel jumbos. A drill jumbo is a portable carriage having one or more carriage having one or more working platform equipped with columns, bars or booms to support and guide the drills, enabling the drills to perform drilling operation at any desired pattern. These platforms have arrangement for supporting the compressed air pipes, water pipes. The booms are operated by hydraulic fluid or air and supports the drifters, and are equipped with control enabling the operator to spot a drill in any desired position conforming to the drilling pattern. The platforms are constructed as per the size of tunnel and can be raised or lowered so as to allow muckers or hauling equipment to pass under the jumbo. Several drills can be operated from each platform for speedy excavation. The jumbos have 1, 2 or 3 booms and have high rate of penetration, any 2 to 3 meter per minute.

The jumbos are mounted either on rails or on pneumatic tyres (Fig. 15.4) depending upon the type of work. The jumbo can be equipped with electricity feeding cables, pneumatic concrete placers etc. Mobile jumbos of modern design with four-wheel drive and centrally articulated steering speeds production and reduces tunnelling costs.

Fig. 15.4 Multiboom drilling jumbo.

Loading and Firing

Details about explosives and firing as described in the chapter on 'drilling and blasting equipment' are equally applicable in driving tunnel. However, in tunnels the holes should be fired in the sequence as given in the drilling pattern. Drilling pattern when followed produces most economical and efficient breakage of rock for a given tunnel, and is determined by conducting tests using different patterns. Electronic detonators are used and supplied with built-in fuses and with leads of varying lengths to suit the length of holes in use in the particular tunnel.

Explosives selected for working in tunnels should have low fumes characteristics. Ammonium Nitrate explosives are therefore preferred over dynamites due to less toxic blast fumes (Ref. Fig. 14.5).

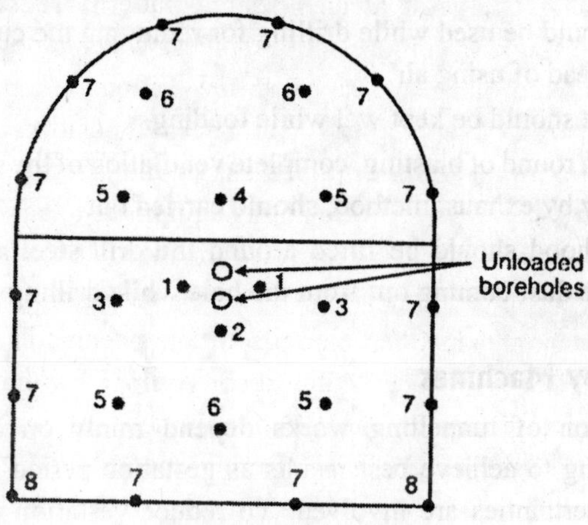

Fig. 15.5 Firing pattern.

Ventilating and Removing the Dust

Main objects of ventilation system in a tunnel are :

(i) To provide fresh air for workers.

(ii) To remove poisonous gases and fumes produced by explosion.

(iii) To remove the dust caused by drilling, blasting, mucking and other operations performed in the tunnel.

If a pilot or a drift is driven in the tunnel from portal, sufficient natural ventilation shall be available. When natural ventilation is not adequate, a mechanical method is provided. Mechanical ventilation is provided by one or more electric-motor-driven fans, which may blow fresh air in the tunnel or exhaust the dust and foul gases from the tunnel. Air is known into the tunnel through a light weight pipe or a fibre duct, whereas if the air is exhausted, the duct should be of sufficient strength so that it may not collapse under partial vacuum.

Tunnel may have both blower and exhaust system. When fresh air is blown into the tunnel, it is released near the working face, and as it flows towards the portal it carries the dust and fumes with it. While exhaust system is used, dust and foul air is drawn keeping the duct opening at about 50 to 60 m from working face. Thereby causing the fresh air to flow into the tunnel, from the portal. The system should be such that, it provides minimum of 6 to 8 cum m of fresh air per workers, while dust and fumes should be removed within 20 minutes of blasting. Air is generally supplied at a discharge velocity of about 9 m/min at the end of the duct. As tunnelling work progresses and length of air duct increases, blowing power of the electric fans should be increased.

Dust Control

As we know that dust is created by drilling, blasting, loading the muck and is serious health hazard to the workers, hence it is necessary to control the amount of dust in the air in a tunnel. Some of the steps which can reduce the dust are listed below :

(i) Water should be used while drilling for removing the cuttings from drilled holes instead of using air.

(ii) Muck pile should be kept wet while loading.

(iii) After each round of blasting, complete ventilation of the space near the face, preferably by exhaust method, should carried out.

(iv) Vacuum hood should be fitted around the drill steel at the rock face to collect the dust coming out from the hole while drilling.

15.7 Tunnelling by Machines

Faster implementation of tunnelling works depend minly on careful equipment selection and planning to achieve best results as gestation period in such projects is more and lot of uncertainties are involved. To reduce gestation period, one of the remedy is to adopt state-of-art technology and equipment for execution of underground structures like tunnels, shafts, underground caverns etc.

The latest trends in India suggests use of fast track equipments like use of 2/3 boom Drilling Jumbos, Boomers, Tunnel Boring Machines, Road Headers and raise borers for rock excavation, mechanised rock bolting equipment and wet shotcreting machines for support systems besides telescopic concreting gantry, concrete pumps etc. for concrete lining.

Tunnelling started firstly with "drill and blast" techniques and finally culminated in the development of boom type road headers and full face tunnel boring machine (TBM). Frequently changing ground conditions and the adoption of the conventional drill-and blast method have been mainly responsible for very slow rate of tunnelling. It is natural, therefore, to think of adopting machine tunnelling to achieve a faster rate of tunnelling.

Besides a rapid and regulated advance, machine tunnelling has many other advantages over the conventional drill-an-blast method. These include continuous excavation, improved strata conditions and tunnel-profile control with smooth walls, minimum interactions with nearby structures, increased safety, reduced ground vibrations, improved environment for workforce, and greater cost-effectiveness.

Types of Tunnelling Machines

Mechanical moles though can be classified in many ways, namely; according to the type of material to be mined, or cutting principle employed, or cutter head movement, but mainly fall under following two categories based on the action of their cutter-heads :

1. Rotary type 2. Oscillating type.

Rotary type moles consists of a wheel fitted with either teeth of disc cutters or roller bits which revolves in either direction ground the central shaft. These are primarily used in firm underground formations including hard rock applications.

Oscillating type of mechanical moles are generally used for soft or semistable formations, *i.e.,* in clays, sands and gravels. These machines are used in changeable ground conditions or where underground formations vary.

Special openings in the cutter arms and bulkhead can be controlled by the operator while using the machines in varying formations, in order to facilitate varying amount of cuttings, through the bulk head. The cutting arms operate like wipers in the automotive vehicles, and are mounted on separate shafts close to the centre.

Tunnelling machines can generally be grouped into following main groups :

1. Road heading machines
2. Reaming machines
3. Shield tunnelling machine
4. Partial face/Mini rock tunnelling machine
5. Full face tunnelling machine or tunnel boring machine (TBM).

1. Road Headers

Road headers can be used in rock strain of any type. Road headers are available for tunnels of any diameter or even heading and benching method can also be adopted with this machine for larger diameter tunnels. It can be used in parts, *i.e.,* heading and benching separately. The efficiency of these machines are very high and are most

Fig. 15.6 Road header (Courtesy : Mitsui, Japan).

suited for Indian conditions as rock strata especially in Himalayan regions are most unpredictable. However, the road headers are used for cutting only and shovels is employed for much loading.

Road headers are equipped with telescopic boom which eliminates machine movements and maintains floor in good conditions. Its speed of cutting motor can be changed as per the type of strata (as per geological conditions). These can be operated from safe distance by remote control unit for safety in hazardous areas.

"Road header" is a boom type track-mounted machines which cut and load material. Road headers or different types are available depending upon various applications.

2. Reaming Machines

The principle of reaming machine is to drive only moderate size tunnel and, if desired be enlarged by fixing a larger boring head on the shaft. Thus this concept is used in large diameter machine-bored tunnels.

3. Shield Tunnelling Machines

Tunnelling shields are specifically designed and employed where geological conditions throughout the tunnel vary substantially in unstable and loose ground, where rock pressure and water inflow are considerable. These machines are particularly useful in construction where no setting of the ground surface can be tolerated, *e.g.*, underground railway tunnel and hydraulic engineering construction.

The main function of the shield is to support the sides of a tunnel until supports are erected. The cutter head and cutter head support are contained within the shield. The thrust is reacted through the shield to the tunnel lining system. The shield is a casing or a rigid steel cylinder open at both ends to be forced forward. The front end has the excavating facilities and the rear and has mechanism to handle and erect heavy tunnel supports. The operations that are involved in a shield tunnelling include excavation of the front face, travel of shield and installation of permanent lining.

4. Partial Face/Mini Rock Tunnelling Machines

This machine is used as a full-face tunnel borer for small sized tunnels for watermains, gas ducts, electric and communication cables, sewer lines etc., where these services pass through rock formations and beneath built-up areas where cut and cover methods are impracticable and blasting is prohibited.

These machines were developed in nineteen seventees by different companies as mini full-facer in different designs, and different sizes and shapes of tunnels such as arch-shaped, rectangular, and circular. The shapes and sizes are programmed and controlled by hydraulic mechanism.

15.8 Muck Loading (Mucking)

Mucking is the operation of loading the broken rock or earth for removal from a tunnel. Mucking is done by hand in small tunnels, drifts and pilot tunnels. Mucking operations can be performed by power shovels, tractor loader, mucking machines, etc.

Power Shovels : Power shovels with short booms and dipper sticks are used for mucking in large tunnels. If the tunnel is small in length, and if there is no problem of ventilation, a diesel engine powered shovel may be used, otherwise an electric motor powered shovel is used.

Tractor Loaders : Wheeled or crawler type tractor loaders are used with diesel engine or electric motor or air motor prime-movers of different bucket capacities. The wheeled tractor loaders are articulated and have front end buckets. The bucket is filled during forward motion and then lifted over the tractor to discharge the load into a dumper. Tractor loaders powered by compressed air or by electric motors are commonly used. Use of diesel engine prime movers is restricted to tunnels of very small lengths.

Mucking Machines (Muckers) : These machines operated on rails and are available in different dipper capacities. The dipper is loaded by pushing it into the pile of much either in the front or on sides. These are operated by electric motors. The machine is designed to discharge onto a conveyor belt attached to the rear of the machine which in turn discharges into a much car. Air operated numbers are also used.

15.9 Muck Hauling Equipment

Mucking involves loading of blasted rock on the haulers and its transportation out of tunnel to disposal areas. Excavated rock is required to be hauled out of the tunnel in an effective and efficient manner so that the work of excavation continues uninterrupted. Muck-hauling equipment is selected depending upon excavating equipment, tunnel diameter, gradients etc. Following equipment are used for much hauling :

(i) **Front end loaders** can be used for this purpose for a short leads of about 30 meters or so.

(ii) **Small diesel trucks/tippers** are suitable for a short lead of about 1 to $1\frac{1}{2}$ kms in the tunnels of smaller diameters of about 4 meters or so.

(iii) **Rear dump trucks** are used for tunnels having 5 to 10 meters diameter and a haul distance of about 3 kms. For longer hauls these are not generally used due to smoke problem.

(iv) **Belt conveyors** are used for hauling the excavated muck where steep gradients are involved. Now-a-days these are becoming more popular due to economy and efficiency. This system proves to have low maintenance cost and has high capacity for muck hauling.

(v) **Pumps and pipelines** are used to remove the muck as a slurry where the tunnels are driven through the earth. Since this requires less space, hence are most useful for small to medium diameter tunnels of 2.5 to 4 meters.

(vi) **Rail haulage equipment**. These equipment include much train, muck cars, locomotives etc. These move on a narrow gauge track prepared by having the steel rails on solid ground. The muck cars are pulled by electric locomotives etc. The much cars are generally side dumping type having low height. Batteries are mounted on the loco and are recharged after 8 hours of working. Recharging requires 8 hours for the batteries to become fit for use. Therefore, 2 sets of batteries are sufficient for continuous use. The size of the locomotives are indicated by weight in tonnes which can be hauled by it.

It small dia tunnels the loading units could be small overhead loaders or convey muckers. While using type mounted equipment, the loading unit could be a hydraulic excavator with short boom or stick or front end loader or side dump loaders.

15.10 Tunnel Boring Machines (TBMs)

At present tunnelling in our country is being mostly done by conventional drilling and blasting method which is very time consuming. In hydro-electric projects, construction of tunnels is one of the most critical activities and has led to delays in commissioning of projects. In drilling and blasting technique, it has been experienced that only 25 percent of explosive energy is utilised in actual rock breaking process and the rest is dissipated through surrounding medium.

There is, therefore, a pressing need for employing tunnel boring machines for driving tunnels for speedy, economic and timely completion of hydro-electric, underground metro rail and other projects requiring tunnelling work. Use of tunnel boring machines have revolutionised and tunnelling practices in Europe. The tunnels which would have been completed in years are executed in months.

Tunnel boring machines were initially developed for boring soft rock formations. Now machines capable of boring much stronger rocks are available. Machines ranging in capacity from Miniborers, 2.10 m to those capable of boring tunnels upto 11.5 m in diameter, provided with a cutter head for a pilot hole of lesser diameter and enlarging cutter to bore tunnels upto 15 m diameter (multi-stage machines) are available. Correct alignment of boring is obtained with a laser type directional control.

Tunnel Boring Machines (TBMs) also known as Moles are the recent developments in the tunnel driving techniques. The function of TBM is to loosen the earth of break the rock continuously in the entire section of the tunnel, into cuttings and convey to the rear of the machine, where it can be loaded into muck cars or dumpers or onto conveyor belts for the transportation to the ultimate disposal site. The moles are transported to the site of work in parts and then assembled at the project site either outside the tunnel portal, if space for assembly is available, or inside the tunnel by driving the tunnel, sufficient in lengths for enabling its assembly using conventional method. For proper operation of the moles, auxiliary services like workshop facilities,

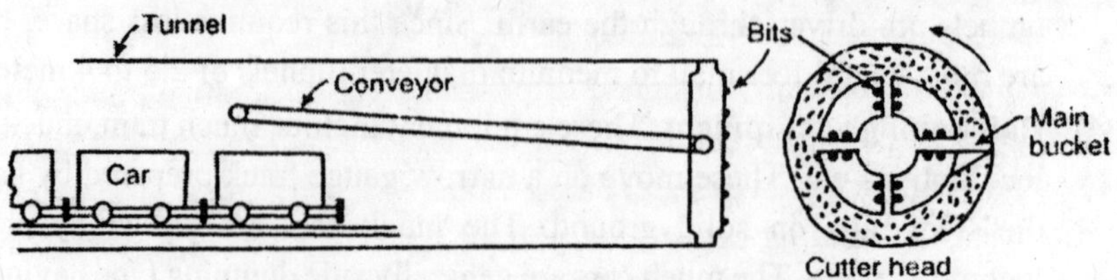

Fig. 15.7 Tunnel boring machine (TBM).

electric power, lighting, ventilation, drainage, compressed air and water supply etc. be provided.

Working Principle and Constructional Features of TBM

Depending on the manufacturer and the type of service to be provided, essential parts of mole might include the items as shown in Fig. 15.8.

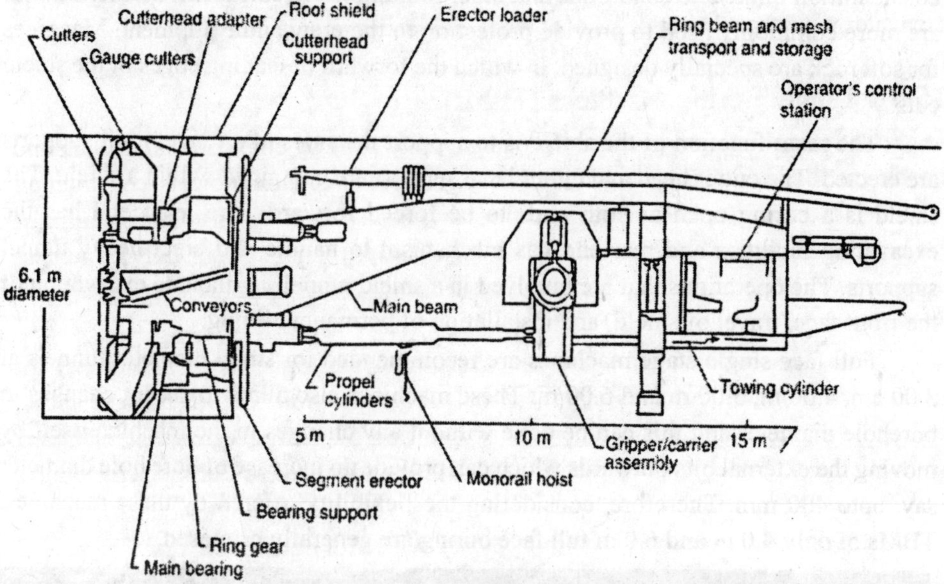

Fig. 15.8 Components of a typical tunnel boring machine.

These machines perform the boring operation through rotation of the front head against the rock face. the mole has circular cutter head in the front provided with fixed cutters of desired shape. The cutter head while rotating is pressed against the rock to cut or pulverize it. The cuttings while falling down is collected in the buckets provided around the cutter-head periphery. These buckets discharge the muck into a hopper to ıeed it into the belt conveyor leading to the rear of the machine. This conveyor then discharges the muck either into the mine car or to another belt conveyor leading to the portal of the tunnel. The mine cars are hauled by using the loco. The muck of cuttings can also be disposed off by using the slurry pipelines after mixing the fine muck into water to form slurry.

The tunnel boring machines are of two types :

(i) Single stage machine—Full fact TBM.

(ii) Multi-stage machine—Reaming TBM.

The machines are basically designed to penetrate the rock strata continuously using cutting tools fixed to a retaining head. The cutter head may be a single full diameter or cutter head for a pilot of lesser diameter and enlarging cutter to bore tunnels of bigger diameter. On rotating cutter head various types of cutters can be mounted depending on the type of rock to be excavated. The buckets attached to the cutter head elevate the cuttings and deposit them on a belt conveyor that transports them to the rear of the machine.

The physical characteristics of the rock to be excavated influence the selection of type of machine whether single stage or multi-stage, and type of cutters. The decision to use single stage or multi-stage driving can be reached only after careful consideration of the site conditions and other limitations. In soft rock, shield machines are more commonly used to provide protection to the crew and equipment. Machines for soft rock are specially designed, in which the forward or leading edges of the shield cuts.

The main function of the shield is to support the sides of a tunnel until supports are erected. The cutter head and cutter head support are contained within a shield. The shield is a casing open at both ends to be forced forward. The front end has the excavating facilities and rear end has mechanism to handle and erect heavy tunnel supports. The operations that are involved in a shield tunnelling include excavation of the front face, travel of shield, and installation of permanent lining.

Full face single stage machines are recommended for small diameter tunnels at 3.00 am, 4.00 m, 5.00 m and 6.00 m. These machines also allow to accept changes in borehole diameter and this can be done without any changes in the machine itself by moving the external bits outwards which can provide an increase of bore hole diameter say, upto 400 mm. Therefore, considering the flexibility offered by these machines, TBMs of only 4.0 m and 6.0 m full face boring are generally proposed.

Fig. 15.9 Tunnel boring machine.

For driving through full-face on full-face TBMs number of cutter heads are mounted on a drum. The drum when rotates in one direction, the individually driven cutterhead having projected tungsten carbide tipped tools can be rotated in another direction and the drum advances into the tunnel face, by providing a thrust with the help of hydraulic system. The tips of the tools when worn out can be easily replaced. The tips are kept cooled by spraying a mixture of water and compressed air into the cutting area. This also suppress the dust formed during cutting.

Operation of TBM

When a mole is in position to operate, the cutter head and discs are pressed against the face of the tunnel. As this thrust is maintained, the cutter head is rotated and the muck is delivered to the rear of the mole. When the cutter head reaches the end of the advance stroke, the rear legs are extended downward to support the machine. The clamp legs are retracted to free the main frame and the thrust move the frame forward. The clamp legs are then extended to anchor the mole in position for the beginning of the nest cycle.

Different steps of TBM operations are shown in Fig. 15.10.

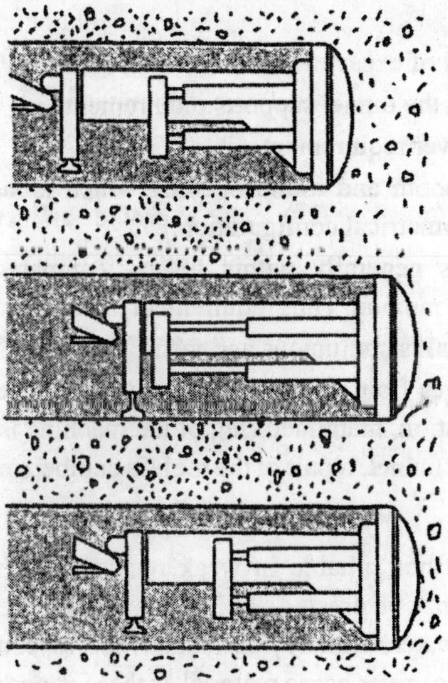

Fig. 15.10

1. Machine Advance Cycle

Start of Boring Stroke :

1. Grippers set on tunnel wall
2. Rear support legs raised
3. Thrust cylinders energized
4. Cutterhead and conveyor running.

Retract After Stroke Completed :

1. Cutterhead and conveyor stopped
2. Rear support legs lowered

3. Thrust cylinders full extended, then
4. Retract thrust cylinders, gripper assembly.

Reset for New Boring Stroke :

1. Grippers reset on tunnel wall
2. Rear support legs raised
3. Cutterhead and conveyor started
4. Thrust cylinders energized.

Advantages of Tunnel Boring Machines

(i) There is very less danger of fall outs in machine bored tunnels, since adjacent or surrounding rocks are undisturbed as no blasting is done.

(ii) Mucking is also safe and convenient, since muck is conveyed from the face of the rear of the machine and is loaded automatically by means of the belt conveyors.

(iii) Higher speed of excavation.

(iv) Reduction in the tunnel supports requirement.

(v) Less manpower requirement.

(vi) Produces smooth and round opening which is supposed to be strongest available geometrical configuration.

(vii) Overbreak is generally within 5% as compared to 25% obtained by conventional method. Thus requirement of cement concrete is also reduced.

(viii) Muck removal is continuous and fast.

Major disadvantages from TBMs are high investment cost, long delivery period in purchase and importation, manufacturing of the machine is required to be done for the exact diameter of the tunnel, repair of the mole is cumbersome and time consuming.

Application

Full face TBM is not suitable in weak rock strata conditions, as immediate support at the face can not be erected. TBM may also not be suitable where there is continuous ingress of water, chimney formation due to continuous flowing of the rock-mass and presence of river borne material as these zones may cave in and thereby jam the entire cutter head of the TBM. These are also not useful where there is continuous squeering pressure from all sides of the tunnel, presence of shear zones with high plastic seams.

TBMs are available for boring tunnels of 2.1 m to 11.5 m in dia. They are also provided with a cutter head or a pilot hole of lesser dia and enlarging cutter to bore tunnels upto 15 m diameter.

TBMs are available either for single stage machine, *i.e.*, full face tunnel boring, or multistage tunnel boring. In first case cutter head is of a single full diameter, while in later case it is for a pilot of lesser diameter and enlarging cutter to bore tunnels of bigger diameter.

15.11 Safety in Tunnel and Shaft Excavation

1. Frequent careful inspection of tunnel walls and roof and thorough sealing or removal of loose rock and necessary to prevent rock falls, ample illumination, good housekeeping, and safe walkways are important factors in the prevention of accidents.
2. All persons working (or entering) in the tunnel should wear hard hats and hardtoe shoes.
3. In every shaft and tunnel sufficient safe means of access should be provided.
4. After every blasting operation, roof and walls of the tunnel and sides of the shaft should be carefully inspected.
5. Motive power, other than electric should not be used. Every locomotive should have headlights on each end. It should also be equipped with whistles or born.
6. The ventilation system should be adequate to maintain circulation of air in all parts of tunnels and shafts.
7. All electric wiring shall be extra-heavy insulated and to sufficient capacity supported on insulators and not looped on or tied to spikes or other makes shift supports.
8. No inflamable materials or oil and grease should be stored inside or near the tunnel or shaft.
9. In case of shaft excavation, all sheaves should be of the proper diameter of the cable or hoist rope and should be amply strong, properly mounted and frequently inspected. All hoisting equipment including ropes and cables should be thoroughly inspected atleast once a weak and maintained in a good condition.
10. Telephone system should be established in the tunnels and shafts.
11. Following safety precautions should be followed in case of gaseous tunnels :
    (a) Regular checking of methane gas by methane detector.
    (b) No entry of lighters, match boxes etc. inside by workers etc.
    (c) To detect carbon dioxide formation safety lamps be provides.
    (d) Regular checking of gas at the faces should be done before each shift.
    (e) The gas percentage should be checked regularly.
    (f) Rescue apparatus shall be provided, and some personnel should be trained to handle them.

QUESTIONS

1. Enumerate the purposes where tunnelling equipment are required.
2. List the equipment used in underground works.
3. Discuss the methods used for (i) tunnelling construction, and (ii) tunnel driving.
4. Discuss the following in brief :
   (a) Intermediate tunnel entrances
   (b) Shapes of tunnels
   (c) Heading and benching.
5. Discuss the factors to be considered for selecting the equipment for underground works.
6. Discuss the method of tunnelling by "drill and blast".
7. Discuss different types of machines used for tunnelling.
8. Explain the following in brief with regards to tunnelling :
   (a) Drill jumbo
   (b) Ventilation and removal of dust
   (c) Vertical/inclined shafts
   (d) Caverns.
9. What is grouting? Discuss the necessity in underground works.
10. What is tunnel boring machine? Explain its importance in tunnel construction.
11. Explain the construction and working of TBM.
12. Explain the applications of TBM and discuss the advantages and disadvantages of use of TBM in tunnelling.

Chapter 16

Pumping and Dewatering Equipment

16.1 Introduction

Almost all construction projects require water for different purposes such as water supply for human consumption or for other processes as for aggregate washing, curing, jetting etc. The pump is the basic equipment in the operation of a water handling system.

In excavating below the ground surface, construction often encounter groundwater prior to reaching the required depth of excavation. Dewatering, temporarily lowering the level of groundwater, is necessary for construction activities. After the construction operation are completed, the dewatering action can be discontinued and the groundwater will then return to its normal level. While planning for dewatering, the planner should consider that groundwater levels change from season to season.

The water from excavated areas are diverted into sumps from where it can be removed by pumping. The pumps are used mainly for following important operations :

1. Removing water from pits, tunnels and other excavations.
2. Lowering water table for enabling excavation.
3. Dewatering coffer dams.

The pumps in construction works are generally used under severe conditions, such as those resulting from (a) variations in the pumping head, or (b) from handling muddy water, or (c) highly corrosive water.

Factors for Selecting Pumps

Factors to be considered in selecting pumps for construction works are :

1. Dependability.
2. Availability of spare parts for repair and maintenance.
3. Easy repair and maintenance.
4. Less installation and operation costs.
5. Power efficient, *i.e.*, lesser power consumption.

Information Required for Selecting a Pump

Following informations should be considered for selecting a pump :

1. The type of fluid to be pumped.
2. Height of lift from the existing water inlet to the point of discharge.
3. The rate at which the water is to be pumped.
4. The altitude of the project.
5. The suction head.
6. The variation in water level at suction and discharge.
7. The pressure head at discharge.
8. The size of pipe (at suction and delivery).
9. The type, sizes, number of fittings and valves to be used in the pipe line and length of pipe.

16.2 Pumps

Pump is a mechanical device to increase the pressure energy of a fluid. The pumps are used as water-handling device in construction projects. The water is required to handle for human consumption, drainage and dewatering. The liquid handled by the pumps may be water, oil, sludge etc. In construction works the water may be pure or dirty.

Pumps are extensively used in construction projects and are required to perform various operations such as :

(a) Removing of water from pits, tunnels etc.

(b) Unwatering cofferdams.

(c) Lowering the water table for excavation.

(d) Supply of water for many types of utility services.

These pumps are required to perform their functions under severe conditions and handling of water which may be muddy, sandy or corrosive. The pump selected should, therefore be able to handle all these types of works and dependable.

Types of Pumps : Pumps are of following types :

1. **Positive displacement pumps :** These may be :
   (a) Reciprocating pumps.
   (b) Rotary Pumps : These may be gear pumps, vane pumps, screw pumps etc.
2. **Rotodynamic pumps :** These may be volute pumps, circular pumps, diffuser pumps, vertical turbine pumps, centrifugal, mixed flow and propeller type of pumps.

16.3 Reciprocating Pumps

Reciprocating pump is also known as a "positive displacement pump" because in it liquid is pushed out of the cylinder by the actual displacement of the piston or plunger.

A reciprocating pump is driven by power available from an external source and consists of a cylinder in which piston or plunger reciprocates. This movement of the piston or plunger creates alternatively vacuum pressure and positive pressure in the cylinder which raises the water.

If the water acts only on one side of the piston, the pumps is known as "single acting pump". These pumps suck the water into the cylinder during outward stroke. In this stroke atmospheric pressure acting on the surface of the water helps to push the water into the cylinder. During inward stroke the suction valve closes and the water is forced up in the delivery pipe. The construction and working of a single acting reciprocating pump is shown in Fig. 16.1.

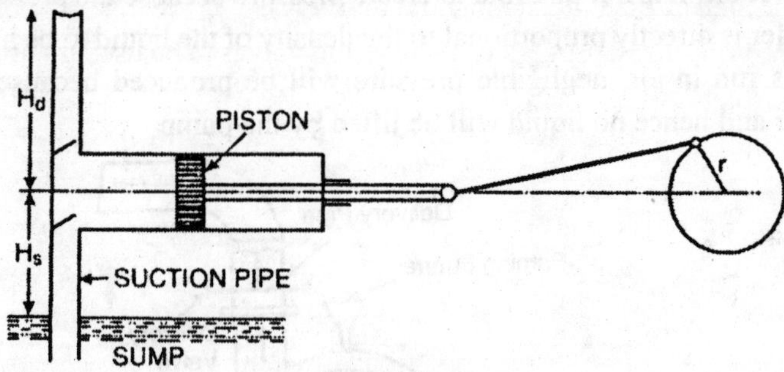

Fig. 16.1

The working of a reciprocating pump can easily be understood with the help of above figure. The piston moves backward and forward in the cylinder due to the rotation of the crank. During outward (suction) stroke, piston moves to the right. This movement of the piston causes vacuum in the cylinder. The atmospheric pressure on the water surface forces the water into the cylinder through the suction pipe This force of water opens the suction valve which is a non-return valve. On the inward stroke, pressure of water closes the suction valve and opens the delivery valve. In this stroke water is forced up the delivery pipe and so water is raised to the required height or pressure.

In "double action pumps" water acts on both the sides of the piston. Fluid is sucked on one side and delivered on the other side during each stroke.

Types of Reciprocating Pumps

The classification may be :

(a) According to the action of water :

(i) Single acting (ii) Double acting

(b) According to the number of cylinders :

(i) Single cylinder (ii) Double cylinder

(iii) Triple cylinder etc.

(c) According to the existence of air vessel :

(i) With air vessel (ii) Without air vessel

16.4 Centrifugal Pumps

A centrifugal pump is a hydraulic machine used to raise the liquids from a lower to higher level by creating a required pressure by means of centrifugal action. Centrifugal pumps are the machines which increases the pressure energy of a fluid. These may either lift the fluid or just boost the pressure in a pipe line.

Working of Centrifugal Pump

Fig. 16.2 explains in detail the working of a centrifugal pump. Before starting a pump, priming is done. In priming, water is filled in the suction pipe, casing and into a portion of delivery pipe upto delivery valve. This is done for the removal of air. With the presence of air, it is not possible to create pressure because the pressure generated by the impeller is directly proportional to the density of the liquid to be handled. Thus, if impeller is run in air, negligible pressure will be produced because of very less density of air and hence no liquid will be lifted by the pump

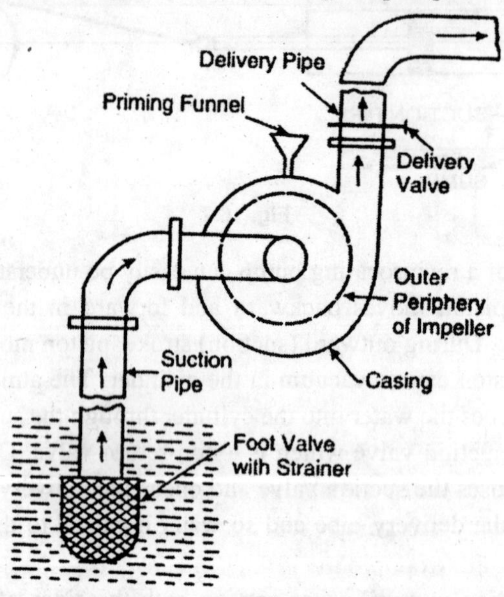

Fig. 16.2

Thus, it is very essential to prime the pump properly and it should be noted that during priming delivery valve is kept closed. The various methods of priming will be discussed in this chapter later on.

After priming, the delivery valve is kept still closed and prime mover (generally electric motor or diesel engine) is started to rotate the impeller. The rotation of impeller in the casing full of liquid produces centrifugal head in the liquid and thus pressure in whole of the liquid is increased.

After a short period, when pump attains, a constant speed, delivery valve is gradually opened and thus liquid is allowed to flow in a radially outward direction through the impeller vanes and attains a higher velocity and pressure at the outer periphery. With the help of special shape of casing (Volute, Vortex or Diffuser) this high velocity energy is converted into pressure energy and reduces high velocity. Now this water at higher pressure rises through the delivery pipe into a desired height. At the same time centrifugal action creates partial vacuum at the centre of impeller, known as EYE. The partial vacuum cause the water to rush through the suction pipe towards the impeller eye, to take the place of water which has left the impeller vanes, from the sump (where the pressure is atmospheric).

Thus, in this way water reaches and leaves the impeller continuously and water is raised to a certain height at constant rate.

Number of Impellers

According to the number of impellers provided, the pumps may be classified as single stage or multi-stage pumps.

In single stage pumps, only one impeller is fitted (Fig. 16.3) while in multi-stage pumps two or more than two impellers are fitted on the shaft either in series or in parallel.

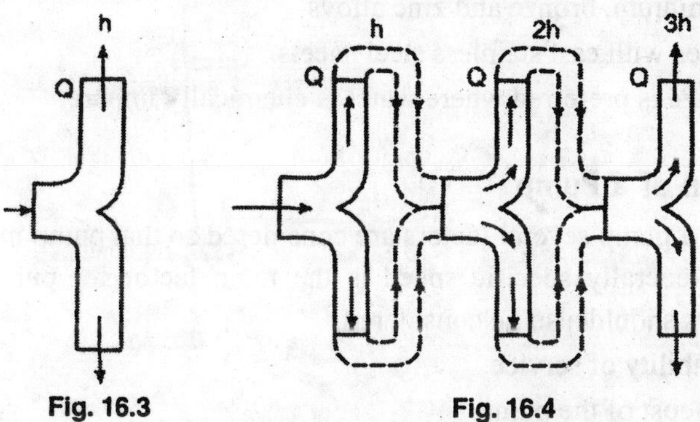

Fig. 16.3　　Fig. 16.4

(a) **In Series :** When two or more than two impellers are in series, head produced by the pumps will be the sum of the head produced in each impeller. For example if h is the head developed by one impeller then total head (H) produced by n impellers to series will be $n \times h$. As shown in Fig. 16.4 the discharge from one impeller is allowed to enter in the next impeller. Thus, the total discharge will be equal to the discharge through single impeller. Therefore, when impeller are connected in series, the discharge remains the same but the head increases as the number of impellers increase.

(b) **In Parallel :** As shown in Fig. 16.5 when the impellers are connected in parallel, the discharge of each impeller enters a common delivery pipe. Thus total discharge will be equal to the number of impellers multiplied by the discharge of one impeller. Here the total head produced will be equal to as that produced by a single impeller.

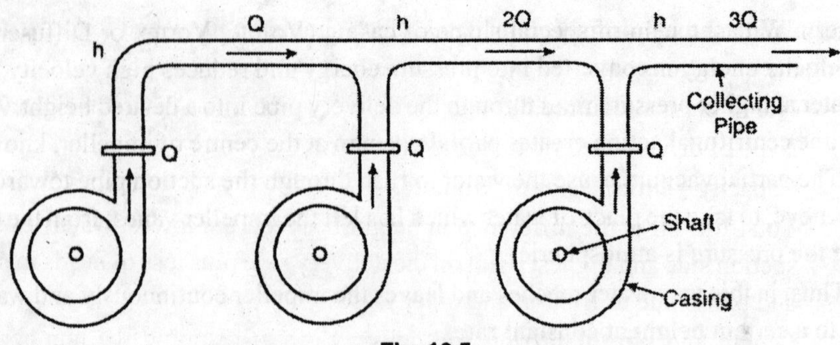

Fig. 16.5

Generally, the term multi-stage pump is known for two or more impellers connected in series which are used for producing high heads.

Impellers are made of following materials :

(i) Low carbon steels coated with stainless steel.

(ii) Stainless steel. (cr-12 to 13% and Ni-1%).

(iii) Aluminium, bronze and zinc alloys.

(iv) Blades with cast stainless steel sheets.

(v) Bronze is preferred where water is chemically impure.

16.5 Selection of a Pump

While selecting a pump several factors are considered so that pump may fulfill all the requirements. Generally specific speed is the main factor for pump selection but following factors should also be considered :

(a) Reliability of service.

(b) First cost of the pump.

(c) Efficiency of the pump

(d) Depreciation and life of the pump.

(e) Cost of energy which is to be consumed in running of the pump.

(f) Maintenance cost.

(g) Properties of liquid to be pumped.

(h) Temperature of the liquid to be handled.

(i) Specific gravity of the liquid.

(j) Suspended impurities in the liquid.

(k) Capacity.

(l) Suction head, and total head.

(m) Friction head.

(n) Discharge pressure required.

(o) Length and dia. of suction, as well as of delivery pipe.

(p) Type of power available.

(q) Location and altitude where the pump to be installed.

Following are the most important datas which should be furnished for ordering or for calling the quotations :

1. No. of pumps required.
2. Type of drive—electric material/oil engine.
3. Capacity—litres/sec or m^3/minute.
4. Total lift—It is the difference in height between the lowest water level on suction side and highest point on the delivery side plus loss of heads in pipes and pump due to friction and other losses.
5. Length and size of suction and delivery pipes including the number and sizes of bends, tees, valves etc.
6. Type of pump—horizontal or vertical.
7. Type of liquid to be handled.
8. Place of application : Irrigation, condenser circulation, boiler, feed and deep well, interlifting and dewatering in construction field etc.

16.6 Axial Flow or Propeller Pumps

This type of pump resembles to a reversed propeller turbine. This pump is fitted with an axial flow impeller in which water enters and leaves the impeller axially. In such pumps no centrifugal head is created in water but pressure is developed during the flow of liquid over the blades. Fig. 16.6 shows a line diagram of this type of pump. These pumps have vertical shafts.

As shown in the figure a small length of suction pipe at its upper end, ends in a casting in which a boss carrying about 4 vanes is provided. The boss is rotated by a motor connected at the top of boss shaft. Sucked liquid passed through a set of single blades into the boss vanes, where it gets pressure energy. Then liquid passes through another set of guide blades into the delivery pipe.

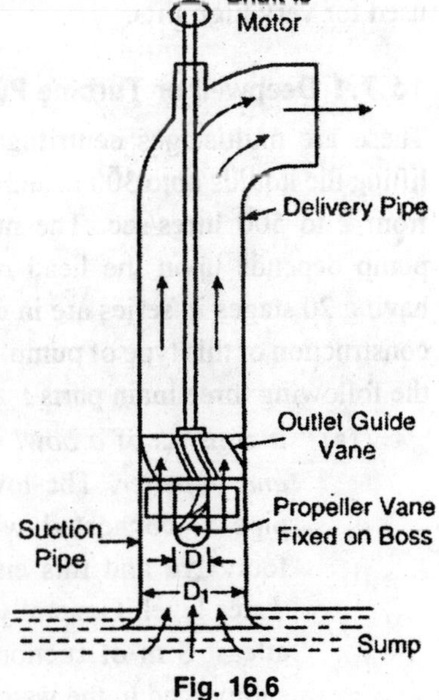

Fig. 16.6

The first set of inlet guide blades, guides the incoming water axially without any velocity or whirl into the impeller. Guide blades at the outlet takes the whirl action again. (This whirl velocity is imparted by impeller blades). Thus allowing the water to flow axially in delivery pipe.

These pumps are suitable for very large discharge against small heads (generally 9-12 m). As the speeds of these pumps are high hence danger of cavitation is more and, therefore, very low suction is kept.

These pumps are used in sewage handling, land drainage, flood control, condenser circulation in power houses and irrigation etc.

Axial Thrust

Axial thrust is a force acting parallel to the axis of the pump shaft. This is caused due to the (i) water rotation with a forced vortex while passing through the impeller, and (ii) water ente4ring the pump axially and then changing its path to a radial direction. This causes a force to act in the direction of flow at inlet. In order to enable the pump to withstand this thrust the small pumps are provided with a thrust bearings, while large pumps use double suction impeller, where suction on two sides of the impeller neutralises the thrust. In multistage pumps inlet of half the impellers are arranged in opposite direction.

16.7 Deepwell or Borehole Pumps

These pumps are used where water or any other liquid like oils etc. are required to be raised from a larger depth. These are generally used for pumping from depths more than 6 to 7 m. Special type of pumps can lift the oils even from a depth of 3000 m but generally ordinary deepwell pumps can lift upto 300 m. These pumps can have capacities upto 500 lit/sec and have pipe dia upto 0.6 m nearly.

These pumps can be plunger pumps, multistage centrifugal pumps, jet pumps and air lift pumps etc. Out of these, plunger and multistage vertical type turbine pumps (centrifugal type) are most common. Plunger pumps are reciprocating pumps and are used for very high lifts.

16.7.1 Deepwell or Turbine Pump

These are multistages centrifugal pumps and used for lifting the liquids upto 300 m and have a capacity varying from 2 to 500 litres/sec. The number of stages in the pump depends upon the head required. These pumps, having 20 stages in series are in use. Fig. 16.7 shows the construction of this type of pump. These pumps consist of the following three main parts :

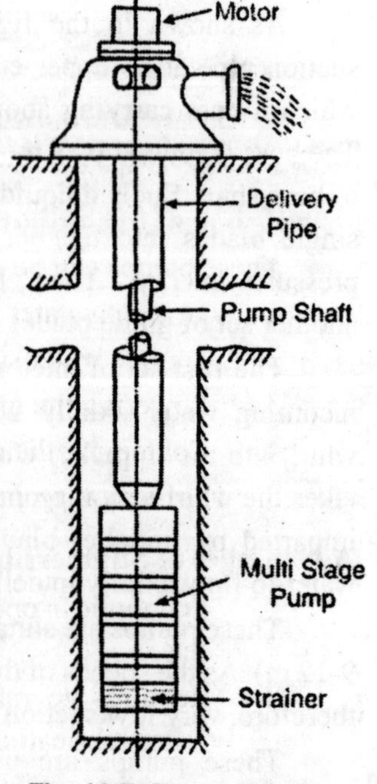

Fig. 16.7 Deepwell pump.

(a) It consists of *a bowl which has suction case and impeller*. The lower end of the suction pipe is connected with the strainer at the footvalve and this end is placed below the water level. Generally all the impellers have atleast 3 m of suction with strainer remains submerged in the water. Water enters the first impellers through suction pipe and then passes through all the impellers, thus gaining head one after the other.

(b) *Rising main* is the second part, the lower end of which is connected to the outlet of the impellers and the upper end of these is connected to be driving head (Prime mover).

(c) The third main part is the *driving head or the prime mover*, which is generally an electric motor. This is placed at the top of the line shaft usually on the ground level and is directly coupled with the long vertical shaft of impellers. The electric motor is properly protected against water.

The pump shaft and line shaft are coupled together and are enclosed in the rising main. These shafts are supported at suitable intervals with the rubber bearings. The bearings are lubricated by the delivery water passing through the rising main. Upper end of the line shaft is fitted with thrust bearing to carry the weight of all the impellers at the shaft.

16.7.2 Submersible Pump

This is the modification on the deepwell pump explained above. As the name indicates, in this electric motor and pump both are submerged in the water. By submerging electric motor, large economy can be made by avoiding long shaft, large number of bearings and large sized rising main etc. The complications due to thrust (arising due to the weight of the shaft and impeller etc.) are also avoided.

Since the motor is submerged in water, the only problem is to prevent the motor windings and other electrical connections to be spoiled by water coming in contact. For this purpose either of the following two solutions can be made :

(i) To use a normal type of motor but to prevent the water from reaching it by enclosing in a water-tight diving ball. This system of enclosing is known as "Dry motor" type system.

(ii) To allow the water to have more or less free contact with motor windings but to give them special protection by suitable type of insulation. This is known "Wet motor" type system.

Application of the Submersible Pumps

These pumps can be used for :

1. Drinking water supply installations for cities and rural areas.
2. Service water supply installations for industry and commerce.
3. Lowering the ground water level on building sites.
4. Containing the ground water level in mines.
5. For irrigation purposes.

Advantages of Submersible Pumps

1. Economic in operation, because of high overall efficiency of these pumping sets.
2. Requires no maintenance, because of its glandless construction and its water lubrication.
3. Can be easily installed in crooked wells.

4. It is compact, comparatively light to weight, has no longdrive shaft and no coupling.
5. Due to submerged installations, priming of the pump is not required (after once it is installed), and since foot valve is not required, hence no suction trouble.
6. Low noise level because of journal bearing.

16.8 Rotary Pumps

Rotary pumps are the positive displacement type pumps having circular motion, and are without valves and can deliver a constant capacity against variable pressure. These are generally used for producing pressure upto 25 kg/cm^2. These are suited for handling viscous fluids, maintain high volumetric efficiency, require very less clearance between rubbing surfaces. Although used successfully for clean water and gasoline, their field of application is primarily in pumping oils or other liquids having some lubricating qualities and sufficient viscosity to prevent excessive leakages. Air leakage into the oil pump should be prevented, as entrance of air causes foaming which present a difficult problem when these lubricating oils are for bearings, gears, and similar other services. Oil foaming can be prevented by (i) low velocities in suction and discharge, (ii) low suction lifts, and (iii) preventing air leakage.

Classification : Mainly these are of two types :

1. *Constant Delivery Pump* : This type includes :
   (a) Gear pump (b) Screw pump
   (c) Vane pump (d) Radial piston pump
2. *Variable Delivery Pump* : This type includes :
   (a) Rotary piston pump (sliding piston pump).
   (b) Radial or seated valve piston pump.

"Constant" delivery pump is a pump in which there is continuous discharge of liquid at a uniform rate of flow, whereas a "variable" delivery pump is a pump in which there is a continuous discharge of liquid at varied rate of flow.

16.9 Air-Lift Pumps

In this pump compressed air is used to lift the water up. Here the function of air is to mix the water and to reduce the mixture density so that the weight of a given column of mixture is less than the weight of a much shorter column of "solid water".

The air is passed through one or more nozzles at the bottom into the water at the foot of the rising main fixed in a wall. As soon as the column in the rising main has become impregnated with the bubbles, the pressure due to the column of length L is less than that due to the

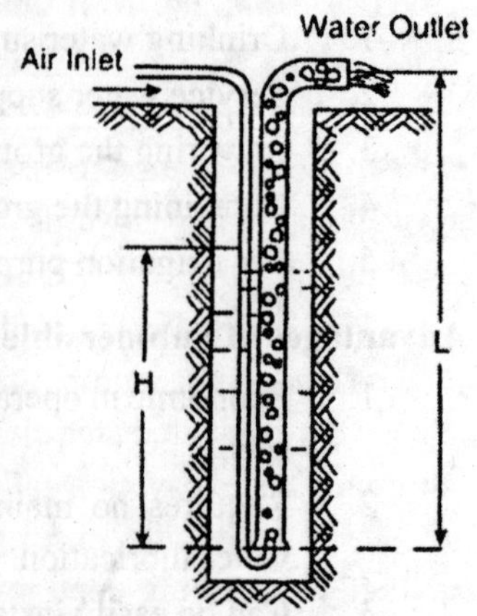

Fig. 16.8 Air lift pump.

static pressure H, thus causing the flow water and air issue from the top of the rising main so long as the supply of air is continued. Fig. 16.8 shows a line diagram of this type of pump.

To obtain better results the useful lift $(L - H)$ is less than the submergence H. The ratio $\left(\frac{L}{L-H}\right)$ vary from 4 when H is about 30 m to 1 when H is about 90 m.

Advantages

1. As it has no moving parts below water level, therefore, can not be damaged by solids suspended in the water.
2. It can raise more water through a bore-hole of given diameter than any other form of pump.

Limitation : Its efficiency is low say 20 to 40%.

16.10 Dewatering System

Seepage of water in excavation sometimes becomes most difficult problem. Since heavy and continuous pumping in such cases is not only a costly item but may also cause settlement of adjacent structures, and may also result in erosion or collapse of the sides of open excavation. Many times it so happens that after an excavation is started ground water is met in too large quantities than anticipated. Such heavy inflow of water may cause collapsing with danger to adjoining structures. In these circumstances installation of bored well system or a well point system is the only solution.

Methods of Ground Water Control

Following methods of ground water control are adopted :

1. Pumping from open sumps.
2. Pumping from well points.
3. Pumping from bored wells.

16.10.1 Pumping from Open Sumps

This method is most commonly used where area is large enough for allowing excavation to be cut back to stable slopes and where there are no important structures close to the excavation to affect their stability by settlement resulting from erosion due to water flowing towards the sump. This method is also applicable for rock excavations.

This method costs comparatively low for installation and maintenance. In this method one or more sumps are made below the general level of the excavation. In order to keep the excavated area clear of standing water, a small grip or ditch is cut around the bottom of the excavation falling towards the sump. Safeguard against erosion can be achieved by providing check weirs (boards placed across the ditch), stones or concrete paving, or by laying open jointed pipes surrounded by graded stones or gravel filter material.

The depth to which the water table may be lowered by the open sump method is not more than 8 m below the pump. For greater depths of excavation the pump should be reinstalled at a lower level or sinking pump is used or submersible deepwell pump suspended by chains and progressively lowered down. Pumps suitable for operating from open sumps are : Pneumatic sump pumps, self priming centrifugal pumps, monopump, sinking pumps.

Such pumping is simple and less expensive, but has serious limitations. When fine sand or cohesionless soil lie below the water table, this type of pumping removes the fine material from the surrounding soil and results in settlement of adjacent structures. To protect it, sumps lined with gravel filter are sometimes used.

16.10.2 Pumping from Wellpoints

This system comprises the installation of a number of filter wells (also known as well points), generally 1 m long, around the excavation. These filter wells are connected by vertical riser pipers to a large dia header main at ground level which is under vacuum from a pumping unit. The water flows to the filter well by gravity and then drawn by the vacuum upto the header main and discharged through the pump. This system has the advantage that the water is filtered as it is removed from the ground and carries almost no soil with it once steady discharge conditions are attained. This system has the limitation of limited suction lift (generally upto about 5 m below pump level). Therefore, for deeper excavations the wellpoints are installed in two or more stages.

The filter wells or well points (refer Fig. 16.9) are usually 1 m long and 60 to 75 mm dia gauge screen surrounding a central perforated riser pipe. The capacity of a single wellpoint with 50 mm riser is about 10 lit/min. Spacing between two wellpoints depends on the permeability of the soil and on the time available to effect the draw

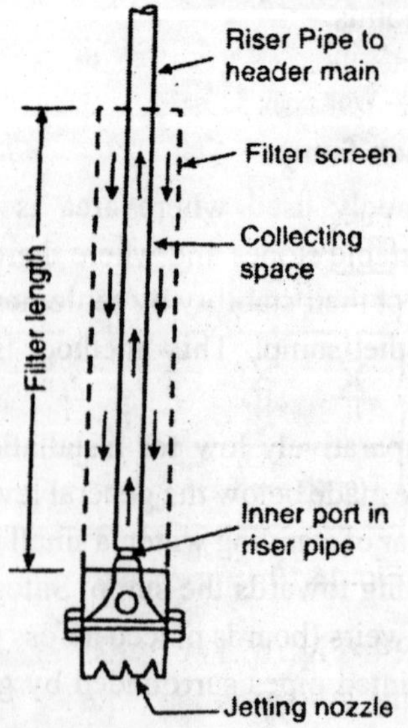

Fig. 16.9 Well point arrangement.

down. In fine coarse sand or sandy gravels a spacing of 0.75 to 1 m is required, while in silty sands of low permeability a 1.5 m spacing is sufficient. In permeable course gravels spacing should be as low as only 0.3 m. A normal set of wellpoint system comprises 50 to 60 points is a single 150 or 200 mm pump with a separate 100 mm jetting pump.

Types of Wellpoint System

Wellpoint systems are installed in two ways :

(a) Line system (b) Ring system.

(a) Line System : (Refer Fig. 16.10). This system is employed when excavation area is long. The header (a larger diameter pipe) is laid out along the sides of the excavation, and the pumping is continuously in progress in one length as further points are jetted ahead of the pumped down section and pulled up from the completed and back filled lengths and repeated till entire length is completed. For narrow excavations, like trenches, header is laid only on one side, while for wide excavations, the headers are required to be placed on both sides of the area.

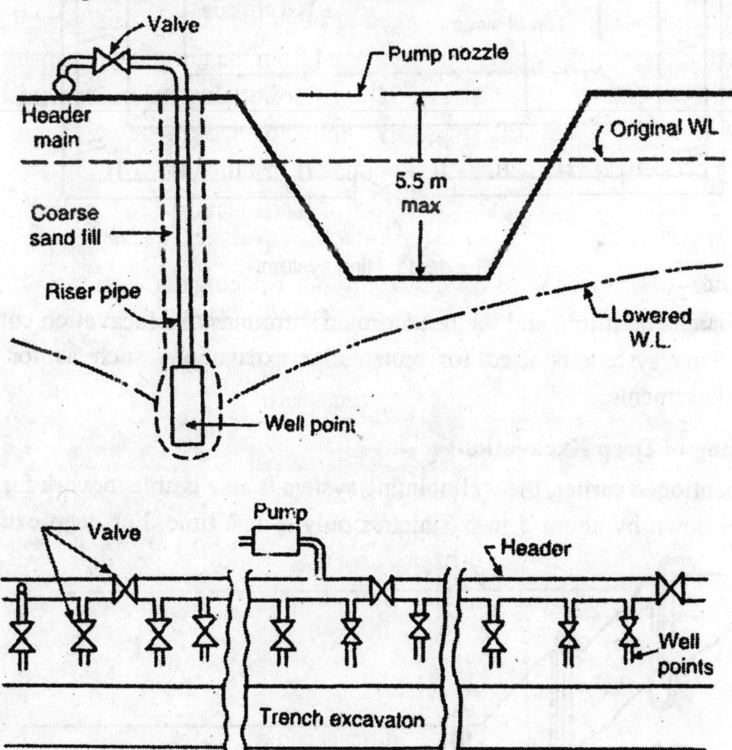

Fig. 16.10 Line system.

(b) Ring System : (Refe4r Fig. 16.11). When excavation is done in area of appreciable width, line system is inadequate. The ring system is used in

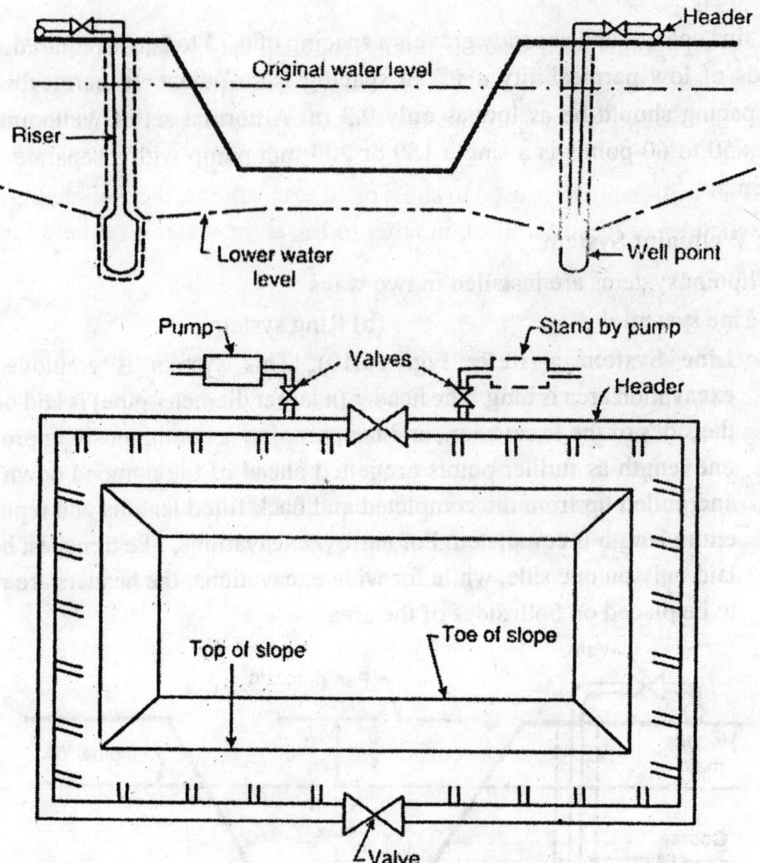

Fig. 16.11 Ring system.

such condition, and the header main surrounds the excavation completely. This system is used for rectangular excavations such as for piers or basements.

Wellpointing of Deep Excavations

As mentioned earlier, the wellpointing system is able is able to work for bringing water level down by about 5 to 5.5 metres only at one time. For deep excavations,

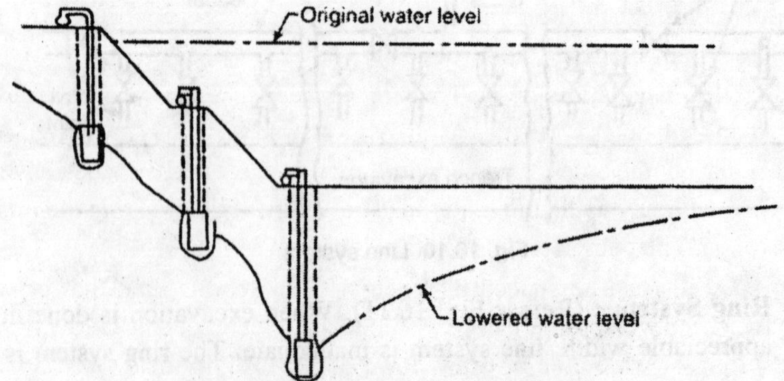

Fig. 16.12 A three stage well point installation.

multistage wellpoints with separate pumps for each stage must be provided. A three stage installation is shown in Fig. 16.12. Although deeper depths can be excavated by adopting multistage wellpoints, but the overall width of excavation at ground level become very large.

When well pointing is used in sheet piled excavations, the well points are placed close to the toes of the sheet piles, in order to lower the water level between the sheet pile rows.

Wellpoint Operation

For efficient working of the system, riser pipes must run full so that air is not sucked into them. This can be achieved by adjusting the stop cock, provided at the top of riser pipes. To prevent leakage in the headers, air tight joints are necessary. For small leakage sealing compound is used for repair, while large leakages need welding for repairs. In order to achieve effective vacuum header pipes most be kept at intake level of the pump and at the level of tops of risers. For efficient working 50 to 60 well points are connected to each pumping set. These are generally placed at an interval of 0.6 to 1 m.

16.10.3 Pumping from Bored Wells

Pumping from wells, for draw-down depth of less than 8 meters can be undertaken by surface pumps with their suction pipes installed in bored wells.

When dewatering is required to be undertaken from a considerable depth, electrically driven submersible pumps are installed in deep bore holes with rising main to the surface. Since heavy boring equipment are used, installation of wells can be done in all ground conditions including boulders and rocks. Due to higher costs or installation, this method is adopted where construction period is long and other methods of dewatering are not possible.

Installation of bore well consists of sinking of casing having a dia of about 20-30 cm larger than the inner well casing. The dia of inner well casing depends on the size of submersible pump. This inner well casing is inserted after complete sinking of borehole screen over the length where dewatering of the soil is required and it terminates in a 3-5 m length of unperforated pipe to act as a sump to collect any fine material which may be drawn through the filter mesh. Screen having slots are preferable to holes, since there is less risk of blockage from round stones.

After the installation of well casing, graded gravel filter material is placed between it and the outer borehole casing over the length to be dewatered. As the filter material is placed, the outer casing is withdrawn in stages. The space above the screen is backfilled with any available material. The submersible pump is then installed and commissioned. The completed installation if shown in Fig. 16.13.

Bored wells can be spaced at much wider intervals than that of well points, because the bored well pumps can be installed at a greater depths below the excavation level, resulting in wide area of draw down for each individual well. Spacing of the

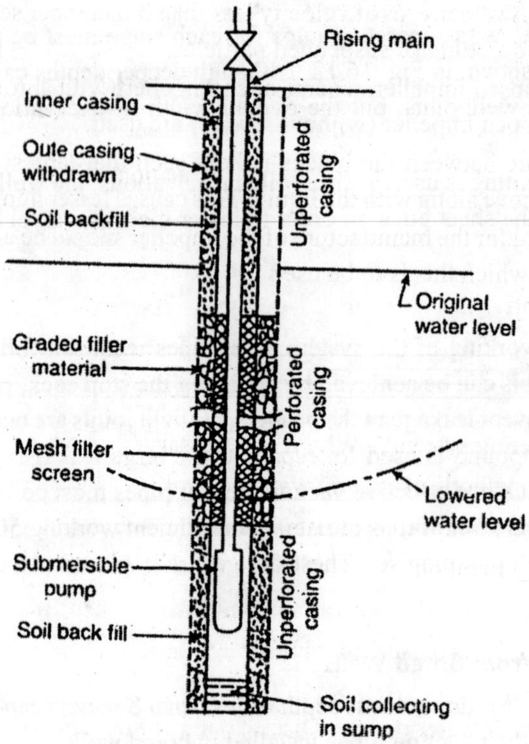

Fig. 16.13 Bored well installation.

wells should be such that, due to shutting of an individual pump for repair and maintenance; water level does not rise above excavation level.

16.11 Mining Pumps

Mine waters are generally abrasive, acidic or alkaline, and corrosive. Mining pumps are required to remove water continuously and generally in large quantities. Therefore, low speed pump with more number of stages are employed, but this arrangement poses problem of shaft, deflection. Due to development of new abrasion resistant materials (Austenitic stainless steels, martensitic stainless steels, and their alloys) higher speeds upto 3000-3600 rpm are successfully employed. This enhances the pump reliability and strength, and pumps with lesser number of stages can be made.

16.12 Non-Clog Pumps

These pumps are used to handle liquids having suspended impurities and even solids. These are also used for transport of coal slurries, sewerage disposal etc. These pumps take care of abrasive, clogging and chemical effect.

In designing such pumps following guiding factors are considered :

1. Arrangement for clearing the clogging passages quickly.
2. Arrangement for easy replacement of parts subjected to high wear.

3. Keeping high velocity, as at velocity less than 3 meter per second there is a tendency of desetting of suspended particles.
4. Instead of closed impeller, a semi-open impeller (with shroud on one side only) or an open impeller (without shroud) are used.
5. Pitch distance between the blades is kept such that largest possible solid matter can move along with the liquid. This causes lesser number of blades.
6. Material used for the manufacture of the impeller should be according to the purpose for which this is to be used.

QUESTIONS

1. What is a "dewatering system"? Why it is necessary?
2. Discuss different methods of ground water control.
3. Describe line system and well system of wellpoint dewatering system.
4. Discuss wellpoint operation system.
5. Explain 'wellpoint' method of dewatering with neat sketch.
6. What factors should be considered while selecting a water pump for dewatering purposes?
7. Give classification of water pumps. Discuss their applications.
8. Discuss the working and advantages of the following pumps :
   (a) Reciprocating pump (b) Centrifugal pump
9. Write short notes on the following :
   (a) Multi-stage pump (b) Submersible pump
   (c) Deepwell pump
10. What is a pump? Discuss applications of pumps in construction works.
11. Discuss important components of a centrifugal pump.
12. Explain the working of centrifugal pump.
13. What is priming? Discuss different methods of priming the pumps.
14. What is cavitation? How it can be prevented?
15. Explain in brief :
    (a) Axial flow pump (b) Air lift pump
    (c) Bored-well pump (d) Non-clog pumps

Chapter **17**

Pile Driving Equipment

17.1 Introduction

A pile is a structural member and is used to transmit the load of a structure through a stratum of low bearing value; protect bridge foundations from possible scour by flash floods; anchor structures against uplift, overturning and the effects of earthquake stresses etc.

Where the subsoil has poor or uncertain bearing capacity or where there is likely to be appreciable ground movement as with block cotton soil or shrinkable clay, it is often economical to use piles for foundation.

A pile therefore is a column either cast-in-situ or driven into ground to transfer loads through the poor bearing soil to a more stable stratum. The piles may support RCC column, beam frame structure, and bridge structure. The pile foundation is designed in such a way that the load from the structure it supports can be transmitted to soil without causing any soil failure and without causing any damage or functional distress to the distance due to settlements.

A pile is relatively a small diameter shaft driven into the ground by a suitable equipment. Pile foundations are usually adopted for multistoreyed buildings, or for bridges etc. where moderate to heavy loadings are expected. The design of piles involve the study of the principles of soil mechanics as well as those of structural engineering.

17.2 Piles Classification

Piles can be classified in the following ways :

17.2.1 On Function Basis

(i) Load bearing piles (b) Sheet piles

1. Load Bearing Piles

These behave like loaded columns and are stressed axially along their length. When the surface of the ground below the structure is not strong enough to bear the load directly, then the pile carry the load to a firm strata, where it resists or distributes the load along its length through skin friction between the pile surface and immediately

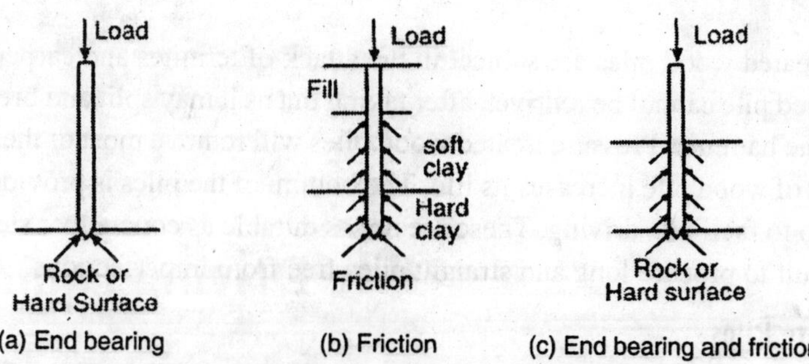

(a) End bearing (b) Friction (c) End bearing and friction

Fig. 17.1 Load transform bearing piles to surrounding soil.

surrounding soil. Friction and end bearing piles are shown in Fig. 17.1. In practice, piles are based on combination of friction and load bearing.

Load bearing piles, support the foundation loads, either by transferring the load the structure bearing on them, to a stronger in compressible layer below the end of a pile, just like a column (Refer Fig. 17.1(a)) or by transferring the load essentially to the soil surrounding the height (*i.e.*, length) of the pile,which in turn, supports the load through the development of shearing resistance between the soil elements (refer Fig. 17.1(b)). The pile, in the former case, is called an end bearing pile, whereas, in the latter case, a friction pile.

Therefore, friction pile is driven through the soft soils, and develop bearing pressure on the circumference; whereas, end pile is driven through poor soil strata on a firm incompressible stratum such as rock, developing the bearing pressure at its base, and passing it to that firm stratum.

In general practice a pile behave both as a friction pile as well as an end bearing pile, developing its load bearing capacity on the base as well as on the sides.

2. Sheet Piles

These are used to resist flow of underground water or loose soil or of both. These are adequately sized to resist bending, abrasion, and other stresses which may arise in use. Sheet piles are of three types : wooden or steel or concrete sheet piles.

17.2.2 On Material Basis

The piles are also classified on the basis of materials from which they are constructed. Following are four principal types of piles : wood, concrete, steel and composites of two or more of these materials.

1. Timber Piles

These are being used since olden days. If properly used and not too heavily loaded, wooden piles are often economical where suitable woods are available. The strength of timber piles depend on the species of wood, and its wearing qualities. Wood is resilient and will bend under load or impact, where other materials will break. These are light handles easily and resist driving stresses within normal design loads.

Untreated wood piles are subject in the attack of termites and carpenter ants etc. An untreated pile cannot be redriven after taking out as it may split and break under the blows of the hammer. Pressure treated wood piles will remove most of these problems. Treatment of wood pile increases its life. The bottom of the piles is provided with steel point or tip to facilitate driving. These are not as durable as concrete or steel piles. It is also difficult to procure long and straight piles free from imperfections.

2. Concrete Piles

Concrete piles are of two types, namely precast and cast-in-place. These may be tapered or parallel. The concrete piles are characterised by their high structural strength high load capacity. These can act as the columns supporting the bridge seat. Concrete piles are durable, resistant to chemical and biological attacks and are made in square, octagonal and round sections, suitably reinforced. Since handling of these piles is difficult and may lead to damages, precast piles are casted near the site only. Concrete piles cast in place are constructed by depositing concrete in metallic shell driven into the ground to required depth. The shell may then either be left in place or withdrawn as the concrete is poured and fills into the hole.

Precast piles are generally made of steel, concrete, timber etc., which are driven into the ground by hammering; whereas, **cast-in-situ piles** are of concrete or R.C.C., laid into the hole drilled or bored into the ground. Precast concrete piles are only occasionally used, as there is always a problem of their carriage and handling at site for driving them with hammering. Another problem in the use of precast piles is the difficulty to cut them when full length can not be driven at site, or the length can not be increased, when it becomes short at site.

Cast-in-situ concrete piles are, therefore, usually adopted in actual practice. They may be driven or bored.

Driven piles are those in which casings are used, which are driven into the ground by hammering. The casing may be either left or removed after filling with concrete, and accordingly they are termed as **cased** or **uncased piles**. These cast-in-situ driven piles are constructed by first driving a hollow thin metal steel casting, and then filling the casing with concrete after removing the coil, either keeping the casing in position or removing it step by step.

The other form of such case-in-situ piles is a **boared pile**, in which a bore is first made by drilling, and then filling it with concrete. This is generally done in rocky or firm soils, in which bore can stand of its own or with the support bentonite slurry. A special type of a bored pile, known as **under-reamed pile**, which is normally reinforced concrete pile, contains one or more enlargements, called bulbs, formed by enlarging the bore holes at the base and or above, by a special tool, called an under reamer. These under-reamed piles are useful and economical for soils, which shrink and swell largely, such as the black cotton soils.

Following are the **advantages of cast-in-place** concrete piles :

(i) Light weight shells can be handled and driven easily.

(ii) The length of the shell can be increased or decreased easily.

(iii) No problem of handling and stress caused by handling.

(iv) The shells can be transported in small lengths and assembled at the site.

(v) The danger of breaking while driving is eliminated.

Following are the **disadvantages of cast-in-place** concrete piles as compared to precast concrete piles :

(i) A slight movement of the earth around on unreinforced pile may break it.

(ii) The bottom of the pile may not be symmetric.

(iii) An uplifting force acting on the shaft of an uncased and unreinforced pile may cause it to fail in tension.

3. Steel Piles

Steel is generally used for piling in various shapes including H-shapes, pipe shape and various steel section. It can take hard driving and has high load bearing capacities. To protect the pile from rust and corrosion, special, coating are given to the steel piles. These piles are easy to join by welding to form long lengths.

Compared to concrete piles, **steel H piles** generally have better driving characteristics and can be installed to great depths. These are used as point-bearing piles with typical lengths of 20 m to 60 m. These piles can be susceptible to deflection on striking boulders, obstructions, or can inclined rock surface. These are widely used because of their ease of handling and driving. These piles can be driven in short lengths, and additional lengths are then welded on the top of the previously driven section. They can be utilized more readily in situations where there are height restrictions.

Steel pipe piles are the most efficient as friction piles as they have substantial surface area that interacts with the surrounding soil to provide significant frictional load resistance. If it is necessary to increase the length of a pile, two or more sections may be added by welding or by connecting by using an inside sleeve for each joint. The soil can be removed from inside after driving the pipe to be required depth. Soil removal methods include (i) bursts of compressed air, (ii) a mixture of water and compressed air, (iii) the use of an earth auger. The follow steel pipe is then filled with concrete.

4. Composite Piles

Composite piles are formed of two or more materials. It may be either reinforce concrete pile or the steel pipe filled with concrete. Ordinarily, composite pile is termed to the pile which has its lower part of one material and the upper part of another. The joint between the two materials should be permanent and mechanically made so that it may not be separated during driving or thereafter. The joint must be able to avoid bending. Composite piles are generally of following three types :

(a) Wood and Concrete Composite Piles : These have lower section of wood and upper section of concrete (either precast or cast-in-place).

(b) Wood and Steel Composite Piles : These have lower section of wood and upper section of steel or *vice-versa*.

(c) Steel and Concrete Composite Piles : These have a lower section of steel (either H section or pipe) and an upper section of concrete (either cast-in-place or concrete pipe or a precast concrete section). These are used to support high loads.

17.3 Bearing Capacity of Piles

The piles are seldom used as single individual member, but are generally used in groups. A number of piles (generally a minimum of three), are installed at distance $2B$ to $4B$ (B being the width of dia of a single pile), and joined at the top by a slab, known as **the pile cap.**

After making the pile cap, the soil between the individual piles may become "locked in" due to densification from driving, and the group may tend to behave as a unit or an equivalent single large pile (Fig. 17.2). Densification and improvement of soil surrounding the group may also occur. These factors may increase the group capacity to be greater than the sum of the capacities of the individual piles.

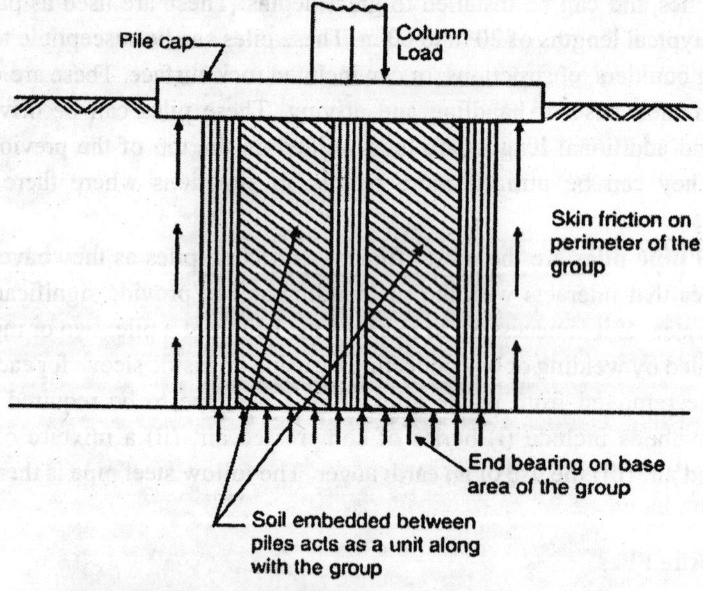

Fig. 17.2 Single equivalent large pile concept for a group.

The load carrying capacity of the equivalent large pile is computed by determining the skin friction resistance around the embedded perimeter of the group, and adding the end bearing resistance formed by this block.

The efficiency of the group depends upon the parameters, such as the type of soil in which the piles are embedded and on which they rest, method of installation, and spacing of the piles.

17.4 Selection of Piles

For any structure selection of piles is done considering following main factors :

(i) Amount of load to be supported.
(ii) Depth at which adequate support is available.
(iii) Physical and chemical properties of the soil strata.
(iv) Type of equipment used for driving.
(v) Stresses likely to be developed while driving the pile.
(vi) Comparative cost of different piles and their durability.
(vii) Cost economy is considered by calculating the cost of piling in case two or more type of piles are found suitable for the job.

17.5 Pile Driving Equipment

Pile driving process involves lifting and holding the pile into position and driving until it stops due to hard strata or reaches to a specified depth. The pile is cut on the top, if it is more than required after driving or to add in length by splicing if they are short. The depth upto which the pile is to be derived is determined by using pile driving formula.

The driving is done by hammering the pile at the top with a hammer. The driving plant should be able to deliver the greatest amount of useful hammer energy to the pile for penetration. Too hard strokes may damage the pile top or may bend if it meets any obstruction, whereas light strokes may result in very little or no penetration of pile.

To hold the pile into position during driving, pile drivers are used. These are the rigs which are stable and heavy enough to handle both pile and hammers with obvious movement.

The *equipment and accessories used for pile driving* are described in the following paragraphs :

Pile driving equipment consist of pile driving hammers, pile driver and accessory tools such as jets, spuds, pre-excavators etc.

17.5.1 Pile Driving Hammers

The energy required to drive the pile into soil is provided by the pile driving hammer. For an ordinary hammer,

$$\text{Energy} = \text{Weight of ram} \times \text{Fall of hammer}$$

Thus the stroke or fall of the hammer ram and the weighty of the ram are important factors. Pile hammers are rated in terms of m-kg of energy delivered per blow. A heavy ram impact hammer working on a short stroke is more effective in driving a pile than a light ram long stroke hammer. A hammer blow causes a temporary compression at the pile head. The compression travels the length of the pile in the form of a wave and when reaches to the point it moves the pile forward into the soil. The friction between the ground and the pipe provides some resistance to the downward motion of the pile. Energy of small hammer is thus completely absorbed by this friction along with in elastic energy absorption within the pile. Therefore, it is very essential to use the heavy ram hammers for the driving of long piles. In order to get deeper pile penetration heaviest ram hammer, that will not cause permanent damage to the pile, should be employed. The heavy hammers also reduce losses due to the rebound of the hammer. As a thumb rule, a ram weighing equal to the weight of the pile will transfer energy quite efficiently and effectively to the pile during driving.

Following are the main types of pile driving hammers :

1. Drop hammers,
2. Single acting hammers,
3. Double acting hammers,
4. Differential acting hammers,
5. Diesel hammers,
6. Hydraulic hammers,
7. Sonic or vibratory hammers.

1. Drop Hammer

This type of driving hammer is an oldest and simplest form of hammer and does not require any external source of power. It is basically a block of cast iron, and is lifted to the desired height of fall with the help of a winch and then release to fall freely under the act of gravity. The weight of a hammer generally varies between 1/2 to about 3 tonnes although larger sized hammers are also specially constructed by the manufacturers. Height of fall is varied depending upon the energy required per blow.

These pile driving hammers employed with a suitable combination of hammer weight and stroke for a particular type of pile and condition of soil. These are very suitable when a source of energy (steam or compressed air supply) is not available.

A drop hammer has following limitations :

(i) The rate of driving is low, hence require more time.

(ii) To increase the rate of driving, there is a tendency to let the hammer fall from a great height, which causes fraction of head or to cause breakage of the pile.

(iii) Cannot be used for underwater driving unless the head is kept out of water using along pile or a follower is used so as to keep hammer out of water.

(iv) Cannot be used for underwater driving unless the head is kept out of water using long pile or a follower is used so as to keep hammer out of water.

Therefore, the drop hammers are suitable for lighter piles, and when only few piles are to be driven in a remote place and sufficient time is available for driving.

2. Single Acting Hammer

In single acting pile driving the ram of the hammer is raised by the steam or compressed air when works on the underside of the piston. When the ram reaches the top of the upward stroke, the pressure of the seam or air is released, which results in the fall of the hammer by gravity. The falling hammer gives a blow to the anvil block located at the pile head. The weight of the ram of these hammers are generally available in the range of 1.5 to 10 tonnes, thus making the overall weight of hammer between 2 to 20 tonnes. The number of blows per minute are generally around 60.

These hammers can also be used under water, where the hammers are lifted and dropped in an enclosed casing. Thus these can be used without long piles or followers, as in the case of drop hammers. Since they use heavy hammers, therefore it is possible to drive heavier piles in stiff clays and dense cohesionless formations. As they deliver heavy blows at faster speed, the time required for driving operation is lesser as compared to the drop hammers.

The speed of driving is slower than that of double-acting hammer hence it is less suitable where very fast driving of lighter piles is required. Although these hammers cost less than a double acting hammer, but need more investments and are costlier to operate and maintain than that of drop hammers.

3. Double Acting Hammers

Double acting pile driving hammers is similar to single acting hammer except that steam or air acts on both sides of the piston in this type of hammer. Steam or air raises the ram to the top of the driving stroke and then drives it down in its downward stroke. Thus steam or air pushes the ram downward and assist the gravitation force in striking the blow. This also increases the speed of downward motion and thereby increases the member of blows per minute. In single acting hammers there is a provision for admitting the steam or air at the bottom of the cylinder to lift the ram upward, whereas there is no provision for allowing the fluid to enter the fluid from above. In the case of double acting hammer steam or air is admitted above the piston, after the piston reaches to the top during its upward stroke. During the same time the fluid is allowed to escape from the underside of the piston.

In these types of hammers the speed of the ram is about 100 blows per minute as against about 60 of single acting hammers. The energy delivered by each blow is about 20% more due to steam pressure assisted gravitational force during downward stroke. This results in about 90% more energy per minute as compared to the single acting hammer. This enables to drive the pile with faster speed.

Double acting hammers are capable of fast driving of light or medium heavy piles in hard soils. These are also suitable to drive steel sheet piles.

4. Differential Acting Hammer

This type of hammer has a piston of two different diameters, larger one on the top and the smaller one below it. The lifting is affected due to the difference in pressure acting on the two sides, while the ram falls with acceleration resulted due to the force on the larger area on the top of the piston during downward stroke. These hammers are manufactured both in open and enclosed models and are operated by either steam or compressed air. Hammers in large varieties with ram weight ranging from 1.5 to 20 tonnes with speed of 100 to 130 blows per minute are available. Overall weight of the hammer varies between 3.5 to 40 tonnes.

It has an advantage of heavy weight like single acting hammer and higher speed (blows per minute) like double-acting hammer. Due to high speed of blows pile continuously remains in a state of vibration resulting elimination of skin friction, causing better speed of driving the pile. Being costly it is suitable only where piling work involves widely varying conditions of driving.

5. Diesel Hammer

This type of hammer does not require any external power source like steam or compressed air. These forms of energy are delivered by this hammer to the pile for driving it. These are, force of air compressed by descending piston, impact of the piston, and the force of fuel in the combustion chamber.

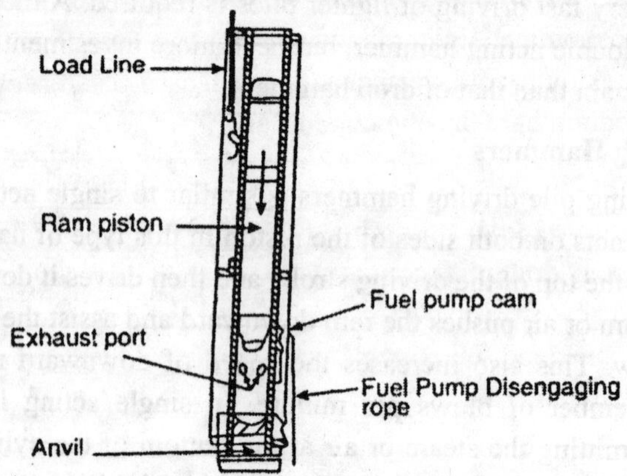

Fig. 17.3 Diesel hammer.

The operation of the hammer is started by raising the ram to the top of the cylinder by a hoist line. This upward movement of the ram compressed the air entrapped above it in the cylinder. The ram is then released from top of the stroke and accelerates downward by the gravitational force. Towards the end of the downward stroke the descending piston closes off the exhaust parts and compresses the trapped air in the cylinder, between the bottom of the ram and the top of the anvil. The anvil is fitted to the lower end of the cylinder over which the blow is struck by downward motion of the piston. This compression of air at the bottom of cylinder exerts a pre-loading force on the anvil and the pile. At the end of the down stroke the diesel is injected in the automated state at a high pressure by a fuel pump into the combustion chamber provided on the top of the anvil. The ram strikes the anvil at the end of the stroke and deliver the impact energy to the pile and also to ignite the combustible gases. This causes the explosion and drives the ram upward and the pile downward. The rebounce of the ram due to striking on the anvil combined with the force of this explosion is sufficient to return the ram to its maximum height is the cylinder. Upward motion of the ram uncovers the exhaust ports and allows burst gases to escape. This after the first blow, the diesel hammer will continue to operate as long as fuel is injected.

The above procedure thus drives the pile by :

(i) Preloading force of the compressed air on the anvil and the pile.

(ii) Impact of the ram due to striking on the anvil at the end of downward stroke.

(iii) Explosion of fuel forces the pile downward. Thus the downward force is exerted on the pile head for a large part of the hammer cycle; which keeps the pile continuously in downward motion and also reduces the frictional resistance during driving. This enables faster speed of the pile during operation. This type of hammer is lighter in weight for same energy of blow with other type of hammers.

These hammers are available in range of 1 to 30 tonnes with a speed of ram varying from about 50 blows per minute to about 100 blows per minute. These hammers are very economical, lighter in weight for same energy per blow. These have limitations of use in extreme cold weather and also in hard driving conditions. It is very much suitable in medium hard driving conditions.

6. Hydraulic Hammers

These hammers are of recent origin and are based o the principle of differential hammer but utilises hydraulic fluid in place of steam or compressed air. These hammers utilise high pressure (upto 350 kg/sq m) hydraulic fluid, provided by a system consisting of an oil pump and fluid lines. Due to very high pressure, equivalent driving force can be obtained with economy in size, space and cost.

In previous methods of pile driving, we face environmental constraints of noise, vibration and smoke. Some countries have been banned diesel pile drivers and put check on noise level. Computer installations, now common in offices, are extremely vibration sensitive, and pose serious problems for engineers and contractors working close to existing building.

The hydraulic hammer gives maximum driving efficiency, reduced air pollution, noise and vibration levels. These are completely under operator control, and economical. Although hydraulic hammers work in the same way as diesel and winch powered free fall or drop hammers, their advantage is that three key operating parameters—stroke, blow rate, and dwell on the pile cap—are totally and automatically controllable. This makes it easier to exactly match performance to piling and soil conditions.

Other advantages of hydraulic hammers are lower set up, lower expenditure in shifting, saving in time due to absence of of boiler or air compressor, fast work and less energy consumption.

7. Vibrating Hammers

In pile driving methods described earlier, hammer blows are struck on the pile head with certain frequency. Each time with the blow, pile moves down from a state of rest. During the period of interval between two blows soil friction is build up around the pile surface. Out of the energy given by each blow, some of the energy is consumed in moving the pile against this frictional resistance. This extra energy can be saved if pile is kept in continuous state of motion.

To achieve this object pile is set under vibration, to eliminate frictional resistance and to save energy required for meeting this resistance. Thus the driving becomes very fast and requires less efforts.

These types of hammers comprise a vibratory unit to produce vibrations to the pile. These vibrations are generated either by internal combustion engine or with electric meters. Since in the vibrating hammer friction is eliminated due to vibration, small hammer blow can give a considerable penetration without any danger of deforming the pile.

The vibratory hammers are best suited to drive light piles in sandy, non-cohesive soils. The speed of pile driving by vibrating hammers may be as high as four times the speed achieved by double acting hammers. Since vibratory hammers operate at low noise level and with less shock to adjacent ground, these can be used in busy locations.

Latest development in the field of vibratory hammers is 'Sonic Hammers'. It works on the vibration principle with some modifications that the principle of vibrations used in driving a pile is at its resonant frequency.

17.5.2 Selection of Pile Driving Hammers

Following are the few factors which should be considered while selecting the most suitable pile hammer :

(i) Size and type of piles.
(ii) Number of piles.
(iii) The character of the soil.
(iv) The location of the project.
(v) The topography of the site.
(vi) The type of rig available.
(vii) Whether driving will be done on land or water.

Generally, a contractor selects a pile hammer out of the few sizes and types available with him, unless it is necessary or economical to secure additional size or type. The selection becomes more important when a project requires several hundred piles, as compared to that of a project requiring only a few piles.

Generally a hammer selected is of largest size that can be used without-over stressing or damaging a pile. As, a major portion of the energy is effective in driving a pile, when a larger hammer is used, resulting in higher operating efficiency.

17.5.3 Pile Extractors

Piles are sometimes required to be pulled out of the soil for replacement by another pile, inspection or reuse. Sheet piles are generally extracted after they fulfill the task of ground water control during construction works. For the purpose of extraction, the pile is kept under vibration to eliminate the frictional resistance around the surface of the pile, and an upward pull is applied to pull out the loosened pile.

Pile extractors are used to produce the upward blows and are similar to the double acting hammers turned upside down. Double-acting hammers are reversed and fitted with extraction to work as extractors. These are operated with either steam or compressed air.

17.5.4 Pile Driving Rigs

As mentioned earlier the process of pile driving involves lifting the pile into position, holding it and then driving it upto specified depth or upto a hard strata where it cannot be driven further. The driving operation is done through hammering the pile top with a hammer suitable for the purpose as described above. Whereas the operation of lifting and holding the pile to position and guiding it accurately, is performed by the mechanism provided on the driving rig.

This rig is used to support the winch boom, driving hammer and various other accessories. The height of the boom should be such that sufficient space should be left above the pile head for the pile driving hammer to work conveniently. The rig should be stable and heavy enough to handle both pile and hammer without obvious movement.

Types of Pile Driving Rigs

There are mainly two types of pile driving rigs, namely land drivers and floating drivers.

1. **Land drivers** are mainly mobile crawler crane type. However, a light weight skid drivers and the large roller rigs are also used. Amongst crane type rigs truck chassis with a swinging deck are also employed for lighter works. Mobile crawler crane type driving rigs are fully revolving units and are very useful and efficient, where large number of piles are required to be

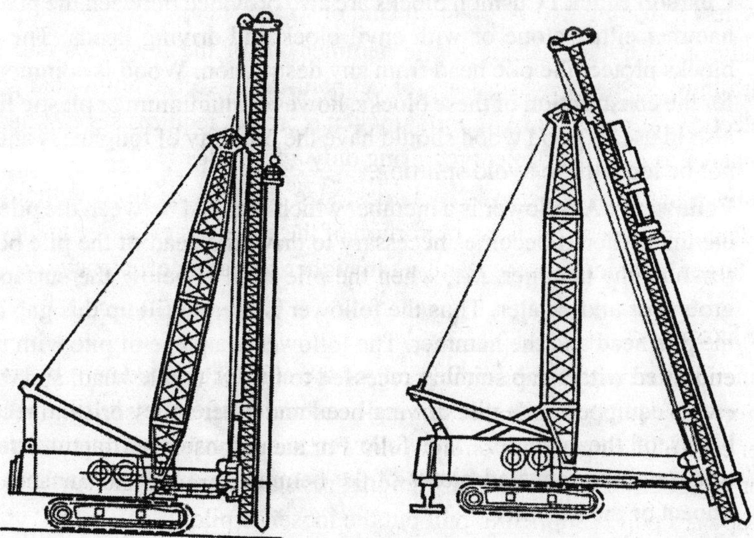

Fig. 17.4 Pile driver (Courtesy : Liebherr).

driven with in a small area. These can drive a number of piles with in the reach of the boom while the crane is stationed at one place.

2. **Floating drivers** are assembled by placing a land driver on suitable barge and adding winch engines for the fore, apt, port and starboard lines. These floating driving rigs are used for driving the piles under standing water. These may be self-propelled type or towed with tug type.

17.5.5 Pile Driving Equipment Accessories

Following are the common accessories used with pile driving equipment :

1. Pile driving heads	2. Anvil blocks
3. Cushion blocks	4. Followers
5. Spuds	6. Pre-excavator

1. **Pile Driving Head :** Driving head distributes the blow of the hammer uniformly over head of the pile and, when used with cushion block, softens the sharp impact of the hammer blow which otherwise may damage the pile. Driving heads also known as 'driving rings' or 'driving caps' or 'helmets' are made in different sizes and shapes by fabricating the forged cast steel. Care should be taken that base of the driving head be shaped to fit the particular pile or sheeting to avoid damages which may lead the pile to become beyond repairs, in addition, properly seated driving head may transmit the hammer blow to the pile with maximum efficiency.

2. **Anvil Block :** Anvil blocks are provided to transmit the blow of hammer to the pile and spread the blow over the whole part of pile top. The anvil blocks are available in various sizes and shapes to suit the section of the pile being driven. These are very effective when the soil where pile is being driven is hard.

3. **Cushion Block :** Cushion blocks are also provided between the pile and the hammer either alone or with anvil block and driving heads. The cushion blocks protect the pile head from any destruction. Wood is commonly used for the construction of these blocks, however aluminium or plastic fibres are also in use. A good wood should have the property of toughness and should not be too hard to avoid splitting.

4. **Followers :** A follower is a member which is added between the pile and the hammer when it becomes necessary to drive the head of the pile below the reach of the hammer, *i.e.*, when the pile head is below the surface of the ground or underwater. Thus the follower is used to fill up this gap between the pile head and the hammer. The follower is a piece of pile with its lower end fitted with a cap suitably recessed to fit on the pile head, and the upper end is equipped with pile driving head and other accessories to receive the blows of the hammer. The follower should have sufficient strength to withstand the repeated blows of the hammer and able to transmit the full impact of the hammer.

5. **Spuds :** Spuds are used where piles are driven through an accumulation of debris and rubbish fill or where boulders are present above soft or loose

materials. The spud (the diameter of which should be about 65 per cent bigger than that of pile) is driven at the proposed pile location to push these obstruction aside, which otherwise may damage or direct the pile.

6. **Pre-Excavator :** These are similar to spuds, and are used either to remove material which may give a false bearing value for the pile or to isolate the pile permanently from an undesirable soil or to act as a form for a sand or concrete encasement for the pile. The casing and mandrel is driven into the ground location, displacing all the soil. The inner mandrel is then withdrawn and the pile is driven through this open casing till the desired depth. Therefore, any one of the following courses is adopted :
   (a) The casing is withdrawn, leaving the soil to move back around the pile; or
   (b) Casing is filled with sand or good soil to prevent a bond between the original soil (which is undesired) and pile, and when the casing is withdrawn; or
   (c) The casing is filled with concrete and then withdrawn leaving the pile in the ground with concrete protection; or
   (d) Leaving the unfilled casing permanently in the ground and thus isolating the pile completely from the undesired soil.

17.6 Sheet Piles

Sheet piles are mainly used to retain or support earth where excavation depths or soil conditions require temporary or permanent bracing to support the lateral loads imposed by the soil or by the soil and adjacent structures. These are also used to check erosion of soil below hydraulic structures. These, as explained earlier also resist flow of underground water or loose soil or of both.

Sheet piles are generally driven with the help of vibrating hammer and a guide frame. The height of guide frame should be at least half of the sheet pile. The pile should remain in plumb in both the directions.

Driving Sheet Piles

While driving sheet piles, following points should be taken care of :

1. Sheet pile being driven should be straight and undamaged, as it is difficult to drive a damaged pile.
2. Interlocks must be cleaned so as to keep free them from any dirt, sand or the debris.
3. While driving a sheet pile, a guide frame is used to keep the sheet pile to plumb when an obstruction in encountered or excessive driving conditions exist.
4. When ever possible sheet piles should be driven in pairs.
5. The length of the boom of the crane should be twice the length of the pile plus few meters.
6. Sheet piles should never be over-driven. Bending, bouncing or vibrating with no penetration is the indication of over driving.

17.7 Supporting and Positioning Piles During Driving

For driving a pile it is necessary to have an arrangement that will position the pile in proper location with the required alignment and that will support the pile during driving. Some common methods for this purpose are discussed hereunder :

1. **Fixed Leads :** Fixed leads consists of a three-sided steel lattice frame with one side open. The open side allows positioning of the pile in the leads and under the hammer. This offer a good control of the pile position and keep the pile in correct alignment with the hammer. The leads have a set of rails or guides for the hammer. During driving, the hammer descends along the load rails as the pile moves downward into the ground. When driving **batter piles**, the leads are positioned at an angle. A pile driven at an inclination from the vertical to provide more stability, is known as batter pile.
2. **Hydraulic Leads :** To control and support the pile in position, hydraulic leads use an arrangement of hydraulic cylinders are connected between the bottom of the leads and the driving rig. This arrangement helps in positioned the pile very quickly and accurately. Since this arrangement adjust the angle of leads rapidly and easily, hydraulic leads are very useful in driving batter piles.

17.8 Jetting the Piles

Jetting requires a plenty of water, through a jet pipe varying in size from 5 to 10 mm in diameter with a nozzle, at a pressure high enough to loosen the soil and in remove it from the hole ahead of the penetration of the piles. This is effective in driving piles into sand or fine gravel to enhance the speed of the driving operation.

The jetting is applicable for all types of piles and is based on reducing the friction during driving and thereby avoiding the need for increased driving weight. For driving a pile into hard soils, high-pressure jetting is required.

The jetting method for final penetration is not advisable because it is not possible in determine the safe supporting capacity of a pile driven in this way. Therefore, it is essential that piles should be driven the last one meter minimum without jetting (*i.e.*, use of pile hammer for last one meter is essential).

17.9 Safety Aspects

17.9.1 General Safety Provisions

1. All pile driving equipment should be of good design and sound construction taking into account the ergonomic principles and properly maintained.
2. A pile driver shall be firmly supported on a heavy timber sill, concrete bed or other secured foundation.
3. In case a pile driver is required to be erected in dangerous proximity to an electrical conductor, all necessary precautions shall be taken to ensure safety.
4. The hoses of hammer shall be securely lashed to such hammer so as to prevent them from whipping in case of connection or break.

5. Adequate precautions shall be taken to prevent the pile driver from over-turning and hammer from missing the pile.
6. A responsible competent person should inspect the pile-driving equipment before taking it into use and takes all appropriate measures as required for the safety of workers before commencing piling work by such equipment.
7. Where there is any question of stability of a structure for its adjoining areas to be piled, such structure shall be supported, where necessary, by underpinning, sheet piling, shoring, and bracing or by other means safety and stability of such structure and to prevent injury to any person.
8. The operator every pile driving equipment shall be protected from falling objects, cinders or water by suitable means.
9. Every worker working on a pile driving equipment should be given instructions regarding safe working procedure to be followed in piling operation and shall be supervised by a responsible person through out such work.
10. It should be ensured to prevent the entry of unauthorized persons at a construction site of all piling areas where pile-driving equipment is in use are effectively cordoned off.

17.9.2 Safety of Pile Driving Equipment

1. Pile driving equipment should not be taken into use until it has been inspected by a responsible person and found to be safe for such use.
2. These equipment alongwith all pipe lines and pulley blocks should be inspected at regular intervals by a responsible person.
3. Only experienced and trained workers should be allowed to operate pile driving equipment so as to avoid any probable danger from such operations.
4. Every worker employed in pile driving operation or in the vicinity of such operation should wear ear protection and safety helmet or hard had and safety shoes.
5. When a pile driver is not in use, the hammer of such pile driving is blocked at the bottom of the heads of such pile driver.
6. Pile driver equipment and devices used in connection with pile driving work should be constructed, installed, inspected, maintained and operated so as to prevent danger.
7. A safety lashing shall be provided for all hose connections to pile driver hammers, piles ejectors or jet pipes.
8. Hanging or swinging leads of pile drivers should have fixed ladders. Employees should be prohibited from remaining on leads or ladders while pile or being driven.
9. Every pile driver should be firmly supported on heavy wood sills or substantial cribbing should be securely and safety guyed at all times and when air hammers used, the hose should be securely lashed to the hammer to prevent it from slipping, if a connection break.

QUESTIONS

1. What is a pile? Describe different types of piles used in the foundation.
2. What are the factors that control the selection of the type of pile on a particular job?
3. Give a brief account of pile driving equipment.
4. What are the various types of pile driving equipment? Explain their working.
5. Enumerate and describe briefly various pile driving hammers.
6. How will you classify piles?
7. Name the constituents of a pile driving rig.
8. Name different types of hammers used for pile driving and explain any two of them.
9. Explain the working of drop hammers for pile driving with its advantages and disadvantages.
10. Compare the working of single setting and double acting pile driving hammers.
11. Discuss the working and advantages of diesel hammer for pile driving.
12. Explain the vibratory pile hammer in detail.
13. What is a sheet pile? Where it is used? Explain the method for driving the sheet pile.
14. What do you understand by bearing capacity of group of piles?
15. Explain different types of concrete piles giving their advantages and disadvantages.
16. Explain the following in brief :
    (a) Application of piles.
    (b) Types of load bearing piles.
    (c) Cast-in-situ piles.
    (d) Difference between bored piles and under-reamed piles.
17. (a) Explain the steel pipe piles.
    (b) What is a pile cap?
    (c) List out the points to be considered for driving sheet piles.
18. Write short notes on :
    (a) Jetting the piles (b) Precast piles (c) Pile driving
19. Explain any two common methods for supporting and positioning piles during driving.
20. Explain important pile driving equipment accessories.

Part - V

MATERIALS HANDLING EQUIPMENT

Chapter 18

Introduction to Materials Handling

18.1 Materials Handling

The basic function of materials handling—the movement of materials—is as old as men, but the need of materials handling developed from the development of factory system, which started from the industrial revolution which took place in late eighteenth and early nineteenth centuries. The industries, supermarket, offices, construction projects and the banks—all are engaged in moving things. In early days man was physically handling the materials, however over a period of years he started applying mechanical principles like lever, wheel, pulley etc.

The materials handling, though does not add value to a product, it generally adds significant elements of cost. Materials handling generally costs between 20 to 35% of the cost of the product, with certain exceptions. Earlier, it was a general belief that most of this cost is inevitable and can not be easily avoided, but now-a-days need for reduction in materials handling cost through systems approach is being realised. Not only cost, majority of production time is also consumed in handling material before, during and after the manufacture. The materials handling time and cost can be reduced by proper selection, operation, maintenance and layout of these handling devices.

The materials handling problem must be studied at the time of planning of various machines and tools to be required and before the erection of factory building. Materials handling is a prime consideration in designing new plants, and existing plants can also be modified by the application of modern material handling devices. These devices increase output, improve quality, speed up the deliveries and therefore, produces the production cost.

The main objective of the efficient material handling is to save costs. Material handling equipment are not the production machinery. These are auxiliary equipments which improve the flow of materials which in turn reduce stoppages in production machines and thus increases their production.

Material handling devices are used for following main **functions** :

(i) Movement and positioning of the construction material.

(ii) Lifting a load, and landing it down at desired place, may be at certain distance away or at a particular height.

(iii) Loading of material into transportation equipment.

(iv) Unloading of material from transportation equipment.

Definition

There is no hard and fast definition of materials handling, however attempts have been made to define this term. Materials handling is the science and art both involving the moving, packing and storing of substance in any form, and includes the preparation, placing and positioning the material to facilitate their movement or storage.

Materials handling occurs whenever a material a moved, may be in a manufacturing distribution (warehouse), or office environment. Materials handling also occurs during preparation for shipment, transportation may be by sea, air or land, and moving material in and out of carriers.

International Materials Management Society has defined the Materials Handling as : "Materials handling is an art and science involving the movements, packaging, and storing of substances in any form". Materials handling is concerned with the following :

(i) **Movement :** Materials handling involves movement of materials mechanically or manually in batches or one by one within the plant. Movement of materials may be materials handling engineer is to find out most efficient manner as to how raw materials reach operator and how finished or processed articles are removed from the work-station. He is also concerned to find out as to how parts, materials, and finished products must be moved from location to location.

(ii) **Time :** Materials must arrive at its place at right time. Materials handling must ensure that no production process or customer (internal as well as external) need is hampered due to late or early arrival of material at each location.

(iii) **Quantity :** Materials handling must ensure that each location continually receives the right quantity of materials (parts, raw material or semi-finished/ processed item).

(iv) **Spae :** Space requirements are influenced by the materials handling flow pattern. Space is required for storage of raw materials, parts and semi-finished or finished products.

Symptoms of Inefficient Materials Handling

1. Backtracking in material flow.
2. Congested aisles.
3. Bottlenecks or hindrances in material flow.
4. Disorganised storage or piled up materials on floor.
5. Excessive handling.
6. Excessive movement.
7. Lack of use of gravity.

8. Long hauls.
9. Idle machines.
10. Materials handling by skilled labour.
11. Lack of supplies.
12. Overcrowding.
13. Damages in products.
14. Repetitive handling.

Advantages of Good Handling System

1. Better use of the floor space and facilities.
2. Increased production due to reduced manufacturing cycle time and faster movement of materials.
3. Reduced material handling time and indirect labour cost.
4. Improved inventory control.
5. Less fatigue of workers.
6. Reduced inventory in process.
7. Greater industrial safety and elimination of accident potential and disruption of work.
8. Better working conditions.
9. Better protection of materials being handled.
10. Help in manufacturing the quality standards.
11. Improved morale of workers.
12. Reduced cost of transportation.

18.2 Principles of Materials Handling

(A) Principles Related to Planning

1. **Planning Principle :** All material handling activities should be planned.
2. **Systems Principle :** Handling activities be integrated and coordinated. Handling activities are : receiving, storage, in-process handling, inspection, packaging, warehousing, shipping and transportation.
3. **Simplification Principle :** Reduce, combine or eliminate unnecessary movements and/or equipment.
4. **Material Flow Principle :** Material flow pattern must be determined by operation sequence and pattern of equipment arrangement.
5. **Gravity Principle :** Utilize gravity where possible.
6. **Unit Size Principle :** Increase size, quantity, weight of the load handled.
7. **Space Utilisation Principle :** Optimum utilisation of building space.
8. **Safety Principle :** Safe handling methods and equipment for better working conditions and to avoid unsafe conditions.

(B) Principles Related to Equipment

9. **Mechanisation Principle :** For increasing efficiency use mechanised handling equipment but to the desired extent only.
10. **Flexibility Principle :** Equipment capable of handling variety of tasks be used.
11. **Equipment Selection Principle :** Select equipment very carefully considering all aspects of materials, movements and the method.
12. **Standardisation Principle :** Standardise equipment as well as methods.
13. **Light Weight Principle :** Reduce weight of equipment.
14. **Motion Principle :** The handling equipment should be kept in motion, *i.e.*, minimum period for loading,unloading or other idleness.
15. **Idle-Time Principle :** Reduce idle and unproductive time.
16. **Obsolescence Principle :** Obsolete methods and equipment be replaced by efficient methods and equipment.
17. **Maintenance Principle :** Preventive maintenance practices be adopted for handling equipment.

(C) Principles Related to Operation

18. **Control Principle :** Control production and inventory through materials handling equipment.
19. **Capacity Principle :** Production capacity should be fully achieved.
20. **Performance Principle :** Performance of handling be measured in terms of cost per unit handled, safe working condition, increase in production rate or reduced manpower for handling.

18.3 Unit Load Concept

Principle of unit load states that, "it is quicker and economical to move a lot of items at a time rather to move each one of them individually". In other words this principle suggested that,the larger the load handled, the lower the cost per unit handled. For small parts, or parts where machines are engaged for handling, movements are made in containers.

Unit load principle implies that materials should be handled in most efficient, maximum size unit, mechanical means to reduce the number of moves needed for a given amount of materials.

Characteristics of a Unit Load

- There should be minimum number of handlings.
- Manual handling should be eliminated.
- Materials are assembled into a unit—load for economy of handling and storage.

- Redesign packages, containers etc. for better assembly into unit—loads and retain them to prevent product damage.
- Unit—load should be as large as possible within the constraints of building, equipment etc.

Advantages of Unit Load Concept

- Possible to handle large loads.
- Reduce handling cost of one unit.
- Reduces packaging cost.
- Maximise space usilisation.
- Faster movement of materials.
- Reduces loading and unloading time.
- Reduces pilferage/damage during transit or storage.
- Safer handling.
- Reduces cost of transportation.

18.3.1 Types of Unit Loads

Types of unit loads are the key to most unit load applications, and are made of wood, plywood, steel, light weight metals, plastic etc. These are constructed either a rigid one or collapsible to permit their return by common carrier in a minimum space.

Unit Load on a Platform

(i) **Pallet :** Pallet is a horizontal portable platform device used as a base for handling materials in a unit load. Pallet is basically a portable platform, with or without superstructure, and consists of two decks separated by bearers or a single deck supported by small feet and handled by means of fork lift trucks and pallet trucks. The pallets may be flat pallets, box pallets and post pallets (Refer Fig. 18.1). For details refer 'transport equipment' section in the chapter on "Handling Equipment".

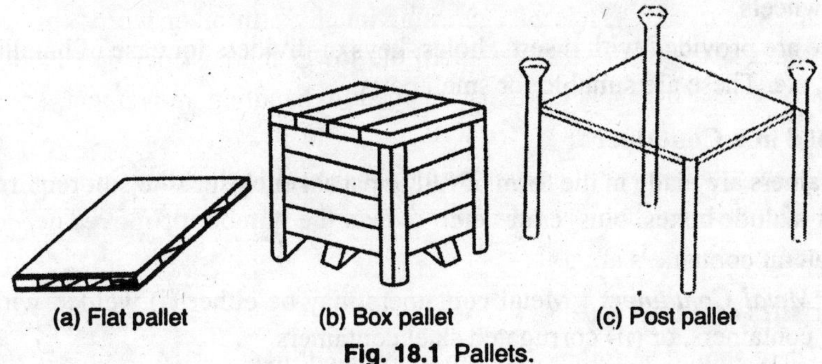

Fig. 18.1 Pallets.

(ii) **Skid :** These are non-stackable, single-faced device elevated above the floor to allow lifting by lift trucks. Goods may be loaded on the skids and then picked up with lift trucks. The skid can be loaded as a unit and

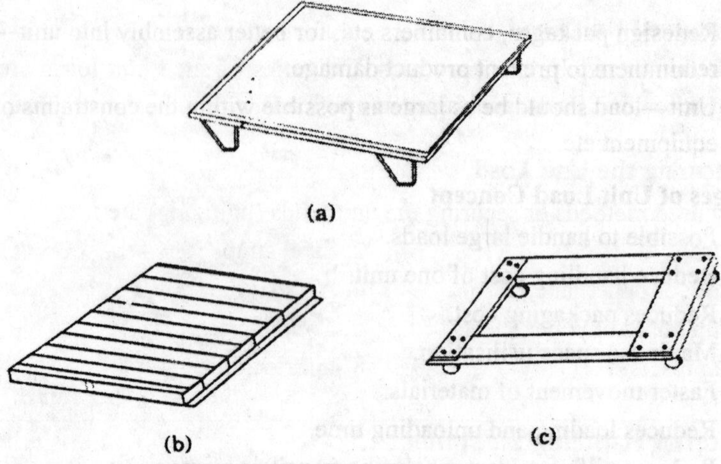

Fig. 18.2 Skids (a and b); Dolly (c).

transferred from position to position without subsequent loading and unloading like pallets (Refer Fig. 18.2). For details chapter on "Handling Equipment" may be referred.

(iii) **Dollies** are the small, plain, low platform equipped with rollers, wheels etc. A unit load is assembled on a pallet resting on the dolly. These are meant for infrequent movement of loads and demand relatively smooth surface.

2. Unit Load on a Sheet

(i) **Flat Sheets :** The sheet maybe plain or corrugated, and made of cardboard, chip board or plywood.

(ii) **Molded Sheets :** These are especially formed to facilitate building of load. These sheets are made in such a way that they have hollow spaces for fork entry.

3. Unit Load on a Rack or Trays

These racks, tote box or trays are designed to hold parts in a desired position and may have wheels.

These are provided with inserts, holes, keys or dividers for ease of handling and inspection, etc. These are suitable for small parts.

4. Unit Load in a Container

Containers are made in the form of full or partial enclosures to suit requirements. Containers include boxes, bins, crates etc.

Important containers are :

(a) *Metal Containers* : Metal containers may be either (i) welded wire mesh containers, or (ii) corrugated steel containers.

(b) *Wooden Containers* : Wood containers with standard pallet base can be used for mechanical handling or storage for products.

(c) *Corrugated Cardboard Containers* : These offer a wide range of economical solutions for packing or material handling problems.

5. Self-Contained Unit Load

These do not require auxiliary aids. Examples of such unit loads are bundles, bales, interlocked unit loads, and fastened unit loads.

18.3.2 Securing the Unit Load

Commonly used methods or securing the unit loads (unitizing) are :

1. Wire,
2. Steel strap,
3. Cloth or paper lake,
4. Adhesive,
5. Chip board or paper sheets,
6. Containers,
7. Clamps, and
8. Interlocking.

18.4 Material Handling Equipment

Material handling had always, been a major task in construction work. Even in the days of Yore, the pyramids of Egypt were constructed with blocks of stones each weighing several tonnes and were raised to heights of hundred metres or more. Today the material handling means a wide spectrum of sophisticated operations using complicated modern machinery. Today a large variety of material handling equipments are needed to support construction industry and their extensive and intensive use is accelerated by the escalation of labour costs and problems of labour management. The demand to handle more and more material for the growing needs of construction projects and mining activities gave impetus to developing and refining methods, machinery and systems for material handling. The post world-war II era is the most significant for such growth and this resulted in increasing the variety of machines and the complexity of their systems through the use of improved designs, material and interdisciplinary approach. These equipments are operated mechanically, hydraulically, pneumatically or electrically or in their combinations.

Need for the present day is fort the construction equipments to handle heavy loads with fast speed, reliability, safety and economy. Construction of multipurpose irrigation-power projects, dams, big buildings, industrial plants, roads, canals, and mining inaustry requires handling of huge construction materials. In order to meet the variety of requirement, equipments of different type and sizes have been developed and are manufactured.

Material handling equipment is mechanical equipment used for the movement, storage and protection of materials, goods and products through out the process of manufacturing/construction, distribution, consumption, disposal.

18.5 Mechanisation Guidelines

Here we shall discuss the circumstances as to when equipment should be used and when they should not be used. Equipments for this purpose can be categorised as : manual equipment, mechanized equipment and automated equipment.

1. Circumstances when no equipment should be used :

(i) Low volume.
(ii) Rate of flow is low.
(iii) Flow is not uniform.
(iv) Small items.
(v) Short distances.
(vi) Limited area.
(vii) Occasional handling.
(viii) Varying paths.
(ix) Complex flow pattern.
(x) Obstacles in flow path.

2. Circumstances when equipment are used :

(i) Loads over 22 kg.
(ii) Travel time exceeds lifting and placing time.
(iii) Unused space above floor is available.

(A) For Manual Equipment :

(i) Relatively light loads.
(ii) Limited volume.
(iii) Limited capital.
(iv) Low cost operation.
(v) Minimum maintenance facilities.
(vi) Wide variety of small or infrequent handling.
(vii) Complex flow-pattern..

(B) For Mechanized Equipment :

(i) High volume.
(ii) Continuous movement.
(iii) Much handling.
(iv) More capacity.
(v) Need for controlled rate of flow.
(vi) Hazardous materials.
(vii) Unit loads practicable.
(viii) Flexible type of equipment adoptable to handling tasks.

(C) For Automated Equipment :

(i) High volume.
(ii) High percentage of handling in operation.
(iii) Uniform product, material.
(iv) Practicable to combine movement with production.
(v) Maintain process control.
(vi) Reduce cost.

(vii) Limited number of paths.

(viii) Relatively fixed movements.

(ix) Fixed materials flow pattern.

18.6 Selection of Material Handling Equipment

Material handling devices,should be able to give maximum efficiency, economy, life and reliability of service. Under-utilisation and faulty selection of the material handling equipment is an expensive luxury which give rise to increase in operating costs. The equipment selected should be according to the requirement of the job in respect to the size, shape, weight, material to be handled etc.

The selection of the material handling devices depend upon the following factors :

(A) Factors Related to the Material :

(i) Type of material to be handled :

(a) Bulk or units (b) Large or small

(b) Heavy or light (d) Shape

(e) Rough or fragile

(ii) Volume of material.

(iii) Distance over which transported.

(iv) Height to which lifted/lowered.

(v) Method of construction.

(vi) Space available for the equipment.

(vii) Number of times materials are to be handled.

(B) Factors Related to the Equipment :

(i) Type and kind suitable for the job.

(ii) Size and capacity of equipment.

(iii) Number of hours it is expected to work.

(iv) Adoptability to other service.

(v) Electric power availability.

(vi) Ease of operation and maintenance.

(vii) Expected life of the equipment.

(viii) Comparison of various equipments available in the market with respect to cost of installation, operation and maintenance; its ease in operation, reliability and other requirements of economy and feasability.

18.7 Types of Material Handling Equipment

There can be divided into following categories :

1. Hoisting (Lifting and Lowering) Equipment

(i) Block and tackle.

(ii) Winches.
(iii) Power hoists.
(iv) Elevators.
(v) Jacks.
(vi) Lifts.
(vii) Cranes.

2. Transportation Equipment (Horizontal Motion)

(i) Wheel barrows and hand trucks.
(ii) Narrow gauge rail road.
(iii) Skids.
(iv) Pipe line.
(v) Trucks, tractors and trailers.

3. Combination Equipment (Lifting, Lowering Plus Transportation)

(i) Chutes.
(ii) Crane trucks.
(iii) Conveyours.
(iv) Fork lift trucks.

4. Aerial Transport

(i) Cableways.
(ii) Ropeways.

Various types of material handling equipment are being discussed in detail in next few chapters.

Material handling equipment can also **classified as per use of power** as under :

1. **Non-Powered Equipment :**

   These are the equipment which are manually operated and are not taken in the category of mechanical equipment.

   Commonly used non-powered (manual) equipment :

   (i) Hand truck.
   (ii) Hand cart.
   (iii) Dolly.

2. **Mechanised Equipment :**

   These equipment are used under following circumstances :

   - Loads are over 22 kg.
   - Travel time exceeds lifting and placing time.
   - Unused space above floor is available.

Points of favour of mechanised material handling :

1. It can handle tough works which can not be performed by manual labour.
2. It is cheaper when quantum of work is more and material is required to be transported for long distances.

3. It delivers safe and better quality of work.
4. Time-bound targets are easily achievable with mechanised equipment.
5. Lesser number of persons are required. Seasonal fluctuations of manpower availability will not effect the progress of work.

Commonly used mechanised equipment are :

1. Gravity conveyor, chute.
2. Power conveyors (belt or roller).
3. Power truck (using pallet, skid, platform etc.).
4. Tractor-trailer.
5. Train.
6. Overhead travelling crane.
7. Stacker crane.
8. Monorail hoist.

3. **Automatic Equipment :**

Automation in material handling means maximum amount of practicable mechanisation plus total self-regulating control of the functions. This not only imply mechanized handling operations but also the information aspects including feedback. In actual practice automation is less than the theoretical one. Commonly used automated equipment are :

- Tilting cars/trucks.
- Gravity, power conveyors.
- Automated trains.
- Automated overhead cranes.
- Automated hoists.

QUESTIONS

1. Propose suitable materials handling equipment required in the stores of major construction project.
2. Discuss factors affecting the selection of materials handling equipment in a major hydropower project.
3. Write short notes on :
   (a) Selection of material handling equipment.
   (b) Types of materials handling equipment.
4. How will you classify material handling equipment?
5. Explain characteristics of good material handling devices.
6. What do you understand by material handling? What factors should be considered while selecting a material handling equipment?

7. Define 'materials handling'. Explain why material handling is important in construction.
8. Explain objectives of materials handling.
9. Describe various functions of materials handling in brief.
10. Explain various principles of materials handling.
11. Write an essay on "unit load concept" in materials handling.
12. Explain different types of unit loads.
13. Write short notes on :
    (a) Characteristics of a unit load.
    (b) Advantages and disadvantages of mechanical handling.
    (c) Advantages of unit load concept.
    (d) Securing the unit load.

Chapter **19**

Hoisting Equipment

19.1 Introduction

Hoisting is the operation of lifting a load, handling them in suspension, and lowering and placing them at required locations.

Hoists are device for lifting or lowering the loads, suspended from a hook on the end of retractable chains or cables. The loads are generally supported from overhead by a hook or travelling on a track.

The hoisting equipment are of following types :

(i) Block and tackle (ii) Winches

(iii) Power hoists (iv) Elevators

(v) Jacks (vi) Lifts

(vii) Cranes of different types.

Components of a Hoisting Equipment

Hoisting equipment include following components :

1. Flexible hoisting appliances (chains and ropes).
2. Pulleys, pulley systems, sprockets and drums.
3. Load handling attachments.
4. Stopping and braking devices.
5. Drivers (motors).
6. Transmissions.
7. Transmission components (axles and shafts, bearings, clutches etc.)
8. Rails and travelling wheels.
9. Machine structures (crane frame).
10. Control devices.

19.2 Block and Tackle (Pulley System)

Fig. 19.1 shows a block and tackle arrangement of lifting loads through a vertical distance. This is one of the oldest and simplest device. It is still used today for moving men and in hoisting machinery into position. It depends on manual power and gives only the mechanical advantages that is possible for the various rope formations. It is the most inexpensive in cost but the most wasteful of manpower.

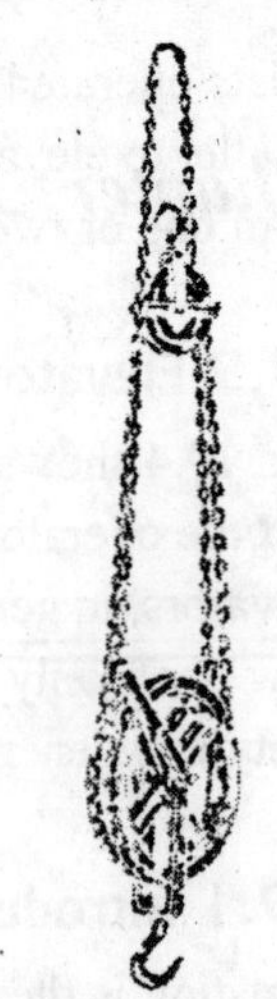

Fig. 19.1 Block and tuckle.

A unit consisting of one or more sheaves (pulleys) mounted in a frame is known as 'block'. Block is mostly equipped with an eye, a hook or some similar device at one or both ends of the frame, by which objects can be attached. In pulley system fixed or movable pulleys are connected in different combinations.

19.3 Winches

Fig. 19.2 shows a winch. This is used to lift loads vertically by winding the rope or cable on a drum. Here, it is possible to use manpower, to get a much greater mechanical advantage than with a block and tackle. It is frequently used in loading heavy equipment into ships, construction of buildings and in similar jobs.

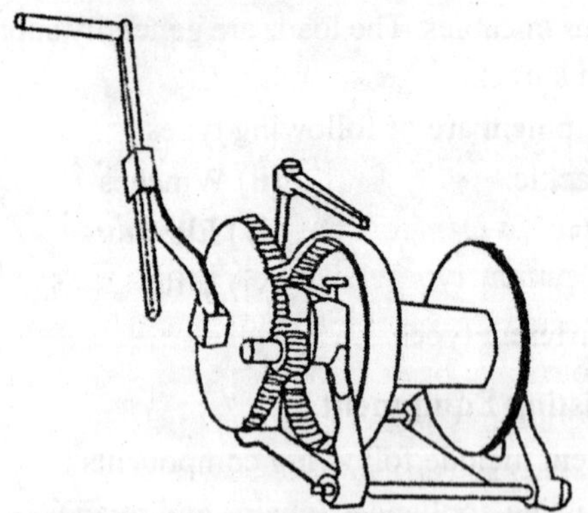

Fig. 19.2 Winch.

Capacity of a winch can be increased by increasing the number of gear trains. These are very useful, simple and how cost equipment for lifting heavy loads. Ratchet, brakes may be fitted on the winch to hold a suspended load and to prevent reverse travel of gears and thus provide safety against accidental dropping of load.

19.4 Power Hoists

Fig. 19.3 show a power hoist, which is often operated between fixed guide rails, for lifting things vertically. There is an infinite variety of hoists suitable for different purposes. The simplest is the chain hoist, which is operated by hand. There are

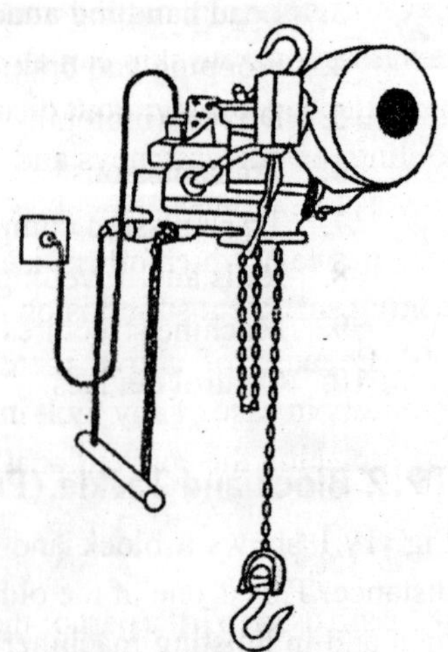

Fig. 19.3 Power hoist.

hoists operated by compressed air, diesel engine or by electric power. The hoidss are smaller to elevators except that, a hoist does not carry the operator in it, but is operated from one or two other points.

19.5 Elevators

Fig. 19.4 shows a hydraulic type elevator. This is differentiated from hoists by the fact that the operator rides with the load. Although there are many types of drives for such elevators, in general the only important type is the electric one. Hydraulic elevators are now used only where it is dangerous to take the chance of an electric spark, as in acetylene generator houses.

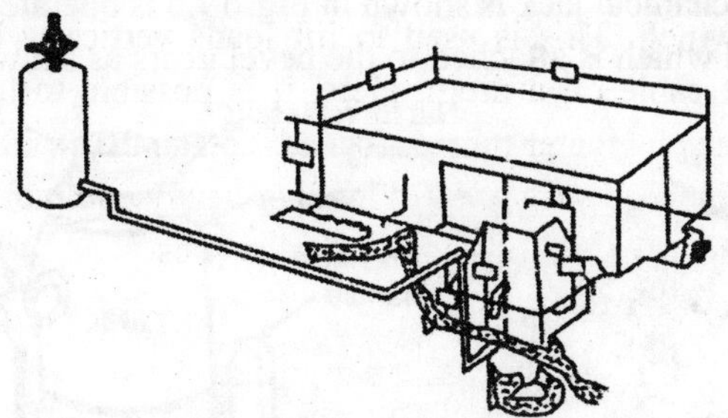

Fig. 19.4 Hydraulic elevator.

Recent development in elevators have replaced conventional rope type ordinary elevators by rack and pinion type elevators. Earlier elevators (rope type) required machinery room for housing the machinery and could be used only after the complete building and the lift room have been made, which is a permanent installation. Present day elevators, rack and pinion type can stand on their own base and go upto 18 meters without any support, and hence can start working right from the very first day the work on the construction site starts. This can stop anywhere in-between levels or wherever we want to stop it; while conventional elevator stops only at predetermined levels. New elevator is simple, rugged and easy to maintain. Using the same tower of this type of elevator, concrete skip can also be provided on the other side of the tower, which can run independently without disturbing the passenger cage. For very high structures like cooling towers, chimneys and T.V. towers these can go upto a height of 600 meters.

By using these elevators speed of work enhances considerably, and supervision becomes easy which otherwise by climbing such a height becomes difficult and hence making sufficient supervision as almost impossible.

Because of above mentioned advantages along with safety, as these stops smoothly in case of any fault in the system, the rack and pinion type elevator hoists are fast replacing the conventional rope type elevator hoists.

19.6 Jacks

Jacks are used to lift a part of the equipment by either mechanical or hydraulic means to a sufficient height to enable the removal of the flat tyred wheel and put on a space wheel or for servicing. These work on the principle of the lever. These may be classified as follows :

1. With respect to method of operation : Mechanical or hydraulic.
2. With respect to the lifting mechanism : Ratchet, friction, screw, scissor, geared.

(a) Mechanical Jacks

These may be ratched type, screw type, scissor type, or geared type. Geared types are generally used for construction equipments, whereas others mentioned above are used for lift works.

The geared mechanical jack is shown in Fig. 19.5 is operated by a lever having a pawl and ratchet and which is attached to the bevel gears as shown.

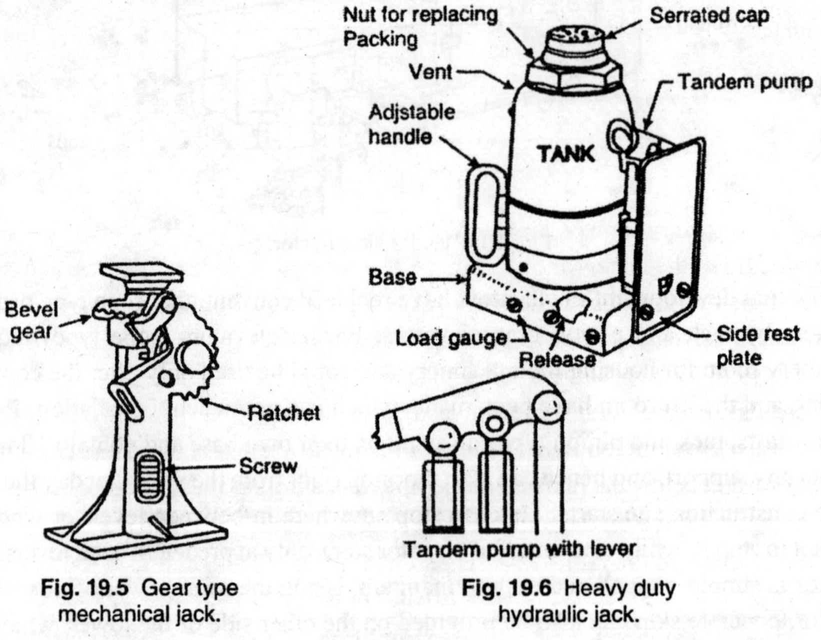

Fig. 19.5 Gear type mechanical jack.

Fig. 19.6 Heavy duty hydraulic jack.

(b) Hydraulic Jacks

Hydraulic jacks work on the principle that, the pressure exerted by liquid on a surface, is proportional to the area of the surface. Due to this principle, jacks are capable of lifting great weight. Surface pressure exerted by a liquid depends upon the ratio of face areas of the ram and plunger.

Hydraulic jack works on the same principle as that of hydraulic press. These are used to lift loads, and are commonly used for lifting automobiles to facilitate cleaning and repair work. These are used to lift heavy loads through a short distance.

Fig. 19.7 shows a simple hydraulic jack. It is provided with plunger on one side. This plunger is reciprocated by a handle attached to it. Another side of the jack is provided with a ram, by means of which loads are lifted.

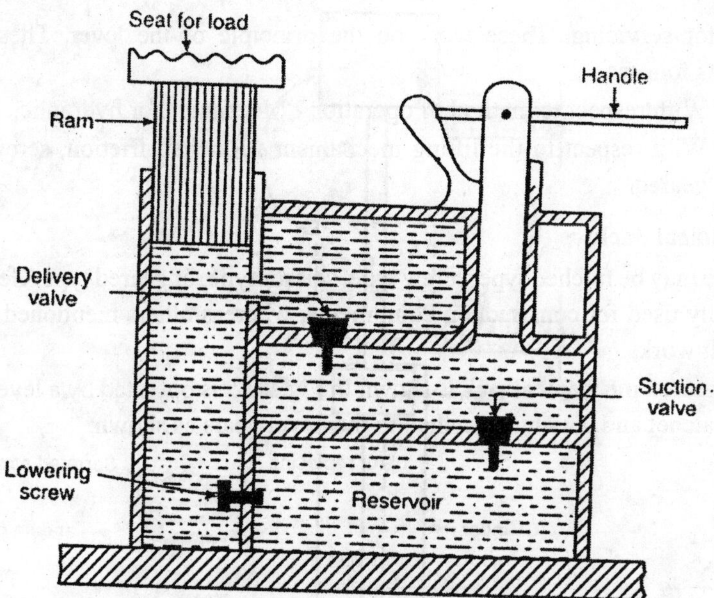

Fig. 19.7 Hydraulic jack principle.

Up and down motion of the handle reciprocates the plunger. This movement of the plunger draws the water (or oil) from the reservoir and delivers to the cylinder fitted with the lifting ram through the delivery valve. Both the suction and delivery valves are the non-return valves. Addition of high pressure water at the bottom of the ram causes it to move upward. Loads can be lifted if placed at the top of the ram.

Load is lowered with the help of a lowering screw. By unscrewing it, high pressure water from the bottom of the ram rushes to the reservoir, thus reducing the pressure of water below the ram and causes the ram and hence the load to come down.

Theoretical force on the ram = Force on the plunger × Ratio of areas

Actual force on the ram = Theoretical force × Efficiency

$$\text{Velocity ratio of jack} = \frac{\text{Area of ram}}{\text{Area of plunger}} \times \text{Leverage}$$

19.7 Lifts

It consists of a cylinder and a ram. A platform or a cage is fitted as the top of the ram. Load or the persons are carried from one floor to another floor by means of these platform or cages. Water under pressure enters the bottom of the cylinder and pushes the ram upward. Thus ram moves up along with a case, in which load and persons may be there. In this type of lift (known as direct acting lift) stroke of the ram is equal to the lift of the cage. The cage moves between guides and can be stayed at any level so that one can get in or out of the cage to the floor. For lowering it high pressure water is gradually taken out. Such type of lift is shown in Fig. 19.8 in which dotted line indicates the initial position while firm line indicates final position.

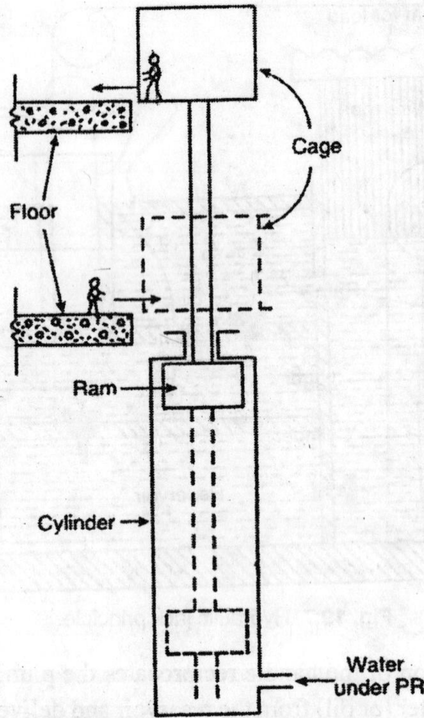

Fig. 19.8 Hydraulic lift principle.

Let, d = Ram dia in cm

p = Pressure of water in kg/cm^2

W = Total load of ram, cage and its contents in kg

a = Cross-section area of ram $= \frac{\pi}{4} d^2$.

Then, neglecting friction etc.

$$W = p \times a = p \times \frac{\pi}{4} d^2$$

Thus dia of ram is designed, considering the maximum weight likely to be lifted.

Direct acting lifts require deep wells for the ram and cylinder. To overcome this difficulty modified form of hydraulic lifts fitted with jigger are common. By providing jigger these lifts require small ram and cylinder and thereby reduces the cost of construction. The cage is suspended with the wire rope and gets its motion by means of a jigger, in the same way as that of hydraulic cranes. Such type of lifts are commonly known as suspended type of lifts, and is shown in Fig. 19.9.

Now-a-days electric lifts are very common and hydraulic lifts are not so common. But hydraulic lifts are very useful at the places where electric supply is not available.

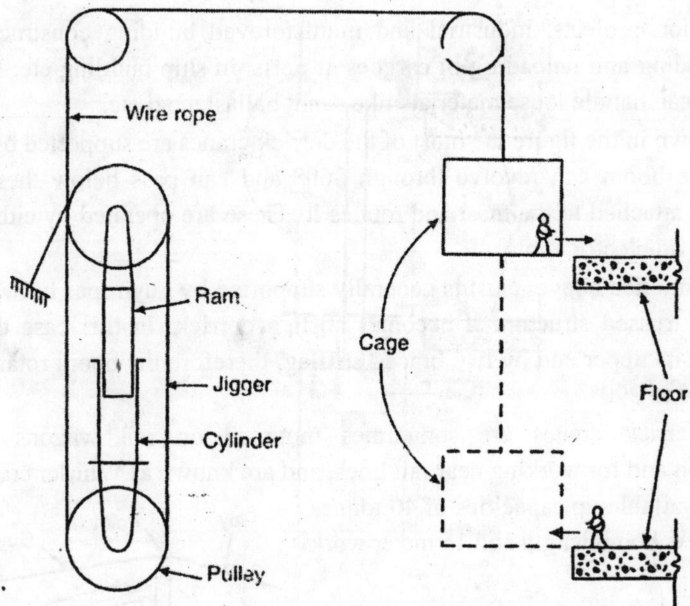

Fig. 19.9 Hydraulic lifts with jigger.

19.8 Cranes

Cranes have wide application in construction projects, industries and in shipping etc. These are used for lifting the loads (may be construction materials, loose materials, packages, containers, finished and semifinished products in industries etc.) and placing them at desired place. For this purpose the cranes have three motions in general, namely hoisting, *i.e.*, lifting or lowering, derricking and slewing. The cranes are generally electrically operated, diesel operated or may have diesel-electric drive.

The cranes are very much useful to pick up a load at one point and be able to deposit it at another point within a restricted area. These are used for loads that are heavy for other types of equipment. Each type of crane is designed and manufactured to work economically in specific site situations : modern-day sites often employ more than one type of crane and more than one crane of the same type. Construction cranes are generally classified into two major families, namely mobile cranes and tower cranes.

The cranes can be classified in following classes :

1. Derrick cranes
2. Mobile cranes.
3. Hydraulic cranes
4. Overhead cranes, also known as Gantry cranes.

19.8.1 Derrick Cranes (Stationary Cranes)

Derrick cranes consist of a mast, a boom, bullwheel on which it rotates about a vertical axis, and supporting members (also known as guys). These cranes are very widely used in construction projects, industrial and multistoreyed building construction, plant erection, loading and unloading of cargoes at ports, in ship building etc. When used with grab it can handle loose materials like sand, ballast, coal etc.

As shown in the figure the most of the derrick cranes are supported by a number of guys. The boom can revolve through 360° and can pass below these guys. A bullwheel is attached to the mast and rotates it. These are operated by either a diesel engine or by an electric motor.

As mentioned above, mast is generally supported by guy ropes but when this is replaced by trussed structure it becomes stiffleg derrick. In this case the mast is supported at its upper end by two braced stiffleg, therefore the boom rotates through angle of 270° to 290°.

The derrick cranes are sometimes mounted on rail wagons for quick transportation and for working near rail lines, and are known as Whirler cranes. These cranes are available up capacities of 40 tonnes with 25 meters boom length and 15 meter work radius.

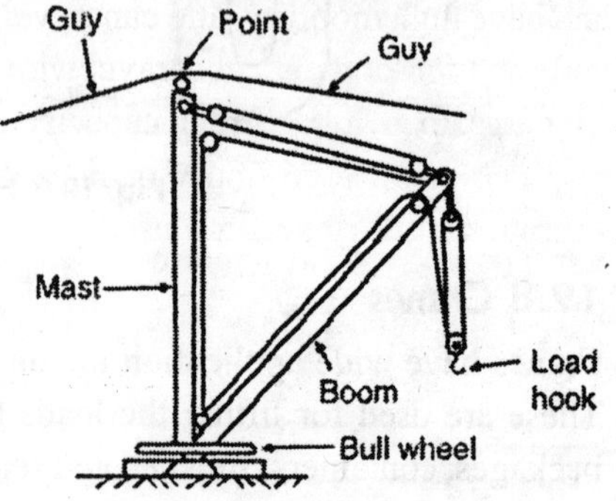

Fig. 19.10 Derrick crane.

The Derrick cranes can be used as Tower cranes for the purpose of erection of high industrial and residential buildings of height 100 meter or above. The Derrick cranes are also designed to work as port tower cranes (for use in ports for container and general cargo handling), as shipyard cranes (for use in ship building and ship repairing works with longer capacities and larger working radii).

19.8.2 Mobile Cranes

The mobile cranes have four motions *viz.*, hoisting, derricking, slewing and travelling. Thus it has travelling motion as an extra feature as compared to Derrick cranes.

Mobile cranes are either crawler mounted or wheel mounted.

1. Crawler mounted cranes are highly manoeuverable and have the ability to operate on unmade ground. Long wide crawler mountings and wide crawler shoes give low ground bearing pressures and they can travel with their maximum load suspended from the hook. This improves crane stability. Since these move slowly, they are used in rough terrain where truck mounted cranes can not travel and hence are economically used where ground conditions are poor and required to operate in a limited area.

The boom of these cranes comes in sections which are joined by pin connections. The straight boom thus formed can lift loads over a radius of 30 to 40 metres.

The full revolving super structure of crawler crane is mounted on a pair of continuous, parallel crawler tracks. Many manufacturers have different option packages available that enable configuration of the crane to a particular application. The crawlers provide the crane with good travel capability around the job site. Shifting

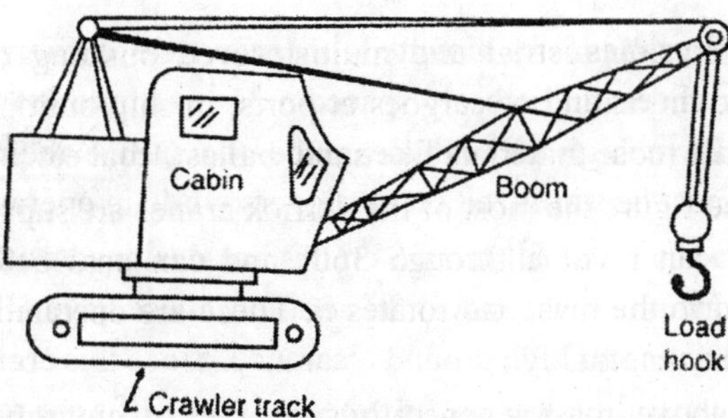

Fig. 19.11 Crawler crane.

a crawler crane between projects requires that it be transported by the truck, rail or barge. As the size of the crane increases, the time and cost to dismantle and load the crane, investigate the haul routes, and assemble the crane will also increase.

2. Wheel mounted mobile cranes are generally truck mounted or self-propelled and have high mobility, and can travel upto 70 to 75 km per hr on good roads. These are designed for long distance travel with high road speeds. The number of axles and drive depends upon load lifting capacity and the length of the boom. These cranes can operated on firm ground. For increasing base width and to improve stability during operations, out-riggers are used.

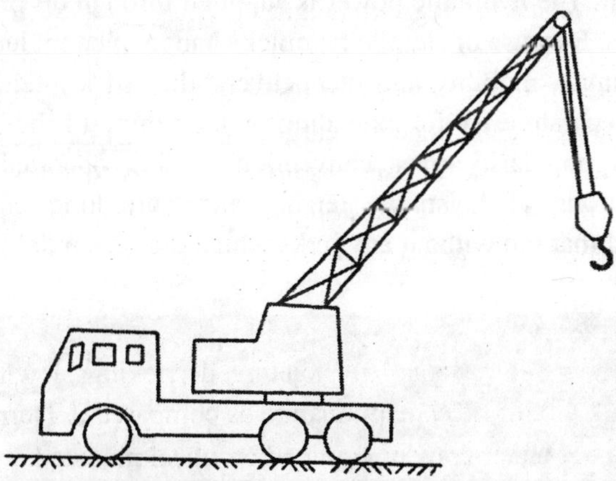

Fig. 19.12 Truck mounted crane.

Self-propelled rubber-tyred wheel cranes have greater mobility over hard surface and are widely used for shifting and transporting light loads over short distance, and for off-loading of medium to heavy loads.

Truck-mounted cranes are available with telescopic-jib and strut-jib. Telescopic-jib cranes provide flexibility in adjusting distances and heights of lifts. These have greater mobility on roads than other cranes. Strut-jib, cranes are suitable for shifting small loads at a distance, where ground obstruction restricts the utility of the crane.

Telescopic-boom mobile cranes can travel on public highways between projects under their own power.

Rough-terrain cranes are mounted on two axle carriers. These units are equipped with large wheels and closely spaced axles to improve manoeuverability at the job site. These have high ground clearance. To utilize their maximum lifting capacity the cranes must be stabilized on outriggers while in operation.

All-terrain cranes : The all-terrain cranes are designed with an undercarriage capable of long-distance highway travel. In addition, these have all-axle drive and all wheel steering, large tyres and high ground clearance. Since this crane has both job-site mobility and transit capability, it is useful when multiple lifts are required at scattered project sites or multiple work locations on a single project.

Rail-mounted cranes are also manufactured to move on rail tracks. Such cranes are used in steel industry, dockyards and railways. These cranes can be driven by stream engines, by diesel engines or by electricity. These are designed to suit the railway gauge clearances available, so as to enable negotiating while travelling, to lift high loads such as required for salvage operations after accidents etc.

19.8.3 Hydraulic Cranes

Hydraulic cranes are usually truck-mounted cranes. All operations of these cranes are hydraulically powered including extension and retraction of out-riggers, extension and shortening of boom. The hydraulic power is supplied through oil pressure, generated by rotary oil pumps. Because of simplicity, quick change of boom length and easy and quick change of angle, mobility and manoeuverability of the telescopic boom, no requirement of a separate crew for extending or shortening of the boom, these have attained the wide popularity over conventional cable operated, latticed boom. Besides,the operations of hoisting, slewing and derricking can be performed simultaneously and that too without any jerks which the unavoidable in conventional cranes.

Fig. 19.13 Mobile hydraulic crane on outriggers.

Since ground contact of most cranes is longer than its width, they have greater stability in front and rear than off the sides. The balance of a crane can be improved by (i) adding counterweight (but not much, to avoid straining to its structure), (ii) by raising the boom to bring the load closer, or (iii) by using outriggers.

Hydraulic cranes consist of two main parts :

(i) Jigger, and (ii) Craning arrangement.

(i) Hydraulic Jigger : It is an arrangement of pulleys for increasing the velocity ratio. It consists of a fixed cylinder in which a ram moves (Refer Fig. 19.14). A number of pulleys (2 to 6 lifted side by side) are fixed on the top of a ram and similar number is fixed at the end of the cylinder. A wire rope, with one end fixed to a point on the cylinder, is taken round all the pulleys on ram and cylinder alternatively and finally to the other end is taken round a pulley fixed at the top of the mast (hollow vertical post) of the craning arrangement. It is then taken down after passing through a pulley fixed at the junction of jib and tie rods. At the free end, a hook is provided for hanging loads. Jigger may be kept either horizontally or vertically.

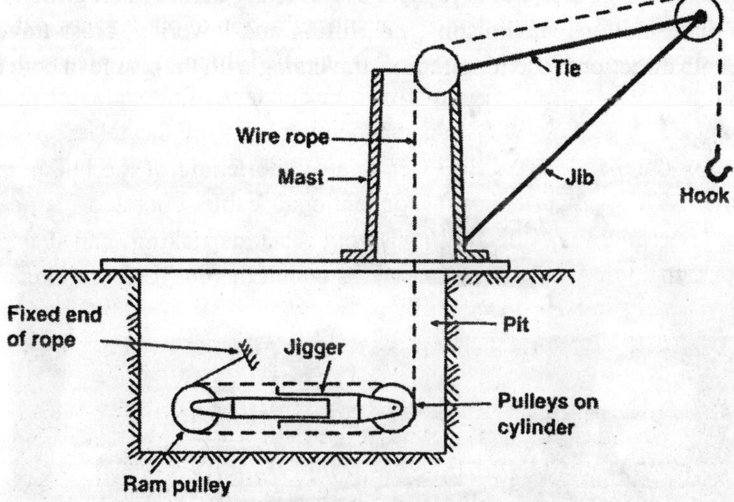

Fig. 19.14 Hydraulic crane.

(ii) Craning arrangement : The crane consists of a hollow vertical post (known as mast) to which a jib and a tie is attached as shown in Fig. 19.14. The mast is supported on a bearing and can be revolved with its vertical axis, so that load from all directions can be handled. The jib can be raised or lowered together with the load.

Working : When the ram is at the end of the inward stroke, water under pressure is admitted in the cylinder. This water forces the ram to go in outward direction. While ram is making outward stroke, the wire rope is pulled and the heavy weight hanged with the hook will be lifted upward. The mast can be revolved in a desired direction, for placing load, water from the cylinder is then taken out and ram makes inward stroke. Thus the hook with load comes down on the ground.

Velocity ratio : The velocity ratio of crane hook to the ram depends upon the number of sets of pulleys. If there be *n* pulleys on the ram and similar number of pulleys on the cylinder, them load will move through a distance which will be 2*n* times the travel of ram, *i.e.*, velocity ratio = 2*n*.

19.8.4 Overhead (Gantry) Cranes

These are used for handling loads over a long rectangular area in factories, power stations, in shipyards and in workshops. The simplest form mainly consists of (i) structural bridge support on elevated tracks, and (ii) supporting a lifting block or hoist trolley. Control is from a cabin on the bridge or by pendant at floor level. Due to freedom from floor obstructions, these are widely used in erection, foundries, steel plants, power houses, shipyards etc.

The bridge consists of two main girders which are fixed at the end and supported on tram wheels and can more on gantry rails. The hoist trolley also known as crab is supported on these girders and is capable of travelling across main girders. Thus load hook has three motions *viz.* hoisting, *i.e.*, lifting and lowering; cross travelling with trolley in both directions; and longitudinal traversing with the bridge in both directions.

Fig. 19.15 Travelling bridge crane.

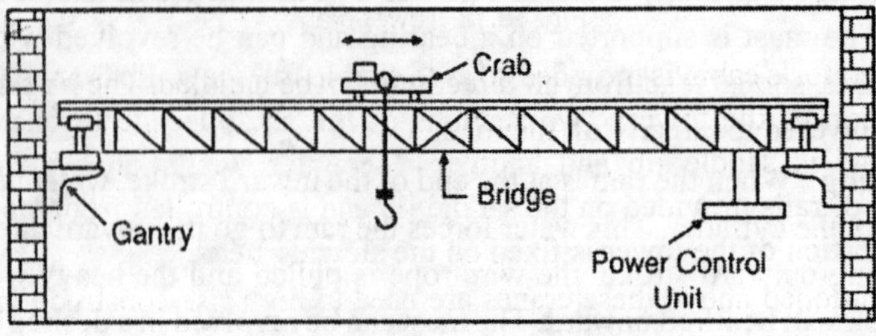

Fig. 19.16 Overhead crane.

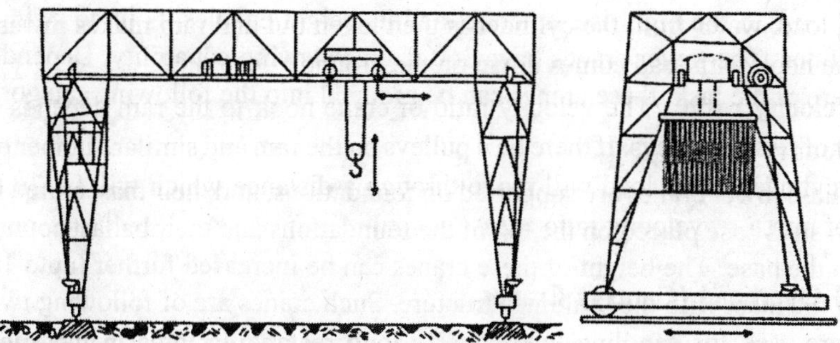

Fig. 19.17 Gantry crane.

19.8.5 Tower Cranes

Tower cranes are used in various construction projects of high buildings, bridges, cooling towers, television towers or power plants. The construction of the tower crane is such that it can work and then dismentled in restricted space. The tower has a truss structure welded from angle bars and channels. Tower extension pieces are available to increase the height as per requirement. Ladder are provided inside the whole height of the tower.

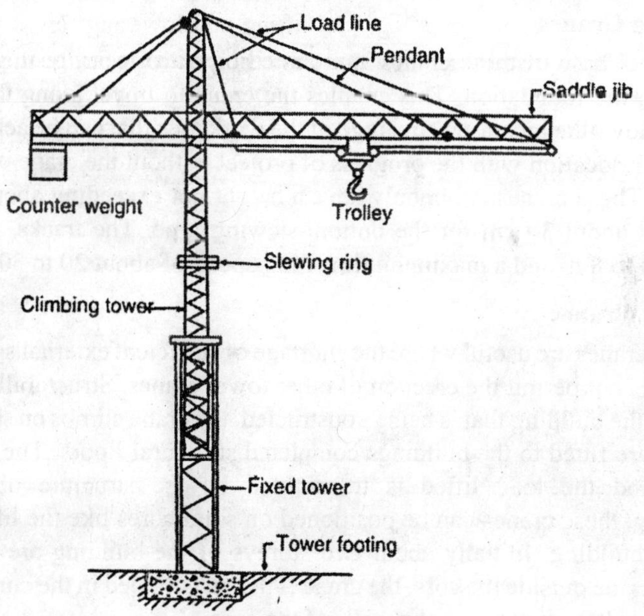

Fig. 19.18 Tower crane.

An operator's cabin is provided so as to enable full view. Jib is attached to the last highest section of the tower. Two sections of the jib, opposite to one another, are provided, one is saddle jib and another is counter weight jib. A saddle moves horizontally or rails provided on the saddle jib and is controlled from the hook block. The upper portion of the lower is fixed on the slowing head.

As mentioned above these cranes are used in high rise construction sites where concentration is in a limited area. The tower crane configuration enables the crane to be

erected close to the high rise structure, and its height enables its jib to swing clear of obstructions. The tower cranes have 360 degree slewing capability. Depending upon the nature of the task, these cranes can be grouped into the following categories :

1. Stationary Cranes

These tower cranes are supported on foundations, and their mast bolted to a fixed position steel base placed on the top of the foundations and their ballast counterweight rests on the base. The height of these cranes can be increased further (upto 100 m) by bracing the mast with the building structure. Such cranes are of following two types :

(a) *Top slewing tower cranes* : These have a fixed tower and a swing circle mounted at the top, allowing only the jibs, tower top and operator cabin to rotate.

(b) *Bottom slewing tower cranes* : These tower cranes have the swing circle located under a slewing platform, and both the tower and jib assembly rotate relative to the base chassis. In this case the entire ballast is placed on the revolving base platform. In these cranes, the tower is essentially a telescopic mast for medium and large cranes. The smallest, hollow-section models is often of the folding type, and not telescopic type.

2. Travelling Cranes

The steel base of these cranes is mounted on travel-gear, resting on rail-tracks embedded to the foundation. This enables the crane to travel along the track with a load. This allows the increased coverage of the work area that can be achieved and also to enable its relocation with the progress of project without the crane dismantling and reassembly. These cranes commonly have a height not exceeding about 70 m for top slewing, and about 30 cm for the bottom-slewing type. The tracks, generally have width of 4 m to 8 m and a maximum travelling speed of about 20 to 30 m/min.

3. Climbing Cranes

These cranes are useful where the shortage of sufficient external space around the building does not permit the erection of other tower cranes. Structurally supported by the floors of the building that is being constructed, the crane climbs on special climbing collars that are fitted to the buildings completed structural floors. The weight of both the crane and the load lifted is transmitted be the structure of the building. Alternatively, these cranes can be positioned on solid cores like the lift shaft inside a multistorey building. Initially about two storeys of the building are constructed by placing the crane outside the core. the crane is then positioned in the core by securing it with special collars, resting on the walls of the core.

These cranes have only a relatively small mast because it moves upward with vertical construction progress. This climbing movement which causes work on the height of the mast employed. At the end of the construction, the tower crane is at the top of the structure. Its removal is then planned by using a derrirk, which is placed on the roof such that it can dismantle the tower crane, and then it is dismantled itself by using the hand tools, and its parts are then taken down in the elevator of of building.

From the above, it is clear that the selection and use of a tower crane requires considerable planning, because of its fixed position, its mast ability to cover all points from where the loads are to be lifted and to reach all the locations where the loads must be placed. The tower cranes are selected for use based on following factors :

(i) Weight, dimensions and lift and of the heavy loads.
(ii) Maximum free-standing height of the crane.
(iii) Maximum braced height of the crane.
(iv) Crane climbing arrangement.
(v) Weight of the crane to be supported by the structure.
(vi) Area that must be reached.

19.9 Safety Precautions

19.9.1 General Precautions for Lifting Appliances

1. Every lifting appliance and every part thereof including all working gear and all plants or gears used for anchoring or fixing such appliances shall.
   (a) Be of good mechanical construction, sound material, adequate strength and free from patent defects;
   (b) Be properly maintained; and
   (c) As far as construction permits, be inspected at least once every week by a competent person and a report of the result of inspection entered in a register maintained for the purpose.
2. *Erection and dismantling* :
   (a) When lifting and hoisting machinery is to be erected at site, proper procedures specified by the manufacturers shall be followed during erection and dismantling operations at site, particularly with reference to correct assembly and the sequence or the operations by identification of different parts and components, which make assembly.
   (b) The erection and dismantling operation shall be carried out under the supervision of a competent person.
   (c) The erection crew shall wear safety helmets.
3. *Drum* : Every chain or rope which terminates at the winding drums of lifting appliances shall be properly secured thereto and at least two turns of such chain or rope shall remain on the drum in every operating position of the appliance.
4. *Brakes, controls and other safety devices* :
   (a) Every crane, crab and winch shall be provided with an efficient brake, or brakes and dogs or pawls or other safety devices which will prevent the fall of the load when suspended, and by which load can be effectively controlled whilst being lowered.
   (b) While a load is suspended from a crane, hoist or derrick, the operator shall not leave his position at the control until the load has been lowered to the ground.
   (c) Side pulls shall not be made with cranes or derricks. The crane or derrick book shall be directly over the load to be lifted.

(d) Riding on loads, hooks, hammers, materials hoists, or buckets shall not be permitted. Loads, boom and buckets shall not be swung over the head of the workmen.

5. *Competent persons for operation* :
   (a) Lifting appliance shall not be operated except by a person trained and competent to operate that appliance except that for the purpose of training it shall be permissible for any person to operate the appliance provided such a person is under the direct supervision of a competent person.
   (b) If the person operating a lifting appliance has no clear view of the load, there shall be appointed signalers to give signals to the operator.
   (c) The crane operator should recognize signals from only one person designated as signalman.
   (d) Every crane operator and rigger should be made familiar with the rules and regulations for cranes operations and standard crane signals for the safe operation of the crane.
6. *Testing and examination* :
   (a) All lifting appliance shall be tested and thoroughly examined once in every period of four years and thoroughly examined once every year by a competent person.
   (b) Any lifting appliance, to which any substantial alteration has been carried out, shall not be taken into use unless it is tested and throughly examined by a competent person.
   (c) Results of all tests and thorough examinations shall be entered in a register to be maintained by the occupier.
7. *Loads* :
   (a) The safe working load or safe working loads and a means of identification shall be plainly marked :
      - Upon every crane, crab and winch; and
      - Upon every pulley block, gin wheel, shear legs or derrick pole or mast used in the raising or lowering of any load.
   (b) The lifting appliance, shear legs or derrick pole or mast or any part there of shall not be loaded beyond the safe working load except for the purpose of testing when it may be loaded to such amount as may be decided by a competent person for carrying out such test.
   (c) Before lifting, the load shall be checked to ensure that it is secure.
   (d) The slinger or other persons shall stand well clear of the load and shall not walk, crawl or stand under the suspended load.

19.9.2 General Precautions for Cranes

1. Crane rails, where used, shall be installed on firm ground and shall be properly secured. In case of tower cranes, it shall be ensured that the level difference between the two rails remains within the limits prescribed by the manufacturer to safeguard against toppling of the crane.

2. All practicable steps shall be taken to prevent the cranes being operated in dangerous proximity to a live overhead power line. In particular, no member of the crane shall be permitted to approach within the distance of overhead power lines.
3. Cranes shall not be used at a speed, which causes the boom to swing.
4. A crane shall be thoroughly examined at least once in a period of 6 months by a competent person who shall record a certificate of the check. A crane, including all ropes, clamps and hook shall be inspected by a responsible person and defective ropes, clamps, hooks, etc., replaced before taken into use every time.
5. Unauthorized persons shall not be allowed to move near and around the crane. No person shall be lifted or transported by the crane on its hook or boom.
6. Concrete buckets handled by crane or overhead cableway shall be suspended from deep-throated hooks, preferably equipped with a swivel and safety latch. In the concrete buckets, both bottom drop type and side drop type, closing and locking of the exit door of the bucket shall always be checked by the man in charge of loading concrete in the bucket to avoid accidental opening of the exit door and consequent falling of concrete.
7. The driver of every power driven lifting appliance shall be provided with a suitable cabin for protection from the weather and it should be so constructed as to afford ready and safe access to parts of the lifting appliance in the cabin which required periodic inspections and maintenance and it shall not be so placed that it prevents the driver from having clear and unrestricted view of all lifting operations out side the cabin.
8. Mobile lifting appliance shall not be used on soft or uneven surface or on a slope in circumstances in which the stability of appliance is likely to be affected unless adequate precautions are taken to ensure its stability.
9. No fixed crane shall be used unless it is securely anchored or adequately weighted as to secure stability.
10. Every travelling jib crane on rails shall be provided with guards to remove any loose material from the track, which shall be provided with effective stops at the end.
11. Cranes shall be so operated as not to be liable to over turning particularly the following misadventures :
    (i) By taking load in excess of the safe working load.
    (ii) By rapid deceleration of slowing motion by severe application of brake.
    (iii) By braking too hard in order to arrest descending load.
    (iv) By sudden release of a heavy load.
    (v) By pulling loads from the sides.
    (vi) By operating the crane without sufficient counter-weight.
    (vii) By positioning the crane at a steep slope.
12. When a crane is used at different times with jibs of different lengths, particulars of the lengths and the appropriate safe working loads shall be plainly markeu in a prominent place on the crane and each driver,

authorized to work, shall be certified after a regular test, that he understands the limitations of each conditions of the working of the crane.

13. No crane shall, except for the purpose of test, be loaded beyond the safe working load, and for this purpose, either a table showing the safe working loads at different radii of the jib shall be displayed in a prominent place or an automatic safe load indicator which takes into account both the radii of the jib and the weights of the loads being lifted, with both visible and audible warnings shall be provided. Whenever possible, automatic device for cutting off power to hoisting and derricking motions when the safe working load is exceeded shall also be provided.
14. No load which lies in the angle between the back stays of the scotch derrick crane shall be moved by the crane.
15. No crane shall be used for lifting a load which is in excess of maximum load marked on the crane. Use only one hook to lift the load, when more than one hook are provided.
16. The crane operator should test the brake for full load capacity, at least, once a week while the crane is in use. Such testing everyday, before the work is started, is recommended.

19.9.3 Specific Precautions for Different Types of Cranes

(A) Tower Cranes

1. No person other than the operator trained and capable to work at heights shall be employed to operate tower cranes.
2. The ground on which a tower crane stands shall have adequate bearing capacity.
3. Bases for tower cranes and trucks for rail mounted tower cranes shall be firm and developed and such cranes erected at a reasonably safe distance from excavations and operated within gradient limits as specified by the manufacturer of such cranes.
4. Tower cranes shall be sited where there is a clear space available for erection, operation and dismantling of such cranes.
5. Tower cranes shall be sited in such a way that the loads on such cranes shall not be handled over any occupied premises, public thoroughfares, failways or near power cables, other than construction works for which such cranes are used.
6. Where two or more tower cranes are sited and operated, every care shall be taken to ensure positive and proper communication between operators of such cranes to avoid any danger or dangerous occurrences.
7. Tower cranes shall not be used for loading magnet, or demolition ball service, piling operation or other similar operations which could impose excessive load stresses on the crane structure of such cranes.
8. The instruction of the manufacturer of a tower crane and standard safe practices regarding such cranes shall be followed while operating or using such cranes.

9. In case of mobile tower cranes, their movement shall be preferably on a level track. If there has to be a gradient in the track this shall be with in the permissible limits as specified.

(B) Mobile Cranes

1. When travelling up a gradient, the load shall be derricked out and when travelling down a gradient, the load shall be derricked into the minimum radius, and this position shall be corrected on reaching level ground. Cranes shall not move down the hill when the engine off or with the engine out of gear.
2. The mobile cranes shall be fitted with suitable horn, head lights, side lamps, rear and stop lights and flashing directional indicator.
3. On cranes with cantilever type jib, when travelling without load, the jib shall be lowered to a horizontal position.
4. When a load to be handled at a particular radius exceeds the rated load, the out riggers shall be used and blocked.
5. During operation of the rubber tyred crane, air brakes shall be put in 'ON' position.
6. The pneumatic tyres shall be maintained at the correct pressure at all times.
7. When the crane moves down the hill, its engine should be kept running with the gear on.
8. It is advisable to equip the crane with the following accessories :
   (a) Anemometer to indicate wind pressure.
   (b) Anchors for rail amounted cranes.
   (c) Limiter to prevent failure of ropes.
   (d) Safety stops to restrict crane travel.
   (e) Swinging radius indicator to indicate safe load at a given radius.
   (f) Heel indicators to control crane heeling.
   (g) Electrical/mechanical safe limits to compare the weight actually hoisted and the load admissible at various swing radii.

(C) Derricks

The guy derrick consists of a boom and a mast supported by wire rope guys. These derricks are generally used in the erection of multi-story buildings.

The boom of guy derrick must be shorter than the mast, the latter supported by wire ropes and secured tightly.

The stiff leg derrick is the most versatile of derrick used in steel erection. It is essentially a mast and boom, with two sloping fixed legs to support the mast. The legs are relatively short. Stiff legs are used on yard derricks for unloading and storing materials and for bridge erection when mounted on a frame.

19.9.4 Precautions for Winches

These are used for hoisting (vertical lift) and hauling (horizontal or inclined pulls). They may be powered hydraulically, electrically, pneumatically, or by diesel engine. The most commonly used winches in construction are electric operated. In construction these are used to :

(a) Pull electrical cables (b) Move heavy machinery
(c) Lift vessels (d) Install structural steel

These are often used with other rigging attachment like snatch block, sheaves,and rollers.

Some of the important safety measures related to the winches are :

1. Winches shall not be used if their control levers operate with excessive friction or play.
2. Double gear winches shall not be used unless a positive means of locking the gear-shift is provided.
3. There shall be no load other than the fall and the hook assembly on the winch while changing gears on a two-gear winch.
4. Adequate protection shall be provided to the winch operator against abnormal weather.
5. Temporary seats or shelters for winch operators that may pose hazard to the winch operator or any other building worker shall not be allowed to be used.
6. Control levers shall be secured in the neutral position and, whenever possible, the power shall shut off if the winch is left unattended.
7. In use of every electric winch, no building workers shall be permitted to transfer, after or adjust electric control circuits in case of any defect in such winch.
8. Electric winches shall not be used for building work where :
   (a) The electromagnetic brake is unable to hold the load; or
   (b) One or more control points either hoisting or lowering are not operating properly.

QUESTIONS

1. Describe different types of hoisting equipment.
2. Explain different types of lifting devices.
3. Write short notes on :
   (a) Gantry crane (b) Power winch
   (c) Power hoist (d) Elevators
4. Explain following in brief :
   (a) Pillar crane (b) Overhead crane
   (c) Screw jack (d) Hydraulic jack
5. (a) Indicate three lifting and lowering devices.
   (b) Explain pneumatic and hydraulic conveyors.
6. Describe construction, working and application of tower crane.
7. Classify crane on the basis of broad construction features. Explain the application of each type and its method of operation.
8. Explain a gantry crane. Explain its applications.

Chapter 20

Transportation Equipment for Materials Handling

20.1 Introduction

These are the equipment (devices) which are used for horizontal motion on level or nearly level routes by pulling or pushing. We have already discussed hauling equipments like trucks, tippers, dumpers etc. in a separate chapter in the book. Here we are concentrating on transportation equipment used for materials handling.

Transport equipment can be categorized into following categories :

(i) Non-powered equipment.

(ii) Powered equipment.

20.2 Non-Powered Transport Equipment

These are the equipment operated manually. Following are some of the common non-powered, *i.e.*, manually operated equipment :

1. Wheel Barrows

These have single or double wheel fitted generally in the front, and pushed by a man as shown in the Fig. 20.1.

Fig. 20.1 Double wheeled barrow.

2. Hand Trucks

The simplest transporting devices are wheel barrows and hand trucks. These are used by a number of stores and other works. Fig. 20.2(a) shows a hand truck, while Fig. 20.2(b) shows a wheeler used to carry materials inside the shops, building etc.

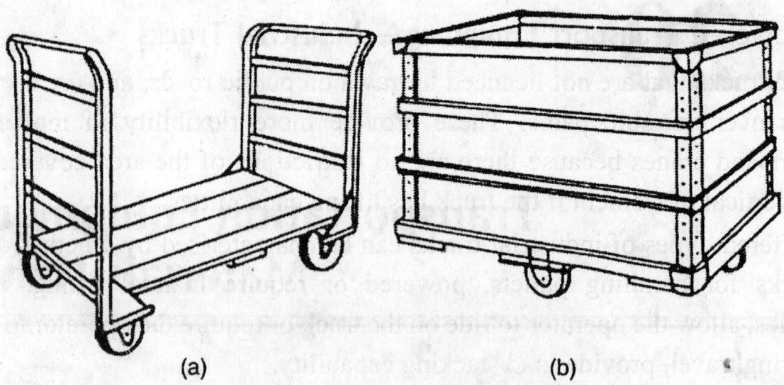

(a) (b)

Fig. 20.2 Hand trucks.

Dollies for carrying the pallet have already been discussed in chapter on "Introduction to Material Handling".

All such equipments involve a large amount of manpower for a relatively small load. The chief advantages of this equipment is its very low cost, great flexibility and easy portability from one job to another.

Fig. 20.3 Platform trucks/trollies.

3. Platform Trolley

This is a small low platform type load carriers with one or more small rollers or wheels. These are used to carry low volumes for short distances and variable paths and are suitable for large variety of loads.

4. Stockpickers' Trucks

These are used for picking and collecting store items (generally small items). These are shown it Fig. 20.4. The equipment mentioned above are also known as "non-powered industrial trucks".

(a) Stockpicker's Trucks

(b) Shelf Stockpicker's Trucks

Fig. 20.4

20.3 Powered Transport Equipment—Industrial Trucks

These are trucks that are not licenced to travel on public roads, and are used to move materials over variable paths. These provide more flexibility in movement then conveyors and cranes because there are no restrictions of the area covered and they provide vertical movement if the truck has lifting capabilities.

Different types of industrial trucks can be characterised by whether or not they have forks for handling pallets, powered or require manual lifting, and travel capabilities, allow the operator to ride on the truck or require the operator to walk with truck during travel, provide load stacking capability.

We have already discussed non-powered hand trucks including carts, dollies, platform trucks trollies, and stockpickers' trucks. All these equipment are known as non-powered industrial trucks.

Now in this section we shall discuss powered industrial trucks, such as, pallet lift truck, and fork lift truck. Powered industrial trucks can be broadly classified as (i) electric powered (battery operated), (ii) I.C. engine powered (diesel or petrol operated), and (iii) gasoline powered.

The industrial powered trucks can also be classified as (a) a walkie truck, where the operator guides the truck by means of a handle, while walking along the truck, and (b) a truck, with provision of a seat for operator or a provision to stand on it.

20.3.1 Pallet Lift Trucks

The lifting feature in lift trucks provide clearance in the floor to lift the skids and permits horizontal transportation. These are generally operated by battery or diesel engine (Refer Fig. 20.5). Hydraulic lift trucks are also known as jack trucks having wheeled platform that can be rolled under a pallet or skid and are equipped with a lifting device a hydraulic lift trucks also use forks for lifting the load.

Fig. 20.5 Platform lift truck.

These are also used for loading or unloading carriers and supplementing powered trucks, spotting loads. There lift trucks may be low lift trucks (upto 1.5 m) or high lift trucks (more than 2 meters). These may have multiple telescopic mast for lifting load even upto 4 meters.

Fig. 20.6 Hydraulic operated pallet truck (Courtesy : Mahendra Stiller Auto Trucks Ltd.).

20.3.2 Fork Lift Trucks

These trucks have tail board called 'fork' which will receive the load at ground level and elevate it hydraulically to the level of the ceiling heights, so that all manual lifting is avoided (Fig. 20.7). When the load is to be shifted from one shop to another, fork trucks are used. These trucks do not require any extra man, and driver operating the truck can lift, carry, unload, stack, unstack, lower the materials. Self-loading and unloading can be carried out by providing a fork at the front end of the truck.

Fig. 20.7 16 tons capacity forklift trucks for stacking of containers (Courtesy : Godrej).

Front attachment of the truck varies with the type of load to be lifted and may consist of crane scoop, hydraulic clamp, hydraulic wood clamp, hydraulic pipe clamp or hydraulic bucket etc. instead of the fork.

Fork lift trucks are widely used in workshops, stores and in construction works. These are used for handling cartons, boxes, crates, bags etc. and by using various attachment they can also be utilised for timber handling including logs, heavy coils, sheet metal, large size tyres, drums etc.

Most fork lift trucks are powered, like pallet lift trucks, by internal combustion engines (diesel or petrol) or battery operated. These trucks have 'fork' as the loading engagement device. Generally fork is 10-15 cm urde, about 1 m long and 2.5 cm thick. Forks are available in a number of variations with chieseled ends, full bottom taper and spark resistant materials.

Fig. 20.8 Power-operated fork lift truck.

Fork lift trucks can do any job that can be done by platform truck or pallet lift truck and is far more versatile. These can also be used without pallets for piling and unpiling large packages, large bales, boxes, crates etc.

20.4 Other Powered Transport Equipment

20.4.1 Narrow Gauge Rail Road

In general, little use a made of such equipment because it requires a heavy investment in the roadbed and tracks, has little flexibility and is difficult to change at a later date. These are used in the days before the development of rubber-tired equipment. They are still found in metal-working industries (blast furnaces, copper refineries and steel-rolling operations) and in mining, quarrying and tunnelling activities, where it is cheaper or more desirable to lay tracks than to pave the entire area.

20.4.2 Crane Trucks

Small crane trucks (Fig. 20.9) operate on the same principle as lift trucks. They are used for materials that cannot be put on skids, or not available for skids at the present time, or

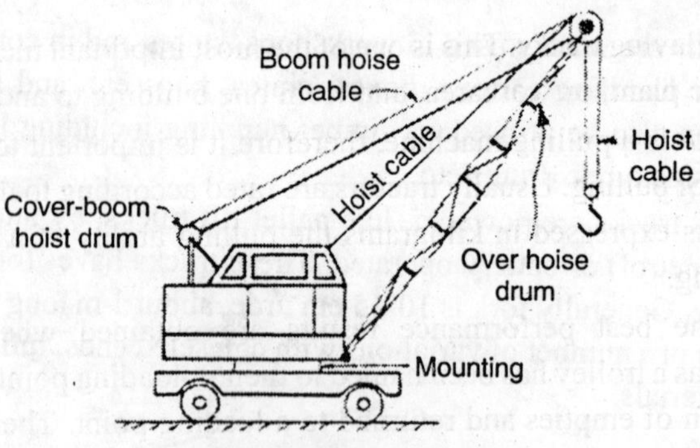

Fig. 20.9 Crane truck.

too much heavy to handle in the lift trucks. This moves quickly over smooth, even and hard ground. This can be carried at will and to any place. In these cranes the solid rubber tyres are used.

The cranes are rotary type, so that the load can be lifted from any position.

Different types of cranes have already been discussed in detail in the previous chapter.

20.4.3 Tractors and Trollies

These are one of the most common modes of horizontal transportation. Great flexibility is achieved as tractors can be used to haul such a variety of different types of trailers. Trailers can be lift-loaded and can be picked up by different tractors. This system has the advantage of great flexibility plus all the advantages of industrial railways and there

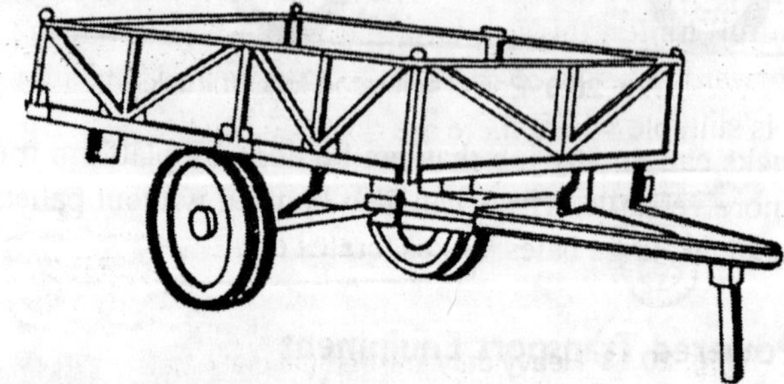

Fig. 20.10 2-wheel trolley.

Fig. 20.11 4-wheel trolley.

Fig. 20.12 4-wheels hydraulic tripping trailer.

is no investment in laying tracks. This is one of the most important methods of handling materials inside the plant, or workarea, and from one building to another.

Since a tractor is a pulling machine, therefore it is important to know as to how much it is capable of pulling. Usually tractors are rated according to their drawbar pull. The drawbar pull is expressed in kilograms the pulling ability of a tractor before its wheels start slipping.

Generally, the best performance results are obtained when the tractor is uncoupled as soon as a trolley has been hauled to their unloading point. The tractor then is coupled to a train of empties and returned to a loading point. There the trollies are uncoupled and another loaded trolley is picked up. This reduces the lost time of the tractor at terminal points to a minimum. Tractors should be kept transporting rather than waiting for trollies to be loaded or unloaded.

20.4.4 Trailers

These are the load carrying platforms mounted on four or more wheels. These are towed by a prime mover, and steered either through turn table or through wheels.

Two types of trailers are used namely, full trailers and half (semi) trailers. Full trailers, also known as wagons, are self supported and are provided with a swivelling axle and a drawbar for connecting to the prime mover. Semi-trailers are supported on their own wheels only at the rear, while front end is supported on the prime mover. The semi-trailers have more manoeuverability as compared to full trailers. The front end of the semi-trailers has a goose neck resting on the rear of the prime mover (driving unit). These semi-trailers can be turned and operated in a more limited space than that needed for a truck or for a full trailer, this can turn upto 90° either to the right or to the left without moving forward. This is of more importance in tunnel work or on narrow mountain roads. It is suitable where there are no steep grades.

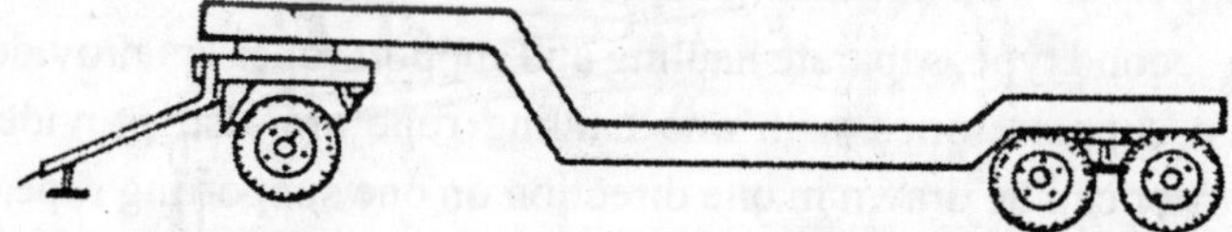

Fig. 20.13 Heavy duty low bed flat deck trailer.

20.5 Aerial Transport

Aerial ropeway is generally used for transporting of material and passenger traffic in mountaneous areas. Ropeway and cableway are very cheap in mountains and are used as aerial transport. Whereas, cableway is a single span overhead conveying system, ropeway having two or more spans. The ropeways are becoming very popular means of transportation in construction of irrigation, power projects, mining etc.

1. Cableways

In cableway, while traversing, load can be raised or lowered at any point. This is very useful in excavation work in dams, workpits, quarries etc. Where loads are hoisted and moved horizontally. These are also used for transporting and then placing the concrete in concrete structure.

A cableway is supported on two end supports and consists of the track cable, the carriage, the traction rope and the hoist rope as shown in Fig. 20.14. One support having an operating gear is known as head tower, while the other is known as tail tower. A track cable (strong steel cable) is **stratched** over these two end towers. The carriage is attached to a endless traction rope, which passes over sheaves on the two towers and is finally wound over the traction drum under the head tower. The hoist rope is supported, between the carriage and the head tower, on the carriers hanging from the traction rope. The cableways generally operate at speeds between 150 to 400 metres per minute during travel, and between 30 to 100 metres per minutes during lifting and lowering, and usually carry a carriage load between 3 to 10 tons.

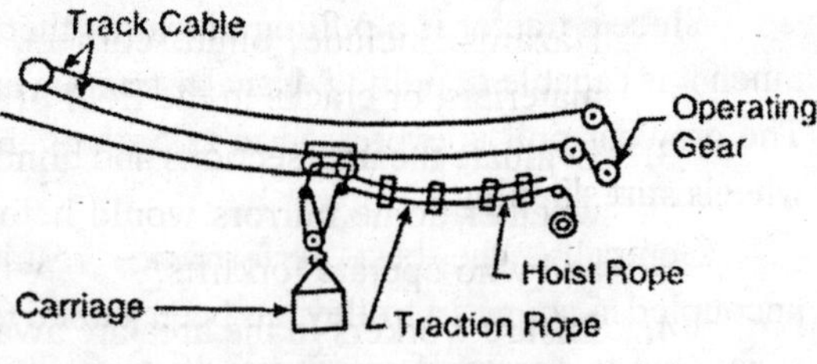

Fig. 20.14 Cableway.

2. Ropeways

As mentioned earlier these are used for long distance. Ropeways have two end towers and rest intermediate lowers, the number depends upon the distance. Ropeways are of following two types :

(i) In first type, endless rope runs over pulleys or horizontal sheaves at the two end towers and is supported along its length on a series of pulleys mounted on intermediate towers. These are rotated by a diesel engine or electric motor at a speed of 5 to 6 km/hr. In this system same rope is acting as a support as well as hauling rope for the carriers.

(ii) In second type, separate hauling and support ropes are provided. Sometimes two support ropes with one hauling rope are also provided so that one carrier can be drawn in one direction on one supporting rope, while another carrier is drawn in opposite direction on second supporting rope. Though this system is more expensive in initial cost, but due to large carrying capacities, higher speeds (6 to 10 km/hr), and lesser wear and tear the system is economical and hence widely used as compared to that of first type.

20.6 Safety Aspects

Safety for Industrial Trucks/Forklift Trucks :

1. Fall, struck-by incidents and overturned machinery are the most common causes of injury and death in forklift operations. Many of these deaths and injuries can be prevented by ensuring machine operators are trained and the work area is safe.

Worksite :

2. Routinely inspect the work area to make sure it is safe for forklift use. Hazards include blind corners, obstructed paths, improperly stored materials, or cracks in the floor or loading docks.
3. Evaluate the intersections and blind corners in your workspace to determine whether dome mirrors would help improve visibility for workers on foot and who operate forklifts.
4. Ensure workers in the area are aware of safe procedures when forklifts are operating.
5. Whenever possible, separate vehicular traffic from foot traffic. Consider establishing certain aisles or walkways as "machine only" and "worker only".
6. Limit forklift use in times and places where employees are most likely to be on the floor, including the start and end of shifts, and near break rooms or time clocks.
7. When foot traffic and forklift traffic are working simultaneously, be certain workers are aware of the forklift's presence. Hence, back-up alarms and flashing lights should be used to alert workers of forklifts.

Operators :

8. Ensure forklifts are only operated by employees who have been extensively trained and licensed. Operator training should cover factors that can affect forklift stability, such as weight and symmetry of the load, speed of travel, operating surface, tire pressure, and driving behaviour.
9. In the event of a forklift turnover, employees operating sit-down forklifts should be instructed to remain inside and lean in the opposite direction of the overturn. Restraint systems can greatly reduce injuries and fatalities.
10. Operators should be aware of the capacity of the forklift and be trained in how to handle unbalanced loads.
11. If forklifts are used to lift employees, operators should know how to perform this act safety. Workers should never be lifted on the forks—only a secure lifting platform should be used fo this purpose.
12. Other workers should never be allowed to ride in or on a forklift unless there is a separate seat with a proper restraint available.

QUESTIONS

1. Explain construction and working of 'fork-lift truck'. Discuss their applications.
2. Write short notes on :
   (a) Cable-ways (b) Pallets
   (c) Rope-ways

3. How will you classify transport equipment for materials handling?
4. Explain different types of non-powered equipment.
5. Discuss different types of hand-trucks.
6. Explain construction and working of platform trolleys with the help of a sketch.
7. Write short notes on :
   (a) Dolleys (b) Wheeled barrow
   (c) Stockpickers' trucks
8. Discuss about 'Industrial trucks' in detail.
9. Differentiate between powered pallet lift trucks and forklift trucks.
10. Explain the construction and working of forklift trucks. Also discuss its applications.
11. Explain about different types of tractors and trollies. Also explain about their applications.
12. Write short notes on :
    (a) Trailers (b) Crane trucks
    (c) Narrow-gauge rail road
13. Discuss about safety aspects of 'forklift trucks'.

□□□

Chapter 21

Conveying Equipment

21.1 Introduction

If the path for the flow of material is fixed, then the provision of the conveyor at suitable level eliminates a good deal of lifting and lowering of materials. Conveyors require no stopping or starting but is continuous in operation. In these, transportation is affected by friction between materials being transported and the belt. These conveyors have the advantage that they largely save labour cost, but have disadvantage that they take up considerable space, are relatively fixed and in most cases the investment cost is high. Conveyors may be used for horizontal, vertical (also known as elevators) or inclined conveying of materials.

Conveyors are of several kinds, which can be divided into following two groups :

1. Traction Type Conveyors :

(i) Belt conveyors.

(ii) Roller conveyors.

(iii) Chain conveyors.

(iv) Bucket elevators.

2. Tractionless Typ[e Conveyors :

(i) Gravity type conveyors.

(ii) Chutes.

(iii) Screw or spiral conveyors.

(iv) Hydraulic conveyors.

(v) Pneumatic conveyors.

(vi) Vibrating and oscillating conveyors.

21.2 Belt Conveyors

Belt conveyor is one of the most common form of material handling system used in mining industries and in construction projects. Heavy industries like steel, fertiliser, chemical and cement etc. can not function without the belt conveyors. In construction projects the belt conveyors are used for handling the materials in Asphalt plants. Aggregate mixing plants etc. In coal mining and other mining industries these are used for handling of coal or other raw material. The belt conveyors are capable of conveying large quantities of material continuously over long distances at a fast speed.

For transporting the material for short distance, conveyor may be a portable or a fixed unit. When a belt conveyor system is used to transport materials for a considerable distance, upto several kilometres in some cases, the system consists of a number of flights. Each flight is complete conveyor unit discharging its load onto the tail end of the successive unit.

Belts used in the system are costly and perishable item and hence need to be carefully maintained. The belts are generally made of rubber covered over cotton or rayon laid up in plies. The strength of a rubber belt depends on number of plies. Canvas plies, woven wire mesh and steel belts are also used depending upon the strength required for the conveyors to convey various type of materials, their temperature, quantity to be transported etc. Belts are specified by width, number of plis, and weight of each layer of ply.

Belt conveyors consist of a belt running over drums or pulleys provided at the end and are supported at intervals by a series of rollers known as idlers. These idlers are supported on the conveyor frame, and help to support the conveyors and reduce the sag of the belt and prevent the loose material from spilling. These 3 idlers are free to move on bearings. Since 1000 to 1200 idlers per kilometre of belt length are provided, it is important to design, select and maintain them for maximum life and to give best performance. Selection of proper bearings with minimum friction value, standardisation, strict quality control and proper finish/tolerance of shifting is essential. The dust proof bearings packed with lubricant with efficient seals, require no further attention for years. The spacing of idlers depend upon the weight of the material handled, if the idlers are widely spaced, the sag between them becomes excessive, which will result in wastage of power, increase in belt wear, chances for spillage of material due to impact at each idlers.

Advantages : Following are the main advantages of belt conveyors :

(i) It is capable of handling light or heavy, fine or coarse, wet or dry material.

(ii) It can handle, thousands of tons of material per hour for several kms.

(iii) It can handle hot materials upto 160°C or so.

(iv) It is higher in weight, and consumes less power.

(v) It operates without noise.

(vi) It gives a continuous discharge and quantity of which can be varied by varying the speed of conveyor belt.

(vii) It can carry the material horizontally or in an inclination.

(viii) It is used for carrying the material over rough country, where use of other means is difficult and costly.

Economical Aspects

To assess the economy of a belt conveyor as compared to that of trucks for hauling, it is desired to estimate the cost of transportation by each method. To assess the cost of the conveyor system, its installation, maintenance, repair, electric energy, labour, depreciation, interest on investment, taxes, insurance must all be considered. Then unit cost of moving the material be calculated.

Whereas to assess the cost of transportation the materials by truck, the cost of truck, its depreciation, maintenance, repair, interest on investment, etc. and cost of constructing and maintaining haul road be considered. Then the unit cost of moving the material be calculated and compared with that obtained for belt conveyor system, in order to take decision about the economy of either of the system.

Belt Conveyor Components

Following are the main components in a belt conveyor system :

(i) **Belt :** Rubber belt is the costliest single component in the system. Conveyor belt consists of a carcass imbedded in rubber. The carcass is made up of plies or layers of fabric (cotton or synthetic) bonded together and carried tension and absorbs impact. The rubber compound may be natural, synthetic or a blend. Steel-wire stranded cables are now-a-days also used in place of fabric yarn in carcass to have higher tensile strength. Vulcanizing or mechanical fasteners are used in make the conveyor belts endless at the job site. Mechanical fastener are also used for quick repairs of cuts and rips in conveyor belting in an emergency.

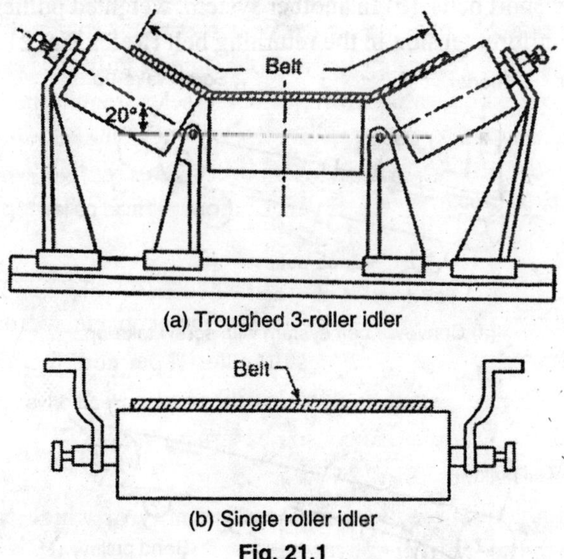

(a) Troughed 3-roller idler

(b) Single roller idler

Fig. 21.1

(ii) **Pulleys and Idlers :** Pulleys are generally located at the terminals of belt conveyors, where they support the belt and transmit driving power. The conveyor belts are supported on **idlers**, between the terminals. The idlers are generally of the three-roll type, with the centre roll horizontal and the two side rolls inclined to form a trough. This angle is generally kept at 20°. The idler rolls are made up of steel tubing, with welded end discs which house antifriction bearings.

The idler supporting the loaded strand of the belt is known as super idler and the one which is supporting the return belt is called as lower idler. The upper idler are 3 roller type or single roller type, but lower idler always have single roller. The belt runs flat on a single roller,while takes the shape of a trough on multi-roller idlers.

(iii) Drives : Nearly all belt conveyors are driven by electric motors. Speed reduction may be achieved by chain and sprockets, 'V' belts or gearing. The drives are generally located at the discharge ends or inclined conveyors.

(iv) Motors and Controls : Squirrel-cage and wound-rotor type motors are commonly used in conveyors. The motor for a conveyor belt drive must have sufficient torque to overcome the starting friction of the system. Which consists of moving endless belt and carries materials within supporting frames.

(v) Conveyor Belt Take-ups : Take-ups are provided to adjust for the increase in length of the belt due to its elongation after it is put into operation. Take ups are of two types : (a) Screw take-ups, which are used to increase the length of the conveyor by moving the head or tail pulley. This system is used for short belts. (b) In another system, weighted pullies are provided to create uniform tension in the returning belt (Refer Fig. 21.2).

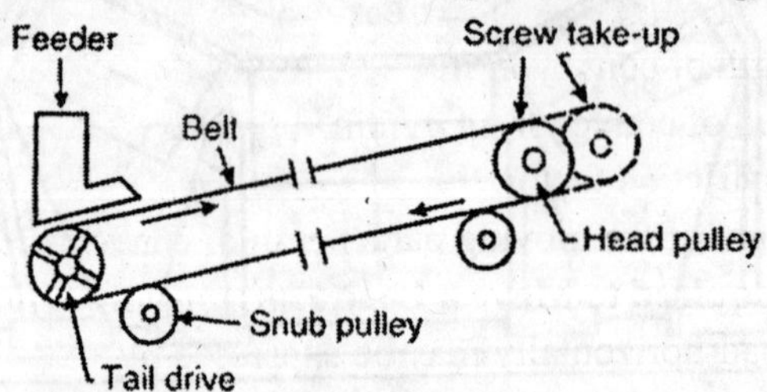

(a) Conveyor belt system with screw take-up

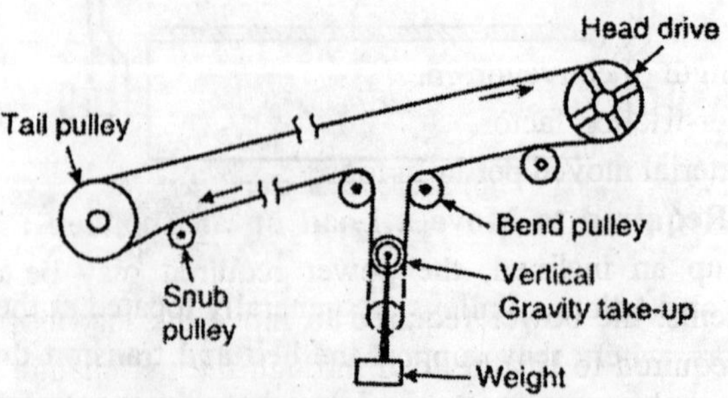

(b) Conveyor belt with weighted take-up

Fig. 21.2 Main components of conveyor belt system.

(vi) **Hold Backs :** Hold backs are provided on the driving pulley to prevent the load from causing the belt to run backward in the event of a power failure, if the belt is operating on an incline. Holdbacks are mechanical devices which allow the driving pulley to rotate only in normal direction and prevents it from rotating in the opposite direction.

(vii) **Feeders :** These are used to deliver the material to a belt at a uniform rate. It may deliver the material onto the belt either directly or through a chute in order to reduce the impact of falling material.

Power Required to Move a Belt-Conveyor

Belt conveyor system required external power for following purposes :

(a) To move the empty belt over the idlers.

(b) To move the load (i) horizontally, and (ii) vertically.

(c) To rotate all pulleys.

(d) To compensate for friction and other losses.

The total external power required to drive a belt conveyor system is the algebraic sum of the power required for all the above functions.

(a) **Power Required o Move an Empty Belt :** Horse power, required to move an empty belt is given by the equation :

$$P = \frac{LSCW}{4500}$$

where,

L = Length of conveyor, m.

S = Speed of conveyor, in m/min.

C = Idler-friction factor.

W = Weight of the moving parts per m of conveyor.

(b) **Power Required to Move a Load Horizontally :** Horse-power required to move a load-horizontally may be expressed by,

$$P = \frac{LCT}{3600}$$

where,

L = Length of conveyor, m.

C = Idler-friction factor.

T = Material moved per hr in tons.

(c) **Power Required to Move a Load up an Inclined :** When the load is moved up an inclined, the power required may be divided into two components, the power required to move the load horizontally, and the power required to lift the load through the net change in elevation. The power required for earlier component can be determined using the expression given at (b) above, while that for later component, *i.e.*, to lift the load through the net change in elevation is determined as follows :

$$P = \frac{TH}{3600}$$

where,

T = Material moved in tons/hr.

H = Net change in elevation in meters.

21.3 Roller Conveyors

Fig. 21.3 shows this type of equipment. This is used to transport various shapes of products such as boxes or materials, which extend over several rollers. This type consists of rollers supported in framers over which materials are allowed to move. They are allowed to move. They are driven by power or gravity. These are of different varieties and an move materials in horizontal direction as well as from the upper floor to lower floor etc.

Roller conveyors are used for relatively short distances as compared to belt conveyors. Roller conveyors using gravity are known as **gravity roller conveyors,** while those operated by power are known as **powered roller (or live rollers) conveyors.**

Roller conveyors have long life, readily assembled and installed, easy to adjust and used for handling large variety of loads. Loads with rigid and smooth base are moved on the roller conveyors, other items can be moved ·fter placing them on flat boards. Pitch of the llers should be such that minimum of 3 llers must remain under load at all times.

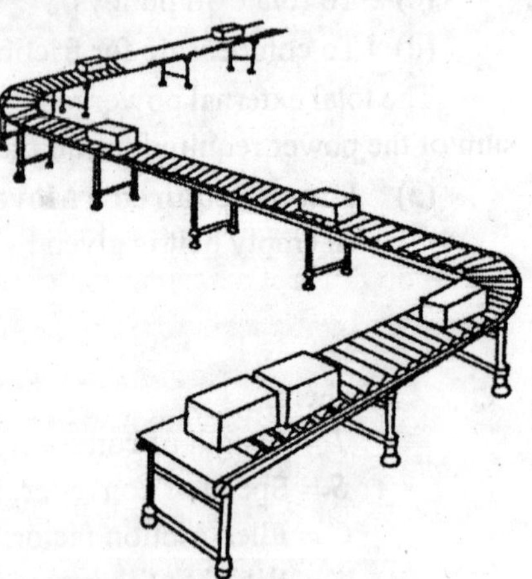

Fig. 21.3 Roller conveyor.

Spacing is generally kept at 8 cms, 10 cms or 15 cms. Rollers generally range from 2 cms to 8 cms in diameter with length governed by load. The rollers are made of cylindrical tubing with a bearing on each end. Generally, tapered rollers are provided at the turns.

21.4 Chain Conveyors

These are, moved by chains for cables in horizontal direction and installed flush with floor or a little above it. This is used for moving barrels and heavy boxes. This is also used for moving grates of big boilers.

Chain conveyors employ continuous chains wrapped around head and tail end sprockets. These are generally operated by motor drive, attached to the head drive shaft. Materials can be carried directly on aprons or pushed in a trough by flights attached to the chain. The conveyor units can be arranged for operation horizontally, inclined or in combination. These can be designed to operate upto 45° inclination.

21.5 Bucket Elevators (Elevating Conveyors)

The elevating conveyors are used for transporting dry granular materials (the material that will not stick to the buckets) in the vertical direction with the help of buckets and trays. These are also known as bucket elevating conveyors or bucket elevators and carry the material in bucket to vertical or near vertical positions. These are either (i) Chain bucket elevator in which buckets are attached to one or two chains which move on two end wheels, or (ii) Belt bucket elevator in which buckets are attached to the belt moving on pulleys provided at two ends.

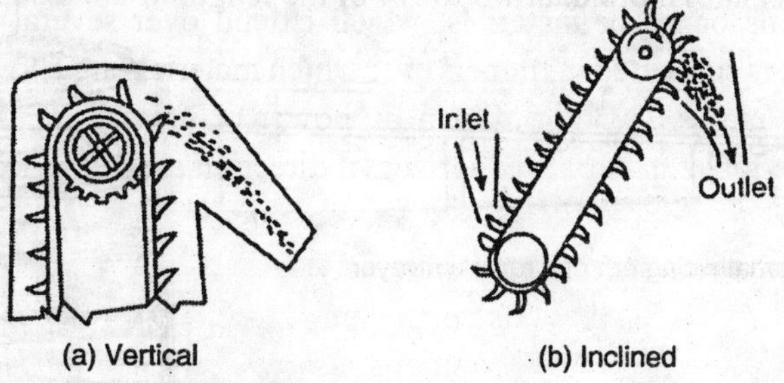

Fig. 21.4 Bucket elevator.

Bucket elevators, also known as elevating conveyors, are operated between head and foot terminal machinery in a supporting fame. Buckets are loaded by scoop action at foot end or by a chute above.

These consists of an endless chain of buckets which elevates the minerals. The elevators are usually enclosed in a sheet of metal casing with necessary inlet and outlet openings and chutes.

Normal operating speeds of these conveyors is between 0.15 and 0.5 m/sec. These conveyors are usually variable upto 400 tons/hr and normal lifts upto 30 meters.

21.6 Gravity Type Conveyors (Sliding Friction Gravity Conveyors)

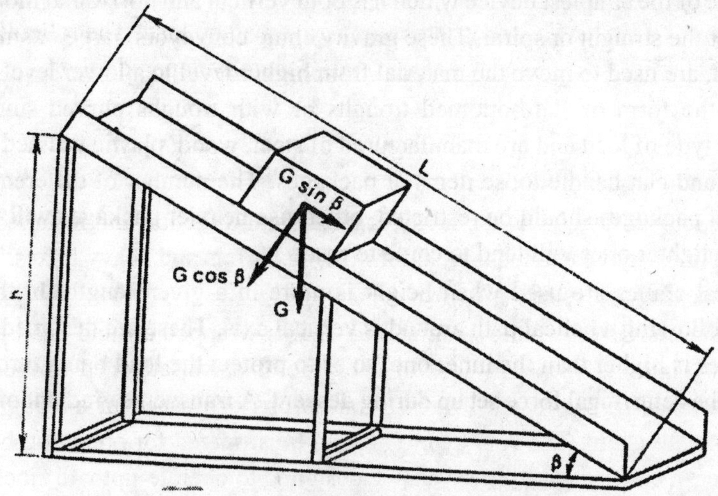

Fig. 21.5 Forces coming into play on a slide.

This type of conveyors depend on gravitation to perform its function. The most common are slides, chutes and tubes arranged so as to enable the load to slide down. In these conveyors, bulk or unit loads move on a declined surface under the force of gravity. The angle of inclination is determined by the coefficient of friction for the material of its surface and the material conveyed as well as by the angle of repose.

Gravity roller conveyor is a material handling installation in which the bed consists of rolls fitted to a frame. These are equally suitable for the handling of unit loads and containerized high volume materials. Smooth operation is obtained by spacing the rollers not more than 1/3 to 1/4 of the length of the load.

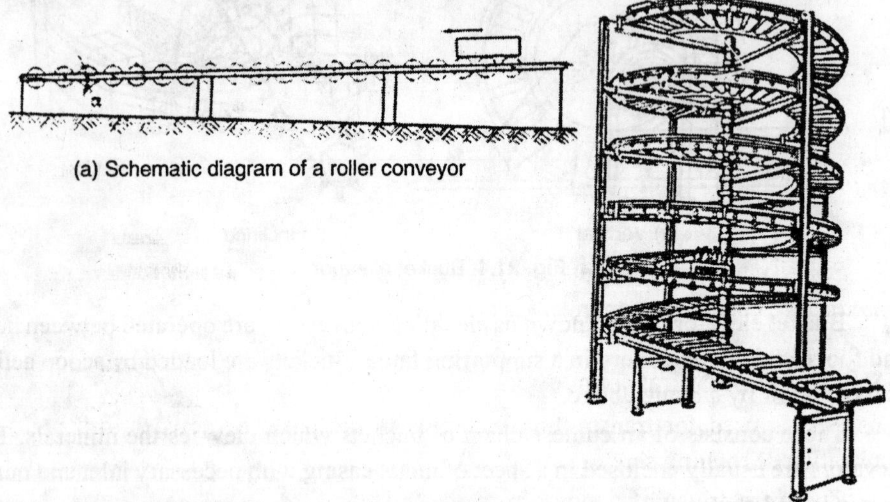

(a) Schematic diagram of a roller conveyor

(b) Roller spiral chute

Fig. 21.6 Gravity roller conveyors.

21.7 Chutes

This is one of the simplest device which has both vertical and horizontal motion. These may either the straight or spiral. These gravity chute conveyors, large or small, curved or straight, are used to move the material from higher level to a lower level. These are either in the form of flat-bottomed troughs or with troughs curved suitable for a particular type of load and are manufactured of steel, wood, plastic or lined with other materials and can handle loose items or packages. The number of different sizes and weights of packages should be restricted, otherwise heavier packages will travel very fast while lighter ones will tend to come to rest.

Spiral chutes are used when height is more in a given length. In this, load is lowered following a helical path around is vertical axis. These are designed so that the outer edges is higher than the inner one, so as to protect the load being thrown off the chute by the centrifugal force set up during descent. A transverse gradient of 10° to 15° is normal.

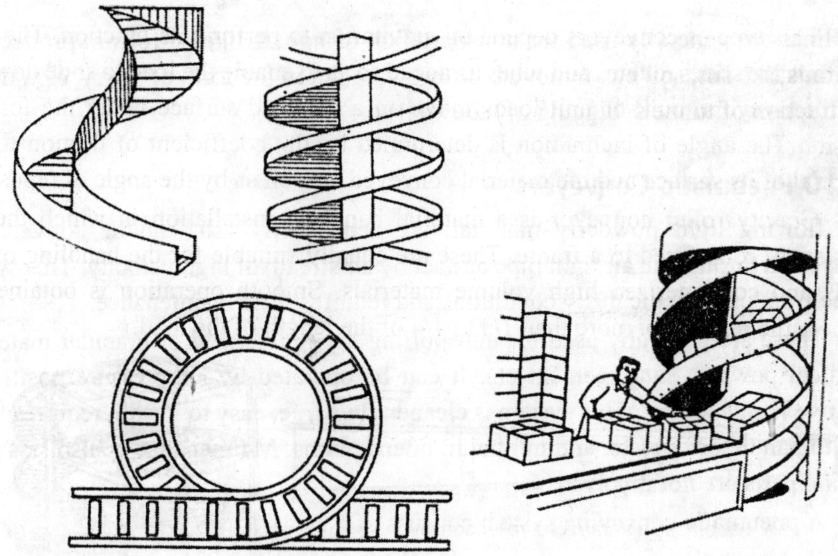

Fig. 21.7 Spiral chutes.

Spiral chute has advantage of low price due to no power requirement, low maintenance cost, and economical use of space.

21.8 Screw or Spiral Conveyors

This type is used for transmitting materials in the paste or powder form with the application of rotating screw.

These are driven by a motor from one end, and consists of a helix mounted on bearings at the ends, and also at intermediate points. This type of conveyor is also dust free by enclosing it. The material enters from one end and is carried to the other by the screwing action. Screw conveyors can also be used for handling pulverised coal (for feeding into the furnace) or other granular materials.

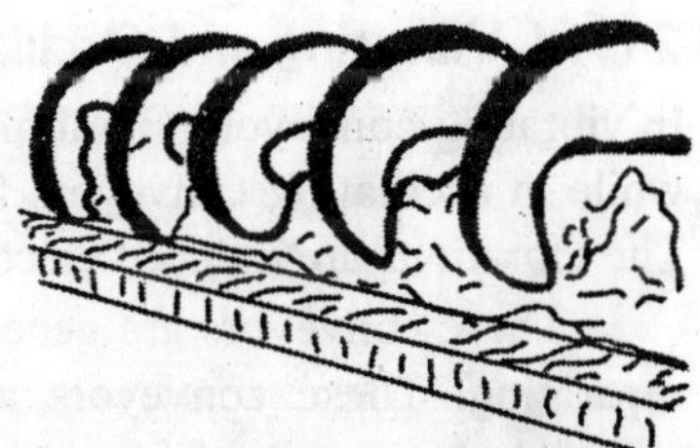

Fig. 21.8 Screw conveyor.

These conveyors consist of a screw rotating in a stationary trough or tube. As the shaft on which screw type spiral blades are fitted, rotates, the spiral blade causes the material to be pushed forward along the trough. These can operate in a horizontal, inclined or even vertical upward direction. While the materials are being moved, the screw conveyors can also be used to perform the process of blending and mixing of materials.

21.9 Hydraulic Conveyors

In hydraulic transport installations bulk loads are carried in a pipe or trough by the stream of a liquid (usually water). The mixture of material with water, is carried by gravity or due to the pressure of the liquid created by a pump. Hydraulic pumps and pipe lines are generally used for transportation of liquids like petroleum products, or materials like silt, soil etc. removed for throwing out in the form of slurry, *e.g.*, during construction of tunnels, digging of tube wells etc.

21.10 Pneumatic Conveyors

Free flowing light powderly material like cement, fly ash, can be conveniently transported through an air tight pipe or duct by air stream of high velocity. This system is free from unhygienic dusty conditions and requires little maintenance.

These are generally used for transporting dry, pulverized or granular materials, chemical powder, sand, cement etc. It can be operated by air pressure positive or negative (*i.e.*, suction). This system is cleaner, dust free, easy to install, requires lesser staff to handle or operate, and minimum interruptions. Maintenance is also less since moving parts are not involved.

A pneumatic conveying system consists of :

(a) air supply unit, (b) feeder unit,

(c) pipe lines, and (d) separation unit

This type of conveyor system is economical because of the :

(i) the saving in the cost of bags or other packages,

(ii) less expenses on bulk handling,

(iii) less labour costs, and

(iv) no chance of damage, spillage or residual materials in the discarded bags.

21.11 Vibrating and Oscillating Conveyors

In vibrating conveyors vibrations are created at high frequency and small amplitude, while in oscillating conveyors frequency is relatively lower and amplitude is larger. The vibrations are induced electrically or mechanically.

These conveyors are generally used as a feeder, and for screening, blending or separating. These conveyors are fitted with metal or plastic trough over which materials consisting of fragments of varying sizes are kept, which while moving are separated, larger ones travel at a higher speed then those of smaller ones. For designing a vibrating conveyor, it is essential to specify nature of material to be handled indicating density, grain size and other characteristics.

Vibratory conveyors are used for handling abrasive, hot, jagged materials, sand, grit etc. These are widely used in screening plants and aggregate hoppers in aggregate mixing plants, asphalt plants, and concrete mixing plants.

21.12 Safety Aspects

Common safety measures taken in conveyors are :

1. All conveyors shall be regularly inspected, repaired and maintained.
2. Belt conveyors shall not be overloaded to the point where material fall off the belt. The walkway along the belt shall be kept free of materials. Where

the walkway is one meter or more above the ground, a standard guardrail shall be installed.

3. Oilers shall never attempt to clean rollers while the belt is in motion. All oil and grease cups shall be so located that the oiler can service the cups without exposing himself to danger.

4. Following are the maximum allowable speeds of conveyor belts carrying sand, gravel and earth :

Width of Belt (cm)	*Speed (meters per min)*
40 to Less	80
40 to 60	130
60 or More	180

If the materials includes abrasive lumps such as crushed rock, the speed should be reduced 15 meters per minute on narrow belts and by 30 meters per minute on wide belts of 60 cms more in width.

5. Where trippers are used to control the discharge from the belt, a device for throwing the propelling mechanism into neut4ral gear shall be installed at each end of the runway.

6. Whenever the belt crosses over a travelled way, either public or private, trays, shall be installed to catch all spillage from the belt. The trays and their supports shall be of ample strength to support a heaped load of wet materials and the estimated weight of the cleaning crew. The trays shall not be so allowed to fill and patrolmen shall be particularly alert to prevent any spillage on travel ways.

7. Crossovers or underpasses with proper safeguards shall be provided for passage over or under all conveyors, as necessary. Crossing over or under conveyors except where safe passageways are provided is prohibited.

8. All conveyor systems shall be equipped with such emergency signal devices that will provide reasonable safe control at all time. A system of signals to indicate the stopping or starting of belt shall be installed.

9. On all conveyors where reversing or runaway presents a hazards "anti-runway" or "backup" stops or other safeguards shall be installed to protect persons and property from injury and damage.

10. Riding on conveyors shall be prohibited.

11. Baffles shall be placed across belts installed on steel grades to prevent materials from rolling or bouncing off. The baffles shall be placed at intervals of about 30 meters on level belts.

12. Where conveyors are operated in tunnels, pits and similar enclosures, ample room shall be provided to allow safe access way and operating space for all workmen. Tunnels, pits and similar enclosures shall be provided with

adequate drainage, lighting, ventilation and emergency controls including escape ways where it is necessary for person to work in or enter such areas.

13. All openings to hoppers, chutes, bins, etc., shall be protected to prevent unauthorized entry or persons from stepping or falling into them.

QUESTIONS

1. Explain different types of conveyors in brief.
2. Write an essay on belt conveyors.
3. Explain the following in detail :
   (a) Roller conveyors, and
   (b) Chian conveyors.
4. Explain (a) gravity, and (b) screw type conveyors.
5. What are conveyors? Name different types of conveyors in use in construction industry.
6. Describe a belt conveyor. State its advantages.
7. Explain (a) Screw, and (b) elevating conveyors.
8. Explain pneumatic and hydraulic conveyors.
9. Write short notes on :
   (a) Traction type conveyors.
   (b) Tractionless type conveyors.
10. Discuss vibrating and oscillating conveyors. Give its applications.
11. Explain gravity type conveyors and chutes. Discuss their advantages over traction conveyors.
12. Explain bucket elevators in detail.

□□□

Chapter 22

Latest Developments in Construction

22.1 Introduction

As, construction has become the basic input for socio-economic development, in addition, construction industry provides a growth impetus to other sectors through backward and forwarded linkages. The upswing in the Indian economy has enhanced the demand for the construction and material handling equipment. The demand for these equipment is correlated with the growth of other segments.

During last 3 to 4 decades construction industry has made enormous progress and has grown both in terms of size and diversity. Construction equipment plays a significant role in the execution of modern high cost time bound construction projects. These produce output at accelerated speed and enable completion of tasks in a limited time. The equipment saves manpower which is becoming scarce, costly and more demanding day-by-day. In addition, equipment improves the productivity, quality and safety. Thus, the construction equipment have become indispensable item of resources and their role continues to grow steadily. The equipment are also being introduced in new areas of application in different fields of construction.

During the last about two decades, construction industry has made enormous progress and has grown in terms of size and diversity due to large scale developments in the field of infrastructure and housing sectors.

The construction industry has a long Turn Around Time (TAT) due to human-based work environment. Further, lack of skilled labour, increase in labour cost and technological advances are forcing rapid changes in various fields of construction.

The construction projects of today has made the contractors to equip their construction so as to perform the highest output with minimum construction cost. In order to have highest output, parameters like accuracy, precision, quality and cycle time have to be optimized. This is possible either by having highly skilled manpower or by automating system.

Intense competition, shortage of skilled labour and technological advances are forcing rapid changes in the construction industry encouraging its automation. In order to have highest output, as discussed above, the parameters like accuracy, precision, quality, cycle time have to be optimized. This optimization is possible either by having a skilled manpower, or automating the system, but in the case of even employing highly skilled manpower, continuously doing the same kind of work for long time will cause fatigue resulting in lower efficiency. Thus, only alternative would be automate the system, especially when work is of repetitive nature and involve large construction.

With the automation it is also possible to have higher efficiency, accuracy and quality along with safety of workers for which the contractors and the society is concerned. The automation also provides a solution on the safety aspects of both workers and the machines.

Here, in this chapter we are discussing the equipments which are being in the advance stage of development in the construction industry, such as plastering machines, use of drones, and use of robots.

22.2 Wall Plastering Machines

Due to manual process of wall plastering on construction site, there is very large requirement of labour and hence the labour cost is responsible for increasing the price of construction projects. The quality of work is mostly depending on the skill of the labour in manual plastering process.

The automation of plastering process is the solution to these problems, further, there will be a saving of construction period and cost. It will also give good plaster finishing to the walls.

Presently the plastering work is being done manually, which required large time for their completion. Due to which the cost of the project is very high, and therefore, efforts are being made to automate the plastering process.

All these factors are forcing rapid changes in building construction, which mainly consists of commercial infrastructure and residential complexes, where plastering work is necessary. The introduction of new plastering machine can help to reduce the time. Some plastering machines have been developed, though they are yet to pick-up by the major building contractors.

In construction of buildings, apartments, complexes, shops, malls, and homes plastering is necessary for decorating the wall. Plastering refers to the ornamental work done with plaster, such as a layer of plaster on the walls or plaster decorative mouldings on ceilings. Plastering is therefore used to get smooth and finished wall surfaces and also to give specified strength to the walls. It protects the wall from moisture from both the sides, besides giving a good look. But in present days this work is being done with the help of manual labour, which is a lengthy and time consuming. Therefore efforts are being made to develop a good and reliable automatic (or semi-automatic) plastering machine. The plastering machines are portable, easy to operate and maintain.

22.2.1 Objectives

Main objectives of plastering machines are :

- To reduce the human work involved in plastering.

- To render the plaster on walls mechanically.
- Reducing the requirement of trained workers.
- Higher excellence/finish of the plaster can be achieved.
- It helps in reducing the labour cost and reduces the time required to complete the project substantially.
- It avoid wastage of cement and other materials, which enables in saving of materials cost.

22.2.2 Construction and Working

1. Construction

The plastering machine consists of the motor pump to push the cement mix, funnel to load the cement mix, flexible pipe to bear the cement blend to the hopper, horizontal bar guide to move the plastering unit horizontally, horizontal top to grasp the vertical bar guide to move in the horizontal direction. It also has a rail guide to move the hopper vertically, vertical head to grasp the hopper, cylinder slot to discharge the cement consistently with the pressure from the pump present in hopper, metal sheet to evenly distribute the cement on the walls.

The hopper box containing the cement mix is lowered to the required height. The cement mix when fall on the blade surface, while the blades rest upon the wall surface, the upward motion causes the mix to be pasted on the wall surface.

2. Working of the Machine

Initially, the plastering machine should be brought closed to the wall to be plastered and positioned. The mortar of cement and sand in requisite proportion (generally 1 : 4) is poured into the hopper-tray, which is lifted by some mechanism (generally by means of a rope or through a lead screw coupled to the motor). The mortar (cement-sand mix) flows downwards due to gravitational force. The wedge plate applies pressure on to the cement mixture so that the cement adheres to the wall.

The clearance between the wall and the plastering machine can be adjusted as per the thickness of the plaster. When the carriage moves upward, the mortar gets applied, and the downward movement sees that the finishing of the plaster is done. The quality achieved with the machines are within 3 mm deviation in surface alignment in 1200 mm radius.

22.2.3 Advantages

Following are the main advantages of using the plastering machines :

(i) The plastering machines can achieve any thickness uniformly.

(ii) The wastage of mortar is negligible.

(iii) The machines need very less time to complete the plastering work.

(iv) There is no need to employ skilled labour.

(v) The quality of plastering is batter than manual plastering.

(vi) Plastering by machines have low cost than manual plastering.

(vii) Less risk of accident (more safety) during plastering by machines.

(viii) Plastering by machines is more reliable than conventional process.

(ix) It has more productivity.

(x) It saves labour and material cost.

22.2.4 Disadvantages/Limitations

Plastering machines have mainly following disadvantages/limitations :

1. The plastering machines can be used for straight walls and are not suitable for the construction of curved or inclined walls.
2. It is also not suitable for plastering the corners and for joining of two walls.
3. The plastering machines are subjected to break-down at one time or another time. The more the sophisticated more the chances of breakdowns. The breakdown results in delay in completion of work and this may cause in increase in cost.
4. As manual labour enhances the expertise of an individual. Some people believe that plastering is an art with plasters producing magnificent works of art. Dependence on automated plastering machine would deter a creative mind and result loss of interest in the art of plastering.

22.2.5 Future Scope of Work

As mentioned earlier, the plastering machines are in developing stage and still there use is very limited. A lot of improvements are required so as to make it popular. The present models are semi-automatic and these machines do not have automatic loading of mortar. Therefore loading the mortar has to be automated.

The present machines can plaster straight walls and are suitable only for buildings which have large walls. There is need to upgrade these machines to handle walls which are curved.

22.3 Use of Drones in Construction Industry

Drones were originally used in military. These are also known as **"Unmanned Aerial Vehicles (UAVs)"**. In recent past these have seen many technological advancements. Today's drones are more lightweight, more agile and can stream live video, while being operated by a pilot on ground.

'Drone Systems' generally consist of an operator, control system, ground and satellite equipment, communication links and the drone itself. Drones are now-a-days being used in various ways on construction sites.

UAVs can be equipped with infrared cameras, radar and other technology that enhances their surveillance capabilities on a job site. This information is useful for tracking not only construction progress but also workers, equipment and material on a jobsite.

The emerging uses of UAVs in the construction industry range from aiding with construction project planning by aerial mapping of a construction site to extending the actual building of structures.

UAVs can monitor construction sites, especially large sites or those spread out over several locations more quickly and efficiently than on-the ground construction management.

Here, it is necessary to mention that drone industry is still in its infancy stage.

Drone systems can also be used to inspect remote sites for hazardous conditions or unstable structures without placing the workers at risk, especially for awkward and difficult to reach locations such as tall structures, on and under bridges and along busy highways.

22.3.1 Benefits of Drones in Construction

Use of drones have following benefits in the field of construction :

1. **Time, money and hard labour is saved** by using commercial drones instead of the traditional methods.
2. It is possible, for the builders, with a drone to develop work plans, track progress and monitor, and check for problems along the highways.
3. These are cheaper than the flying manned aircraft.
4. An inspection job of an high rise structure, would require several days for setting up extensive scaffolding or bringing a huge crane, can now be completed quickly using drones.
5. Drones can investigate and inspect a problem onsite and **reach high-risk areas quickly and safely.**
6. Drones can be easily programmed to fly to the same exact location over and over again to **show project progress as needed with superior image resolution.**
7. Surveying applications have been made easier because data collection is now quicker, more accurate and less expensive using drone.
8. Monitor the progress of construction work and jobsite logistics without disrupting ongoing work.
9. Identify problems before they develop through the use of maintenance assessments.
10. Facilitate surveillance.
11. Assist search and rescue operations.

12. Document jobsite conditions from beginning to end.
13. By using drones project management can increase the scope and frequency of inspections.
14. Drones can be useful in applications where worker access is an issue and in spaces that are too small for humans.
15. In the case of highway work zones, drone can inspect the entire length of road or an adjacent structures when fast moving traffic presents a serious hazard for workers.

22.3.2 Drone Applications in Construction

Following are the some of the construction activities where drones are replacing the traditional manual way of working :

1. Mapping of Construction Site

Mapping a construction site has traditionally been a long, labour-intense process that requires a lot of time, skill and money. For large projects, drones can be hired to fly over the site and take photographs. By capturing the footage and other informations, company can save a lot of effort and money.

2. Site Inspection of Construction Site

Construction sites which are dangerous or difficult to inspect, use of drones is very useful. Drones can carry out a visual inspection of high-risk areas which reduces health and safety risks, as site managers by using drones can watch the footage while sitting in their site offices.

3. Monitoring for Spread out Sites

The drones (UAVs) can monitor large construction sites or those sites which are spread out over several locations more quickly and efficiently than on-the-ground construction management. These drones can be equipped with infrared cameras, radar and other technology that enhances their surveillance capabilities on a construction site. This is useful for tracking not only construction progress but also workers, equipment and material on the work site.

22.3.3 Limitations/Challenges in the Use of Drones

The use of UAVs for construction work, though has many advantages, there are a few challenges/limitations, such as :

1. Use of drones may pose several **hazards to workers**, which include overhead hazards, if a drawn falls form the sky due to low battery power or strikes a stationary object while flying.
2. Its use may open employers to **privacy concerns** depending upon how they are used on the site.
3. These are susceptible to **cyber attacks** just like virtually all the other network connected devices we use.

4. Two people are required for operating a commercial drone, who should be experienced and knowledgeable in this field. They should be familiar with important aspects of the drone, such as drones sensor and should also be able to retrieve the best possible footage and informations.
5. Drones are costly to purchase, though they may be economical in long-run. However, it is believed that the costs will come down in future as technology evolves and their demand and production will increase.

Drone adoption by the construction industry is continuously growing as is the development of drones to suit various needs.

22.3.4 Legal Aspects in the Use of Drones

The drone operators should be aware of the following rules for safe operation :

1. The drone should be registered with FAA (Federal Aviation Administration). Its FAA registration number should be labelled on the drone.
2. Fly the drones at or below 120 meters height only.
3. Drone should be kept within the line of sight.
4. Be aware of FAA airspace restrictions.
5. Respect the privacy of others.
6. Never fly near other aircraft, especially near airports.

22.3.5 How to Start Using a Drone

To start the use of drones, the companies have two options as under :

1. **Hire a subcontractor** having a drone for doing the work. This enables the company to start using drone services quickly. Selection of right subcontractor requires some home work. The operator should have experience, proper certification, adequate equipment and the adequate and correct type of insurance needed to protect the clients. The operator should have a remote pilot's license. It should also be made sure that drone operator has the right equipment and right operators for commercial applications.
2. Second option for starting the **use of own drones** require several months for selection of right drone and its purchase before starting its use. It also require selection of right experienced operators. For successful drone programme requires good equipment (drone) good experienced operator and good internal process for using drone.

   As discussed, training and certifications are the next steps All commercial operators are required to have the right type of FAA license. Remote pilot is required to pass an aeronautical test administered by the FAA. The drone training schools are available, which offer comple' integration programme solutions.

22.3.6 Future of Drones

Drones are being developed incorporating, X-ray technology and to have ability to create high resolution '3D' maps of objects. The technology is also being developed to create models of unknown areas behind walls or for structural monitoring of dangerous buildings, bridges etc.

Drones can be used in variety of ways so as to help to keep workers safe. These could soon be common on construction sites. As drone technology continues to advance, their uses in the construction industry is expected to increase by improving worker safety, boost work site efficiency and reduce cost.

22.4 Use of Robots in Construction

Robots are used today in several manufacturing industries, the most common amongst them are car industry, forging, where they replace workers engaged in intensive manual labour, or where safety in hazardous environment is most essential. **These are mostly used especially for repetitive tasks.** If robotics aims to replace men with machines, then the construction industry still require lot of developments in technology for its applications.

Robots on Building Sites

When considering using robots for construction at building site, the final products are not considered repetitive, since each project is unique. A large number (hundreds) of different activities are carried out on building sites, with little repetition.

Building sites are relatively dynamic places, with systematic changes of jobs and the surrounding environment. Building sites are hostile as they are full of obstacles, uneven surfaces, ladders etc. These sites are unstructured in the sense that they are not set up to have known references for the movement of robots. The building sites are since unstructured areas, they present considerable challenge to mobility and recognition of the workplace environment.

For the success and effectiveness of robots for use in building construction it is necessary that :

(a) Robots should be able to move about with a certain degree of "intelligence". This situation is not possible for real building sites where surfaces are not smooth and are littered with rubbish, obstacles etc.

(b) The robots cannot be used in hostile environments i.e. in unprotected and unexpected conditions such as falling from heights of materials, impacts etc.

(c) Handling of unwieldy or heavy loads. **The use of robots in such circumstances are not economically viable.** The example of unwieldy or heavy loads are beams.

From the above we can say that the **greatest advantage of robots lies in carrying out repetitive tasks on a large scale and with a fixed job, in a factory situation.**

Robots in Pre-fabrication Work

In view of the above discussions, preparation of the works on site would thus become more important in execution, with the prior manufacture of components to be incorporated into the job, construction would increasingly become an assembly industry.

With respect to the economic viability of producing the elements to be incorporated into buildings, construction would be more and more reliable. The robotic systems have the potential for immediate use in the environment of pre-fabrication for the construction industry. Further advancement of robotics technology could make it applicable in many construction processes.

Another area being developed for the use of robots is in welding in metal structures. The personal computer with suitable software are used for controlling, programming and monitoring the robot. This enable to achieve welding of constant quality, within pre-defined ranges.

In case of welding by using robots, a database is used which contains all the variables of the welding process and the dimensions of the places to be welded, the weld points programmed for the beginning and end of the operation. This database will help to reduce the work time related to changing the product, adjusting and programming the robot. For the purpose of welding by robot, the user sends the full details of the task, including welding spots and parameters, type of trajectory and precision etc.

All these informations are stored in a file in the personal a computer. These informations can be reused countless times, forming production routines that the operator can use whenever the components to be welded have the same characteristics.

Future Aspects

Thus, the pre-fabricated elements produced by robots can be manufactured in a workshop (not on building site) in controlled environment can be incorporated in building.

While research continues in the use of robots in building construction, the implementation will increase in fields where productivity gains outweigh the equipment and implementation costs.

QUESTIONS

1. Discuss the need for wall plastering machine in plastering of buildings.
2. What are the objectives of plastering machines?
3. Explain the construction and working of a plastering machine.
4. Discuss the advantages of using a plastering machine.
5. Discuss various limitations and disadvantages in the use of wall plastering machine.

6. Write a short note on :
   (a) Future scope of wall plastering machine.
   (b) Comparison of manual plastering and plastery by machines.
   (c) Elements in a "drone system".
7. Discuss in detail about the use of drones in construction industry.
8. Explain benefits of drones in construction.
9. Discuss important applications of drones in construction industry.
10. Explain various limitations in the use of drones.
11. Discuss various legal aspects related to the use of drones.
12. Write short notes on :
    (a) Steps involved in hiring of drones.
    (b) Future of drones in construction industry.
13. What steps would you like to take for starting the use of your own drone in construction projects?
14. Write an essay on use of robots in the field of construction.
15. Explain as to why it is not possible to use robots at construction site in a housing project.
16. Discuss the use of robot in prefabrication works for a housing project.
17. "Robots are useful and economically viable in repetitive works." Discuss the statement with reference to construction of buildings.

□□□

Appendices

Appendix - I : Economic Life of Equipment

Economical life of any equipment vary depending upon the terrain, working conditions, climate etc. however to have a general idea, economic life generally considered is given below :

Vehicles

1.	Water browser	10,000 hrs or 200,00 kms
2.	Diesel carrier	10,000 hrs or 300,00 kms
3.	Diesel distributor	10,000 hrs or 200,00 kms
4.	Bitumen carrier	10,000 hrs or 250,00 kms
5.	Bitumen distributor (*i.e.*, sprayer)	8,000 hrs or 200,00 kms
6.	Dump truck (off-highway)	12,000 hrs
7.	Dump truck (on-highway)	15,000 hrs or 300,00 kms
8.	Trailor self propelled with prime mover	18,000 hrs or 3500,00 kms
9.	Mobile workshop trailor	15,000 hrs or 300,00 kms
10.	Recovery vehicle	10,000 hrs or 200,00 kms
11.	Tractors (wheeled)	10,000 hrs or 200,00 kms
12.	Mobile crane	12,000 hrs
13.	(a) Truck mounted concrete mixer	10,000 hrs or 150,00 kms
	(b) Portable concrete mixers	6,000 hrs
14.	Concrete dump truck	6,000 hrs
15.	Self propelled concrete mixer	8,000 hrs
16.	Cement carrier	12,000 hrs or 250,00 kms
17.	Light motor vehicle (Jeeps cars, pickups, station wagons)	160,000 kms

Other Equipments/Plants

1.	Dozers	
	(a) 300 HP and above	12,000 hrs
	(b) Below, 300 HP	10,000 hrs
2.	Scraper, motorised	10,000 hrs

3.	Scraper, towel	15,000 hrs
4.	Pay loader	12,000 hrs
5.	Motor grader	12,000 hrs
6.	Stone crushing and screening plant	16,000 hrs
7.	Aggregate mixing plant	16,000 hrs
8.	Hot mix asphalt plant	16,000 hrs
9.	Cold mix asphalt plant	8,000 hrs
10.	Excavator	10,000 hrs
11.	Draglines and shovels	16,000 hrs
12.	Bucket wheel excavator	40,000 hrs
13.	Road rollers	10,000 hrs
14.	Paver finishers	8,000 hrs
15.	Air compressors	10,000 hrs
16.	Self propelled power blower	8,000 hrs
17.	(a) Generating set 200 kVA and above	14,000 hrs
	(b) Generating set upto 200 kVA	12,000 hrs
18.	Road marking machine	8,000 hrs
19.	Concrete vibrator	
	(a) With petrol engine	5,000 hrs
	(b) With electric motor	6,500 hrs
20.	Pile driving hammers	8,000 hrs
21.	Trenching machine	6,000 hrs
22.	Drill blast hole, core wagon	10,000 hrs
23.	Tower crane	30,000 hrs
24.	Ropeway and cable ways	40,000 hrs
25.	Jack hammers, paving breakers	4,000 hrs

Appendix - II : Trouble Shooting

S. No.	Faults		Reasons
	Engine Problems		
1.	Engine starting difficulty		
	(a) Engine does not crack	(i)	Weak battery.
		(ii)	Disconnected, loose or corroded battery terminals.
		(iii)	Starting switch defective.
		(iv)	Starter defective.
		(v)	Piston seizure.
		(vi)	Bearing seizure.
		(vii)	Injection pump plunger seized.
	(b) Engine cracks	(i)	Fuel level too low or clogged.
		(ii)	Air in fuel lines.
		(iii)	Clogged fuel filter.
		(iv)	High pressure injection line connection loose.
		(v)	Injection nozzle or pump faulty.
		(vi)	Fuel injection timing improper.
		(vii)	Air cleaner clogged.
		(viii)	Low compression.
		(ix)	Water in fuel.
2.	Engine stalls at low speed	(i)	Fuel pump governor out of adjustment.
		(ii)	Fuel pump rack and pinion malfunctioning.
		(iii)	High pressure injection pipe clogged.
		(iv)	Injection nozzle defective.
3.	Engine lacks power	(i)	Insufficient fuel supply : clogged fuel line or air in the system, clogged fuel filter, insufficient, injection, injection nozzle defective, nozzle spray incorrect or improper injection timing.
		(ii)	Clogged air cleaner.
		(iii)	Intake valve tappet improperly adjusted.
		(iv)	Low compression.
		(v)	Engine overheating.
4.	Engine overheating	(i)	Cooling system defective : Radiator cap defective, clogged radiator, less water in radiator. Thermostat defective, loose fan belt, defective coolant pump, sediment in water jacket.

(Contd...)

		(ii)	Defective fuel injection system : Incorrect timing, excessive fuel injection, defective nozzle.
		(iii)	Defective lubrication system : Engine level too low, oil pump defective, engine oil deteriorated.
		(iv)	Carboned cylinder.
		(v)	Under inflated tyres.
		(vi)	Gas leak from cylinder head gasket.
		(vii)	Brakes dragging.
		(viii)	Excessive mechanical resistance in transmission.
		(ix)	Cylinder head cracked.
5.	Engine knocking	(i)	Improper fuel injection timing.
		(ii)	Uneven injection.
		(iii)	Incorrect nozzle spray.
		(iv)	Fuel cetane value too low.
		(v)	Oil leaking into combustion chambers.
		(vi)	Lack of compression.
		(vii)	Excessive worn cylinder and piston.
		(viii)	Worn crank shaft and connecting road bearing.
		(ix)	Incorrect value clearance.
	Improper exhaust gas colour		
	(a) White smoke	(i)	Delayed fuel injection timing.
		(ii)	Water in the fuel.
		(iii)	Oil leaking into combustion chamber.
	(b) Black smoke	(i)	Advance fuel injection timing.
		(ii)	Nozzle spray incorrect.
		(iii)	Compression pressure insufficient.
7.	Excessive fuel consumption	(i)	Fuel leakage.
		(ii)	Poor fuel quality.
		(iii)	Clogged air cleaner.
		(iv)	Low tire pressure.
		(v)	Injection pump or nozzle defective.
		(vi)	Incorrect injection timing.
		(vii)	Incorrect valve timing.
		(viii)	Excessive friction either in engine parts of in wheel bearings.
		(ix)	Clutch slipping.
		(x)	Brake dragging.

8.	Excessive engine oil consumption	(i)	Improper oil, oil level too high or oil leak.
		(ii)	Engine overheating.
		(iii)	Worn cylinders, pistons and rings.
	Gear Problems		
1.	Hard shifting gear	(i)	Play in gear shift lever.
		(ii)	Loose shifter shaft.
		(iii)	Clutch dragging.
		(iv)	Gear tooth cracked or foreign matter in the gear.
		(v)	Clutch shaft and pilot bearing seizure.
		(vi)	Excessive viscosity for gear oil.
	Clutch Problems		
1.	Slipping clutch	(i)	Worn lining.
		(ii)	Glazed lining.
		(iii)	Grease or oil on the lining.
		(iv)	Installation of improper type of lining.
		(v)	Lack of free play in the clutch pedal.
		(vi)	Weak or broken pressure springs.
		(vii)	Worn splines in clutch shaft.
		(viii)	Warped pressure plate or flywheels.
2.	Grabbing and chattering clutch	(i)	Glazed or hardened lining or grease on the lining.
		(ii)	A bent or tight release shaft.
		(iii)	Cracked or damaged pressure plate or ply.
		(iv)	Too much clay between gears.
		(v)	Badly tuned engine.
		(vi)	Loose engine support.
3.	Dragging clutch	(i)	Too much pedal free play.
		(ii)	Improper release-lever adjustment.
		(iii)	Warped drive plate.
		(iv)	Tight or burred splines.
		(v)	Loose or worn linkages.
		(vi)	Misalignment or clutch housing.
4.	Rapid wear of lining	(i)	Slipping clutch.
		(ii)	Operator starts the vehicle in higher speeds.
		(iii)	Weak or broken pressure springs.
		(iv)	Badly warped pressure plate.
		(v)	Improperly adjusted lining.

(Contd...)

Steering Problems			
1.	Hard steering	(i)	Tyres under-inflated.
		(ii)	Poorly lubricated steering system.
		(iii)	Improper wheel alignment.
		(iv)	Front spring weakend.
		(v)	Frame bent..
		(vi)	Steering knuckle bent.
2.	Excessive play	(i)	Loose of worn linkages.
		(ii)	Steering gear adjusted too loose or worn.
		(iii)	King pins, steering knuckle bushings and bearings or spherical joints worn.
		(iv)	Front wheel bearings too loose or worn.
		(v)	Steering wheel loose on post.
3.	Steering becomes erratic when breakes are applied	(i)	Brake lining worn or soaked with oil grease or brake fluid.
		(ii)	Poorly adjusted brakes.
		(iii)	Steering knuckle bent.
4.	Vehicle pulls to one side	(i)	Rear wheel not tracking with front wheels.
		(ii)	Wheel bearings too tight.
		(iii)	Upper and lower suspension arm mounting bolts loose.
5.	Steering wheel return poor	(i)	Improper wheel alignment.
		(ii)	Improperly adjusted gear.
		(iii)	Steering system poorly lubricated.
		(iv)	Wheel base unbalanced.
Brake Problems			
1.	Brakes drag	(i)	Too little or no pedal free play.
		(ii)	Incorrect brake fluid that has corroded rubber parts.
		(iii)	Clogged or kinked line leading to master cylinder.
		(iv)	Too tight brakes.
2.	One wheel drags	(i)	Weak or broken brake shoe return spring.
		(ii)	Brake adjusted too tight.
		(iii)	Loose or worn wheel or axle bearing.
		(iv)	Clogged or kinked line.
		(v)	Wheel cylinder piston or cup stuck.
		(vi)	Brake drum out-of-round.

(Contd...)

3.	Springy or spongy brake pedal	(i)	Air in lines.
		(ii)	Poor shoe adjustment.
	Battery Discharges Early		
1.	Battery not charging	(i)	Alternator defective.
		(ii)	Improper adjusted regulated adjustment.
		(iii)	Plates sulfating.
		(iv)	Corroded, disconnected, or loosened battery terminals.
		(v)	Loose fan belt.
2.	Starting current excessive causing early discharge of battery	(i)	Excessive use of starter.
		(ii)	Starter defective.
		(iii)	High mechanical resistance in engine.
3.	Excessive lamp current	(i)	Excessive use of lamps.
		(ii)	Wiring defect.
4.	Other reasons	(i)	Pole plate separator defective.
		(ii)	Switches to electrical equipment.

INDEX

D

E

F

G

H